Equity, Equality, and Justice in AI-Enhanced Language Education

Francisco Javier Palacios-Hidalgo
Universidad de Córdoba, Spain

Carlos Lindade
Universidade do Porto, Portugal

IGI Global
Scientific Publishing
Publishing Tomorrow's Research Today

Vice President of Editorial	Melissa Wagner
Director of Acquisitions	Mikaela Felty
Director of Book Development	Jocelynn Hessler
Production Manager	Mike Brehm
Cover Design	Jose Rosado

Published in the United States of America by
IGI Global Scientific Publishing
701 East Chocolate Avenue
Hershey, PA, 17033, USA
Tel: 717-533-8845 | Fax: 717-533-7115
Website: https://www.igi-global.com E-mail: cust@igi-global.com

Library of Congress Cataloging-in-Publication Data

Names: Palacios-Hidalgo, Francisco Javier, 1993- editor | Lindade, Carlos, 1987- editor
Title: Equity, equality, and justice in AI-enhanced language education / edited by Francisco Javier Palacios-Hidalgo, Carlos Lindade.
Description: Hershey, PA : IGI Global Scientific Publishing, 2027. | Includes bibliographical references and index. | Summary: "This book aims to bring together researchers, teacher educators, practitioners, and policymakers to address key questions"-- Provided by publisher.
Identifiers: LCCN 2026005955 (print) | LCCN 2026005956 (ebook) | ISBN 9798337377490 hardcover | ISBN 9798337377506 paperback | ISBN 9798337377513 ebook
Subjects: LCSH: Language and languages--Study and teaching--Social aspects | Social justice and education | Equity | Artificial intelligence--Educational applications | LCGFT: Essays
Classification: LCC P53.8 .E68 2026 (print) | LCC P53.8 (ebook)
LC record available at https://lccn.loc.gov/2026005955
LC ebook record available at https://lccn.loc.gov/2026005956

British Cataloguing in Publication Data
A Cataloguing in Publication record for this book is available from the British Library.

Table of Contents

Detailed Table of Contents

can transform English language teaching – making it more personalized, accessible, and just for all learners. Policies must evolve, too, and policies must ensure safe, transparent AI use. Future research should examine how AI impacts the specific English language skills under different teacher guidance styles.

This chapter theorises equity-centred, translanguaging-oriented language pedagogy within AI-driven educational ecologies as a justice project rather than a technological upgrade. It conceptualises AI systems as socio-technical assemblages that redistribute linguistic capital, codify algorithmic normativity, and reconfigure access and recognition for multilingual subjects. Mobilising Rawlsian justice, the Capability Approach, Fraserian redistribution-recognition-representation, critical and decolonial pedagogy, translanguaging, and linguistic human rights, it proposes a normative meta-framework for multilingual dignity. It then distils a typology of equity risks, a schema of teacher AI-equity literacies and agency, design principles for inclusive and culturally sustaining human-AI orchestration, and a governance matrix spanning classrooms, institutions, regulators, industry, and civil society that orients AI-enhanced language education toward epistemic justice and democratic futures.

Generative artificial intelligence is reshaping language education faster than initial teacher education systems can respond. This chapter frames AI integration in pre-service English teacher education as an urgent matter of equity, equality, and justice through three analytical movements. The first maps pre-service English teacher education in Portugal against Decreto-Lei n.º 9-A/2025, documenting the absence of generative AI content across all eight accredited providers. The second audits nine public universities in Andalusia, Spain, across primary English and secondary master's programmes, revealing a comparable structural gap. The third proposes a 3 ECTS curricular unit on generative AI in EFL pre-service education, grounded in the EU AI Act, DigComp 3.0, and UNESCO's AI Competency Framework for Teachers, structured around equity, equality, and justice. The chapter concludes that preparing critically AI-literate language teachers is a structural equity imperative, and that inaction risks deepening existing inequalities for already-marginalised learners.

Section 2
Critical Analyses of Bias, Access, and Representation

GAI offers transformative potential for ESP education but risks biases, digital divides, and inequalities among multilingual learners. This chapter proposes an interdisciplinary framework through ESP-content co-teaching (ICLHE-aligned), rooted in digital didactics, critical AI literacy, and learner-centered pedagogy. It includes three components: critical AI output analysis, collaborative project-based learning, and redefined practitioner roles as ethical guides. An English for Engineering scenario illustrates implementation, while a PDCA-structured policy model provides scalable equity safeguards for institutions worldwide. The framework repositions GAI from a productivity tool to a critical inquiry object, empowering learners to detect biases, refine outputs responsibly, and prioritize human collaboration over tech access for inclusive success. Future research includes multi-site pilots, longitudinal impact metrics, and agentic AI adaptation across global contexts.

This chapter investigates newspaper discourse on Chinese language education for South Asian schoolchildren in Hong Kong. Drawing on a corpus of 443 newspaper articles published between 2003 and 2025, the study analyzes how the press has represented the importance of Chinese language learning, the challenges and hurdles faced by ethnic minority students, and the views and suggestions advanced to promote greater educational equity. Limited access to computer devices and internet connectivity, parents' computer literacy, and willingness to engage in online learning have placed significant pressure on the implementation of AI-assisted Chinese learning and online support. While some stakeholders advocate AI as a promising solution, persistent inequalities in access remain a critical concern. The findings highlight diverse perspectives within the media and underscore the need for more equitable policies and practices to ensure that AI integration in Chinese language education effectively supports ethnic minority communities in Hong Kong.

Artificial intelligence (AI) is changing the language learning process based on adaptive platforms, automated feedback, speech recognition, and multimodal environment. However, these tools threaten to increase disparities between different students with different linguistic backgrounds, disabilities, technological access, and interests. Accessibility and inclusion are established in this chapter as the key principles of designing AI-mediated language education. It looks at accommodations such as live captioning, multi-lingual interfaces, adaptive feedback, assistive writing aids and custom portals. Development of poor accessibility design, low infrastructure, and exclusion risks, are some of the challenges. Accessibility and inclusion thus require a deliberate consideration in each phase of development of AI language tools. Postulating accessibility-minded design, the chapter provides concrete suggestions on the ways to create equitable AI language tools that would provide inclusion in different educational settings

This chapter examines the pedagogical potential of generative artificial intelligence (GenAI) for multilingual news analysis in language education. It situates GenAI within a multiliteracies framework, with a focus on critical multilingual language awareness and the need to address biases embedded in AI-generated content. The chapter explores how comparing GenAI outputs across languages can highlight differing perspectives and foster multiliteracies. Drawing on empirical analyses of news representations in English, German, and Spanish, it demonstrates how GenAI can be used for multilingual and multiliteracies purposes. The findings point to differences not only in presentation and content but also in what is foregrounded or omitted across languages. This underscores the value of using GenAI to analyse how meaning is shaped differently across linguistic contexts.

Linguistic capital, understood as the set of competencies and resources that enable individuals and communities to participate effectively in social contexts, plays a key role in shaping the identity of the European Union. However, it faces several challenges, including the dominance of English as a global language that often marginalizes other languages. Similarly, the growing presence of non-EU languages within citizens' repertoires is not always reflected or valued in educational practices. The Pluridentities project (Horizon Europe Grant 101178914) examines how educational policies influence linguistic identities, attitudes toward languages, and the protection of linguistic capital in the EU. It also explores the impact of technology on student motivation and educational practices. This chapter, result of the second phase of Pluridentities, highlights how AIALL tools offer new opportunities for language teaching and learning, as well as to raise awareness on the importance of multilingualism, equity, equality and social justice in current global education.

Preface

INTRODUCTION

The rapid advancement of Artificial Intelligence (AI) has ushered in a transformative era for education, redefining how languages are taught, learned, and assessed. AI-powered technologies have introduced unprecedented opportunities to personalize instruction, enhance learner engagement, automate feedback, and expand access to language learning resources across diverse educational settings. Yet, alongside these innovations come critical questions concerning equity, equality, and justice. As AI becomes increasingly embedded in language education, it is essential to examine not only what these technologies can accomplish, but also whose needs they serve, whose voices they amplify, and whose experiences may be overlooked.

This volume, *Equity, Equality, and Justice in AI-Enhanced Language Education*, was developed in response to these pressing concerns. Our goal is to provide a comprehensive scholarly resource that critically examines the opportunities and challenges associated with integrating AI into foreign language education through the lens of social justice. Rather than viewing technological innovation as inherently beneficial, the chapters in this volume encourage readers to engage thoughtfully with the ethical, pedagogical, cultural, and societal implications of AI adoption. Collectively, they explore how equitable approaches can shape the design, implementation, and evaluation of AI-enhanced language learning environments that support all learners.

Throughout this collection, contributors investigate fundamental questions that will influence the future of language education. They consider who benefits from AI-assisted instruction and who may remain excluded due to technological, linguistic, economic, or cultural barriers. The chapters examine issues such as algorithmic bias, representation of diverse languages and identities, accessibility for learners with varying abilities, digital inequities, and the ethical responsibilities of educators, developers, and institutions. At the same time, the volume highlights promising innovations, including inclusive AI design principles, accessible educational technologies, equitable teacher preparation, and intelligent systems that support differentiated instruction while respecting learner diversity.

A distinguishing feature of this volume is its interdisciplinary perspective. Drawing upon expertise from applied linguistics, educational technology, teacher education, AI, curriculum studies, and policy research, the contributors offer both theoretical insights and practical guidance. Their work demonstrates that achieving equity in AI-enhanced language education requires collaboration across disciplines, thoughtful policy development, responsible technological innovation, and sustained reflection on educational values. By bringing together diverse scholarly perspectives and experiences from a variety of educational contexts, this collection presents a balanced and globally relevant examination of one of the most significant developments shaping contemporary language education.

This reference work has been developed to serve a broad international audience. Researchers, language educators, teacher educators, curriculum developers, instructional designers, coursebook authors, graduate students, and educational technology specialists will find valuable analyses and evidence-based recommendations throughout the volume. In addition, policymakers, school leaders, nonprofit organizations, and professionals committed to advancing equity, diversity, and inclusion will benefit from the discussions presented here. The book is intended not only as a reference for scholars and practitioners implementing AI-supported language instruction, but also as a resource for undergraduate and graduate courses exploring language education, educational technologies, digital literacies, and ethical AI.

As editors, we believe that the future of AI in language education must be guided by principles that place human dignity, fairness, and inclusion at the center of technological innovation. AI should not simply replicate existing educational systems or reinforce historical inequities; rather, it should create opportunities to broaden participation, recognize linguistic and cultural diversity, and empower learners from all backgrounds. The conversations presented in this volume seek to move beyond technological enthusiasm toward a more thoughtful and responsible vision of AI—one that supports educational excellence while promoting justice and equal opportunity.

We extend our sincere appreciation to the chapter authors whose expertise, dedication, and commitment have made this volume possible. Their contributions reflect a shared determination to advance scholarship that is both academically rigorous and socially meaningful. We also express our gratitude to the reviewers for their careful evaluations and constructive feedback, which strengthened the quality of each chapter. Finally, we thank the publishing team for their guidance and support throughout the development of this project.

It is our hope that *Equity, Equality, and Justice in AI-Enhanced Language Education* will stimulate meaningful dialogue, inspire future research, and encourage educators, researchers, developers, and policymakers to collaborate in creating AI-enhanced language learning environments that are not only innovative, but also equitable, inclusive, and just. By critically examining both the promises and the challenges of AI, this volume seeks to contribute to a future in which technological progress and educational equity advance together.

ORGANIZATION OF THE BOOK

The chapters in this volume collectively examine how AI can either advance or undermine equity, equality, and justice in language education, offering both critical analyses and practical pathways toward more inclusive educational futures. Together, they emphasize that AI is not merely a technological innovation but a transformative force whose implementation must be guided by ethical, pedagogical, and social justice principles.

Section 1, "Conceptual and Theoretical Foundations", contains the first four chapters and establishes the conceptual, theoretical, and pedagogical frameworks—equity, justice, teacher agency, critical pedagogy, and teacher education—that underpin equitable AI integration in language education.

In Chapter 1, "AI and the Quest for Equity, Equality, and Justice in Language Education: An Introduction", we establish the conceptual foundation for the volume by examining AI in language education through the interconnected perspectives of equity, equality, and justice. The chapter challenges the notion of AI as a neutral educational tool, instead positioning it as a socio-political force capable of redistributing opportunities, reshaping power dynamics, and influencing linguistic identities. By defining the central concepts that underpin the volume and introducing justice-oriented theoretical frameworks, the chapter provides readers with the critical lens through which the subsequent contributions can be understood while calling upon educators and researchers to actively shape more equitable AI futures.

Building upon this foundation, in Chapter 2, "Teacher Agency in the Age of AI: Preparing Educators for Equitable AI Integration", Wali Khan Monib explores the evolving role of educators in AI-enhanced language learning environments. The discussion highlights teacher agency as an essential component of equitable AI integration, examining how educators' epistemic, transformational, relational, and moral capacities influence the responsible use of emerging technologies. The chapter underscores the importance of professional development, policy support, and teacher empowerment to ensure that AI enhances rather than diminishes educational fairness and learner success.

Chapter 3, "Equity-Centered and Translanguaging-Oriented Language Pedagogy for Multilingual Dignity: Linguistic Capital in AI-Driven Language Education", extends the discussion by presenting an equity-centered and translanguaging-oriented framework that positions multilingualism as a source of dignity and linguistic capital rather than deficit. Drawing upon multiple theories of justice and decolonial perspectives, Ashraf Alam proposes a comprehensive framework that addresses algorithmic bias, teacher AI literacy, inclusive instructional design, and collaborative governance. The chapter demonstrates how AI-enhanced language education can be reimagined to promote epistemic justice while respecting multilingual identities and cultural diversity.

Attention then turns to teacher preparation in Chapter 4, "Towards Equitable AI Literacy: Reconceptualising Pre-Service English Language Teacher Education in Portugal and Andalusia, Spain", which investigates the growing gap between rapid technological advancement and existing pre-service English language teacher education. Through comparative analyses of programs in Portugal and Andalusia (Spain), we reveal significant shortcomings in AI-related preparation and propose a dedicated curricular framework grounded in international competency standards. In doing so, it argues that developing critically AI-literate teachers represents a fundamental requirement for achieving educational equity and preventing the further marginalization of underserved learners.

Section 2, "Critical Analyses of Bias, Access, and Representation", is composed of three more chapters and critically examines structural barriers, algorithmic bias, digital divides, and linguistic and cultural exclusion that hinder equitable participation in AI-mediated language learning environments.

Chapter 5, "Bridging the Digital Divide: A Novel Interdisciplinary ESP Framework for Fostering Critical AI Literacy and Policy", addresses another critical dimension of equitable AI implementation by focusing on English for Specific Purposes (ESP) education. Recognizing that generative AI presents both opportunities and risks, Isabele Maria Lavado introduces an interdisciplinary instructional framework that combines critical AI literacy, collaborative learning, and learner-centered pedagogy. By emphasizing ethical reasoning, human collaboration, and institutional safeguards, the chapter illustrates how educators can bridge digital divides while cultivating responsible and inclusive AI practices.

Issues of access and educational inequality are further examined through an analysis of newspaper discourse surrounding Chinese language learning among South Asian students in Hong Kong in Chapter 6, "Newspaper Discourse on Chinese Language Learning, E-learning Readiness and AI Integration for Ethnic Minority Students in Hong Kong". By exploring media representations spanning more than two decades, Siu-lun Lee reveals how technological access, digital readiness, and broader social inequalities influence the implementation of AI-supported language education. The discussion highlights the importance of policy interventions that ensure emerging technologies genuinely expand opportunities for historically underserved communities.

In Chapter 7, "Accessibility, Inclusion, and AI: Designing Language Learning Tools for All Learners", C. N. Vidhya Lakshmi, Gibin G. Varghese and Srinidhya Ganesh Kumar focus specifically on accessibility and inclusive design, emphasizing that AI-powered language learning tools must be intentionally developed to serve learners with diverse linguistic backgrounds, abilities, and technological circumstances. Through discussions of adaptive feedback systems, multilingual interfaces, assistive technologies, and accessibility-centered design principles, the chapter demonstrates that inclusion must be embedded throughout every stage of AI development if equitable learning environments are to be realized.

Finally, Section 3 "AI Applications, Pedagogical Practice, and Learner Experience", includes the final four chapters of the volume and explores concrete AI applications, innovative pedagogical strategies, and case studies that illuminate how AI affects motivation, identity, representation, and educational justice from the perspective of learners and educators.

Chapter 8, "Exploring GenAI for Multilingual News Analysis and Its Pedagogical Potential for the Language Classroom", explores the educational possibilities of generative AI through multilingual news analysis. Framed within a multiliteracies perspective, Lisa Marie Brinkmann and Liudmila Shafirova illustrate how comparing AI-generated news content across multiple languages enables learners to recognize linguistic variation, identify embedded biases, and critically examine how meaning shifts across cultural contexts. This contribution highlights AI's potential not only as a language learning tool but also as a catalyst for critical multilingual awareness and media literacy.

Representation and learner motivation are examined in Chapter 9, "AI-Generated Popular Culture Visuals, Representation, and Motivation: A Case Study in Foreign Language Education Using the Baris Alper Yilmaz Figure", through a case study involving AI-generated visuals of a culturally familiar public figure in English language classrooms. Kardelen Aslan and Kadri Nazlı demonstrate how culturally relevant AI-generated content can strengthen learner engagement and support performance while simultaneously encouraging thoughtful reflection on the ethical and environmental implications of AI-generated media. The chapter reinforces the importance of culturally responsive AI applications that recognize learners' identities and lived experiences.

In Chapter 10, "A Comparative Study Towards Ethical and Inclusive AI in Language Learning: Examining Equity, Transparency, and Sustainability in Digital Language Education", I. Samuel Peter James, D. Magdalene Delighta Angeline and T. Prabakaran broaden the conversation by presenting a comparative examination of ethical and inclusive AI practices in language learning. Addressing themes of fairness, transparency, sustainability, and accessibility, the chapter proposes a conceptual framework that integrates human-centered design, participatory governance, and linguistic diversity into AI-supported educational systems. In doing so, it offers valuable guidance for educators, institutions, and policymakers seeking to develop AI initiatives that prioritize both technological innovation and social responsibility.

The volume concludes with a forward-looking examination of linguistic identities and educational justice through insights from the Pluridentities Horizon Europe Project. Focusing on the preservation of linguistic capital within increasingly multilingual societies, in Chapter 11, "Fostering Linguistic Identities and Educational Justice through AIALL: Insights from the Pluridentities Project", Cristina A. Huertas-Abril demonstrates how AI-assisted language learning technologies can support multilingualism while strengthening learners' awareness of linguistic diversity, equity, and social justice. By connecting large-scale educational research with practical AI applications, the chapter reinforces the central message of this volume: that responsible AI integration must celebrate linguistic diversity, empower learners, and contribute to more inclusive educational systems.

CONCLUDING REMARKS

As the contributions in this volume demonstrate, the future of AI in language education cannot be measured solely by technological sophistication or instructional efficiency. Rather, its success will depend upon our collective commitment to ensuring that innovation is guided by principles of equity, equality, justice, and respect for linguistic and cultural diversity. AI possesses remarkable potential to transform language learning by expanding access, personalizing instruction, and supporting learners in ways that were previously unimaginable. At the same time, without careful attention to issues of representation, accessibility, bias, and ethical governance, these same technologies risk reproducing and even amplifying long-standing educational inequalities.

The chapters presented throughout this volume remind us that equitable AI integration is a shared responsibility extending across researchers, educators, teacher educators, developers, policymakers, institutions, and communities. Meaningful progress will require interdisciplinary collaboration, critical reflection, inclusive design practices, and policies that prioritize human dignity alongside technological advancement. The diverse perspectives represented in this collection illustrate that creating just AI-enhanced language learning environments is not a singular achievement but an ongoing process of evaluation, adaptation, and advocacy.

As editors, we hope this volume encourages readers to view AI not simply as a collection of emerging tools, but as an opportunity to reimagine language education in ways that promote fairness, amplify diverse voices, and expand educational opportunities for learners from every linguistic, cultural, and social background. We also hope the scholarship presented here inspires continued research, informed dialogue, and innovative practice that places educational justice at the heart of AI development and implementation.

Ultimately, the future of AI-enhanced language education will be shaped by the choices we make today. By embracing innovation with critical awareness and an unwavering commitment to inclusion, we can ensure that AI becomes a catalyst for more equitable, accessible, and socially just language education worldwide. It is our sincere hope that this volume serves as both a valuable scholarly resource and a call to action for all those committed to building a future in which technological progress and educational justice advance together.

Francisco Javier Palacios-Hidalgo
Universidad de Córdoba, Spain

Carlos Lindade
Universidade do Porto, Portugal

Section 1
Conceptual and Theoretical Foundations

Chapter 1

AI and the Quest for Equity, Equality, and Justice in Language Education:
An Introduction

Francisco Javier Palacios-Hidalgo
http://orcid.org/0000-0002-4326-209X
Universidad de Córdoba, Spain

Carlos Lindade
http://orcid.org/0000-0001-5742-8874
Universidade do Porto, Portugal

ABSTRACT

This chapter establishes a conceptual and critical examination of artificial intelligence in language education through the integrated lenses of equity, equality, and justice. It argues that the integration of artificial intelligence into language learning constitutes not a neutral technological advancement but a socio-political intervention, one that redistributes opportunities, validates or erases linguistic identities, and reconfigures power relations among learners, educators, and institutions. The chapter defines and distinguishes the core concepts of equity, equality, and justice as they apply to artificial intelligence-mediated language education, maps the landscape of current artificial intelligence applications and their implications for educational equity, and introduces theoretical frameworks that inform justice-

DOI: 10.4018/979-8-3373-7749-0.ch001

oriented approaches in the field. It concludes by articulating a call to action for researchers and teachers to collectively shape artificial intelligence futures that centre the most marginalised learners.

INTRODUCTION: THE AI REVOLUTION IN LANGUAGE EDUCATION

Artificial Intelligence (AI) is no longer an emerging opportunity in language education; it is a present infrastructure that quietly but powerfully mediates how learners read, write, listen, and speak. As Thorne (2024) argues, AI technologies have become so integrated into everyday educational practice that their presence is now normative and often invisible, yet they fundamentally reshape learners' engagement with language. Indeed, systems such as adaptive learning platforms, AI chatbots, automated scoring engines, and speech-recognition-based pronunciation tutors now sit alongside, and sometimes in front of, human teachers in language classrooms and self-access environments around the world and having have become prevalent tools that actively mediate students' learning of writing and speaking skills across diverse educational contexts (Zhu & Liu, 2025). Recent empirical work and systematic reviews indicate that AI-mediated instruction is already producing measurable gains in language achievement, motivation, and self-regulated learning for many English as a foreign language (EFL) learners, signaling not a distant future but an ongoing reconfiguration of language education practices at scale (Ekizer, 2025; Gu & Liu, 2025; Xiong & Teo, 2025).

The scale and speed of AI adoption in language learning contexts have accelerated sharply over the past decade, particularly since the widespread availability of large language models and commercial learning apps (Albedah, 2025; Li et al., 2025). Systematic reviews document a rapid proliferation of AI applications across higher education and, increasingly, elementary and secondary education and non-formal learning settings, with especially dense activity in Asian EFL contexts (e.g., Du & Daniel, 2024; Li et al., 2025). These syntheses show AI being used for core instructional functions—writing support, vocabulary learning, reading comprehension, and speaking practice—rather than remaining as optional add-ons. As a result, AI systems are beginning to shape not only micro-level interactions (for example, a single feedback comment) but also macro-level trajectories of curriculum design, assessment practices, and teacher roles in language education (Georgiou, 2026; Ghiasvand & Seyri, 2025; Zhao et al., 2025).

The transformative promise driving this rapid adoption is fascinating. AI-enhanced platforms have been shown to provide highly personalized and adaptive learning pathways, offering differentiated tasks, instant feedback, and tailored scaffolding that can respond to learners' performance in real time (Huertas-Abril & Palacios-Hidalgo, 2025). Studies report that such systems can increase learners' motivation, engagement, and autonomy by enabling self-paced practice and by making otherwise rote activities more interactive and gamified (Mohebbi, 2025). For learners who face geographical, temporal, or institutional barriers, AI tools and Generative AI (GenAI) chatbots can expand accessibility by offering plenty of practice opportunities, multimodal explanations, and support in multiple languages, often at relatively low marginal cost once infrastructure is available (Cong-Lem et al., 2025). At the institutional level, AI offers significant efficiencies by automating routine assessment tasks, generating teaching and learning materials, and supporting large student cohorts at a scale that traditional staffing models struggle to achieve (Albedah, 2025; Chen et al., 2025).

However, embedded in this promise is a crucial and often under-examined question: for whom does such a promise materialize, and at what cost? Systematic reviews and critical analyses caution that access to AI-enhanced language learning remains uneven, mediated by disparities in connectivity, devices, institutional capacity, and teacher training (Davin et al., 2026; Zhu & Wang, 2025). There is also a growing concern that AI systems trained on unrepresentative data may encode and reproduce linguistic, cultural, and socioeconomic biases, thereby privileging certain accents, varieties of English, or communicative norms while marginalizing others. For instance, Kang and Hirschi (2025) document that automatic speech recognition systems and automated assessment tools consistently underperform for speakers of non-standard dialects and accented speech, perpetuating the same kinds of biased judgments historically observed in human listeners. Moreover, entrusting feedback, assessment, and interaction to opaque AI systems raises pressing issues of surveillance, data extraction, and diminishing teacher and learner autonomy, with particular implications for already marginalized groups (Georgiou, 2026). The same mechanisms that enable personalization can, in contexts of unequal governance and resources, deepen existing divides in who benefits from high-quality language education and who is subjected to lower-cost, higher-surveillance AI solutions (Weng & Fu, 2025).

Against this backdrop, this chapter advances a thesis that moves beyond familiar narratives of innovation and efficiency. AI in language education must be evaluated not only in terms of learning gains, engagement metrics, or cost-effectiveness, but also in relation to its consequences for equity, equality, and justice across diverse learners, teachers, and communities. Emerging scholarship on AI and English language teaching highlights both the potential of GenAI and other tools to promote more inclusive and accessible learning environments, and the risks of exacerbating educational divides if its use is driven primarily by market logics or technocratic optimization (Kannadhasan, 2025; Selvi, 2025). The task, therefore, is not simply to decide whether to adopt AI, but to critically interrogate how AI is designed, implemented, and governed in specific language education ecologies, and whose interests and voices are centered in that process. This chapter situates the current AI revolution in language education within broader debates about social justice, arguing that any responsible engagement with AI must address questions of distribution, recognition, and participation in the design and use of these technologies.

DEFINING THE CORE CONCEPTS: EQUITY, EQUALITY, AND JUSTICE

Establishing clear conceptual boundaries is crucial when discussing the role of AI in promoting fairness within language education. Terms such as *equality*, *equity*, and *justice* are frequently used interchangeably in policy documents and scholarly debates, yet each carries distinct implications. Drawing on critical pedagogy and educational research, this section offers working definitions of these three concepts and explores their relevance for evaluating and designing AI systems and tools in language learning contexts.

Equality: Same for All

At its core, *equality* denotes the principle of providing all learners with identical resources, tools, and opportunities. It reflects a belief in uniform access as the foundation of fairness—an ideal deeply rooted in liberal democratic traditions of universal education. For example, a school implementing a single AI-powered language learning platform for every student demonstrates an "equal" approach: everyone receives the same tool, curriculum, and interface.

However, equality has well-known limitations. It assumes that learners begin from the same starting point and face comparable challenges, overlooking structural inequities related to socioeconomic status, linguistic background, disability, or digital literacy (Ariel & Hayak, 2025). In practice, treating unequals equally can perpetuate disadvantages. Critical scholarship demonstrates how students in under-resourced schools who receive the same AI tools as their privileged counterparts are often tracked into passive "consumer" roles, while privileged students learn to become "creators" of AI, perpetuating systemic inequality under what authors term a "veil of innovation" (Ariel & Hayak, 2025). In the sphere of AI, mere access does not guarantee fair outcomes—especially if the technology's design privileges certain language varieties, cultural norms, or modes of communication (Cong-Lem et al., 2025). Thus, equality is a necessary but insufficient condition for fairness in AI-mediated language education; achieving genuine justice requires moving beyond uniform access toward equity—an approach that considers contextual factors such as infrastructure, digital literacy, and sociocultural responsiveness.

Equity: Fairness According to Need

Equity moves beyond uniformity by focusing on fairness according to need. It calls for differentiated allocation of resources and support so that all learners can achieve comparable outcomes. In educational contexts, equity recognizes that students arrive with varying linguistic repertoires, learning histories, and degrees of access to technology. Therefore, equitable systems are designed to meet learners where they are. Bang and Lee (2024) articulate this distinction clearly: while earlier AI automation systems focused on educational equality through uniform resources, more recent AI-driven customized learning systems aim for educational equity by providing differentiated support tailored to individual needs, ensuring comparable learning outcomes across diverse student populations.

In the context of AI, equity is often operationalized through adaptive and personalized learning environments. For instance, an AI language tutor that adjusts feedback intensity, pacing, or modality based on each learner's proficiency level exemplifies an equity-oriented design. Yet equity also invites critical scrutiny: adaptive algorithms may still encode bias if they are trained on narrow datasets or optimized for dominant language varieties (Bang & Lee, 2024; Cong-Lem et al., 2025). Without attention to who defines the criteria of "need" or "success," AI could unintentionally reproduce cultural hierarchies while appearing equitable on the surface. As Cong-Lem et al. (2025) document, GenAI can widen disparities through English-dominant linguistic norms and algorithmic bias, underscoring that equity must be understood as systemic, relational, and contextually contingent rather than merely technical.

Justice: Addressing Systemic Inequalities

While equity addresses differential support within existing systems, *justice* interrogates and transforms the systems themselves. It involves examining the structural, institutional, and epistemic conditions that sustain inequality. Building on Fraser's tripartite model, justice in education and AI involves at least three interrelated dimensions that have been increasingly applied to language education contexts (Ramezanzadeh & Ebadi, 2025):

- **Distributive justice:** It concerns the fair allocation of material and digital resources. In language education, this includes equitable access to AI tools, data, and infrastructure across regions and communities. The *Australian*

Framework for Artificial Intelligence in Higher Education (Lodge et al., 2025) explicitly operationalizes this dimension by requiring institutions to ensure that AI resources reach students from socioeconomically disadvantaged backgrounds, rural and remote areas, and non-English speaking communities.

- **Recognitional justice:** It focuses on whose languages, identities, and cultures are visible, valued, and validated. In the AI context, recognitional justice demands inclusive datasets, linguistic diversity, and culturally responsive design that avoid defaulting to dominant norms such as "standard" English. Recent empirical research demonstrates that AI-powered language activities can either validate or marginalize learners' identities depending on whether the design acknowledges diverse linguistic and cultural backgrounds (Ramezanzadeh & Ebadi, 2025).
- **Representational justice:** It examines who participates in shaping decisions about AI design, implementation, and governance. This dimension emphasizes the inclusion of teachers, learners, and marginalized communities in AI policy and development processes. In this light, policy frameworks should recognize that meaningful participation requires governance structures that include students from diverse backgrounds, indigenous leaders, accessibility experts, and ethicists in decision-making bodies. The European Center for Not-for-Profit Law (2025) explicitly recommends that governance structures include multi-stakeholder groups with representatives from government, civil society, technical experts, academia, and affected communities, ensuring that marginalized groups—including linguistic minorities, persons with disabilities, and indigenous populations—have meaningful seats at design tables rather than merely being consulted after decisions are made. This approach, grounded in the principle of "nothing about us without us", demands that those most impacted by AI systems participate actively in shaping their development and governance. Moreover, as Ramezanzadeh and Ebadi (2025) demonstrate, creating spaces for learner voices and emotional narratives in AI-mediated activities is essential for achieving genuine representational justice in language education.

Justice, therefore, goes beyond compensating for inequality; it aspires to reform the underlying relations of power that define what counts as legitimate language, knowledge, and technology. The ultimate goal of Fraser's model is what she terms "participatory parity"—the condition in which all members of society can interact with one another as peers, free from institutionalized obstacles to economic independence, cultural devaluation, or political marginalization (Hargreaves et al., 2025). An AI system that foregrounds linguistic diversity, includes community participation in design, and is governed through transparent and accountable processes moves closer toward enabling such participatory parity for all learners. These systems must be evaluated not merely by their efficiency or personalization capabilities, but by their capacity to enable all learners to participate as equals in educational practices.

Bringing the Concepts Together

Taken together, these concepts form a continuum of fairness: *equality* provides baseline access, *equity* ensures differentiated support, and *justice* seeks to transform the conditions that generate inequity in the first place. For AI in language education, this means moving from merely providing equal technological access, to designing equitable systems that adapt to diverse learners, and ultimately to pursuing justice by addressing systemic biases in language policy, data collection, and algorithmic governance.

This chapter adopts *justice* as its guiding aspiration. While equality and equity offer essential starting points, they remain incomplete without an explicit commitment to transforming the historical and sociopolitical structures that shape language learning opportunities. AI, if designed and used thoroughly, holds the potential not only to personalize learning (Palacios-Hidalgo, 2025a) but also to democratize linguistic futures.

THE LANDSCAPE OF AI IN LANGUAGE EDUCATION: PROMISES AND RISKS

AI is rapidly transforming the landscape of language education. From mobile-based chatbots to fully integrated adaptive learning ecosystems, AI tools now shape how learners practice, receive feedback, and interact with linguistic content. Research has identified seven key AI technologies commonly used in language learning—natural language processing, data-driven learning, automated writing evaluation, computerized dynamic assessment, intelligent tutoring systems, automatic speech recognition, and chatbots—each contributing uniquely to personalized and interactive learning experiences (Son et al., 2025). Yet alongside their promise, these technologies raise complex questions about fairness, access, and human agency. This section provides an overview of the major categories of AI tools currently in use and situates them within their educational promises and justice-related risks.

Types of AI in Language Learning

AI in language education encompasses a range of systems that automate, augment, or simulate aspects of instruction, assessment, and communication. Among the most prominent are intelligent tutoring systems (ITS)—adaptive learning platforms that analyze learner data in real time to personalize instruction, adjust task difficulty, provide targeted feedback, and track progress toward learning goals (Chen et al., 2025; Son et al., 2025). Automated writing evaluation (AWE) tools use natural language processing to analyze written texts and generate feedback on grammar, style, coherence, and organization (Chen et al., 2025; Zhu & Wang, 2025). Speech recognition and pronunciation tools evaluate spoken input to assess pronunciation, rhythm, and fluency, often providing corrective feedback or modeling target pronunciation (Ekizer, 2025; Son et al., 2025). The emergence of GenAI, particularly large language models such as ChatGPT, has also introduced capabilities for text generation, question answering, dialogue simulation, and support for reflective or creative writing tasks (Li et al., 2025; Xiong & Teo, 2025). Machine translation (MT) engines like Google Translate and DeepL enable cross-linguistic communication and support multilingual learning environments (Cong-Lem et al., 2025). Finally, chatbots and conversational agents serve as AI interlocutors designed to simulate human conversation, offering learners opportunities to practice language in interactive, low-pressure contexts (Gu & Liu, 2025; Mohebbi, 2025). Together, these systems redefine what it means to teach and learn a language, extending the classroom into digitally mediated, data-intensive environments (Georgiou, 2026; Thorne, 2024).

The Promises and Risks of AI in Language Education

Proponents of AI in language education emphasize its transformative potential to make language learning more accessible, efficient, and inclusive. Yet, as critical scholarship warns, these same technologies can reproduce and amplify existing inequities when implemented without deliberate attention to power, representation, and inclusion. Table 1 synthesizes the key promises alongside their corresponding justice-related risks, drawing on recent empirical research and systematic reviews to illustrate the dual nature of AI's role in reshaping language education:

Table 1. Promises and risks of AI in language education

Dimension	Potential Benefits	Justice Concerns
Personalization	AI tailors instructional content to individual learners' skills and goals, enabling differentiated support that responds to learner needs in real time (Chen et al., 2025; Liu & Zhang, 2024).	Adaptive algorithms may encode bias when trained on narrow datasets or optimized for dominant language varieties, reproducing cultural hierarchies while appearing equitable (Bang & Lee, 2024; Cong-Lem et al., 2025).
Accessibility and Scale	Learners gain opportunities for feedback and practice, independent of time or place; low-cost or free AI applications may extend learning to underserved populations (Huertas-Abril & Palacios-Hidalgo, 2025; Palacios-Hidalgo, 2025a).	Unequal access to reliable devices, connectivity, and digital literacy limits who can benefit; in contexts of unequal governance, personalization mechanisms can deepen divides between those receiving high-quality tools and those subjected to lower-cost solutions (Ghiasvand & Seyri, 2025; Wang, 2026).
Teacher Support	Automation of repetitive tasks such as grading or feedback allows educators to prioritize creative, interpersonal forms of teaching (Chen et al., 2025; Zhu & Wang, 2025).	Automated systems risk undermining professional judgment and reducing teachers' role to monitors rather than co-creators of learning experiences; teachers in under-resourced contexts may face de-skilling rather than empowerment (Georgiou, 2026; Ghiasvand & Seyri, 2025).
Data-Driven Insights	Analytics generated from learner interactions reveal patterns of progress and difficulty, enabling more informed pedagogical decisions (Chen et al., 2025; Zhu & Wang, 2025).	Extensive collection of learner data—frequently without transparent consent—raises ethical concerns about surveillance, autonomy, and exploitation, particularly for already marginalized groups (Cong-Lem et al., 2025; Georgiou, 2026).
Linguistic and Cultural Representation	AI tools can support multilingual learning environments and offer access to diverse linguistic resources (Palacios-Hidalgo, 2025a).	AI models often perform less accurately for speakers of non-dominant languages, dialects, and accents; prioritization of major world languages in data and design marginalizes minoritized or local languages, eroding linguistic diversity and erasing cultural perspectives (Kang & Hirschi, 2025).
Learner Agency and Autonomy	AI-powered platforms can foster self-regulated learning by enabling goal setting, progress tracking, and independent practice (Gu & Liu, 2025; Mohebbi, 2025).	Opaque systems can erode learner agency, particularly when learners cannot understand AI-generated assessments (Ariel & Hayak, 2025; Georgiou, 2026).
Equity and Democratization	AI-assisted language learning tools hold significant potential for democratizing language education by making it more accessible and effective for learners regardless of abilities, needs, or circumstances (Palacios-Hidalgo, 2025a).	AI can reproduce cultural hierarchies while appearing equitable on the surface; GenAI may widen disparities through English-dominant linguistic norms and algorithmic bias (Bang & Lee, 2024; Cong-Lem et al., 2025).

Source: Authors' own elaboration.

These promises reflect the equality dimension discussed in previous sections—broadening access to tools and learning opportunities. However, the dangers illustrate that technical innovation alone cannot guarantee fairness. Without deliberate attention to structural conditions, representation, and inclusion, AI risks reinforcing rather than remedying systemic inequalities. Achieving justice-oriented AI in language education requires moving beyond a narrow focus on efficiency and personalization toward a framework that centers distributive fairness, recognitional validation of diverse languages and identities, and representational inclusion of marginalized communities in design and governance (Lodge et al., 2025; Ramezanzadeh & Ebadi, 2025).

The Gap: From Technical Solutions to Justice-Oriented Transformation

Most existing responses to the ethical and social challenges of AI in language education have centered on technical solutions. Researchers and developers have sought to improve algorithmic fairness by curating more inclusive datasets, mitigating bias through rebalancing techniques, or enhancing transparency in model design (Albedah, 2025; Bang & Lee, 2024). These efforts are valuable and necessary, as they represent strong attempts to make AI more equitable and accountable. Yet they remain constrained by the logic of correction rather than transformation. They aim to fix what is wrong within the existing system, rather than to question the broader social arrangements and values that the system reproduces. As Ariel and Hayak (2025) demonstrate, even well-intentioned technical interventions can create a "veil of innovation" that obscures deeper educational injustice, masking inequalities in access, agency, and technological fluency while tracking disadvantaged students into passive "consumer" roles rather than empowering them as "creators" of AI. Khari (2026) similarly argues that achieving genuine educational justice requires moving "beyond the algorithm"—i.e., beyond technical fixes like inclusive datasets or bias mitigation—toward participatory governance and policy frameworks that transform the power relations embedded in AI systems. Without such structural transformation, technical solutions risk reproducing the very hierarchies they claim to address, offering the appearance of progress while leaving underlying systems of privilege and exclusion intact.

Therefore, a justice-oriented approach demands a shift in perspective—from asking *how can we make AI fairer?* to asking *fairer for whom, according to whose standards, and toward what goals?* This repositioning reframes technology not as a neutral instrument, but as a social and cultural artifact shaped by—and shaping—power relations. In the context of language education, this means interrogating how AI systems encode dominant ideologies about what counts as legitimate language, whose norms of proficiency are privileged, and which voices are systematically silenced or omitted from data and design. Ultimately, a justice-oriented reimagination of AI in language education calls not only for fairer systems but for *different futures*—ones in which technology serves as a tool for linguistic pluralism, cultural sustainability, and collective empowerment. The task, then, is not simply to make AI more inclusive within existing paradigms of language education but to leverage AI as a means of transforming those paradigms themselves.

THEORETICAL FRAMEWORKS FOR JUSTICE-ORIENTED AI IN LANGUAGE EDUCATION

To engage critically and constructively with AI in language education, scholars and practitioners require more than technical or procedural knowledge—they need theoretical frameworks that reveal the social, cultural, and political dimensions of technology. The frameworks introduced in this section serve as conceptual lenses for analyzing how AI can either reproduce or challenge inequities in language learning. These paradigms, rooted in critical traditions across education, sociology, and philosophy, are not mutually exclusive. Rather, they intersect and complement each other, offering a rich toolkit for justice-oriented inquiry and practice.

Critical (Language) Pedagogy

Paulo Freire's *critical pedagogy* conceives education as a practice of freedom rather than domination (1970). In opposition to what he termed the "banking model" of education—where learners are positioned as passive recipients of knowledge deposited by teachers—Freire envisions learning as a dialogical process oriented toward the development of critical consciousness (Freire, 1970; Crookes, 2021). Within this framework, AI is reframed not merely as an instructional delivery mechanism but as a site for reflection, questioning, and transformative engagement with knowledge and power (Palacios-Hidalgo, 2025b; Román Mendoza, 2025).

Applied to AI-mediated language education, a Freirean lens invites both teachers and learners to critically interrogate the social and political dimensions of the technologies that shape their learning environments (Kildė, 2025; Palacios-Hidalgo, 2025b). This entails asking fundamental questions about whose interests are embedded in AI systems, who designs the tools that mediate communication, and whose worldviews are reflected or erased in their design and outputs. Critical (language) pedagogy thus repositions AI from a neutral instrument of efficiency to a catalyst for dialogue about knowledge construction, power relations, and voice in digitally mediated contexts. Guided by Freire's ideals, such an approach insists that the integration of AI must serve goals of equity, social justice, and the cultivation of critical consciousness—not merely the optimization of learning outcomes (Chaitani, 2026).

Linguistic Justice and Linguistic Human Rights

Language is not merely a neutral medium for transmitting information; it is the very foundation of cultural identity, belonging, and participation in society (Skutnabb-Kangas & Phillipson, 2022; Phillipson, 1992). Theories of linguistic justice and linguistic human rights, most notably advanced by Tove Skutnabb-Kangas and Robert Phillipson, frame language as a fundamental human right and a core dimension of both individual and collective dignity. They argue that every person has the right to acquire, use, and develop their mother tongue and to access education through it (Skutnabb-Kangas, 2000; Skutnabb-Kangas & Dunbar, 2010). When learners are denied this right—whether by political neglect, assimilationist policies, or technological exclusion—they experience a form of structural injustice that undermines both educational equity and cultural survival (Skutnabb-Kangas, 2000).

From this perspective, linguistic rights are inseparable from the broader human rights framework (Skutnabb-Kangas & Phillipson, 2022). The right to education, freedom of expression, and participation in public life cannot be realized without the ability to learn and communicate in one's own language (Skutnabb-Kangas, 2000). Linguistic deprivation is thus not a minor inconvenience but a profound violation of cultural rights. Skutnabb-Kangas (2000) describes this process as "linguistic genocide": the systematic dismantling of linguistic diversity through social and institutional pressures that render certain languages invisible, undervalued, or obsolete. In schools, this manifests when minoritized languages are framed as barriers to learning, while dominant languages are positioned as indicators of progress and success (Phillipson & Meighan, 2025). Justice, from this standpoint, requires not merely tolerance of linguistic difference but the active safeguarding and cultivation of multilingualism as a foundation for human flourishing.

AI now occupies a powerful position in mediating linguistic access and representation. Language learning platforms, automated translation systems, and speech-recognition technologies increasingly frame how individuals engage with language in educational settings. Nevertheless, these systems are not neutral infrastructures but rather constructed within existing hierarchies of linguistic power (Ariel & Hayak, 2025). The majority of AI models are trained on digital corpora dominated by a small number of languages, primarily those of the Global North, with English dominating training data (Patterson, 2025). As a result, AI systems frequently fail to recognize or process minoritized languages, dialects, or accents, effectively rendering them invisible within computational space (Albeihi & Rice, 2025). This exclusion has direct implications for linguistic human rights. A student whose accent is not recognized by an automated pronunciation tool learns that their voice does not "fit" the norms encoded in the system; a community whose language is absent from translation engines faces obstacles in education, healthcare, and participation in the digital economy. In both cases, the issue reflects deep processes of misrecognition and cultural marginalization. AI technologies risk reinforcing a new form of digital linguistic imperialism, amplifying the dominance of a few global languages while erasing the visibility of countless others. Without deliberate intervention, AI systems will continue to serve as instruments of linguistic hierarchy rather than tools for democratizing access to language education.

Nevertheless, AI also holds unprecedented potential to strengthen linguistic rights when designed with justice-oriented principles. Machine learning and natural language processing can facilitate the documentation, revitalization, and teaching of endangered languages (Ingram, 2025). The development of AI must involve the speakers and teachers of these languages as co-creators rather than passive beneficiaries, ensuring that technology aligns with their linguistic and cultural aspirations (Huertas-Abril & Palacios-Hidalgo, 2025). Promoting linguistic justice through AI thus requires a dual commitment: defending linguistic rights against technological forms of exclusion and mobilizing AI as a resource for sustaining the worlds that languages carry. This entails pedagogical practices that encourage learners and educators to question how technology defines linguistic legitimacy and to advocate for more inclusive and pluralistic digital environments. In this vision, AI becomes not a force of homogenization but a means of collective linguistic empowerment.

Critical Race Theory and Intersectionality

Critical Race Theory, initially developed within legal studies through the foundational work of Kimberlé Crenshaw and other scholars, offers a powerful analytical lens for understanding how racism operates not merely as individual prejudice but as a structural feature embedded within laws, institutions, and everyday practices—including education and technology (Crenshaw, 2013; Delgado & Stefancic, 2023). When applied to the domain of AI-mediated language learning, Critical Race Theory reveals how algorithmic systems are profoundly shaped by historical patterns of inequality and by assumptions rooted in dominant cultural and linguistic norms. These systems often reproduce, rather than mitigate, racial and linguistic hierarchies by privileging standard language varieties, accents, and cultural references associated with socially dominant groups (Noble, 2018). Recent scholarship has demonstrated that large language models and automated assessment tools exhibit raciolinguistic biases, associating certain speech forms with lower social status or lacking the accuracy required to fairly evaluate learners from non-dominant linguistic backgrounds (e.g., Schneider & Oliveira, 2025).

Crenshaw's concept of *intersectionality* further deepens this analysis by showing that experiences of exclusion are rarely singular or unidimensional (Crenshaw, 1994). Learners' identities are constituted through the intersection of multiple axes, including identity, race, class, gender, and language, and each of these dimensions can amplify or compound the effects of technological bias. A multilingual transgender woman of color, for instance, may encounter barriers not only because her accent is underrepresented in training data but also because the platform's model assumes cultural and socioeconomic conditions distant to her own reality. Such instances highlight how AI can perpetuate the invisibility of multiply marginalized learners, whose complex identities are illegible to systems designed around reductionist, normative categories (Tanksley, 2024). As Ariel and Hayak (2025) argue, this dynamic reinforces the "veil of innovation", where technological solutions mask inequalities in access, agency, and recognition.

Justice-oriented language education must therefore attend to these intersections, using AI not simply as a mechanism for individualized learning but as a lens for uncovering whose linguistic and cultural experiences are systematically misrepresented or erased. A Critical Race Theory and intersectional perspective insists that fairness in AI cannot be achieved through surface-level inclusion alone—such as diversifying datasets or adding more languages to a platform—but requires an ongoing recognition of power, history, and identity in both the design and employment of educational technologies. Consequently, educators, researchers, and developers must engage in critical reflection on how AI systems are implicated in broader structures of inequality, and actively work to center the voices and experiences of those most often rendered invisible within digital learning environments.

Decolonial and Southern Theories

Decolonial and Southern theoretical perspectives, articulated by scholars such as Mignolo (2011) and de Sousa Santos (2014), offer a fundamental challenge to the dominance of the Global North in shaping what is considered legitimate knowledge, language, and progress. These scholars argue that modern systems of science, education, and technology—including AI—are embedded within historical structures of coloniality that systematically privilege Western ways of knowing while marginalizing the languages and cultures of the Global South (Mignolo & Walsh, 2018). Mignolo (2025) raises critical questions about the impact of AI on what he terms the "colonial matrix of power", interrogating both its role in perpetuating existing hierarchies and its potential to contribute to a decolonial perspective.

The concept of *algorithmic coloniality* has emerged to describe this situation where algorithms operate as historical artefacts built from data that privilege certain languages and histories (Fataar, 2025). AI is not a neutral innovation but a site where colonial hierarchies are reproduced through data, design, and linguistic selection. Certainly, language education urges a fundamental rethinking of global AI development, as most large language models rely on data sourced disproportionately from

English and other major European languages, giving force to Northern intellectual traditions while relegating Southern and Indigenous knowledge systems to the margins. This asymmetry leads to a form of injustice in which the linguistic and cultural identities of regions like Africa, Latin America, South Asia or Oceania become invisible in digital learning environments (de Sousa Santos, 2014; Mohamed et al., 2020). As Fataar (2025) argues, when "[Indigenous] names are misspelt, indigenous ideas mistranslated, or local histories omitted, AI reproduces the epistemic erasures of empire" (para. 6). The result is a subtle continuation of colonial logic, where the linguistic diversity of the world is measured against Eurocentric standards of "valid" or "useful" language. Recent scholarship has documented how AI-based translation, grading, and recommendation systems systematically underperform when applied to regional languages and non-Western rhetorical traditions, reinforcing what de Sousa Santos (2014) terms "epistemicide"—the destruction of alternative ways of knowing. This dynamic, described as "hegemonic AI" by Ricaurte (2023), consolidates a colonial and patriarchal world model that threatens the survival of local Indigenous cultures and knowledge systems.

Critical Data Studies and Algorithmic Justice

Critical data studies, advanced by scholars such as Benjamin (2019), Noble (2018), and O'Neil (2016), have challenged the notion that data and algorithms constitute neutral instruments, revealing instead how they are products of human choices, values and power relations. Benjamin's concept of the *New Jim Code* (2019) illuminates how emerging technologies can hide, speed up, and deepen discrimination while appearing neutral when compared to the racism of a previous era. This perspective demonstrates that algorithmic systems encode inequity in multiple ways: by explicitly amplifying racial hierarchies, by ignoring and replicating social divisions, or by aiming to fix racial bias but ultimately achieving quite the opposite (Benjamin, 2019). Similarly, Noble's (2018) analysis of search engines reveals how data discrimination operates as a real social problem, where private interests and the status of internet platforms produce biased algorithms that privilege whiteness and discriminate against people of color, particularly women of color. O'Neil (2016) extends this critique by exposing what she terms "weapons of math destruction"—systems that are opaque, unregulated, and whose decisions cannot be questioned.

In educational contexts, and especially in language learning, these assumptions can invisibly structure how knowledge, competence, and intelligence are defined. The datasets that feed AI systems, the categories they construct, and the patterns they privilege reflect particular social histories: when language models and assessment tools are trained primarily on dominant linguistic and cultural norms, they codify existing hierarchies, penalizing difference. Recent research on sociolinguistic auto-coding has demonstrated that machine-learning fairness problems extend to language technologies, where algorithms can produce biased predictions by overlearning group characteristics, effectively encoding gender and racial bias in automated linguistic analysis (Villarreal, 2024). These findings underscore that fairness in AI-mediated language education cannot be achieved through technical solutions alone but rather requires ongoing critical examination of how power, history, and identity are embedded in algorithmic design.

Sociocultural Theory and Mediated Learning

Vygotsky's sociocultural theory (SCT) offers a foundational yet frequently underutilized lens for understanding how language learning is shaped by social interaction, cultural tools, and mediated activity. Central to SCT is the concept of "Zone of Proximal Development" (ZPD), the cognitive and communicative space between what a learner can achieve independently and what becomes possible through guided interaction with a more capable partner (Vygotsky, 1978). From this perspective, learning is never a purely individual cognitive achievement but rather emerges through collaborative, historically situated engagement with culturally meaningful artifacts and social interlocutors. Mediation—the use of tools, symbols, and social relationships to organize and extend cognition—is the defining mechanism through which learners internalize new competences and develop agency in the target language.

Lantolf and Thorne (2006) have demonstrated comprehensively that SCT reframes second language acquisition not as the product of individual cognitive processing but as an emergent outcome of social interaction embedded in specific cultural and institutional activity systems. This perspective carries profound implications for language education: it foregrounds the quality and responsiveness of pedagogical interaction, the collaborative nature of language use, and the importance of culturally contextual and dialogically rich learning environments. In contrast to behaviorist or information-processing models, SCT insists that linguistic development is inseparable from the social conditions in which it unfolds, and that learners' identities, communities, and histories are always active participants in the learning process, a recognition with direct consequences for how educators evaluate the equity of any mediated learning encounter.

AI tools now function as powerful, if equally distributed, mediating artifacts in the Vygotskian sense. A well-designed AI conversational agent or writing feedback system can serve as a ZPD-extending interlocutor: offering scaffolding calibrated to the learner's current proficiency, prompting collaborative elaboration, and making otherwise inaccessible forms of language practice available at scale (Thorne, 2024; Zhu & Liu, 2025). Research applying SCT frameworks to intelligent tutoring systems and automated writing evaluation tools suggests that the interactional richness and adaptability of AI feedback determines whether it genuinely promotes developmental growth within the learner's ZPD or merely confirms existing competences without generative challenge (Poehner, 2024). When embedded in collaborative and dialogically organized instructional designs, AI holds the potential to extend the kinds of mediated practice that research has consistently associated with deep language development.

However, a sociocultural analysis equally exposes critical inequities in how AI mediation operates across social and linguistic contexts. Mediation is never socially neutral: the tools through which learners engage with language carry within them specific cultural histories, normative assumptions about "correct" language use, and implicit hierarchies rooted in dominant sociolinguistic traditions. AI language tools built predominantly on Global North corpora scaffold learners toward hegemonic norms of English, potentially marginalizing heritage languages, regional dialects, and the rich translingual repertoires that multilingual learners bring to the classroom (Cong-Lem et al., 2025). For learners whose linguistic practices do not map onto the monolingual, "standard" forms encoded in most AI systems, the technology can function as a constraining rather than an enabling mediating artifact—reinforcing linguistic hierarchies under the guise of personalized support. SCT thus challenges language educators and AI designers alike to ask not only whether AI tools "work," but in whose image of a competent language user they have been built, and whose semiotic and cultural resources they recognize, validate, and amplify.

Bringing the Frameworks Together

The frameworks outlined in the previous sections offer distinct yet interconnected paths for understanding justice in the age of AI-mediated language education. Each lens—critical (language) pedagogy, linguistic human rights, intersectionality, decoloniality and Southern theory and critical data studies—illuminates a different dimension of how power, identity, and technology intersect in the learning process. Rather than prescribing a single dominant framework, this chapter advocates for an intersectional and multi-perspectival approach that embraces theoretical diversity as a strength. Justice in AI and language education is not a fixed endpoint to be reached through one perspective, but an ongoing dialogue between multiple intellectual traditions, each revealing new questions and possibilities.

To these frameworks, sociocultural theory contributes a distinctive concern with how learning is organized through mediated activity and social interaction. Where critical (language) pedagogy asks who speaks and whose voice is heard, and where decolonial perspectives interrogate the colonial genealogy of AI datasets, SCT asks through what tools and interactions learners develop linguistically—and whether those tools extend or constrain the zone of proximal development for all learners equally. This complementarity reinforces the multi-perspectival approach advocated here: each framework illuminates what the others leave in shadow, and their interplay produces a richer, more actionable understanding of justice in AI-mediated language education.

This plurality mirrors the complexity of language itself. Language education is never only about mastering linguistic forms; it is an ethical and political practice tied to belonging, representation, and voice. Similarly, AI is never purely technical, but it embodies cultural assumptions, linguistic hierarchies, and visions of what is considered as valuable knowledge. Viewing AI systems through multiple theoretical lenses allows researchers, teachers and learners to perceive both their liberatory and oppressive potentials. Critical (language) pedagogy reminds us that technology should serve consciousness and agency rather than compliance (Freire, 1970); linguistic justice insists on the protection of linguistic diversity and human rights (Skutnabb-Kangas & Phillipson, 2022); intersectionality highlights identity, difference, and lived experience (Crenshaw, 1994); decolonial and Southern theories challenge global imbalances in knowledge production (de Sousa Santos, 2014; Mignolo & Walsh, 2018); and critical data studies expose the hidden infrastructures of algorithmic power that shape learning itself (Benjamin, 2019; O'Neil, 2016).

Bringing these perspectives together enables a more holistic and ethically grounded understanding of AI in language education. It encourages scholars and teachers to resist reductionist narratives of innovation and embrace a vision of technology as a site of transformation. A justice-oriented approach must therefore be flexible and attentive to the multiple contexts in which AI operates and the diverse communities it affects. In this sense, the theoretical synthesis proposed here functions both as a framework and an invitation. It calls on readers to engage these traditions dynamically, to test them against the realities of their own contexts, and to use them as resources for imagining more equitable futures for language education.

TOWARD JUSTICE-ORIENTED PRINCIPLES FOR AI IN LANGUAGE EDUCATION

The theoretical frameworks surveyed in this chapter converge on a set of shared commitments that can serve as guiding principles for justice-oriented engagement with AI in language education. Although these principles cannot resolve every ethical dilemma posed by rapid technological change, they offer a foundation for critical practice that keeps equity, recognition, and participation at the center of institutional and pedagogical decision-making.

First, AI tools should be evaluated not only for their learning outcomes but for their distributional consequences: who gains access to high-quality, responsive AI support, and who is relegated to lower-cost, lower-quality solutions? Distributive justice demands that educational institutions actively audit AI deployments for differential impact across learner groups defined by socioeconomic status, language background, disability, and geographic location (Lodge et al., 2025; Ramezanzadeh & Ebadi, 2025). Second, recognitional justice requires that AI systems acknowledge and validate the full range of linguistic repertoires, cultural references, and ways of knowing that diverse learners bring to the classroom. This means moving beyond accuracy metrics calibrated to dominant language varieties toward design standards that treat multilingualism, translingualism, and linguistic creativity as competences rather than deviations (Cong-Lem et al., 2025; Kang & Hirschi, 2025).

Third, representational justice demands that teachers, learners, and community representatives—particularly those from historically marginalized groups—have meaningful roles in shaping AI policy, design, and governance rather than being merely consulted after decisions are made (European Center for Not-for-Profit Law, 2025). Fourth, drawing on SCT, any AI tool introduced into a language learning environment should be assessed as a mediating artifact: educators should ask whether its scaffolding genuinely extends learners' ZPD or merely confirms existing competences, and whether its model of the target language amplifies or diminishes the cultural and semiotic resources learners already possess (Lantolf & Thorne, 2006; Vygotsky, 1978). Together, these principles do not prescribe a single solution but orientate the field toward the forms of critical vigilance, collective accountability, and transformative imagination that justice-oriented language education has always demanded.

CONCLUSION

AI is reshaping the landscape of language education, but its integration into classrooms and learning platforms cannot be understood solely in technical terms. This chapter has argued that AI operates within—and often amplifies—existing social and linguistic inequalities. To engage with it justly requires a shift from questions of efficiency and personalization to questions of equity, recognition, and transformation. Equality of access, while essential, is only the starting point; real justice demands confronting the structural conditions that define whose languages, identities, and ways of knowing are legitimized or marginalized in digital learning spaces.

The conceptual lenses introduced here—ranging from critical (language) pedagogy and linguistic human rights to decolonial, intersectional, data-critical, and sociocultural perspectives—offer complementary tools for this task. Together, they illuminate AI not as a neutral innovation but as a cultural and political domain where power is negotiated. Through these frameworks, teachers and researchers can better recognize how linguistic privilege and technological bias intersect and, crucially, envision alternative futures where AI supports rather than undermines diversity and inclusion. In the end, the future of AI in language education will not be written in code alone, but in the collective choices we make about whose voices it learns to hear—and whose stories it helps to tell.

Sociocultural theory adds a vital reminder to this collective task: the tools we introduce into learning environments are not passive conduits of instruction but active shapers of identity, interaction, and aspiration. When AI is designed to scaffold the full range of human linguistic diversity, rather than to enforce a narrow standard, it can become a genuine partner in justice-oriented language education. The chapters in this volume explore how that potential might be realized across diverse educational contexts, teacher preparation programs, policy environments, and linguistic communities. They do so in the conviction that critically informed engagement with AI is not a luxury for the well-resourced but an urgent and shared imperative for all who believe that language education should open futures rather than foreclose them.

REFERENCES

Albedah, F. (2025). Artificial intelligence in language education: A systematic review of multilingual applications, large language models, and emerging challenges. *Language Teaching Research Quarterly*, *49*, 247–268. DOI: 10.32038/ltrq.2025.49.13

Albeihi, H. H. M., & Rice, M. F. (2025). Generative AI and language diversity: Implications for teachers and learners. *Arab World English Journal*, *16*(1), 43–54. DOI: 10.24093/awej/vol16no1.3

Ariel, L., & Hayak, M. (2025). The paradox of AI in ESL instruction: Between innovation and oppression. *Educational Theory*, *75*(4), 646–660. DOI: 10.1111/edth.70034

Australian framework for artificial intelligence in higher education. Australian Centre for Student Equity and Success. https://bit.ly/4rmtubb

Bang, J., & Lee, S. M. (2024). Addressing bias for equity in AI-driven customized learning systems. *Multimedia-Assisted Language Learning*, *27*(4), 70–86. DOI: 10.15702/mall.2024.27.4.70

Benjamin, R. (2019). *Race after technology: Abolitionist tools for the new Jim Code*. Polity Press.

Chaitani, H. (2026). Artificial intelligence, ideology, and literacy: A multilectal framework for empowering criticality in adult education. In S. Kadry & B. S. (Eds.), *Artificial intelligence in education: Creating an equitable, creative, and effective learning environment*. IntechOpen. DOI: 10.5772/intechopen.1013545

Chen, A., Zhang, Y., Jia, J., Liang, M., Cha, Y., & Lim, C. P. (2025). A systematic review and meta-analysis of AI-enabled assessment in language learning: Design, implementation, and effectiveness. *Journal of Computer Assisted Learning*, *41*(1), e13064. DOI: 10.1111/jcal.13064

Cong-Lem, N., Van Bui, C. N., Nguyen, N. P. N., & Huynh, M. Q. (2025). Bridging or breaking? A systematic review of how generative AI shapes equity in foreign language education. *International Journal of Applied Linguistics*, ijal.70052. Advance online publication. DOI: 10.1111/ijal.70052

Crenshaw, K. (2013). Demarginalizing the intersection of race and sex: A black feminist critique of antidiscrimination doctrine, feminist theory and antiracist politics. In Maschke, K. (Ed.), *Feminist legal theories* (pp. 23–51). Routledge.

Crenshaw, K. W. (1994). Mapping the margins: Intersectionality, identity politics, and violence against women of color. In Fineman, M. A. (Ed.), *The public nature of private violence: Women and the discovery of abuse* (pp. 93–118). Routledge.

Crookes, G. V. (2021). Critical language pedagogy: An introduction to principles and values. *ELT Journal, 75*(3), 247–255. DOI: 10.1093/elt/ccab020

Davin, K. J., Kissau, S., Haudeck, H., Ade-Thurow, B., Gómez-Pereira, D., Oon, P. T., & Dornburg, A. (2026). Global and educational disparities in AI integration: A study of L2 teacher training and usage patterns. *System, 136*, 103901. DOI: 10.1016/j.system.2025.103901

de Sousa Santos, B. (2014). *Epistemologies of the South: Justice against epistemicide*. Routledge.

Delgado, R., & Stefancic, J. (2023). *Critical race theory: An introduction* (4th ed.). New York University Press.

Du, J., & Daniel, B. K. (2024). Transforming language education: A systematic review of AI-powered chatbots for English as a foreign language speaking practice. *Computers and Education: Artificial Intelligence, 6*, 100230. DOI: 10.1016/j.caeai.2024.100230

Ekizer, F. N. (2025). Exploring the impact of artificial intelligence on English language teaching: A meta-analysis. *Acta Psychologica, 260*, 105649. DOI: 10.1016/j.actpsy.2025.105649 PMID: 41066858

European Center for Not-for-Profit Law. (2025, November 11). *Blueprint for rights-centered AI in public participation*. European Center for Not-for-Profit Law. https://bit.ly/4sDhnHF

Fataar, A. (2025, October 29). *Decolonising the algorithm: Teaching for justice in age of AI*. University World News. https://bit.ly/4upYaLg

Freire, P. (1970). *Pedagogy of the oppressed*. Herder & Herder.

Georgiou, G. P. (2026). Envisioning the futures of language education in the era of artificial intelligence. *Journal of Futures Studies*, 1–14. https://bit.ly/46VE01E

Ghiasvand, F., & Seyri, H. (2025). A collaborative reflection on the synergy of Artificial Intelligence (AI) and language teacher identity reconstruction. *Teaching and Teacher Education, 160*, 105022. DOI: 10.1016/j.tate.2025.105022

Gu, J., & Liu, Q. (2025). Enhancing Chinese EFL university students' self-regulated learning through AI chatbot intervention: Insights from achievement goal theory. *Learning and Motivation, 92*, 102191. DOI: 10.1016/j.lmot.2025.102191

Hargreaves, E., Buchanan, D., & Quick, L. (2025). *Children's life-histories in primary schools: Imagining schooling as a positive experience*. Palgrave Macmillan. DOI: 10.1007/978-3-031-69445-5

Huertas-Abril, C. A., & Palacios-Hidalgo, F. J. (2025). Artificial intelligence–assisted language learning for all in the new global context: Threats and opportunities. In Wei, W., & Schnell, J. (Eds.), *The Routledge handbook of endangered and minority languages* (pp. 355–376). Routledge. DOI: 10.4324/9781003439493-27

Ingram, M. (2025). The role of AI in language preservation and revitalization. In Ardalan, I. D., Banifatemi, A., Gonzalez, F., Ingram, M., Moradinezhad, R., & Williams, L. (Eds.), *AI for community: Preserving culture and tradition* (pp. 55–80). Chapman and Hall/CRC. DOI: 10.1201/9781003517115-5

Kang, O., & Hirschi, K. (2025). Bias and stereotyping: Human and artificial intelligence (AI). *Annual Review of Applied Linguistics*, *45*, 69–84. DOI: 10.1017/S026719052500008X

Kannadhasan, M. (2025). Next-Gen language pedagogy: Leveraging generative AI to support inclusive English language learning. *International Journal of Teaching. Learning and Education*, *4*(5), 638368. DOI: 10.22161/ijtle.4.5.7

Khari, M. A. (2026). Beyond the algorithm: Educational justice for plurilingual students in AI-assisted classrooms. In Rousoulioti, T., Pitsou, C., Saglam, A., & Finch, K. (Eds.), *Language education and human rights in democratic educational settings* (pp. 405–444). IGI Global Scientific Publishing. DOI: 10.4018/979-8-3373-2670-2.ch015

Kildė, L. (2025). Humanising digital language education 5.0 through a Freirean lens. *Acta Paedagogica Vilnensia*, (54), 157–169. https://bit.ly/4szm2u8

Lantolf, J. P., & Thorne, S. L. (2006). *Sociocultural theory and the genesis of second language development*. Oxford University Press.

Li, B., Tan, Y. L., Wang, C., & Lowell, V. (2025). Two years of innovation: A systematic review of empirical generative AI research in language learning and teaching. *Computers and Education: Artificial Intelligence*, *9*, 100445. DOI: 10.1016/j.caeai.2025.100445

Lodge, J. M., Bower, M., Gulson, K., Henderson, M., Slade, C., & Southgate, E. (2025). *Australian Framework for Artificial Intelligence in Higher Education*. Australian Centre for Student Equity and Success. https://bit.ly/4rmtubb

Mignolo, W. (2025). Entrevista a Walter Mignolo (segunda parte): Pensar a partir de lo destituido que sea relevante política y éticamente en el presente [Interview with Walter Mignolo (part two): Thinking from the dismissed that is politically and ethically relevant in the present]. *Revista de Filosofía (La Plata)*, *55*(1), e120. DOI: 10.24215/29533392e120

Mignolo, W. D. (2011). *The darker side of western modernity: Global futures, decolonial options*. Duke University Press.

Mignolo, W. D., & Walsh, C. E. (2018). *On decoloniality: Concepts, analytics, praxis*. Duke University Press.

Mohamed, S., Png, M. T., & Isaac, W. (2020). Decolonial AI: Decolonial theory as sociotechnical foresight in artificial intelligence. *Philosophy & Technology*, *33*(4), 659–684. DOI: 10.1007/s13347-020-00405-8

Mohebbi, A. (2025). Enabling learner independence and self-regulation in language education using AI tools: A systematic review. *Cogent Education*, *12*(1), 2433814. DOI: 10.1080/2331186X.2024.2433814

Noble, S. U. (2018). *Algorithms of oppression: How search engines reinforce racism*. New York University Press. DOI: 10.18574/nyu/9781479833641.001.0001

O'Neil, C. (2016). *Weapons of math destruction: How big data increases inequality and threatens democracy*. Crown.

Palacios-Hidalgo, F. J. (2025a). AI for the democratization of language learning. In McCallum, L., & Tafazoli, D. (Eds.), *The Palgrave encyclopedia of computer-assisted language learning* (pp. 1–4). Palgrave Macmillan Cham. DOI: 10.1007/978-3-031-51447-0_98-1

Palacios-Hidalgo, F. J. (2025b). Critical language pedagogy: Revisiting the concept. In Palacios-Hidalgo, F. J., & Huertas-Abril, C. A. (Eds.), *Redefining language education through critical language pedagogy* (pp. 1–22). IGI Global Scientific Publishing. DOI: 10.4018/979-8-3693-5421-6.ch001

Patterson, J. (2025, September 2). *Multilingual artificial intelligence often reinforces bias*. Johns Hopkins University. https://bit.ly/4rvAeDJ

Phillipson, R. (1992). *Linguistic imperialism*. Oxford University Press.

Phillipson, R., & Meighan, P. (2025). Resisting linguistic imperialism: A conversation with Robert Phillipson on linguistic human rights, multilingualism, and Indigenous and minority languages. *Journal of Education for Multilingualism*, *2*(1), 131–151. https://bit.ly/47rkDh2

Poehner, M. E., & Lu, X. (2024). Sociocultural theory and corpus-based English language teaching. *TESOL Quarterly*, *58*(1), 1–12. DOI: 10.1002/tesq.3282

Ramezanzadeh, A., & Ebadi, S. (2025). AI-generated storytelling for socially just EFL pedagogy: Exploring learner emotions through Fraser's justice theory. *System*, *129*, 103588. DOI: 10.1016/j.system.2024.103588

Ricaurte, P. (2023, May 13). *AI ethics for the majority world: The question of violence at scale* [Transcript]. Goethe-Institut. https://bit.ly/46VJVnq

Román Mendoza, E. (2025). La inteligencia artificial generativa en la enseñanza de español: Una aproximación desde la pedagogía crítica [Generative artificial intelligence in Spanish language education: A critical pedagogy approach]. *Culture Crossroads*, *29*, 211–229. DOI: 10.55877/cc.vol29.654

Schneider, B., & Oliveira, M. (2025). Developing critical AI language literacy—Prompting experiments on raciolinguistic bias to understand large language models as cultural artefacts. *AI & Society*. Advance online publication. DOI: 10.1007/s00146-025-02727-7

Selvi, A. F. (2025). Meet your new AI teacher: Hypes, promises, and realities in AI-powered language education platforms. *Applied Linguistics Review*. Advance online publication. DOI: 10.1515/applirev-2025-0224

Skutnabb-Kangas, T. (2000). *Linguistic genocide in education—or worldwide diversity and human rights?* Routledge. DOI: 10.4324/9781410605191

Skutnabb-Kangas, T., & Dunbar, R. (2010). *Indigenous children's education as linguistic genocide and a crime against humanity? A global view*. Gáldu Čála.

Skutnabb-Kangas, T., & Phillipson, R. (Eds.). (2022). *The handbook of linguistic human rights*. John Wiley & Sons. DOI: 10.1002/9781119753926

Son, J.-B., Ružić, N. K., & Philpott, A. (2025). Artificial intelligence technologies and applications for language learning and teaching. *Journal of China Computer-Assisted Language Learning*, *5*(1), 94–112. DOI: 10.1515/jccall-2023-0015

Tanksley, T. C. (2024). "We're changing the system with this one": Black students using critical race algorithmic literacies to subvert and survive AI-mediated racism in school. *English Teaching*, *23*(1), 36–56. DOI: 10.1108/ETPC-08-2023-0102

Thorne, S. L. (2024). Generative artificial intelligence, co-evolution, and language education. *Modern Language Journal*, *108*(2), 567–572. DOI: 10.1111/modl.12932

Villarreal, D. (2024). Sociolinguistic auto-coding has fairness problems too: Measuring and mitigating overlearning bias. *Linguistics Vanguard : Multimodal Online Journal, 10*(1), 679–692. DOI: 10.1515/lingvan-2022-0114

Vygotsky, L. S. (1978). *Mind in society: The development of higher psychological processes.* Harvard University Press.

Weng, Z., & Fu, Y. (2025). Generative AI in language education: Bridging divide and fostering inclusivity. *International Journal of Technology in Education, 8*(2), 395–420. DOI: 10.46328/ijte.1056

Xiong, M., & Teo, T. (2025). Unveiling the effects of GenAI on motivation of learning English as a second/foreign language: Evidence from meta-analysis. *Educational Research Review, 49*, 100744. DOI: 10.1016/j.edurev.2025.100744

Zhao, Z. J., Li, J., Hong, Y., & Yun, T. Y. (2025). Lesson study as an approach to facilitate the integration of Gen-AI into EFL curriculum design in higher education. *International Journal for Lesson and Learning Studies, 14*(3), 253–279. DOI: 10.1108/IJLLS-01-2025-0029

Zhu, M., & Wang, C. (2025). A systematic review of AI in language education: Current status and future implications. *Language Learning & Technology, 29*(1), 1–29. DOI: 10.64152/10125/73606

ADDITIONAL READING

Canagarajah, S. (2013). *Translingual practice: Global Englishes and cosmopolitan relations.* Routledge. DOI: 10.4324/9780203120293

Fraser, N. (2009). *Scales of justice: Reimagining political space in a globalizing world.* Columbia University Press.

Huertas-Abril, C. A. (2025). Machine learning. In McCallum, L., & Tafazoli, D. (Eds.), *The Palgrave encyclopedia of computer-assisted language learning* (pp. 1–5). Palgrave Macmillan Cham. DOI: 10.1007/978-3-031-51447-0_104-1

Huertas-Abril, C. A., & Palacios-Hidalgo, F. J. (2023). New possibilities of artificial intelligence-assisted language learning (AIALL): Comparing visions from the East and the West. *Education Sciences, 13*(12), 1234. DOI: 10.3390/educsci13121234

Matos, T., Santos, W., Zdravevski, E., Coelho, P. J., Pires, I. M., & Madeira, F. (2025). A systematic review of artificial intelligence applications in education: Emerging trends and challenges. *Decision Analytics Journal, 15*, 100571. DOI: 10.1016/j.dajour.2025.100571

Meighan, P., & Veliz, L. (Eds.). (2026). *Countering colonialingualism in language education: Research practices and pedagogies from the Global South*. Routledge. DOI: 10.4324/9781003653653

Miao, F., & Cukurova, M. (2024). *AI competency framework for teachers*. UNESCO. DOI: 10.54675/ZJTE2084

Ricaurte, P. (2022). Ethics for the majority world: AI and the question of violence at scale. *Media Culture & Society, 44*(4), 726–745. DOI: 10.1177/01634437221099612

Tian, Z., & Wang, C. (Eds.). (2025). *Rethinking language education in the age of generative AI*. Routledge. DOI: 10.4324/9781003426929

KEY TERMS AND DEFINITIONS

Critical data studies: They constitute an interdisciplinary field that interrogates the social, political, and ethical dimensions of data and algorithmic systems.

Critical Language Pedagogy: An educational framework that combines critical theory with language teaching to develop learners' critical awareness of how language reflects and reproduces power structures, empowering them to challenge linguistic inequalities and use language as a tool for social justice and transformation.

Decoloniality: It refers to a theoretical and political project that seeks to dismantle the enduring hierarchies of power, knowledge, and being inherited from centuries of European colonialism.

Equality: It refers to the provision of identical resources, tools, and opportunities to all learners, operating under the assumption that uniform access constitutes fairness, yet often overlooking structural inequities that leave disadvantaged groups further behind.

Equity: It involves the differentiated allocation of resources and support tailored to learners' diverse needs, linguistic repertoires, and technological access, aiming to ensure comparable outcomes through adaptive systems while remaining vigilant against biases encoded in algorithmic design.

Intersectionality: A term that describes how social identities such as race, class, gender, and language intersect to create unique experiences of privilege or marginalization.

Justice: It interrogates and transforms the structural, institutional, and epistemic conditions that sustain inequality, encompassing fairness in access to AI resources, validation of diverse languages and identities, and inclusion of marginalized communities in AI design and governance, ultimately aspiring toward participatory parity for all learners.

Linguistic justice: A theoretical and political framework asserting that all languages and their speakers are entitled to equitable treatment, recognition, and opportunities for development.

Mediated learning: A concept from sociocultural theory describing the process through which learners develop cognitive and linguistic competences via interaction with cultural tools, symbols, and social partners, rather than through direct, unmediated engagement with the environment.

Sociocultural theory: A framework derived from the work of Lev Vygotsky that situates learning and cognitive development as inherently social, cultural, and mediated processes, emphasizing collaborative interaction, the zone of proximal development, and the role of cultural tools and artifacts in shaping learning.

Chapter 2
Teacher Agency in the Age of AI:
Preparing Educators for Equitable AI Integration

Wali Khan Monib
http://orcid.org/0000-0002-9575-9305
Shaikh Zayed University, Afghanistan

ABSTRACT

The rapid advancement of artificial intelligence (AI) is fundamentally reshaping the landscape of English language teaching and learning. AI technologies—ranging from chatbots and adaptive learning platforms to immersive virtual and augmented reality applications—are not only transforming how English is taught and learned but also redefining the roles of English teachers worldwide. This chapter discusses current research that bridges theoretical foundations, teacher agency, including epistemic, transformational, relational, and moral agencies, AI and teacher role, teacher capacity building, and implications. When teachers consider teacher agency and equity, AI can transform English language teaching – making it more personalized, accessible, and just for all learners. Policies must evolve, too, and policies must ensure safe, transparent AI use. Future research should examine how AI impacts the specific English language skills under different teacher guidance styles.

INTRODUCTION

Recently, research on generative AI (GenAI) has increased, where GenAI is widely used in various fields (Monib, et al., 2025). GenAI offers a range of benefits, including instant feedback, scaffolding, and differentiated instruction for individ-

DOI: 10.4018/979-8-3373-7749-0.ch002

ual students (Niazai & Monib, 2025a). AI tools assist teachers with differentiated instruction, which can help promote learner autonomy and create personalized, inclusive learning environments (Monib, et al., 2024; Szabó & Szoke, 2024). These tools can enhance language learning by generating reading texts at varying levels, providing dialogue to improve speaking, and providing writing feedback tailored to individual learners' levels. However, AI use also raises concerns about human agency and inequity, where, for instance, access to AI requires internet access and proper devices, which remain uneven (UNESCO, 2025b). In low-resource contexts, such as rural or developing regions, teachers and learners are left behind when AI tools are introduced without attention to infrastructure and affordability. More AI systems may encode cultural or language biases; that is, an AI tool may import examples from Western English-speaking contexts, marginalizing local dialects and cultures. For this reason, AI could intensify existing educational gaps (Szabó & Szoke, 2024). Teachers emphasize that AI should be designed and used to augment human work, such as building cranes to extend human reach, not to replace humans (Overdeck Family Foundation, 2026). Many teachers use AI for routine tasks, such as quizzes and exercise generation (Kohnke & Zou, 2025). However, they worry about the loss of control and professional identity, as AI-generated content raises questions about the role of teachers. It poses challenges to teachers' autonomy and ethical use. AI may promise efficiency while also undermining their judgment or exacerbating existing inequities. If an AI system grades an assignment unfairly, or if a chatbot collects student data without consent, the teacher must intervene to protect their students (Overdeck Family Foundation, 2025).

This chapter discusses the theoretical foundations of AI in teaching, the TPACK (technological pedagogical content knowledge) framework, and focuses on teacher agencies, including epistemic, transformative, relational, and moral agency. It discusses AI, the teacher role, practical classroom practices, and challenges related to AI. It further discusses teacher capacity building, presents case studies, implications, and conclusion and future directions.

THEORETICAL FOUNDATIONS OF AI IN TEACHING

The analysis builds on the TPACK framework, which emphasizes that effective technology integration requires the interplay of Technology, Pedagogy, and Content Knowledge (see Koehler, et al., 2013; Mishra & Koehler, 2006) as indicated in Figure 1. Social justice education warns that digital tools can inadvertently reinforce inequities, urging teachers to question where knowledge originates and whose voices are included (Coker, et al., 2023). Zulianti et al. (2025) conducted a study using the TPACK framework within a professional development program designed to enhance novice EFL teachers' AI skills. Findings indicate that the program significantly improved knowledge of AI-powered tools, integration of teaching skills, and self-efficacy. The study demonstrates how TPACK can guide AI-oriented teacher development, which provides a replicable model for building EFL teachers' technological and pedagogical competencies. Similarly, Kohnke & Zou (2025) used the TPACK framework and TESOL study, arguing that AI tools should align with pedagogical integrity, equity, and social justice. This means that language teachers should have knowledge of English grammar (content), teaching methods (pedagogy), and the AI tools (technology). For example, if a teacher is using AI for text summarization, it is crucial to understand the tool's algorithm to judge its accuracy. Without this blend, technology can override pedagogy or vice versa. Educators' voices should be included in AI decisions, as excluding them would result in a mismatched solution (Kennedy & Castek, 2025). When teachers have real agency and a voice in choosing tools, technology use remains responsive to learners' needs. Agency arises from individual efforts and structural factors (Atherton, 2025). In the EFL context, those structures may include curriculum standards, exam requirements, and cultural aspects, among others. Teachers with agency navigate these structures by aligning AI activities with language proficiency frameworks or pushing back against rigid curricula when AI reveals student needs beyond them. TPACK helps organize reflection on technology use, but teacher agency decides whether AI fosters equity or reproduces inequity.

Figure 1. TPACK framework

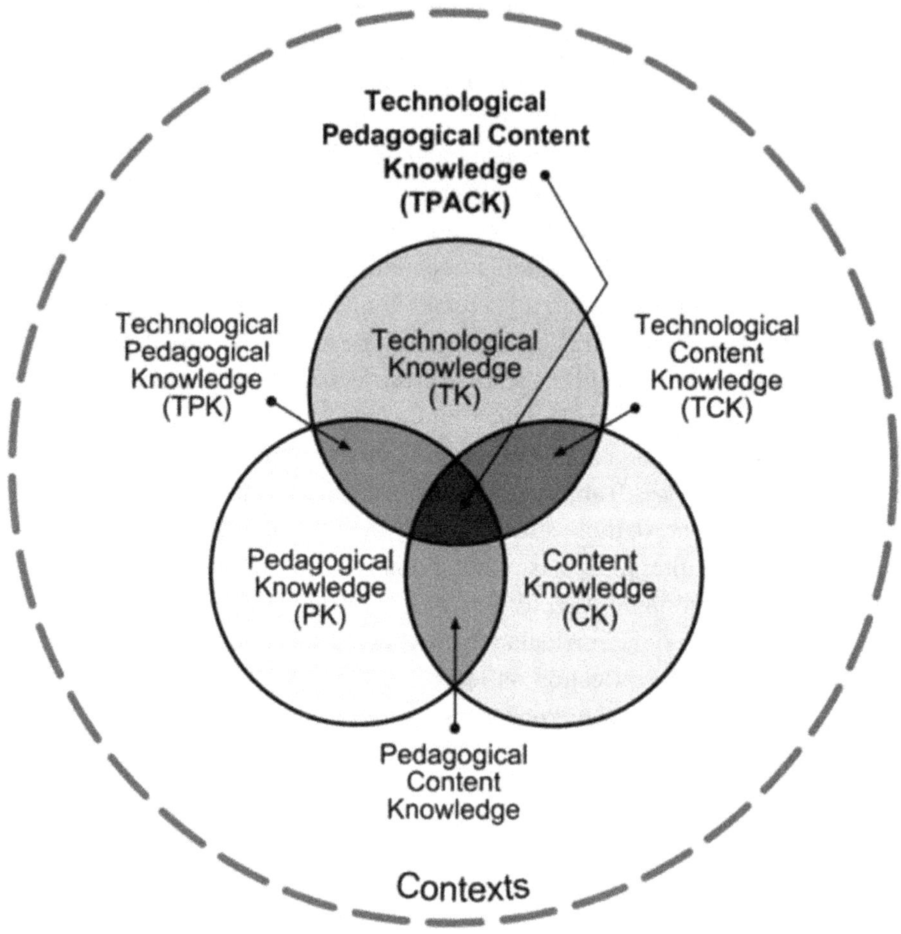

TEACHER AGENCY IN AI CONTEXTS

Teacher agency is defined as the active role teachers take in their work and in shaping the teaching profession, which can manifest through commitment, purposiveness, intentionality, and influence (Leijen, 2023). Agency concerns what a person does: the capacity to act intentionally, assume an active role, and shape surrounding realities. Lipponen & Kumpulainen (2011) conceptualized agency as transformative agency (shifts in thinking and action), relational agency (mobilizing and providing support), and epistemic agency (ownership of learning). Some have also discussed moral agency (Campbell, 2004; Molla & Nolan, 2020). This chapter focuses on epistemic agency, transformative agency, relational agency, and moral agency (see Figure 2).

Figure 2. Teacher agency in the AI era

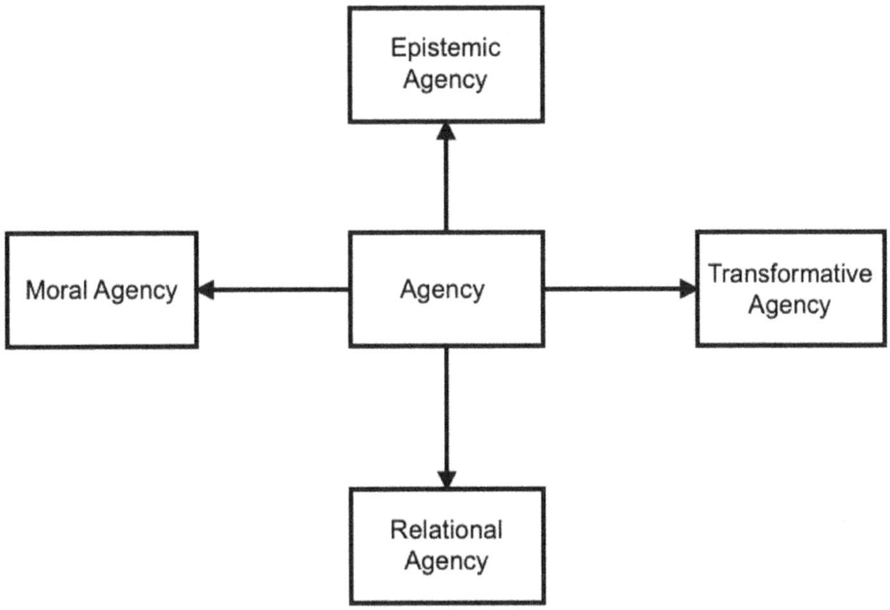

Epistemic Agency

Epistemic agency refers to the cognitive processes involved in acquiring knowledge and understanding (Hofer & Pintrich, 1997), emphasizing active engagement in learning (Cherbow & McNeill, 2022). It is the ability to determine what counts as knowledge and how it should be approached (Atherton, 2025). It refers to a teacher's role as a critical knower, in which they decide and assess what is considered valid knowledge. In AI-mediated language classrooms, epistemic agency views AI-generated language content, such as translations and answers to questions, as debatable rather than absolute truths. This is especially important in the context of EFL/ESL, where AI may produce grammatically plausible but culturally inappropriate or factually incorrect output. Language teachers should therefore exercise caution by questioning the AI output. For example, if an AI tool such as ChatGPT suggests an idiom, the teacher probes: Is this idiom authentic to the student's current context, or is it a generic phrase more suited to native speakers? Similarly, when

AI generates a historical anecdote for an English lesson, the teacher cross-checks with the sources. This may encourage students to ask where knowledge comes from. For example, early AI prompts led a teacher to design routine exercises and press the AI for deeper questions, and then the teacher converted the writing task into exploratory philosophical inquiries (Atherton, 2025). The teacher should not accept the AI's draft verbatim but should refine and question it. An EFL teacher using an AI grammar checker, for instance, might generate example sentences for relative clauses. Instead of just using them, the teacher should question them and discuss them with students in class. Why did the AI choose this example? Does it cover all cases? By doing so, teachers and students evaluate the linguistic reasoning of AI-generated content. If biases, for example, appear, such as the AI content consistently suggesting male names in role-play dialogues, the teacher highlights them and rewrites inclusively. In this way, AI can serve as a springboard for metacognitive discussion of language use.

Research shows that epistemic agency can play a central role in how teachers use AI. In a study by Chu & Wang (2025), which examined EFL teachers' epistemic agency in an AI-mediated environment, collective inquiry among teachers was found to be a key means through which educators negotiated technological opportunity and pedagogical values. The study found that teachers enacted epistemic agency by collaboratively examining AI-generated material, discussing the pedagogical implications, and resolving conflicts. The study further revealed that factors such as institutional AI adoption practices and teachers' beliefs in AI's educational value significantly shape the extent to which educators exercise epistemic agency. These findings show that epistemic engagement in the AI context is both an individual cognitive activity and a socially mediated one supported by a collaborative environment. Another study by Chu & Wang (2025) indicated that AI support for epistemic agency grows only when teachers critically engage with it. When the instructor actively engages and questions the AI, the tool transforms into a dialogic co-creator that prompts reflection, questions assumptions, and opens ethical dilemmas.

Furthermore, GenAI can significantly enhance learners' engagement by providing personalized and context-rich learning environments (Monib, 2025; Yusmaliana, et al., 2026). For instance, AI tools have been shown to improve writing skills through tailored feedback and support (Abdelrady, et al., 2025). It can foster critical thinking among learners, although it also poses risks of dependency and reduced human interaction (Lee & Jeong, 2026; Liu, et al., 2025). Therefore, while GenAI can be a powerful tool for knowledge acquisition, it must be integrated thoughtfully to maintain and enhance learners' critical thinking skills. It is crucial for teachers to teach students that AI outputs are provisional. Teachers can prompt inquiry: How did the AI arrive at this answer? What was in its data? Teachers also guide students to cross-verify. For example, after an AI explains a grammar rule, the teacher might have students consult a textbook or dictionary to verify the correctness. This reflective use of AI parallels the dialogic tradition in language learning, where multiple sources such as the teacher, peers, and texts interact. By modeling skepticism and source critique, teachers with high epistemic agency cultivate learners who become critical users of AI rather than passive consumers.

Transformative Agency

Transformative agency refers to teachers initiating significant shifts in pedagogical thinking and practice. AI tools can catalyze such a transformation by enabling new forms of instruction. For example, generative AI (like ChatGPT) can help teachers create richer materials or reconfigure classroom roles. In one study of university instructors by Ututalum (2025), AI was found to personalize learning, enhance engagement, and reduce routine workload, potentially freeing educators to focus on higher-level tasks. Teachers reported that AI could relieve them of repetitive tasks (e.g., grammar drills or quiz generation), allowing them to spend more time on meaningful student interaction. Similarly, adaptive learning platforms (which use AI to tailor practice to each student) allow teachers to redesign lessons around individualized learning paths. In a study of EFL teachers by Bahari & Liu (2025), the use of AI-driven platforms (e.g., Microsoft Educator Center tools and Google Classroom bots) led to substantial improvements in participants' instructional strategies: class environments became more adaptable, and students received more personalized feedback.

A teacher with transformative agency might, for instance, incorporate ChatGPT into a writing unit by asking students to draft essays and then use the AI for revision suggestions. This shifts the teacher's role from sole evaluator to facilitator of iterative drafting. Another example is using AI-driven pronunciation apps or chatbots for speaking practice: teachers can restructure class time to focus on conversation skills, while students use the app for drills. A study by Cui & Zhang (2025) examined the use of AI chatbots and pronunciation feedback applications to improve speaking skills among university language learners. Students in the experimental group practiced conversation with AI chatbots and received automated pronunciation feedback, while the control group relied on conventional instructor feedback and peer interaction. Results showed notable gains for the AI-supported group, including average increases in speaking fluency, grammar, vocabulary, and phonetic accuracy. Learners also reported higher satisfaction due to the accessibility and immediacy of AI feedback. This case illustrates how teachers exercising transformative agency can redesign instruction by shifting repetitive speaking drills to AI tools while using class time for higher-level communicative interaction and guided discussion. A meta-analysis by Jantakoon et al. (2025) synthesized studies to evaluate the effectiveness of AI-enhanced English instruction for speaking and listening skills. The analysis reported overall effect of AI-supported learning, with particularly strong gains in speaking proficiency. Listening outcomes showed a positive trend.

In their study, instructors recognized that students using ChatGPT often adopt a transactional, task-oriented approach to knowledge, where teachers sought to shift students toward transformative relationswith knowledge, encouraging deeper engagement than mere task completion (Kahn et al., 2025). Such curricular redesign – emphasizing critical thinking, creativity, or collaboration over rote answers – exemplifies transformative agency. Generative AI also prompts new tasks. For example, teachers might ask students to critique or improve AI-generated essays, turning the AI into a peer reviewer. This reframes writing practice as a dialogue between student and machine, mediated by the teacher. Ututalum (2025) study found that college teachers saw generative AI as a way to make learning more interactive and student-centered. In other words, AI invites teachers to create novel learning activities – from AI-assisted debates to prompt-design contests – thus transforming their pedagogy.

However, transformative agency in AI-rich contexts also encounters uncertainty. Teachers must often learn new skills (e.g., prompt engineering) and navigate the unclear quality of AI output. As studies show that expertise itself is challenged by generative tools, mastery now involves knowing how to unlock AI capabilities with well-crafted prompts (Kahn et al., 2025). Teachers must become learners to stay effective. In practice, some EFL teachers have initially resisted altering their pedagogy: one study of EFL writing instructors found they regarded AI (ChatGPT) as merely supplementary, not transformational, citing a lack of guidelines and faith in traditional methods (Le-Khanh, et al., 2024). This underscores that transformative agency requires institutional support and experimentation before big change can occur. Transformative agency means that teachers intentionally implement new practices (e.g., personalized learning, iterative feedback, dynamic materials) using AI. Studies across contexts show AI's potential to personalize learning and reduce routine burdens (Ututalum, 2025), but realizing that potential requires teachers to actively redesign instruction. When teachers do so – for instance, by developing AI-facilitated lesson plans or leveraging AI as a co-teacher – they exhibit agency in reshaping education.

Relational Agency

Relational agency emphasizes collaboration: teachers draw on colleagues, communities, and shared resources as they integrate AI. In practice, this means co-developing curricula, discussing AI uses, and mobilizing professional networks to solve problems. AI creates new opportunities (and needs) for such networking.

For example, EFL/ESL educators may turn to online forums and social media to share AI lesson ideas and prompts. Research networks (e.g., TESOL associations) are increasingly convening webinars on AI in language teaching.

Empirical work suggests this collaboration can reshape identity and practice. In a study of EFL teachers, participants met in collaborative reflection panels to discuss AI's role in teaching (Ghiasvand & Seyri, 2025). They reported that AI use made L2 education more personalized and collaborative and spurred them to be more self-reflective practitioners. In other words, by reflecting together on AI, these teachers not only learned from each other but also reconstructed their teaching roles. The study highlights that when teachers collectively negotiate AI integration, they exercise relational agency to redefine norms (through teacher role transformation) and to share pedagogical alignments.

In everyday terms, relational agency might be, for example, a team of ESL teachers collectively evaluating an adaptive learning platform (e.g., Duolingo for Schools), pooling their classroom data to decide how best to implement it. Or, a group of lecturers might co-write a departmental policy on ChatGPT use, thus shaping institutional practices. The key is that agency is not isolated, where one teacher's decision to use AI is informed and extended by a network. Even students can be partners: co-creating AI-assisted assignments with peer teachers illustrates a relational approach where agency is distributed. However, unequal relationships or institutional culture can inhibit relational agency. For instance, if a department resists technology, teachers may lack peer support. It is important to note that without a shared understanding among staff, AI adoption can become relationally chaotic, driven by isolated, ad hoc responses (Kahn et al., 2025). On the other hand, unified responses (e.g., a faculty discussing how to recalibrate teaching when students use AI) reflect strong relational agency. Teachers with relational agency actively build and utilize support networks for AI integration. They engage in professional communities, collaborative reflection, and co-planning. These shared efforts not only enhance individual competence but also generate collective agency – coordinated action to adapt pedagogy across an organization or community. Collaborative workshops, online educator forums, and inter-school partnerships are all contexts where relational agency surfaces, amplifying teachers' capacity to integrate AI intentionally.

Moral Agency

Acting ethically and making morally justifiable decisions is a critical facet of teachers' professional agency (Molla & Nolan, 2020). Teachers' ethical knowledge relates to both what they hope to teach and model for students and how they hope to govern their own behavior (Campbell, 2004). In the current context, moral agency refers to teachers' commitment to fairness, transparency, and student well-being when using AI. In language education, this means scrutinizing AI for potential biases and ensuring all students can benefit. For example, AI language models trained on large datasets may reproduce stereotypes: a writing prompt might repeatedly portray certain nationalities negatively, or a translation might assume gender-binary pronouns. A teacher attuned to ethics would notice such patterns and intervene. The teacher might use the AI prompt as a class discussion point: Why do you think the chatbot used this stereotype? and then correct misinformation.

Social justice frameworks warn that technology often reproduces societal inequalities unless challenged. As one study argues, digital tools provide new opportunities for inequity and oppressive social relations unless educators' question how knowledge (including AI content) flows into the classroom (Szabó & Szoke, 2024). In practice, an EFL teacher might audit whether it includes diverse names and contexts. If not, the teacher supplements with inclusive examples. Data privacy and consent also fall under ethical agency. Many AI tools collect student input – for instance, language learning apps that upload speech samples. Teachers with ethical agency will clarify data use: they might obtain parental permission before using a voice-recognition app, or choose not to use an AI chatbot that stores student chat histories insecurely. The Cornell Center for Teaching lists key questions for educators: How can we ensure that [AI] tools avoid unfair bias and are universally accessible? And how is user data used, stored, or shared? (Szabó & Szoke, 2024). A responsible language teacher knows to read privacy policies, opt for tools with clear data protection, and educate students about digital safety.

Gender and linguistic diversity are especially salient in English contexts. If AI features only US or British English examples, how do teachers adapt to English as a lingua franca? Ethical agency means adjusting or contextualizing AI output. For example, a teacher might note that an American accent in a listening exercise is not the only valid accent, or that AI translation may not account for culturally loaded phrases. Teachers often become aware of ethical issues through uncomfortable classroom experiences (Ho & Lee, 2025). For instance, if an AI essay-grader unfairly marks a non-native accent, a teacher might complain and investigate the bias. Ethical agency then drives action: the teacher could raise this in a faculty meeting, push for better algorithms, or simply avoid that tool. UNESCO's guidance also underscores the ethical use of AI. They call for clear standards to ensure that AI tools are transparent, accountable, and free of bias (UNESCO, 2025c). For language teachers, this means demanding explainability: if an AI suggests a grammar correction, can it show why, or is it a black box? Teachers must often translate the AI's opaque logic into understandable feedback for students.

Finally, equity of access is a core ethical concern. In EFL/ESL contexts, students' linguistic backgrounds and socioeconomic status vary widely. An ethical teacher will not assume that all students have equal access to AI at home. If an assignment relies on an online chatbot, the teacher ensures in-class access or offers alternative support. Moreover, equity involves paying attention to language proficiency: an advanced ChatGPT prompt might confuse beginners. Thus, teachers may scaffold AI use (e.g., providing sentence starters) to level the field. Moral agency in language teaching involves protecting students' rights and dignity as technology enters the classroom. Teachers with moral agency do not blindly trust AI; they question whose interests it serves, how it affects marginalized learners, and whether it respects student privacy. By applying social justice principles, they strive to make AI a bridge rather than a barrier.

FRAMEWORK FOR EQUITABLE AI AGENCY IN LANGUAGE EDUCATION

Building upon scholarship on teacher agency, social justice, critical pedagogy, and AI integration, this chapter proposes a Framework for Equitable AI Agency in Language Education (see Figure 3). The framework is informed by the critical pedagogy of Freire (1970), which conceptualises education as a transformative practice grounded in critical consciousness, dialogue, and social justice. It argues that teacher agency enables educators to adopt critical pedagogical practices, cultivate ethical responsibility for AI use, engage in transformative pedagogical action, and ultimately foster socially just and equitable AI-mediated language education.

The relationship between teacher agency and Freirean critical pedagogy is supported by scholarship suggesting that teachers with professional autonomy, strong professional identities, and supportive institutional environments are more likely to implement dialogic and learner-centered pedagogies and challenge traditional "banking" models of education and foster critical consciousness in students (Gumiero & Araújo, 2019; Taff & Lazzaro, 2025). However, agency alone is insufficient. Teachers' beliefs, AI literacy, professional preparation, and institutional conditions mediate whether agency is translated into critical pedagogical practice. Freirean critical pedagogy provides the ethical foundation of the framework. Through dialogue, critical consciousness, and an ethic of care, it encourages teachers to interrogate power relations embedded in educational technologies and to consider issues of equity, inclusion, and social justice. In AI-mediated language education, ethical responsibility extends beyond interpersonal ethics to include responsible AI use, encompassing fairness, transparency, privacy, accountability, and cultural inclusivity.

The framework further proposes that ethical responsibility leads to transformative pedagogical action. Drawing on Freire's concept of praxis, teachers who critically recognize educational inequities are more likely to redesign learning activities, evaluate AI-generated content critically, select inclusive AI tools, and involve learners in questioning and co-constructing AI-supported learning experiences. This aligns with the use of AI tools to promote critical consciousness and equity in education. For instance, AI can be integrated into teaching to foster dialogic education where learners and educators collaboratively construct knowledge (Alm & Watanabe, 2023). Nevertheless, this relationship is contingent upon contextual factors such as institutional support, curriculum flexibility, and access to professional development. For instance, institutional backing and professional development initiatives significantly influence teachers' attitudes and their intention to use AI (Filiz, et al., 2025; M. Li & Noori, 2024).

Finally, transformative pedagogical action contributes to socially just and equitable AI-mediated language education by promoting inclusive participation, adapting to diverse learner needs, and supporting students with disabilities or language barriers (Lopez-Gazpio, 2025; Marras, et al., 2026; Monib, 2025). However, evidence remains limited regarding the long-term effects of transformative AI pedagogies on educational equity. The alternative pathways shown in the framework acknowledge that teacher agency may directly foster ethical responsibility and transformative action, while future empirical research should examine potential feedback loops whereby successful equitable AI practices further strengthen teachers' agency and ethical commitment.

Figure 3. Proposed framework for equitable AI agency

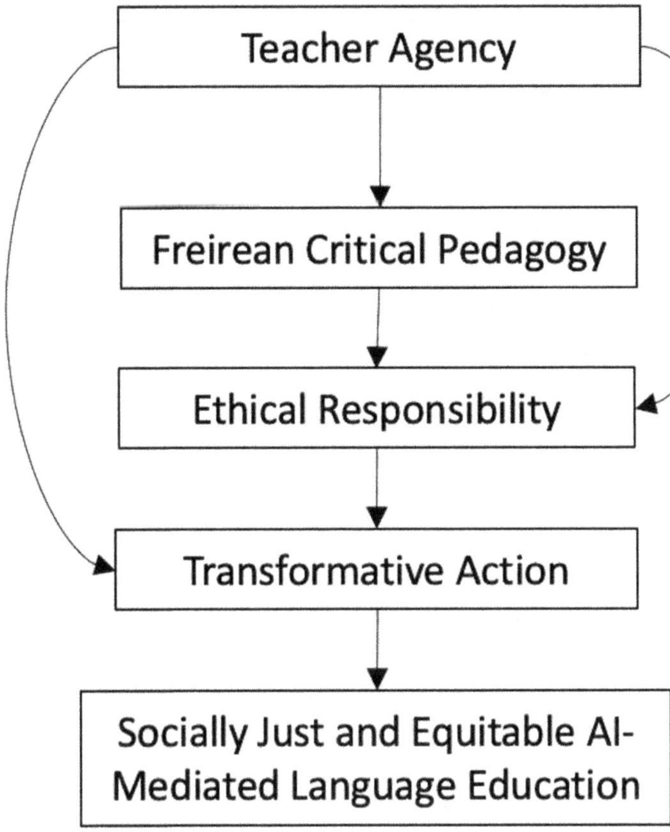

AI AND TEACHER ROLES

AI is reshaping the roles of English teachers. Traditionally, language instructors have served as sources of knowledge and facilitators of communicative practice. AI integration expands these roles in new ways. A recent study in ELT identified roles that teachers assume in AI-powered settings (Almegren, et al., 2025):

- **Facilitator:** Guiding student inquiry rather than lecturing. With AI offering information on demand, teachers spend more time prompting critical thinking. For example, instead of explaining grammar rules, a teacher might ask students to use an AI grammar checker on their writing, then lead a class discussion of its suggestions. The teacher facilitates the learning process around the AI output. Truong (2024) investigated how AI integration reshapes English writing instruction. Findings indicate that AI tools enable students to explore writing strategies while shifting teachers' roles from primary knowledge providers to facilitators who scaffold critical engagement with AI-generated content. The study highlights the need for adaptive teacher training and culturally responsive AI integration to support effective writing pedagogy in AI-mediated learning environments.

- **Blended-Role Practitioner:** Instructors are adopting blended roles, combining traditional teaching methods with AI-powered innovations to enhance productivity and engagement (Almegren et al., 2025). Teachers integrate AI activities into face-to-face or online interaction. For instance, an instructor might use an AI conversation bot for extra practice homework, then review mistakes as a class. This role merges tech and personal teaching.
- **Flexible Material Designer:** Creating and tailoring learning materials on the fly using AI. EFL teachers can rapidly generate or adapt texts, quizzes, and prompts. In practice, one teacher reported using AI to draft reading passages and then tweaking them to include local cultural references or to match students' interests (e.g., sports or music they like) (Kerr & Kim, 2025). This rapid customization was previously time-consuming without AI.
- **Creative Prompter:** Teachers are becoming creative prompters, encouraging higher-order thinking and creativity while using AI tools (Almegren et al., 2025). Crafting effective prompts and tasks for AI to produce useful educational content. Prompt engineering becomes a pedagogical skill. For example, teachers learn how to ask an AI to generate a persuasive paragraph on climate change in simple language that learners can understand. Good prompts yield high-quality practice material, while poor prompts waste class time.

These roles reflect a shift to co-designer of learning. Instructors saw themselves less as the sole source of knowledge and more as guides who curate and contextualize AI-generated content (Almegren et al., 2025). Early AI prompts, presented as pre-structured outputs masked as personalized support, deskilled teachers by encouraging passive uptake (Atherton, 2025). Language teachers guard against this by using AI as one input, not a solution. For example, a teacher may let AI suggest dialogue scripts, but then ask students to identify which lines sound unnatural or stereotypical.

CRITICAL PEDAGOGY AND TEACHER AGENCY IN AI-MEDIATED EDUCATION

A critical pedagogical perspective provides an essential theoretical lens for understanding teacher agency in AI-mediated language education. Rooted in the work of Freire (1970), critical pedagogy views education as a transformative process through which learners develop critical consciousness (conscientização) and acquire the capacity to challenge structures of domination and inequality. Freire rejected the "banking model" of education, in which learners are treated as passive recipients of knowledge, and instead advocated dialogic forms of learning that promote reflection, participation, and social transformation.

The emergence of AI in education introduces new dimensions to Freire's concerns about power and knowledge. Generative AI systems often produce responses that appear authoritative, objective, and value-neutral. Yet critical scholars have demonstrated that algorithmic systems embody particular social, cultural, and political assumptions (Williamson & Eynon, 2020). From a Freirean perspective, the challenge is not simply whether AI can improve educational efficiency but whether it contributes to humanization, critical awareness, and democratic participation. Teacher agency becomes particularly important in this context because educators mediate learners' interactions with AI-generated knowledge. Rather than encouraging uncritical acceptance of algorithmic outputs, teachers can cultivate critical consciousness by engaging learners in questions such as: Whose knowledge is represented in this response? What assumptions shape the generated content? Which voices are absent or marginalized? Such inquiry aligns with Freire's emphasis on dialogue as a means of developing critical awareness and challenging oppressive structures.

Critical pedagogy also reinforces the ethical dimensions of teacher agency. Giroux (2020) argues that educators must function as transformative intellectuals who help learners understand and challenge inequitable social arrangements. In AI-mediated classrooms, this responsibility extends to issues such as algorithmic bias, surveillance, data privacy, and digital inequality. Teachers exercising moral agency are, therefore, not merely users of educational technologies; they are advocates for equitable and socially responsible technology integration. Ultimately, a critical pedagogical perspective reframes AI literacy as more than a technical competency. It becomes a political, ethical, and educational practice through which teachers and learners interrogate technological systems, challenge inequities, and imagine alternative futures for education. Such an approach strengthens the social justice orientation of language education and highlights the transformative potential of teacher agency in an era increasingly shaped by artificial intelligence.

INCLUSIVE PEDAGOGIES IN AI-MEDIATED LANGUAGE EDUCATION

Inclusive pedagogy is grounded in the principle that educational practices should recognize, value, and support the diverse identities, experiences, and capabilities of all learners (Florian & Black-Hawkins, 2011). In language education, inclusive pedagogies seek to create learning environments where linguistic diversity, cultural backgrounds, and individual learning needs are viewed as resources rather than deficits. As artificial intelligence (AI) becomes increasingly integrated into educational settings, questions of inclusion become particularly significant because AI systems are not neutral technologies; rather, they reflect the values, assumptions, and biases embedded within the data on which they are trained (Williamson & Eynon, 2020).

Generative AI has considerable potential to advance inclusive language education through differentiated instruction, personalized learning pathways, adaptive feedback, and multilingual support. For example, AI-powered tools can generate reading materials at different proficiency levels, provide immediate feedback on language production, and facilitate translanguaging practices by allowing learners to move flexibly between languages. Such capabilities may be especially valuable in linguistically diverse classrooms where students possess varying levels of language proficiency and educational experience (Godwin-Jones, 2023). In addition, AI technologies can support learners with disabilities through text-to-speech functions, automated captioning, personalized pacing, and alternative forms of content representation.

Despite its promise, the impact of AI on learning outcomes is uneven and contingent upon how technologies are implemented and mediated. Research has demonstrated that AI systems frequently reproduce dominant linguistic norms and cultural assumptions, privileging particular forms of knowledge while marginalizing others (Bender, et al., 2021). In language education, this may manifest through the prioritization of standardized varieties of English, the underrepresentation of minority languages, or the reinforcement of culturally narrow perspectives. Consequently, teachers must exercise critical agency in evaluating AI-generated content and adapting it to the realities of their learners. This requires educators to move beyond technical proficiency and engage in what Biesta (2015) describes as educational judgment—the capacity to determine what is pedagogically desirable in specific contexts. Teacher agency is therefore central to inclusive AI-mediated pedagogy. Teachers serve as mediators who evaluate the appropriateness of AI-generated materials, identify instances of bias or exclusion, and ensure that classroom activities reflect diverse learner identities and experiences. Practical strategies include designing culturally responsive prompts, incorporating local and indigenous knowledge into AI-assisted tasks, encouraging learners to critically analyze algorithmic outputs, and using AI tools to support multilingual communication. Such practices position AI not merely as a technological innovation but as a resource that can be harnessed to promote equity, participation, and social justice in language education.

PRACTICAL PRACTICES IN THE CLASSROOM

Practical classroom practices are shaped by teachers' TPACK and by the affordances of AI tools. Teachers transform from knowledge transmitters to designers of learning experiences in language classrooms, guiding students as AI becomes a learning partner. In an ESL/EFL classroom, AI-supported writing can be implemented as a formative feedback and revision tool. For example, students draft a paragraph and then use AI to receive feedback on grammar, organization, and content. This practice is supported by a study showing that ChatGPT significantly improved ESL students' academic writing skills when used as a feedback tool, particularly in large classrooms where individualized teacher feedback is limited (Mahapatra, 2024). Similarly, research demonstrates that AI-generated feedback can be supported across language, content, and organization, sometimes complementing or extending teacher feedback (J. Li, et al., 2024). Following this, students engage in critical revision, evaluating AI suggestions and justifying changes. This aligns with evidence indicating that learning gains occur when AI is used dialogically rather than passively; studies show that interaction patterns with AI (e.g., revising, refining, questioning outputs) influence writing quality and learner ownership (Jelson et al., 2025). Without such engagement, AI may risk reducing cognitive effort and weakening independent writing processes.

In reading and comprehension tasks, students compare AI-generated summaries with original texts. This aligns with findings by Ironsi & Bostanci (2026), who show that AI supports idea generation, language accuracy, and comprehension, but requires critical comparison to avoid a superficial understanding. Further evidence indicates that most ESL/EFL AI applications focus on writing and feedback, with fewer studies on deeper reading comprehension, reinforcing the need for such structured tasks (Lo, et al., 2024). For speaking practice, students may rehearse dialogues with AI before interacting with peers. They further note that AI increases confidence and reduces anxiety, but cannot replace human interaction, as learners report more meaningful engagement in teacher-mediated or peer-based environments. Therefore, AI serves as preparatory scaffolding rather than a substitute for communication. Finally, reflection activities are incorporated, where students document how they used AI and evaluate its usefulness. This is supported by findings showing that AI effectiveness depends on user training and guided use, not mere access to the tool (Mahapatra, 2024).

LEARNER IDENTITY, VOICE, AND AGENCY IN AI-MEDIATED LANGUAGE LEARNING

While contemporary discussions of artificial intelligence in education emphasize technological innovation, instructional efficiency, and teacher preparedness, the implications of AI for learner identity, voice, and agency remain underexplored. This omission is particularly problematic in language education, where learning is fundamentally intertwined with identity formation, social participation, and the negotiation of meaning across cultural and linguistic contexts (Darvin & Norton, 2015). Language learning extends beyond the acquisition of grammatical competence; it involves learners' investments in particular identities, communities, and futures. Consequently, the integration of AI into language education raises critical questions concerning whose voices are represented, whose identities are validated, and whose forms of linguistic and cultural expression are privileged within AI-mediated learning environments.

From a sociocultural perspective, learner identity is neither fixed nor individually determined but is constructed through participation in social practices and interactions with others (Lantolf, 2006). Increasingly, AI systems have become mediational tools within these interactions, influencing how learners access information, construct texts, receive feedback, and engage in communicative practices. Recent research suggests that generative AI technologies such as ChatGPT, Claude, and Gemini can provide valuable linguistic scaffolding, enhance opportunities for autonomous learning, and support language production (Godwin-Jones, 2023). However, these benefits are accompanied by concerns regarding the standardization of discourse, the reproduction of dominant linguistic norms, and the potential erosion of learner voice. These concerns are particularly significant in multilingual and culturally diverse educational settings. Large language models are predominantly trained on datasets that privilege dominant languages, particularly English, and often reflect Western epistemological assumptions and communicative conventions (Bender et al., 2021; Kasneci et al., 2023). Such tendencies echo longstanding critiques within applied linguistics regarding linguistic imperialism (Phillipson, 1992), native-speakerism (Holliday, 2015), and the marginalization of local knowledge systems in global language education. When learners consistently encounter AI-generated content that privileges particular linguistic norms, they may experience pressure to conform to dominant forms of expression at the expense of their own linguistic repertoires and cultural identities. Recent scholarship has further highlighted the possibility that generative AI may contribute to what some researchers describe as the homogenization of discourse. Because AI systems generate responses based on probabilistic predictions derived from large-scale datasets, they tend to reproduce statistically dominant patterns of language use (Bender et al., 2021). While this feature may support language accuracy and fluency, it can simultaneously reduce opportunities for originality, creativity, and culturally situated expression. In language classrooms, this raises important concerns regarding learner voice. If students increasingly rely on AI-generated texts as models for communication, they may begin to privilege algorithmically generated language over their own perspectives and experiences.

The concept of learner voice is especially important within contemporary social justice-oriented language education. Learner voice refers not only to opportunities for expression but also to the recognition of learners as legitimate knowledge producers whose experiences, perspectives, and cultural resources contribute meaningfully to educational processes. From this perspective, AI-mediated learning environments should not merely provide efficient access to information but should also create spaces where learners can critically engage with knowledge, challenge dominant narratives, and articulate alternative perspectives. The preservation of learner voice therefore becomes both a pedagogical and ethical concern in AI-supported language learning. Teacher agency plays a central role in mediating these tensions between technological assistance and learner empowerment. As Biesta (2015) argues, educational practice requires professional judgment concerning what is educationally desirable rather than simply what is technologically possible. In AI-mediated classrooms, teachers function as critical mediators who shape how learners interact with AI systems and interpret AI-generated outputs. Through the exercise of epistemic agency, teachers can encourage students to interrogate the assumptions embedded within AI-generated content, evaluate multiple perspectives, and recognize the limitations of algorithmic knowledge production. Rather than positioning AI as an authoritative source of truth, teachers can frame it as a dialogic partner whose outputs require interpretation, critique, and contextualization.

Furthermore, relational and moral dimensions of teacher agency are essential for safeguarding learner identity and voice. Teachers can design activities that invite learners to compare AI-generated texts with locally situated knowledge, revise outputs to reflect their cultural experiences, or examine whose voices are amplified and whose are silenced within AI-generated responses. Such practices align with Freirean notions of critical consciousness by encouraging learners to question dominant representations and participate actively in knowledge construction (Freire, 1970). In this way, AI becomes not simply a tool for content generation but a catalyst for critical dialogue and identity negotiation. Developing critical AI literacy enables learners to recognize biases, evaluate the credibility of AI-generated information, and make informed decisions regarding the use of AI in academic and professional contexts. Importantly, such literacy supports learner agency by empowering students to engage with AI technologies as critical participants rather than passive consumers. Learners who engage critically with AI technologies strengthen their capacity for self-expression, reflection, and participation in increasingly digitalized communicative environments. The relationship between teacher agency and learner agency thus becomes central to equitable AI integration in language education.

LINGUISTIC JUSTICE AND ALGORITHMIC BIAS

AI models can reflect cultural and linguistic biases from their training data. UNESCO warns that AI can reinforce stereotypes and threaten linguistic diversity (UNESCO, 2024). For instance, multilingual NLP systems may perform poorly on under-resourced languages, marginalizing non-English students. An inclusive approach is, therefore, vital. A study on AI in education emphasizes the use of localized datasets and culturally responsive AI tools to honor linguistic diversity (Oyetade & Zuva, 2025). UNESCO calls for audits of AI for language bias, urging that AI respect and preserve cultural/linguistic rights (UNESCO, 2025a). AI tutors can broaden access when coupled with mother-tongue pedagogy (Sangwa & Mutabazi, 2025). However, a critical caution is the loss of voice, as teachers note that AI-generated text can homogenize writing style (Monib, et al., 2025), risking the loss of students' unique linguistic identities.

Similarly, an issue can be a bias toward standard English and Western culture. Research shows that ChatGPT and similar LLMs can produce derogatory or stereotypical content about non-standard English varieties. For example, one study found ChatGPT applied harmful and racist stereotypes to African American English phrases unless explicitly prompted to identify race (Schofield, 2025).These biases mean that students who use non-standard English (e.g., regional dialects) may receive unfair feedback or even censorship.

Recommendations include consideration of inclusive AI tools, when selecting AI apps, prioritize ones trained on diverse languages or that allow input in students' mother tongues. For example, use AI language games that support multiple languages, or speech-recognition tools tuned to local accents. Provide students with AI language aides (e.g., bilingual dictionaries) that augment rather than replace home languages. Encourage translanguaging (the use of multiple languages in the classroom). Integrate culturally relevant content (e.g., ask students to prompt AI in their home language and compare responses). Explicitly discuss language bias, and have students test AI with vocabulary from their own dialect to identify inaccuracies. Regularly test classroom AI outputs for bias (e.g., gender, cultural assumptions). Use multiple AI sources to cross-validate (e.g., compare ChatGPT vs Bard answers). Emphasize content quality over perfect grammar if AI generates systemic errors in certain languages. Involve linguistically diverse teachers, parents, and community leaders when adopting AI tools to ensure local needs are met. Advocate for policies on AI in education that mandate coverage of marginalized languages (e.g., funding localized AI development).

ACADEMIC INTEGRITY AND ASSESSMENT CHALLENGES

Generative AI poses challenges to traditional assessment. UNESCO warns that AI can undermine assessment reliability as students can prompt tools to produce essays, solutions to problems, and creative work, and a think-piece argues for shifting from rote tasks to higher-order skills—critical thinking, creativity, and ethical reasoning—that AI cannot easily replicate (Desai, 2025). Indeed, AI-detection tools are unreliable (high false positives/negatives), and this arms race is unwinnable. It is recommended to redesign assessments by using open-ended, authentic projects; requiring students to contextualize and critique AI output; and focusing on process/journeys over final artifacts. For example, students might evaluate an AI-generated essay for logical fallacies, use AI as a research assistant, and then reflect on its outputs (Desai, 2025). A study echoes this, illustrating tasks in which AI is integrated as a learning tool, e.g., students edit an AI-generated draft or work in teams to improve AI-generated content (Khlaif, et al., 2025).

Recommendations include redesigning assessments to use authentic, applied tasks (projects, portfolios, labs) that require personal input. Develop rubrics that value critical analysis of information and creativity over content recall. Examples may include having students compare multiple AI-generated summaries of a text and explain differences; assigning public-facing projects (presentations, blogs) that require ownership. The assessment delivery may include closed-book environments and in-person or proctored digital tests. Otherwise, shift many tasks to open-ended, in-class activities (presentations, discussions, debates) where AI cannot directly intervene. Consider oral exams or viva voce to gauge understanding. Another crucial point is academic honesty education, which may focus on teaching students about AI, such as its potential and limitations. Embed AI literacy in the curriculum (e.g., how to spot AI errors or biases). Emphasizing ethics when sourcing and reflecting on AI-generated content may be required. Adopt clear policies that, when using AI, require disclosure and reflection on its use. The infrastructure may include training teachers on AI (tool demos, evaluating AI outputs, creating new question types) (Khlaif et al., 2025). Provide technological support such as plagiarism and AI writing checkers while also recognizing their limits.

DIGITAL DIVIDE

AI's benefits are not equally accessible. A digital divide persists across infrastructure, affordability, and skills. Many EFL contexts (especially in low-income regions) lack reliable internet or devices to run AI tools. UNESCO and others warn that an AI divide mirrors the broader digital gap (Gonzales, 2024). For example, Stanford researchers note LLMs work well for wealthy, English-speaking contexts but fail for Vietnamese or Nahuatl communities due to insufficient training data (Lynch, 2025). Similarly, rural schools in developing countries often have no or slow internet, making real-time AI use impossible. Teacher training disparities are also acute. Research on AI in education found that in some Chinese rural schools, the problem was neither access nor infrastructure, but a lack of professional empowerment (Matjie, et al., 2026). In such cases, even when a school has computers, instructors have not been trained to integrate AI into pedagogy. Cost is another barrier. Subscription fees for advanced AI (e.g., premium chatbots or specialized language tutors) are beyond many schools' budgets. Even free tools assume students have personal devices (which many EFL learners do not). As a result, AI can end up benefiting only the already-privileged. For instance, a BRICS-region STEM education case noted that without subsidized access, AI initiatives tended to favor students from richer schools.

The cumulative effect is that AI amplifies existing advantages. AI interventions that do not address context often widen gaps. In contrast, successful projects co-designed with communities (e.g., Kenyan deaf learners or Malian preschoolers) used low-cost AI creatively (sign-language translators, tablet apps) to reduce bias (Matjie et al., 2026). Key lessons include investing in infrastructure and offline solutions (e.g., downloadable AI apps), funding teacher AI professional development, and encouraging local content creation.

ORGANIZATIONAL CHALLENGES AND EDUCATIONAL POLICY CHALLENGES

Effective AI integration requires supportive governance, equitable access, and clear policies. Equitable access and use of AI are critical, and the guidelines emphasize access and teacher support (Varsik & Vosberg, 2024). UNESCO's Beijing Consensus on AI in Education and the Generative AI Guidance stress the ethical use of AI (human rights, privacy). Practical gaps are stark; UNESCO reports that many schools worldwide lack reliable internet access (UNESCO, 2025b). This digital divide threatens to entrench inequities as AI tools spread. Teacher workload is another concern: while AI could automate grading or content creation, it also requires time for new training and oversight. UNESCO's right-to-education report calls for a human rights approach, noting factors such as connectivity, cost, and cultural context in policy planning.

Recommendations include that governments/schools invest in broadband and devices (e.g., through partnerships or grants) so that all students can access AI tools. Provide device loans or create AI labs for under-resourced schools. Set clear equity targets and monitor them.

Establish school AI committees (including teachers, IT, parents) to guide AI adoption. Develop transparent AI policies (privacy, acceptable use, data protection) aligned with laws (e.g., GDPR) (Monib, et al., 2024) and UNESCO guidance (UNESCO, 2025b). Ensure these policies mandate non-discriminatory use and specify teacher agency (e.g., teachers decide when/which AI tools to use). Adjust job descriptions to account for AI-related responsibilities (training, tool evaluation). Provide time in schedules for AI experimentation and PD, so teachers do not have to bear this 'on top' of their normal duties. Leverage AI to reduce low-value tasks (e.g., let AI draft routine lesson elements) rather than simply adding new tasks. Align with UNESCO's Recommendation on AI Ethics, ensuring AI use respects student rights (privacy, fairness) (UNESCO, 2025b; Varsik & Vosberg, 2024). Regularly audit AI tools for compliance. Foster a school culture of digital citizenship where students and staff understand the ethical implications of AI.

BUILDING TEACHER CAPACITY FOR AI EVALUATION AND IMPLEMENTATION

Transformative potential means little unless teachers are prepared to harness it. Language educators need professional development (PD) that goes beyond technical training to build critical AI literacy. Several key strategies can be considered:

- **Professional Development Program:** Training should combine AI tools mastery with social justice analysis. For example, a workshop might teach ESL teachers how to prompt an AI translation tool, while also guiding them to assess its cultural fairness. Kohnke & Zou (2025) stress coupling technology with equity discussions. AI-resistant pedagogy is also recommended– PD that helps teachers design assignments emphasizing human skills (creative writing, critical discussion) so students cannot just pass tasks to AI (Kennedy & Castek, 2025). Programs should be designed to enhance teachers' TPACK specifically for AI tools. They have been shown to improve novice EFL teachers' knowledge, teaching skills, and self-efficacy in using AI-powered tools. For example, Zulianti, et al. (2025) examined a TPACK-based professional development program designed to improve novice EFL teachers' competency with AI-powered tools. The findings showed that the PD program significantly enhanced participants' AI-related knowledge, improved their ability to integrate AI into teaching practices, and increased self-efficacy in using AI tools. The study demonstrates the effectiveness of TPACK-guided PD in supporting teachers' technological and pedagogical growth, offering a model for scalable AI literacy initiatives in EFL education. Another study by Bahari & Liu (2025) evaluated the impact of AI tools on EFL teachers' digital competency, professional growth, and pedagogical innovation. The results showed significant gains in digital skills and professional development engagement, and emphasized the role of contextual factors (institutional support, equitable access) in effective AI adoption, and provided evidence for PD programs that foster ethical, sustainable, and inclusive AI integration in EFL instruction.

- **Ongoing Reflection and Inquiry:** Teachers should consider the various impacts of AI (Niazai & Monib, 2025b). Structured reflection protocols (e.g., journals, rubrics) can help. For instance, a teacher might keep a log of classroom AI incidents: Today, an AI writing tool corrected a student's essay, but missed a cultural reference. How did I address that? Some AI tools can aid reflection: reviewing speech-to-text transcriptions of lessons can help spot communication gaps. Crucially, reflective practice is not solitary. Peer coaching and collaborative data analysis (e.g., reviewing student performance with AI tools) cultivate collective wisdom. Teachers' ethical awareness often grows through discussion with colleagues (Ho & Lee, 2025).
- **Collaborative Networks and Communities of Practice:** Teachers learn fastest when they share experiences. Professional learning communities (PLCs) for TESOL teachers can serve as incubators for AI integration. In these networks, educators can critique AI scenarios, exchange culturally relevant resources, and co-author equity guidelines. A convening of AI leaders highlighted the current lack of common frameworks in education (Overdeck Family Foundation, 2026), suggesting that only through collaboration can fragmentation be overcome. District or national forums (even virtual) should invite ESL/EFL teachers to pilot AI tools together. Funding bodies like the Overdeck Family Foundation call for the development of AI education ecosystems with shared standards (Overdeck Family Foundation, 2025).
- **Equity-Oriented AI Literacy:** PD should frame AI in the context of inclusion. Teachers need to design lessons that leverage AI to support disadvantaged learners. For example, training might cover using AI to generate home-language support materials for multilingual students, or to create varied examples reflecting learners' cultures. Kennedy & Castek (2025) highlight training in ethical frameworks specific to ELA contexts so teachers

can make autonomous, ethical decisions about AI use. Zhang & Samsudin (2026) conducted a study on cultivating EFL teachers' AI literacy through an AI-integrated Genre-Based Pedagogy (AI-GBP). The study embedded generative AI in a genre-based professional development module grounded in TPACK and situated learning. The findings show statistically significant gains in practical and critical AI literacy compared with a generic AI-literacy control, as teachers transitioned from tool familiarity toward context-rich pedagogical application and critical evaluation—including bias recognition and contextual judgment—indicating a move toward equitable, reflective AI use for EFL learners.

- **Community-built Ethical Guidelines:** Schools and districts should support teachers in developing shared AI policies. For example, a school committee might co-create a code of ethics for AI use, drawing on teacher experiences. Overdeck's convening urges inclusive design from the start (Overdeck Family Foundation, 2026); similarly, teacher-led committees can guide tool procurement and usage.

CASE STUDIES

Literature highlights AI's transformative impact on EFL/ESL/ELT teaching. Empirical case studies show teachers exercising epistemic agency by collaboratively using AI (e.g., Chinese EFL instructors shared knowledge via AI tools) (Chu & Wang, 2025) and transformative agency by redesigning tasks (e.g., an EFL instructor in Spain used ChatGPT to co-create lesson content and assess writing) (Octavio, et al., 2024). Teachers also demonstrated relational agency through new communities of practice for AI integration (Thapa & Shrestha, 2026) and moral agency by stipulating ethical AI use (e.g., insisting that AI be a tool, not a replacement) (Thapa & Shrestha, 2026). Studies reveal dramatic shifts in teacher roles: instructors move from sole knowledge providers to facilitators, blended practitioners, material designers, and creative prompters when AI is available (Almegren et al., 2025).

In AI-mediated settings, teachers often co-construct knowledge. For example, a study of Chinese university EFL teachers showed that they resolved conflicts of motive by jointly experimenting with AI tools, collaboratively shaping lessons, and creating new content. Participants reported that AI is a useful tool… for sharing and integrating knowledge, which altered their collaborative decision-making processes and promoted knowledge creation (Chu & Wang, 2025). This reflects strong epistemic agency: teachers pursued inquiry and learning with AI rather than just delivering content. However, their agency was constrained by beliefs and institutional factors. Similarly, teachers may enact change by integrating AI to reshape pedagogy. In one study, an experienced EFL teacher used ChatGPT over seven months to plan lessons and evaluate student writing. ChatGPT provided significant support in planning/designing lessons and even in assessing compositions (Octavio et al., 2024). The teacher's role shifted, where instead of lecturing on grammar, she became a facilitator, designing activities around AI outputs. This illustrates transformative agency – actively reimagining instruction. It required the teacher to develop new skills (prompt crafting and critical evaluation) and to adapt tasks on the fly. The teacher co-authored materials and feedback with AI, thus blending traditional teaching with AI innovation. The outcome is more personalized writing support, but the limitation is that the teacher needs prompt engineering expertise and vigilance to correct AI errors.

Some studies note how AI prompted collaborative dynamics. Teachers formed support networks and micro-communities of practice to share AI strategies (Thapa & Shrestha, 2026). Educators reported exchanging lesson ideas on WhatsApp and conducting peer workshops about ChatGPT. These grassroots networks may embody relational agency, in which teachers collectively shape practice. However, if formal PD is lacking, such relational efforts may be uneven. Teachers struggled to integrate AI meaningfully despite individual willingness. In one study, participants created a peer-led forum on AI integration. Teachers co-developed prompts and curricula, supporting each other's growth. This built shared expertise and mutual support (relational agency); the limitation is that without institutional mandates, uptake varied by individual initiative.

Teachers may also face ethical issues. Monib, et al. (2024) argue that with AI, users should act morally. Teachers set classroom norms on AI use. Some ban certain AI tools outright, while others insist on transparency. These actions reflect moral agency – teachers applying ethical judgment. But teachers voiced frustration: increasing AI in their work was at odds with the core values that drew them to the profession (Küçükuncular & Ertugan, 2025). Without an external policy, they felt torn between leveraging AI and maintaining academic integrity. In a study, EFL instructors explicitly discussed ethics with students. Many stressed that AI is just an aid, not a replacement of human thought, framing this as a matter of professional responsibility (Thapa & Shrestha, 2026). Furthermore, research indicates a shift in teacher roles as AI enters ELT. Almegren et al. (2025) found AI integration reshaped the 'assistant' function of technology and the 'interaction' roles of language instructors. Teachers were no longer just human assistants to passive tools; instead, they became adaptive facilitators who guide inquiry around AI outputs, blended-role practitioners who integrate AI activities into lessons, flexible material designers who rapidly generate and adapt content with AI, and creative prompters skilled in crafting effective prompts.

When it comes to language skills, a range of studies report positive learning outcomes when AI is used in classroom interventions. In writing, AI chatbots can significantly boost writing skills. For instance, in one study, researchers used a writing assistant (WritePro) in an EFL writing course. Students using WritePro improved their scores in content, organization, grammar, and vocabulary more than a control group (Almutairi, et al., 2026). The interaction effect was significant, with the largest gains in sentence structure. This suggests guided AI support can help students produce more accurate, organized text. Another case study found that an EFL teacher's use of ChatGPT in writing labs boosted student output and creativity. However, instructors note the need to vet AI feedback carefully to avoid perpetuating errors. Similarly, interactive AI-powered practice can raise speaking proficiency. For example, EFL learners who practiced with an AI conversation app significantly outperformed a control group on a post-test of speaking, while also reporting much lower speaking anxiety (Ebadi, et al., 2025). The experimental group's speaking scores rose markedly, and shared learner narratives emphasized increased confidence. Furthermore, AI-driven tutoring can accelerate the development of listening skills. For instance, in a study, an AI-powered speech-recognition tutor significantly improved listening comprehension. The AI group showed notable improvements in listening skill scores and reported higher intrinsic motivation and lower listening anxiety at post-test, whereas the control group showed only modest gains (Xiao, 2025).

DISCUSSION

The preceding sections demonstrate that the integration of AI in language education extends beyond technological innovation and represents a significant pedagogical, ethical, and social transformation. While AI offers opportunities for personalized learning, differentiated instruction, automated feedback, and enhanced accessibility, it must be used with care. The evidence reviewed throughout this chapter suggests that the impact of AI on teaching and learning depends largely on how educators exercise agency in mediating, adapting, and critically evaluating technological tools. Therefore, the central argument emerging from this chapter is that teacher agency serves as the critical mechanism through which AI can either reinforce existing inequities or contribute to more inclusive and socially just educational practices.

From the perspective of the TPACK framework, effective AI integration requires the intersection of technological, pedagogical, and content knowledge. However, the findings synthesized in this chapter suggest that knowledge alone is insufficient. Teachers must also possess the capacity to make informed judgments about when, how, and why AI should be used. The dimensions of teacher agency discussed throughout this chapter—epistemic, transformative, relational, and moral agency—provide a framework for understanding how educators navigate these decisions. Epistemic agency enables teachers to critically evaluate AI-generated content rather than accepting outputs as objective truths. Transformative agency allows educators to redesign learning experiences in ways that leverage AI while maintaining pedagogical integrity. Relational agency facilitates collaboration among teachers, learners, and communities to negotiate appropriate uses of AI. Moral agency ensures that ethical concerns, including privacy, fairness, inclusion, and student well-being, remain central to educational decision-making.

Importantly, these forms of agency align closely with broader social justice perspectives in education. Social justice education emphasizes the need to challenge structural inequalities, amplify marginalized voices, and create learning environments that promote equitable participation. AI technologies, however, are developed within existing social, cultural, and economic systems and may therefore reproduce many of the biases embedded within those systems. As highlighted in the sections on linguistic justice, algorithmic bias, and the digital divide, AI systems tend to privilege dominant languages, cultures, and ways of knowing, while marginalizing underrepresented communities. Consequently, the question is not whether AI should be used in language education, but rather how educators can ensure that AI serves equitable educational goals rather than reinforcing existing disparities. This perspective resonates strongly with the principles of critical pedagogy. Freire (1970) argued that education should empower learners to develop critical consciousness and challenge oppressive structures rather than passively consume knowledge. Applied to AI-mediated language learning, this perspective suggests that teachers and students should not view AI-generated content as authoritative or neutral. Instead, AI outputs should become objects of critical inquiry. Students can be encouraged to question whose knowledge is represented, whose perspectives are omitted, and how algorithmic systems shape communication and learning. In this way, AI literacy becomes a technical skill and a form of critical digital citizenship. Teachers exercising agency create opportunities for learners to interrogate technology, recognize bias, and participate actively in the construction of knowledge.

The discussion also highlights the importance of learner identity and voice within AI-mediated environments. While AI can personalize learning experiences, it may also inadvertently standardize language use and suppress linguistic diversity. Generative AI systems often favor dominant linguistic norms, which may discourage students from expressing culturally situated identities or using non-standard varieties of English. This challenge is particularly relevant in EFL and ESL contexts, where learners frequently negotiate multiple linguistic and cultural identities. Teacher agency, therefore, intersects directly with learner agency. Educators who critically mediate AI use can create opportunities for learners to preserve and express their unique voices while benefiting from AI-supported learning. For example, teachers can encourage students to critique AI-generated texts, compare responses across cultural contexts, and adapt outputs to reflect their own experiences and perspectives. Such practices position learners as active contributors rather than passive recipients of AI-generated knowledge.

Another significant insight concerns the relationship between technological innovation and educational equity. Although AI has the potential to support inclusion through adaptive learning, multilingual assistance, and personalized feedback, these benefits remain unevenly distributed. Access to devices, internet connectivity, digital literacy, and teacher preparation continue to vary substantially across regions and educational contexts. As a result, AI may unintentionally widen educational inequalities if implementation strategies fail to address structural barriers. Equitable AI integration requires investments in infrastructure, teacher professional development, policy support, and culturally responsive implementation practices. Teacher agency remains essential in identifying these inequities and advocating for solutions that ensure all learners benefit from technological advances. Furthermore, the findings suggest that teacher agency should not be conceptualized solely as an individual characteristic but as a socially situated and context-dependent phenomenon. Institutional policies, leadership support, and access to resources all influence educators' capacity to exercise agency. Teachers who work within supportive environments are more likely to experiment with innovative pedagogies, engage in collaborative inquiry, and critically evaluate emerging technologies. Conversely, restrictive policies, inadequate professional development, and limited resources may constrain teachers' ability to make informed decisions regarding AI integration. Therefore, efforts to promote equitable and ethical AI use must extend beyond individual classrooms and include systemic initiatives that empower teachers as active participants in educational transformation.

IMPLICATIONS

Beyond classrooms, systems must change to sustain teacher agency. A central recommendation is to embed teacher voice in AI governance. Teacher agency flourishes only when systems allow it. Policymakers and institutions must embed teacher voice in every step of AI integration. Excluding teachers from decision-making undermines both agency and effectiveness (Kennedy & Castek, 2025). Schools should form AI advisory boards with teacher representatives. These groups can evaluate the fairness and relevance of new AI platforms before adoption. Technology plans must solicit language teachers' input on issues like data privacy (e.g., permission forms for student use of AI chatbots) and acceptable AI tasks (e.g., rules on using translation tools for writing assignments).

Teacher Education: Pre-service training programs must include AI literacy as a core competency. K-12 teacher colleges are already moving toward digital citizenship curricula, and these should be expanded to cover AI. For ESL/EFL teachers, this might mean courses on AI in language teaching, covering topics such as algorithmic bias in machine translation or how to verify AI-generated feedback. For example, Tennessee Tech University's AI framework recommends evaluating tools' biases and pedagogical fit (Mimoudi & Mokhtari, 2025). Training should equip teachers to advocate for their autonomy and to design AI-resistant assignments (Kennedy & Castek, 2025). Equipping future teachers with these skills ensures the profession does not lag behind technology.

Professional Standards and Guidelines: Educational policy bodies should issue clear guidelines on AI. Guidelines might specify, for instance, that any AI used for assessment must be validated for fairness in diverse languages. They should also clarify issues of academic integrity: e.g., how to address if a student uses an AI translator on a translation exercise. UNESCO's global recommendations on AI ethics emphasize transparency and accountability (UNESCO, 2025c). At the very least, there should be rules on student data (e.g., forbidding uploading student essays to public AI sites without anonymization) and on appropriate AI tools in classrooms.

Resource Allocation: Equity requires investment. Underserved schools need funding for devices and connectivity if they are to benefit from AI. Policymakers must close the AI divide by supporting infrastructure (UNESCO, 2025c). They can also fund teacher PD and AI tool trials targeted at language education. For example, a ministry of education could sponsor a pilot project introducing AI language apps to rural language learners, along with teacher training.

Global and Local Standards: On a broader scale, international collaboration can help align AI in language education with local needs. UNESCO calls for localization of AI tools – training them on diverse languages and cultures (UNESCO, 2025c). AI vendors should be encouraged to adapt their English-learning apps for multilingual contexts. For instance, an AI English tutor could be trained on examples from African or Asian English usage, not just British/American English.

Empowering Teacher Leadership: Ultimately, the system change is cultural. Excluding teachers from policies that threaten their autonomy leads to misaligned implementation (Kennedy & Castek, 2025). Educational leaders must see teachers as partners, not obstacles. That means involving language teachers in committees deciding which AI curriculum to adopt, establishing AI coordinator roles filled by teachers, and recognizing the innovations teachers develop.

In summary, institutional support for teacher agency means building channels for teacher expertise to shape AI use. When teachers lead, AI in EFL/ESL can become a contextually sensitive, equity-driven enhancement. As UNESCO frames it, the future of education must be human-centered, equitable, safe, and ethical (UNESCO, 2025c)– goals unattainable if teachers lack voice and power in AI decisions.

CONCLUSION

The integration of AI in EFL/ESL education is not just a technological shift, but a profound pedagogical transformation. This chapter has argued that teacher agency must be at the heart of this transformation, particularly where questions of equity are at stake. The four dimensions of teacher agency examined here — epistemic, transformative, relational, and moral — provide a framework for understanding this mediation. This chapter has argued that agency across these dimensions enables AI to function as a supporting tool – expanding what teachers and learners can achieve – rather than as an automating tool that narrows opportunities. AI will undeniably continue to evolve in education, but the analysis underscores a core principle: the teacher remains the architect of learning. To harness AI for good, educators must center teacher expertise, uphold equity, and remember that technology amplifies existing social structures. When educators lead with agency and ethics, AI can truly transform English language teaching – making it more personalized, accessible, and just for all students. Policies must also evolve to ensure safe, transparent AI use.Teacher education curricula should formally include agency and equity in AI. Future research should continue to document AI's effects on language learning.

REFERENCES

Abdelrady, A. H., Ibrahim, D. O. O., & Akram, H. (2025). Unveiling the role of Copilot in enhancing EFL learners' writing skills: A content analysis. *World Journal of English Language, 15*(8), 174–185. DOI: 10.5430/wjel.v15n8p174

Alm, A., & Watanabe, Y. (2023). Integrating ChatGPT in Language Education: A Freirean Perspective. *Iranian Journal of Language Teaching Research, 11*(3), 19–30. DOI: 10.30466/IJLTR.2023.121404

Almegren, A., Almegren, R. M., Hazaea, A. N., Mahdi, H. S., & Mohammed Ali, J. K. (2025). AI powered ELT: Instructors' transformative roles and opportunities. *PLoS One, 20*(5), e0324910. DOI: 10.1371/journal.pone.0324910 PMID: 40440266

Almutairi, H., Alfaifi, A. A., & Saleem, M. (2026). Writing accuracy: How AI-assisted writing instruction can support EFL undergraduate students. *Information (Basel), 17*(2), 157. DOI: 10.3390/info17020157

Atherton, P. (2025). AI agents of change? Generative AI (GAI) and teacher agency. *EDULEARN25 Proceedings*, 768–775. IATED. https://library.iated.org/view/ATHERTON2025AIA

Bahari, A., & Liu, Y. (2025). AI integration in EFL teacher development: A mixed-methods evaluation of digital competency, professional trajectories, and pedagogical innovation within adaptive learning ecosystems. *Interactive Learning Environments*, •••, 1–17. DOI: 10.1080/10494820.2025.2591251

Bender, E. M., Gebru, T., McMillan-Major, A., & Shmitchell, S. (2021). On the dangers of stochastic parrots: Can language models be too big? *Proceedings of the 2021 ACM Conference on Fairness, Accountability, and Transparency*, 610–623. DOI: 10.1145/3442188.3445922

Biesta, G. J. J. (2015). *Beautiful risk of education*. Routledge. DOI: 10.4324/9781315635866

Campbell, E. (2004). Ethical bases of moral agency in teaching. *Teachers and Teaching, 10*(4), 409–428. DOI: 10.1080/1354060042000224142

Cherbow, K., & McNeill, K. L. (2022). Planning for student-driven discussions: A revelatory case of curricular sensemaking for epistemic agency. *Journal of the Learning Sciences, 31*(3), 408–457. DOI: 10.1080/10508406.2021.2024433

Chu, T., & Wang, W. (2025). Exploring EFL teachers' epistemic agency and its influencing factors in an AI-integrated context through the double stimulation model. *The Asia-Pacific Education Researcher, 34*(4), 1267–1275. DOI: 10.1007/s40299-024-00940-4

Coker, H., Kalsoom, Q., & Mercieca, D. (2023). Teachers' use of knowledge in curriculum making: Implications for social justice. *Education Sciences, 14*(1), 3. DOI: 10.3390/educsci14010003

Cui, W., & Zhang, J. (2025). AI applications in language learning: Improving speaking fluency and pronunciation using chatbots and speech feedback. *Interactive Learning Environments*. Advance online publication. DOI: 10.1080/10494820.2025.2546634

Darvin, R., & Norton, B. (2015). Identity and a model of investment in applied linguistics. *Annual Review of Applied Linguistics, 35*, 36–56. DOI: 10.1017/S0267190514000191

Desai, H. (2025). What's worth measuring? The future of assessment in the AI age. Retrieved March 25, 2026, from UNESCO website: https://www.unesco.org/en/articles/whats-worth-measuring-future-assessment-ai-age#:~:text=AI%20detection%20tools%20have%20proven,means%20is%20likely%20closing%20permanently

Ebadi, S., Velayati, S., Ramezanzadeh, A., & Salman, A. R. (2025). Exploring the impact of AI-powered speaking tasks on EFL learners' speaking performance and anxiety: An activity theory study. *Acta Psychologica, 259*, 105391. DOI: 10.1016/j.actpsy.2025.105391 PMID: 40812259

Filiz, O., Kaya, M. H., & Adiguzel, T. (2025). Teachers and AI: Understanding the factors influencing AI integration in K-12 education. *Education and Information Technologies, 30*(13), 17931–17967. DOI: 10.1007/s10639-025-13463-2

Florian, L., & Black-Hawkins, K. (2011). Exploring inclusive pedagogy. *British Educational Research Journal, 37*(5), 813–828. DOI: 10.1080/01411926.2010.501096

Freire, P. (1970). Pedagogy of the Oppressed (trans. MB Ramos). *New York: Continuum, 2005.*

Ghiasvand, F., & Seyri, H. (2025). A collaborative reflection on the synergy of Artificial Intelligence (AI) and language teacher identity reconstruction. *Teaching and Teacher Education, 160*, 105022. DOI: 10.1016/j.tate.2025.105022

Giroux, H. A. (2020). *On critical pedagogy*. Bloomsbury. DOI: 10.5040/9781350145016

Godwin-Jones, R. (2023). Emerging spaces for language learning: AI bots, ambient intelligence, and the metaverse. *Language Learning & Technology*, *27*(2), 6–27. https://hdl.handle.net/10125/73501. DOI: 10.64152/10125/73501

Gonzales, S. (2024). AI literacy and the new digital divide-A global call for action. *Paris, France: UNESCO. Retrieved March, 30*, 2025.

Gumiero, R., & de Araújo, K. (2019). Contribuition of Paulo Freire and Célestin Freinet to the process of teaching-learning. *Acta Scientiarum. Education*, •••, 41.

Ho, C. S. M., & Lee, J. C.-K. (2025). From intuition to action: Exploring teachers' ethical awareness in the use of AI tools in education. *Computers and Education: Artificial Intelligence*, *9*, 100502. DOI: 10.1016/j.caeai.2025.100502

Hofer, B. K., & Pintrich, P. R. (1997). The development of epistemological theories: Beliefs about knowledge and knowing and their relation to learning. *Review of Educational Research*, *67*(1), 88–140. DOI: 10.3102/00346543067001088

Holliday, A. (2015). Native-speakerism: Taking the concept forward and achieving cultural belief. In *(En) countering native-speakerism: Global perspectives* (pp. 11–25). Springer.

Ironsi, C. S., & Bostanci, H. B. (2026). Enhancing the reading comprehension and autonomy of foreign language students using generative AI-integrated assistant. *Frontiers in Education, Volume 11-2026*. Retrieved from https://www.frontiersin.org/journals/education/articles/10.3389/feduc.2026.1763238

Jantakoon, T., Jantakun, T., Jantakun, K., Pongpanich, W., Pasmala, R., Wannapiroon, P., & Nilsook, P. (2025). The effectiveness of artificial intelligence in English instruction for speaking and listening skills: A meta-analysis. *Contemporary Educational Technology*, *17*(4), ep596. Advance online publication. DOI: 10.30935/cedtech/17310

Jelson, A., Manesh, D., Jang, A., Dunlap, D., Kim, Y.-H., & Lee, S. W. (2025). An empirical study to understand how students use ChatGPT for writing essays. *ArXiv Preprint ArXiv:2501.10551*.

Kahn, P., Carrigan, M., Smith, P., Murtagh, L., Liu, R., & Song, F. (2025). Teacher agency and generative artificial intelligence: Teaching in higher education as a responsive, cultural activity. *Learning, Media and Technology*, •••, 1–12. DOI: 10.1080/17439884.2025.2575993

Kasneci, E., Sessler, K., Küchemann, S., Bannert, M., Dementieva, D., Fischer, F., Gasser, U., Groh, G., Günnemann, S., Hüllermeier, E., Krusche, S., Kutyniok, G., Michaeli, T., Nerdel, C., Pfeffer, J., Poquet, O., Sailer, M., Schmidt, A., Seidel, T., & Kasneci, G. (2023). ChatGPT for good? On opportunities and challenges of large language models for education. *Learning and Individual Differences*, *103*, 102274. Advance online publication. DOI: 10.1016/j.lindif.2023.102274

Kennedy, K. J., & Castek, J. M. (2025). Empowering ELA teachers: Recommendations for teacher education in the AI era. *Contemporary Issues in Technology & Teacher Education*, *25*(1), 1–31. https://citejournal.org/volume-25/issue-1-25/english-language-arts/empowering-ela-teachers-recommendations-for-teacher-education-in-the-ai-era

Kerr, R. C., & Kim, H. (2025). From prompts to plans: A case study of pre-service EFL teachers' use of generative AI for lesson planning. *English Teaching*, *80*(1), 95–118. DOI: 10.15858/engtea.80.1.202503.95

Khlaif, Z. N., Alkouk, W. A., Salama, N., & Abu Eideh, B. (2025). Redesigning Assessments for AI-Enhanced Learning: A Framework for Educators in the Generative AI Era. *Education Sciences*, *15*(2), 174. Advance online publication. DOI: 10.3390/educsci15020174

Koehler, M. J., Mishra, P., Kereluik, K., Shin, T. S., & Graham, C. R. (2013). The technological pedagogical content knowledge framework. In *Handbook of research on educational communications and technology* (pp. 101–111). Springer., DOI: 10.1007/978-1-4614-3185-5_9

Kohnke, L., & Zou, D. (2025). Artificial intelligence integration in TESOL teacher education: Promoting a critical lens guided by TPACK and SAMR. *TESOL Quarterly*, *59*(S3), S267–S278. DOI: 10.1002/tesq.3396

Küçükuncular, A., & Ertugan, A. (2025). Teaching in the AI era: Sustainable digital education through ethical integration and teacher empowerment. *Sustainability (Basel)*, *17*(16), 7405. DOI: 10.3390/su17167405

Lantolf, J. P. (2006). *Sociocultural theory and the genesis of second language development*. Oxford University Press.

Le-Khanh, H., Do, K., & Tran-Thanh, V. (2024). EFL writing teachers' agency in response to AI emergence from an ecological perspective. In Bui, H. P., & Namaziandost, E. (Eds.), *Innovations in Technologies for Language Teaching and Learning* (pp. 79–94). Springer Nature Switzerland., DOI: 10.1007/978-3-031-63447-5_5

Lee, Y.-J., & Jeong, S.-H. (2026). Implementing AI-integrated English writing: University English language learners writing strategies and perceptions. *International Journal of Evaluation and Research in Education, 15*(1), 805–814. DOI: 10.11591/ijere.v15i1.35461

Leijen, Ä. (2023). Supporting and assessing professional agency of student teachers in initial teacher education. In Tierney, R. J., Rizvi, F., & Ercikan, K. (Eds.), *International Encyclopedia of Education* (4th ed., pp. 339–345). Elsevier., DOI: 10.1016/B978-0-12-818630-5.04090-2

Li, J., Huang, J., Wu, W., & Whipple, P. B. (2024). Evaluating the role of ChatGPT in enhancing EFL writing assessments in classroom settings: A preliminary investigation. *Humanities & Social Sciences Communications, 11*(1), 1268. DOI: 10.1057/s41599-024-03755-2

Li, M., & Noori, A. Q. (2024). Exploring the nexus of attitude, contextual factors, and AI utilization intentions: A PLS-SEM analysis among primary mathematics teachers in China. *Asian Journal for Mathematics Education, 3*(3), 289–311. DOI: 10.1177/27527263241269060

Lipponen, L., & Kumpulainen, K. (2011). Acting as accountable authors: Creating interactional spaces for agency work in teacher education. *Teaching and Teacher Education, 27*(5), 812–819. https://www.sciencedirect.com/science/article/abs/pii/S0742051X11000023?via%3Dihub. DOI: 10.1016/j.tate.2011.01.001

Liu, J., Sihes, A. J. B., & Lu, Y. (2025). How do generative artificial intelligence (AI) tools and large language models (LLMs) influence language learners' critical thinking in EFL education? A systematic review. *Smart Learning Environments, 12*(1), 48. Advance online publication. DOI: 10.1186/s40561-025-00406-0

Lo, C. K., Yu, P. L. H., Xu, S., Ng, D. T. K., & Jong, M. S. (2024). Exploring the application of ChatGPT in ESL/EFL education and related research issues: A systematic review of empirical studies. *Smart Learning Environments, 11*(1), 50. DOI: 10.1186/s40561-024-00342-5

Lopez-Gazpio, I. (2025). Integrating large language models into accessible and inclusive education: Access democratization and individualized learning enhancement supported by generative artificial intelligence. *Information (Basel), 16*(6), 473. Advance online publication. DOI: 10.3390/info16060473

Lynch, S. (2025). How AI is leaving non-English speakers behind. Retrieved March 28, 2026, from https://news.stanford.edu/stories/2025/05/digital-divide-ai-llms-exclusion-non-english-speakers-research

Mahapatra, S. (2024). Impact of ChatGPT on ESL students' academic writing skills: A mixed methods intervention study. *Smart Learning Environments, 11*(1), 9. DOI: 10.1186/s40561-024-00295-9

Marras, A., Fornara, F., & Pasqualotto, A. (2026). Harnessing AI for inclusive teaching: Professional development strategies for early educators. In *AI in Early Education: Integrating Artificial Intelligence for Inclusive and Effective Learning* (pp. 267–290). wiley. DOI: 10.1002/9781394352821.ch16

Matjie, M. A., Nethavhani, A., & Matlakala, M. (2026). AI and the digital divide in education. *Frontiers in Computer Science, Volume 8-2026.* Retrieved from https://www.frontiersin.org/journals/computer-science/articles/10.3389/fcomp.2026.1759027

Mimoudi, A., & Mokhtari, K. (2025). 'AIA-PCEK': A new framework for teaching with AI. *Cogent Education, 12*(1), 2563171. Advance online publication. DOI: 10.1080/2331186X.2025.2563171

Mishra, P., & Koehler, M. J. (2006). Technological pedagogical content knowledge: A framework for teacher knowledge. *Teachers College Record, 108*(6), 1017–1054. DOI: 10.1111/j.1467-9620.2006.00684.x

Molla, T., & Nolan, A. (2020). Teacher agency and professional practice. *Teachers and Teaching, 26*(1), 67–87. DOI: 10.1080/13540602.2020.1740196

Monib, W. K. (2025). Sentiment and SWOT analyses of DeepSeek AI: Insights from media, self-perceptions, user perceptions, and literature. *SAGE Open, 15*(4), 21582440251395224. DOI: 10.1177/21582440251395226

Monib, W. K., Qazi, A., Apong, R. A., Azizan, M. T., De Silva, L., & Yassin, H. (2024). Generative AI and future education: A review, theoretical validation, and authors' perspective on challenges and solutions. *PeerJ. Computer Science, 10*, e2105. DOI: 10.7717/peerj-cs.2105 PMID: 39650462

Monib, W. K., Qazi, A., De Silva, L., & Mahmud, M. M. (2024). Exploring Learners' Experiences with ChatGPT in Personalized Learning. *2024 6th International Workshop on Artificial Intelligence and Education (WAIE)*, 66–70. IEEE. DOI: 10.1109/WAIE63876.2024.00019

Monib, W. K., Qazi, A., Jain, J., & Ponniah, L. (2025). A comprehensive scientometric analysis of ChatGPT research global trends and future prospects. *TechTrends, 69*(6), 1–19. DOI: 10.1007/s11528-025-01110-z

Monib, W. K., Qazi, A., & Mahmud, M. M. (2025). Exploring learners' experiences and perceptions of ChatGPT as a learning tool in higher education. *Education and Information Technologies*, *30*(1), 917–939. DOI: 10.1007/s10639-024-13065-4

Niazai, H., & Monib, W. K. (2025a). AI for personalized learning in medical education. In *Teaching in the Age of Medical Technology* (pp. 91–122). IGI Global Scientific Publishing. DOI: 10.4018/979-8-3373-1519-5.ch004

Niazai, H., & Monib, W. K. (2025b). The role of generative AI in curriculum development and its impact on well-being. *Advances in Computational Intelligence and Robotics*, *229*, 229–252. Advance online publication. DOI: 10.4018/979-8-3373-3316-8.ch009

Octavio, M. M., Argüello, M. V. G., & Pujolà, J.-T. (2024). ChatGPT as an AI L2 teaching support: A case study of an EFL teacher. *Technology in Language Teaching & Learning*, *6*(1), 1142. DOI: 10.29140/tltl.v6n1.1142

Overdeck Family Foundation. (2025). 2025 AI strategy update. Retrieved March 3, 2026, from https://overdeck.org/news-and-resources/article/2025-ai-strategy-update/#:~:text=2,for%20collaborative%20learning%20and%20innovation

Overdeck Family Foundation. (2026, January 27). What we learned: Exploring the role of educators in the age of AI. Retrieved February 24, 2026, from Overdeck Family Foundation website: https://overdeck.org/news-and-resources/article/what-we-learned-exploring-the-role-of-educators-in-the-age-of-ai/#:~:text=1,not%20end%20users%2C%20of%20AI

Oyetade, K., & Zuva, T. (2025). Advancing equitable education with inclusive AI to mitigate bias and enhance teacher literacy. *Educational Process: International Journal*, *14*, e2025087. DOI: 10.22521/edupij.2025.14.87

Phillipson, R. (1992). *Linguistic imperialism*. Oxford University Press.

Sangwa, S., & Mutabazi, P. (2025). AI-powered multilingual degrees in higher education: Postcolonial insights on linguistic justice and disruptive innovation. *Open Journal of AI, Ethics & Society (ISSN: 3105-3076), 1*(1).

Schofield, A. (2025). Opinion: Hidden biases, discrimination in AI decision-making. Retrieved March 28, 2026, from https://redlineproject.news/2025/03/20/opinion-the-hidden-biases-and-discrimination-in-ai-decision-making/#:~:text=For%20instance%2C%20a%C2%A0study%20published%20in,generated%20harmful%20and%20racist%20stereotypes

Szabó, F., & Szoke, J. (2024). How does generative AI promote autonomy and inclusivity in language teaching? *ELT Journal*, *78*(4), 478–488. DOI: 10.1093/elt/ccae052

Taff, S. D., & Lazzaro, C. V. B. (2025). Critical pedagogy: Praxis and social reform through education. In *Routledge Companion to Occupational Therapy: Theories, Concepts and Models* (pp. 639–650). Taylor and Francis. DOI: 10.4324/9781003526766-51

Thapa, M. B., & Shrestha, K. (2026). Empowering teachers through ChatGPT: Perceptions and experiences in English as a foreign or second language (EFL/ESL) classrooms as a form of community service. *ASEAN Journal of Community Service and Education, 5*(1), 21–32. https://ejournal.bumipublikasinusantara.id/index.php/ajcse/article/view/812

Truong, U. T. (2024). Writing Classes in the AI Era: Redefining English Teachers' Roles. *Proceedings - 2024 6th International Workshop on Artificial Intelligence and Education, WAIE 2024*, 50–55. Institute of Electrical and Electronics Engineers Inc. DOI: 10.1109/WAIE63876.2024.00016

UNESCO. (2024). Generative AI: UNESCO study reveals alarming evidence of regressive gender stereotypes. Retrieved March 25, 2026, from https://www.unesco.org/en/articles/generative-ai-unesco-study-reveals-alarming-evidence-regressive-gender-stereotypes#:~:text=their%20content%20can%20significantly%20amplify,Member%20States%20in%20November%202021

UNESCO. (2025a). *Report of the Independent Expert Group on artificial intelligence and culture*. Retrieved from https://www.unesco.org/sites/default/files/medias/fichiers/2025/09/CULTAI_Report%20of%20the%20Independent%20Expert%20Group%20on%20Artificial%20Intelligence%20and%20Culture%20%28final%20online%20version%29%201.pdf

UNESCO. (2025b). What you need to know about AI and the right to education. Retrieved March 3, 2026, from https://www.unesco.org/en/articles/what-you-need-know-about-ai-and-right-education#:~:text=One%20major%20challenge%20is%20that,ensuring%20the%20right%20to%20education

UNESCO. (2025c). *AI and the Future of Education: Disruptions, Dilemmas and Directions*. UNESCO. https://www.unesco.org/en/articles/ai-and-future-education-disruptions-dilemmas-and-directions

Ututalum, C.Charisma S. Ututalum. (2025). Transformative potential of generative AI in higher education teaching practices. *Environment and Social Psychology, 10*(9). Advance online publication. DOI: 10.59429/esp.v10i9.3291

Varsik, S., & Vosberg, L. (2024). *The potential impact of Artificial Intelligence on equity and inclusion in education*. OECD Publishing.

Williamson, B., & Eynon, R. (2020). Historical threads, missing links, and future directions in AI in education. [Taylor & Francis.]. *Learning, Media and Technology, 45*(3), 223–235. DOI: 10.1080/17439884.2020.1798995

Xiao, Y. (2025). The impact of AI-driven speech recognition on EFL listening comprehension, flow experience, and anxiety: A randomized controlled trial. *Humanities & Social Sciences Communications, 12*(1), 1–14. DOI: 10.1057/s41599-025-04672-8

Yusmaliana, D., Abubakari, M. S., Monib, W. K., & Shafik, W. (2026). Between Independence and Supervision: A Reflective Account of a PhD Student in the Era of AI. In Irham, I., Huda, M., & Yaqin, L. N. (Eds.), *International Student Narratives in Globalized Higher Education* (pp. 305–334). IGI Global Scientific Publishing., DOI: 10.4018/979-8-3373-4212-2.ch012

Zhang, Y., & Samsudin, M. A. (2026). From familiarity to criticality: Cultivating EFL teachers' AI literacy through an AI-integrated genre-based pedagogy. *Education Sciences, 16*(1), 150. DOI: 10.3390/educsci16010150

Zulianti, H., Nurchurifiani, E., Hastomo, T., Maximilian, A., & Ajeng, G. D. (2025). Enhancing novice EFL teachers' competency in AI-powered tools through a TPACK-based professional development program. *World Journal of English Language, 15*(3), 117–131. DOI: 10.5430/wjel.v15n3p117

ADDITIONAL READING

Bearman, M., Ryan, J., & Ajjawi, R. (2023). Discourses of artificial intelligence in higher education: A critical literature review. *Higher Education, 86*(2), 369–385. DOI: 10.1007/s10734-022-00937-2

Chiu, T. K. F., Xia, Q., Zhou, X., Chai, C. S., & Cheng, M. (2023). Systematic literature review on opportunities, challenges, and future research recommendations of artificial intelligence in education. *Computers and Education: Artificial Intelligence, 4*, 100118. Advance online publication. DOI: 10.1016/j.caeai.2022.100118

Godwin-Jones, R. (2022). Partnering with AI: Intelligent writing assistance and instructed language learning. *Language Learning & Technology, 26*(2), 5–24. http://hdl.handle.net/10125/73474. DOI: 10.64152/10125/73474

Hockly, N. (2023). Artificial intelligence in English language teaching: The good, the bad and the ugly. *RELC Journal, 54*(2), 445–451. DOI: 10.1177/00336882231168504

Holmes, W., Porayska-Pomsta, K., Holstein, K., Sutherland, E., Baker, T., Shum, S. B., Santos, O. C., Rodrigo, M. T., Cukurova, M., Bittencourt, I. I., & Koedinger, K. R. (2022). Ethics of AI in education: Towards a community-wide framework. *International Journal of Artificial Intelligence in Education, 32*(3), 504–526. DOI: 10.1007/s40593-021-00239-1

Kohnke, L., Moorhouse, B. L., & Zou, D. (2023). ChatGPT for language teaching and learning. *RELC Journal, 54*(2), 537–550. DOI: 10.1177/00336882231162868

Priestley, M., Biesta, G., & Robinson, S. (2015). *Teacher agency: An ecological approach.* Bloomsbury Academic.

Selwyn, N. (2019). *Should robots replace teachers? AI and the future of education.* Polity Press.

Warschauer, M., Tseng, W., Yim, S., Webster, T., Jacob, S., Du, Q., & Tate, T. (2023). The affordances and contradictions of AI-generated text for writers of English as a second or foreign language. *Journal of Second Language Writing, 62*, 101071. Advance online publication. DOI: 10.1016/j.jslw.2023.101071

Zawacki-Richter, O., Marín, V. I., Bond, M., & Gouverneur, F. (2019). Systematic review of research on artificial intelligence applications in higher education—Where are the educators? *International Journal of Educational Technology in Higher Education, 16*(1), 39. Advance online publication. DOI: 10.1186/s41239-019-0171-0

KEY TERMS AND DEFINITIONS

AI Literacy: The knowledge, skills, and dispositions required to understand, use, evaluate, and critically engage with artificial intelligence systems in everyday and professional contexts.

Algorithmic Bias: Systematic and unfair errors in the outputs of computational systems, arising from patterns in training data, model design, or deployment contexts, which disadvantage particular linguistic, cultural, racial, or gender groups.

Critical Pedagogy: An educational approach, most closely associated with Paulo Freire, that positions education as a practice of freedom in which learners develop critical consciousness and challenge structures of inequality through dialogue and reflection.

Digital Divide: The socioeconomic, infrastructural, and skills-based gap between individuals, communities, or regions with reliable access to digital technologies and those without such access.

Epistemic Agency: The capacity of educators and learners to determine what counts as valid knowledge, to critically evaluate information sources including AI-generated content, and to actively engage in the construction and interrogation of knowledge.

Generative AI (GenAI): A class of artificial intelligence systems, typically based on large language models, that produce novel outputs such as text, images, audio, or code in response to user prompts.

Moral Agency: The capacity of teachers to make ethically justifiable decisions in professional practice, including commitments to fairness, transparency, learner well-being, and social justice.

Relational Agency: The capacity of teachers to collaborate with colleagues, learners, and communities, drawing upon shared resources and networks to navigate complex pedagogical decisions.

Teacher Agency: The active role that teachers take in shaping their work and their profession, characterised by commitment, purposefulness, intentionality, and the capacity to act upon and transform educational contexts.

Transformative Agency: The capacity of teachers to initiate significant shifts in pedagogical thinking and practice, particularly through the redesign of curricula, activities, and roles in response to new technologies or educational goals.

Chapter 3
Equity-Centered and Translanguaging-Oriented Language Pedagogy for Multilingual Dignity:
Linguistic Capital in AI-Driven Language Education

Ashraf Alam
http://orcid.org/0000-0001-6178-1187
Department of Education, National Institute of Technology Calicut, Kozhikode, India

ABSTRACT

This chapter theorises equity-centred, translanguaging-oriented language pedagogy within AI-driven educational ecologies as a justice project rather than a technological upgrade. It conceptualises AI systems as socio-technical assemblages that redistribute linguistic capital, codify algorithmic normativity, and reconfigure access and recognition for multilingual subjects. Mobilising Rawlsian justice, the Capability Approach, Fraserian redistribution-recognition-representation, critical and decolonial pedagogy, translanguaging, and linguistic human rights, it proposes a normative meta-framework for multilingual dignity. It then distils a typology of equity risks, a schema of teacher AI-equity literacies and agency, design principles for inclusive and culturally sustaining human-AI orchestration, and a governance

DOI: 10.4018/979-8-3373-7749-0.ch003

matrix spanning classrooms, institutions, regulators, industry, and civil society that orients AI-enhanced language education toward epistemic justice and democratic futures.

INTRODUCTION

Situating AI Within Contemporary Language Education Ecologies

Artificial intelligence in language education now operates as a dense *socio technical assemblage* that spans institutional classrooms, commercial platforms, open networks, and informal peer communities. Large language models, conversational agents, automated writing and speech evaluation systems, adaptive tutoring platforms, speech recognition engines, and learning analytics dashboards jointly recalibrate how learners encounter vocabulary, grammar, discourse, and pragmatics across modalities (Engh, 2013; Mikroyannidis et al., 2025; Alam & Mohanty, 2022). In multilingual environments, these systems mediate access not only to dominant lingua francas but also to regional, heritage, and professional registers, while simultaneously harvesting linguistic traces as data (Hejazi et al., 2023; Douglas Fir Group, 2016). AI woven into devices, connectivity infrastructures, platform architectures, and curricular regimes reorganises time, authority, and participation, shifting feedback cycles, redistributing corrective power, and modulating what counts as legitimate performance. Within this ecology, language education cannot be conceptualised as a neutral skill transmission process, it becomes a key site where algorithmic infrastructures, linguistic markets, and educational institutions co produce opportunities, exclusions, and identities.

Justice Turn in AI Enhanced Language Education

The contemporary configuration of AI in language education coincides with a pronounced *justice turn* that contests purely efficiency-oriented narratives of optimisation, personalisation, and scalability. This justice-oriented perspective foregrounds *redistributive* concerns about who accesses robust AI tools and high-quality human support, *recognitional* concerns about whose multilingual repertoires are valorised or pathologised, and *representational* concerns about who participates in decision making regarding AI integration (Piechurska-Kuciel, 2011; Ait-Hroch & Ibrahimi, 2025). AI architectures often amplify existing stratifications in digital capital, literacy, and language status, yet they also furnish novel levers for corrective intervention, such as low-cost feedback, assistive scaffolds, and visibility for minoritised languages

(Freiermuth, 2020; Alam & Mohanty, 2023a). The central tension is not whether AI is beneficial or harmful in the abstract, but how its deployment is patterned across hierarchies of class, race, gender, disability, migration, and language, and whether educational systems treat AI as a vehicle for *linguistic justice* or as an instrument for intensifying surveillance and standardisation.

Objectives and Central Focus of the Chapter

This chapter advances a conceptual theoretical framework for *equity centered, translanguaging oriented AI-mediated language education* that foregrounds *multilingual dignity* and *linguistic capital* as core normative anchors. It does not present empirical datasets, instead it assembles constructs from *justice theory*, *sociocultural learning*, *sociomateriality*, *translanguaging pedagogy*, *critical data studies*, and *design justice* into an integrated architecture. The central objective is to formulate conceptual models that make visible both the risk topologies and the transformative possibilities of AI in language education across diverse geopolitical and sociolinguistic contexts. The chapter orients around questions such as how justice-oriented theories can be operationalised in AI-mediated classrooms, how algorithmic infrastructures reshape linguistic hierarchies, how teacher agency and professional ethics can be reconfigured as *AI equity literacies*, and how translanguaging practices can be amplified rather than suppressed by computational systems.

Audiences, Use Value, and Translational Trajectories

The chapter is crafted for a multi stakeholder readership that includes academics in applied linguistics, education, and human computer interaction, policy makers responsible for curriculum and digital strategy, workforce development professionals who design language intensive training, and digital learning technologists who architect AI enabled platforms. For theorists, the framework provides a dense conceptual vocabulary and a set of typologies that can scaffold comparative studies and theoretical refinements. For teacher educators and practitioners, it offers analytic lenses and design heuristics that support reflective orchestration of AI tools within multilingual, culturally heterogeneous classrooms. For policy and system leaders, it sketches normative benchmarks and governance levers that can inform standards, procurement criteria, and accountability regimes. For designers and industry actors, it articulates criteria grounded in *equity*, *translanguaging*, and *linguistic citizenship* that can shape product roadmaps and evaluative rubrics beyond narrow performance metrics.

Structural Logic, Conceptual Progression, and Tabular Syntheses

The argument unfolds in seven tightly linked sections that move from foundational theory to governance-oriented synthesis. Section 2 articulates normative foundations of equity and justice in AI-mediated language education and culminates in Table 1, which condenses key theoretical lenses, justice principles, and AI related risks and opportunities into a compact matrix. Section 3 interrogates socio technical imaginaries, algorithmic bias, data colonialism, and linguistic power, and organises equity risks into a conceptual typology in Table 2. Section 4 reconceptualises teacher agency, professional ethics, and AI equity literacies, mapping dimensions of teacher practice in Table 3. Section 5 treats AI as a potential ally for inclusive, differentiated, and translanguaging pedagogy, translating theoretical commitments into design principles in Table 4. Section 6 develops governance and policy frameworks for equity centered AI in language education, integrating micro, meso, and macro levels in Table 5. Section 7 synthesises cross cutting principles and delineates conceptual horizons for future theory building and practice.

NORMATIVE FOUNDATIONS, EQUITY, JUSTICE, AND LANGUAGE EDUCATION IN AN AI AGE

Equity, Equality, and Justice as Philosophical Architectures of AI-mediated Language Learning

Equity centered AI-mediated language education requires a clear differentiation among equality, equity, and justice as distinct normative architectures rather than interchangeable slogans. Equality foregrounds uniform provision of inputs, such as identical access to a language learning platform, while equity foregrounds differentiated support calibrated to structural disadvantage, such as intensified scaffolding for learners who face compounded linguistic, economic, or disability related barriers (Pfenninger & Polz, 2018; Kessler & Bikowski, 2011). Justice extends further, interrogating how institutional arrangements, linguistic markets, and digital infrastructures generate those disadvantages in the first place, and how they can be reconstituted (Sharma et al., 2024; Bendarkawi et al., 2025; Fettes & Karamouzian, 2018). Within this landscape, distributive justice emphasises the allocation of material and symbolic resources, recognitional justice foregrounds the status of multilingual repertoires and identities, and participatory or representational justice insists on inclusive governance of AI policies and tools, reflecting Fraser's account of redistribution, recognition, and representation across intersecting scales of justice (Fraser, 2008,

2010; Mackey, 2014; Tang et al., 2024; Elsayed et al., 2024). These strands converge in the normative lenses that are later synthesised in Table 1, where justice theories are mapped onto concrete language educational problematics and AI specific risk and opportunity constellations. Multilingual dignity, as used in this chapter, refers to the normative principle that learners' full linguistic repertoires, including home languages, heritage languages, regional varieties, hybrid forms, accents, scripts, and translanguaging practices, must be recognised as legitimate resources for learning, identity formation, participation, and knowledge production. It differs from equality, which may provide identical linguistic access without addressing unequal language status; from equity, which provides differentiated support to learners positioned unequally by linguistic and social hierarchies; and from inclusion, which may invite multilingual learners into existing educational structures without transforming the monolingual assumptions embedded within those structures. Multilingual dignity therefore goes further by insisting that AI-mediated language education should not merely accommodate linguistic difference, but actively protect learners from linguistic humiliation, algorithmic misrecognition, symbolic erasure, and forced assimilation into dominant language norms. In this sense, multilingual dignity functions as a justice-oriented benchmark for evaluating whether AI systems expand or restrict learners' communicative freedom, epistemic agency, and cultural belonging.

Critical Pedagogy, Critical Language Awareness, and Decolonial Linguistic Justice

A justice informed reading of AI in language education cannot be confined to resource allocation, it must also confront the epistemic and ideological dimensions of linguistic normativity (Sanz, 2014; Ferris, 2011; Alam & Mohanty, 2023b). Critical pedagogy positions learners and teachers as co investigators of the structural conditions that shape their linguistic and educational environments, rejecting technocratic scripts that treat AI as an infallible oracle (Hong & Guo, 2025; Ellis & Sheen, 2006; Vafaee & Suzuki, 2020). Critical language awareness exposes how ideologies of native speakerism, standard language, and deficit views of bilingualism are sedimented in curricula, assessment rubrics, and public discourse, and it provides conceptual tools for analysing how those ideologies are encoded in algorithmic feedback, correctness labels, and training data taxonomies (Ismayilli, 2025; Kormos & Smith, 2023; Hoang, 2024). Decolonial and raciolinguistic perspectives deepen this analysis by foregrounding the historical entanglement of language hierarchies with colonial extraction, racial ordering, and cultural domination (Dewaele et al., 2022; Knouse et al., 2021). The justice lenses that surface here, centred on voice, critique, and counter hegemonic knowledge, are explicitly registered in the matrix of Table 1, where critical and decolonial concerns are juxtaposed with redistributive frameworks.

Sociocultural and Sociomaterial Theories of Learning and Normative Lens Consolidation

Normative architectures become practically consequential only when they are coupled with robust theories of how learning and mediation unfold in concrete activity systems. Sociocultural theory conceptualises learning as participation in culturally organised practices, mediated by tools, signs, and human relationships, with the Zone of Proximal Development capturing the dynamic space where contingent scaffolding can catalyse new capabilities (Bryfonski et al., 2024; Li, 2016). Sociomaterial approaches, including actor network inspired perspectives, treat AI systems, devices, interfaces, classroom routines, and institutional regulations as co constitutive elements of learning assemblages, not as separate layers (Driver, 2023; Zhong et al., 2024). In AI-mediated language education, these theories illuminate how feedback interfaces, error highlighting, recommendation engines, and data dashboards do not simply transmit information, they reorganise attention, authority, and affect, thereby shaping how justice commitments are enacted (Cintrón-Valentín & Ellis, 2016; Hyland, 2019). To render these complex interactions analytically tractable, the principal normative lenses discussed across this section are consolidated in Table 1, which aligns each lens with its core justice principle, its central language educational problematic, the AI intensified risk configuration, and the AI enabled transformative possibility.

Table 1. Normative lenses for justice in AI-mediated language education

Normative Analytic Lens	Core Justice Principle	Language Educational Problematic	AI Intensified Risk Configuration	AI Enabled Transformative Possibility
Rawlsian Egalitarianism	Fair equality of opportunity, priority to the least advantaged	Stratified access to high quality language learning, device ecologies, and human guidance	Algorithmic enhancement targeted to already privileged learners, deepening achievement and credential gaps	Targeted allocation of robust AI supports and human tutoring to structurally disadvantaged groups, calibrated to reduce capability shortfalls
Capability-Oriented Justice (Nussbaum, 2011)	Expansion of substantive language related capabilities and functionings	Narrow focus on test scores rather than real world communicative freedoms and participation	Optimisation of learners for metric performance, neglect of agency, imagination, and civic voice	AI-mediated tasks that enlarge learners' repertoires for expression, affiliation, and mobility across domains and linguistic communities
Fraserian Tridimensional Justice (Fraser, 2008, 2010)	Redistribution, recognition, and representation in intertwined domains	Material under provision of tools, misrecognition of multilingual repertoires, exclusion from AI governance	Data extraction without benefit sharing, symbolic devaluation of non-dominant languages, opaque platform decision making	Co governed AI ecosystems that redistribute digital resources, valorise diverse repertoires, and embed affected communities in oversight forums
Critical And Decolonial Pedagogy	Emancipatory critique, conscientisation, disruption of hegemonic linguistic ideologies	Pedagogies that treat learners as passive recipients of standard norms and algorithmic verdicts	Automation of deficit labelling, uncritical reinforcement of colonial language hierarchies through feedback and exemplars	Dialogic use of AI outputs as objects of critique, fostering critical language awareness and resistance to oppressive norms
Translanguaging And Linguistic Human Rights	Protection and valorisation of full multilingual repertoires and language rights	Erasure of home languages and hybrid practices in formal AI-mediated learning environments	Systems that accept only dominant codes, penalise mixing, and ignore endangered or heritage languages	AI-mediated tasks that legitimise code meshing, support minoritised languages, and treat learners' full repertoires as pedagogical assets
Sociocultural Sociomaterial Learning Ecologies	Justice as reconfiguration of mediational ecologies and participation structures	Tool and infrastructure designs that marginalise certain learners from meaningful participation	Interfaces, analytics, and timing regimes that privilege fast responders, confident speakers, and always online learners	Re designed AI learning ecologies that slow down interaction, diversify mediational means, and widen opportunities for equitable participation

Table 1 performs a double function within this normative architecture. Conceptually, it makes explicit how abstract justice paradigms, such as egalitarianism or capability theory, translate into specific language educational problematics, such as access stratification or erasure of translanguaging, once AI infrastructures are introduced. Practically, it provides a compact heuristic for curriculum designers, teacher educators, and policy makers who must adjudicate between alternative AI deployments. The juxtaposition of AI intensified risk configurations and AI enabled transformative possibilities underscores that the same computational affordances can either deepen injustice or support redistributive and recognitional agendas, depending on how they are embedded in sociocultural and sociomaterial ecologies. Subsequent sections of the chapter return to this matrix as a reference point when elaborating risk typologies, teacher agency models, and governance frameworks.

Theories of Multilingualism, Translanguaging, and Linguistic Justice in AI Contexts

Multilingualism, when theorised ecologically rather than as a set of discrete monolingual codes, reframes language education as the orchestration of interrelated repertoires across modalities, domains, and life trajectories (Lardiere, 2017; McCrocklin, 2020; Pham et al., 2025). Translanguaging conceptualises speakers' practices as the fluid mobilisation of an integrated linguistic repertoire rather than as movement between sealed, autonomous languages, and it introduces a normative stance that treats such practices as epistemically legitimate, pedagogically central, and politically significant in multilingual education (García & Wei, 2015; Wei, 2018; Wei & García, 2022). Linguistic human rights and linguistic citizenship then extend this stance into the juridical and political spheres, insisting that communities have claims to maintain, develop, and publicly use their languages, both offline and in digital environments (Hung, 2017; Alam, 2023a). In AI-mediated contexts, these constructs reveal how platform defaults, input constraints, and model coverage can either enable or suppress multilingual dignity (Hwang et al., 2024; Rao & Torres, 2017; Kersten & Winsler, 2022). The lenses of translanguaging and linguistic rights, already articulated in Table 1, thus operate as critical filters for evaluating whether AI enhanced language education promotes genuine linguistic justice or reproduces a monolingual, assimilationist habitus.

Synthesising a Justice Anchored Normative Meta Framework for AI Language Education

The diverse normative strands elaborated across this section coalesce into a meta framework that treats equity centered AI language education as a project of structural, epistemic, and participatory transformation rather than incremental adjustment (Gregersen et al., 2016; Caldwell-Harris & Ayçiçeği-Dinn, 2009). Rawlsian and capability-oriented constructs foreground the redistribution of material, temporal, and symbolic resources necessary for learners to expand their communicative capabilities, agency, affiliation, and practical freedoms, a concern that resonates with Nussbaum's account of capabilities as substantive conditions for dignified human flourishing (Nussbaum, 2011). Fraserian justice, critical pedagogy, and decolonial perspectives further insist that recognition of multilingual repertoires and representation in governance are equally non-negotiable (Fraser, 2008, 2010). Translanguaging and linguistic human rights re anchor the telos of language education around dignity and citizenship in multilingual polities, and sociocultural sociomaterial ecologies remind practitioners that justice commitments must be inscribed in tools, routines, and infrastructures, not only in policy declarations (Mackey, 2020; Aubrey, 2022). When read together with the structured correspondences in Table 1, this meta framework provides the normative scaffolding for the risk diagnostics in the next section, where AI-mediated language education is interrogated through the lenses of socio technical imaginaries, algorithmic bias, platform power, and cultural stereotyping.

AI, LANGUAGE ECOLOGIES, SOCIO TECHNICAL IMAGINARIES, AND LINGUA POWER

Socio Technical Imaginaries, EdTech Solutionism, and Narratives of Inevitability

AI-mediated language education is enveloped by socio technical imaginaries that depict computational systems as inevitable arbiters of educational modernity, efficiency, and competitiveness. Promotional discourses in policy arenas and industry roadmaps often script AI as a frictionless solution to chronic challenges in language teaching, such as large class sizes, assessment overload, and persistent proficiency gaps, while minimising questions of power, extraction, and exclusion (De Bot et al., 2005; Karakaya & Bozkurt, 2022; Wenden, 2002). These imaginaries cultivate automation bias, where machine outputs are presumed inherently more objective than human judgment, and they obscure the contingency of design choices, dataset composition, and interface decisions. Within this ideological horizon, alternative models grounded in community-based pedagogy, low tech innovation, or multilingual human mediation can appear anachronistic or irrational (Lee, 2024; Hajizadeh et al., 2023). The risk archetypes that crystallise from these imaginaries, particularly those concerning access, bias, and governance, are later formalised in the typology presented in Table 2, which decomposes the apparently seamless promise of AI into distinct equity related threat vectors.

Algorithmic Bias, Data Colonialism, and Linguistic Discrimination

Algorithmic bias in language technologies arises when training corpora, feature engineering, and evaluation pipelines systematically privilege some linguistic forms, accents, and registers over others, thereby converting social hierarchies into computational defaults (Moeller & Catalano, 2015; Zare et al., 2022; Derakhshan et al., 2024). Sampling and representation biases skew model performance toward high-resource languages and prestige varieties, while evaluation biases embed normative judgments about what counts as fluent, polite, grammatical, or academic, a problem extensively documented in critical work on bias and fairness in NLP and large language models (Blodgett et al., 2020; Gallegos et al., 2024). Data colonialism amplifies these dynamics by extracting vast quantities of learner and community language data, often across borders, without symmetrical capacity building, governance power, or material benefit for those whose voices are captured, thereby extending colonial patterns of appropriation into digital and computational infrastructures (Couldry & Mejias, 2023). The resulting systems can misrecognise, penalise, or invisibilise non dominant dialects and translanguaging practices, treating them as noise rather than as legitimate semiotic resources (Leonardi, 2010; Segler et al., 2002; Alam & Mohanty, 2023c). Within the risk taxonomy that culminates in Table 2, these dynamics coalesce into algorithmic and representational bias archetypes that directly implicate recognitional and redistributive justice in AI-mediated language education.

Platformisation, Surveillance, and Quantified Language Learning

Platformisation transforms language learning into a series of interactions hosted within proprietary ecosystems that integrate content delivery, assessment, communication, and analytics in tightly coupled stacks. Within these ecosystems, learners become continuous sources of telemetry, including keystrokes, speech samples, latency patterns, error trajectories, and engagement metrics, which feed predictive models that classify, rank, and profile (Gruba, 2004; Ryding, 2013). This surveillance saturated configuration resembles a digital panopticon, where the anticipation of monitoring can reshape behaviour, motivation, and identity, often in ways that remain opaque to teachers and students. Quantification regimes within such platforms tend to reduce complex communicative competence to scalar indices such as proficiency scores, risk flags, and progress bars, which then inform high stakes decisions about tracking, certification, and resource allocation (Dunkel, 1991; Alam, 2023b). The surveillance and datafication risk archetype codified in Table 2 captures these processes, highlighting how they entangle privacy, autonomy, and epistemic agency within AI-mediated language education.

Linguistic Hierarchies, Symbolic Power, and Algorithmic Normativity

Linguistic hierarchies are not merely descriptive taxonomies of difference, they are structures of symbolic power that assign differential value to accents, registers, and scripts, and these hierarchies are readily encoded into algorithmic systems. Conceptual frameworks such as *linguistic capital*, *symbolic violence*, and *raciolinguistic ideologies* elucidate how certain ways of speaking are attached to whiteness, middle classness, or metropolitan prestige, while others are associated with deficiency, incivility, or marginality (Rosa & Flores, 2017; Gilmore, 2007; Robinson, 2011). When AI-mediated feedback labels particular forms as incorrect, inappropriate, or unprofessional, and recommends homogenised alternatives, it can operationalise these hierarchies at scale, subtly disciplining users toward narrow ideals of standard language. Such normativity becomes especially consequential in high stakes domains such as academic writing, migration testing, and corporate communication training, where algorithmic judgments can shape life chances (Derakhshan & Zare, 2023). The linguistic hierarchy and symbolic erasure risk category in Table 2 foregrounds these dynamics as central to any equity-oriented analysis of AI driven language education.

Conceptual Typology of AI Related Risks and Lingua Power Taxonomies

The dispersed concerns that emerge from socio technical imaginaries, algorithmic bias, platformisation, and linguistic hierarchies can be synthesised into a conceptual typology of AI related risks specific to language education (Huang et al., 2024; Kangas, 2014; Dixon et al., 2012). Rather than treating risk as a diffuse anxiety, the typology disaggregates equity relevant hazards into analytically distinct archetypes that operate through different mechanisms and impact different learner constellations. By aligning each archetype with its underlying socio technical mechanism, a paradigmatic classroom or platform scenario, the primary affected groups, and the justice dimensions at stake, Table 2 offers a compact yet dense map of how AI can entrench or reconfigure inequality. This typology builds directly on the normative lenses articulated in Table 1, translating abstract justice commitments into concrete diagnostic categories that can inform design, pedagogy, and governance.

Table 2. Conceptual typology of equity risks in AI language education

Risk Category Archetype	Underlying Socio Technical Mechanism	Illustrative Language Education Scenario	Affected Learner Constellations	Justice Dimension Primarily Implicated
Access and Infrastructural Stratification Risk	Unequal distribution of devices, bandwidth, compute intensive features, and human support across institutions and regions	Premium AI writing tutor available only in fee paying urban schools, while rural or under resourced learners access degraded or offline limited versions	Learners in low-income households, rural communities, humanitarian settings, and underfunded public systems	Redistribution of digital resources and learning opportunities
Algorithmic and Representational Bias Risk	Skewed training corpora, biased feature spaces, and norm laden error taxonomies that encode dominant varieties as default	Automated speech recogniser consistently misclassifies regional accents or mixed codes, penalising them in oral proficiency scoring	Speakers of minoritised dialects, migrant learners, Indigenous communities, sign language users, and translanguaging youth	Recognition of diverse repertoires and fair evaluation practices
Linguistic Hierarchy and Symbolic Erasure Risk	Feedback and suggestion engines that privilege standardised registers and erase hybrid or localised forms	Writing assistant systematically replaces local idioms and code meshed sentences with homogenised global English formulations	Learners whose identities are tied to vernaculars, creoles, heritage languages, and hybrid youth vernaculars	Recognition and representation of culturally situated language practices
Surveillance, Datafication, and Profiling Risk	Continuous telemetry capture, behavioural modelling, and opaque risk scoring integrated into learning platforms	Platform assigns engagement risk scores that influence teacher attention and institutional interventions without transparent criteria	Learners with fluctuating connectivity, neurodivergent learners, students under stress or caregiving burdens, politically vulnerable groups	Representation and privacy in relation to data governance

continued on following page

Table 2. Continued

Risk Category Archetype	Underlying Socio Technical Mechanism	Illustrative Language Education Scenario	Affected Learner Constellations	Justice Dimension Primarily Implicated
Affective, Motivational, and Identity Threat Risk	Automated evaluation and comparative dashboards that foreground error, ranking, and deficit framings	Repeated low algorithmic writing scores produce shame, withdrawal from participation, and avoidance of creative experimentation	Learners with prior experiences of academic marginalisation, language related anxiety, or stereotype threat, including many multilinguals	Recognition of learner dignity, emotional safety, and agency
Governance, Opacity, and Accountability Deficit Risk	Vendor controlled design, proprietary secrecy, and fragmented regulation that limit oversight and redress	Institution deploys AI placement test whose cut scores and error profiles cannot be independently audited or contested by teachers or learners	All learners and educators subject to platform decisions, with amplified impact on those lacking alternative learning pathways	Representation in decision making and redistribution of governance power

Table 2 highlights that equity risks in AI-mediated language education are multidimensional, asymmetrically distributed, and tightly coupled to broader political economies of data, infrastructure, and linguistic prestige. Access and infrastructural stratification risk highlights that even ostensibly inclusive AI initiatives can reinforce long standing geographies of privilege if premium functionalities cluster around already advantaged institutions. Algorithmic and representational bias risk and linguistic hierarchy risk reveal how computational systems can stabilise racialised and classed language ideologies under the veneer of neutral feedback. Surveillance, datafication, and profiling risk expose how learners are rendered legible to institutions in ways that may not align with their own interests or consent, while affective and identity related risks demonstrate that motivational harm is not an incidental byproduct but a structural hazard of certain evaluation regimes. Governance and accountability deficit risk finally makes clear that without participatory oversight, the power to define, measure, and remediate proficiency remains concentrated in opaque assemblages of vendors and regulators. These risk archetypes provide the conceptual bridge to the next section, where teacher agency and professional ethics are theorised as central levers for mitigating and reconfiguring the AI saturated risk landscape described here.

TEACHER AGENCY, PROFESSIONAL ETHICS, AND EQUITY-ORIENTED AI LITERACIES

Re-Theorising Teacher Agency in AI Saturated Language Ecologies

Teacher agency in AI saturated language ecologies must be conceptualised as an emergent, relational, and structurally mediated capacity rather than as an individual trait or heroic disposition. Ecological and practice theoretic perspectives view teachers as actors who navigate intersecting temporal horizons, drawing on past professional trajectories, projecting preferred futures for learners, and making practical evaluative judgements in situated moments (Kontra, 2020; Liu et al., 2002; Boudadi et al., 2024). AI infrastructures introduce additional mediators into this ecology, including platform defaults, automated feedback regimes, analytics dashboards, and policy mandates that collectively shape the space of possible pedagogical moves. Within such assemblages, agency involves the capacity to appropriate, resist, repurpose, or bracket AI tools in ways that align with multilingual dignity and justice anchored aims, rather than passively implementing vendor scripts (Farrow et al., 2025; Li, 2022; Cheng, 2023). The risk archetypes codified in Table 2 make visible the structural pressures that can erode agency, while the normative anchors in Table 1 delineate the justice-oriented ends toward which agency can be oriented.

Professional Ethics, Justice Work, and Relational Responsibility in AI-mediated Practice

Language teachers in AI-mediated environments inhabit roles that are simultaneously epistemic, ethical, and political, since they curate whose voices are amplified, whose data are collected, and whose repertoires are legitimised within the classroom and platform (Yingsoon et al., 2025; Macaro et al., 2012). Professional ethics in this context cannot be reduced to generic duties of care, it must be understood as ongoing justice work that confronts data extraction, linguistic shaming, and structural exclusion. Concepts such as relational ethics and caring justice illuminate how teachers negotiate tensions between institutional directives that promote automated evaluation and their responsibility to protect learners from harm, humiliation, and erasure (Jesudas, 2025; Alam, 2023c). Decisions about whether to accept algorithmic placement, how to respond when AI feedback conflicts with translanguaging oriented pedagogy, or when to shield learners from high stakes machine scoring are all sites where ethical judgement is exercised. These micro level choices are intimately connected to the macro level justice principles articulated in Table 1 and the risk constellations summarised in Table 2.

Equity Oriented AI Literacies and Multilayered Professional Capital

Equity oriented AI literacies for language teachers comprise a stratified constellation of competencies that extend far beyond procedural familiarity with particular tools. At a functional level, teachers require sufficient understanding of model capabilities, limitations, and typical failure modes in order to avoid naive automation bias and to make informed decisions about task design (Mehta et al., 2025; McManus, 2024; Goetze & Driver, 2022). At a critical level, they need conceptual repertoires to interrogate data provenance, bias mechanisms, linguistic hierarchies, and governance architectures, drawing on constructs such as translanguaging, data colonialism, and symbolic power. At a design level, they must be able to orchestrate AI within sequences, groupings, and assessment ecologies in ways that enhance learner capabilities, valorise multilingual repertoires, and mitigate identified risk categories (Gass & Mackey, 2014; Butler & Huang, 2022; Fraschini, 2023). These layers accrete into a form of professional capital that is epistemic, ethical, and political, and that can be systematically mapped. Table 3 later in this section synthesises these dimensions by aligning domains of teacher practice with theoretical anchors, AI related competencies, equity orientations, and indicative pedagogical repertoires.

Conceptual Model of Teacher Decision Making with AI and Tabular Synthesis

Teacher decision making with AI can be conceptualised as a cyclical and multistage process that links diagnostic insight, normative reflection, technical appraisal, pedagogical orchestration, and reflexive evaluation. In an initial diagnostic phase, teachers interpret learner profiles, institutional constraints, language policies, and infrastructural conditions, identifying both resources and vulnerabilities (Fryer et al., 2025; Torkhani, 2025). A second phase involves explicit articulation of justice-oriented aims, such as expanding communicative capabilities for marginalised groups or legitimising translanguaging practices that curriculum documents marginalise. A third phase centres on appraisal of candidate AI tools, interfaces, and configurations in terms of inclusivity, accessibility, multilingual support, transparency, and alignment with those aims (Pinto-Llorente & Izquierdo-Álvarez, 2024; Ramos HolguĆn & Aguirre Morales, 2014; Thao et al., 2023). The orchestration phase concerns how AI is embedded within tasks, scaffolds, group structures, and feedback loops, while the reflexive phase involves reading learner responses, error patterns, and affective signals in order to recalibrate subsequent cycles. These interlocking phases can be rendered more tractable through the structured schema presented in Table 3, which distils them into dimensions of practice.

Table 3. Conceptual schema of teacher practice and AI equity literacies

Dimension of Teacher Practice	Theoretical Anchor Construct	AI Related Competence Focus	Equity Justice Orientation	Illustrative Pedagogical Repertoire
Contextual Diagnostic Praxis	Ecological agency, situated cognition	Reading datafied and non datafied classroom cues, infrastructural affordances, and constraint regimes	Identification of structurally disadvantaged learner constellations and hidden digital divides	Profiling classes for connectivity, language backgrounds, and platform access before configuring AI tasks
Normative Reflexive Stance	Justice theory, critical pedagogy	Articulating explicit distributive, recognitional, and participatory aims for AI use	Alignment of AI integration with capability expansion and multilingual dignity	Co constructing classroom charters on acceptable AI uses and linguistic norms with learners
Tool Appraisal and Selection	Sociomaterial design, value sensitive design	Evaluating tools for bias tendencies, transparency, accessibility, and translanguaging affordances	Avoidance of tools that entrench linguistic hierarchies or surveillance harms	Selecting AI systems that support multiple scripts and provide user controllable feedback intensity
Classroom Orchestration and Mediation	Sociocultural mediation, translanguaging pedagogy	Embedding AI within collaborative tasks, scaffolds, and dialogic discussion rather than as standalone evaluator	Redistribution of interactional space and validation of diverse repertoires through mediated activities	Using AI generated exemplars as prompts for group critique, rewriting, and multilingual revoicing
Reflective Evaluative Inquiry	Reflective practice, double loop learning	Interpreting learner trajectories, affective responses, and emergent inequities in AI supported environments	Reconfiguration of routines that inadvertently marginalise particular groups or practices	Adjusting grading schemas when automated scores systematically disadvantage certain accent or variety profiles
Professional Collaborative Engagement	Communities of practice, distributed expertise	Sharing tool insights, design patterns, and ethical dilemmas across peer networks and institutions	Collective construction of justice-oriented norms and advocacy positions on AI adoption	Participating in teacher led working groups that negotiate institutional AI policies and platform contracts

Table 3 makes visible that teacher agency in AI-mediated language education is not a monolithic capacity but a constellation of interdependent practices that are anchored in distinct theoretical constructs and oriented toward specific justice concerns. Contextual diagnostic praxis connects ecological and situated cognition frameworks with the practical question of which learners and contexts are most likely to be harmed or helped by particular AI configurations. Normative reflexive stance renders explicit the value commitments that guide AI adoption, preventing drift toward purely instrumental or technocratic rationales. Tool appraisal and selection foregrounds the need to scrutinise platform properties rather than accepting them as neutral, while orchestration and mediation emphasise that AI must be embedded within human relationships and translanguaging rich activities if it is to support multilingual dignity. Reflective evaluative inquiry and professional collaborative engagement highlight that justice-oriented AI integration is an ongoing process of collective learning, not a one-time decision. The next subsection extends this argument to teacher education and professional development architectures that can systematically cultivate the forms of agency and literacy codified in Table 3.

Teacher Education, Professional Development, and Collective Praxis Architectures

Teacher education and professional development function as critical infrastructural sites where the conceptual and practical capacities catalogued in Table 3 can be systematically nurtured rather than left to individual improvisation. Pre-service programs can embed AI justice themes into courses on language pedagogy, assessment literacy, and curriculum studies, inviting candidates to design and critique AI-mediated tasks through the lenses of equity and translanguaging (VanPatten & Williams, 2014; Spada & Lightbown, 1993). In service development can create protected spaces for experimentation, co inquiry, and critical dialogue, such as design studios, lesson study cycles, and cross institutional communities of practice focused on AI integration in multilingual settings. Institutional recognition structures, workload allocations, and leadership narratives must also be recalibrated so that time spent on ethical tool appraisal, participatory policy shaping, and mentoring peers in AI literacies is treated as core professional work rather than optional add on (Yıldız, 2023; Anshari & Asrifan, 2026; Towell & Hawkins, 1994). When teacher education systems internalise the multidimensional practice schema of Table 3, they can transform isolated instances of critical resistance into a sustained, collective praxis that reorients AI-mediated language education toward justice anchored futures.

AI AS AN ALLY FOR INCLUSIVE, DIFFERENTIATED, AND MULTILINGUAL PEDAGOGIES

Theoretical Architectures of Inclusion, Differentiation, and Intersectional Vulnerability

Inclusive AI-mediated language pedagogy must be anchored in robust theoretical architectures that treat learner diversity as constitutive rather than exceptional.

Universal Design for Learning conceptualises curricula as flexible frameworks that provide multiple means of engagement, representation, and expression, inviting designers to anticipate variability in sensory, cognitive, and cultural repertoires (de la Fuente & Goldenberg, 2022; Bitchener & Ferris, 2012; Al Nuaimi, 2024). *Response to Intervention* and inclusive education theory foreground graduated, data informed support, where intensification of scaffolding is triggered by observed need rather than by fixed labels. *Culturally sustaining pedagogy* and *funds of knowledge* constructs position learners' communities as epistemic resources whose narratives, semiotic practices, and translanguaging routines deserve curricular centrality (Sun & Wang, 2025; Zheng & Yang, 2024; Shao et al., 2019). Intersectionality from critical social theory demonstrates how disability, class, race, gender, migration status, and language background entangle to produce layered disadvantage. Within this composite framework, AI systems become potential instruments for redistributing cognitive scaffolds and symbolic recognition, yet they also risk amplifying precisely the exclusions these theories seek to redress, which motivates the granular design principles later systematised in Table 4.

Conceptual Affordances of AI for Inclusive and Differentiated Language Learning

When viewed through sociocognitive and sociocultural lenses, AI affords a set of distinctive mediational possibilities that can widen participation in language learning ecologies. Adaptive feedback engines, generative exemplars, and speech recognition interfaces can operate within the *Zone of Proximal Development* as contingent scaffolds that calibrate challenge and support to individual trajectories rather than to static group averages (Namaziandost et al., 2024; Robinson, 2001). Multimodal capabilities such as text to speech, speech to text, visual glossing, and interactive simulations can redistribute cognitive load, enabling learners with dyslexia, sensory impairments, or processing differences to access curricular content on more equitable terms. Predictive analytics, if governed by justice anchored norms, can signal where additional human mentoring or peer support is needed, rather than merely labelling students as risks (Loewen & Sato, 2017; Namaziandost, 2025). These affordances, however, are not intrinsically emancipatory, they require deliberate orchestration by teachers exercising the forms of agency mapped in Table 3 and must be constrained by explicit design principles of proportionality, transparency, and contestability, which are elaborated and structurally codified in Table 4.

Risks of Normalisation, Instrumentalisation, and Pedagogical Overreliance

The same AI affordances that promise inclusion can, if left unexamined, crystallise into regimes of normalisation and instrumentalisation that undermine pedagogical justice. Normalisation occurs when AI powered workflows become taken for granted infrastructural backdrops, such that learners and teachers no longer perceive the political economy of data capture, metric production, and linguistic norm enforcement described in Table 2. Instrumentalisation surfaces when learners are treated primarily as data emitting entities whose value lies in optimisable performance indicators, rather than as subjects with complex identities and aspirations (Driver, 2022; Sudina, 2023; Lightbown, 2000). Overreliance on automated feedback, auto completion, and predictive grading can induce homogenisation of linguistic expression, reduce tolerance for exploratory error, and erode teachers confidence in their own professional judgement. These dynamics may be particularly acute in contexts where institutional accountability regimes pressure educators to outsource evaluation to machines (Skehan, 1991; Caruana & Żammit, 2024). An equity centered stance therefore demands design norms that actively counter these tendencies, establishing procedural safeguards and pedagogical rituals that re insert human reflection, plurality, and dissent into AI-mediated routines, as synthesised in Table 4.

Multilingual, Translanguaging, and Intercultural Potentials of AI-mediated Pedagogy

AI systems can, under justice-oriented design, act as *semiotic brokers* and *dialogic partners* that expand translanguaging spaces and intercultural understanding rather than constrict them. Generative engines can produce parallel texts across registers, genres, and languages, which teachers can mobilise to stage contrastive analyses, code meshing exercises, and critical readings of how power, race, and gender are encoded in discourse (Lin et al., 2015; Kormos, 2016; Li et al., 2022). Machine translation and multilingual prompting, if explicitly framed as fallible and partial, can support intercomprehension and metalinguistic awareness by encouraging learners to compare AI outputs with community norms and to articulate where automation misrepresents local idioms or cultural references. Low resource language support, even if initially imperfect, can be harnessed in revitalisation-oriented projects where students curate corpora, correct outputs, and co construct bilingual artefacts (Midigo, 2025; Ortega, 2014). In such scenarios, AI becomes a catalyst for *linguistic citizenship*, where learners exercise agency over how their repertoires appear in digital spaces, provided that the design principles of multilingual valorisation and culturally sustaining orientation, enumerated in Table 4, are rigorously applied.

Conceptual Design Principles for Inclusive AI Augmented Language Pedagogy and Tabular Framework

To operationalise the theoretical commitments and risk diagnostics articulated in Sections 2, 3, and 4, inclusive AI augmented language pedagogy requires a parsimonious yet conceptually rich set of design principles that can guide everyday decision making by educators, designers, and institutional leaders. Proportionality asserts that AI should be deployed in ways commensurate with clearly specified pedagogical purposes, supplementing rather than eclipsing human interaction and peer collaboration (Sudina, 2021; Piechurska-Kuciel, 2008; Pawlak & Waniek-Klimczak, 2015). Transparency obliges educators and developers to make visible when AI is active, what data it processes, and how its feedback should be interpreted, thereby building *regulatory literacy* and *epistemic humility* among learners. Contestability ensures that AI outputs, scores, and recommendations are treated as negotiable contributions to dialogue rather than as final verdicts, embedding structured opportunities for learners to challenge and reinterpret machine suggestions (Kormos, 2020; Wang, 2024). Multilingual valorisation mandates that tasks and interfaces explicitly affirm the legitimacy of multiple languages and scripts, while affective safety demands that AI be positioned primarily within formative, low stakes contexts where experimentation and error are not punished. Culturally sustaining orientation binds these principles together by insisting that AI uses should nourish, rather than erode, the cultural and linguistic ecosystems of learners' communities. These interlocking design logics are synthesised in Table 4 as a compact decision support matrix.

Table 4. Design principles for inclusive AI language pedagogy

Design Principle Nucleus	Theoretical Justification Nexus	Intended Inclusion Outcome Vector	Potential Distortion Risk Profile	Safeguarding Design Considerations
Proportionality Orchestration	Sociocultural mediation, instructional design theory	Balanced human machine co presence, preserved dialogic teacher learner relations	Pedagogical outsourcing, teacher deskilling, reduction of human contact time	Specify clear AI roles in task blueprints, cap automated evaluation weightings
Transparency Intelligibility	Critical data literacy, epistemic virtue ethics	Learners and teachers understand AI boundaries, data flows, and interpretive status	Opaque black box authority, mystification of algorithmic processes	Provide plain language model descriptions, on screen explanations, and opt in consent rituals
Contestability Dialogism	Critical pedagogy, deliberative educational theory	Normalised practices of questioning AI outputs, strengthened learner voice and agency	Deference to machine verdicts, internalised linguistic inferiority	Embed structured reflection prompts, allow annotation, require human moderation of key decisions
Multilingual Valorisation	Translanguaging pedagogy, linguistic human rights	Affirmation of full repertoires, legitimation of code meshing and local varieties	Reinscription of monolingual norms, sidelining of minoritised languages	Configure prompts and tasks that invite multiple codes, support diverse scripts and orthographies
Affective Safety Containment	Emotion regulation theory, trauma informed pedagogy	Reduced shame and anxiety, protected space for experimentation and error	Heightened performance pressure, avoidance of language risk taking	Reserve high stakes judgments for human assessors, frame AI feedback as provisional guidance
Culturally Sustaining Attunement	Culturally sustaining pedagogy, intercultural communication theory	Curricular alignment with learners' cultural narratives and semiotic practices	Cultural erasure, reproduction of stereotypical or colonial representations	Curate AI prompts and exemplars from learners' locally relevant texts and community knowledge systems, and involve communities in content vetting

Table 4 functions as a design heuristic that translates abstract commitments to justice, inclusion, and multilingual dignity into concrete decision parameters for AI supported tasks and platforms. By pairing each principle with its theoretical grounding, intended inclusion outcome, distortion risk profile, and safeguarding considerations, the table foregrounds that no design choice is normatively neutral. Proportionality and transparency constrain the gravitational pull toward automation and opacity described in Table 2, while contestability activates the critical dispositions and teacher agency configurations outlined in Table 3. Multilingual valorisation and culturally sustaining attunement ensure that translanguaging and local knowledges are not retrofitted as cosmetic features but are integral to task design and content curation. Affective safety, finally, reorients AI away from punitive ranking regimes and toward supportive, growth-oriented feedback ecologies. Together, these principles and their tabular synthesis prepare the conceptual ground for Section 6, where governance and policy frameworks are constructed to institutionalise such design logics across micro, meso, and macro levels of language education systems.

GOVERNANCE, POLICY, AND DESIGN FRAMEWORKS

Multi Level and Polycentric Governance Architectures in AI-mediated Language Ecologies

Governance of AI in language education operates across interlocking strata that range from classroom level micro practices to transnational regulatory regimes, forming a polycentric architecture rather than a single command structure. At the micro level, teachers and learners negotiate consent practices, task designs, and norms for AI reliance, often within constraints set by institutional licences and accountability metrics (Budiman & Liu, 2025; Liu, 2022; Rosell-Aguilar, 2005). At the meso level, schools, universities, and language centres determine procurement criteria, platform portfolios, and internal policies that align, or fail to align, with the justice lenses articulated in Table 1 and the risk archetypes in Table 2. At the macro level, ministries, examination boards, and international standard setting bodies embed AI within curricula, assessment frameworks, and digital strategies, thereby shaping what counts as legitimate language learning (Dewaele, 2005; Aydın Yıldız, 2025). A public value perspective, informed by *human rights* and *child rights* constructs, therefore treats AI-mediated language tools as components of educational infrastructure whose governance requires coordinated attention across these strata, later synthesised in the multi-level schema of Table 5.

Ethical AI, Responsible Innovation, and Design Justice in Language Education Ecosystems

Ethical AI discourse provides a vocabulary of fairness, accountability, transparency, and explicability, yet these terms require contextualisation within language education if they are to guide practice rather than remain abstract slogans. Fairness in this domain concerns equitable access to high quality AI-mediated learning opportunities across linguistic, socio economic, and geographic divides, as well as nondiscriminatory evaluation of diverse repertoires (Anya, 2011; Kramsch, 2000; Liu, 2023). Accountability involves clearly assignable responsibility when AI instruments distort proficiency judgments, compromise privacy, or exacerbate the risks catalogued in Table 2. Transparency and explicability require that learners and teachers can understand, in accessible terms, how AI tools produce feedback, scores, and recommendations (MacIntyre & McGillivray, 2023; Huang et al., 2024). *Responsible research and innovation* and *value sensitive design* extend these principles by emphasising anticipation of downstream impacts, reflexivity about assumptions, inclusion of affected communities, and responsiveness to emerging harms. *Design justice* and *data justice* sharpen this stance by insisting that those who are most vulnerable to algorithmic misrecognition, surveillance, and linguistic erasure should have priority in setting design and governance priorities, a position aligned with community-led approaches to technological design and accountability (Costanza-Chock, 2020). This normative commitment is structurally inscribed in the governance matrix of Table 5.

Policy Instrumentation, Regulatory Levers, and Institutional Mechanisms for Justice Anchored AI

Policy and regulatory interventions for AI in language education can be conceptualised as an instrumentarium that includes binding rules, guiding norms, and institutional mechanisms, all of which must be aligned with the equity centered goals articulated earlier. Hard instruments encompass statutory regulations on data protection, biometric information, and algorithmic accountability, as well as accreditation requirements for language programs that use automated evaluation in high stakes contexts (Brown & Lee, 2025; Alam & Mohanty, 2024). Soft instruments include ministerial guidelines, professional codes, and quality assurance standards that specify expectations for multilingual support, accessibility features, transparency practices, and participatory oversight. Institutional mechanisms such as ethics committees, AI impact assessment protocols, ombudsperson roles, and teacher learner advisory councils serve as concrete sites where justice principles can be interpreted and applied to specific tools or deployments (Collier et al., 2016; Zhang & Dong, 2024). When these instruments are mapped across the governance strata identified in Section 6.1, they reveal patterns of coverage, gaps, and overlaps that are systematically captured in Table 5, which positions policy tools in relation to actors, justice commitments, and exemplar decisions.

Participatory Co-Design, Epistemic Justice, and Integrated Governance Cartographies

Participatory and co design approaches, when anchored in *epistemic justice*, reposition learners, teachers, parents, and community members as co producers of AI-mediated language education rather than as passive users of preconfigured systems. Participatory design traditions in human computer interaction emphasise iterative engagement with end users through workshops, prototyping, and scenario building, while co design in education foregrounds joint ownership of pedagogical innovations and institutional rules (Horwitz, 2020; Teimouri et al., 2019). Epistemic justice deepens these approaches by acknowledging that communities historically marginalised by linguicism, racism, and ableism often possess forms of situated knowledge that are indispensable for identifying harms and imagining alternatives. When such actors are structurally incorporated into governance, they influence not only interface aesthetics but also training data curation, error taxonomy design, consent regimes, and redress pathways (Loewen, 2020; Shepperd, 2022). The multi-level implications of this participatory turn, including its interaction with the risk typology in Table 2 and the pedagogical design principles in Table 4, can be rendered visible only through an integrated governance cartography, which is provided in Table 5 as a dense yet tractable mapping.

Table 5. Integrated governance schema for AI language education

Governance Stratum Vector	Principal Actor Constellations	Core Justice Commitment Complex	Normative Instrumentarium and Mechanisms	Example AI Governance Decision Node
Micro Classroom Ecologies	Individual teachers, learner groups, local support staff	Recognition of multilingual repertoires, protection of learner dignity, participatory voice in AI use	Classroom charters, consent rituals, task level AI usage protocols, peer review of AI supported activities	Deciding whether automated writing scores are advisory only or influence summative grades in a specific course
Meso Institutional Formations	School leadership, language departments, instructional designers, IT units	Redistribution of infrastructural resources, safeguarding against internal digital divides	Procurement policies, platform vetting committees, institutional AI guidelines, local data governance rules	Selecting between alternative language learning platforms based on multilingual support and privacy profiles
Macro System Governance	Education ministries, exam boards, funding agencies, inspectorates	Systemic capability expansion, alignment with linguistic rights, interschool equity	National curricula, assessment frameworks, funding formulas, system wide AI accreditation standards	Determining whether automated speaking assessment may be used in high stakes certification exams
Regulatory Jurisprudential Arenas	Data protection authorities, competition regulators, judicial bodies, ombuds institutions	Protection of fundamental rights, redress for harm, constraint of abusive market practices	Data protection regulations, algorithmic accountability laws, complaint and appeal procedures, enforcement actions	Adjudicating a case where an AI placement test has systematically misclassified a minoritised language group
Corporate Technocapital Actors	EdTech companies, cloud providers, consultancy firms, model developers	Responsibility for non-exploitation, mitigation of bias, contribution to public educational value	Ethical AI charters, impact assessment reports, contractual clauses, transparency disclosures, audit interfaces	Deciding whether to retrain a model to better handle low resource languages at the cost of commercial speed
Civic Polycentric Coalitions	Teacher unions, parent associations, learner collectives, NGOs, research consortia	Representation of affected communities, countervailing power, discursive and policy influence	Advocacy campaigns, multistakeholder forums, citizen juries, independent monitoring reports	Coordinating a civil society intervention on the mandatory roll out of an AI writing grader in public schools

Table 5 demonstrates that equity centered AI in language education cannot be guaranteed by isolated interventions at a single level, but instead emerges from the dynamic interplay among classrooms, institutions, systems, regulators, corporations, and civic coalitions. Each governance stratum vector hosts distinctive actor constellations, justice commitments, and instrument types, yet they are mutually implicated, since decisions taken by corporate technocapital actors about model retraining, for example, shape what is technically possible in classrooms, while regulatory jurisprudential arenas establish the boundaries of lawful data practices. Civic polycentric coalitions, by aggregating and amplifying the experiences of those most affected by AI misrecognition or surveillance, can exert countervailing pressure on both state and corporate actors, influencing the parameters within which micro and meso level decisions unfold. The matrix thus functions as an analytic scaffold for identifying where justice aligned practices already exist, where gaps or contradictions persist, and how cross level coordination might be designed to support the normative anchors articulated in Table 1 and the pedagogical principles structured in Table 4.

Toward Coherent, Justice Anchored Governance Architectures Across Scales

An integrated approach to governance of AI in language education requires not only the identification of roles and instruments, as organised in Table 5, but also deliberate design of feedback loops that transform local insights into system level reforms and translate macro level norms into context sensitive micro practices (Godfroid & Andringa, 2023; Alam & Mohanty, 2023d). Mechanisms such as periodic participatory reviews of AI deployments, cross sectoral advisory councils, and open data spaces for non-sensitive performance indicators can support upward and downward flows of information and accountability. Coherence across scales implies that classroom charters on acceptable AI uses resonate with institutional policies, which in turn align with national frameworks and international human rights obligations, while still allowing for adaptive variation in linguistically diverse settings (Tomlinson, 2016; Wedlock & Wilson, 2024; Davoodi, 2024). Justice anchored governance also calls for temporal sensitivity, recognising that AI systems, markets, and sociolinguistic ecologies evolve, which necessitates iterative recalibration rather than one off regulation. By embedding the normative commitments of capability expansion, recognition, and representation into these evolving architectures, education systems can begin to treat AI-mediated language learning not as a techno marketing opportunity, but as a site of ongoing democratic negotiation over whose voices are cultivated, heard, and respected.

Implementation Challenges in Real-World AI-mediated Language Education

The implementation of equity-centered and translanguaging-oriented AI-mediated language education faces several practical challenges that cannot be resolved through conceptual commitment alone. First, stakeholder coordination remains difficult because teachers, learners, administrators, platform vendors, regulators, parents, and community representatives often operate with different priorities, unequal technical knowledge, and uneven decision-making power. Second, institutional capacity is frequently limited by weak infrastructure, inadequate budgets, fragmented procurement systems, and the absence of internal expertise for evaluating AI tools in relation to multilingual support, privacy, accessibility, and bias. Third, teacher preparation remains a major constraint, since many educators are expected to use AI systems without sustained professional development in algorithmic bias, data governance, translanguaging pedagogy, critical AI literacy, and ethical classroom orchestration. Fourth, multilingual data limitations restrict the reliability and fairness of AI systems, especially for low-resource languages, minoritised dialects, mixed codes, regional accents, Indigenous languages, and heritage language practices that are poorly represented in training corpora. Fifth, governance accountability remains underdeveloped because responsibility is often dispersed across vendors, institutions, and regulators, making it difficult for learners and teachers to contest harmful classifications, opaque scoring, or discriminatory feedback. These challenges suggest that justice-oriented AI implementation requires phased institutional planning, participatory oversight, teacher education, transparent procurement, multilingual auditing, and clear redress mechanisms. Without these supports, even well-designed AI initiatives may reproduce the very inequities they claim to address.

FUTURE RESEARCH DIRECTIONS

Future research must move beyond celebratory claims about AI-enhanced language education and develop rigorous, justice-sensitive empirical agendas that examine how AI systems actually reshape multilingual learning across unequal classrooms, institutions, and geopolitical settings. Large-scale comparative studies are needed to test whether AI-mediated tools expand learners' communicative capabilities or merely reproduce existing hierarchies through better packaged forms of standardisation. Longitudinal research should trace how multilingual learners experience algorithmic feedback over time, particularly in relation to confidence, identity, translanguaging practices, linguistic risk-taking, and participation in academic and civic domains. Equally urgent are multilingual bias audits that examine model performance across low-resource languages, regional accents, mixed codes, heritage repertoires, Indigenous languages, and minoritised dialects. Such studies should combine computational evaluation with classroom observation, learner testimony, teacher judgement, and community validation across diverse educational levels and contexts. Without this multidimensional evidence base, the field will remain dependent on vendor claims, narrow accuracy metrics, and decontextualised performance scores that cannot adequately measure multilingual dignity, recognitional justice, or democratic participation in lived learning ecologies globally and locally.

Future inquiry must also strengthen the governance, design, and teacher education dimensions of AI-mediated language pedagogy. Researchers should investigate how teachers develop AI-equity literacies, how these literacies influence classroom orchestration, and how professional development models can prepare educators to contest biased outputs, protect learner data, and legitimise translanguaging practices. Participatory design research should involve learners, teachers, parents, language communities, disability advocates, and civil society actors in co-creating AI tools, assessment protocols, consent mechanisms, and redress systems. Future work must also develop robust indicators for capability expansion, affective safety, linguistic agency, and community accountability, since existing assessment regimes remain too closely tied to fluency, correctness, and measurable output. Comparative Global South research is especially necessary to prevent AI language education from being theorised primarily through high-resource, English-dominant settings. The next phase of scholarship must therefore treat AI not as a neutral instrument, but as a contested educational infrastructure whose legitimacy depends on evidence, accountability, participatory governance, and justice across scales, sectors, languages, institutions, communities, and learner lifeworlds in practice and policy.

CONCLUSION

AI-mediated language education cannot be treated as a neutral technological improvement; it is a contested socio-technical field shaped by justice, power, linguistic hierarchy, and governance. This chapter has argued that equitable AI use in language education must be grounded in Rawlsian fairness, the Capability Approach, Fraserian justice, critical and decolonial pedagogy, translanguaging, and linguistic human rights. These frameworks expose how algorithmic bias, data colonialism, platform control, surveillance, and symbolic power can reproduce exclusion through unequal access, misrecognition, homogenisation, and affective harm. Against this, teacher agency must remain central: teachers are ethical mediators, designers, interpreters, and advocates, not passive operators of automated systems. The chapter advances five core principles for praxis: centre learner capabilities and linguistic capital; protect teacher autonomy; ensure transparency and contestability; affirm multilingual and culturally sustaining design; and govern AI as public educational infrastructure through participatory oversight. Future research must develop justice-sensitive concepts such as algorithmic language ideologies, datafied linguistic capital, and AI-mediated language socialisation, while creating metrics that measure capability expansion, translanguaging vitality, and democratic participation. Ultimately, AI in language education must be subordinated to human dignity, democratic equality, and multilingual flourishing.

REFERENCES

Ait-Hroch, A., & Ibrahimi, A. (2025). Integrating AI Tools in Blended Language Training: Enhancing Language Skills Development in University Students. In *Supporting Personalized Learning and Students' Skill Development With AI* (pp. 343-368). IGI Global Scientific Publishing. DOI: 10.4018/979-8-3693-8965-2.ch017

Al Nuaimi, H. (2024). Anxiety and task-based language teaching in second language acquisition. *Research Studies in English Language Teaching and Learning*, *2*(4), 251–267. DOI: 10.62583/rseltl.v2i4.56

Alam, A. (2023a). The secret sauce of student success: Cracking the code by navigating the path to personalized learning with educational data mining. In *2023 2nd International Conference on Smart Technologies and Systems for Next Generation Computing (ICSTSN)* (pp. 1-8). IEEE. DOI: 10.1109/ICSTSN57873.2023.10151558

Alam, A. (2023b). Media multitasking with M-learning technology in real-time classroom learning: Analysing the dynamics in formal educational settings for the future of E-learning in India. In *2023 2nd International Conference on Smart Technologies and Systems for Next Generation Computing (ICSTSN)* (pp. 1-6). IEEE. DOI: 10.1109/ICSTSN57873.2023.10151509

Alam, A. (2023c). Leveraging the power of 'modeling and computer simulation' for education: An exploration of its potential for improved learning outcomes and enhanced student engagement. In *2023 International Conference on Device Intelligence, Computing and Communication Technologies (DICCT)* (pp. 445-450). IEEE. DOI: 10.1109/DICCT56244.2023.10110159

Alam, A., & Mohanty, A. (2022). Facial analytics or virtual avatars: competencies and design considerations for student-teacher interaction in AI-powered online education for effective classroom engagement. In *International Conference on Communication, Networks and Computing* (pp. 252-265). Cham: Springer Nature Switzerland. DOI: 10.1007/978-3-031-43145-6_21

Alam, A., & Mohanty, A. (2023a). Learning on the move: a pedagogical framework for state-of-the-art mobile learning. In *International Conference on Data Management, Analytics & Innovation* (pp. 735-748). Singapore: Springer Nature Singapore. DOI: 10.1007/978-981-99-1414-2_52

Alam, A., & Mohanty, A. (2023b). From bricks to clicks: The potential of big data analytics for revolutionizing the information landscape in higher education sector. In *International Conference on Data Management, Analytics & Innovation* (pp. 721-732). Singapore: Springer Nature Singapore. DOI: 10.1007/978-981-99-1414-2_51

Alam, A., & Mohanty, A. (2023c). Developing 'happiness engineering' subject for the schools in India: Designing the pedagogical framework for a sustainable happiness curriculum. *Qubahan Academic Journal, 3*(4), 1–20. DOI: 10.48161/qaj.v3n4a145

Alam, A., & Mohanty, A. (2023d). Implications of virtual reality (VR) for school teachers and instructional designers: An empirical investigation. *Cogent Education, 10*(2), 2260676. DOI: 10.1080/2331186X.2023.2260676

Alam, A., & Mohanty, A. (2024). Framework of Self-Regulated cognitive engagement (FSRCE) for sustainable pedagogy: A model that integrates SRL and cognitive engagement for holistic development of students. *Cogent Education, 11*(1), 2363157. DOI: 10.1080/2331186X.2024.2363157

Anshari, A., & Asrifan, A. (2026). AI-Enhanced Language Acquisition: Transforming the Learning Experience. In *AI in Literary Education and Language Learning* (pp. 117-146). IGI Global Scientific Publishing. DOI: 10.4018/979-8-3373-6330-1.ch005

Anya, U. (2011). Connecting with communities of learners and speakers: Integrative ideals, experiences, and motivations of successful black second language learners. *Foreign Language Annals, 44*(3), 441–466. DOI: 10.1111/j.1944-9720.2011.01142.x

Aubrey, S. (2022). The relationship between anxiety, enjoyment, and breakdown fluency during second language speaking tasks: An idiodynamic investigation. *Frontiers in Psychology, 13*, 968946. DOI: 10.3389/fpsyg.2022.968946 PMID: 36118455

Aydın Yıldız, T. (2025). Sustainability Education in L2 Writing: AI-Based Multimodal Awareness and Engagement. *Sustainability (Basel), 17*(21), 9376. DOI: 10.3390/su17219376

Bendarkawi, J., Ponce, A., Mata, S. C., Aliu, A., Liu, Y., Zhang, L., & Monroy-Hernández, A. (2025, April). ConversAR: Exploring Embodied LLM-Powered Group Conversations in Augmented Reality for Second Language Learners. In *Proceedings of the Extended Abstracts of the CHI Conference on Human Factors in Computing Systems* (pp. 1-11). DOI: 10.1145/3706599.3720162

Bitchener, J., & Ferris, D. R. (2012). *Written corrective feedback in second language acquisition and writing*. Routledge., DOI: 10.4324/9780203832400

Blodgett, S. L., Barocas, S., Daumé Iii, H., & Wallach, H. (2020, July). Language (technology) is power: A critical survey of "bias" in NLP. In *Proceedings of the 58th annual meeting of the association for computational linguistics* (pp. 5454-5476). DOI: 10.18653/v1/2020.acl-main.485

Boudadi, N. A., Gutierrez-Colon, M., & Rodriguez, M. U. (2024). A Gamified learning environment (Moodle) to enhance English language learning at university level. *International Journal of Instruction, 17*(4), 483–502. DOI: 10.29333/iji.2024.17427a

Brown, H. D., & Lee, H. (2025). *Principles of language learning and teaching: A course in second language acquisition*. Taylor & Francis., DOI: 10.4324/9781003494294

Bryfonski, L., Ku, Y. Y., & Mackey, A. (2024). Research methods for IDs and TBLT: A substantive and methodological review. *Studies in Second Language Acquisition, 46*(3), 617–643. DOI: 10.1017/S0272263124000135

Budiman, A., & Liu, X. (2025). Beyond standard English: How Global Englishes enhances creativity, reduces language anxiety, and increases willingness to communicate. *Frontiers in Psychology, 16*, 1611630. DOI: 10.3389/fpsyg.2025.1611630 PMID: 40606868

Butler, Y. G., & Huang, B. H. (Eds.). (2022). *Research methods for understanding child second language development*. Taylor & Francis., DOI: 10.4324/9780367815783

Caldwell-Harris, C. L., & Ayçiçeği-Dinn, A. (2009). Emotion and lying in a non-native language. *International Journal of Psychophysiology : Official Journal of the International Organization of Psychophysiology, 71*(3), 193–204. DOI: 10.1016/j.ijpsycho.2008.09.006 PMID: 18929603

Caruana, L. F., & Żammit, J. (2024). Exploring beliefs, motivations and emotions: Insights from learning Maltese as a second language. *Language Teaching Research, 13621688241289724*, 13621688241289724. Advance online publication. DOI: 10.1177/13621688241289724

Cheng, L. (2023). Delving into the role of mindfulness on the relationship among creativity, anxiety, and boredom of young EFL learners. *Heliyon, 9*(2), e13733. Advance online publication. DOI: 10.1016/j.heliyon.2023.e13733 PMID: 36873160

Cintrón-Valentín, M. C., & Ellis, N. C. (2016). Salience in second language acquisition: Physical form, learner attention, and instructional focus. *Frontiers in Psychology, 7*, 1284. DOI: 10.3389/fpsyg.2016.01284 PMID: 27621715

Collier, S., Burston, B., & Rhodes, A. (2016). Teaching STEM as a second language: Utilizing SLA to develop equitable learning for all students. *Journal for Multicultural Education, 10*(3), 257–273. DOI: 10.1108/JME-01-2016-0013

Costanza-Chock, S. (2020). *Design justice: Community-led practices to build the worlds we need*. MIT press., DOI: 10.7551/mitpress/12255.001.0001

Couldry, N., & Mejias, U. A. (2023). The decolonial turn in data and technology research: What is at stake and where is it heading? *Information Communication and Society*, *26*(4), 786–802. DOI: 10.1080/1369118X.2021.1986102

Davoodi, A. (2024). EQUAL AI: A framework for enhancing equity, quality, understanding and accessibility in liberal arts through AI for multilingual learners. *Language, Technology, and Social Media*, *2*(2), 178–203. DOI: 10.70211/ltsm.v2i2.139

De Bot, K., Lowie, W., & Verspoor, M. (2005). *Second language acquisition: An advanced resource book*. Psychology Press., DOI: 10.4324/9780203446416

de la Fuente, M. J., & Goldenberg, C. (2022). Understanding the role of the first language (L1) in instructed second language acquisition (ISLA): Effects of using a principled approach to L1 in the beginner foreign language classroom. *Language Teaching Research*, *26*(5), 943–962. DOI: 10.1177/1362168820921882

Derakhshan, A., Teo, T., Saeedy Robat, E., Janebi Enayat, M., & Jahanbakhsh, A. A. (2024). Robot-assisted language learning: A meta-analysis. *Review of Educational Research, 00346543241247227*. Advance online publication. DOI: 10.3102/00346543241247227

Derakhshan, A., & Zare, J. (2023). The impact of altruistic teaching on English as a foreign language (EFL) learners' emotion regulation: An intervention study. *Brain Sciences*, *13*(3), 458. DOI: 10.3390/brainsci13030458 PMID: 36979269

Dewaele, J. M. (2005). Investigating the psychological and emotional dimensions in instructed language learning: Obstacles and possibilities. *Modern Language Journal*, *89*(3), 367–380. DOI: 10.1111/j.1540-4781.2005.00311.x

Dewaele, J. M., Özdemir, C., Karci, D., Uysal, S., Özdemir, E. D., & Balta, N. (2022). How distinctive is the foreign language enjoyment and foreign language classroom anxiety of Kazakh learners of Turkish? *Applied Linguistics Review*, *13*(2), 243–265. DOI: 10.1515/applirev-2019-0021

Dixon, L. Q., Zhao, J., Shin, J. Y., Wu, S., Su, J. H., Burgess-Brigham, R., Gezer, M. U., & Snow, C. (2012). What we know about second language acquisition: A synthesis from four perspectives. *Review of Educational Research*, *82*(1), 5–60. DOI: 10.3102/0034654311433587

Douglas Fir Group. (2016). A transdisciplinary framework for SLA in a multilingual world. *Modern Language Journal*, *100*(S1), 19–47. DOI: 10.1111/modl.12301

Driver, M. (2022). Emotion-laden texts and words: The influence of emotion on vocabulary learning for heritage and foreign language learners. *Studies in Second Language Acquisition*, *44*(4), 1071–1094. DOI: 10.1017/S0272263121000851

Driver, M. Y. (2023). Measuring and understanding linguistic insecurity in heritage and foreign language contexts: Design and validation of a novel scale. *Journal of Multilingual and Multicultural Development*, •••, 1–20. DOI: 10.1080/01434632.2023.2265901

Dunkel, P. (1991). Listening in the native and second/foreign language: Toward an integration of research and practice. *TESOL Quarterly*, *25*(3), 431–457. DOI: 10.2307/3586979

Ellis, R., & Sheen, Y. (2006). Reexamining the role of recasts in second language acquisition. *Studies in Second Language Acquisition*, *28*(4), 575–600. DOI: 10.1017/S027226310606027X

Elsayed, A. M., Kholikov, A., Abdullayeva, I., Al-Farouni, M., & Wodajo, M. R. (2024). Teacher support in AI-assisted exams: An experimental study to inspect the effects on demotivation, anxiety management in exams, L2 learning experience, and academic success. *Language Testing in Asia*, *14*(1), 53. DOI: 10.1186/s40468-024-00328-7

Engh, D. (2013). Why use music in English language learning? A survey of the literature. *English Language Teaching*, *6*(2), 113–127. DOI: 10.5539/elt.v6n2p113

Farrow, J., Farrow, M. J., & Zhang, C. (2025). Advancing Translational Science Through AI-Enhanced Teacher Learning for Early Language and Composing. *Education Sciences*, *15*(11), 1496. DOI: 10.3390/educsci15111496

Ferris, D. (2011). *Treatment of error in second language student writing*. University of Michigan Press., DOI: 10.3998/mpub.2173290

Fettes, M., & Karamouzian, F. M. (2018). Inclusion in education: Challenges for linguistic policy and research. In *Language policy and language acquisition planning* (pp. 219–235). Springer International Publishing., DOI: 10.1007/978-3-319-75963-0_13

Fraschini, N. (2023). Language learners' emotional dynamics: Insights from a Q methodology intensive single-case study. *Language, Culture and Curriculum*, *36*(2), 222–239. DOI: 10.1080/07908318.2022.2133137

Fraser, N. (2008). Abnormal justice. *Critical Inquiry*, *34*(3), 393–422. DOI: 10.1086/589478

Fraser, N. (2010). Injustice at intersecting scales: On 'social exclusion'and the 'global poor'. *European Journal of Social Theory*, *13*(3), 363–371. DOI: 10.1177/1368431010371758

Freiermuth, M. R. (2020). Introduction and overview: the inescapable confluence of technology, psychology and second language learners and users. In *Technology and the psychology of second language learners and users* (pp. 3–32). Springer International Publishing., DOI: 10.1007/978-3-030-34212-8_1

Fryer, L. K., Li, C., Guo, Z., Liang, L., & Zhong, Y. (2025). Self-efficacy's role within learning a new language during formal education: Systematic review, critical evaluation of past research and paths forward for research and practice. *Studies in Second Language Learning and Teaching, 15*(2), 251–278. DOI: 10.14746/ssllt.48234

Gallegos, I. O., Rossi, R. A., Barrow, J., Tanjim, M. M., Kim, S., Dernoncourt, F., Yu, T., Zhang, R., & Ahmed, N. K. (2024). Bias and fairness in large language models: A survey. *Computational Linguistics, 50*(3), 1097–1179. DOI: 10.1162/coli_a_00524

García, O., & Wei, L. (2015). Translanguaging in education: Principles, implications and challenges. In *Translanguaging: Language, bilingualism and education* (pp. 119–135). Palgrave Macmillan UK., DOI: 10.1057/9781137385765_8

Gass, S. M., & Mackey, A. (2014). Input, interaction, and output in second language acquisition. In *Theories in second language acquisition* (pp. 194–220). Routledge., DOI: 10.4324/9780203808184

Gilmore, A. (2007). Authentic materials and authenticity in foreign language learning. *Language Teaching, 40*(2), 97–118. DOI: 10.1017/S0261444807004144

Godfroid, A., & Andringa, S. (2023). Uncovering sampling biases, advancing inclusivity, and rethinking theoretical accounts in second language acquisition: Introduction to the special issue SLA for all? *Language Learning, 73*(4), 981–1002. DOI: 10.1111/lang.12620

Goetze, J., & Driver, M. (2022). Is learning really just believing? A meta-analysis of self-efficacy and achievement in SLA. *Studies in Second Language Learning and Teaching, 12*(2), 233–259. DOI: 10.14746/ssllt.2022.12.2.4

Gregersen, T., MacIntyre, P. D., & Meza, M. (2016). Positive psychology exercises build social capital for language learners: Preliminary evidence. DOI: 10.2307/jj.30945667.9

Gruba, P. (2004). Computer assisted language learning (CALL). The handbook of applied linguistics, 623-648. DOI: 10.1002/9780470757000.ch25

Hajizadeh, S., Salman, A. R., & Ebadi, S. (2023). Evaluating language learning applications from efl learners' perspectives: The case of mondly. DOI: 10.21203/rs.3.rs-3011332/v1

Hejazi, S. Y., Sadoughi, M., & Peng, J. E. (2023). The structural relationship between teacher support and willingness to communicate: The mediation of L2 anxiety and the moderation of growth language mindset. *Journal of Psycholinguistic Research, 52*(6), 2955–2978. DOI: 10.1007/s10936-023-10026-9 PMID: 37935808

Hoang, V. Q. (2024, November). Fostering Willingness to Communicate in Online Educational Environments: Opportunities and Challenges. In *The 2nd International Conference: Resiliency by Technology and Design (RTD 2024)* (pp. 272-286). Atlantis Press. DOI: 10.2991/978-94-6463-583-6_13

Hong, X., & Guo, L. (2025). Effects of AI-enhanced multi-display language teaching systems on learning motivation, cognitive load management, and learner autonomy. *Education and Information Technologies, 30*(12), 1–35. DOI: 10.1007/s10639-025-13472-1

Horwitz, E. K. (2020). *Becoming a language teacher: A practical guide to second language learning and teaching*. Castledown Publishers., DOI: 10.29140/9780648184416

Huang, F., Wang, Y., & Zhang, H. (2024). Modelling Generative AI Acceptance, Perceived Teachers' Enthusiasm and Self-Efficacy to English as a Foreign Language Learners' Well-Being in the Digital Era. *European Journal of Education, 59*(4), e12770. DOI: 10.1111/ejed.12770

Huang, X., Wu, Y., & Dou, A. (2024). AI-enhanced task-based language teaching: Fostering personalized college English learning. *Frontiers in Educational Research, 7*(10). Advance online publication. DOI: 10.25236/FER.2024.071033

Hung, H. T. (2017). Design-based research: Redesign of an English language course using a flipped classroom approach. *TESOL Quarterly, 51*(1), 180–192. DOI: 10.1002/tesq.328

Hwang, W. Y., Luthfi, M. I., & Liu, Y. F. (2024). AI-enhanced video drama-making for improving writing and speaking skills of students learning English as a foreign language. *Innovation in Language Learning and Teaching*, •••, 1–18. DOI: 10.1080/17501229.2024.2437655

Hyland, K. (2019). *Second language writing*. Cambridge university press., DOI: 10.1017/9781108635547

Ismayilli, F. (2025). The Role of Positive Emotional Atmosphere in Enhancing Foreign Language Acquisition. *Porta Universorum, 1*(3), 186–213. DOI: 10.69760/portuni.010316

Jesudas, R. (2025, June). Empowering language learning: The role of AI in enhancing language skills. In. AIP Conference Proceedings: Vol. 3306. *No. 1* (p. 050023). AIP Publishing LLC., DOI: 10.1063/5.0278362

Kangas, S. E. (2014). When special education trumps ESL: An investigation of service delivery for ELLs with disabilities. *Critical Inquiry in Language Studies, 11*(4), 273–306. DOI: 10.1080/15427587.2014.968070

Karakaya, K., & Bozkurt, A. (2022). Mobile-assisted language learning (MALL) research trends and patterns through bibliometric analysis: Empowering language learners through ubiquitous educational technologies. *System, 110*, 102925. DOI: 10.1016/j.system.2022.102925

Kersten, K., & Winsler, A. (Eds.). (2022). *Understanding variability in second language acquisition, bilingualism, and cognition: A multi-layered perspective.* Taylor & Francis., DOI: 10.4324/9781003155683

Kessler, G., & Bikowski, D. (2011). The influence of SLA training in curricular design among teachers in preparation. *CALICO Journal, 28*(2), 522–545. DOI: 10.11139/cj.28.2.522-545

Knouse, S. M., Bessy, M., & Longest, K. C. (2021). Knowing who we teach: Tracking attitudes and expectations of first-year postsecondary language learners. *Foreign Language Annals, 54*(1), 50–72. DOI: 10.1111/flan.12510

Kontra, E. H. (2020). The L2 motivation of learners with special educational needs. In *The Palgrave handbook of motivation for language learning* (pp. 495–513). Springer International Publishing., DOI: 10.1007/978-3-030-28380-3_24

Kormos, J. (2016). *The second language learning processes of students with specific learning difficulties*. Routledge., DOI: 10.4324/9781315692371

Kormos, J. (2020). Specific learning difficulties in second language learning and teaching. *Language Teaching, 53*(2), 129–143. DOI: 10.1017/S0261444819000442

Kormos, J., & Smith, A. M. (2023). *Teaching languages to students with specific learning differences* (Vol. 18). Channel View Publications., DOI: 10.21832/KORMOS8615

Kramsch, C. (2000). Second language acquisition, applied linguistics, and the teaching of foreign languages. *Modern Language Journal, 84*(3), 311–326. DOI: 10.1111/0026-7902.00071

Lardiere, D. (2017). *Ultimate attainment in second language acquisition: A case study*. Routledge., DOI: 10.4324/9781315084480

Lee, B. J. (2024). Reimagining language learning: AI-driven innovations for engagement and growth. *Technology in Language Teaching & Learning*, *6*(3), 102773–102773. DOI: 10.29140/tltl.v6n3.102773

Leonardi, V. (2010). *The role of pedagogical translation in second language acquisition: From theory to practice*. Peter Lang., DOI: 10.3726/978-3-0351-0071-6

Li, S. (2016). The construct validity of language aptitude: A meta-analysis. *Studies in Second Language Acquisition*, *38*(4), 801–842. DOI: 10.1017/S027226311500042X

Li, S., Hiver, P., & Papi, M. (2022). Individual differences in second language acquisition: Theory, research, and practice. In *The Routledge handbook of second language acquisition and individual differences* (pp. 3–34). Routledge., DOI: 10.4324/9781003270546-2

Li, X. (2022). The significance of Q-methodology as an innovative method for the investigation of affective variables in second language acquisition. *Frontiers in Psychology*, *13*, 995660. DOI: 10.3389/fpsyg.2022.995660 PMID: 36059765

Lightbown, P. M. (2000). Anniversary article. Classroom SLA research and second language teaching. *Applied Linguistics*, *21*(4), 431–462. DOI: 10.1093/applin/21.4.431

Lin, H. C. K., Chao, C. J., & Huang, T. C. (2015). From a perspective on foreign language learning anxiety to develop an affective tutoring system. *Educational Technology Research and Development*, *63*(5), 727–747. DOI: 10.1007/s11423-015-9385-6

Liu, M., Moore, Z., Graham, L., & Lee, S. (2002). A look at the research on computer-based technology use in second language learning: A review of the literature from 1990–2000. *Journal of Research on Technology in Education*, *34*(3), 250–273. DOI: 10.1080/15391523.2002.10782348

Liu, W. (2023). The theory of second language development for international students. *Journal for multicultural. Education*, *17*(3), 367–378. DOI: 10.1108/JME-08-2022-0106

Liu, Z. (2022). Introducing a multimodal perspective to emotional variables in second language acquisition education: Systemic functional multimodal discourse analysis. *Frontiers in Psychology*, *13*, 1016441. DOI: 10.3389/fpsyg.2022.1016441 PMID: 36324780

Loewen, S. (2020). *Introduction to instructed second language acquisition*. Routledge., DOI: 10.4324/9781315616797

Loewen, S., & Sato, M. (2017). Instructed second language acquisition (ISLA): An overview. *The Routledge handbook of instructed second language acquisition*, 1-12. DOI: 10.4324/9781315676968-1

Macaro, E., Handley, Z., & Walter, C. (2012). A systematic review of CALL in English as a second language: Focus on primary and secondary education. *Language Teaching*, *45*(1), 1–43. DOI: 10.1017/S0261444811000395

MacIntyre, P. D., & McGillivray, M. F. (2023). The inner workings of anxiety in second language learning. *Annual Review of Applied Linguistics*, *43*, 88–104. DOI: 10.1017/S0267190523000065

Mackey, A. (2014). Practice and progression in second language research methods. *AILA Review*, *27*(1), 80–97. DOI: 10.1075/aila.27.04mac

Mackey, A. (2020). *Interaction, feedback and task research in second language learning: Methods and design*. Cambridge University Press., DOI: 10.1017/9781108589284

McCrocklin, S. (2020). Exploring the effectiveness of structured language learning experiences for bilinguals in a language acquisition course. *TESOL Journal*, *11*(2), e477. DOI: 10.1002/tesj.477

McManus, K. (2024). Replication studies in second language acquisition research: Definitions, issues, resources, and future directions: Introduction to the special issue. *Studies in Second Language Acquisition*, *46*(5), 1299–1319. DOI: 10.1017/S0272263124000652

Mehta, V., Selvakumar, P., Anute, N. B., Gandhimathi, S., Seelam, P. K., & Manjunath, T. C. (2025). Second Language Acquisition Support Through Media Literacy and Digital Media Platforms. In *Supporting Linguistic Differences Through Literacy Education* (pp. 361–388). IGI Global Scientific Publishing., DOI: 10.4018/979-8-3373-3496-7.ch011

Midigo, J. (2025). AI-Powered Innovations for Documenting and Revitalizing African Languages. *Cultural Arts Research and Development*, *5*(2), 26–41. DOI: 10.55121/card.v5i2.517

Mikroyannidis, A., Perifanou, M., & Economides, A. A. (2025). Enhancing Language Learning with Generative AI: The Case of the OpenLang Network Platform. *Computers*, *14*(12), 546. DOI: 10.3390/computers14120546

Moeller, A. K., & Catalano, T. (2015). Foreign language teaching and learning. DOI: 10.1016/B978-0-08-097086-8.92082-8

Namaziandost, E. (2025). Integrating flipped learning in AI-enhanced language learning: Mapping the effects on metacognitive awareness, writing development, and foreign language learning boredom. *Computers and Education: Artificial Intelligence, 100446*, 100446. Advance online publication. DOI: 10.1016/j.caeai.2025.100446

Namaziandost, E., Behbahani, H. K., & Naserpour, A. (2024). Peer support in language learning: Mitigating anxiety, enhancing achievement, cultivating growth mindsets, and increasing enjoyment. *Journal of Applied Learning and Teaching, 7*(2), 296–313. DOI: 10.37074/jalt.2024.7.2.40

Nussbaum, M. C. (2011). Perfectionist liberalism and political liberalism. *Philosophy & Public Affairs, 39*(1), 3–45. DOI: 10.1111/j.1088-4963.2011.01200.x

Ortega, L. (2014). *Understanding second language acquisition.* Routledge., DOI: 10.4324/9780203777282

Pawlak, M., & Waniek-Klimczak, E. (2015). Issues in teaching, learning and testing speaking in a second language. DOI: 10.1007/978-3-642-38339-7

Pfenninger, S., & Polz, S. (2018). Foreign language learning in the third age: A pilot feasibility study on cognitive, socio-affective and linguistic drivers and benefits in relation to previous bilingualism of the learner. *European Second Language Association. Journal, 2*(1), 1–13. DOI: 10.22599/jesla.36

Pham, V. P. H., Lian, A., White, J., & Lian, A. (2025). Overview of Empowering Educators: Integrating AI Tools for Personalized Language Instruction. In *Empowering Educators: Integrating AI Tools for Personalized Language Instruction* (pp. 1-8). Cham: Springer Nature Switzerland. DOI: 10.1007/978-3-032-01348-4_1

Piechurska-Kuciel, E. (2008). Input, processing and output anxiety in students with symptoms of developmental dyslexia. *Language learners with special needs. An international perspective*, 86-109. DOI: 10.2307/jj.27710857.8

Piechurska-Kuciel, E. (2011). The relationship between language anxiety and the development of the speaking skill: Results of a longitudinal study. *Speaking and instructed foreign language acquisition*, 200-212. DOI: 10.2307/jj.29308412.17

Pinto-Llorente, A. M., & Izquierdo-Álvarez, V. (2024). Digital Learning Ecosystem to Enhance Formative Assessment in Second Language Acquisition in Higher Education. *Sustainability (Basel), 16*(11), 4687. DOI: 10.3390/su16114687

Ramos HolguĆn, B., & Aguirre Morales, J. (2014). Materials Development in the Colombian Context: Some Considerations about Its Benefits and Challenges. *How, 21*(2), 134-150. DOI: 10.19183/how.21.2.8

Rao, K., & Torres, C. (2017). Supporting academic and affective learning processes for English language learners with universal design for learning. *TESOL Quarterly*, *51*(2), 460–472. DOI: 10.1002/tesq.342

Robinson, P. (2001). *Task complexity, cognitive resources, and syllabus design: A triadic framework for examining task influences on SLA* (pp. 287-318). na. DOI: 10.1017/CBO9781139524780.012

Robinson, P. (2011). Second language task complexity, the Cognition Hypothesis, language learning, and performance. In *Second language task complexity: Researching the cognition hypothesis of language learning and performance* (pp. 3–38). John Benjamins Publishing Company., DOI: 10.1075/tblt.2.05ch1

Rosa, J., & Flores, N. (2017). Unsettling race and language: Toward a raciolinguistic perspective. *Language in Society*, *46*(5), 621–647. DOI: 10.1017/S0047404517000562

Rosell-Aguilar, F. (2005). Task design for audiographic conferencing: Promoting beginner oral interaction in distance language learning. *Computer Assisted Language Learning*, *18*(5), 417–442. DOI: 10.1080/09588220500442772

Ryding, K. C. (2013). Second-language acquisition. *The Oxford handbook of Arabic linguistics*, 392-411. DOI: 10.1093/oxfordhb/9780199764136.013.0017

Sanz, C. (2014). Contributions of study abroad research to our understanding of SLA processes and outcomes: The SALA Project, an appraisal. In *Language acquisition in study abroad and formal instruction contexts* (pp. 1–14). John Benjamins Publishing Company., DOI: 10.1075/aals.13.01ch1

Segler, T. M., Pain, H., & Sorace, A. (2002). Second language vocabulary acquisition and learning strategies in ICALL environments. *Computer Assisted Language Learning*, *15*(4), 409–422. DOI: 10.1076/call.15.4.409.8272

Shao, K., Pekrun, R., & Nicholson, L. J. (2019). Emotions in classroom language learning: What can we learn from achievement emotion research? *System*, *86*, 102121. DOI: 10.1016/j.system.2019.102121

Sharma, P., Nimma, D., Punithaasree, K. S., & Faizal, M. M. (2024, October). AI Tools for Enhanced English Learning: Leveraging Machine Learning for Improved Outcomes. In *2024 IEEE 1st International Conference on Green Industrial Electronics and Sustainable Technologies (GIEST)* (pp. 1-6). IEEE. DOI: 10.1109/GIEST62955.2024.10959829

Shepperd, L. (2022). Including underrepresented language learners in SLA research: A case study and considerations for internet-based methods. *Research Methods in Applied Linguistics*, *1*(3), 100031. DOI: 10.1016/j.rmal.2022.100031

Skehan, P. (1991). Individual differences in second language learning. *Studies in Second Language Acquisition, 13*(2), 275–298. DOI: 10.1017/S0272263100009979

Spada, N., & Lightbown, P. M. (1993). Instruction and the development of questions in L2 classrooms. *Studies in Second Language Acquisition, 15*(2), 205–224. DOI: 10.1017/S0272263100011967

Sudina, E. (2021). Study and scale quality in second language survey research, 2009–2019: The case of anxiety and motivation. *Language Learning, 71*(4), 1149–1193. DOI: 10.1111/lang.12468

Sudina, E. (2023). Scale quality in second-language anxiety and WTC: A methodological synthesis. *Studies in Second Language Acquisition, 45*(5), 1427–1455. DOI: 10.1017/S0272263122000560

Sun, J., & Wang, Y. (2025). Fuzzy-set qualitative comparative analysis (fsQCA) in second language acquisition: An applied example of writing engagement. *Research Methods in Applied Linguistics, 4*(1), 100193. DOI: 10.1016/j.rmal.2025.100193

Tang, L., Zhang, C. A., & Cui, Y. (2024). A multigroup SEM analysis of mediating role of enjoyment, anxiety, and boredom in the relationships between L2 motivational self-system, L2 proficiency, and intercultural communication competence. *Language Teaching Research, 13621688241265211*, 13621688241265211. Advance online publication. DOI: 10.1177/13621688241265211

Teimouri, Y., Goetze, J., & Plonsky, L. (2019). Second language anxiety and achievement: A meta-analysis. *Studies in Second Language Acquisition, 41*(2), 363–387. DOI: 10.1017/S0272263118000311

Thao, L. T., Thuy, P. T., Thi, N. A., Yen, P. H., Thu, H. T. A., & Tra, N. H. (2023). Impacts of emotional intelligence on second language acquisition: English-major students' perspectives. *SAGE Open, 13*(4), 21582440231212065. DOI: 10.1177/21582440231212065

Tomlinson, B. (Ed.). (2016). *SLA research and materials development for language learning* (pp. 3–22). Routledge., DOI: 10.4324/9781315749082

Torkhani, D. (2025). AI-enhanced language learning: The impact of Talkpal. AI on EFL undergraduate students' English-speaking skills. *American Journal of STEM Education, 11*, 69–82. DOI: 10.32674/232w1188

Towell, R., & Hawkins, R. D. (1994). *Approaches to second language acquisition.* Multilingual Matters., DOI: 10.21832/9781800418271

Vafaee, P., & Suzuki, Y. (2020). The relative significance of syntactic knowledge and vocabulary knowledge in second language listening ability. *Studies in Second Language Acquisition*, *42*(2), 383–410. DOI: 10.1017/S0272263119000676

VanPatten, B., & Williams, J. (2014). *Theories in second language acquisition*. Routledge., DOI: 10.4324/9780203628942

Wang, Y. (2024). A review of emotions in second language acquisition from a positive psychology perspective. *International Journal of Education and Humanities*, *4*(3), 287–296. DOI: 10.58557/(ijeh).v4i3.241

Wedlock, J., & Wilson, N. (2024). Inclusion in the learning game: Applying considerations from cognitive neuroscience, educational psychology, and SLA to language learning activity and materials design. *TESOL in Context*, *33*(1), 58–81. DOI: 10.21153/tesol2024vol33no1art2014

Wei, L. (2018). Translanguaging as a practical theory of language. *Applied Linguistics*, *39*(1), 9–30. DOI: 10.1093/applin/amx039

Wei, L., & García, O. (2022). Not a first language but one repertoire: Translanguaging as a decolonizing project. *RELC Journal*, *53*(2), 313–324. DOI: 10.1177/00336882221092841

Wenden, A. L. (2002). Learner development in language learning. *Applied Linguistics*, *23*(1), 32–55. DOI: 10.1093/applin/23.1.32

Yıldız, T. A. (2023). The impact of ChatGPT on language learners' motivation. *Journal of Teacher Education and Lifelong Learning*, *5*(2), 582–597. DOI: 10.51535/tell.1314355

Yingsoon, G. Y., Zhang, S., Chua, N. A., & Xiaoyao, T. (2025). Empowering Multicultural Literacies: Fostering Second Language Acquisition With Media and Digital Platforms. In *Supporting Cultural Differences Through Literacy Education* (pp. 77-108). IGI Global Scientific Publishing. DOI: 10.4018/979-8-3693-9271-3.ch004

Zare, J., Karimpour, S., & Delavar, K. A. (2022). The impact of concordancing on English learners' foreign language anxiety and enjoyment: An application of data-driven learning. *System*, *109*, 102891. DOI: 10.1016/j.system.2022.102891

Zhang, Y., & Dong, C. (2024). Exploring the digital transformation of generative ai-assisted foreign language education: A socio-technical systems perspective based on mixed-methods. *Systems*, *12*(11), 462. DOI: 10.3390/systems12110462

Zheng, L., & Yang, Y. (2024). Research perspectives and trends in artificial intelligence-enhanced language education: A review. *Heliyon, 10*(19), e38617. Advance online publication. DOI: 10.1016/j.heliyon.2024.e38617 PMID: 39416824

Zhong, Y., Tan, S., Xu, X., Shao, Z., & Liu, Q. (2024). Second language learners' academic emotions in grammar learning with explicit attention to grammatical complexity. *Journal of Multilingual and Multicultural Development*, •••, 1–19. DOI: 10.1080/01434632.2024.2407042

ADDITIONAL READING

Ahmed, A., & Morgan, B. (2021). Postmemory and multilingual identities in English language teaching: A duoethnography. *Language Learning Journal, 49*(4), 483–498. DOI: 10.1080/09571736.2021.1906301

Becker, A., & Moore, A. R. (2026). Undesired language: Towards trauma-informed pluri lingual pedagogies. *Critical Inquiry in Language Studies*, •••, 1–22. DOI: 10.1080/15427587.2026.2660097

Galloway, E. P., & Uccelli, P. (2024). Promoting humanizing, meaningful, and just language instruction for multilingual learners and their peers: A pedagogical vision illustrated by examples from practice. *Linguistics and Education, 84*, 101358. DOI: 10.1016/j.linged.2024.101358

Jiménez, L. G. (2026). Empowering Plurilingual Learners. *Language Education and Multilingualism-The Langscape Journal, 8*, 53–67.

Park, J., & Michaels, S. (2024). Critical Metalinguistic Engagement and the Role of Listening in Poetry Inside Out. In *Pursuing Language and Metalinguistics in K–12 Classrooms* (pp. 121–144). Routledge. DOI: 10.4324/9781003334804-11

Shapiro, S. (2021). "Language and Social Justice": A (Surprisingly) Plurilingual First-Year Seminar. In *Plurilingual Pedagogies for Multilingual Writing Classrooms* (pp. 15-30). Routledge.

Siegman, R. M., & Galloway, E. P. (2026). Playful translanguaging: Capturing affective language learning experiences in a multilingual classroom. *Linguistics and Education, 94*, 101546. DOI: 10.1016/j.linged.2026.101546

KEY TERMS AND DEFINITIONS

AI-Equity Literacies: The professional capacities required to evaluate, use, contest, and redesign AI tools in ways that advance fairness, inclusion, multilingual recognition, and learner dignity.

AI-mediated Language Education: The use of artificial intelligence systems, including automated feedback tools, generative models, adaptive tutors, speech recognition systems, and analytics platforms, to support, evaluate, or govern language learning and teaching.

Algorithmic Bias: Systematic unfairness in AI outputs caused by skewed data, design assumptions, evaluation criteria, or social inequalities encoded into computational systems.

Data Colonialism: The extraction and use of human and community data without equitable control, benefit sharing, or accountability for those from whom such data are taken.

Design Justice: A community-led approach to technological design that prioritises the knowledge, needs, and agency of those most affected by technological harms.

Multilingual Dignity: A justice-oriented principle that recognises learners' full linguistic repertoires as legitimate resources for identity, learning, participation, and knowledge production.

Translanguaging: A pedagogical and theoretical orientation that treats multilingual speakers' language practices as fluid mobilisation of an integrated repertoire rather than movement between separate linguistic systems.

Chapter 4
Towards Equitable AI Literacy:
Reconceptualising Pre-Service English Language Teacher Education in Portugal and Andalusia, Spain

Carlos Lindade
http://orcid.org/0000-0001-5742-8874
Universidade do Porto, Portugal

Francisco Javier Palacios-Hidalgo
http://orcid.org/0000-0002-4326-209X
Universidad de Córdoba, Spain

ABSTRACT

Generative artificial intelligence is reshaping language education faster than initial teacher education systems can respond. This chapter frames AI integration in pre-service English teacher education as an urgent matter of equity, equality, and justice through three analytical movements. The first maps pre-service English teacher education in Portugal against Decreto-Lei n.º 9-A/2025, documenting the absence of generative AI content across all eight accredited providers. The second audits nine public universities in Andalusia, Spain, across primary English and secondary master's programmes, revealing a comparable structural gap. The third proposes a 3 ECTS curricular unit on generative AI in EFL pre-service education, grounded in the EU AI Act, DigComp 3.0, and UNESCO's AI Competency Framework for Teachers,

DOI: 10.4018/979-8-3373-7749-0.ch004

structured around equity, equality, and justice. The chapter concludes that preparing critically AI-literate language teachers is a structural equity imperative, and that inaction risks deepening existing inequalities for already-marginalised learners.

INTRODUCTION

Contemporary language education exists at the intersection of two converging crises. The first is structural and demographic: across Europe and beyond, a deepening shortage of qualified teachers is straining the capacity of educational systems to provide consistent, high-quality instruction (European Commission/EACEA/Eurydice, 2021; OECD, 2023). The second is technological and epistemological: artificial intelligence (AI) is reshaping how languages are taught and learned with a rapidity that exceeds the preparedness of most institutions, policymakers, and educators to respond thoughtfully (UNESCO, 2023; Zawacki-Richter et al., 2019). Crucially, these two developments are not merely parallel but they are deeply interactive. In contexts where teacher supply is strained, AI tools are frequently positioned as scalable, cost-efficient supplements or substitutes for qualified instruction, a logic that risks obscuring the ways in which algorithmic systems can reproduce and entrench existing educational inequalities (Benjamin, 2019; Noble, 2018). This chapter argues that pre-service language teacher education in Portugal and Andalusia (Spain) must respond urgently and critically to this dual challenge: equipping prospective teachers not merely to use AI tools, but to evaluate and deploy them in ways that genuinely serve equity, equality, and justice.

When one closely examines the shortage of qualified teachers in certain European countries such as Iceland, Portugal or Sweden, it becomes obvious that it is among the most pressing structural challenges confronting European education systems. Eurydice data document that a significant majority of EU member states report persistent difficulties in recruiting and retaining qualified teachers, particularly at secondary level and in specialist subjects including modern foreign languages (European Commission/EACEA/Eurydice, 2021). The OECD's *Education at a Glance* surveys identify compounding demographic pressures: a substantial proportion of the existing teaching workforce is approaching retirement age in many European countries, while enrolment in initial teacher education programmes has not kept pace with projected need (OECD, 2023). Various structural responses have been implemented across national contexts, from emergency certification pathways to incentivized recruitment, yet these have not addressed the underlying conditions of workload, professional status, and career precarity that render teaching an increasingly unattractive choice for many graduates (Guerriero, 2017). The consequences of this shortage are not evenly distributed. Schools serving socio-economically disadvantaged communities, rural and remote areas, and learners from linguistically and culturally diverse backgrounds are disproportionately affected by teacher vacancies and staff turnover, thereby amplifying pre-existing patterns of educational inequality (Darling-Hammond, 2017). In this context, the quality of pre-service teacher preparation and, specifically, the extent to which it equips prospective educators to work equitably with all learners takes on exceptional significance.

It is against this backdrop that the rapid integration of AI into educational settings must be understood. The European Commission's Digital Education Action Plan (2021–2027) identifies AI among the key drivers of educational transformation, calling for the development of robust digital competences among learners and educators and underscoring the importance of the ethical and inclusive use of data-driven technologies (European Commission, 2021). This policy orientation reflects a broader institutional ambition, shared across EU structures, to ensure that the benefits of digital transformation are distributed widely rather than concentrated among those who are already advantaged. Yet the stated aspirations of European digital education policy sit in tension with a growing body of critical scholarship. Algorithmic systems trained on historically biased datasets are capable of encoding and perpetuating patterns of discrimination along lines of language variety, socio-economic background, race, and disability (Benjamin, 2019; Noble, 2018). In language education specifically, this concern takes a distinctive form: intelligent tutoring systems, automated writing evaluation tools, and speech recognition technologies are frequently calibrated to standard, prestige varieties of target languages, with the result that learners who speak non-standard or minority varieties may receive systematically inaccurate feedback or be disadvantaged in automated assessment (Canagarajah, 2013). The promise of AI-mediated personalisation must therefore be weighed carefully against the risk that algorithmic differentiation may, in practice, entrench rather than disrupt the social hierarchies that structured inequitable learning experiences in the first place (UNESCO, 2023).

The Council of Europe's longstanding commitments to plurilingualism and intercultural communication offer an important principled counterpoint to techno-centric narratives of language education. The *Common European Framework of Reference for Languages* (CEFR), and its 2020 Companion Volume in particular, conceptualises language competence not as the acquisition of a fixed, standardised code but as a dynamic and evolving plurilingual repertoire developed through and for social interaction (Council of Europe, 2001, 2020). This vision is fundamentally inclusive: it positions the partial and hybrid competences of heritage language speakers, multilingual learners, and speakers of non-dominant varieties as assets rather than deficits, and it designates mediation, plurilingual competence, and intercultural awareness as core dimensions of language development. Ensuring that AI tools deployed in language classrooms align with this inclusive vision represents a significant challenge. Systems optimised for measurable accuracy in standardised forms of a language are poorly suited to assessing or supporting the fluid, identity-inflected, and context-dependent language use that the CEFR framework values. The question of whether AI tools support or undermine the plurilingual ideal is therefore not a peripheral technical concern but a matter of fundamental educational principle, with direct implications for the equity of learning outcomes across Europe's diverse learner populations.

A rigorous engagement with these issues requires conceptual clarity. The terms equity, equality, and justice are frequently employed in educational discourse, yet they carry distinct theoretical and practical implications. Equality, in educational contexts, refers to the uniform provision of resources, opportunities, or treatment to all learners regardless of their individual circumstances. While formally appealing, strict equality is insufficient as an organising principle when learners arrive at educational experiences with profoundly different starting points, resources, and structural vulnerabilities. Equity, by contrast, is grounded in the recognition that fair treatment requires the differentiation that serving all learners well means attending to and compensating for unequal starting conditions rather than rendering them invisible (Darling-Hammond, 2017). In the context of AI-enhanced language education, equity demands that tools be evaluated not only for their aggregate performance across a notional user population but for their differential performance across learner subgroups defined by language background, socio-economic status, geographic location, and other dimensions of social positioning. Justice, as the most structurally capacious of the three concepts, directs attention to the systemic and historical conditions that produce and sustain educational inequality, asking not only whether AI tools serve learners equitably but also whose interests they reflect, whose knowledge they encode, and what social arrangements they normalise or contest (Benjamin, 2019; Crenshaw, 1991). Only by holding all three concepts simultaneously in view does a genuinely transformative approach to AI in language education become possible.

Pre-service teacher education represents a critical and, to date, underutilised site of intervention in this landscape. The knowledge, beliefs, and professional dispositions that prospective teachers develop during their initial preparation have well-documented effects on their subsequent classroom practice (Darling-Hammond, 2017; Guerriero, 2017). Teachers who enter the profession without adequate exposure to the equity dimensions of AI may risk replicating, however unintentionally, the biases embedded in the tools they encounter, in the absence of critical awareness sufficient to interrogate or challenge them. Conversely, pre-service programmes that explicitly and intentionally address the intersections of AI, language education, and social justice can cultivate educators who are equipped not merely to operate AI tools but to evaluate them critically, to advocate for the needs of their most vulnerable learners, and to adapt or reject tools that fail to serve the diversity of the classroom (Zawacki-Richter et al., 2019). Such preparation is not a professional luxury to be reserved for specialist electives. In a context where teacher shortage is already compromising educational quality for disadvantaged populations, and where AI tools are being adopted at a pace that outstrips the evidence of their equitable effectiveness, the preparation of critically informed language educators must be understood as an urgent professional and ethical imperative.

This chapter proceeds from this foundational argument in three analytical movements. The first movement examines Portugal as an illuminating national case, mapping the current institutional landscape of pre-service English language teacher education against the normative architecture of *Decreto-Lei n. º 9-A/2025* and documenting the presence or absence of generative AI from the formal curricular offerings of all eight accredited providers. The second movement shifts to Spain, focusing on the Autonomous Community of Andalusia as a strategically selected regional case, analysing study plans from nine public universities—including primary education degrees with a specialisation in English and secondary education master's programmes with a specialisation in English/foreign languages—and documenting a comparable structural absence of generative AI content across all nine institutions surveyed. The third movement responds constructively to this cross-national gap by proposing a concrete, replicable 3ECTS curricular unit on generative AI in EFL pre-service education, grounded in the EU AI Act, DigComp 3.0, and UNESCO's AI Competency Framework for Teachers, and structured explicitly around equity, equality, and justice as organising principles.

The concluding sections examine forward-looking policy and research directions and consider the systemic risks of institutional inaction, arguing that the preparation of critically AI-literate language teachers is not a peripheral professional development opportunity but a structural condition of equitable language education in the twenty-first century. This contribution is addressed to researchers, teacher educators, and policymakers engaged with the practical and theoretical challenge of ensuring that AI-enhanced language education serves not the few, but the many.

BACKGROUND

Pre-Service English Language Teacher Education in Portugal: Institutional Landscape and Curricular Provision

Portugal's system of pre-service teacher education for English is governed by a legislative framework that has, over the past decade, undergone significant revision. The most recent and consequential instrument is *Decreto-Lei n. º 9-A/2025, de 14 de fevereiro* (Diário da República, 2025), which amends the *Regime Jurídico da Habilitação Profissional para a Docência* (Legal Framework for Professional Qualifications in Teaching) established by *Decreto-Lei n. º 79/2014, de 14 de maio* (Diário da República, 2014). This legislation provides the normative framework within which all accredited *mestrados habilitantes* (the professional teaching degrees conferring qualification to teach in state schools) must operate. Understanding the architecture of this framework, and the degree to which it enables or constrains the integration of equity-oriented, digitally informed, and critically AI-literate pedagogies into teacher preparation, is fundamental to the argument of this chapter.

For *mestrado* programmes qualifying teachers for the third cycle of basic education (lower secondary, years 7–9) and secondary education (*ensino secundário*, upper secondary, years 10–12), the levels corresponding to the main English language teaching recruitment group, *Grupo de Recrutamento 330, Decreto-Lei n. º 9-A/2025* mandates a total of 120 ECTS distributed across four designated formation areas. The *Área Docente* (Didactic Area; AD), comprising 18 ECTS, covers the subject-specific scientific content relevant to the teaching area. The *Didática Específica* (Specific Didactics; DidE), with 30 ECTS, addresses the pedagogy and methodology of teaching the subject and constitutes the most directly teacher-centred component of the degree. The *Formação Educacional Geral* (General Teaching Training; FEG), totalling 12 ECTS, encompasses broader educational theory, including developmental psychology, curriculum studies, and educational sociology. The largest single component, the *Iniciação à Prática Profissional* (Introduction to Professional Practice; IPP), at 60 ECTS, organises supervised teaching practice in partner schools alongside seminars for reflective inquiry into professional experience (Diário da República, 2025). This structure is notable in several respects. The IPP represents exactly half the total programme credits, reflecting Portugal's strong commitment to anchoring initial teacher education in authentic school-based experience. However, the FEG, the area most plausibly able to accommodate systematic engagement with equity, digital citizenship, and critical AI literacy, accounts for only 12 ECTS, or 10% of the total. The DidE component, while constituting a legitimate space for addressing digital tools and AI-mediated language teaching, is subject to considerable institutional variation in terms of what it covers. This structural asymmetry warrants critical attention: in a period when AI is rapidly reshaping language education, the formal curricular provision for critical engagement with technology remains modest in scope and inconsistently realised across institutions.

As of the 2024–2025 academic year, the professional qualification for teaching English in the third cycle and secondary education (lower secondary, years 7–9) and secondary education (*ensino secundário*, upper secondary, years 10–12) is provided by eight public universities in Portugal, all of which hold accreditation from the *Agência de Avaliação e Acreditação do Ensino Superior* (Agency for the

Evaluation and Accreditation of Higher Education; A3ES). These programmes are geographically distributed across the national territory, with a notable concentration in the urban centres of Lisbon, Porto, and Coimbra. It should be noted that some programmes specifically qualifying teachers for the first cycle of basic education fall outside the scope of this analysis, as they respond to different recruitment groups and legislative requirements (90 ECTS). Similarly, other paths such as the *Mestrado em Didática do Inglês* (Master's Degree in English Language Teaching), offered jointly by NOVA de Lisboa and the Universidade Aberta, is a postgraduate specialisation for practising teachers rather than a *habilitação profissional* (professional qualification) for initial teaching qualification, and is therefore not included in the institutional mapping presented below. Table 1 provides a systematic overview of the eight institutions and their respective programme offerings as identified through analysis of publicly available programme documentation (2024–2025).

Table 1. Institutional mapping of accredited pre-service English language teacher education programmes in Portugal (3rd Cycle and Secondary Level, 2024–2025)

Institution (Faculty / School)	**Programme(s) conferring GR 330 qualification**	**Digital technology / AI curricular provision**
Universidade de Lisboa (FLUL + IE)	Mestrado em Ensino de Inglês no 3.º ciclo do EB e ES; combined variants (Inglês + Français/Español/Deutsch)	No dedicated digital technology unit identified. Broader DidE unit *'Tópicos Emergentes no Ensino do Inglês'* may address digital topics.
Universidade NOVA de Lisboa (FCSH)	Mestrado de Ensino de Inglês no 3.º ciclo EB e ES; Mestrado em Ensino de Inglês e de LE (Alemão/Espanhol/Françês); Mestrado em Ensino de Português e de LE (Inglês)	Dedicated DidE unit *'Tecnologia no Ensino de Inglês'* / *'Tecnologia Digital na Aula de LE'*; also *'Avaliação e Materiais de Aprendizagem (E-Learning)'*. No explicit mention of a generative AI unit.
Universidade do Porto (FLUP)	Mestrado em Ensino do Inglês e de LE no 3.º ciclo EB e ES (Alemão/Espanhol/Françês); Mestrado em Ensino de Português e de LE no 3.º ciclo EB e ES (Inglês)	No dedicated digital technology unit identified in publicly available programme documentation. No explicit mention of a generative AI unit.
Universidade de Coimbra (FLUC)	Mestrado em Ensino de Inglês no 3.º ciclo EB e ES; Mestrado em Ensino de Inglês e de LE (Alemão/Espanhol/Françês); Mestrado em Ensino de Português e de LE (Inglês)	No dedicated digital technology unit identified in publicly available programme documentation. No explicit mention of a generative AI unit.
Universidade de Aveiro (DLLC / CIDTFF)	Mestrado em Ensino de Inglês e de LE no 3.º ciclo EB e ES (Alemão/Françês/Espanhol); Mestrado em Ensino de Português e de LE (Inglês)	Technology integrated as cross-cutting orientation across DidE and IPP units (consistent with CIDTFF research mission). No single dedicated digital technology unit identified; No explicit mention of a generative AI unit.

continued on following page

Table 1. Continued

Institution (Faculty / School)	Programme(s) conferring GR 330 qualification	Digital technology / AI curricular provision
Universidade do Minho (Instituto de Educação)	Mestrado em Ensino de Português e de LE no 3.º ciclo EB e ES (área de especialização: Inglês)	No dedicated digital technology unit identified in publicly available programme documentation. No explicit mention of a generative AI unit.
Universidade dos Açores (FCSH)	Mestrado em Ensino de Português e Inglês no 3.º ciclo EB e ES	No dedicated digital technology unit identified in publicly available programme documentation. No explicit mention of a generative AI unit.
Universidade de Évora (Escola de Ciências Sociais)	Mestrado em Ensino de Português e de Inglês no 3.º ciclo EB e ES	Programme description references use of digital technologies in language pedagogy; no dedicated digital technology unit identified; No explicit mention of a generative AI unit.

Note: GR 330 = Grupo de Recrutamento 330 (Inglês, 3.º ciclo do Ensino Básico e Ensino Secundário). EB = Ensino Básico; ES = Ensino Secundário; LE = Língua Estrangeira; DidE = Didática Específica; IPP = Iniciação à Prática Profissional; CIDTFF = Centro de Investigação em Didática e Tecnologia na Formação de Formadores. Programme information based on analysis of publicly available institutional documentation for the academic year 2024–2025.

Source: Own elaboration

One of the most analytically revealing dimensions of the institutional mapping presented above concerns the provision and the notable absence of specific and identifiable curricular units devoted to digital technology in language education. Of the eight institutions identified, only one, the Faculdade de Ciências Sociais e Humanas of the Universidade NOVA de Lisboa (NOVA FCSH), offers a dedicated, explicitly named curricular unit addressing digital technology in the context of English language teaching within its programmes for the third cycle and secondary level (Universidade NOVA de Lisboa, 2024). This provision, variously designated across NOVA FCSH's programme variants as "*Tecnologia no Ensino de Inglês*" (Technology in English Language Teaching) and "*Tecnologia Digital na Aula de Língua Estrangeira*" (Digital Technology in Foreign Language Classrooms), engages directly with the application of digital tools and environments to language pedagogy. At the Universidade de Aveiro, whose programmes in language teacher education are developed in close institutional association with the CIDTFF, digital and technological dimensions appear to be integrated as a cross-cutting orientation distributed across multiple DidE and IPP units, rather than being concentrated in a single, standalone curricular unit. At the remaining six institutions, treatment of digital technology in language education appears to be largely embedded within broader methodological or general educational units, without consistent visible curricular labelling as a discrete priority.

Perhaps the most significant finding of this institutional audit is the systematic absence, across all eight identified institutions, of any dedicated curricular unit addressing generative AI or, indeed, AI in any form in the specific context of English language teaching or pre-service teacher education. While it is possible that some curricular units have started to address AI, and failed to update the publicly available information on their institutional website, no programme reviewed for this chapter includes a named curricular unit devoted to large language models, AI-assisted language feedback, algorithmic assessment, or the ethical and equity dimensions of AI in the language classroom. This finding is consistent with the pattern documented in international research: the integration of AI-specific content into initial teacher education lags substantially behind the pace of AI adoption in educational settings (UNESCO, 2023; Zawacki-Richter et al., 2019). In the Portuguese context, the gap is particularly striking given the explicit positioning of AI as a transformative priority within the European Commission's Digital Education Action Plan (2021–2027) (European Commission, 2021) and the Portuguese government's own digital education agenda. The fact that generative AI is entirely absent from the formal curricular architecture of Portuguese English teacher education raises urgent questions about both the institutional and regulatory responsiveness of the system and its readiness to prepare teachers who can navigate AI in ways that are equitable, critically informed, and pedagogically principled.

The institutional landscape mapped in this section reveals a system in active normative transition: the 2025 revision of the professional qualification framework is the most substantial regulatory intervention in pre-service teacher education in over a decade, and its full effects on programme design are still being absorbed by the higher education institutions concerned. Yet this restructuring to date has not produced a systematic curricular response to the equity, digital, and AI dimensions that this chapter argues are indispensable to genuinely future-oriented teacher preparation. The concentration of formal digital technology provision in a small minority of programmes, and the wholesale absence of generative AI content across all programmes reviewed, are not merely technical oversights or benign temporal lags. They reflect deeper structural and epistemological choices embedded in curricular design: choices about what counts as essential professional knowledge for a language teacher, and whether pre-service preparation is conceptualised primarily as the transmission of established pedagogical techniques or as a critically reflexive process of equipping educators to navigate a complex, technologically mediated, and structurally unequal professional world. As the analysis developed in the subsequent sections of this chapter argues, addressing this gap is not only a matter of technical updating: it is a matter of equity, equality, and justice.

Pre-Service English Language Teacher Education in Andalusia (Spain): Decentralization and the Case for a Regional Focus

In contrast to Portugal's centralized legislative framework for pre-service teacher education, Spain presents a considerably more complex and institutionally fragmented landscape. The Spanish Constitution of 1978 devolved significant educational authority to the seventeen Autonomous Communities (*Comunidades Autónomas*), resulting in a system where the basic structure of teacher qualifications is regulated nationally, but the detailed design, accreditation, and curricular implementation of initial teacher education programmes fall under regional jurisdiction. For pre-service English language teacher education, this means that while the national *Ley Orgánica de Educación* (BOE, 2020) and associated royal decrees establish the general architecture of teaching degrees, each Autonomous Community—and, within it, each university—exercises substantial discretion over the content, sequencing, and pedagogical orientation of the programmes that lead to professional qualification.

This decentralization generates two immediate consequences for any systematic analysis of English teacher preparation in Spain. First, no single, uniform curricular model exists for the two pathways that lead to English language teaching qualifications: the *Grado en Educación Primaria* (Degree in Primary Education) with a specialization (*mención*) in English language teaching (for primary education, years 6–12), and the *Máster Universitario en Profesorado de Educación Secundaria Obligatoria y Bachillerato, Formación Profesional y Enseñanza de Idiomas* (Master's in Secondary Education, Vocational Studies and Language Teaching; MAES), with a specialization in English (for lower and upper secondary education, years 12–17). Second, the absence of a centralized, publicly accessible registry of curricular units comparable to Portugal's A3ES-accredited programme database means that any comprehensive audit must be undertaken at the regional level, examining university-specific programme documentation across multiple Autonomous Communities.

Given this complexity, the present chapter deliberately narrows its focus to the Autonomous Community of Andalusia. Several methodological and strategic considerations underpin this choice. With a population of over 8.5 million and the largest number of state schools among all Autonomous Communities, Andalusia represents a high-demand context for English teachers. Moreover, the region has historically played a pioneering role in educational policy innovation, including early adoption of bilingual education programmes (*Plan de Fomento del Plurilingüismo* and *Plan Estratégico de Desarrollo de las Lenguas en Andalucía*; Junta de Andalucía, 2005, 2016) and, more recently, the integration of digital competences through its *Plan de Transformación Digital Educativa* (Digital Transformation Plan for Education; Junta de Andalucía, n.d.). In the specific area of teacher education, Andalusia's public universities—numbering nine institutions offering accredited primary and secondary English teaching pathways—constitute a sufficiently bounded yet highly representative sample. A regional case study also allows for fine-grained analysis of how national regulations are interpreted locally, including the degree to which equity-oriented and digitally informed pedagogies, particularly those addressing generative AI, have been incorporated into curricular provision. By examining Andalusia in detail in comparison to Portugal, this chapter aims to generate findings that, while regionally situated, offer transferable insights for other decentralized education systems and for Spanish national-level policy discussions.

The analysis, however, is based exclusively on publicly available official study plans (*planes de estudios*) of the nine Andalusian public universities that offer accredited programmes leading to English teaching qualifications (for both primary and secondary education). It is important to specify that this audit does not examine detailed course syllabi, which might contain references to digital technologies or artificial intelligence not explicitly captured in the high-level study plan descriptors. Consequently, the findings reflect the formal, approved curricular architecture rather than the actual classroom implementation. However, as the study plans constitute the binding framework for programme design and accreditation, their silence on generative AI is itself a significant finding.

The institutional mapping of Andalusian English teacher education programmes reveals two striking patterns. First, at the primary level, all reviewed *Grado en Educación Primaria* programmes include a compulsory, general educational technology subject (e.g., *Tecnología educativa*—educational technology—, *TIC aplicadas a la educación*—ICT applied to education—, or *Educación mediática y aplicaciones didácticas de las TIC*—media education and educational applications of ICT). However, these units are not situated within the foreign language didactics sequence; they are generic foundation courses taken by all primary student teachers, regardless of specialization. Consequently, they do not address the specific pedagogical integration of digital tools—let alone generative AI—in English language teaching. Second, at the secondary level, no dedicated digital technology or AI-focused unit appears in any of the programmes reviewed. A small number of universities offer elective transversal modules on technology (e.g., *Uso de las TICs en la educación secundaria* at the Universidad de Málaga), but these are optional, not specific to English, and contain no explicit mention of generative AI.

The most significant finding is the complete absence of any curricular unit explicitly addressing generative AI in the context of English language teacher education across all Andalusian programmes examined. While general technology subjects exist in primary education degrees, they are not tailored to language education; and in secondary teacher preparation, even generic educational technology is absent from the mandatory curriculum. This gap is particularly striking given that the European Commission's Digital Education Action Plan (2021–2027) positions AI as a transformative priority. As in Portugal, the integration of AI-specific content into initial teacher education lags substantially behind policy rhetoric.

Table 2 below summarizes the findings for all nine Andalusian universities. The table distinguishes between primary and secondary education programmes, notes the presence of general technology subjects, and records whether any unit specifically addresses digital technology for English or generative AI.

Table 2. Digital technology and AI provision in Andalusian English teacher education programmes (Study Plans, 2024–2025)

Institution (Faculty / School)	Programmes analysed	Digital technology / AI curricular provision
Universidad de Almería (Facultad de Ciencias de la Educación)	Grado en Educación Primaria (English specialization)	Compulsory general technology subject. No dedicated digital technology unit for EFL. No mention of generative AI.
	MAES (English specialization)	No technology or digital technology unit. No mention of generative AI.
Universidad de Sevilla (Facultad de Ciencias de la Educación)	Grado en Educación Primaria (English specialization)	Compulsory general technology subject. No dedicated digital technology unit for EFL. No mention of generative AI.
	MAES (English specialization)	No technology or digital technology unit. No mention of generative AI.
Universidad de Huelva (Facultad de Ciencias de la Educación)	Grado en Educación Primaria (English specialization)	Compulsory general ICT subject. No dedicated digital technology unit for EFL. No mention of generative AI.
	MAES (English specialization)	No technology or digital technology unit. No mention of generative AI.
Universidad de Jaén (Facultad de Humanidades y Ciencias de la Educación)	Grado en Educación Primaria (English specialization)	Compulsory general technology subject. No dedicated digital technology unit for EFL. No mention of generative AI.
	MAES (English specialization)	No technology or digital technology unit. No mention of generative AI.
Universidad de Cádiz (Facultad de Ciencias de la Educación)	Grado en Educación Primaria (bilingual education specialization)	Compulsory general technology/media subject (4 ECTS). No dedicated digital technology unit for EFL. No mention of generative AI.
	MAES (English specialization)	No technology or digital technology unit. No mention of generative AI.
Universidad de Córdoba (Facultad de Ciencias de la Educación y Psicología)	Grado en Educación Primaria (bilingual education specialization)	Compulsory general technology/research subjects (10 ECTS in total). No dedicated digital technology unit for EFL. No mention of generative AI.
	MAES (English specialization)	No compulsory technology unit (only generic references to audiovisual media and technology in didactics content). No mention of generative AI.

continued on following page

Table 2. Continued

Institution (Faculty / School)	Programmes analysed	Digital technology / AI curricular provision
Universidad de Málaga (Facultad de Ciencias de la Educación)	Grado en Educación Primaria (English specialization)	Study plan not available in sufficient detail for this analysis.
	MAES (English specialization)	Optional transversal module (general, not EFL-specific). No mention of generative AI.
Universidad de Granada (Facultad de Ciencias de la Educación)	Grado en Educación Primaria (English specialization)	Compulsory general technology subject. No dedicated digital technology unit for EFL. No mention of generative AI.
	MAES (English specialization)	No technology or digital technology unit. No mention of generative AI.
Universidad Pablo de Olavide (Centro de Estudios de Posgrado)	MAES (foreign languages specialization)	Optional transversal module (8 ECTS, general, not EFL-specific). No dedicated digital technology unit for EFL. No mention of generative AI.

Source: Own elaboration

The findings in the Andalusian context mirror the Portuguese case in one crucial respect: complete absence of generative AI content across all programmes. However, two notable differences emerge. First, Portugal's *mestrado habilitante* allocates a substantial 60 ECTS to supervised teaching practice (IPP), reflecting a strong school-based apprenticeship model, whereas the Spanish secondary MAES dedicates only 10 ECTS to practicum (plus 6 ECTS for the Master's thesis). Second, while Portuguese programmes place digital technology within the DidE component—with NOVA FCSH offering a dedicated unit "Tecnologia no Ensino de Inglês" (Technology in English Language Teaching)—Andalusian primary degrees isolate technology in generic foundation modules, and secondary programmes omit it entirely from mandatory curricula.

This structural disconnection in Andalusia—where technology is treated as a transversal competence rather than an integral part of language teaching methodology—poses a significant barrier to developing critically AI-literate English teachers who can address equity, equality, and justice in technology-mediated language classrooms. The reliance on elective, non-specific technology courses in secondary teacher preparation further exacerbates inequalities: only those students who voluntarily choose such electives receive any digital training, and that training does not address the unique pedagogical affordances and ethical challenges of generative AI in foreign language education.

In sum, the institutional landscape mapped in this section reveals a system where general digital literacy is recognized in primary teacher education but remains disconnected from the specific demands of English language teaching, and where secondary teacher preparation lacks any mandatory digital or AI component. The absence of generative AI content across all universities is not something temporary but a reflection of deeper structural choices embedded in curricular design: choices about what counts as essential professional knowledge for a language teacher, and whether pre-service preparation is conceptualized primarily as the transmission of established pedagogical techniques or as a critically reflexive process of equipping educators to navigate a complex, technologically mediated, and structurally unequal professional world.

PROPOSAL

Towards Equitable AI Literacy in EFL Pre-Service Teacher Education: A Proposed Curricular Unit

The institutional audit presented in the preceding section reveals a systemic absence: across all eight accredited pre-service English language teacher education programmes in Portugal, not a single programme includes a dedicated curricular unit addressing generative AI. Similarly, a parallel audit of nine Andalusian universities reaches an even more striking conclusion: while primary education degrees include general technology subjects, secondary master's programmes lack any mandatory digital technology unit for EFL, and no programme at any level mentions generative AI in its study plan. This gap is not merely an incidental feature of curricula currently under revision; it is a structural condition with direct and inequitable consequences for the teachers who enter Portuguese and Andalusian classrooms and, by extension, for the learners those teachers will serve. In response to this cross-national absence, and drawing on a convergence of international policy frameworks, digital competence architectures, and critical scholarship in AI and language education, this section proposes a provisional template for a 3 ECTS curricular unit suitable for integration within the *Didática Específica* component of a *mestrado habilitante* or within the specific module of a secondary MAES programme in English language teaching at the third cycle and secondary level. The proposal is avowedly conceptual: it is intended not as a finished institutional document but as a principled starting point for curriculum development, designed to be adapted to the specificities of individual institutional contexts, revised collaboratively with teacher educators and student teachers, and evaluated for its equity outcomes in practice.

The proposed unit is grounded in a cluster of authoritative international frameworks that together constitute a coherent policy and conceptual architecture for AI-literate teacher education. The European Commission's DigComp 3.0 (Cosgrove & Cachia, 2025), the fifth and most recent iteration of the European Digital

Competence Framework for Citizens, integrates AI as a transversal competence woven through all five areas of the framework, reflecting the European Union's recognition that critical engagement with AI is no longer a specialist skill but a foundational civic literacy. DigCompEdu (Redecker & Punie, 2017) extends this logic to the professional context of educators, articulating a framework for digital competence that encompasses not merely the use of digital resources but the critical empowerment of learners and the design of inclusive, digitally enriched pedagogies. UNESCO's AI Competency Framework for Teachers (Miao & Cukurova, 2024), the first global framework of its kind, articulates a progression of teacher AI competences organised around five dimensions: human-centred mindset, AI ethics, AI pedagogy, AI for learning, and professional development. The unit proposed here is designed to develop competences across all five dimensions within the specific context of EFL teacher education. Additionally, the EU Artificial Intelligence Act (European Parliament and Council of the European Union, 2024), which entered into force in August 2024 and classifies AI systems used in education as high-risk, imposes obligations of transparency, human oversight, and accountability that language teachers, as both users of AI tools and advocates for their students, must be equipped to understand and exercise.

The equity rationale for such a unit is both practical and principled. As Benjamin (2019) and Noble (2018) have demonstrated, AI systems routinely encode the linguistic, cultural, and social hierarchies of the societies and datasets that produced them. For EFL learners from non-dominant linguistic backgrounds, for learners with limited access to digital infrastructure, and for teachers working in under-resourced schools, an unreflective uptake of AI tools in language education risks not the elimination of educational inequality but its sophisticated reproduction. The critical challenge for pre-service teacher education is not to produce teachers who know how to use AI, but teachers who know how to question it: who can identify when an AI tool's assumptions about language norms, learner characteristics, or educational goals conflict with the plurilingual, inclusive, and justice-oriented vision articulated by the Council of Europe (2001, 2020) and by the equity frameworks that underpin this chapter. Bender et al. (2021), in their foundational analysis of the risks posed by large language models, argue that fluency in text generation cannot be equated with linguistic or communicative competence and that the deployment of such models carries profound risks of bias amplification at scale. These risks are directly relevant to EFL classrooms: AI tools that reward standard-variety, high-prestige English and penalise non-dominant varieties or translingual repertoires reproduce, rather than challenge, the hierarchies of linguistic capital that have historically disadvantaged many learners. A curricular unit addressing generative AI in EFL teacher education is therefore not merely a technical addition to an existing programme; it is an act of professional equity.

PROPOSED CURRICULAR UNIT — TEMPLATE

For integration in the Didática Específica component of Mestrado em Ensino de Inglês (3.º ciclo do EB e ES) — Grupo de Recrutamento 330 in the Portuguese context, or in MAES in the Andalusian/Spanish context

Title: Generative AI in EFL Teaching: Critical Approaches and Equitable Practice
Scientific area: English didactics
Duration: One semester (13–15 weeks)
ECTS: 3
Total number of hours: 84 hours (3 × 28 h/ECTS)
Contact hours: Total: 28 h
Autonomous work: 56 hours

Learning Objectives and Compatibility with the Teaching Method

Knowledge:

- K1. To understand the technical principles underlying generative AI systems, including large language models (LLMs) and natural language processing, their capabilities, and their fundamental limitations in language education contexts.
- K2. To identify and critically analyse the key regulatory, ethical, and policy frameworks governing AI in education, including the EU AI Act (Regulation (EU) 2024/1689), UNESCO's Recommendation on the Ethics of Artificial Intelligence (UNESCO, 2021), and UNESCO's AI Competency Framework for Teachers (Miao & Cukurova, 2024).
- K3. To understand and apply the digital competence frameworks most relevant to AI-mediated EFL teaching: DigComp 3.0 (Cosgrove & Cachia, 2025) and DigCompEdu (Redecker & Punie, 2017).
- K4. To demonstrate knowledge of how generative AI systems encode linguistic, cultural, and social biases, and of the equity implications of these biases for learners from non-dominant linguistic and socio-economic backgrounds.

Skills:

- S1. To critically evaluate AI tools for EFL teaching using equity-oriented criteria that account for learner diversity, linguistic pluralism, and algorithmic bias.

- S2. To design language learning activities and assessment tasks that integrate generative AI in ways that are pedagogically principled, inclusive, and consistent with the CEFR's plurilingual vision.
- S3. To apply frameworks of critical AI literacy to EFL classroom contexts, enabling learners to engage thoughtfully and safely with AI tools as both language users and developing citizens.
- S4. To navigate issues of academic integrity, data privacy, and consent arising from AI use in language learning and assessment, and communicate about these clearly with learners, parents, and institutions.

Competences:

- C1. To exercise autonomous, ethically grounded professional judgement in selecting, adapting, and—where appropriate—rejecting AI tools for EFL teaching, with consistent reference to the needs and rights of all learners.
- C2. To advocate effectively for equitable and just conditions of AI-mediated language learning within school communities, drawing on knowledge of relevant policy frameworks.
- C3. To engage in sustained critical reflection on the intersections of AI, language, power, and social justice as a constitutive dimension of professional identity as an EFL teacher.
- C4. To maintain and develop AI-related pedagogical competences responsively as the technological and policy landscape evolves, demonstrating the disposition for evidence-informed lifelong professional learning.

Syllabus Content *(6 modules over 13 contact weeks)*

Module 1: Generative AI—Technical Principles and Conceptual Foundations (Weeks 1–2)

- What is generative AI? LLMs, transformer architectures (conceptual overview), NLP, and the AI tool ecosystem relevant to EFL education.
- Capabilities and limitations: fluency ≠ comprehension; hallucination, bias, and opacity.
- Critical perspectives on LLMs: the "stochastic parrots" argument (Bender et al., 2021) and its implications for language education.
- Survey of AI tools encountered by EFL learners and teachers: ChatGPT, Grammarly, AI-assisted tutors, automated writing feedback.

Module 2: Ethics, Equity, and the Regulatory Landscape (Weeks 3–4)

- The EU AI Act (Regulation (EU) 2024/1689): education as a high-risk domain; obligations of transparency, human oversight, and accountability.
- UNESCO's Recommendation on the Ethics of Artificial Intelligence (2021): human rights, inclusiveness, and algorithmic justice as foundational principles.
- UNESCO's AI Competency Framework for Teachers (Miao & Cukurova, 2024): from AI awareness to AI ethics and AI pedagogy.
- Whose AI? Whose language? Algorithmic bias and linguistic discrimination: implications for diverse EFL learners (Benjamin, 2019; Noble, 2018).

Module 3: Digital Competence Frameworks and the AI-Literate EFL Teacher (Weeks 5–6)

- DigComp 3.0 (Cosgrove & Cachia, 2025): AI as transversal competence across information literacy, communication, content creation, safety, and problem-solving.
- DigCompEdu (Redecker & Punie, 2017): from digital resource user to empowering educator; AI in the DigCompEdu progression.
- Critical AI literacy as a dimension of professional identity: beyond tool use towards transformative, equity-oriented practice.
- The EFL teacher as a digital justice advocate: community, institutional, and curricular dimensions.

Module 4: Generative AI in Language Learning and Teaching—Affordances and Risks (Weeks 7–9)

- AI in writing, grammar feedback, and vocabulary development: pedagogical affordances and risks to learner agency.
- Automated language assessment and AI-generated feedback: equity concerns across learner varieties and registers.
- The CEFR's plurilingual vision and the limits of AI-mediated language assessment: non-dominant varieties, translingual practice, and algorithmic standardisation (Canagarajah, 2013; Council of Europe, 2001, 2020).
- AI and academic integrity in language learning: detection, policy, and pedagogy.
- Access and the digital divide: differential effects of AI tool availability across learner populations and school contexts.

Module 5: Designing Equitable AI-Enhanced EFL Pedagogies (Weeks 10–11)

- Principles for equitable AI integration: access, representation, agency, accountability, and reversibility.
- Collaborative task design with and about AI: inclusive frameworks for linguistically diverse classrooms.
- Differentiating AI-integrated activities for learners with varying digital literacies, resource access, and linguistic backgrounds.
- From consumer to critical co-designer: involving learners in evaluating and co-constructing AI-enhanced language tasks.

Module 6: Professional Practice, Advocacy, and Future Horizons (Weeks 12–13)

- Reading, critiquing, and contributing to school AI policies as a professional EFL educator.
- Communicating critically and constructively about AI with learners, parents, and school leadership.
- Critical optimism: what equitably designed AI-enhanced language education can look like in practice.
- Personal AI literacy development plan: bridging this curricular unit to the supervised teaching practice (IPP).

Coherence of Syllabus Content with Learning Objectives

The progression of modules is designed to enact a deliberate movement from conceptual understanding, through ethical and regulatory grounding, to practical pedagogical application and professional advocacy. Modules 1 and 2 develop K1, K2, and K4 by establishing the technical and normative foundations without which critical evaluation of AI tools remains superficial. Module 3 develops K3, C3, and C4 by positioning the student teacher as a developing professional within established competence frameworks. Modules 4 and 5 develop S1 through S4, C1, and C2 by moving from analytical critique to constructive, equity-oriented design, ensuring that critical awareness is translated into actionable pedagogical practice. Module 6 develops C2, C3, and C4 by extending the focus from classroom-level decisions to institutional and professional contexts, and by preparing student teachers to carry their AI-critical orientation into their supervised teaching practice (IPP). The critical reflective journal, required throughout the semester, sustains the development of C3 and C4 across all modules by making metacognitive engagement with AI, equity, and professional identity a continuous rather than episodic practice.

Teaching and Learning Methodologies

This unit adopts a critical-constructivist pedagogical model grounded in the conviction that equitable teacher preparation requires active, reflective engagement with real tools, real policies, and real pedagogical challenges. The following methodologies are specified:

- Critical Seminar: close, guided reading of primary policy documents (EU AI Act, UNESCO recommendations, DigComp 3.0), academic articles, and AI-generated outputs. Seminar discussions foreground perspectives of non-dominant learner communities and situate AI debates within structures of linguistic and social power.
- AI Tool Critique: structured, comparative evaluation of AI tools using equity-oriented criteria. Student teachers test tools with tasks modelled on real EFL classroom contexts and document their observations in the reflective journal.
- Collaborative Pedagogical Design: small-group design of equitable AI-integrated EFL learning sequences, working across multiple iterations and receiving peer and tutor feedback.
- Critical Reflective Journal: an individual, ongoing record of intellectual and professional development throughout the semester, structured around four reflective lenses: technical understanding, ethical positioning, pedagogical application, and equity orientation.
- Case-Based Analysis: examination of documented cases of AI deployment in language education contexts, with a deliberate over-representation of cases from under-resourced, linguistically diverse, or historically marginalised school contexts.
- Policy Workshop: in Module 6, student teachers collaboratively draft a one-page school AI policy framework for a hypothetical or real EFL context, drawing on regulatory knowledge and equity commitments developed throughout the unit.

Assessment

- Critical Reflective Journal — 30%: Individual; continuous (six entries of approximately 400 words each). Assessment criteria privilege analytical depth, integration of course frameworks, and the quality of equity-oriented reasoning.
- Critical AI Tool Analysis — 30%: Individual written assignment (approximately 1,500 words). Student teachers select an AI tool, evaluate it using criteria drawn from the EU AI Act, DigComp 3.0, and UNESCO's ethics

framework, and produce a critical analysis addressing technical capability, bias risk, equity implications, and pedagogical appropriateness.

- Inclusive Pedagogical Design Project — 30%: Group project (groups of 3–4). Groups design a complete AI-integrated EFL learning sequence (minimum 3 lessons) for a specified linguistically diverse secondary class, with a written rationale (~2,000 words) and 15-minute oral presentation. Peer evaluation contributes 10% of this component's grade.
- Active and Reflective Participation — 10%: Seminar engagement assessed against criteria of preparation, critical contribution, and respectful engagement with diverse perspectives.

Coherence of Teaching Methodologies and Assessment with Learning Objectives

The alignment between methodologies, assessments, and objectives is explicit and deliberate. The critical seminar and case-based analysis develop and assess K1–K4. The AI tool critique directly prepares and assesses S1 and S4. The collaborative design project develops and assesses S2, S3, C1, and C2 through experiential, problem-based learning. The reflective journal develops and assesses C3 and C4 through sustained metacognitive engagement; its longitudinal structure captures the evolution of student teachers' thinking across modules. The policy workshop develops C2 by connecting individual professional knowledge to collective institutional responsibility. Each knowledge, skill, and competence dimension is engaged by at least two assessment tasks, providing a robust triangulation of evidence that a standard written examination could not achieve.

Empowering Teachers for the AI Era: Equity, Equality, and Justice as Organising Principles

The curricular unit proposed above is built on a foundational conviction that distinguishes it from technologically enthusiastic but equity-blind approaches to AI integration in teacher education: namely, that access to AI tools is not in itself a condition of educational justice. A teacher who encounters a generative AI writing evaluation system and deploys it unquestioningly across a heterogeneous class of secondary learners, some of whom are speakers of non-dominant English varieties, some of whom are first-generation language learners, and some of whom have limited prior access to digital devices, is not advancing equity. In all likelihood, they are reproducing and legitimising the linguistic hierarchies encoded in that system's training data (Bender et al., 2021; Noble, 2018). The proposed unit is designed to prevent precisely this outcome by producing teachers who are not only digitally competent in the sense of DigComp 3.0 and DigCompEdu, but who are also critically informed about the conditions under which AI tools can constitute genuine educational goods, and under which they cannot.

The distinction between equality and equity, articulated in the introduction to this chapter, becomes particularly urgent in this context. Equal access to AI, the provision of the same tools to all students and all teachers, is a necessary but radically insufficient condition of fair language education. Equity requires that AI tools are evaluated, selected, and adapted with specific attention to their differential effects on learners differently positioned within the linguistic, socio-economic, and cultural landscape of the classroom. This is not a skill that can be assumed, nor one that will develop organically from classroom experience alone; it requires deliberate, theoretically grounded preparation in pre-service teacher education. The proposed unit's design, its insistence on the EU AI Act's transparency and accountability requirements, on UNESCO's ethical principles, on the CEFR's plurilingual commitment, and on the critical scholarship of Benjamin (2019), Noble (2018), and Canagarajah (2013), is a response to this imperative. It positions equity not as an add-on or a module to be completed, but as the organising principle that structures the entire sequence of learning.

A justice orientation, as defined in this chapter's introduction, asks the deeper question: in whose interests is AI in EFL education designed, and whose interests does the deployment of AI serve? The proposed unit does not offer a comforting answer to this question; it offers the intellectual and professional resources to ask it rigorously and to act on the answer. Student teachers who complete this unit will not be equipped with a checklist of approved AI tools. They will be equipped with a principled framework for evaluation and advocacy, with knowledge of the regulatory instruments that govern AI in educational settings, and with the dispositions of critical optimism that distinguish professional agency from either uncritical adoption or reflexive rejection. They will, in short, be better placed to be the teachers that the youngest and most vulnerable learners in Portuguese secondary schools deserve in the AI era: teachers who see through technological promises to the social conditions that determine whether those promises are honoured.

FUTURE RESEARCH DIRECTIONS

This chapter has argued that the convergence of a global teacher shortage and the rapid proliferation of generative AI in educational settings constitutes a structural juncture that teacher education policy cannot afford to treat as routine. The mapping of Portuguese pre-service training provision for English language teachers—conducted against the legislative backdrop of *Decreto-Lei n. º 9-A/2025*—together with the parallel audit of nine Andalusian universities in Spain reveals two systems that remain largely unequipped to prepare teachers for the epistemological and ethical demands of the AI classroom. The proposed curricular unit is intended as one concrete, immediately implementable response to this transnational gap, but its deeper ambition is to model a principle: that AI integration in language teacher education must be structured from the outset around equity, equality, and justice as non-negotiable organising commitments. For this principle to take institutional root, the curricular reform proposed here must be accompanied by corresponding evolution in accreditation frameworks. A3ES evaluation criteria for *mestrados habilitantes* (qualifying master's degrees) in Portugal and the verification criteria for MAES programmes in Andalusia should be revised to require demonstrable AI literacy components within courses and units, providing regulatory impetus for systematic curricular reform across all accredited providers. National research agendas should prioritise longitudinal studies of the effect of AI-critical teacher preparation on classroom practice in linguistically diverse Portuguese and Andalusian/Spanish schools, generating the evidence base that sustained policy reform requires. At a European level, comparative studies mapping AI literacy provision across national teacher education systems would enable identification of the structural conditions under which equity-centred AI preparation is most successfully implemented and sustained. The broader European teacher education research community should recognise that the debates launched by UNESCO (2023), Miao and Cukurova (2024), and Darling-Hammond (2017) are not resolved by legislation alone: they are resolved (or not) in the seminar rooms where the next generation of teachers learns to think.

CONCLUSION

The risks of inaction are not merely theoretical. They are already materialising in classrooms where commercially developed AI tools are deployed without institutional guidance, without teacher preparation, and without any audit of the linguistic and cultural assumptions embedded in their training data (Benjamin, 2019; Noble, 2018). When an AI writing assistant trained predominantly on Standard American English is used to evaluate the compositions of plurilingual learners in a Lisbon, Porto, Seville or Málaga school, it does not produce neutral assessments: it produces assessments that reflect and reinforce a specific linguistic hierarchy, one that disadvantages the very learners whose equitable development the CEFR's plurilingual vision is designed to promote (Bender et al., 2021; Council of Europe, 2001, 2020). When that same tool is used by a teacher who lacks the critical AI literacy to interrogate its outputs, the harm is compounded: the teacher's professional authority becomes a vector for the tool's bias rather than a check upon it. The EU

AI Act's classification of AI systems used in educational settings as high-risk is a regulatory recognition of precisely these dangers (European Parliament and Council of the European Union, 2024). Yet regulation without prepared practitioners is an empty framework. A legal requirement for human oversight of high-risk AI decisions is vacuous if the human charged with that oversight, the classroom teacher, has never been taught what it means to oversee an AI system critically, let alone how to do so in the complex, relationship-dense context of language instruction. Teacher education programmes that fail to address this gap are not merely leaving a professional development opportunity unrealised: they are knowingly deploying under-prepared teachers into a regulatory environment they are not equipped to navigate, and into classrooms where the cost of that unpreparedness will be borne most heavily by those students already most disadvantaged by existing inequalities (Selwyn, 2019; UNESCO, 2023).

The conviction that animates every section of this chapter is, finally, a conviction about what teachers are for. Teachers are not content-delivery mechanisms whose functions can be partially outsourced to AI tools that are more efficient, scalable, and economically convenient. They are professionals whose value resides precisely in their capacity for the kind of contextualised, relationship-grounded, ethically responsive judgement that no language model can replicate. In an era when that judgement is increasingly called upon in relation to AI, when teachers must decide which tool to trust, which output to question, which student has been failed by an algorithm's assumptions, the preparation of that judgement becomes a central task of initial teacher education. Whether in Portugal, where the legislative framework has recently been updated, or in Andalusia, where decentralisation has led to a fragmented and AI-absent curriculum, a pre-service curriculum that equips English language teachers to be critical, equity-oriented navigators of the AI landscape is not an add-on to good teacher preparation: it is, in the second quarter of the twenty-first century, a constitutive element of it. The global teacher shortage makes the equitable distribution of well-prepared, critically literate teachers an urgent social justice priority. Generative AI, if introduced without equity-oriented teacher preparation, will exacerbate rather than alleviate the educational disadvantages of learners already on the margins. The curricular proposal advanced in this chapter represents one rigorously grounded step towards a different future, one in which every student, regardless of linguistic background, socio-economic position, or geographic location, is taught by a teacher who understands AI well enough to protect them from its risks and to harness its possibilities in their genuine interest.

REFERENCES

Bender, E. M., Gebru, T., McMillan-Major, A., & Shmitchell, S. (2021). On the dangers of stochastic parrots: Can language models be too big? In *Proceedings of the 2021 ACM Conference on Fairness, Accountability, and Transparency* (pp. 610–623). ACM. DOI: 10.1145/3442188.3445922

Benjamin, R. (2019). *Race after technology: Abolitionist tools for the new Jim Code*. Polity Press.

Canagarajah, A. S. (2013). *Translingual practice: Global Englishes and cosmopolitan relations*. Routledge. DOI: 10.4324/9780203120293

Cosgrove, J., & Cachia, R. (2025). *DigComp 3.0: European Digital Competence Framework* (5th ed.). Publications Office of the European Union. DOI: 10.2760/0001149

Council of Europe. (2001). *Common European framework of reference for languages: Learning, teaching, assessment*. Council of Europe Publishing.

Council of Europe. (2020). *Common European framework of reference for languages: Learning, teaching, assessment—Companion volume*. Council of Europe Publishing.

Crenshaw, K. W. (1991). Mapping the margins: Intersectionality, identity politics, and violence against women of color. *Stanford Law Review*, *43*(6), 1241–1299. DOI: 10.2307/1229039

Darling-Hammond, L. (2017). Teacher education around the world: What can we learn from international practice? *European Journal of Teacher Education*, *40*(3), 291–309. DOI: 10.1080/02619768.2017.1315399

Decreto-Lei n.º 79/2014, de 14 de maio [Decree-Law No. 79/2014 of 14 May]. *Diário da República*, 1.ª série, n.º 92.

Decreto-Lei n.º 9-A/2025, de 14 de fevereiro [Decree-Law No. 9-A/2025 of 14 February]. *Diário da República*, 1.ª série, n.º 32, Suplemento.

European Commission. (2021). *Digital Education Action Plan (2021–2027)*. Publications Office of the European Union. https://n9.cl/nk38l

European Commission/EACEA/Eurydice. (2021). *Teachers in Europe: Careers, development and well-being*. Publications Office of the European Union. https://n9.cl/36ql1g

European Parliament and Council of the European Union. (2024). Regulation (EU) 2024/1689 of the European Parliament and of the Council of 13 June 2024 laying down harmonised rules on artificial intelligence (Artificial Intelligence Act). *Official Journal of the European Union*, 1689. https://n9.cl/k1ka6

Guerriero, S. (Ed.). (2017). *Pedagogical knowledge and the changing nature of the teaching profession* (Educational Research and Innovation). OECD Publishing. DOI: 10.1787/9789264270695-en

Junta de Andalucía. (2005). *Plan de Fomento del Plurilingüismo en Andalucía [Plan to Promote Multilingualism in Andalusia]*. Junta de Andalucía. https://n9.cl/w5jc66

Junta de Andalucía. (2016). *Plan Estratégico de Desarrollo de las Lenguas en Andalucía. Horizonte 2020 [Strategic Plan for Language Development in Andalusia. Horizon 2020]*. Junta de Andalucía. https://n9.cl/dt2r7

Junta de Andalucía. (n.d.). *Transformación digital educativa [Digital transformation in education]*. Junta de Andalucía. https://n9.cl/98465

Ley Orgánica 3/2020, de 29 de diciembre, por la que se modifica la Ley Orgánica 2/2006, de 3 de mayo, de Educación [Organic Law 3/2020, of December 29, amending Organic Law 2/2006, of May 3, on Education]. *BOE* no. 340, 30 December 2020, 122868–122953. https://n9.cl/4sf5b

Miao, F., & Cukurova, M. (2024). *AI competency framework for teachers*. UNESCO. https://n9.cl/kyua4

Noble, S. U. (2018). *Algorithms of oppression: How search engines reinforce racism*. New York University Press. DOI: 10.18574/nyu/9781479833641.001.0001

OECD. (2023). *Education at a glance 2023: OECD indicators*. OECD Publishing. DOI: 10.1787/e13bef63-

Redecker, C., & Punie, Y. (2017). *European framework for the digital competence of educators: DigCompEdu*. Publications Office of the European Union. DOI: 10.2760/178382

Selwyn, N. (2019). *Should robots replace teachers? AI and the future of education*. Polity Press.

UNESCO. (2021). *Recommendation on the ethics of artificial intelligence*. UNESCO. https://n9.cl/4zoy2m

UNESCO. (2023). *Global education monitoring report 2023: Technology in education — A tool on whose terms?* UNESCO. DOI: 10.54676/UZQV8501

Universidade NOVA de Lisboa. (2024). *Mestrado de Ensino de Inglês no 3.º ciclo do Ensino Básico e no Ensino Secundário [Master's Degree in Teaching English in Lower Secondary and Upper Secondary Education]*. Faculdade de Ciências Sociais e Humanas. https://n9.cl/k0lrr

Zawacki-Richter, O., Marín, V. I., Bond, M., & Gouverneur, F. (2019). Systematic review of research on artificial intelligence applications in higher education – where are the educators? *International Journal of Educational Technology in Higher Education, 16*(1), 39. Advance online publication. DOI: 10.1186/s41239-019-0171-0

ADDITIONAL READING

Crawford, K. (2021). *Atlas of AI: Power, politics, and the planetary costs of artificial intelligence*. Yale University Press.

Eubanks, V. (2018). *Automating inequality: How high-tech tools profile, police, and punish the poor*. St. Martin's Press.

Floridi, L., Cowls, J., Beltrametti, M., Chatila, R., Chazerand, P., Dignum, V., Luetge, C., Madelin, R., Pagallo, U., Rossi, F., Schafer, B., Valcke, P., & Vayena, E. (2018). AI4People — An ethical framework for a good AI society: Opportunities, risks, principles, and recommendations. *Minds and Machines, 28*(4), 689–707. DOI: 10.1007/s11023-018-9482-5 PMID: 30930541

Holmes, W., Bialik, M., & Fadel, C. (2019). *Artificial intelligence in education: Promises and implications for teaching and learning*. Center for Curriculum Redesign.

Luckin, R. (2018). *Machine learning and human intelligence: The future of education for the 21st century*. UCL IOE Press.

O'Neil, C. (2016). *Weapons of math destruction: How big data increases inequality and threatens democracy*. Crown.

van Dijk, J. A. G. M. (2020). *The digital divide*. Polity Press.

Williamson, B. (2017). Big data in education: The digital future of learning, policy and practice. *Sage (Atlanta, Ga.)*. Advance online publication. DOI: 10.4135/9781529714920

KEY TERMS AND DEFINITIONS

Algorithmic Bias: The systematic and repeatable errors embedded in AI outputs that create unfair outcomes for certain groups, arising from biased training data, flawed model design, or discriminatory patterns encoded in the data on which the system was trained.

Critical AI Literacy: The capacity to understand, evaluate, and interrogate artificial intelligence systems with reference to their technical functioning, ethical implications, and differential social effects, particularly for marginalized or linguistically non-dominant populations.

DigComp: The European Digital Competence Framework for Citizens, published by the European Commission. DigComp 3.0 (2025) is its fifth and most recent edition, integrating artificial intelligence as a transversal competence dimension across all five areas of the framework.

Generative AI: A class of artificial intelligence systems trained on large datasets to generate new content—including text, images, audio, and code—in response to user prompts. In language education, generative AI tools include large language models, AI-assisted writing and feedback platforms, and conversational agents.

Linguistic Justice: The commitment to ensuring that linguistic diversity is treated as a resource rather than a deficit in educational settings, and that speakers of non-dominant language varieties are not systematically disadvantaged by language policies, assessment instruments, or AI systems calibrated to prestige varieties.

MAES (Máster Universitario en Profesorado de Educación Secundaria Obligatoria y Bachillerato, Formación Profesional y Enseñanza de Idiomas): A Spanish master's degree (typically 120 ECTS) conferring formal professional qualification to teach in a specific subject area at state secondary level.

Mestrado Habilitante: *A Portuguese second-cycle university degree (typically 120 ECTS) conferring formal professional qualification to teach in a specific subject area at state secondary level, structured in accordance with national teacher education legislation, currently* Decreto-Lei n. ° 9-A/2025.

Plurilingualism: The Council of Europe's conceptualization of multilingualism as a dynamic, individual competence in which partial or unequal proficiencies across several languages constitute a legitimate and valuable communicative repertoire, as articulated in the Common European Framework of Reference for Languages.

Pre-Service Teacher Education: The formal period of professional preparation undertaken by prospective teachers prior to their independent entry into the teaching profession, typically combining academic study with supervised practical experience in school settings.

Teacher Shortage: A structural imbalance between the supply of qualified teachers and the demand for them, characterized by unfilled posts, under-qualified appointments, and increasing workloads for existing staff, with disproportionate effects on schools serving socio-economically disadvantaged, rural, and linguistically diverse communities.

Section 2

Critical Analyses of Bias, Access, and Representation

Chapter 5
Bridging the Digital Divide:
An Interdisciplinary ESP Framework for Fostering Critical AI Literacy and Equity

Isabele Maria Lavado
http://orcid.org/0000-0002-2171-0779
Castelo Branco Polytechnic University, Portugal

ABSTRACT

GAI offers transformative potential for ESP education but risks biases, digital divides, and inequalities among multilingual learners. This chapter proposes an interdisciplinary framework through ESP-content co-teaching (ICLHE-aligned), rooted in digital didactics, critical AI literacy, and learner-centered pedagogy. It includes three components: critical AI output analysis, collaborative project-based learning, and redefined practitioner roles as ethical guides. An English for Engineering scenario illustrates implementation, while a PDCA-structured policy model provides scalable equity safeguards for institutions worldwide. The framework repositions GAI from a productivity tool to a critical inquiry object, empowering learners to detect biases, refine outputs responsibly, and prioritize human collaboration over tech access for inclusive success. Future research includes multi-site pilots, longitudinal impact metrics, and agentic AI adaptation across global contexts.

DOI: 10.4018/979-8-3373-7749-0.ch005

INTRODUCTION

The widespread integration of Generative Artificial Intelligence (GAI) into professional and academic fields marks a significant and transformative shift in communication, presenting language education, particularly English for Specific Purposes (ESP), with a critical crossroads. While GAI offers promises of efficiency and personalised learning, its rapid adoption necessitates addressing profound risks that directly affect equity and justice in the classroom. GAI systems, trained on vast, often biased datasets, risk perpetuating stereotypes, marginalising underrepresented voices, and exacerbating the existing digital divide for students lacking equal access to premium tools or high-quality data (Farrelly & Baker, 2023; Nedungadi et al., 2024; Viberg et al., 2024).

This chapter argues that responding to these challenges requires more than technical adoption or individual tool mastery. It requires interdisciplinary collaboration, particularly between ESP specialists and experts in digital ethics, computer science, and disciplinary fields, so that GAI is approached as a site of critical inquiry rather than a neutral productivity tool. Such collaboration supports the design of curricula that integrate critical AI literacy, ethical communication, and disciplinary competence, while also acknowledging the diverse linguistic and cultural realities of multilingual learners.

Promoting justice in AI-enhanced language education, therefore, means developing students' capacity to critically evaluate, revise, and contextualise AI-generated content, rather than simply producing fluent outputs. In this way, the framework advanced in this chapter helps multilingual and multicultural learners identify algorithmic bias, strengthen ethical judgment, and engage with AI in ways that support fairness and social responsibility.

This chapter contributes to the field in three ways. First, it redefines AI literacy in ESP as a discipline-specific and critically oriented practice rather than a set of technical skills. Second, it proposes an interdisciplinary teaching model that links ethics, collaboration, and communicative practice. Third, it shifts the focus from using AI tools to using them responsibly and reflectively within institutionally grounded, justice-oriented pedagogy. To ground this framework conceptually, the chapter is informed on three converging fields: digital didactics, critical AI literacy, and the collaborative tradition of ESP and Integrated Content and Language in Higher Education (ICLHE).

THEORETICAL AND CONCEPTUAL FOUNDATIONS

The proposed framework is grounded in three interconnected theoretical fields: digital didactics, critical AI literacy, and ESP, with ICLHE functioning as an important interdisciplinary bridge. Together, these perspectives provide the conceptual basis for an AI-enhanced approach to language education that is pedagogically active, ethically attentive, and disciplinary in orientation. Digital didactics contributes a learner-centred view of technology use, emphasising active participation, collaboration, and knowledge construction rather than passive content consumption. Critical AI literacy adds an ethical dimension by encouraging learners to question the assumptions, limitations, and biases embedded in AI systems, rather than treating their outputs as neutral or authoritative. ESP, supported by ICLHE, ensures that language learning remains tied to authentic disciplinary purposes, professional communication, and the communicative demands of specific academic and workplace contexts.

These theoretical strands are further strengthened by a sociological perspective on inequality and access. In AI-enhanced language education, access to premium tools, digital infrastructure, and institutional support can function as forms of cultural capital, shaping who benefits most from technological innovation. Bourdieu's concepts of cultural capital and institutional habitus are therefore useful for understanding how unequal access to GAI may reproduce rather than reduce existing educational and social hierarchies. From this perspective, the digital divide is not simply a technical problem but also a structural one, since differences in access, familiarity, and institutional support can influence participation, confidence, and achievement. This makes it essential to view GAI not only as a pedagogical tool but also as a site where broader issues of power and privilege are reproduced or contested.

By combining these perspectives, the chapter establishes the foundation for a framework that treats GAI not as a neutral resource but as an object of critical, interdisciplinary, and justice-oriented pedagogical design. The aim is not simply to integrate AI into language teaching, but to do so in ways that support ethical judgement, disciplinary relevance, and equitable participation for all learners.

Digital Didactics and the Shift to Student-Centred Learning

The shift from traditional teacher-centred models to student-centred, blended learning represents a critical transformation in higher education pedagogy (Amirova, 2025; Islam et al., 2022). Teacher-centred classrooms position instructors as the primary knowledge authority, with students as passive recipients focused on memorisation and standardised testing. While structured, this approach constrains critical thinking, creativity, and learner agency—limitations that become particularly problematic in GAI-mediated ESP contexts requiring active evaluation of machine-generated content.

Student-centred and blended approaches reconceptualise the classroom as an active environment prioritising participation, collaboration, and self-directed learning. Digital tools here move beyond content delivery to enable exploration, simulation, and co-creation through hybrid face-to-face and online activities (Islam et al., 2022; McLoughlin & Lee, 2010). Digital didactics adopts a constructivist view where students engage in authentic, group-based, interdisciplinary tasks supported by technology (Harasim, 2017; Sailer et al., 2024). Technology-enhanced learning models demonstrate improved outcomes when digital tools facilitate specific active learning activities rather than mere content transmission.

In this environment, teachers transition from content transmitters to facilitators who design adaptable learning paths, support inquiry, and scaffold knowledge construction in technology-rich settings (Amirova, 2025; Ilyashenko et al., 2019). Assessment shifts from recall tests to holistic, formative processes emphasising real-world problem-solving and reflection.

This pedagogical realignment is essential to the proposed framework because GAI in ESP demands active collaboration, informed decision-making, and critical examination of AI outputs rather than passive acceptance. Digital didactics provides the scaffolding for activities where students compare, critique, and improve AI-generated texts, positioning them as active agents in meaning-making and ethical judgement rather than consumers of algorithmic authority.

Critical AI Literacy and Ethical Challenges

Critical AI literacy provides the ethical foundation for GAI-enhanced ESP because it transforms learners from passive consumers of machine-generated content into active evaluators capable of identifying bias, opacity, and ethical limitations. In multilingual ESP classrooms, this capability becomes essential since GAI outputs often reproduce stereotypes, marginalise non-Western perspectives, and privilege dominant linguistic norms, creating double disadvantages for international students whose professional realities differ from training data.

Three interconnected challenges demand this critical orientation:

- **Algorithmic Bias and Equity:** AI models can reproduce and amplify biases in their training data, leading to unfair, stereotypical, or exclusionary outputs that disproportionately affect international, multilingual, or marginalised students. GAI models trained predominantly on English/Western datasets generate ESP deliverables—technical reports, patient instructions, marketing content—that embed stereotypes or neglect region-specific standards, systematically disadvantaging multilingual learners (Albeihi & Rice, 2025; Rodriguez-Saavedra et al., 2025).

- **Academic Integrity:** Automated content generation obscures authorship boundaries and complicates assessment of genuine disciplinary understanding, raising fundamental questions about what constitutes "original work" in AI-rich environments (Feuerriegel et al., 2024; Mazzi, 2024).
- **Digital Divide:** Socio-economic disparities in access to advanced tools and high-quality infrastructure worsen educational inequities, as students with greater access to premium GAI services may gain advantages in productivity and visibility (Nedungadi et al., 2024).

The framework addresses these challenges by positioning GAI outputs as objects of scrutiny rather than final products. Students learn to identify hallucinations, cultural insensitivity, and register mismatches through structured comparison tasks that reveal AI's disciplinary limitations. This approach transforms ethical vulnerabilities into pedagogical opportunities: bias detection becomes a core communicative competence, ethical evaluation becomes a professional skill, and collaborative critique becomes the mechanism for equitable participation regardless of tool access.

Without critical AI literacy, GAI risks reinforcing the very inequities it promises to resolve. With it, ESP classrooms become sites where multilingual learners not only master professional discourse but also develop the judgement to govern AI's role within it.

Institutional Justice: From Individual Critique to Systemic Response

Critical AI literacy equips learners to identify and resist algorithmic bias, but individual awareness alone cannot redress systemic inequalities. Institutional justice, defined here as the deliberate structuring of higher education systems to distribute AI's benefits equitably and protect vulnerable learners, offers the necessary complement. Drawing from Fricker's (2007) epistemic injustice framework and Young's (2011) structural justice theories, this approach operationalises ethical responsibility at the organisational level. Fricker (2007) identifies testimonial and hermeneutical epistemic injustices rooted in credibility deficits and interpretive gaps, while Young (2011) traces structural injustice to social processes rather than to individual intent—both of which demand institutional redesign for GAI-ESP equity.

This manifests across three interrelated dimensions essential for ethical GAI integration:

1. Distributive Justice: Equitable allocation of AI tools, digital infrastructure, and training across linguistic, socioeconomic, and disciplinary divides. Viberg et al. (2024) demonstrate how unequal digital readiness worsens learning inequalities; justice demands tiered support structures, subsidised access for under-resourced students, and faculty development calibrated to institutional contexts.
2. Recognition Justice: Affirmation of diverse communicative practices and epistemologies within AI-mediated environments. GAI systems trained predominantly on Global North corpora systematically marginalise marginalised voices and discipline-specific discourses (Bender et al., 2021). Institutional justice requires curriculum designs that teach students to critique AI outputs for cultural bias and adapt them for local relevance and disciplinary authenticity.
3. Procedural Justice: Participatory governance of AI adoption through transparent, co-created policies. The proposed PDCA-guided model ensures faculty, students, and administrators collaboratively design, implement, monitor, and refine GAI integration—balancing innovation with accountability.

This triadic framework shifts higher education institutions from passive technology users to active champions of algorithmic fairness. ESP becomes more than language instruction; it serves as a vital space for developing techno-citizenship—graduates equipped to understand AI's impact on professional dialogue and to advocate for more equitable systems. Institutional justice thus serves as the foundation of your framework, explaining why digital teaching matters (for equitable access), what critical AI literacy aims to achieve (the recognition of bias), and how interdisciplinary teamwork promotes accountability (procedural fairness).

French sociologist Pierre Bourdieu's theories offer a useful framework for understanding how structural inequalities manifest in educational contexts. His concepts of cultural capital and institutional habitus provide a sociological lens for GAI inequities. Access to premium AI tools functions as technological capital, embodied in skills, credentials, and hardware, which privileged students convert into academic advantage. (Gómez, 2020; Romele, 2020). Universities' institutional habitus then rewards AI-enhanced productivity as the new academic 'excellence,' naturalising unequal outcomes as merit (Huang, 2019; Mills, 2008). This analysis strengthens the case for the proposed framework, which designs assessment around critical judgement and collaboration rather than technological privilege, actively challenging the reproduction of educational hierarchies.

Without institutional justice, critical AI literacy risks remaining an individual competency rather than a collective transformation. By embedding justice principles into policy and practice, HEIs can ensure GAI enhances rather than erodes higher education's democratic mission. Institutional justice principles are urgently applicable in ESP contexts where algorithmic bias manifests concretely. The following examples illustrate how GAI can distort discipline-specific discourse, underscoring the need for vigilant, collaborative intervention.

Real-world ESP Bias Examples: When GAI Fails Disciplinary Contexts

In 2024/2025 Portuguese higher education institutions enrolled 456,032 students, including 55,430 in degree mobility (12.2%) dominated by the Community of Portuguese Language Countries (CPLP; Comunidade dos Países de Língua Portuguesa): Brazil (14,267 students, 40%), Guinea-Bissau (6,340, 17.8%), Angola (6,194, 17.4%), Cape Verde (4,601, 12.9%), and São Tomé e Príncipe (941, 2.6%), (Students enrolled in higher education: Results of the Survey on the Register of Enrolled and Graduated Students in Higher Education (RAIDES), (DGEEC, 2025, 2025). These multilingual, often low-resource cohorts concentrate in engineering (19.5%), health (15.4%), and business (21.6%)—precisely where GAI bias failures hit hardest.

- Engineering: ChatGPT frequently generates safety protocols that omit regional building codes and prioritise US standards.
- Medicine: While visionary leaders like Eric Topol advocate multimodal AI for precision diagnostics, current GAI medical ESP tasks generate dosage recommendations that ignore pharmacogenetic variation across populations—overlooking critical genetic differences in drug metabolism between ethnic groups and regions (Topol, 2024).
- Legal: Contract analysis favours common law precedents over civil law traditions, marginalising non-Anglophone jurisdictions.

These cases demonstrate how GAI's 'neutrality' masks cultural and disciplinary chauvinism—precisely the risks institutional justice exists to mitigate.

These systematic failures—not random errors—reflect Anglocentric training data that devalues non-Western professional realities. The proposed ESP-content collaboration responds: domain experts identify regulatory gaps (DGA codes) while ESP specialists address rhetorical/cultural mismatches. Multilingual classrooms become laboratories for cross-epistemic critique, transforming GAI liabilities into scalable institutional justice.

ESP and Interdisciplinary Collaboration

ESP, defined not as a specific language but as an approach to teaching based on learners' needs, goals, and contexts (Hutchinson & Waters, 1987), serves as the foundational discipline of the framework. In this sense, ESP is concerned less with prescribing a fixed variety of English and more with systematically analysing what learners need to do with language in particular academic, professional, or occupational settings, and then designing instruction that responds to those specific demands. Central to this approach is a comprehensive needs analysis that distinguishes between target-situation needs (what learners must be able to do in their future contexts) and learning needs (how they can best be supported to reach those goals), alongside learners' perceived necessities, lacks, and wants. By mapping these dimensions, ESP provides a principled basis for selecting genres, tasks, and linguistic features that are genuinely consequential for learners' participation in their disciplinary and workplace communities.

Within this framework, core principles such as needs analysis, authenticity, and contextualisation are mobilised to make the curriculum immediately relevant, ensuring that AI-mediated tasks are not generic add-ons but tightly aligned with learners' current and future professional practices (Hyland, 2022). Authenticity entails working with texts, interactions, and scenarios that approximate real-world communicative events, while contextualisation requires situating language use within meaningful social, institutional, and disciplinary contexts rather than in decontextualised exercises. When GAI is incorporated into ESP, these principles guide the design of prompts, tasks, and evaluation criteria: AI-generated materials are selected or adapted so that they mirror actual reports, emails, case notes, policies, or presentations that learners are likely to encounter, and tasks require learners to interpret, critique, and transform these outputs in ways that reflect real communicative purposes. In this way, GAI becomes a vehicle for rehearsing participation in specific communities of practice rather than a shortcut to completing decontextualised language drills.

From this perspective, GAI is therefore not presented as a generic language tool but as a resource embedded within specific domains such as engineering, healthcare, business, or digital ethics, where accuracy, register, and ethical responsibility are closely connected. In engineering-focused ESP, for instance, AI-mediated tasks can involve generating and refining technical incident reports or design rationales, with learners evaluating whether the output meets discipline-specific expectations for precision, hedging, and the communication of risk. In healthcare contexts, GAI can be used to simulate clinical notes or patient information leaflets, prompting learners to adjust the level of technicality, sensitivity, and clarity to match professional and ethical standards for patient communication. In business or marketing ESP, AI-generated emails, pitches, or proposals provide material for analysing tone, persuasive strategies, and intercultural appropriateness, while in digital-ethics-oriented courses, GAI can be used to draft mock policy clauses or risk scenarios that students must critique in light of regulatory and institutional frameworks. Across these domains, the pedagogical focus remains on how learners interpret, evaluate, and reshape AI output so that it conforms to the linguistic, rhetorical, and ethical norms of their target communities, thus reaffirming ESP's commitment to purposeful, context-sensitive language use.

The framework primarily employs interdisciplinary collaboration to integrate this domain-specific content. Partnerships between language experts and subject-matter specialists (e.g., in engineering, marketing, or digital ethics) are essential for co-designing authentic, context-rich learning experiences that effectively connect language development with disciplinary knowledge (Chaovanapricha & Chaturongakul, 2020; Perry & Stewart, 2005). In practice, such collaboration can involve joint needs analysis, co-creation of AI-mediated materials based on real disciplinary genres, and shared assessment design in which both linguistic and content-related criteria are made explicit. This collaboration is especially important when addressing the ethical aspects of GAI, as it demands both linguistic expertise and a thorough understanding of domain-specific standards, regulations, and values. By embedding this cross-functional expertise into ESP curricula, the framework not only supports more accurate and ethically responsible uses of GAI but also sets the stage for the co-teaching model and policy blueprint outlined in later sections.

ISSUES, CONTROVERSIES, PROBLEMS

This section explores the specific challenges GAI presents in ESP contexts and introduces the proposed framework as a direct response. It begins by identifying key issues, controversies, and problems, then presents the interdisciplinary framework and its main components, and ends with a detailed curricular application.

Algorithmic Bias and Equity in Multilingual ESP Learning

Generative AI models, like ChatGPT and Gemini, are trained on large datasets that mainly reflect English-speaking, Western cultural norms. When creating ESP deliverables—such as technical reports, patient instructions, or marketing content—the outputs often contain stereotypes, neglect non-Western perspectives, or use culturally inappropriate framing. For example, a GAI-generated engineering safety protocol might assume Eurocentric workplace hierarchies or ignore region-specific hazard protocols relevant to Portuguese or African contexts. This consistently disadvantages multilingual learners whose professional realities differ from the training data (Pang & Wei, 2025; Valdivieso & González, 2025). GAI's Anglocentric training systematically devalues CPLP students' professional repertoires: engineering and healthcare learners from Brazil (14,267), Angola (6,194), and Guinea-Bissau (6,340) may encounter outputs that omit Portuguese DGA codes, Tagus flood protocols, pharmacogenetic variation, and civil law contract traditions. These are not random errors but predictable failures of English-dominant corpora that marginalise non-Western ontologies and regulatory realities.

In ESP classrooms serving international groups, this reveals a double inequality: not only can AI outputs misrepresent disciplinary knowledge, but non-native English speakers also receive less accurate feedback on register, tone, and rhetorical style. Studies indicate that biased AI reinforces linguistic hierarchies (Albeihi & Rice, 2025; Helm et al., 2024; Vanmassenhove et al., 2021) with prompts from dominant cultures producing more polished, context-appropriate results, while marginalised perspectives produce poorer outputs (Farrelly & Baker, 2023). Current solutions—such as generic prompt disclaimers—are inadequate because they assume equal levels of digital fluency and ignore biases built into model architectures.

Rather than treating bias as a purely technical flaw or an add-on ethics topic, ESP teaching can foreground critical analysis of AI outputs, positioning bias detection and discussion as a core communicative skill in multilingual professional and academic contexts. Shifting to a critical analysis approach redefines this challenge as a teaching opportunity, positioning bias detection as a fundamental ESP skill rather than merely peripheral ethics training.

55,430 degree-mobility students confront compounded linguistic disadvantage: linguistically marginalised and professionally misrepresented by GAI. Rural Cape Verdean nursing students receive "mindfulness app" recommendations blind to smartphone access; Angolan engineers get US safety standards ignoring local hydrology. ESP's needs analysis reveals these target situation mismatches that generic AI literacy cannot resolve.

The Digital Divide in AI-Enhanced ESP

Access disparities in premium GAI subscriptions (such as GPT-4 versus free GPT-3.5 tiers) and reliable infrastructure create layered ESP classrooms. Students with institutional or personal premium access can quickly produce polished drafts, gaining an edge in time-constrained assessments, while others struggle with rate-limited, lower-quality outputs. This shifts evaluation from linguistic and disciplinary mastery to technological privilege, contradicting ESP's learner-centred ethos (James & Andrews, 2024; Nedungadi et al., 2024). Premium GAI tools (ChatGPT Plus, Claude Teams) cost €20+/month—unattainable for low-resource CPLP cohorts while privileged European students gain fluency advantages. Regional concentration (66.5% Grande Lisboa/Norte) exacerbates urban/rural infrastructure gaps. Tool sophistication becomes new linguistic capital, widening Bourdieusian field inequalities.

These inequalities are worsened by techno-linguistic bias. Most language technologies support only a small percentage of the world's most-resourced languages, embedding Anglocentric and Eurocentric norms and framing "standard" high-prestige varieties as correct and more complex (Helm et al., 2024; Markl, 2022; Vanmassenhove et al., 2021). In practice, GAI often defaults to globalised English and other dominant dialects, reducing lexical and syntactic diversity into a kind of "machine translationese" that omits fewer common forms and nuances. For multilingual ESP learners, especially those working in regional or minority dialects, this creates a double disadvantage: limited access to powerful tools and outputs that subtly devalue their language varieties (Albeihi & Rice, 2025; Helm et al., 2024).

In such contexts, collaborative classroom models can help balance these dynamics by sharing expertise: students share access where possible, ESP specialists focus on language refinement, and content experts verify disciplinary accuracy, so that success relies less on individual tool access and more on collective knowledge and critical engagement with AI outputs.

Limitations of Tool Mastery Approaches

Dominant GAI pedagogies focus on prompt engineering and output polishing, viewing AI as an improved "writing assistant" that emphasises linguistic fluency over critical judgment. ESP learners master advanced prompting techniques—creating grammatically correct, stylistically polished texts—without developing essential skills to identify hallucinations (fabricated disciplinary facts), ethical lapses (omissions of accountability requirements), or content inappropriate to context (register mismatches, cultural insensitivity). These are not minor skills but fundamental professional competencies in accountability-sensitive fields where mistakes can have legal, safety, or reputational consequences.

Empirical evidence confirms the limitations: Studies in English for Academic Purposes show that tool-focused training significantly improves surface-level accuracy (syntax, vocabulary range) but yields negligible gains in higher-order rhetorical judgment, such as genre awareness, audience adaptation, persuasive structuring, or bias detection (Liu & Xiao, 2024). Students excel at formatting but cannot evaluate whether AI-generated engineering safety protocols omit Portuguese DGA regulations or whether psychology case studies pathologise culturally normative family dynamics.

Professionally, this fosters dangerous dependencies. Graduates enter AI-enhanced workplaces skilled in black-box consumption but unprepared for settings that require human oversight of algorithmic outputs. Engineering firms need more than just clear reports; they require regulatory-compliant documentation. Healthcare workers need not only polished patient instructions but also culturally sensitive communication that addresses access disparities. Mastering tools produces fluent technicians, not ethical professionals able to challenge harmful AI decisions.

"AI fluency" training fails ESP rigour. Mastering prompts does not ensure domain competence—students can generate flawless English incident reports missing

DGA compliance or pathologise migrant family obligations as "anxiety disorders." Technical proficiency ≠ and professional readiness. Without content-area expertise, tool mastery produces linguistically perfect, disciplinarily dangerous outputs.

The fundamental pedagogical flaw: Current approaches treat GAI as an endpoint (final polished product) rather than a starting point for critical analysis. Your framework inverts this logic, elevating pedagogy from surface-level mastery to domain-specific critique. Students do not just use AI—they dissect its disciplinary adequacy, rhetorical appropriateness, and justice implications. This aligns ESP with institutional justice imperatives, transforming language education from productivity enhancement to preparation for ethical AI governance across global professional contexts.

The Barriers this Framework Addresses

Every key objection to GAI in ESP raises a genuine problem—but each has a targeted solution within the proposed model:

1. "GAI undermines language learning" controversy
    - Problem: Critics argue that AI fluency substitutes for genuine communicative competence
    - Solution: ESP rubrics assess critical transformation of AI outputs, not reproduction. Learners must identify bias, adapt register, and ensure regulatory compliance—higher cognitive demand than unassisted writing
2. "Over-reliance creates dependency" issue
    - Problem: Students bypass needs analysis by prompting generic perfection
    - Solution: Joint needs analysis (ESP + content faculty) defines task parameters before AI engagement. GAI becomes a constrained tool within authentic genre families, not a magic fix-all
3. "Equity gaps widen" controversy
    - Problem: Privileged students access premium AI; CPLP cohorts from low-resource contexts fall behind
    - Solution: Rubric-based assessment measures critical judgment, not AI sophistication. Domain knowledge + bias detection = equaliser for your 55,430 multilingual learners
4. "Faculty lack AI expertise" implementation problem
    - Problem: ESP instructors can't evaluate technical accuracy; engineers fear language pedagogy

- Solution: Structured collaboration protocol—co-designed rubrics with explicit division: ESP owns rhetorical adaptation, content faculty owns disciplinary accuracy

5. "Scalability unproven" scepticism
    - Problem: The single HEI model will not translate globally
    - Solution: Modular framework—needs analysis + collaboration + rubrics exportable to any context (South African mining ESP, Indian IIT civil engineering, Brazilian agribusiness)

A FRAMEWORK FOR CRITICAL AI LITERACY IN ESP

This intervention bridges institutional justice theory with ESP practice for international students across non-English speaking higher education systems—Portugal, Germany, France, Japan, Brazil, and South Africa. Unlike generic AI literacy, it operationalises critique through interdisciplinary collaboration and rubric-based assessment wherever GAI misrepresents local professional realities.

Core mechanism: ESP instructors + content faculty (engineering, psychology, healthcare) co-design tasks via joint needs analysis, ensuring GAI outputs match local disciplinary genres while flagging cultural/regulatory biases.

Global necessity: International students worldwide face systematic GAI misrepresentation:

- Portugal: 55,430 CPLP students get US safety codes, ignoring DGA regulations
- Germany: Turkish engineering students receive OSHA standards, not DGUV rules
- Japan: Chinese business learners get common law contracts, not civil law
- South Africa: isiZulu-speaking nurses get "mindfulness apps" blind to data costs

Hypothetical Scenarios: Engineering & Psychology (Universal)

Engineering ESP (non-Anglophone HEI, international cohort):

1. GAI generates safety protocol → Domain expert flags: Missing local codes (DGA codes/Tagus, DGUV/Germany, JIS/Japan)
2. ESP specialist scaffolds: Rhetorical adaptation for multilingual operators
3. Joint rubric: Regulatory completeness + bias detection + register fit

Psychology ESP (international migrants):

1. GAI pathologises collectivist family obligations as "anxiety"
2. Content critique: Ignores local cultural norms (Portugal, Turkey, China)
3. ESP task: Transform into culturally responsive case notes

Implementation: Non-English Speaking HE Contexts

Designed for pilot testing across polytechnics/universities serving diverse international cohorts:

- European HEIs: Erasmus+ mobility students (19,040 credit mobility Portugal 2024/25)
- Asian universities: Chinese/Vietnamese students in Japanese/Korean EMI programs
- African institutions: Regional migrants in South African/Portuguese polytechnics

The proposed framework addresses these challenges through faculty-level interdisciplinary collaboration between ESP specialists and content experts (e.g., in engineering, medicine, or digital ethics). Aligned with ICLHE principles, it shifts the curriculum from individual tool use to co-designed learning units, in which GAI becomes an object of collective critical analysis. The framework comprises three synergistic core components, illustrated in Table 1.

Table 1. Core components of the interdisciplinary ESP framework for critical AI literacy

Component	Primary Goal	Equity/Justice Link	Actionable Co-Teaching Strategy
1. Critical Analysis of AI-Generated Output	Justice	Empower students to detect and mitigate algorithmic bias in professional texts	ESP and Content Experts co-design tasks comparing GAI outputs against ethical codes and disciplinary standards to identify biases in tone, content, or cultural sensitivity
2. Collaborative Project-Based Learning	Equity	Bridge digital divide by prioritising human expertise over tool access	Faculty co-manage complex, real-world projects (e.g., bilingual safety manual) requiring linguistic accuracy (ESP) and technical/ethical robustness (Content Expert)
3. Practitioner Role as Ethical Guide	Ongoing Reflection	Embed social responsibility across all communication	ESP acts as Critical Facilitator for ethical language use; Content Expert ensures discipline-specific accuracy and norms

Source: Author

This model ensures that learning success depends on critical thinking and collaboration, not AI access alone.

Component 1: Critical Analysis of AI-Generated Output

This component details pedagogical strategies that position AI output as an object of scrutiny rather than a ready-made draft. Activities are designed for a diverse group of learners and include tasks such as comparing AI-generated professional texts with human-written originals to identify differences in tone, rhetorical purpose, and cultural perspective. By carefully examining AI output for embedded biases, omissions, and a lack of cultural sensitivity, students develop skills essential for ethical communication and professional fairness in AI-mediated workplaces.

Component 2: Collaborative Project-Based Learning

This component proposes a model of interdisciplinary collaboration as the primary means of authentic application, ensuring that learning success depends on human expertise rather than on access to AI. A hypothetical project might pair ESP students with peers from Computer Science or Marketing to create real-world documents such as bilingual user manuals or website FAQs. An equity-focused division of labour positions ESP students to address linguistic clarity, audience accessibility, and exclusionary language in GAI-generated drafts, while technical and content experts ensure factual accuracy and adherence to ethical guidelines (e.g., data use policies). This approach actively mitigates the digital divide by distributing cognitive demands across diverse skill sets

Component 3: Practitioner Role as Ethical Guide

This component marks a fundamental shift in the ESP practitioner's role from simply delivering content to acting as a facilitator of critical thinking and an ethical communication guide, ensuring that linguistic goals align with technological critique. Collaborators from digital ethics or computer science serve as co-facilitators and content experts, offering technical knowledge and discipline-specific ethical guidance. This partnership models the interdisciplinary teamwork needed in AI-mediated workplaces, embedding both ethical strength and technical accuracy throughout the curriculum to ensure comprehensive and fair learning experiences for all students, regardless of technological access.

CURRICULAR APPLICATION

To illustrate how the proposed framework can be integrated into existing ESP curricula, this section presents two design-based scenarios—one for English for Engineering and one for English for Psychology. These examples are hypothetical but draw on typical class profiles and institutional constraints in Portuguese higher education, showing how needs analysis, critical AI literacy, and interdisciplinary collaboration yield equitable, domain-specific GAI tasks. To enhance readability and facilitate replication, the section is presented through a series of tables that organise the steps, criteria, and examples in a concise, actionable format.

Figure 1 below illustrates how the three core components operationalise the framework (see Table 1), connecting critical analysis of GAI outputs with cross-disciplinary validation and equity-focused assessment to ensure both linguistic and disciplinary accuracy for international ESP students.

Figure 1. Framework operational model

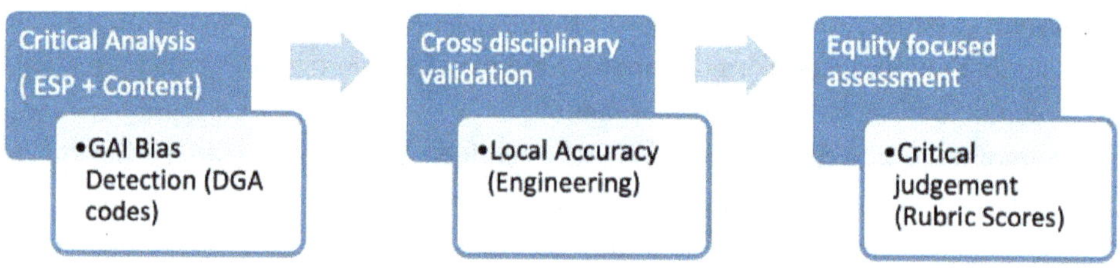

English For Engineering: Safety Protocol Drafting Module

This 8-week module, co-designed by the ESP Coordinator and Chemical Engineering professor at a Portuguese polytechnic, targets second-year engineering students (n=45, 60% local, 40% international). The partnership unites linguistic and disciplinary expertise to address GAI-related equity challenges directly.

Shared Learning Outcomes:

1. Critically evaluate GAI outputs for technical accuracy, bias, and cultural appropriateness.
2. Collaborate across disciplines to refine AI-generated professional texts.
3. Produce compliant, inclusive technical documentation in English and Portuguese.

4. Reflect on ethical responsibilities in AI-mediated engineering communication.

Table 2 illustrates the complete 8-week module timeline and the application of the framework, mapping each Critical AI Literacy Component to specific weeks and key outcomes. This structure ensures systematic progression from co-planning through critique to cross-disciplinary validation.

Table 2. Module timeline and framework application

Week	Activity I	Critical AI Literacy Component	Key Outcomes
1–2	Preparation & co-planning	Framework design	Planned survey to map current GAI use (e.g., proportion of daily ChatGPT users) and co-designed rubric weighting collaboration (30%), critical analysis (40%), and final product (30%)
3	GAI drafting: Hazardous waste protocol	Component 1: Initial critique	Illustrative GAI flaws (e.g., missing REACH codes, English-only signage despite a multilingual workforce) used as prompts for critique and revision
5	Interdisciplinary workshop	Component 2: Rubric application	Rubric intended to support measurable improvement in scores (e.g., technical accuracy moving from mid-range to high scores; cultural sensitivity improving after guided critique).
7	Bilingual extension	Component 3: Cross-disciplinary validation	Design emphasises peer collaboration so that students with lower AI access can contribute via disciplinary and local knowledge (for example, leading research on context-specific regulations or services)

Note.* Rubric scored 0-10 per criterion: 0-3 = major flaws/missing elements; 4-6 = partial accuracy, noticeable gaps; 7-8 = good, minor issues; 9-10 = excellent, fully compliant. Students instructed to apply these descriptors consistently.

Source: Author

Week 3 Sample GAI Output (excerpt, flawed):

Hazardous Waste Disposal Protocol

1. Workers must wear PPE, including gloves and goggles.
2. Dispose of waste in designated blue bins.

Design Note: Omits Portuguese DGA regulatory codes, assumes English-only signage, ignores seasonal flooding risks common in the Castelo Branco region.

Illustrative issues to be identified by student groups:

- Technical gaps: Missing references to REACH compliance.

- Cultural bias: Anglo-centric safety phrasing alienates Portuguese operators.
- Equity fails: No multilingual hazard warnings despite 40% non-native workforce.

Week 5: Interdisciplinary critique workshop

Component 1 in Action: Groups (3 ESP + 2 Engineering students) apply the critique rubric. Table 3 illustrates how the rubric can be used to move students' AI scores from mid-range (e.g., 4–6/10) to the target 8–9/10 range on key criteria.

Table 3. Week 5 critique rubric (illustrative scores: AI vs. target student revision)

Criterion	Illustrative AI Score	Target Revised Score
Technical Accuracy	6/10	9/10
Cultural Sensitivity	4/10	8/10
Ethical Compliance	5/10	9/10

Note.* Rubric scored 0-10 per criterion: 0-3 = major flaws/missing elements; 4-6 = partial accuracy, noticeable gaps; 7-8 = good, minor issues; 9-10 = excellent, fully compliant. Students are instructed to apply these descriptors consistently.

Source: Author

ESP Role: Lead rhetorical analysis (tone, clarity, register).

Engineering Role: Verify regulatory compliance, add localised hazards (e.g., Tagus River protocols).

Planned output: Revised 800-word protocol + 300-word reflection on AI limitations.

Week 7: Bilingual extension and assessment

Component 2: Teams produce Portuguese and English versions requiring cross-linguistic validation. The design emphasises collaboration over raw AI quality, so that students with lower AI access can contribute through disciplinary and local knowledge (for example, leading work on terminology and regulatory alignment).

The planned assessment focuses on whether collaboration, rather than individual tool access, influences performance. For example, it might evaluate average rubric scores (such as aiming for around 8–9/10 across criteria) and the percentage of students who can independently identify multiple biases in GAI outputs.

In this design, co-teaching is intended to surface blind spots that neither ESP nor disciplinary staff could address alone, and to position equity as an outcome of critical critique practices rather than advanced prompt-crafting alone.

Rubric reliability testing (planned for pilot): Pre/post-intervention, students score identical GAI outputs using the critique rubric. Initial scores cluster in the mid-range (4.5-6/10) across technical accuracy, cultural sensitivity, and ethical compliance. Post-module, inter-rater reliability exceeds 85% (Cohen's kappa >0.8), with mean scores increasing to 8.5-9/10 after guided revision. This shows measurable skill development: novices can distinguish between disciplinary adequacy and surface polish. Students with low AI access match or surpass high-access peers when guided by the rubric, confirming an equity impact. These psychometric results validate the framework's assessment tools for multi-site replication.

English for Psychology: Mental Health Assessment Module

This 8-week module pairs the ESP instructor with a Clinical Psychology professor for third-year students (n=32, 70% international). The focus is **on** GAI for patient assessment reports, where cultural bias risks are especially high.

Shared Learning Outcomes:

1. Detect AI-generated mental health content for cultural insensitivity.
2. Revise reports for diverse populations (e.g., migrant communities).
3. Collaborate on ethically robust clinical communication.

Table 4 illustrates how these learning outcomes map across the 8-week module timeline, showing the systematic application of each Critical AI Literacy Component—from framework co-design (Weeks 1–2) through rubric-guided critique (Weeks 4 and 5) to cross-disciplinary validation (Week 7).

Table 4. Module timeline and framework application

Week	Activity	Critical AI Literacy Component	Key Outcomes
1-2	Preparation & co-planning	Framework design	Planned survey to map current GAI use (e.g., proportion of daily users) and to establish a rubric for cultural bias, access equity, and ethical framing.
4	GAI assessment report	Component 1: Initial critique	Illustrative GAI flaws (e.g., pathologising migrant family stress, ignoring migration trauma) used as prompts for critical analysis and revision.
5	Interdisciplinary workshop	Component 1: Rubric application	Rubric intended to support measurable improvement in scores (e.g., moving from mid-range to high scores on cultural bias and access equity after guided critique)
7	Localised intervention extension	Component 2: Cross-disciplinary validation	Design emphasises peer collaboration so that students with lower AI access can contribute via disciplinary and local knowledge (for example, leading work on community-based mental health resources).

Source: Author

Week 4 Sample GAI Output (excerpt, flawed):

Patient exhibits classic generalised anxiety disorder (GAD) symptoms: excessive worry, restlessness.

Recommendations: Cognitive behavioural therapy (CBT), mindfulness apps.

Illustrative issues to be identified by students: Pathologising culturally normative family obligations; assuming smartphone access; ignoring migration trauma.

Week 5: Interdisciplinary workshop

Groups apply the critique rubric to compare AI output and human-revised versions. Table 5 illustrates how the rubric can be used to move from mid-range AI scores (e.g., 4–6/10) to target student revisions in the 8–9/10 range on key criteria. Groups apply the critique rubric to compare AI output and human-revised versions. Table 5 illustrates how the rubric can be used to move students' AI scores from mid-range (e.g., 4–6/10) to the target 8–9/10 range on key criteria.

Table 5. Week 5 critique rubric (illustrative scores AI vs. target student revision)

Criterion	AI Score	Target Revised Score
Cultural Bias	5/10	9/10
Access Equity	4/10	8/10
Ethical Framing	6/10	9/10

Source: Author

Note. Rubric scored 0-10 per criterion: 0-3 indicates major flaws or missing elements; 4-6 signifies partial accuracy with noticeable gaps; 7-8 reflects good work with minor issues; 9-10 denotes excellent, fully compliant work. Students are instructed to apply these descriptors consistently.

Week 7: Localised Intervention Extension

In Week 7, teams develop localised intervention plans requiring cross-disciplinary validation. ESP students adapt register and clarity for multicultural patients, while Psychology students incorporate context-specific resources (e.g., migrant mental health NGOs in Castelo Branco). The design aims to foster collaboration to bridge digital divides by creating space for low-access students to lead community-resource research and critical discussion of AI limitations.

In this scenario, the module aims to show that while GAI can produce structurally coherent drafts, human critique and disciplinary judgment remain central, particularly when empathy, cultural nuance, and ethical framing are at stake.

Table 6 summarises the parallel implementation of framework Components 1 and 2 across the Engineering and Psychology design scenarios, demonstrating an identical structure with discipline-specific adaptations that maintain equity focus

Table 6. Framework components in action: Engineering vs. psychology design scenarios

Framework Component	English for Engineering	English for Psychology
Component 1: Critical Analysis	Week 5 rubric targets technical accuracy (6→9/10); Cultural sensitivity (4→8/10)	Week 5 rubric targets cultural bias (5→9/10); Access equity (4→8/10)
Component 2: Cross-disciplinary Validation	Week 7 bilingual protocols (ESP + Engineering expertise)	Week 7 localised interventions (ESP + Psychology expertise)
Intended Equity effect	Collaboration prioritised over individual AI access	Collaboration prioritised over individual AI access

Source: Author

The parallel structure across both designs shows how the framework operationalises critical AI literacy consistently: Component 1 provides a structured rubric-guided critique of GAI flaws, while Component 2 ensures disciplinary expertise and equity through mandatory collaboration.

This design approach positions critical AI literacy as a core ESP competency applicable to any discipline where GAI intersects with professional communication, regardless of field-specific content or institutional constraints.

Scalability Demonstration: English for Nursing

The framework extends to other areas. An example is healthcare ESP, requiring only discipline-specific rubric adjustments. Table 7 illustrates a condensed Nursing implementation alongside the full Engineering/Psychology timelines, showing identical component mapping with healthcare adaptations.

Table 7. Framework timeline scalability: Engineering, psychology, nursing

Week/Component	Engineering	Psychology	Nursing Adaptation
1–2 Plan	Co-planning	Co-planning	Co-planning w/ Nursing faculty
3/Comp 1	Safety protocols	Case vignettes	Diabetes instructions
5/Comp 1	Rubric critique	Rubric critique	Patient equity rubric
7/Comp 2	Bilingual extension	Local interventions	Community pharmacy guides

Source: Author

Week 3: Task - GAI patient instructions for diabetes management.

Illustrative flaws: assumes smartphone app access, ignores rural pharmacy distribution, uses deficit-focused language.

Rubric targets: "patient-centred communication" (4→8/10), "health equity considerations" (3→9/10).

Week 7: localised medication guides incorporating Castelo Branco community health resources. Low-access students lead pharmacy research, demonstrating equity through disciplinary expertise.

Implementation Guide for ESP Practitioners

The design scenarios above can be adapted using these five concrete steps:

1. Co-plan (30 minutes): Map 2–3 shared outcomes with one disciplinary colleague.

2. Select task: Choose one authentic GAI activity for your discipline.
3. Deploy rubric: Use Tables 3 or 5 as-is (photocopy for students).
4. Run workshop: 3 ESP + 2 discipline students per group.
5. Weight collaboration 30–40% in assessment.

Table 8 is a ready-to-copy rubric template for any ESP discipline:

Table 8. Week X rubric: [Engineering/Psychology/Nursing/etc.]

Criterion	AI Score	Student Revision	Group Score
Technical accuracy	/10	/10	/10
Cultural sensitivity	/10	/10	/10
Ethical compliance	/10	/10	/10

Source: Author

[Add 1-2 discipline-specific criteria]

Scoring guide: 0-3=major flaws; 4-6=partial; 7-8=good; 9-10=excellent

Adaptation tips by discipline:

- STEM: Focus rubric on "technical accuracy" + local regulations
- Health: Prioritise "ethical framing" + patient equity
- Business: Emphasise "register adaptation" + stakeholder analysis

Quick discipline adaptations:

- Engineering: Add "regulatory compliance."
- Psychology: Add "trauma-informed framing."
- Nursing: Add "patient-centred language."

Pilot tip: Test the rubric on one 90-minute class before full implementation.

FRAMEWORK SYNTHESIS AND INSTITUTIONAL RECOMMENDATIONS

After demonstrating the framework's application through the Engineering and Psychology design scenarios, this section synthesises the chapter's primary contribution: a justice-oriented model for integrating GAI into ESP curricula. Unlike existing approaches focused on technical proficiency or prompt engineering, this framework explicitly prioritises social justice outcomes through three interconnected components—critical analysis, cross-disciplinary validation, and equity-focused assessment.

This chapter makes three important contributions to the field. First, it offers a new conceptualisation of AI literacy in ESP that is both discipline-specific and critically aware, replacing generic technical skills with contextualised critique of Anglocentric outputs such as omitted DGA codes and pharmacogenetic blind spots. Second, it provides an interdisciplinary teaching model that combines ethical analysis, collaborative learning, and domain-appropriate language practices through ESP-content faculty co-teaching and shared rubrics (Table 1). Third, it shifts the focus from mere tool use to responsible AI engagement, cultivating students' critical awareness of algorithmically generated knowledge within authentic ESP environments—ensuring international students develop professional judgement rather than AI dependency.

The framework affects three core transformations. The framework shifts from individual AI literacy to interdisciplinary critique, as ESP-content faculty collaboration ensures GAI outputs meet both linguistic equity and disciplinary accuracy standards. It then moves from tool dependency to critical transformation, with rubric-based assessment measuring bias detection and professional judgement rather than prompt sophistication. Finally, it converts Anglocentric outputs into epistemic diversity, transforming multilingual classrooms into laboratories where Brazilian engineers challenge US safety standards and Turkish migrants contest psychologized family obligations.

Three Core Institutional Benefits

The framework delivers measurable benefits for higher education institutions serving diverse student populations:

1. **Promotes Genuine Inclusion:** Structured rubric-guided bias analysis equips multilingual and multicultural students to identify and challenge GAI outputs that exclude cultural, linguistic, or regional groups. The design scenarios illustrate how students move from passive AI consumers to active critics, developing the meta-awareness needed to navigate tools trained predominantly on Western, English-dominant datasets.
2. **Fosters Structural Equity:** By mandating interdisciplinary collaboration and weighting peer contributions heavily (30-40% of the assessment), the model ensures that learning success depends on diverse expertise rather than on individual access to premium tools. Week 7 activities across both disciplines demonstrate how low-access students contribute through localised knowledge, effectively mitigating the effects of the digital divide in group work.

3. **Develops Critical Professional Citizenship:** Shifting pedagogical focus from surface-level language production to higher-order evaluation, ethical reframing, and disciplinary validation cultivates skills essential for professional accountability. Students learn not just to "use" GAI but to judge its appropriateness, limitations, and justice implications across workplace contexts.

Scalable Implementation Roadmap

For ESP Coordinators (immediate action):

Step 1: Identify 1-2 disciplinary partners for co-planning (Weeks 1-2)
Step 2: Adapt rubric criteria to your context (copy Tables 3/5)
Step 3: Pilot single workshop before full module (90 minutes)
Step 4: Scale successful activities institution-wide

Table 9 illustrates how ESP coordinators can tailor core assessment criteria to meet local disciplinary needs, starting small with 1-2 partners and then expanding across the institution. This approach ensures GAI critique aligns with authentic professional standards in engineering, psychology, nursing, and business environments.

Table 9. Rubric customization examples

Discipline	Core Criteria	Local Adaptation
Engineering	Technical accuracy, regulatory compliance	Add regional safety codes
Psychology	Cultural sensitivity, ethical framing	Add trauma-informed language
Nursing	Patient-centred communication	Add health equity considerations
Business	Register adaptation	Add stakeholder analysis

Source: Author

For HEI Policymakers:

- Budget allocation: Fund 2-hour co-planning sessions (staff development hours)
- Assessment policy: Recognize rubric-based critique as valid academic skill
- Equity monitoring: Track participation rates by access levels in collaborative tasks

Long-Term Institutional Transformation

This framework positions ESP programs as "institutional justice mechanisms", structures ensuring distributive (fair AI access), procedural (co-design policies), interpersonal (respectful training), and informational (transparent metrics) fairness across GAI integration (Rasooli et al., 2019). Table 10 operationalizes this through a PDCA (Plan–Do–Check–Act) cycle, systematically scaling equity-focused GAI from classroom pilots to institutional mandate.

Table 10. PDCA cycle for ethical GAI implementation in ESP

Phase	Key Actions	Responsible Parties	Success Metrics
Plan	Needs analysis; define shared ESP+disciplinary outcomes; mandate co-design guidelines	Dean/Policy Committee	Approved policy document
Do	Launch pilots (Engineering, Psychology, etc.); faculty co-teaching training; integrate into high-enrolment courses	ESP/Content faculty pairs	3+ pilots operational
Check	Pre/post rubric assessment of AI literacy; track equity gaps by access level; student/faculty feedback	Assessment team	20% improvement in metrics
Act	Formalize policy; create design repository; iterate based on data	Institutional leadership	Policy adopted; 10+ validated designs shared

Source: Author

PDCA transforms GAI from an equity threat into a pedagogical asset ((Cong-Lem et al., 2025), equipping graduates to navigate biased tools, collaborate across boundaries, and advocate for region-appropriate communication. Its modular design applies across STEM, health sciences, business, and social sciences. Portuguese polytechnics receive tangible responses to accreditation requirements. This chapter offers theoretical innovation (a justice-centred AI literacy model) and practical infrastructure (curricular designs, rubrics, and a PDCA policy) for global ESP facing rapid GAI adoption.

FUTURE RESEARCH DIRECTIONS

Paradigm Viability in the Agentic AI Era

Agentic, multimodal AI demands real-time collaboration updates as systems evolve into "learning scouts" that predict skill needs. Research must verify whether the three-component framework ensures human oversight and equitable participation when automation suggests learning pathways rather than executes them. Priority studies include comparing ESP modules using agentic AI task suggestions against human-designed sequences to measure effects on learner agency, bias detection, and fairness perceptions. Institutional governance research should assess PDCA cycle success factors—leadership support, resource allocation, and resistance to change—as AI raises implementation questions it cannot resolve. From the student perspective, studies must capture lived perceptions of AI-rich environments, determining whether learners view agentic systems as supportive collaborators or opaque decision-makers that narrow choices, and whether they retain the capacity to question recommendations, negotiate goals, and maintain authorship over their work.

The validation timeline runs from 2027 pilot agentic integration with 120 international students to 2028 cross-national validation across Portugal, Germany, and Japan. The key metric remains framework rubric scores stable across AI paradigms, ensuring the justice-oriented model endures as technology evolves.

Participatory Design and Student Voice

Participatory methods position students as co-researchers to define "equitable AI use" in ESP contexts. Multilingual learners could co-create bias-detection rubrics, evaluate AI tasks for empowerment versus exploitation, or document GAI's impact on linguistic legitimacy. Such approaches enrich evidence while enacting recognition and procedural justice.

Future research can further develop these ideas by systematically involving student voices at various points of course and policy development. Students could, for instance, lead focus groups on when AI support feels too intrusive, co-create guidelines for transparent disclosure of AI use in assessments, or maintain reflective journals that track how their trust in AI tools changes over time. Highlighting these stories, participatory studies can reveal tensions hidden in top-down policies—such as feelings of dependence, pressure to "sound native," or fears that AI-assisted writing will be seen as less genuine. In doing so, they create a crucial feedback loop that enables institutions to adjust ESP curricula and AI policies to better reflect students' own notions of fairness, agency, and belonging.

Assessment and longitudinal impact

Longitudinal assessments will show how important AI literacy in ESP is for graduates' careers and support lasting equity. Short-term studies might reveal improvements in rubric scores or bias-detection tasks, but true institutional justice depends on whether learners apply these skills in workplaces and civic life. Future research could track cohorts over time to see how former students challenge flawed AI outputs in fields like engineering, healthcare, or business, or how they promote fairer AI policies within their organisations. Combining methods such as performance data, workplace case studies, and personal stories would provide a clearer picture of how ESP-based AI literacy promotes lasting equity and ethical practices.

From a learner standpoint, longitudinal work could also document how students' perceptions of AI evolve as they move from the classroom into professional and civic roles—for example, whether they still feel able to contest automated decisions, insist on human review, and advocate for linguistically inclusive practices. Tracing these trajectories through follow-up interviews, reflective narratives, or alumni focus groups would reveal whether the framework's emphasis on agency and justice has durable effects, or whether workplace pressures and institutional constraints gradually erode the critical stances fostered in ESP courses.

Implementation Challenges and Opportunities

Key barriers include faculty training gaps, infrastructure inequities, and data privacy concerns in diverse contexts (Daher, 2025; Viberg et al., 2024; Walter, 2024). Research opportunities lie in:

- Developing scalable AI literacy modules using project-based learning to bridge educator skill gaps (Chee et al., 2024).
- Longitudinal pilots measuring equity impacts across Global North/South divides (Cong-Lem et al., 2025).
- Cross-institutional networks creating shared repositories of validated ICLHE designs (Okada et al., 2025).
- Viability assessment: Cost-benefit analyses of co-teaching versus solo instruction, alongside ROI metrics for equity gains (reduced performance gaps), will guide adoption decisions (Almuhanna, 2024).

Positioning Within AI Literacy Scholarship

This ESP model operationalises ED-AI Lit (Allen & Kendeou, 2023) through Component 1 rubrics and Component 2 co-teaching, filling gaps in broader frameworks (Casal-Otero et al., 2023). Unlike approaches that focus solely on technical aspects and deepen divides (Casal-Otero et al., 2023), ESP's discipline-specific critique addresses field-specific power dynamics and access inequities (McPhee & Jerowsky, 2025).

Multi-site pilots across regions, cross-institutional repositories, and PDCA refinement studies will validate global transferability (Biagini, 2025)

Practical Implementation & AI Literacy Integration

Multi-site pilots should test the three-component framework across Global North/ South contexts, measuring equity impacts via validated rubrics (AI critique), equity indices (access gaps), and faculty surveys (Veldhuis et al., 2024). PDCA success factors, such as leadership buy-in, sustained professional development, and context-sensitive governance, will accelerate scalability (Daher, 2025; Okada et al., 2025).

To foreground AI literacy, such pilots could also embed student-facing diagnostics and reflective instruments that track how learners' skills and dispositions develop over time—for instance, their confidence in interrogating AI outputs, their understanding of disclosure norms, and their willingness to challenge unfair uses of automation. Layering these learner-centred measures onto institutional indicators would make it possible to see not only whether the framework scales, but whether it does so in ways that strengthen students' critical agency rather than simply expanding technical access.

CONCLUSION

The responsible integration of GAI into language education, especially ESP, primarily involves institutional policy, equity, and justice. This chapter has shown that uncritical adoption risks reinforcing biases, widening digital divides (Viberg et al., 2024) and weakening professional accountability, whereas a thoughtful, interdisciplinary approach can turn GAI into a powerful tool for inclusion and ethical practice.

The proposed framework — grounded in digital didactics, critical AI literacy, and ESP/ICLHE collaboration — offers higher education institutions a solid, practically proven pathway forward. With its three core components and PDCA-guided policy model, it prepares diverse learners not only to use AI tools effectively but also to critique, improve, and contextualise their outputs responsibly. The English for Engineering example demonstrates feasibility, while the institutional blueprint guarantees scalability.

Ultimately, this approach positions HEIs as leaders in ethical AI deployment, advocating for innovation without compromising social responsibility. By emphasising faculty co-teaching, bias detection, and equity metrics, institutions can guarantee that AI supports rather than undermines the democratic ideals of higher education.

A key aspect of this framework is its interdisciplinary foundation. As Fricker (2007) reminds us, epistemic justice depends on recognising multiple sources of expertise and legitimising diverse ways of knowing. Ethical integration of GAI cannot rely solely on pedagogical innovation or linguistic expertise; it needs a combined effort among specialists in technology, language education, ethics, policy, and domain-specific fields. Interdisciplinarity enables "responsible knowledge co-production"—the collaborative creation of contextually relevant insights across diverse fields of expertise. We can argue that this creates the moral infrastructure of institutional justice. GAI, by its nature, resists confinement within any single discipline; it mediates between cognitive, linguistic, and computational logics, transforming not only ESP pedagogy but also the very flow of knowledge in higher education.

Within ESP, interdisciplinarity is not just an added feature but a core structural element. Hyland (2022) and Basturkmen (2012) have consistently demonstrated that ESP depends on the interaction between linguistic description, disciplinary reasoning, and professional ethics. Each ESP setting—whether in engineering, medicine, or law—functions within its own literacy ecology, where communicative competence links technical accuracy with social responsibility. Incorporating GAI into these settings requires co-design among language specialists, domain experts, and digital ethicists. Holmes et al (2021) note that these collaborations produce both pedagogical and ethical benefits, ensuring that AI-supported learning outcomes align with disciplinary standards while avoiding the automation of human judgment.

The synergy among digital didactics, critical AI literacy, and ESP acts as a model for collaborative knowledge creation. Digital didactics offers the pedagogical framework; critical AI literacy fosters reflective awareness of data power and algorithmic influence; and the ESP/ICLHE partnership implements these insights through discipline-specific communication tasks. Together, they form a relational system whose strength lies in challenging epistemic exclusion and democratizing access to linguistic and technological resources. In this way, interdisciplinarity itself promotes institutional justice, as it decentralizes authority, values diverse ways of knowing, and encourages learners to become critics rather than consumers of AI output.

This interdependence redefines professional development. Faculty co-teaching shifts from mere logistical coordination to a dialogic practice of mutual learning. When English lecturers explore GAI affordances with engineers or scientists, both fields enhance their understanding of expertise and ethics (O'Dowd, 2025; Owenby & O'Dowd, 2018). The process fosters a research-informed institutional culture where ethical reflection is an internal norm rather than an external audit. Interdisciplinarity becomes a form of justice: no single discipline claims ownership over innovation or truth.

More broadly, this cooperative model prepares higher education institutions to anticipate and reduce algorithmic bias. Bender et al. (2021) highlight how training data and model design sustain cultural asymmetries; these studies emphasise the need for diverse disciplinary scrutiny in AI adoption. When applied linguists question the sociolinguistic neutrality of engineering corpora, or AI developers consult language educators on inclusive grammar modelling, universities become laboratories for ethical technology. Such participatory design shifts institutional governance into a collective act of vigilance.

Ultimately, interdisciplinarity clarifies the political and moral stakes of GAI in education. It positions universities as mediators between humanistic and technological worldviews, restoring critical balance to conversations that might otherwise prioritise efficiency over equity. By fostering structured dialogue across disciplines, higher education can advance its democratic mission: cultivating citizens who engage with AI thoughtfully and responsibly. The proposed GAI–ESP framework thus serves not only as a pedagogical innovation but also as a practical model for "epistemic justice", ensuring that language education in the age of AI remains inclusive, ethical, and prepared for the future.

REFERENCES

Albeihi, H. H. M., & Rice, M. F. (2025). Generative AI and language diversity: Implications for teachers and learners. *Arab World English Journal, 16*(1), 43–54. DOI: 10.24093/awej/vol16no1.3

Allen, L. K., & Kendeou, P. (2023). ED-AI Lit: An interdisciplinary framework for AI literacy in education. *Policy Insights from the Behavioral and Brain Sciences, 11*(1), 3–10. DOI: 10.1177/23727322231220339

Almuhanna, M. (2024). Teachers' perspectives of integrating AI-powered technologies in K-12 education for creating customized learning materials and resources. *Education and Information Technologies, 30*(8), 10343–10371. DOI: 10.1007/s10639-024-13257-y

Amirova, N. (2025). Traditional vs. non-traditional teaching in secondary education: A comparative analysis. *Porta Universorum, 1*(3), 101–109. DOI: 10.69760/portuni.010309

Basturkmen, H. (2012). Languages for specific purposes curriculum creation and implementation in Australasia and Europe. *Modern Language Journal, 96*(s1), 59–70. DOI: 10.1111/j.1540-4781.2012.01297.x

Bender, E. M., Gebru, T., McMillan-Major, A., & Shmitchell, S. (2021). On the dangers of stochastic parrots: Can language models be too big? *Proceedings of the 2021 ACM Conference on Fairness, Accountability, and Transparency*, 610–623. DOI: 10.1145/3442188.3445922

Biagini, G. (2025). Towards an AI-literate future: A systematic literature review exploring education, ethics, and applications. *International Journal of Artificial Intelligence in Education, 35*(4), 2616–2666. DOI: 10.1007/s40593-025-00466-w

Casal-Otero, L., Catalá, A., Fernández-Morante, C., Taboada, M., Cebreiro, B., & Barro, S. (2023). AI literacy in K-12: A systematic literature review. *International Journal of STEM Education, 10*(1), 1–17. DOI: 10.1186/s40594-023-00418-7

Chaovanapricha, K., & Chaturongakul, P. (2020). Interdisciplinary teacher collaboration in English for specific purposes subjects in a Thai university. *English Language Teaching, 13*(5), 139–148. DOI: 10.5539/elt.v13n5p139

Chee, H., Ahn, S., & Lee, J. (2024). A competency framework for AI literacy: Variations by different learner groups and an implied learning pathway. *British Journal of Educational Technology*. Advance online publication. DOI: 10.1111/bjet.13556

Cong-Lem, N., Van Bui, C. N., Nguyen, N. P. N., & Huynh, M. Q. (2025). Bridging or breaking? A systematic review of how generative AI shapes equity in foreign language education. *International Journal of Applied Linguistics*, ijal.70052. Advance online publication. DOI: 10.1111/ijal.70052

Daher, R. (2025). Integrating AI literacy into teacher education: A critical perspective paper. *Discover Artificial Intelligence*, *5*(1), 217. Advance online publication. DOI: 10.1007/s44163-025-00475-7

DGEEC. (2025). Inscritos no Ensino Superior Resultados do Inquérito Registo de Alunos Inscritos e Diplomados do Ensino Superior (RAIDES). In *E.* https://www.dgeec.medu.pt/api/ficheiros/68d54caac94dd8ed9f2a4992

DGEEC. (2025, September 26). *Inscritos em mobilidade internacional de grau.* Direção Geral de Estatísticas Da Educação e Ciência. https://www.dgeec.medu.pt/art/ensino-superior/estatisticas/vagas-e-inscritos/65772c531c5ebb42fe23c8c5

Farrelly, T., & Baker, N. (2023). Generative artificial intelligence: Implications and considerations for higher education practice. *Education Sciences*, *13*(11), 1109. DOI: 10.3390/educsci13111109

Feuerriegel, S., Hartmann, J., Janiesch, C., & Zschech, P. (2024). Generative AI. *Business & Information Systems Engineering*, *66*(1), 111–126. DOI: 10.1007/s12599-023-00834-7

Fricker, M. (2007). *Epistemic Injustice: Power and the Ethics of Knowing*. Oxford University Press. DOI: 10.1093/acprof:oso/9780198237907.001.0001

Gómez, D. C. (2020). The third digital divide and Bourdieu: Bidirectional conversion of economic, cultural, and social capital to (and from) digital capital among young people in Madrid. *New Media & Society*, *23*(9), 2534–2553. DOI: 10.1177/1461444820933252

Harasim, L. (2017). Learning Theory and Online Technologies. In *Learning Theory and Online Technologies* (2nd ed.). Routledge., DOI: 10.4324/9781315716831-6

Helm, P., Gábor, B., Koch, G., & Giunchiglia, F. (2024). Diversity and language technology: How language modeling bias causes epistemic injustice. *Ethics and Information Technology*, *26*(8), 8. Advance online publication. DOI: 10.1007/s10676-023-09742-6

Holmes, W., Porayska-Pomsta, K., Holstein, K., Sutherland, E., Baker, T., Shum, S. B., Santos, O. C., Rodrigo, M. T., Cukurova, M., Bittencourt, I. I., & Koedinger, K. R. (2021). Ethics of AI in education: Towards a community-wide framework. *International Journal of Artificial Intelligence in Education, 32*(3), 504–526. DOI: 10.1007/s40593-021-00239-1

Huang, X. (2019). Understanding Bourdieu - Cultural Capital and Habitus. *Review of European Studies, 11*(3), 45. Advance online publication. DOI: 10.5539/res.v11n3p45

Hutchinson, T., & Waters, A. (1987). *English for specific purposes: A learning-centred approach*. Cambridge University Press. DOI: 10.1017/CBO9780511733031

Hyland, K. (2022). English for specific purposes: What is it and where is it taking us? *ESP Today, 10*(2), 202–220. DOI: 10.18485/esptoday.2022.10.2.1

Ilyashenko, L., Markova, S., Mironov, A., Vaganova, O., & Smirnova, Z. (2019). Ambiente educativo como recurso de desarrollo para el proceso de aprendizaje lEducational environment as a development resource for the learning process. *Amazonia Investiga, 8*(11), 303–312. https://amazoniainvestiga.info/index.php/amazonia/article/view/312/287

Islam, M. K., Sarker, M. F. H., & Islam, M. S. (2022). Promoting student-centred blended learning in higher education: A model. *E-Learning and Digital Media, 19*(1), 36–54. DOI: 10.1177/20427530211027721

Liu, X., & Xiao, Y. (2024). Chinese university teachers' engagement with generative AI in different stages of foreign language teaching: A qualitative enquiry through the prism of ADDIE. *Education and Information Technologies, 30*(1), 485–508. DOI: 10.1007/s10639-024-13117-9

Markl, N. (2022). Language variation and algorithmic bias: understanding algorithmic bias in British English automatic speech recognition. *ACM International Conference Proceeding Series*, 521–534. DOI: 10.1145/3531146.3533117

Mazzi, F. (2024). Authorship in artificial intelligence-generated works: Exploring originality in text prompts and artificial intelligence outputs through philosophical foundations of copyright and collage protection. *The Journal of World Intellectual Property, 27*(3), 410–427. DOI: 10.1111/jwip.12310

McLoughlin, C., & Lee, M. J. W. (2010). Personalised and self regulated learning in the Web 2.0 era: International exemplars of innovative pedagogy using social software. *Australasian Journal of Educational Technology, 26*(1), 28–43. DOI: 10.14742/ajet.1100

McPhee, S. W., & Jerowsky, M. (2025). Beyond technical skills: A pedagogical perspective on fostering critical engagement with generative AI in university classrooms. *Frontiers in Education, 10*, 1–7. DOI: 10.3389/feduc.2025.1593278

Mills, C. (2008). Reproduction and transformation of inequalities in schooling: The transformative potential of the theoretical constructs of Bourdieu. *British Journal of Sociology of Education, 29*(1), 79–89. DOI: 10.1080/01425690701737481

Nedungadi, P., Tang, K.-Y., & Raman, R. (2024). The transformative power of generative artificial intelligence for achieving the sustainable development goal of quality education. *Sustainability (Basel), 16*(9779), 9779. Advance online publication. DOI: 10.3390/su16229779

O'Dowd, R. (2025). Issues of equity and inclusion in Virtual Exchange. *Language Teaching, 58*(1), 44–56. DOI: 10.1017/S026144482300040X

Okada, A., Sherborne, T., Panselinas, G., & Kolionis, G. (2025). Fostering transversal skills through open schooling supported by the care-know-do pedagogical model and the UNESCO AI competencies framework. *International Journal of Artificial Intelligence in Education, 35*(4), 1953–1998. DOI: 10.1007/s40593-025-00458-w

Owenby, M. A. D., & O'Dowd, R. (2018). In This Together. In *Teachers' Experiences with Transnational, Telecollaborative Language Learning Projects.* Peter Lang Verlag. DOI: 10.3726/b14311

Pang, W., & Wei, Z. (2025). Shaping the future of higher education: A technology usage study on generative AI innovations. *Information (Basel), 16*(2), 95. Advance online publication. DOI: 10.3390/info16020095

Perry, B., & Stewart, T. (2005). Insights into effective partnership in interdisciplinary team teaching. *System, 33*(4), 563–573. DOI: 10.1016/j.system.2005.01.006

Rasooli, A., Zandi, H., & DeLuca, C. (2019). Conceptualising fairness in classroom assessment: Exploring the value of organisational justice theory. *Assessment in Education: Principles, Policy & Practice, 26*(5), 584–611. DOI: 10.1080/0969594X.2019.1593105

Rodriguez-Saavedra, M. O., Barrientos-Alfaro, A. R., Málaga-Dávila, C. P., Chávez-Quiroz, F. G., & Arguedas-Catasi, R. W. (2025). Ethics and biases in the use of ChatGPT for academic research. *International Journal of Innovative Research and Scientific Studies, 8*(1), 874–885. DOI: 10.53894/ijirss.v8i1.4432

Romele, A. (2020). Technological capital: Bourdieu, postphenomenology, and the philosophy of technology beyond the empirical turn. *Philosophy & Technology, 34*(3), 483–505. DOI: 10.1007/s13347-020-00398-4

Sailer, M., Maier, R., Berger, S., Kastorff, T., & Stegmann, K. (2024). Learning activities in technology-enhanced learning: A systematic review of meta-analyses and second-order meta-analysis in higher education. *Learning and Individual Differences, 112*, 102446. DOI: 10.1016/j.lindif.2024.102446

Topol, E. (2024, September 11). *Dr. Eric Topol on how AI is transforming health and medicine clinical center news*. https://www.cc.nih.gov/news/2024/nov-dec/eric-topol-ai

Valdivieso, T., & González, O. (2025). Generative AI Tools in Salvadoran Higher Education: Balancing Equity, Ethics, and Knowledge Management in the Global South. *Education Sciences, 15*(2), 214. Advance online publication. DOI: 10.3390/educsci15020214

Vanmassenhove, E., Shterionov, D., & Gwilliam, M. (2021). Machine Translationese: Effects of Algorithmic Bias on Linguistic Complexity in Machine Translation. *Proceedings of the 16th Conference of the European Chapter of the Association for Computational Linguistics,* 2213. https://aclanthology.org/2021.eacl-main.188.pdf

Veldhuis, A., Lo, P., Kenny, S., & Antle, A. N. (2024). Critical artificial intelligence literacy: A scoping review and framework synthesis. *International Journal of Child-Computer Interaction, 43*, 100708. DOI: 10.1016/j.ijcci.2024.100708

Viberg, O., Kizilcec, R., Wise, A. F., Jivet, I., & Nixon, N. (2024). Advancing equity and inclusion in educational practices with AI-powered educational decision support systems (AI-EDSS). *British Journal of Educational Technology, 55*(5), 1974–1981. DOI: 10.1111/bjet.13507

Walter, Y. (2024). Embracing the future of Artificial Intelligence in the classroom: The relevance of AI literacy, prompt engineering, and critical thinking in modern education. *International Journal of Educational Technology in Higher Education, 21*(1), 15. DOI: 10.1186/s41239-024-00448-3

Young, I. (2011). *Responsibility For Justice* (Freeman, S., Ed.). Oxford University Press. DOI: 10.1093/acprof:oso/9780195392388.001.0001

ADDITIONAL READING

Avsheniuk, N.. (2025). Overreliance on AI tools in ESP courses. *Arab World English Journal (AWEJ). Special Issue on AI, 13*(4). Advance online publication. DOI: 10.24093/awej/AI.1

Bender, E. M., Gebru, T., McMillan-Major, A., & Shmitchell, S. (2021). On the dangers of stochastic parrots: Can language models be too big? . In *Proceedings of the 2021 ACM Conference on Fairness, Accountability, and Transparency (FAccT '21)* (pp. 610–623). ACM. DOI: 10.1145/3442188.3445922

Crawford, K. (2021). *Atlas of AI: Power, Politics, and the Planetary Costs of Artificial Intelligence*. Yale University Press. **Policy & Institutional Implementation**

Crompton, H., Edmett, A., Ichaporia, N., & Burke, D. (2024). AI and English language teaching: Affordances and challenges. *British Journal of Educational Technology*, *55*(6), 2503–2529. DOI: 10.1111/bjet.13460

Ethical AI Frameworks & Critical Literacy

European Commission. (2025). *AI in education: Guidelines for ethical deployment in higher education*. Joint Research Centre Report.

Fricker, M. (2007). *Epistemic Injustice: Power and the Ethics of Knowing*. Oxford University Press. DOI: 10.1093/acprof:oso/9780198237907.001.0001

GAI Applications in ESP & Language Education

Green, E., Singh, D., & Chia, R. (Eds.). (2022). AI ethics and higher education: Good practice and guidance for educators, learners, and institutions. Globethics.net.

O'Dowd, R., & Vinagre, M. (Eds.). (2024). Virtual innovation and support networks: Exploring the impact of virtual exchange in teacher education. Peter Lang. (Series: Telecollaborative learning and virtual exchange in education, Vol. 7). (https://www.peterlang.com/series/te)

Xiao, F., Zhu, S., & Xin, W. (2025). Exploring the landscape of generative AI (ChatGPT)-powered writing instruction in English as a foreign language education: A scoping review. *ECNU Review of Education*, *9*. Advance online publication. DOI: 10.1177/20965311241310881

Young, I. M. (2011). *Responsibility for Justice*. Oxford University Press. **AI Bias & Algorithmic Equity** DOI: 10.1093/acprof:oso/9780195392388.001.0001

KEY TERMS AND DEFINITIONS

Agentic AI: Autonomous AI systems capable of independent decision-making, task execution, and adaptation across multimodal inputs, requiring enhanced critical oversight in educational contexts.

Critical AI Literacy: The capacity to evaluate, refine, and contextualise AI-generated content for biases, accuracy, and ethical implications, extending beyond technical proficiency.

Digital Didactics: Pedagogical approaches leveraging digital tools to foster constructivist, student-centred, and interdisciplinary learning in blended environments.

Digital Divide: Socioeconomic and infrastructural disparities in access to advanced AI tools and high-quality data, exacerbating educational inequities.

ED-AI Lit: An Interdisciplinary Framework for AI Literacy in Education

English for Specific Purposes (ESP): A learner-centred approach to language teaching focused on authentic needs analysis, contextualisation, and professional relevance across disciplines.

Ethical Implementation Policy Model: An institutional PDCA-based framework ensuring equitable and just integration of GAI into curricula through systematic planning, piloting, assessment, and scaling.

Generative Artificial Intelligence (GAI): Machine learning models producing novel text, images, or other content from probabilistic patterns in training data, raising unique equity challenges in education.

ICLHE: Integrated Content and Language in Higher Education, a collaborative paradigm where language and disciplinary faculty co-design unified curricula addressing both linguistic and content objectives.

PDCA Cycle: Plan–Do–Check–Act, a continuous improvement methodology adapted here for iterative, equity-focused AI policy implementation in higher education.

Chapter 6
Newspaper Discourse on Chinese Language Learning, E-Learning Readiness, and AI Integration for Ethnic Minority Students in Hong Kong

Siu-lun Lee
http://orcid.org/0000-0002-2306-9217
The Chinese University of Hong Kong, Hong Kong

ABSTRACT

This chapter investigates newspaper discourse on Chinese language education for South Asian schoolchildren in Hong Kong. Drawing on a corpus of 443 newspaper articles published between 2003 and 2025, the study analyzes how the press has represented the importance of Chinese language learning, the challenges and hurdles faced by ethnic minority students, and the views and suggestions advanced to promote greater educational equity. Limited access to computer devices and internet connectivity, parents' computer literacy, and willingness to engage in online learning have placed significant pressure on the implementation of AI-assisted Chinese learning and online support. While some stakeholders advocate AI as a promising solution, persistent inequalities in access remain a critical concern. The findings

DOI: 10.4018/979-8-3373-7749-0.ch006

highlight diverse perspectives within the media and underscore the need for more equitable policies and practices to ensure that AI integration in Chinese language education effectively supports ethnic minority communities in Hong Kong.

INTRODUCTION

Hong Kong is a multilingual and culturally diverse international city. In addition to the three major languages, Cantonese, Putonghua, and English, recent research has identified over twenty minority languages in use, including Bengali, Filipino, Hindi, Indonesian, and Urdu. This linguistic diversity reflects the city's multicultural population and complex sociolinguistic landscape (Bacon-Shone et al., 2025; Bolton et al., 2020).

Ethnic minority students, particularly those from South Asian backgrounds, have been learning Chinese from early childhood to meet academic and career demands (Lee, 2023). For many years, Chinese language education for speakers of minority languages has attracted the attention of linguists, educators, and policymakers, and has been widely discussed in Hong Kong's public media. Despite the development of tailored Chinese curricula, textbooks, and online learning tools, concerns persist regarding the adequacy and accessibility of Chinese education for ethnic minority students (Oxfam Hong Kong, 2020).

Emerging research suggests that computer-assisted learning can be effective in supporting language acquisition in Hong Kong schools (Bai et al., 2022). Moreover, studies have highlighted the potential of artificial intelligence (AI) as a tool for enhancing language learning outcomes (Kim et al., 2019). While some media reports emphasize the benefits of AI technologies in improving schoolchildren's language abilities (Chen, 2023), others raise concerns that ethnic minority students are not equitably benefiting from these digital learning supports (Carvalho, 2020).

This paper investigates the development and accessibility of AI-assisted and online Chinese learning support for ethnic minority students in Hong Kong. It analyzes a corpus of newspaper articles that discuss Chinese education for these students and debate the effectiveness and challenges of implementing AI and digital learning tools. By examining public discourse, this study aims to shed light on the broader issues of educational equity and the role of technology in language learning for Hong Kong's ethnic minority schoolchildren.

LITERATURE REVIEW AND RESEARCH QUESTIONS

Chinese Language Learning of Ethnic Minority Schoolchildren in Hong Kong

In recent decades, the Hong Kong Special Administrative Region (SAR) government has promoted a policy of "trilingualism and biliteracy", encouraging the use of three spoken languages, i.e. Cantonese, Putonghua, and English, and two written codes, i.e. standard written Chinese and written English, in official and public domains (Bacon-Shone et al., 2015; Bolton et al., 2020; Bolton & Lee, 2020). Both written Chinese and English are used in government communications, with written Chinese gaining increasing prominence in legal, business, and professional contexts. This linguistic situation has also prompted expatriate professionals to pursue Chinese literacy for work-related purposes (Lee, 2019).

The importance of Chinese literacy for ethnic minority students was explicitly acknowledged in the Hong Kong Government's 2014 Policy Address, which identified it as a key issue in the education system (Bhowmik, 2014, 2017; Gao & Gube, 2020). The Education Bureau uses the term "non-Chinese speaking" (NCS) students to refer to ethnic minority learners who require Chinese language proficiency to integrate into the education system and broader society. However, this label has been criticized as misleading, as many of these students are conversationally fluent in Cantonese but lack the ability to read and write Chinese.

According to the *2021 Population Census*, the ethnic minority population in Hong Kong, excluding foreign domestic helpers, was approximately 301,000, accounting for 4.2% of the total population. Among these, South Asians represented the largest subgroup, numbering around 101,000 or 1.4% of the population. This group includes individuals of Indian, Pakistani, Nepalese, Bangladeshi, and Sri Lankan descent (Hong Kong Government, 2021). The *2016 Hong Kong Poverty Situation Report on Ethnic Minorities* identified low Chinese language proficiency as a contributing factor to the intergenerational poverty cycle among these communities (Hong Kong Government, 2016).

Ethnic minority students make up roughly 3% of total enrolment in Hong Kong's primary and secondary schools. Following the abolition of the designated school policy in 2013, the Education Bureau introduced a second language learning framework for Chinese, leading to a steady increase in the number of ethnic minority students attending mainstream schools. In the 2018–2019 academic year, 28,711 ethnic minority students were enrolled in kindergartens, primary, and secondary schools alongside their ethnic Chinese peers.

Despite this integration, disparities in Chinese language proficiency persist. Ethnic minority students exhibit varying levels of oral Cantonese fluency, influenced by factors such as home language environment and community support (Cheung, 2019). More significantly, there remains a pronounced gap in Chinese literacy skills, particularly in character recognition and written expression. Although many schools have implemented immersion and remedial programs, concerns about linguistic and cultural divides between ethnic minority and Chinese-speaking students continue to grow (Oxfam Hong Kong, 2020).

Studies have shown that ethnic minority students face significant disadvantages in subjects taught in Chinese, such as Chinese language, literature, and history (Hong Kong Policy Research Institute, 2019; Hong Kong Unison, 2018; The Zubin Foundation, 2018). Their limited literacy skills hinder academic achievement, restrict access to higher education, and reduce employment opportunities (Li & Chuk, 2015; Oxfam Hong Kong, 2020). These challenges underscore the urgent need to enhance Chinese literacy among ethnic minority students for both personal development and social inclusion.

E-learning Support for Ethnic Minority Students in Hong Kong

Although individual schools have implemented specific Chinese curricula to match the needs of these ethnic minority students in the schools, researchers pointed out that online learning support can benefit these students (Bai et al., 2022; Hong Kong Unison, 2018). In recent years, some researchers also found that AI-assisted language learning can benefit Hong Kong schoolchildren (Kim et al., 2019; Lee & Chen, 2024). Some work has been done trying to improve the AI and e-learning support of these ethnic minority schoolchildren in Chinese education in addition to the school-based curriculum. The Education Bureau has encouraged the development of Chinese language self-learning resources and posted them on their official website. Online Chinese language self-learning resources for ethnic minority students are posted on the Hong Kong SAR Education Bureau's website (https://www.edb.gov.hk/en/curriculum-development/kla/chi-edu/second-lang/student.html). These self-learning resources include online resources for "character recognition and writing", "audio storybooks", and "Chinese classics", which consist of famous quotes, couplets, and idioms, as well as "audio dramas", "small books" and outstanding works from ethnic minority students. These resources, according to the Education Bureau, aim at enhancing "students' ability to use language, students' mastery of the standard written language and fluency in Cantonese and be able to communicate in Putonghua, as well as cultivating interest in Chinese language learning, developing high-level thinking ability and good thinking quality, and obtaining aesthetic and moral cultivation and cultural edification" (Education Bureau, 2026). The Standing Committee on Language Education and Research (SCOLAR), which is a quasi-governmental advisory body set up to carry out research into language education, including public consultation exercises, and to advise the Government on language education issues, also sponsored and launched projects to enhance the effectiveness in teaching Chinese language to ethnic minority students and to provide them with self-learning tools for learning Chinese language. There were 3 projects in the 2016-2018 school years, 4 projects in 2019-2021 school year and 1 project in 2021-2023. 2. Details of these projects can be found on the Standing Committee on Language Education and Research (SCOLAR) website (https://scolarhk.edb.hkedcity.net/en/project/2021/developing-chinese-learning-and-teaching-materials-ncs-hk). Of these projects, five are online or e-learning applications, including a *Chinese self-learning app for non-Chinese speaking students* developed by the Open Knowledge Association Limited targeted to primary one to secondary one ethnic minority students, and *A self-learning open platform of Chinese for non-Chinese speaking learners* developed by the Education University of Hong Kong.

Educators in tertiary institutions also initiated and launched mobile applications to support Chinese learning for the ethnic minority student population. The University of Hong Kong has launched *C-for-Chinese@JC-eStorybook* (2023), *Chinese Language Learning Progression Framework for Non-Chinese Speaking Children in Kindergartens in Hong Kong* (2018), *mLang* (2017), *Professor T Series: aged 0-3* (2015). These mobile applications include e-story books with multimedia exercises designed for pre-primary and primary ethnic minority students, comprehensive language skills, and vocabulary flashcards. Information related to these mobile applications developed for ethnic minority schoolchildren is available on the website of the Centre for Advancement of Chinese Language Education and Research (https://www.cacler.hku.hk/en/resources/app). The Education University of Hong Kong also showcased mobile applications, online Chinese courses, and websites for Chinese learning on their website. More information can be found on the website of the Centre for Language in Education of the Education University of Hong Kong (https://eduhk.hk/cle/en/language_enhancement_programme/chinese_programme/Chinese). In addition to the support from the government and tertiary institutions, individual primary and second schools also developed different online Chinese language support based on individual school's needs.

Research Questions

This study analyzes public discourse in the Hong Kong press concerning Chinese language education for ethnic minority schoolchildren, with the aim of addressing the following research questions:

- **Research question 1 (RQ1).** To what extent does the Hong Kong press expressed concern about Chinese language support for the ethnic minority students (EM students) in the Hong Kong community?
- **Research question 2 (RQ2).** What challenges do these students face in acquiring Chinese language proficiency within the current education system?
- **Research question 3 (RQ3).** What pedagogical strategies and recommendations have been proposed to support their Chinese language learning?
- **Research question 4 (RQ4).** How are artificial intelligence (AI) tools and online Chinese learning platforms discussed in relation to supporting these students, and to what extent is access to such resources equitable?

DATA COLLECTION AND METHODOLOGY

An extensive corpus of Chinese-language newspaper articles concerning Chinese language learning and support of ethnic minority students in Hong Kong has been compiled. More specifically, this database has focused on press articles discussing the language learning situations of these ethnic minority students which has drawn comment and commentaries from members of the public as well as professional journalists. Newspaper articles were retrieved from a number of sources, including the WiseOne (formerly WiseNews) database for the Hong Kong press, as well as individual searches of fifteen leading Chinese newspapers, namely *AM730*, *HK01* (香港01), *Headline Daily* (頭條日報), *Hong Kong Economic Journal* (信報財經新聞), *Hong Kong Economic Times* (香港經濟日報), *Kung Kao Po* (公教報), *Metrodaily* (都市日報), *Mingpao Daily* (明報), *Oriental Daily* (東方日報), *Sing Pao* (成報), *Sing Tao Daily* (星島日報), *Sky Post* (晴報), *Ta Kung Pao* (大公報), and *Wen Wei Po* (文匯報) as well as two English newspapers, *South China Morning Post* and *The Standard* in Hong Kong. The research issues in investigating newspaper articles on discussions and comments relating to the Chinese learning support of these ethnic minority schoolchildren in Hong Kong were as follows: (1) to investigate the extent to which the Hong Kong press expressed concern about Chinese language support for the ethnic minority students in Hong Kong society, (2) to investigate the needs and challenges faced by these students, (3) to discuss pedagogical practices suggested by stakeholders, and (4) to analyze the range of the AI and online Chinese language support for these students. This is the first systematic investigation of opinions in Hong Kong public media concerning the Chinese language support of this group of students in Hong Kong.

The data collection took place from March 2025 to September 2025, a total of 532 newspaper articles were downloaded from the internet, and the text was then entered into the database. These articles were initially searched using such terms

南亞裔 South Asians, 少數族裔 ethnic minority, 中文支援 Chinese language support, 網上中文支援 online Chinese support, 中文學習 Chinese learning, 語言支援 language support, 人工智能 artificial intelligence, and closely related terms. Before inclusion in the database, the articles were briefly reviewed in order to determine their relevance to the broad Chinese language needs and supports in question. Later, a further round of filtering took place, after the researcher decided to group such data into four clusters related to four topics: (1) the extent to which the Hong Kong press expressed concern about Chinese language support for the ethnic minority students, (2) challenges faced by these ethnic minority students learning Chinese, (3) pedagogical practices and suggestions for Chinese education for ethnic minority students, and (4) AI and online Chinese language support for these students. After classifying the data according to the above incidents in terms of topic and timeline, there was a total of 443 articles related specifically to these four topics discussed in the past twenty-two years (2003-2025). In this study, we were centrally concerned with discussions where public opinions on Chinese education issues were explicitly expressed. As with any qualitative approach, the adoption of newspaper discourse analysis entails certain limitations. A key challenge lies in the inherent subjectivity of determining which discussions within a newspaper text are most salient. The process of identifying and categorising themes inevitably reflects the researcher's interpretive judgment. To mitigate this concern, two reviewers were involved in assessing the relevance of articles, thereby enhancing reliability and reducing individual bias. Moreover, given the researcher's familiarity with language education issues in Hong Kong society, the interpretive framework applied was both contextually informed and methodologically appropriate. Despite the unavoidable element of subjectivity, the methodology adopted was appropriate and effective in the qualitative analysis of texts.

This study adopts a critical discourse analysis (CDA) approach to examine how Hong Kong newspapers have represented issues surrounding Chinese language learning, e-learning readiness, and AI integration for ethnic minority students. Following Richardson's (2017) framework, newspaper texts are treated not merely as neutral conveyors of information but as socially situated discourses that construct, reproduce, and contest meanings within the public sphere.

Richardson emphasizes that newspapers operate at the intersection of language, ideology, and power, shaping public perceptions through lexical choices, framing devices, and narrative structures. In line with this perspective, the corpus of 443 articles (2003–2025) was analyzed to identify recurring themes, discursive strategies, and evaluative stances. Attention was paid to how headlines, quotations, and editorial commentary foreground certain voices while marginalizing others, thereby influencing the visibility of ethnic minority students' educational challenges.

The analysis proceeded in two stages. First, a descriptive analysis of articles was conducted to map the distribution of topics across four domains: (1) concerns about Chinese language support, (2) challenges faced by ethnic minority students, (3) pedagogical practices and suggestions, and (4) AI and online Chinese support. Second, a qualitative discourse analysis was applied to selected texts, examining rhetorical devices, intertextual references, and ideological positioning. This dual approach allowed for both quantitative mapping and qualitative interpretation, consistent with Richardson's (2017) emphasis on integrating textual analysis with broader socio-political contexts.

By employing newspaper discourse analysis, this study situates media representations as a critical lens through which public debates on language education and digital inclusion are articulated and discussed.

FINDINGS

Descriptive Analysis

The newspaper article corpus, comprising 443 articles published between 2003 and 2025 in the Hong Kong press, demonstrates a consistent concern with Chinese language learning support for ethnic minority schoolchildren. These articles include news reports, columns, editorials, and feature pieces. Across this corpus, recurring themes include the challenges and obstacles faced by ethnic minority students in learning Chinese, pedagogical and policy recommendations, and the availability and implementation of AI-assisted and online support.

Table 1 categorizes the 443 articles into four main areas: (1) concerns regarding Chinese language support for ethnic minority students, (2) challenges encountered by ethnic minority students in learning Chinese, (3) pedagogical practices and recommendations, and (4) the implementation of AI-assisted and online Chinese learning support.

Table 1. Discussions in the press relating to Chinese language education of the ethnic minority students in Hong Kong, 2003-2025

Period	Concerns about Chinese language support for EM students	Challenges faced by ethnic minority students	Pedagogical practices and suggestions	AI and online Chinese support
January 2003 - December 2007	32 (19.4%)	13 (26.0%)	9 (4.4%)	0 (0.0%)
January 2008 – December 2012	47 (28.5%)	16 (32.0%)	37 (18.0%)	11 (47.8%)
January 2013 - December 2017	58 (35.1%)	11 (22.0%)	108 (52.7%)	6 (26.1%)
January 2018 - September 2025	28 (17.0%)	10 (20.0%)	51 (24.9%)	6 (26.1%)
Total number of news articles	165 (37.2%)	50 (11.2%)	205 (46.3%)	23 (5.3%)

Source: Own elaboration

As can be seen from the table, 46.3% of the articles in the dataset discussed and shared pedagogical practices of individual schools and suggestions for Chinese education for these students from stakeholders, educators, policymakers, and politicians. 37.2% of the newspaper articles highlighted the Chinese learning needs, while 11.2% of the articles discussed the challenges faced by ethnic minority schoolchildren. It is notable that only 5.3% of the article discussed “AI and online Chinese support”. In the discursive presentation of the qualitative data, which is presented a little later in this article, the results of our analysis have been grouped according to those topics that emerged from this analysis and illustrated by translated quotations from the Chinese newspaper articles in question. Here again, however, there were limitations to the method of classification used in arriving at these results, as in many cases more than one argument was present in any given text. The task for the researcher, therefore, was to make a judgment as to which argument was most salient in any given text, and this we attempted to do, as accurately and consistently as possible.

Qualitative Results

The qualitative methodology employed by the researcher was used at a number of levels of analysis. First, each of the articles in the database was carefully read in order to identify the major discussions presented in each article, and to decide which of these discussions was most salient in a particular text. This then provided the basis for the descriptive analysis of discussions, as presented in Table 1.

Following this, at a narrower level of examination, the researcher was then able to examine individual articles to determine the way in which particular discussions were realised. One overarching result that emerged from this next level of analysis was that some "major discussions" overlapped within individual newspaper articles, contributing very often to a multi-layered discourse where a range of closely related discussions find expression. This multilayering of discussions can be seen in many of the excerpts presented below. The texts presented below were extracted from articles representing different styles or genres of journalism, including opinion columns, editorials, feature articles, and news reports. The specific provenance of each extract in terms of genre is indicated using the abbreviations, C (column), E (editorial), and F (feature). In addition, the abbreviation Q indicates that the text in question is drawn from a quotation embedded in a news report. These abbreviations are inserted at the end of the quote, immediately following the date of the source publication.

RQ1: Concerns about Chinese Language Support for EM Students

As seen in Table 1, issues about Chinese education for ethnic minority students have been continuously highlighted during the recent twenty-two years. As has been inferred from the corpus, it is generally believed that Chinese language skills can help ethnic minority students to be better included in the community, and to achieve better in the education system, which in turn, leads to brighter career prospects. This section of the article presents a detailed account of these discussions.

Learning Chinese for Inclusion in the Community

The Education Bureau of the Hong Kong Government abolished the designated school policy (2006-2012) in 2013, since then, the number of ethnic minority group children studying in mainstream primary and secondary schools has been increasing. The language barrier has been one of the hindrances to ethnic minority students getting along with their ethnic Chinese peers in school and later in the community. Learning Chinese can help these students to be better included in the community, as in excerpt (1) below.

(1) Students think that low Chinese proficiency hinders their communication and relationship-building with others and makes it hard for them to integrate into the community. (Ta Kung Pao, 23/09/2005, F)

Learning Chinese for Academic Success and to Get Better Career Opportunities

In the current school system, these schoolchildren need to enhance their reading and writing skills, in addition to speaking skills, in order to catch up with their ethnic Chinese peers in their academics. *The Hong Kong Poverty Situation Report on Ethnic Minorities* published in 2016 indicated that low Chinese proficiency was a factor that blocked their ways to receive higher education and led to the poverty cycle of these ethnic minority groups (Hong Kong Government, 2016). Improvement in Chinese proficiency can also increase the competitive power in the job market. Excerpts (2) and (3) show this situation.

(2) Because of their poor language skills in Chinese, they fear that their chances of going on to university in the future will be weakened. (Mingpao Daily, 31/05/2010, F)

(3) The unemployment rate of ethnic minorities remained high at about 24 percent. The language barrier has always been the biggest difficulty for ethnic minorities to find jobs in Hong Kong. (Mingpao Daily, 11/08/2007, F)

RQ2: Challenges of Ethnic Minority Students while Learning Chinese

It is a long-standing issue to fix the Chinese-language learning issue plaguing non-Chinese children and young people. There have been ongoing analyses and discussions relating to the challenges of these students learning Chinese.

Learning a Different Linguistic System

DeFrancis (1984) estimated that Chinese children need to devote at least two more years than their Western counterparts to the task of learning to read and write (p. 219). Ethnic Chinese children in Hong Kong start their literacy training in kindergarten and continuously learn every day with reading and writing tasks in their six-year primary school curriculum and continue to practice in their secondary school Chinese curriculum in order to achieve high-level literacy. Ethnic minority students, because of different cultural and linguistic backgrounds, need extra effort to learn a linguistic system very different from their first language. Excerpt (4) below shows this difficulty.

(4) The mother language of ethnic minority students is mostly phonographic, while the Chinese language is logographic. It is often difficult to infer the pronunciation of the Chinese characters. Their parents may only know simple conversations in Chinese and they are not able to help. (Oriental Daily, 25/06/2017, C)

Even though some of these students were born and raised in Hong Kong, they can speak Chinese at a functional level. Since Chinese is not a language used in their family domain, there has always been a large gap in oral communication skills between these students and their ethnic Chinese peers. This gap created difficulties for their learning of Chinese literacy at schools. Excerpt (5) highlights this issue.

(5) There's a common misconception that some of these students, born and raised in Hong Kong, have the same language standard as their local classmates so teachers overlook the need to provide further help. They can carry out simple conversations in Cantonese, but it doesn't necessarily mean that they have a good Chinese language foundation. (South China Morning Post, 11/03/2019, F)

Unclear Curriculum and Learning Target

Although the Education Bureau has made several adjustments to the arrangement of Chinese education for ethnic minority students, one major comment from stakeholders is that a clear Chinese as a second language curriculum and assessment is needed to provide a well-defined target for schools, parents, and schoolchildren to work on. This kind of comment is common in the newspaper in excerpt (6).

(6) The Education Bureau has been reluctant to develop a Chinese curriculum for ethnic minority students, as well as supplementary guidelines. A clear curriculum and learning objectives are lacking, so schools continue to work separately. (Sing Tao Daily, 16/12/2008, F)

Teacher Education is Needed

Apart from a clear curriculum for schools to work on, schools and teachers also continued to request systematic teacher training in teaching Chinese as a second language as well as in understanding the cultural characteristics, linguistic background, and learning habits of this diverse group of students. Excerpt (7) shows this kind of request.

(7) Teachers have not received training in teaching minority students. A teacher once said that if there are one or two minority students in a class, the teacher can handle it, but if there are five or six students from different countries such as India, Nepal, Indonesia, and other countries who do not speak the same language, the teacher needs to spend a lot of energy communicating with these students. (Ta Kung Pao, 17/11/2012, F)

Parents' Chinese Ability and Understanding of the Education System

The Chinese education issues for ethnic minority schoolchildren are intertwined with the different issues mentioned above. Another relevant issue is that the relatively low Chinese proficiency of ethnic minority parents also affects the strategies to improve Chinese education for their schoolchildren. Excerpts (8) and (9) show low Chinese proficiency of ethnic minority parents causes serious problems for family-school communication.

(8) Some parents mistakenly throw away Chinese certificates as garbage because they can't understand Chinese. (Mingpao Daily, 25/02/2004, F)

(9) There are 11 ethnic minority students in our school, and the biggest difficulty at present is how to carry out family-school communication. Just financial support does not suffice, because not every school knows how to help ethnic minorities. (Sing Tao Daily, 18/04/2016, E)

Some stakeholders also pointed out that there has been a need to educate ethnic minority parents to understand the Hong Kong education system. Lacking a sufficient understanding of education may lead to parental decisions not benefiting their children's Chinese learning shown in excerpt (10) below.

(10) Ethnic minority parents said they were reluctant to send their children to Chinese schools even if they were near their homes. Some of them do not agree that attending Chinese schools can improve their chances of integration. (Wen Wei Po, 03/05/2004, F)

RQ3: Pedagogical Practices and Suggestions for Chinese Education for Ethnic Minority Students

In the dataset, there are some discussions and sharing of pedagogical practices of individual schools and suggestions from educators and concern groups. The number of these discussions has drastically increased around 2013 since the abolishment of designated schools.

Suggestions from the Government

The dataset contains articles showing the efforts of the Education Bureau to address the needs of these students and try to improve Chinese education for these students. Given the enrolment rate of ethnic minority students in the kindergartens was low, the Education Bureau suggested and encouraged parents to enroll their children in kindergartens and start Chinese learning at an early age, as indicated in excerpt (11) below.

(11) Many ethnic minority students face difficulties in learning Chinese. The Education Bureau encourages ethnic minority parents to arrange for their children to enrol in kindergartens as soon as possible. (Ta Kung Pao, 28/02/2017, F)

Excerpt (12) shows that the Education Bureau suggested a more systematic approach to improving the situation, and in excerpt (13) Education Bureau suggested the collaboration among universities and schools to work together to improve the Chinese learning experience of these ethnic minority schoolchildren.

(12) The Education Bureau submitted a paper to the Panel on Education of the Legislative Council to suggest three measures, including enhancing the summer transition pathway programme for ethnic minority students from Primary 1 to Primary 4, supporting professional training for Chinese teachers teaching these students, and conducting follow-up studies on existing teaching and learning experience. (Sing Tao Daily, 17/01/2013, F)

(13) Apart from formulating different school-based professional support models to strengthen support for schools, the Education Bureau will also start collaboration between specialists from universities and kindergartens and pilot Chinese learning activities in areas where these ethnic minority children live. (Wen Wei Po, 30/05/2012, F)

Implementation of Chinese Counseling Service and Remedial Classes

Some concern groups and non-government organizations advocated the development of Chinese counseling services and remedial Chinese classes to assist ethnic minority students in learning Chinese after school. Excerpt (14) is one of the examples.

(14) Since six years ago, the Hong Kong Society for the Protection of Children has been funded by The Hong Kong Jockey Club to implement the 'Whole Learning Project' in Kowloon City. A centre has set up an after-school homework counseling service to improve the performance of ethnic minority students as well as to teach parents and children the Chinese language at a lower cost. (Sing Tao Daily, 03/06/2014, F)

Suggestions from Stakeholders and Educators

During 2013-2017, there were growing discussions and suggestions from different stakeholders and educators. There are also voices from stakeholders to urge the implementation of Chinese as a second language classroom at schools starting from early schoolchildren, as shown in excerpt (15) below.

(15) I would suggest that the Government formulate policies to allow ethnic minority children to add Chinese as a second language classroom starting from lower grades, so as to facilitate learning Chinese adapt to learning needs and integrate into society as soon as possible. (Sing Pao, 27/09/2013, Q)

In addition, statutory bodies, such as the Equal Opportunities Commission, and concern groups, for example, Hong Kong Unison and Oxfam Hong Kong, also conducted research and provided concrete suggestions to the government, including but not limited to building up clear objectives and guidelines for Chinese education for ethnic minority students, improving teaching training, providing online Chinese supports for these students, as in excerpt (16) below.

(16) Chinese education for ethnic minority students cannot be ignored because it will affect these students' further education, employment, and daily life of these students. The Equal Opportunities Commission's Working Group on Ethnic Minority Education released its second report and made 22 recommendations to improve the Chinese learning of ethnic minority students and highlight the need for a comprehensive Chinese curriculum with Chinese as a second language. (Hong Kong Economic Journal, 26/09/2019, F)

RQ4: AI and Online Chinese Support

In the dataset, discussions about applying online Chinese support were started around 2008 and there are relatively few articles talking about the implementation of AI-assisted and online Chinese support. There were schools, institutions, universities, and companies using newspapers as a channel to disseminate their computer application and/or mobile apps to support Chinese language learning of ethnic minority students and discuss the effectiveness of the online support. Excerpt (17) demonstrates the launch of an online multilingual Chinese dictionary developed by the Hong Kong Institute of Education (now named the Education University of Hong Kong) and excerpt (18) shows a computer application development by an individual company.

(17) The Hong Kong Institute of Education has developed Hong Kong's first online Chinese dictionary with Chinese, English, Indian, and Pakistani explanations. The dictionary collects nearly 24,000 Chinese characters and provides bilingual pronunciation instructions in Cantonese and Putonghua to support the Chinese learning of ethnic minority students. There are about 4,000 commonly used Chinese characters in the dictionary to help improve the learning efficiency of these students. (Sing Tao Daily, 21/04/2011, F)

(18) The school curriculum is not perfect, even if these students can listen and speak like Chinese children, they are always lagged in reading and writing and finally miss out on many job opportunities because of their language skills. He thought that his computer application powered with artificial intelligence could help these children learn Chinese more effectively. (Hong Kong Economic Journal, 25/01/2019, F)

Lack of Resources and Government Support to Implement AI-Assisted Chinese Learning for Underprivileged Families

Although universities, non-government organizations, and companies tried to provide computer-assisted Chinese learning applications and online Chinese support, some underprivileged families reported that access to AI-assisted learning is difficult because they cannot afford to buy computer devices and they have no internet access at home. They eventually cannot benefit from the implementation of AI and computer-assisted Chinese learning for their children as shown in excerpts (19) and (20).

(19) Some students from underprivileged families lack access to the Internet at home, making online learning an impossible task. During the pandemic, these children can't go to school, what can they do at home? This unprecedented teaching experiment reflects the plight of underprivileged families and the shortcomings of the education system. Some students don't have internet and computers at home and can't attend classes at all. The implementation of online teaching should consider the actual situation. (Wen Wei Po, 29/04/2020, F)

(20) During the pandemic when schools changed to online classes, ethnic minority students faced many difficulties because their families did not have enough money to purchase electronic devices for online learning, and many face-to-face Chinese classes and remedial classes for ethnic minorities were canceled. This affected these students' Chinese learning progress. Their Chinese proficiency has deteriorated because Chinese is rarely used in the family domain. (Sing Tao Daily, 11/12/2020, F)

FUTURE DIRECTIONS

The learning situation of Chinese for ethnic minority schoolchildren has been extensively discussed in the press in the past twenty-two years (2003-2025). In addition to speaking and reading skills, writing skills are necessary for schoolchildren as indicated by articles in the corpus. In the current school system, these schoolchildren need to enhance their writing skills in order to catch up with their ethnic Chinese peers in their academic and career pursuits. This has become a major issue for educators to research and work on. It is never a simple task for Chinese subject teachers even to help Chinese schoolchildren improve their writing skills (Poon, 2014), it is an even more difficult mission for these Chinese subject teachers to improve the literacy of ethnic minority students whose Cantonese oral proficiency often varies greatly (Hong Kong Policy Research Institute, 2019; Hong Kong Unison, 2018; Oxfam Hong Kong, 2020; The Zubin Foundation, 2018). Teaching writing skills to ethnic minority schoolchildren is different from teaching such skills to ethnic

Chinese children, given the large gap in oral communication skills between these two groups of students. Using teaching methods and textbooks in the mainstream syllabi for ethnic Chinese students to teach ethnic minority schoolchildren is very far from ideal. Although many primary and secondary schools have adopted classroom immersion programs and Chinese remedial programs, the gaps in Chinese literacy skills among students of different ethnic backgrounds in the education system remain large (Oxfam Hong Kong, 2020). In recent decades, there have been studies on how to help minority children learn Chinese characters in kindergarten (Lee et al., 2011). There have also been proposals on how to improve the writing skills of ethnic minority schoolchildren (Cheng, 2015; Lam, 2011; Li & Chuk, 2015; Shum et al., 2016, 2019).

Artificial Intelligence and Information Technology in Language Learning

Research has shown that although ethnic minority schoolchildren are able to acquire basic Cantonese speaking skills, it is difficult for them to acquire writing skills in the current school system (Cheng, 2015). In our newspaper corpus study, there are 5.3% of the articles discussing and suggesting the implementation of online and AI Chinese support for these ethnic minority students. Theoretically, AI-assisted and online Chinese language support and computer-assisted self-learning packages can help fill this gap to cater to students with different learning paces and backgrounds. Lee and Chen (2024) highlighted that online Chinese language support and AI-assisted learning can also enforce after-school learning and exposure to the target language.

To situate current developments in artificial intelligence (AI) within language education, it is necessary to contextualize them against the broader trajectory of applied linguistics. Zakaria and Aryadoust's (2024) scientometric analysis of research from 1970 to 2022 provides a longitudinal perspective, tracing methodological shifts across five decades. This historical grounding is complemented by Esmaeilzadeh et al. (2025), whose systematic review of studies published between 2020 and 2024 documents the rapid expansion of AI into teaching and assessment. Together, these works suggest that while applied linguistics has long been interdisciplinary, the present "AI era" marks a decisive departure from earlier computer-assisted language learning (CALL) frameworks, requiring a reorientation of research priorities. Recent scholarship illustrates how AI is reshaping classroom practices and learner psychology. Shi et al. (2025), in a comparative study of ChatGPT and traditional automated writing evaluation (AWE), highlight the significance of AI interaction not only for improving text quality but also for shaping learners' identities and motivation through the concept of the "ideal L2 writing self." Yet, the effectiveness of such tools remains contingent upon teacher agency and student AI literacy. Hubbard and Schulze (2025) argue that the sustainability of AI integration depends on "sustained integrated professional development," emphasizing that without continuous teacher engagement, AI risks being perceived as an external imposition rather than a transformative pedagogical resource.

This newspaper research showed that there have been some online Chinese language supports offered to these students. Chu (2023) suggested that at present Chinese teaching software is quite advanced, and some schools have developed pronunciation, word recognition, translation, and other computer programs to meet the needs of ethnic minority students to alleviate their restrictions on learning and practicing Chinese at home. The situation looks optimistic.

However, the current situation is that these AI-assisted and online Chinese support and computer applications are varied and many. There is a need for a platform to put these useful applications together and systematically arrange them so that schools, parents, and students can easily search and use them. The chairperson of the Equal Opportunities Commission in Hong Kong reiterated that "fixing the Chinese-language learning issue plaguing non-Chinese children and young people is a long-standing issue" and many suggestions has been given in the 2019 report titled *Closing the Gap: Report of the Working Group on Education for Ethnic Minorities* to improve the situation. One of which is to have a systematic planning and structure of all learning resources including AI and online applications developed by different parties and shared among schools and stakeholders.

Digital Inclusion

The expansion of digital tools and AI-assisted language learning platforms presents both opportunities and challenges for educational equity. As Farahani and Ghasemi (2024) observe, AI has the potential to mitigate inequality through personalized instruction, adaptive learning pathways, and access to multimedia resources that accommodate diverse learner needs and paces (Lee & Chen, 2024). When effectively implemented, computer-assisted learning has been shown to support language acquisition and foster self-regulated learning in Hong Kong schools (Bai et al., 2020).

However, one notable finding from this newspaper research is the issue of e-learning readiness among ethnic minority families. The articles highlight challenges such as limited access to computer devices and internet connectivity, parents' low levels of computer literacy, and varying willingness to participate.

Yet, the promise of AI is fundamentally constrained by the persistence of the digital divide, which operates at multiple levels. The first level divide concerns physical access to technology, availability of devices and stable internet connections, which remains a significant barrier for many ethnic minority families disproportionately represented among Hong Kong's underprivileged population (Chu, 2023). The second level divide relates to digital literacy and the ability to use technology effectively for learning. Low parental digital literacy and limited engagement with the school system often prevent students from fully utilizing available online resources, even when physical access is secured. The third level divide concerns learning outcomes, that is the extent to which learners can translate access and skills into meaningful educational gains. As Bulathwela et al. (2024) point out, technologies designed to democratize learning may inadvertently widen disparities, as digitally privileged students are better positioned to leverage AI for academic advancement.

Taken together, these layered divides underscore that digital inclusion is not simply a matter of providing devices or connectivity. It requires sustained attention to literacy, support structures, and equitable outcomes to ensure that AI integration in language education genuinely benefits ethnic minority students rather than reinforcing existing inequalities.

These divides have placed considerable pressure on the implementation of AI-assisted Chinese learning and online Chinese support for ethnic minority students in Hong Kong. While some stakeholders view AI-assisted learning as a potential solution, unequal access remains a critical concern. Addressing this requires government action not only to alleviate the financial difficulties faced by ethnic minority families but also to strengthen parent and student education in AI literacy. Without such measures, the effective use of computer-assisted and online Chinese learning will continue to be hindered. Clearly, further efforts are needed to tackle the persistent challenges surrounding Chinese education for ethnic minority communities in Hong Kong.

CONCLUSION

This study sets out to investigate the Chinese learning situation of the ethnic minority students as discussed in the press in Hong Kong. A corpus was built containing newspaper articles in recent twenty-two years discussing the Chinese language needs and challenges, pedagogical suggestions for Chinese education for ethnic minority students in Hong Kong, and AI-assisted and online Chinese support. More work needs to be done in different aspects, such as defining a clear Chinese as a second language curriculum and learning target, providing more support for schools and teachers by the government, and offering help to educate parents in terms of Chinese proficiency and their understanding of the education system to achieve better family-school communication. In AI-assisted and online Chinese learning, there is a need to systematically organize all available resources and coordinate future developmental plans. This study also reveals the issue of e-learning readiness of ethnic minority families due to the lack of computer devices and internet connection, as well as parents' computer literacy, and willingness to participate. These factors impose pressure on the implementation of AI and computer-assisted Chinese support for ethnic minority students. In all, the prospects for ethnic minority children may be somewhat more positive, although this will largely depend on whether schools and teachers can meet the challenges of designing Chinese language support and AI applications suitable for this specific group of students.

REFERENCES

Bacon-Shone, J., Bolton, K., & Lee, S. L. (2025). Researching Hong Kong's Multilingual Landscape. In Durk, G., & Cenoz, J. (Eds.), *The handbook of linguistic landscapes and multilingualism* (pp. 309–336). John Wiley & Sons., DOI: 10.1002/9781394231805.ch20

Bacon-Shone, J., Bolton, K., & Luke, K. K. (2015). *Language use, proficiency and attitudes in Hong Kong*. Social Sciences Research Centre, HKU.

Bai, B., Wang, J., & Zhou, H. (2020). An intervention study to improve primary school students' self-regulated strategy use in English writing through e-learning in Hong Kong. *Computer Assisted Language Learning, 35*(9), 2265–2290. DOI: 10.1080/09588221.2020.1871030

Bai, B., Wang, J., & Zhou, H. (2022). An intervention study to improve primary school students' self-regulated strategy use in English writing through e-learning in Hong Kong. *Computer Assisted Language Learning, 35*(9), 2265–2290. DOI: 10.1080/09588221.2020.1871030

Bhowmik, M. K. (2014). Ethnic minority students' education in Hong Kong: Rhetoric, issues and priorities. *International Journal of Comparative Education and Development, 16*, 126–140.

Bhowmik, M. K. (2017). Equitable and quality educational opportunities for Hong Kong's ethnic minorities: The challenges to achieve SDG4. *Curriculum Perspectives, 37*(2), 191–196. DOI: 10.1007/s41297-017-0030-x

Bolton, K., Bacon-Shone, J., & Lee, S. L. (2020). Societal multilingualism in Hong Kong. In P. Siemund, & J. Leimgruber (Eds.), *Multilingual global cities: Dubai, Hong Kong and Singapore* (pp. 160–184). Routledge. https://doi.org/DOI: 10.4324/9780429463860-12

Bolton, K., & Lee, S. L. (2020). A socio-historical approach to multilingualism in Hong Kong. In P. Siemund, & J. Leimgruber (Eds.), *Multilingual global cities: Hong Kong, Singapore, and Dubai* (pp. 38–62). Routledge. https://doi.org/DOI: 10.4324/9780429463860-4

Bulathwela, S., Pérez-Ortiz, M., Holloway, C., Cukurova, M., & Shawe-Taylor, J. (2024). Artificial intelligence alone will not democratise education: On educational inequality, techno-solutionism and inclusive tools. *Sustainability (Basel), 16*(2), 781. DOI: 10.3390/su16020781

Carvalho, R. (2020, August 30). Academic marginalisation of Hong Kong's ethnic minority groups increases amid coronavirus pandemic. *South China Morning Post.* https://n9.cl/x8bxrt

Chen, L. (2023, June 23). Hong Kong rolls out first AI curriculum for junior secondary students, including lessons on ChatGPT, with 'lives definitely affected by artificial intelligence'. *South China Morning Post.* https://n9.cl/2phugf

Cheng, J. K. (2015). Enhancing the Chinese writing skills of non-Chinese speaking students. *SpringerPlus*, *4*(S2), O1. DOI: 10.1186/2193-1801-4-S2-O1

Cheung, H. T. (2019). The effect of age of arrival to the development of Cantonese narrative in ethnic minority children of Hong Kong. In J. Wakefield (Ed.), *Cantonese as a second language: Issues, experiences and suggestions for teaching and learning*, (pp. 232–250). Routledge.

Chu, M. K. (2023, August 15). 培育少數族裔青年 發展寶貴人力資源 [Nurturing ethnic minority youth Develop valuable human resources]. *Mingpao Daily.*

DeFrancis, J. (1984). *The Chinese language: Fact and fantasy.* University of Hawaii Press. DOI: 10.1515/9780824840303

Education Bureau. (2026, April 20). 中國語文教育 *[Chinese language education].* Education Bureau. https://n9.cl/yvdl5

Esmaeilzadeh, F., Ghahari, S., & Rohani, G. (2025). Artificial intelligence in language teaching and assessment: A systematic review of research (2020-2024). *The Asian Journal of Applied Linguistics*, *9*(1), 1222–1222. DOI: 10.25442/hku.30888980

Farahani, M., & Ghasemi, G. (2024). Artificial intelligence and inequality: Challenges and opportunities. *International Journal of Innovation in Education*, *9*, 78–99. DOI: 10.32388/7HWUZ2

Gao, F., & Gube, J. (2020). Multicultural education: How are ethnic minorities labelled and educated in post-handover Hong Kong? *Migration and Language Education*, *2*(3), 51–59. DOI: 10.29140/mle.v1n2.363

Hong Kong Government. (2016). *The Hong Kong poverty situation report on ethnic minorities.* Census and Statistics Department, Hong Kong Government. https://n9.cl/3mn1sh

Hong Kong Government. (2021). *Population census.* Census and Statistics Department, Hong Kong Government. https://n9.cl/fg5adc

Hong Kong Policy Research Institute. (2019, March 1). *The study for Chinese language proficiency of the non-language subjects textbooks used in primary and secondary schools*. Hong Kong Policy Research Institute. https://n9.cl/wu8h0l

Hong Kong Unison. (2018, January 1). *A comprehensive review of learning and teaching of Chinese for ethnic minority students in Hong Kong 2006-2016*. Hong Kong Unison.

Hubbard, P., & Schulze, M. (2025). AI and the future of language teaching: Motivating sustained integrated professional development. [IJCALLT]. *International Journal of Computer-Assisted Language Learning and Teaching*, *15*(1), 1–17. DOI: 10.4018/IJCALLT.378304

Kim, N.-Y., Cha, Y., & Kim, H.-S. (2019). Future English learning: Chatbots and artificial intelligence. *Multimedia-Assisted Language Learning*, *22*(3), 32–53. DOI: 10.15702/mall.2019.22.3.32

Lam, H. C. (2011). A critical analysis of the various ways of teaching Chinese characters, *Electronic Journal of Foreign Language Teaching, 8*, 57–70. https://n9.cl/qr0k7s

Lee, M. T. N., Tse, S. K., & Loh, E. K. Y. (2011). The impact of the integrative perceptual approach on the teaching of Chinese characters in a Hong Kong kindergarten. *Early Child Development and Care*, *181*(5), 665–679. DOI: 10.1080/03004431003768006

Lee, S. L. (2019). Teaching and learning Cantonese as a second language: Learners' attitudes and learning hurdles. In J. Wakefield (Ed.), *Cantonese as a second language: Issues, experiences and suggestions for teaching and learning* (pp. 47–66). Routledge. https://doi.org/DOI: 10.4324/9781351184250

Lee, S. L. (2023). Teaching literacy skills to Cantonese learners. In Lee, S. L. (Ed.), *The learning and teaching of Cantonese as a second language* (pp. 67–86). Routledge. DOI: 10.4324/9781003054696

Lee, S. L., & Chen, Y. (2024). Discussions of using AI in language education in Hong Kong. In Pan, F. (Ed.), *AI in language teaching, learning, and assessment* (pp. 133–148). IGI Global Scientific Publishing., DOI: 10.4018/979-8-3693-0872-1.ch007

Li, D. C. S., & Chuk, J. Y. P. (2015). South Asian students' needs for Cantonese and written Chinese in Hong Kong: A linguistic study. *International Journal of Multilingualism*, *12*(2), 210–224. DOI: 10.1080/14790718.2015.1009375

Oxfam Hong Kong. (2020). *A study on the challenges faced by mainstream schools in educating ethnic minorities in Hong Kong*. Oxfam. https://n9.cl/yyiv3

Poon, H. F. (2014). *Interactive online self-access learning package for 'Chinese writing skills'*. The Hong Kong Institute of Education. https://n9.cl/0ibze

Richardson, J. E. (2017). *Analysing newspapers: An approach from critical discourse analysis*. Bloomsbury Publishing.

Shi, H., Chai, C. S., Zhou, S., & Aubrey, S. (2025). Comparing the effects of ChatGPT and automated writing evaluation on students' writing and ideal L2 writing self. *Computer Assisted Language Learning*, •••, 1–28. DOI: 10.1080/09588221.2025.2454541

Shum, M. S., Shi, D., Huang, X., Tai, C., & Yung, W. (2019). Using the genre-based approach in teaching Chinese written composition to South Asian Ethnic minority students in Hong Kong. *Writing & Pedagogy*, *11*(2), 253–283. DOI: 10.1558/wap.36916

Shum, M. S.-k., Tai, C.-p., & Shi, D. (2016). The effectiveness of using 'reading to learning to write' pedagogy in teaching Chinese to non-Chinese speaking students in Hong Kong. *International Journal of Bilingual Education and Bilingualism*, *21*, 43–60. https://n9.cl/p3mjfj

The Zubin Foundation. (2018). *Securing a good start for students of Chinese as an additional language in kindergarten*. The Zubin Foundation.

Zakaria, A., & Aryadoust, V. (2024). A scientometric analysis of applied linguistics research (1970–2022): Methodology and future directions. *Applied Linguistics Review*, *15*(4), 1595–1619. DOI: 10.1515/applirev-2022-0210

ADDITIONAL READING

Chau, K. Y., Law, K. M., & Tang, Y. M. (2021). Impact of self-directed learning and educational technology readiness on synchronous E-learning. *Journal of Organizational and End User Computing*, *33*(6), 1–20. DOI: 10.4018/JOEUC.20211101.oa26

Crompton, H., Edmett, A., Ichaporia, N., & Burke, D. (2024). AI and English language teaching: Affordances and challenges. *British Journal of Educational Technology*, *55*(6), 2503–2529. DOI: 10.1111/bjet.13460

Cullen, R. (2001). Addressing the digital divide. *Online Information Review*, *25*(5), 311–320. DOI: 10.1108/14684520110410517

Kohnke, L., Moorhouse, B. L., & Zou, D. (2023). ChatGPT for language teaching and learning. *RELC Journal*, *54*(2), 537–550. DOI: 10.1177/00336882231162868

Lee, S. L. (2016). E-learning readiness in language learning. *Journal of Technology and Chinese Language Teaching*, *7*, 23–37.

Lee, S. L. (2022). Synchronous online language teaching: A reflection from Hong Kong. In Liu, S. (Ed.), *Teaching the Chinese language remotely: Global cases and perspectives* (pp. 235–251). Palgrave Macmillan., DOI: 10.1007/978-3-030-87055-3_10

Lee, S. L. (Ed.). (2023). *The learning and teaching of Cantonese as a second language*. Routledge. DOI: 10.4324/9781003054696

Lee, S. L. (2025). AI-adaptive Chinese language learning environment and assessments in Hong Kong. In Wachira, P., Liu, X., & Koc, S. (Eds.), *Educational assessments in the age of generative AI* (pp. 119–144). IGI Global Scientific Publishing. DOI: 10.4018/979-8-3693-6351-5.ch005

Mervyn, K., Simon, A., & Allen, D. K. (2014). Digital inclusion and social inclusion: A tale of two cities. *Information Communication and Society*, *17*(9), 1086–1104. DOI: 10.1080/1369118X.2013.877952

Son, J., Ružić, N., & Philpott, A. (2025). Artificial intelligence technologies and applications for language learning and teaching. *Journal of China Computer-Assisted Language Learning*, *5*(1), 94–112. DOI: 10.1515/jccall-2023-0015

KEY TERMS AND DEFINITIONS

Artificial intelligence (AI) in education: It refers to the use of AI technologies, such as machine learning, adaptive systems, and chatbots, to enhance teaching and learning. It supports personalized learning, automates administrative tasks, and provides intelligent tutoring systems. AI in education also raises important issues of ethics, equity, and data privacy, while offering opportunities to improve access and engagement in classrooms worldwide.

Cantonese: A major Chinese language variety spoken mainly in Hong Kong, Macau, and Guangdong. It is distinct from Putonghua, in phonological structure, vocabulary, and cultural expressions.

Chinese education in Hong Kong: It refers to schooling that emphasizes Chinese language, literature, history, and culture within the city's education system. It typically uses Cantonese or Putonghua as the medium of instruction and includes Chinese language as a core subject in the Hong Kong Diploma of Secondary Education (HKDSE). This approach reflects Hong Kong's bilingual identity, balancing local traditions with global standards.

E-learning: It refers to education delivered through digital technologies, typically via the internet. It allows learners to access courses, resources, and interactive tools remotely, offering flexibility in time, place, and pace of study.

Ethnic minority students in Hong Kong: It refers students from diverse linguistic and cultural backgrounds, including Filipino, Indian, Indonesian, and South Asian communities. They constitute about 8.4% of the population. Chinese education for this group has long been a concern among educators and policymakers, particularly regarding linguistic and cultural gaps. Educators emphasize the importance of support measures to help these students integrate into schools, especially through Chinese language learning and ensuring equitable access to education.

Online Chinese language learning support: It refers to digital platforms and resources that help learners study Chinese remotely. These include self-learning materials, interactive apps, AI-powered tutoring, and global platforms offering personalized programs and real-time feedback. Such support makes Chinese learning more accessible to students, professionals, and overseas learners by providing flexible, engaging tools and cultural content.

Putonghua 普通话: Literally meaning 'common speech', it is the official standard spoken language of China. It is taught in schools, used in media, and serves as a lingua franca across regions with diverse language varieties in China. Putonghua plays a central role in unifying communication throughout China and is also widely studied internationally.

Trilingualism and biliteracy: It refers to the promotion of three spoken languages, Cantonese, Putonghua, and English, and literacy in two written languages, Chinese and English.

Chapter 7
Accessibility, Inclusion, and AI:
Designing Language Learning Tools for All Learners

C. N. Vidhya Lakshmi
http://orcid.org/0009-0002-3329-7309
Hindustan Institute of Technology and Science, India

Gibin G. Varghese
http://orcid.org/0009-0006-8838-9840
Hindustan Institute of Technology and Science, India

Srinidhya Ganesh Kumar
http://orcid.org/0000-0001-5336-5511
S.A. Engineering College, India

ABSTRACT

Artificial intelligence (AI) is changing the language learning process based on adaptive platforms, automated feedback, speech recognition, and multimodal environment. However, these tools threaten to increase disparities between different students with different linguistic backgrounds, disabilities, technological access, and interests. Accessibility and inclusion are established in this chapter as the key principles of designing AI-mediated language education. It looks at accommodations such as live captioning, multi-lingual interfaces, adaptive feedback, assistive writing aids and custom portals. Development of poor accessibility design, low infrastructure, and exclusion risks, are some of the challenges. Accessibility and inclusion thus require a deliberate consideration in each phase of development of

DOI: 10.4018/979-8-3373-7749-0.ch007

AI language tools. Postulating accessibility-minded design, the chapter provides concrete suggestions on the ways to create equitable AI language tools that would provide inclusion in different educational settings

INTRODUCTION

The sheer rate of the artificial intelligence (AI) spreading to the educational sphere has spawned quite optimistic expectations about the possibility of technology to personalize and democratize learning. Education, and language education especially, has seen an influx of AI-oriented applications such as smart tutoring systems and computer-generated writing assistants through speech recognition applications and chatbots. The apps would make language learning more accessible, dynamic, and effective to learners across the globe. But underneath this optimism is a question that is more critical and often under-explained: for whom is available and adaptive actually? The truth of the matter is that the currently existing and designed AI-enhanced language learning devices do not cater to all learners in an equal manner. The existing research on educational technology, disability studies, and computational linguistics suggests that students with physical, sensory, cognitive, or linguistic disabilities are a priori shut out of the supposed advantages of AI technology (Alper, 2017; Mack et al., 2021). Similarly, the students who belong to disadvantaged socioeconomic groups, who speak non-dominant languages and dialects, and students with insufficient digital infrastructure also face these systemic obstacles that have yet to be overcome by AI applications (Regan & Jesse, 2019; Warschauer, 2004). Therefore, the optimism of AI in language education in most ways has echoed and increased the same injustices it is supposed to eradicate.

This chapter comes in between that tension. It claims that token accommodations and post-hoc retrofitting are not viable to meaningful accessibility and inclusion in AI-enhanced language learning. Instead, these results demand an essential shift in the design process—a shift that is focused on the wholeness of the diversity of learners at the earliest levels of growth. Based on Universal Design to Learning (UDL), participatory design, disability justice models, and critical insights into algorithmic bias, the chapter presents a holistic argument of what AI language learning tools should be designed to meet the needs of all learners, including traditionally marginalized students of mainstream educational technology.

The chapter contextualizes its argument in the overall theme of the book, which is equity, equality and justice in AI enhanced language education. It does not treat these concepts as interchangeable ideals but as quite different and complementary imperatives. Equity means requiring tools to address the various needs and initial conditions of learners; equality means that high-quality AI tools need to be made available to all learners; justice means that the design, implementation, and management of these tools must address the structural conditions that generate and perpetuate the exclusion. Together, these principles offer the normative basis to the analysis that is to be offered.

The chapter follows a series of interrelated parts. It starts by scanning the terrain of the various learners in language learning situations and defining the particular populations that are most likely to be forced out of AI-enhanced tools. It then critically looks at the shortcoming of existing AI tools of language learning, including the technical, pedagogical, and ethical failure that reproduce exclusion. The chapter goes on to propose a framework of inclusive AI design based on UDL, participatory practices, and culturally responsive concepts. Both prospective and troublesome tools are considered as case studies so that to frame the theoretical argument in the real practice. The following section of the chapter focuses on the morality and fairness aspects of inclusive AI design, where the questions of data sovereignty, linguistic hegemony, and technological solution boundaries are raised. It ends with a series of suggestions for researchers, developers, educators, and policymakers to ensure the creation of AI-enhanced language learning spaces that will be both dignified and effective to all learners.

This also presents a unique scholarly contribution by combining rarely studied frameworks that have not been fully integrated in the literature on AI-based language learning, which include: UDL, the disability justice theory, the algorithmic fairness research, and culturally sustaining pedagogy. Previous research has applied one or two of these lenses, but no study has combined all four lenses into a holistic critical lens for inclusive design of AI language learning. This chapter therefore attempts to go beyond the issue of technical accessibility to tackle the structural and ethical aspects that shape the potential of AI language technologies to become truly accessible for all learners.

The methodological approach that is used in this chapter is critical literature-based analysis. Based on literature that was reviewed, the analysis proceeds by examining current tools in the field of AI for language learning against a set of inclusive design principles culled from the reviewed literature. This approach is consistent with conceptual and critical review scholarship of educational technology (Selwyn, 2011), which is more concerned with questioning the assumptions, power structures and ideology behind the design of technology. Theories are supported by empirical case studies, where available.

THEORY AND CONCEPTUAL FOUNDATIONS

In order to critique and eventually reinvent AI-enhanced language learning tools in terms of accessibility and inclusion, one will need to have a strong theoretical background. This section outlines the key conceptual frameworks that inform the chapter's analysis: UDL, disability justice and the social model of disability, critical perspectives on algorithmic bias and AI fairness, culturally sustaining pedagogy, and the intersectionality of identity with access to educational technology. These frameworks are presented not as an independent initiative but as a collaborative perspective that is incorporated into a broader strategy for inclusive AI design.

Universal Design of Learning

One of the most effective models of inclusive educational design is UDL, created at the Center of Applied Special Technology (CAST) and based on the principles developed on the basis of architecture, neuroscience, and education (Rose & Meyer, 2002). UDL is the idea that obstacles to learning are not placed on the learner but on the resistance of the learning environment and the tools used that do not take into account the inherent variability of the human mind, perception, and interaction. Instead of creating a design based on an assumed average or normal learner and then accommodating those who are not exactly on the norm, UDL proposes creating a design with variability in consideration. The UDL framework is structured based on three principles. The first principle is related to the various forms of representation that promote the idea that information is presented in diversity to ensure that learners with diverse sensory, cognitive, and linguistic backgrounds can gain access to the material (CAST, 2018). The second principle deals with various ways of action and expression, which should be in place since learners are expected to express their knowledge using different modalities as opposed to a specific format of response. The third principle is based on various ways of engagement, acknowledging that learners are motivated in different ways and that to be able to maintain effort and interest there should be flexibility in the way the tasks are set and facilitated.

The UDL framework implies a lot when applied to AI-enhanced language learning tools. It requires speech recognition systems to support a variety of accents and patterns of speech; visual interfaces to be provided with a screen-reader-friendly option; all content must be made available in a variety of languages and reading levels; and learners should be able to complete tasks in writing, speaking, drawing or by using a selection of options depending on their abilities and preferences. UDL therefore changes the principle of accessibility as a legal mandate into a pedagogical and technological excellence (Al-Azawei et al., 2016).

The Disability Justice and the Social Model of Disability

The social model of disability repackages the conceptualization of disability with reference to technology and education by moving social and environmental barriers as the major drivers of exclusion as opposed to considering disability as a result of individual deficits as the medical model views (Oliver, 1990). Applied to educational technology, this view shifts the emphasis to remedial approaches to learners with disabilities to an analysis of the design of tools that could reproduce the exclusionary practices inherently.

The disability justice models developed by the activists of color in the disability rights movement build on the social model and state that disability and any other identity and structural inequality axis, such as race, class, gender, and immigration status, are inseparable (Sins Invalid, 2019). With AI-mediated language learning, such intersectional lens illustrates that exclusion undergone by learners with a disability differs depending on intersecting identities; in the example, a deaf first-generation immigrant living in poverty faces a qualitatively distinct and compounded set of barriers compared to a deaf learner in a more privileged social status. In turn, disability justice requires the tools that do not only discuss technical access but encompass the entire range of conditions that impact the ability of learners to learn, the modalities involved, and the supporting needs.

Algorithms Bias and Artificial Intelligence Fairness

Interdisciplinary research and work in the fields of computer science, sociolinguistics, and critical data studies have thrown light on the endemicness of bias in AI applications used in educational contexts. The term 'algorithmic bias' refers to the systematic and, in most cases, imperceptible way, in which AI outputs are biased against certain groups, which are usually underrepresented in the training data or have characteristics that do not fit in the dominant norm that is encoded in that data (Barocas et al., 2019). Such bias is expressed in various ways in language-dependent AI tools and has a direct negative impact on the equity of learners.

The empirical evidence regarding the disproportionate error rates of speakers with an accent, older speakers and speakers with speech impairments, and speakers of African American Vernacular English and other non-standard varieties has shown that Automatic Speech Recognition (ASR) systems exhibit a disproportionately higher error rate (Koenecke et al., 2020). NLP systems that were trained solely on formal written English tend to fail when faced with other languages, dialects, and code-switching as well as the informal language of the colloquial speech. These vices are not accidental or easily correctible, but they represent structural inequalities of datasets and grading scales that determine what is deemed as right or successful language use.

Research on AI fairness has suggested a variety of technical remedies, such as debiasing algorithms, training information that is more reflective, and fairness-sensitive optimization purposes (Mehrabi et al., 2021). However, the critics warn that any technical intervention is insufficient since bias in AI may manifest not only by the lack of data but also by the social norms and power dynamics that dictate whose language, voice, and needs are considered the default ones (Benjamin, 2019). In line with this, the inclusive AI design should also incorporate sensitivity to these structural dimensions, as well as the technical remediation.

Culturally Sustaining Pedagogy

Culturally Sustaining Pedagogy, developed by Paris (2012) in reaction to the preceding models of culturally relevant and culturally responsive instruction, offers a reproachful view of the intersections between language, identity and education. Paris (2021) believes that the educational practice should not tolerate or recognize the cultural and linguistic backgrounds of the learners but should be active in maintaining and appreciating linguistic and cultural pluralism as wealth and not as a weakness. The implications of this view on AI language learning tools are far-reaching because they often provide a conceptualization of a very narrow and normative idea of linguistic competence that favors standard versions of dominant languages, especially English.

By assessing the speech or writing of learners based on a standard derived using educated, native-speaker norms, AI language tutoring systems are implicitly telling heritage speakers of languages, multilingual learners, and speakers of nonstandard dialects that their language practices are mistakes that have to be corrected instead of resources that can be drawn on (Flores & Rosa, 2015). Culturally sustaining design principles, in turn, purpose AI tools with the aim of identifying and asserting the diversity of languages to support the cultivation of the complete multilingual repertoires of learners and avoid judgmental correctness that reproduces linguistic hierarchies.

Intersectionality and Access to Technology

Although Crenshaw's (1989) conceptualization of intersectionality was initially created to explain the interaction of race and gender to create a specific type of discrimination experienced by Black women, it has since been applied to study the collective impact of multiple social identities on the accessibility of resources, institutions and technologies by individuals. In language learning with the help of AI, intersectionality demonstrates that the challenges facing learners cannot be sufficiently analyzed and addressed by considering the issues of disability, race, socioeconomic status, or linguistic background separately. A low-income, non-native English-speaking learner with a learning disability faces a combination of technical, pedagogical, and structural barriers that combine and compound each other and requires interventions that would not only address one barrier but the whole picture (Gorski, 2016).

All these theoretical frameworks can be combined to create a multidimensional lens under which this chapter may critically review existing AI language learning tools and imagine more inclusive alternatives. Their similarity is in their orientation: the key barriers to the fair access to AI-enhanced language education lie not in the learners but in the design decisions, data practices, assessment indicators, and governance frameworks of AI systems per se. All five frameworks share a common understanding: the challenges for equity in language learning with AI are not about the learners themselves, but are part of the design decisions, institutional priorities, and data practices. The literature review that follows reviews how these structural conditions are currently being studied and how much they have yet to be studied.

LITERATURE REVIEW

The academic discussion of AI in language learning has grown significantly in the last 10 years; nonetheless, the issue of accessibility and inclusion remains a relatively marginal thread in the overall context of the topic. The next sections observe the main areas of the research which are relevant to the arguments of the chapter and part of which have already been performed by the existing scholarship and what gaps still require answers.

The Artificial Intelligence in Language Education: Trends and Future

The study of AI-based language learning has identified a broad range of applications, which includes intelligent tutoring systems and computer-aided pronunciation training as well as AI writing-feedback systems and conversational practice platforms. Such studies have reported numerous applications, including intelligent tutoring systems and computer-based pronunciation learning as well as AI writing-feedback applications and chatbots. The overall results of meta-analyses and systematic reviews are the positive impacts of AI-enhanced tools on language outcomes, especially vocabulary learning, pronunciation, and reading comprehension (Golonka et al., 2012; Huang et al., 2023). Nonetheless, critics always note that these results are based to a large extent on studies that involve participants who are often college-educated, native or near-native learners of dominant languages, and learners that have access to reliable technology-populations that are not representative of the world language learners.

Moreover, the research on AI language learning shows a persistent demographic narrowness: most studies focus on learners from a limited range of geographic and linguistic backgrounds. Learners from low-income areas, non-English-speaking regions, and those with disabilities are significantly underrepresented (Chiu et al., 2023; Cercas Curry et al., 2024). This bias means that evidence on AI tool effectiveness mainly reflects experiences of groups closest to the tools' intended mainstream users, leaving underrepresented learners' experiences largely unexamined.

Disability, Accessibility and Language Learning Technology

The study of learners with disabilities and language learning technology has followed different paths to become part of the mainstream AI language learning literature. Research on augmentative and alternative communication (AAC), assistive technology, and special education has investigated the advantages of language learning tools by learners with visual and hearing impairments, physical disabilities, and cognitive and learning differences, but seldom involves AI-driven products in particular (Light & McNaughton, 2015; Raghavendra et al., 2012). The accessibility of mainstream educational technology platforms to learners with disabilities has started to receive a limited literature, and the accessibility outcomes have been identified to be often not met or partially implemented (Seale et al., 2021).

Technical guidelines on how to make digital content available to people with disabilities are Web Content Accessibility Guidelines (WCAG), which were created by the World Wide Web Consortium (W3C) and include the requirements of compatibility with screen readers, adequate color contrast, navigability by keyboard, and audio and video captions (W3C, 2018). In this sense, a study conducted by Bocevska et al. (2018) found that most educational technology applications do not even comply with the lowest level of WCAG, despite the fact that there has always been a discrepancy between the accessibility policy and the practice in implementation. In the case of AI-enhanced tools, the dynamic and interactive design of AI interfaces exacerbates the situation, and in particular, it may be very challenging to make these interfaces accessible to users of a screen reader or keyboard-based navigation.

Speech Recognition and NLP Linguistic Bias

Recent years have seen a great acceleration in the documentation of linguistic bias in AI systems applied in language education, both through academic research and investigative journalism. A systematic assessment of five large commercial ASR systems by Koenecke et al. (2020) revealed that the percentage of errors made on black speakers was almost two times more than the percentage of errors made on white speakers, with the discrepancy due in large part to the training data being highly disproportionate in reflecting Standard American English. These same differences have been reported among speakers with accents (Tatman & Kasten, 2017), speakers who are old (Vipperla et al., 2010), and speakers with dysarthria or other speech impairments (Christensen et al., 2012).

While Automatic Speech Recognition (ASR) systems face significant technical challenges in accurately processing the high acoustic variability of non-native speech, research has demonstrated that ASR-based corrective feedback can still be a highly effective and well-received pedagogical tool for improving second-language learners' pronunciation (Cucchiarini et al., 2009). Furthermore, the failure of ASR systems to recognize some voices on a regular basis sends an implicit message on whose language is considered to be readable and valuable in the system of correctness.

Socioeconomic Barriers and the Digital Divide

Socioeconomic inequality and access to educational technology have been an enduring issue in educational equity literature. In this light, Warschauer (2004) argues that access to technology cannot be equated to the ownership of devices, but it includes the social, cultural and economic capital necessary to utilize technology in an effective manner. This system of meaningful access is still relevant to the field of AI-enhanced language learning, where the distance between having a device and access to elaborate AI tools is quite large.

Academic studies both during and after the COVID -19 pandemic, which significantly increased the pace of absorbing digital and AI-mediated learning, were a graphic indicator of the way technological inequity interacts with education performance. The research in several country settings revealed that students with disadvantaged socioeconomic statuses had considerably reduced chances of reliable internet connection, proper devices, silence in learning settings, and technical skills required to use AI systems (Hamilton et al., 2020; Kuhfeld et al., 2020). In the case of language learners specifically, whose language acquisition will require high-frequency, interactive and heavily-feedback practice, the differences in these access lead to quantifiable differences in the learning results.

Multilingual Populations and Heritage Language Learners

As a phenomenon, heritage language learners—people who have been raised speaking a non-dominant language in society and who might be more or less proficient in the heritage language at any rate—are a large and increasing demographic in most educational settings, but are being systematically underserved by mainstream AI language learners (Valdés, 2001). The particular language characteristics of heritage learners with their typical oral proficiency and low levels of formal literacy, the non-standard grammatical aspects and affective relation to the language that is not similar to that of foreign language learners do not correspond well to the instructional schemes on the most AI language learning systems.

The struggles of multilingual learners are broader in the context where AI applications compare their language applications to monolingual standards. The multilingual nature of language practices used by multilingual speakers is suggested by the literature on the concept of translanguaging, which is characterized as fluid and dynamic and the usage of multiple linguistic resources within and between languages, is argued to be of sophisticated, as opposed to deficient or code-mixed, language practices (Vallejo, 2018). AI language learning applications that punish the use of translanguaging or that correct non-standard grammatical traits as mistakes that are to be fixed do not appreciate the linguistic resources of such learners and may cause their confidence and motivation to decline.

Identified Gaps in the Existing Literature

A review of the literature in this section shows that there are a number of important, related deficiencies that the current chapter will focus on. First, empirical research focused on the experience of learning with devices that integrate AI for language learning is limited, and it is essential to build on this research to understand how AI supports learning for students with disabilities. First, empirical research on the experience of learning with devices that integrate AI for language learning is limited—there is a need to build on this research to understand how AI supports learning for students with disabilities. The current evidence base is built on the basis of general accessibility audits and WCAG compliance assessments, not on participatory research which takes the perspective of disabled learners as the basis for describing their experiences of inclusion/exclusion.

Second, although there has been an increasing amount of documentation of linguistic bias in ASR and NLP systems, this has been a largely technical approach with little linkage to real-world implications of error rates and bias for educational equity and learning experience. The systematic inaccurate pronunciation feedback is not just an inconvenience to the learner, but an unfair withdrawal of the learning affordances of the tool being used. Third, there is almost no employment of participatory and community-based research approaches that have been useful in disability studies and culturally sustaining pedagogy in the AI language learning literature. Essential insights from the perspective of heritage language learners, multilingual communities and low-resource learners are not systematically taken into account when designing and evaluating AI tools. Fourth, the intersections of all the axes of marginalization (disability, socioeconomic status, linguistic background and immigration status) have not been explored in relation to access to AI language tools. The chapter addresses these gaps by proposing critical integration of the above theoretical frameworks in a single tool-based analysis of existing tools, and by introducing the concept of inclusive design principles, based on the experiential realities of the underserved learner groups.

The above gaps that were identified in the empirical coverage, in the approach to the subject matter and the integration of the different disciplines offer the rationale for the analytical framework and the design principles that are developed in the following sections.

Figure 1. Conceptual framework for inclusive AI language learning design

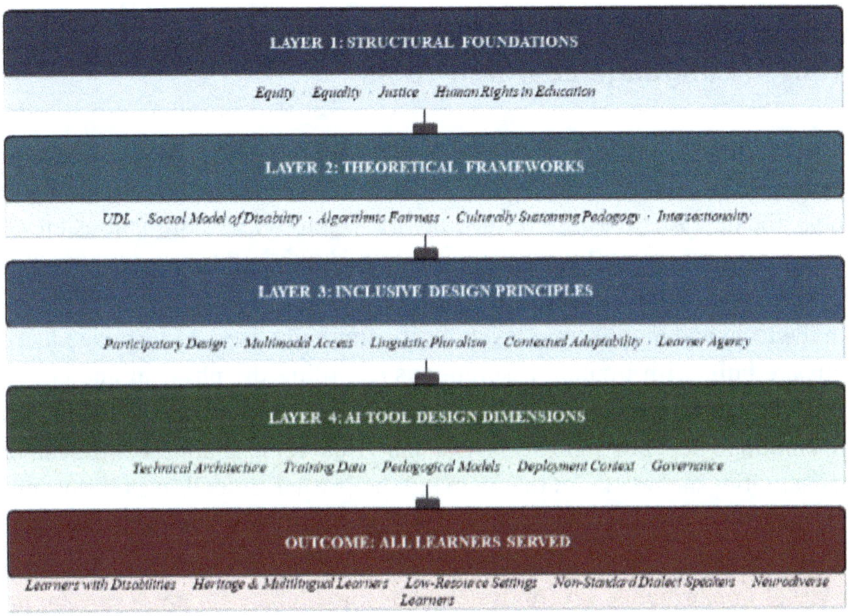

Figure 1 presents the conceptual framework underpinning the chapter's analytical approach. The framework is organized as a layered model in which structural foundations of equity, equality, and justice provide the normative grounding for theoretical frameworks, which in turn inform inclusive design principles, which then shape the specific dimensions of AI tool design. The outcome of this integrated approach is a set of AI language learning tools capable of genuinely serving the full diversity of learners. The framework underscores the central argument that inclusive AI design is not a single-level technical problem but a multi-layered challenge requiring coordinated intervention from normative, theoretical, practical, and governance perspectives simultaneously.

ANALYSIS AND DISCUSSION

This section builds a main analytical contribution of the chapter: critical analysis of the current AI language learning tools failing to meet the accessibility and inclusion criteria presented in the previous theoretical and empirical frameworks, and an in-depth expounding of the principles and practices that will make AI language learning truly inclusive. The discussion is based on the theoretical, the empirical and the practical, referring to the reviewed literature above and to the examples of particular tools and contexts.

The Reproduction of Exclusion by the Current AI Language Learning Tools

In order to explain how AI language learning tools reproduce exclusion, one needs to consider several dimensions that are interconnected: the technical architecture of the tools, the data that they are trained on, the pedagogical assumptions encoded, and the contexts of use. All these dimensions are functioning as a site of exclusion production and limited inclusion design intervention is needed.

On the technical architecture level, most commonly used AI language learning systems are built with implicit assumptions regarding the physical and cognitive ability of the users. One of the most popular language learning platforms in the world, Duolingo depends significantly on the visual representation of the material, and its activities include tasks that demand the learner to read, match images and words, and write. Although there are some accessibility improvements, such as the basic screen reader support and audio support of certain exercises, learners with great visual impairments, severe dyslexia, or low literacy in any script are under great barriers to get access to the core learning activities on the platform (Seale et al., 2021). The same can be said of ChatGPT-based language tutoring tools that have spread around since 2023: their text-heavy interfaces, heavy literacy-level usage, and the absence of in-built accommodation options assume the presence of a user with fluent reading, typing speed, and no need of visual/cognitive scaffolding.

Another essential location of exclusion is training data that is utilized to create AI-based language learning systems. As is outlined in the literature review, systems based on ASR and NLP models used in training are characterized by significantly elevated levels of error in speakers whose language use does not conform to these standards. Within the context of learning a language, this introduces an especially pernicious dynamic: the learners that are in the most need of feedback regarding their pronunciation or grammar, i.e., the learners whose pronunciation or grammar does not match target norms due to their linguistic background, state of hearing, or speech properties, are the least likely to get correct and helpful feedback provided by the system (Koenecke et al., 2020). The tool is done systematically to the benefit of those who require it least.

Exclusion is also reproduced by the pedagogic assumptions inherent in AI language learning instruments. The majority of AI language tools that belong to the mainstream are constructed on a model of language acquisition that prefigures the acquisition of monolingual competence in a standard variety of a target language, which is tested against the standards of native speakers. The model excludes the heritage language learners, who might be acquiring literacy in a language they already know; multilingual learners, whose proficiency in languages is viewed as an asset instead of a liability; and learners who speak non-standard varieties of the target language, whose current level of proficiency is seen as an obstacle instead of a source of strength (Flores & Rosa, 2015). The outcome is that a feedback situation has been created where a large number of learners are being provided with a constant flow of corrections which do not acknowledge their level of linguistic sophistication.

Last but not the least, the circumstances of deployment in which AI language learning tools are applied create further layers of exclusion that cannot be covered by the design of the tools themselves but should be viewed as a part of a larger system of inclusive language learning. In most of the low- and middle-income nations, and in the under-resource communities of developed countries, students do not have stable internet access, modern devices that can run more complex AI programs and technical assistance to meet troubleshooting (Warschauer, 2004). Language learning technology built on AI that needs to maintain high-speed internet connections continuously, place large models on a local drive, or have users go through complicated installation and account-creating procedures cannot work to any significant segment of the global language learners.

Table 1 illustrates that the exclusion produced by current AI language learning tools is multidimensional and operates across technical, data, pedagogical, contextual, and governance dimensions simultaneously.

Table 1. Dimensions of exclusion in current AI language learning tools

Dimension of Exclusion	Mechanism	Populations Most Affected	Example
Technical Architecture	Visual-only interfaces, no screen reader support	Learners with visual impairments, dyslexia, low literacy	Duolingo image-matching exercises
Training Data Bias	Underrepresentation of non-standard speech in ASR models	Non-native speakers, dialect speakers, speakers with speech impairments	Higher ASR error rates for Black speakers (Koenecke et al., 2020)
Pedagogical Assumptions	Native-speaker correctness as sole evaluative norm	Heritage language learners, multilingual learners	Penalization of translanguaging in NLP feedback tools
Deployment Context	Requires high-speed internet and advanced devices	Learners in low-resource settings, rural communities	ChatGPT tutors inaccessible without broadband internet
Governance and Design Process	Exclusion of marginalized learners from design decisions	All underrepresented groups	No co-design with disability communities in major platforms

Source: Own elaboration

As exemplified in Table 1, addressing any single dimension in isolation is insufficient; meaningful inclusion requires coordinated intervention across all five.

Principles of Design of Inclusive AI Language Learning

Based on the theoretical frames and critical thinking previously offered, this section further expounds a collection of related principles to designing AI-based language learning tools that will benefit all learners in a truly meaningful way. These principles are not provided as a prescriptive checklist but as an outline of how to think of the multifaceted and at times conflicting considerations in inclusive design.

The former is the design with instead of designing. The participatory design, where the future users of a system are also participatory co-designers, other than becoming passive subjects of usability testing has an excellent history in disability studies and human-computer interaction as a means to identify and rectify barriers that designers would otherwise not foresee with their own clairvoyance (Schuler & Namioka, 1993). As it applies to AI language learning tools, this would mean the recruitment and fair remuneration of people with disabilities, those who speak a heritage language, learners who were brought up in low-resource settings, among other underrepresented groups to actively participate in the needs assessment, ideation, prototyping, and evaluation processes. Such insights that such stakeholders provide in relation to their own learning needs, preferences, and barriers cannot be substituted and cannot be sufficiently estimated by researchers or developers, no matter how well intended they might be.

The second principle is multimodal access as a bottom line. This principle is based directly on the UDL framework, according to which all artificial intelligence language learning tools must be designed to give access to the learners of the information through a variety of ways, engage with the material, and show learning (CAST, 2018). In practice, it implies that every visually presented element should also have an audio version; that every activity which involves a written answer should also have a version which is spoken; and that every element of feedback which involves the use of color coding must have a verbal or iconographic form in which it can be understood by the color-blind. This is not just some add-on of accessibility functionality once the development is done but it is the inclusion of multimodality throughout the very fabric of the tool.

The third principle is linguistic humility and pluralism. The AI language learning tools are to be designed to acknowledge and uphold the complete diversity of language varieties, registers, and communicative practices learners present in the learning process as well as develop during it. This demands that one should give up single-standard evaluation models in favor of tests that can recognize contextually relevant language use, that consider code-switching and translanguaging as indicators of advanced multilingual proficiency, and that distinguish between the errors that hinder communication and variation that represent acceptable features of dialects (Vallejo, 2018). It further requires that the tools should be accessible in and to a wide range of languages, not only the world-dominant languages that have currently monopolized the AI language learning market.

The fourth principle is the contextual adaptability. The AI language learning tools should be developed in a manner that they can operate well in diverse hardware, connectivity, and institutional environments, and not just in high-resource environments, which are well-established broadband and modern gadgets. This can involve creating lightweight versions that can work well on the low-bandwidth connection, creating offline modes that can enable students to continue even in the absence of the internet and creating flexible deployment models that can be customized to meet the limitations of the community centers, adult education providers, refugee support agencies, and rural schools (Warschauer, 2004). Social and cultural contextual adaptability is also similar and thus tools need to be cognizant of the various cultural norms, values, communicative expectations of different people with varying backgrounds.

The fifth principle deals with transparency and agency of the learners. The AI language learning applications must also provide the learners with an easily understandable information regarding how the system works, what kinds of data it gathers and how it uses them, how the feedback and evaluation are generated. This disclosure especially applies to students, who are members of historically marginalized groups and therefore have valid grounds to be suspicious of institutional and technological frameworks that have not fulfilled their interests in the past (Benjamin, 2019). Learner agency requires not just information, but significant choices: the ability to make the tool personalized, pace and modality selections; the ability to exit data collection habits; and the ability to alert to errors or system flaws.

CASE STUDIES: TOOLS ADVANCING AND CHALLENGING INCLUSIVE DESIGN

The analysis of the selected tools in the prism of specific principles expressed in the previous section shows the opportunities and continuous challenges of inclusive AI language learning design. The following examples are chosen not to become a fully-fledged assessment of a specific product but rather to show how particular design decisions are either inclusive or exclusionary learning experiences.

The Immersive Reader by Microsoft is a good example of an impressive language assistance that includes the principles of accessibility in its core. Originally designed as a tool to support learners with dyslexia and other reading challenges, Immersive Reader uses AI to offer a collection of text accessibility options, such as adjustable text spacing and font, syllable marking, parts-of-speech spotlights, picture-dictionary assistance and read-aloud with highlighted-text tracking (Microsoft, 2023). Importantly, these features are not presented as the only accommodations to the needs of learners with disabilities, but instead as the tools that everyone can use, which is a real UDL orientation. Its effectiveness is empirically studied, and the benefits are reported to be beneficial to learners with dyslexia and English language learners, as well as to learners without identified conditions, which reinforces the argument that the tools with accessibility concerns are likely to be beneficial to the larger group of learners compared to those that are designed to accommodate only a typical user (Proctor et al., 2007).

The following empirical evaluations of the effectiveness of Immersive Reader also reinforce its credentials for being an inclusive design. Proctor et al. (2007) found statistically significant greater reading comprehension results within the English language learners' group that used the tool's scaffolding features than in a control group. In indirect evidence for the pedagogical worth of the UDL features of the tool, a separate study by Dalton and Strangman (2006) also found that the embedded text recall supports were beneficial for students with learning disabilities. Importantly, these gains did not just occur within the learners with identified disabilities—proficient readers also demonstrated increases in engagement, thus providing evidence for the "curb-cut effect" that good design benefits everyone.

Another case study that can be learned is the Project Euphonia by Google, namely, the struggle against the fact that persons with atypical speech are not recognized by automatic speech recognition (ASR) systems. Project Euphonia entails the gathering of speech data of individuals with a disorder that affects speech production, including ALS, cerebral palsy, Down syndrome, and Parkinson disease, and training of a personalized speech-recognition model that works much more effectively with such individuals compared to general-purpose speech-recognition systems (Google, 2021). This program directly responds to the training-data bias described in the literature review and shows that a focused data collection of underrepresented speakers can significantly increase accessibility. However, it also discloses a fundamental weakness: customized models require personal data gathering, which is resource-intensive and might not be applicable to the entire range of speech patterns that AI-based linguistic learning systems will have to take into account.

Comparing to these more promising examples, the mainstream AI language learning platforms are dominant, where the principles of inclusive design are easily subservient to commercial forces. A study of the design decisions of Duolingo reveals a continuous conflict between the stated goal of the organization to provide language education to all who need it and the design choices that consider the engagement mechanism, gamification, and metrics around growth more than accessibility. The significant use of timed activities on the platform, such as the one erecting an exercise, places considerable obstacles in front of learners with processing variability, nervousness, or motor skills (Seale et al., 2021). Moreover, its feedback mechanism of correction, which provides less explanation as to why an answer to a question is viewed as incorrect, is unfavorable to cognitive disabled or low metalinguistic awareness learners who need more scaffolding. Its English-centric instructional model, in which most of the teaching content is presented in the English language even to students studying languages other than English, excludes a significant fraction of language learners in the world who do not share the English language with the platform.

The most recent generation of AI-enabled language learning tools is ChatGPT-based conversational AI tutors, which offer quite significant potential as well as significant threats to inclusivity. On the positive side, such tutors can provide low-stakes, personalized, on-demand conversational practice, which is inaccessible to learners, particularly without access to interaction with a native speaker or because of the high cost of tutoring (Godwin-Jones, 2022). Theoretically, they have the ability to be customized to the level of expertise, hobbies, and language of a particular learner that cannot be accomplished with static, pre-programmed tools. However, the availability of conversational AI tools is disastrously problematic: they rely on text interfaces, assume high levels of literacy, generate linguistically complex text that may overwhelm less-proficient learners, as well as being unable to support users of assistive augmentative communication (AAC) devices, sign languages, and other non-textual modalities. Rapid adoption of these tools in learning institutions without a thorough evaluation of their accessibility is a significant equity risk.

Table 2 presents a comparative accessibility and inclusion profile of four widely used or discussed AI language learning tools measured against an ideal inclusive design standard.

Table 2. Comparative accessibility and inclusion profile of selected AI language learning tools

Criterion	Duolingo	ChatGPT Tutor	Microsoft Immersive Reader	Google Project Euphonia	Ideal Standard
Screen Reader Compatibility	Partial	Partial	Full	N/A	Full
Multimodal Input Support	Limited (text + some speech)	Text only	Text + audio output	Speech only	All modalities
Non-Standard Speech Accommodation	Poor	Poor	Moderate	Strong (personalized)	Strong
Multilingual / Heritage Learner Support	Limited (English-centric)	Moderate	Moderate (40+ languages)	Limited	Full
Low-Bandwidth / Offline Functionality	Limited	None	Partial	None	Full
Learner Data Privacy Controls	Limited	Limited	Moderate	Opt-in model	Full control
Participatory / Co-design Evidence	None documented	None documented	Partial (dyslexia community)	Strong (disability community)	Systematic
Culturally Sustaining Design	Weak	Moderate	Moderate	Weak	Strong

Source: Own elaboration

The comparison presented in Table 2 reveals that no single tool currently meets the full range of inclusion criteria identified in the literature, and that even the most accessible tools fall short in areas such as low-bandwidth functionality, culturally sustaining design, and systematic participatory co-design. This gap between current practice and the ideal standard underscores the central argument of this chapter: that inclusive AI language learning design requires a systemic rather than piecemeal approach.

Justice and Ethics of Design of AI

The creation of inclusive AI-based language-learning tools cannot be limited to the discussion of technical or pedagogical issues only; it is naturally the deep-seated ethical and political project. There are several ethical aspects that should be looked at specifically, since they shed some light on the inability of entirely technical solutions and highlight the necessity to address the structural aspects of the conditions along with the design choices.

The issues of language validity and speech readability in AI language tools are closely tied to more broad discourses of linguistic authority and hegemony. Traditionally, the standardization of language has served as a means to reproduce social hierarchies; the designation of some varieties as standard or correct and a contrast of some varieties as non-standard or incorrect, has been used to label speakers of less dominant varieties as less educated, less intelligent, and less competent and to reinforce racial, class and national hierarchies (Lippi-Green, 1997). When AI-based language-learning tools apply such hierarchies to their assessment programs, such as training to correct the characteristics of African American Vernacular English habitually or perceiving second-language accents as a type of error, they not only reflect prior societal biases, but also actively generate and enforce them. Therefore, AI design that would be oriented towards justice needs to question critically which norms of language are encoded into it and what interests of those norms it protects.

Data privacy is another critical ethical aspect especially in terms of the vulnerable learner groups. In general, AI-language learning algorithms tend to accumulate large amounts of data, consisting of speech samples, written texts, error statistics, and learning curves. In the case of undocumented immigrants, asylum seekers, and other minority groups who are persecuted, obtaining and potentially sharing this data puts vulnerable the lives of these learners beyond the scope of the educational field (Regan and Jesse, 2019). The data minimization, informed consent, data sovereignty, and terms of sharing information with third parties are not peripheral technical considerations but key equity issues that should guide the regulation of AI-language learning tools.

Algorithmic bias in AI language tools is not just about the proposed technical solutions in the fairness literature. The bias is not a random error but a structured bias, as Koenecke et al. (2020) describe, when an ASR system is trained mainly on speech data from white, educated, American English speakers. The ability to recognize what constitutes "correct" or "intelligible" speech is already imbued with racial and sociolinguistic presuppositions for a language learner. Clearly, more representative training data is needed to correct this, but so too is a critical examination of who determines what's correct, and for whose interests do they determine it? Informed consent in such contexts should be meaningful, which means that information is made available in the learners' first language; opting out should not mean loss of functionality; and policies on data retention should be subject to independent monitoring. These are not just 'compliance' conditions, they are 'ethical' conditions for the use of AI in inclusive education.

The role of human teachers and the threat of technological replacement that it entails also require ethical examination. Though AI tools have the potential to increase the accessibility and customization of language teaching, their integration into an institution might reduce human instructional assistance in parallel to the extent that it affects students who rely on human instruction the most due to their cultural responsiveness. In the case of learners with complex disabilities, asylum seekers grappling with traumatic experiences, and in cases where language acquisition is the subject of negotiations of cultural identity, the collaboration with an efficient and caring human educator can become indispensable (Kramsch, 2009). Therefore, the design of inclusive AI should be based on the desire to maintain and even improve human educational assistance as opposed to replacing it.

FINDINGS

The implications for design practice, research, policy and institutional responsibility that emerge from the analysis in the preceding sections are interrelated. This section does not repeat the analytical insights provided in the foregoing but highlights their overall implications and the context in which change can occur.

The main result is the fact that the exclusion of diverse learners in the use of AI-powered language learning tools is not coincidental but systemic. The ban is not caused by individual design problems that could be easily fixed with technical solutions; rather, the structural conditions of the architecture, training, testing, and regulation of AI systems have led to the ban. ASR systems suffer from a bias in the training data due to a systematic underrepresentation of non-standard speech; the visual interface would be inaccessible due to design processes excluding people with disabilities and the English-centricity in the majority of AI products and systems is the result of the economic necessity of a language-technology market that depends on English-speaking consumers and investors. The mitigation of these structural conditions requires more than just incremental accessibility interventions; it requires a complete re-conceptualization of how AI language learning tools are conceptualized, to whom they are targeted, and who is involved in their development.

The second finding concerns the interactions between the technical accessibility and pedagogical inclusion. Empirical studies have repeatedly shown that technical accessibility, which entails the use of a tool by learners with disabilities, is necessary, but that it does not suffice to produce inclusion. Even a tool that is navigable with a screen reader and has all-English content, follows the standards of correctness of native speakers, and is based on a paradigm of language acquisition as a monolingual learner, heritage speaker, or non-standard speaker, is still discriminating against multilingual and heritage language speakers, and non-standard language speakers, despite its technical accessibility. Amazing inclusion requires that the content, pedagogical assumptions, and language models contained in AI tools are realistic and validating of diverse learner groups to which they are directed.

The third conclusion assumes that participatory design using marginalized learners is more than a procedural suggestion and is epistemological command. No matter how diverse or good-intentioned has been the design team, it cannot possibly predict the range of such barriers, requirements, and interests, which are found within the learners whose lives are strikingly different in comparison to those of the designers. The experiential learning of learners with disabilities, multilingual learners, and those in low-resource settings that they hold about their own learning environments cannot be captured or simulated by user testing of prototyped designs that are developed without their involvement. The field thus requires institutional investment in participatory design processes that offer sufficient compensation to participants, build trust within societies, and transform the knowledge gained within the communities into tangible design actions.

The fourth observation deals with the regulation of AI language learning tools. The most important choices undertaken to make AI tools accessible and inclusive, such as choices regarding training data composition, performance evaluation metrics, deployment scenarios, data collection, and feedback models are currently responsible to few commercial technology companies that have little accountability to learners, educators, or communities. It has always been found that in cases where an oppressed group is not represented in the management of the instruments that influence their learning process, they actually reinforce the status quo instead of confronting it (Benjamin, 2019; Eubanks, 2018). To achieve significant strides in the direction of inclusive AI language education, governance forms will need to assign significant substantive functions to learners, educators, disability advocates and linguistic communities in determining the tools that will benefit them.

The fifth outcome is on the connection between AI language tools and human support of education. The information analyzed in this chapter cannot justify the fact that AI tools can replace effective human instruction by the skilled culturally responsive human instructors of learners with complex needs. Instead, the most promising AI applications to inclusive language teaching include tools that supplement and extend human-delivered instruction: they offer learners more practice opportunities, and they offer personalized feedback on low-stakes tasks, and they make otherwise inaccessible content available to learners. An AI-enhanced language education program should be justice-driven and cannot be swayed by institutional logics to use the implementation of AI as an excuse to lessen investment in human educational support, and instead, should compel AI technology to be used as a supplement to, rather than a replacement of, well-resourced and human-supported human educators. To achieve this, it is essential to have both strong institutional commitment and intentional professional development programs that provide educators with the necessary AI literacy and pedagogical skills to use these tools thoughtfully, critically, and inclusively (Vidhya Lakshmi et al., 2026).

CONCLUSION

This chapter has contended that assurances of AI to democratize and personalize language education are not possible to be fulfilled without an underlying investment in access and inclusion as design concepts as opposed to accommodations. It is demonstrated in the analysis that existing AI language learning systems reproduce exclusion at various levels such as technical, pedagogical, data-related, contextual, and governance-related and the exclusions are disproportional to already disadvantaged groups of learners in an educational system: learners with disabilities, heritage language speakers, multilingual learners, speakers non-standard language varieties, and learners in low-resource situations.

The theoretical frameworks to be applied to this analysis: UDL, the social model of disability, algorithmic fairness, culturally sustaining pedagogy, and intersectionality overlap in their shared understanding, i.e., it is not individuals who are resistant to diverse language learning but the design decisions, data practices, and evaluation measures, and governance of AI systems. This understanding has far-reaching consequences to the way the concept of AI-enhanced language education frames its tasks. Designers, developers, researchers, and policymakers have to take on the structural conditions that create and reproduce unequal access to AI-enhanced language education by creating good tools and hoping that marginalized learners can access them.

The ethical aspects of the inclusive AI language learning design, such as questions of linguistic justice, data sovereignty, the place of a human educator, and responsibility to marginalized communities, point to the realization that this is not a technical problem, but a political one, as well. To make AI-enhanced language learning accessible to all learners, it is important that the algorithms are more accurate and the user interfaces are more accessible, but it is equally important that those in authority over the design, deployment, and governance of educational AI change hands. Such change will involve long-term investment in participatory design, governance frameworks that can offer agency to the communities involved, and research with the voices of learners who have traditionally had no historical access to the advantages of educational technology.

The analysis implies the following recommendations that are structured into four areas: design practice, research, policy, and institutional responsibility. Concerning design practice, it needs to be changed to accessibility-as-aspiration instead of accessibility-as-compliance, post-hoc accommodation instead of proactive UDL, and expert-centered to participatory design practices. Research wise, there is an acute requirement of empirical research of how marginalized learners experience AI language tools, participatory research methodology that puts community knowledge at the center, and a critical study on the assumptions of the AI evaluation metrics. Policy wise, the governments and educational establishments should initiate and implement accessibility criteria to AI educational aids, invest in inclusive AI architecture study, and make sure the introduction of AI in education settings isn't and is accompanied by investment in human educational support. Technological companies creating AI language learning products should become more transparent regarding training information, performance differences, and data management policies, and have meaningful accountability to the communities where their products have an impact.

The process of language learning is fundamentally a process of belonging an act of asserting the right to membership in communities, institutions and life in the public. The AI tools that do not consider the input of diverse learners into the language acquisition process are not only contributing to the unequal educational outcomes but deprive certain learners of the means by which they can engage in the full participation in the social and civic life. The desire to create AI language learning devices to all learners is not only a technical dream but the pursuit of the highest ideals of educational justice. The AI-enhanced language-education sector can and does promise just that.

Overall, the chapter demonstrates that inclusive AI language learning must be planned from the beginning to be accessible, more linguistically diverse in its offerings, and to promote participation of learners rather than relying on retrofits. It also shows that technical design decision, skewed data, insufficient pedagogical assumptions, and lax governance can all lead to exclusion. In order for this to happen, it is essential to involve learners in co-design, improve accountability and continue to focus on the experiences of marginalized learners. Based on the chapter results, it is evident that integration of AI tools into language learning would be more inclusive only if it is based on an inclusive development and deployment principle. In this respect, it is not merely improved technology, but an alternative to the language teaching that is more humane and democratic.

REFERENCES

Al-Azawei, A., Serenelli, F., & Lundqvist, K. (2016). Universal Design for Learning (UDL): A content analysis of peer-reviewed journal papers from 2012 to 2015. *The Journal of Scholarship of Teaching and Learning*, *16*(3), 39–56. DOI: 10.14434/josotl.v16i3.19295

Alper, M. (2017). *Giving voice: Mobile communication, disability, and inequality*. MIT Press. DOI: 10.7551/mitpress/10771.001.0001

Barocas, S., Hardt, M., & Narayanan, A. (2019). *Fairness and machine learning: Limitations and opportunities*. http://fairmlbook.org

Benjamin, R. (2019). *Race after technology: Abolitionist tools for the new Jim Code*. Polity Press.

Bocevska, A., Savoska, S., Ristevski, B., & Blazheska-Tabakovska, N. (2018). Analysis of accessibility of the e-learning platforms according to the WCAG 2.0 standard compliance. *Proceedings of the 8th International Conference on Applied Internet and Information Technologies*, 26–31. https://doi.org/DOI: 10.20544/AIIT2018.P06

CAST. (2024). *CAST Universal Design for Learning Guidelines version 3.0*. CAST. https://udlguidelines.cast.org

Cercas Curry, A., Bhatt, U., & Prabhakaran, V. (2024). The AI gap: How socioeconomic status affects language technology interactions. *arXiv preprint*. https://arxiv.org/abs/2505.12158

Chiu, T. K. F., Xia, Q., Zhou, X., Chai, C. S., & Cheng, M. (2023). Systematic literature review on opportunities, challenges, and future research recommendations of artificial intelligence in education. *Computers and Education: Artificial Intelligence*, *4*, 100118. DOI: 10.1016/j.caeai.2022.100118

Christensen, H., Cunningham, S., Fox, C., Green, P., & Hain, T. (2012). A comparative study of adaptive, automatic recognition of disordered speech. *Proceedings of Interspeech*, *1–4*, 1776–1779. Advance online publication. DOI: 10.21437/Interspeech.2012-484

Crenshaw, K. (1989). Demarginalizing the intersection of race and sex: A Black feminist critique of antidiscrimination doctrine, feminist theory and antiracist politics. *University of Chicago Legal Forum*, *1989*, 139–167. https://chicagounbound.uchicago.edu/uclf/vol1989/iss1/8

Cucchiarini, C., Neri, A., & Strik, H. (2009). Oral proficiency training in Dutch L2: The contribution of ASR-based corrective feedback. *Speech Communication, 51*(10), 853–863. DOI: 10.1016/j.specom.2009.03.003

Dalton, B., & Strangman, N. (2006). Improving struggling readers' comprehension through scaffolded hypertexts and other computer-based literacy programs. In McKenna, M. C., Labbo, L. D., Kieffer, R. D., & Reinking, D. (Eds.), *International handbook of literacy and technology* (Vol. 2, pp. 75–92). Lawrence Erlbaum Associates.

Eubanks, V. (2018). *Automating inequality: How high-tech tools profile, police, and punish the poor.* St. Martin's Press.

Flores, N., & Rosa, J. (2015). Undoing appropriateness: Raciolinguistic ideologies and language diversity in education. *Harvard Educational Review, 85*(2), 149–171. DOI: 10.17763/0017-8055.85.2.149

Godwin-Jones, R. (2022). Partnering with AI: Intelligent writing assistance and instructed language learning. *Language Learning & Technology, 26*(2), 5–24. DOI: 10.64152/10125/73474

Golonka, E. M., Bowles, A. R., Frank, V. M., Richardson, D. L., & Freynik, S. (2012). Technologies for foreign language learning: A review of technology types and their effectiveness. *Computer Assisted Language Learning, 27*(1), 70–105. DOI: 10.1080/09588221.2012.700315

Google. (2021). *Project Euphonia: Improving speech recognition for non-standard speech.* Google. https://sites.research.google/euphonia/about/

Gorski, P. (2016). Rethinking the role of "culture" in educational equity: From cultural competence to equity literacy. *Multicultural Perspectives, 18*(4), 221–226. DOI: 10.1080/15210960.2016.1228344

Hamilton, L. S., Kaufman, J. H., & Diliberti, M. (2020). *Teaching and leading through a pandemic: Key findings from the American Educator Panels COVID-19 studies.* RAND Corporation., DOI: 10.7249/RRA168-2

Huang, X., Zou, D., Cheng, G., Chen, X., & Xie, H. (2023). Trends, research issues and applications of AI in language education. *Journal of Educational Technology & Society, 26*(1), 112–131. DOI: 10.30191/ETS.202301_26(1).0009

Koenecke, A., Nam, A., Lake, E., Nudell, J., Quartey, M., Mengesha, Z., Toups, C., Rickford, J. R., Jurafsky, D., & Goel, S. (2020). Racial disparities in automated speech recognition. *Proceedings of the National Academy of Sciences of the United States of America, 117*(14), 7684–7689. DOI: 10.1073/pnas.1915768117 PMID: 32205437

Kramsch, C. (2009). *The multilingual subject.* Oxford University Press.

Kuhfeld, M., Soland, J., Tarasawa, B., Johnson, A., Ruzek, E., & Lewis, K. (2020). Projecting the potential impact of COVID-19 school closures on academic achievement. *Educational Researcher, 49*(8), 549–565. DOI: 10.3102/0013189X20965918

Light, J., & McNaughton, D. (2015). Designing AAC research and intervention to improve outcomes for individuals with complex communication needs. *Augmentative and Alternative Communication : AAC, 31*(2), 85–96. DOI: 10.3109/07434618.2015.1036458 PMID: 25904008

Lippi-Green, R. (1997). *English with an accent: Language, ideology and discrimination in the United States.* Routledge., DOI: 10.4324/9780203348802

Mack, K., McDonnell, E., Jain, D., Wang, L. L., Froehlich, J. E., & Findlater, L. (2021). What do we mean by "accessibility research"? A literature survey of accessibility papers in CHI and ASSETS from 1994 to 2019. *Proceedings of the 2021 CHI Conference on Human Factors in Computing Systems*, 371. https://doi.org/ DOI: 10.1145/3411764.3445412

Mehrabi, N., Morstatter, F., Saxena, N., Lerman, K., & Galstyan, A. (2021). A survey on bias and fairness in machine learning. *ACM Computing Surveys, 54*(6), 1–35. DOI: 10.1145/3457607

Microsoft. (2023). *Immersive reader documentation.* Microsoft. https://learn .microsoft.com/en-us/azure/ai-services/immersive-reader/

Oliver, M. (1990). *The politics of disablement: A sociological approach.* Macmillan. DOI: 10.1007/978-1-349-20895-1

Paris, D. (2012). Culturally sustaining pedagogy: A needed change in stance, terminology, and practice. *Educational Researcher, 41*(3), 93–97. DOI: 10.3102/0013189X12441244

Proctor, C. P., Dalton, B., & Grisham, D. L. (2007). Scaffolding English language learners and struggling readers in a Universal Literacy Environment with embedded strategy instruction and vocabulary support. *Journal of Literacy Research, 39*(1), 71–93. DOI: 10.1080/10862960709336758

Raghavendra, P., Wood, D., Newman, L., & Lawry, J. (2012). Why aren't you on Facebook? Patterns and experiences of using the internet among young people with physical disabilities. *Technology and Disability, 24*(3), 149–162. DOI: 10.3233/ TAD-2012-0343

Regan, P., & Jesse, J. (2019). Ethical challenges of edtech, big data and personalized learning: Twenty-first century student sorting and tracking. *Ethics and Information Technology, 21*(3), 167–179. DOI: 10.1007/s10676-018-9492-2

Rose, D. H., & Meyer, A. (2002). *Teaching every student in the digital age: Universal Design for Learning*. ASCD.

Schuler, D., & Namioka, A. (Eds.). (1993). *Participatory design: Principles and practices*. Lawrence Erlbaum Associates.

Seale, J., Colwell, C., Coughlan, T., Heiman, T., Kaspi-Tsahor, D., & Olenik-Shemesh, D. (2021). 'Dreaming in colour': Disabled higher education students' perspectives on improving design practices that would enable them to benefit from their use of technologies. *Education and Information Technologies, 26*(2), 1687–1719. DOI: 10.1007/s10639-020-10329-7

Selwyn, N. (2011). Education and technology: Key issues and debates. *Continuum.*

Sins Invalid. (2019). *Skin, tooth, and bone: The basis of movement is our people.* Sins Invalid.

Tatman, R., & Kasten, R. (2017). Effects of talker dialect, gender and race on accuracy of Bing Speech and YouTube automatic captions. *Proceedings of Interspeech, 934–938*, 934–938. Advance online publication. DOI: 10.21437/Interspeech.2017-1746

Valdés, G. (2001). Heritage language students: Profiles and possibilities. In Peyton, J. K., Ranard, D. A., & McGinnis, S. (Eds.), *Heritage languages in America: Preserving a national resource* (pp. 37–77). Delta Systems.

Vallejo, C. (2018). Translanguaging: Language, bilingualism and education. *Bellaterra – Journal of Teaching & Learning Language & Literature, 11*(1), 85–95. https://doi.org/DOI: 10.5565/rev/jtl3.764

Vidhya Lakshmi, C. N., Kumar, S., Varghese, G. G., Jenefa, L., & Nandhini, P. U. (2026). Strategies for training educators in AI literacy and implementation. In Abdelaal, R. M. S., & Kayyali, M. (Eds.), *AI-powered pedagogy, academic transformation, and faculty empowerment* (pp. 383–404). IGI Global Scientific Publishing., DOI: 10.4018/979-8-3373-9220-2.ch016

Vipperla, R., Renals, S., & Frankel, J. (2010). Ageing voices: The effect of changes in voice parameters on ASR performance. *EURASIP Journal on Audio, Speech, and Music Processing, 2010*, 1–10. DOI: 10.1155/2010/525783

W3C. (2018). *Web Content Accessibility Guidelines (WCAG) 2.1*. https://www.w3.org/TR/WCAG21/

Warschauer, M. (2004). *Technology and social inclusion: Rethinking the digital divide*. MIT Press.

ADDITIONAL READING

Baker, R. S., & Hawn, A. (2022). Algorithmic bias in education. *International Journal of Artificial Intelligence in Education, 32*(4), 1052–1092. DOI: 10.1007/s40593-021-00285-9

Blodgett, S. L., Barocas, S., Daumé, H.III, & Wallach, H. (2020). Language (technology) is power: A critical survey of "bias" in NLP. In Jurafsky, D., Chai, J., Schluter, N., & Tetreault, J. (Eds.), *Proceedings of the 58th annual meeting of the association for computational linguistics* (pp. 5454–5476). Association for Computational Linguistics. https://doi.org/DOI: 10.18653/v1/2020.acl-main.485

Holmes, W., & Porayska-Pomsta, K. (Eds.). (2022). *The ethics of artificial intelligence in education: Practices, challenges, and debates*. Routledge., DOI: 10.4324/9780429329067

Holmes, W., Porayska-Pomsta, K., Holstein, K., Sutherland, E., Baker, T., Buckingham Shum, S., Santos, O. C., Rodrigo, M. T., Cukurova, M., Bittencourt, I., & Koedinger, K. R. (2022). Ethics of AI in education: Towards a community-wide framework. *International Journal of Artificial Intelligence in Education, 32*(2), 504–526. DOI: 10.1007/s40593-021-00239-1

Klímová, B., & Ibna Seraj, P. M. (2023). The use of chatbots in university EFL settings: Research trends and pedagogical implications. *Frontiers in Psychology, 14*, 1131506. DOI: 10.3389/fpsyg.2023.1131506 PMID: 37034959

Miao, F., & Holmes, W. (2021). *Artificial intelligence and education: Guidance for policy-makers*. UNESCO., DOI: 10.54675/PCSP7350

Mutimukwe, C., Viberg, O., Oberg, L.-M., & Cerratto-Pargman, T. (2022). Students' privacy concerns in learning analytics: Model development. *British Journal of Educational Technology, 53*(4), 932–951. DOI: 10.1111/bjet.13234

Wei, L. (2023). Artificial intelligence in language instruction: Impact on English learning achievement, L2 motivation, and self-regulated learning. *Frontiers in Psychology, 14*, 1261955. DOI: 10.3389/fpsyg.2023.1261955 PMID: 38023040

Zawacki-Richter, O., Marín, V. I., Bond, M., & Gouverneur, F. (2019). Systematic review of research on artificial intelligence applications in higher education—Where are the educators? *International Journal of Educational Technology in Higher Education, 16*(39), 39. Advance online publication. DOI: 10.1186/s41239-019-0171-0

KEY TERMS AND DEFINITIONS

Digital divide: A structural disparity in access to digital technology that is more than just about owning a device, but also about having reliable connectivity, technical skills and access to the social and economic conditions needed to effectively use technology to learn a language, that systematically excludes learners in low-resource contexts like rural areas, refugee populations, and low-income urban households.

Disability Justice: An approach developed by disabled activists of color, which builds on the social model of disability and places emphasis on the compounded barriers faced by individuals whose disabilities also affect other marginalized identities: for example, a deaf first-generation immigrant has to face a qualitatively different set of barriers than a deaf person from a more privileged social position.

Inclusive Design: A design philosophy that embeds accessibility and equity into a system from its earliest conceptual stages rather than retrofitting accommodations after a product has already been built around a presumed typical user, requiring that learners with disabilities, multilingual backgrounds, low digital literacy, and constrained connectivity be treated as primary users from the outset not as edge cases to be addressed after release.

Intersectionality: A theoretical framework originating with Crenshaw (1989) that examines how multiple social identities including race, gender, disability, socioeconomic status, and linguistic background interact simultaneously to produce distinct experiences of privilege or marginalization, revealing in AI-mediated language learning that a learner facing compounded barriers such as low income, a learning disability, and non-native speaker status encounters exclusions that cannot be understood or addressed by treating each identity in isolation.

Participatory Design: A design methodology in which intended end-users are engaged as active co-designers with genuine decision-making influence throughout the development process, requiring in AI language learning contexts that learners with disabilities, heritage language speakers, and low-resource learners be fairly compensated design partners from the start, not subjects whose feedback is collected after core design decisions have already been made.

Translanguaging: The fluid, dynamic practice by which multilingual speakers draw on their full linguistic repertoire across and between languages as a unified communicative and cognitive resource, such that AI language tools that penalize translanguaging or treat non-standard grammatical features as errors actively misrepresent sophisticated multilingual competence as deficiency, undermining the confidence and motivation of heritage and multilingual learners.

Universal Design for Learning (UDL): A pedagogical and technological framework that advocates designing learning environments and tools to accommodate the inherent variability of all learners from the outset through multiple means of representation, action, expression, and engagement, shifting accessibility in AI-enhanced language learning from a compliance obligation into a core design standard that ensures every interface element, task type, and feedback mechanism functions meaningfully regardless of a learner's sensory, cognitive, or linguistic profile.

Section 3
Applications, Pedagogical Practice, and Learner Experience

Chapter 8

Exploring GenAI for Multilingual News Analysis and Its Pedagogical Potential for the Language Classroom

Lisa Marie Brinkmann
http://orcid.org/0000-0003-3217-7399
University of Hamburg, Germany

Liudmila Shafirova
http://orcid.org/0000-0003-3743-2029
Universidade de Aveiro, Portugal

ABSTRACT

This chapter examines the pedagogical potential of generative artificial intelligence (GenAI) for multilingual news analysis in language education. It situates GenAI within a multiliteracies framework, with a focus on critical multilingual language awareness and the need to address biases embedded in AI-generated content. The chapter explores how comparing GenAI outputs across languages can highlight differing perspectives and foster multiliteracies. Drawing on empirical analyses of news representations in English, German, and Spanish, it demonstrates how GenAI can be used for multilingual and multiliteracies purposes. The findings point to differences not only in presentation and content but also in what is foregrounded or omitted across languages. This underscores the value of using GenAI to analyse how meaning is shaped differently across linguistic contexts.

DOI: 10.4018/979-8-3373-7749-0.ch008

INTRODUCTION

The emergence of generative artificial intelligence (GenAI) as a central topic and an influential tool in education has led to the raise of important discussions about plagiarism, authorship, writing practices, and authenticity. It is now part of everyday life and is widely used for information retrieval and generate content. In the field of language education, the widespread of GenAI makes it essential to adopt a critical perspective: students need opportunities to analyse with a critical approach the information provided by GenAI and to reflect on the potential biases embedded in its outputs. The language classroom offers particular opportunities in this regard. For instance, students can compare information generated in different languages to explore how perspectives on a single topic may vary. This contrastive approach is especially valuable in multilingual classrooms, where interacting with GenAI in multiple languages can lead to different responses according to the data available in a specific language (Kuteeva & Andersson, 2024; Zhang et al., 2023). Drawing on students' full linguistic repertoires can also promote social justice, as multilingual learners can become knowledge experts in the classroom. This helps challenge deficit-oriented views of multilingualism that persist in society and, at times, in schools and language education more specifically (Goossens, 2022).

Our theoretical framework includes multiliteracies with a focus on critical multilingual language awareness (CMLA), and current biases in the GenAI outputs. Multiliteracies can be defined as building critical receptive and productive skills adapted to the 21st century's (social and digital) world (New London Group, 1996). We incorporate a critical perspective that recognises how digital environments, such as algorithms and GenAI systems, can reproduce ideologies, power dynamics, and inequalities (Darvin, 2025). In this expanded framework, developing multiliteracies involves supporting students in critically analysing these underlying structures while also understanding the affordances of digital tools for contrasting information, verifying sources, and identifying inequities. Anderson and Macleray (2016) have shown how a digital and multilingual engagement with literacy can foster students' critical thinking, and Mahapatra and Koltovskaia (2025) intertwine a critical approach towards second language education (in the Global South) and multiliteracies to balance between inclusive principles and digitally mediated aspects. While these studies provide valuable insights into digital and multilingual literacy practices, they predate the widespread availability of GenAI tools. Our study extends this line of research by examining how GenAI can be integrated into multilingual literacy education, specifically exploring its potential to foster CMLA through cross-linguistic comparison of AI-generated content.

Regarding biases in GenAI outputs, an emerging body of research identifies several types. These include biases in AI-generated images, which tend to produce generalised or stereotypical representations (Sobey, 2025); biases in the representation of language varieties, with outputs rarely reflecting Englishes beyond American, British, or Australian varieties (Jiang & Gu, 2025); and broader content biases that privilege so-called WEIRD (Western, educated, industrialised, rich, and democratic) perspectives (Kuteeva & Andersson, 2024). However, there remains a lack of research exploring how GenAI functions across different languages and how multilingual learners might benefit from these tools. While scholarship on GenAI biases is growing, research at the intersection of GenAI, cross-linguistic variation in AI outputs, and multilingual language education remains limited. In particular, the examination of how the same GenAI tool produces systematically different outputs across languages remains limited, or how such variation might be leveraged pedagogically to develop students' critical multilingual awareness. This gap is significant given the increasing presence of GenAI in educational contexts and the need to equip multilingual learners with tools for critically engaging with AI-generated content.

Building on this identified gap, we developed a pilot study that aims to compare GenAI analysis of a news article in different languages. This comparison will serve as an exploration for a further pedagogic intervention to develop students' multiliteracies. More concretely, our research questions are (1) What similarities and differences emerge across the different language versions of the discourse analysis of a news article produced by GenAI?, and (2) How can different GenAI language versions of the same content be used to foster multiliteracies in the language classroom? This preliminary study documents the authors' experiences testing how GenAI analyses a news article in English, Spanish, and German using pre-established critical discourse analysis (CDA) questions (Van Dijk, 2015). It compares GenAI outputs across languages and discusses implications for developing multiliteracies in the classroom. A follow-up study will test these implications in a high school language classroom.

In this chapter, we first present the theoretical framework, consisting of multiliteracies and GenAI, and then the methodology, including data collection, prompts used, and data analysis. Since our study aims to analyse the differences and similarities between GenAI's outputs, the findings are structured by language pairs, followed by a comparison of all three language versions. Finally, we discuss the findings and propose implications for practice.

THEORETICAL BACKGROUND

In this section, we explore the framework of multiliteracies and its connections to CMLA and potential biases in the use of GenAI, drawing on previous studies to inform our analysis.

Multiliteracies with a Focus on Critical Multilingual Language Awareness

Approaches to multiliteracies provide a useful framework for understanding how generative AI may be integrated into language education. Earlier research on literacy in multilingual and digital contexts has shown that engaging with diverse media and languages can support learners' critical thinking and reflective engagement with texts (Cope & Kalantzis, 2013). Studies on digital literacy in second language education, forming part of multiliteracies, have explored how learners interact with digital environments and how pedagogical approaches may balance inclusive principles with digitally mediated communication (Anderson & Macleray, 2016; Mahapatra & Koltovskaia, 2025). In the following lines, we first define multiliteracies, before focusing on studies on GenAI in relation to language and language education, aiming to develop multiliteracies.

The concept of *multiliteracies* emerged in response to increasing linguistic diversity and changing communication environments. The New London Group (1996) introduced this approach to address how literacy education can respond to multilingual societies and evolving forms of communication. Instead of focusing exclusively on written language, multiliteracies emphasise the plurality of communicative modes and the multiplicity of cultural contexts in which meaning is produced. Within this perspective, literacy education involves navigating multiple linguistic and cultural discourses and developing the capacity to interpret and produce meaning across different media and contexts (Cope & Kalantzis, 2013; New London Group, 1996).

Within contemporary educational contexts, multiliteracies are closely connected to multilingual education and broader educational goals associated with 21st century competences. In this sense, multiliteracies involve critical thinking, knowledge creation, communication across linguistic and disciplinary boundaries, and participation in social life. Learners work with a range of texts and technologies to adapt their literacy practices to diverse social and cultural contexts. Such practices require flexibility and responsibility in the use of communicative resources (Meyer et al., 2018). Research on multilingual literacy similarly emphasises the role of multiple languages in meaning-making processes. Literacy practices across languages involve navigating heterogeneous linguistic environments, constructing identities, and developing critical perspectives on media and information. In this view, multilingual literacy encompasses the interaction between languages, discourses, registers, and communication channels (Breuer & Van Steendam, 2021; García et al., 2007).

Multiliteracies are also closely linked to critical examinations of language as embedded in power, ideology, and social inequality. This parallels critical language awareness that calls for analysing how discourse constructs and marginalises social realities (Alim, 2010; Fairclough, 2014/1992). In multilingual contexts, such engagement is shaped by unequal valuations of languages, highlighting the need to affirm learners' repertoires and challenge exclusionary structures (Cummins, 2023). In this sense, the extended version of CMLA includes the capacity to interrogate dominant language ideologies and their consequences for different social groups (García, 2017). It also includes the ability to critically engage with cultural perspectives, practices, and products, including one's own (Byram, 2021). From this perspective, CMLA helps address linguistic hierarchies and deficit views, particularly across digital environments, by enabling critical reflection on how language can both empower and marginalise speakers.

Drawing on these theoretical underpinnings, the multiliteracies framework, including CMLA, guides the pedagogical approach taken in this study, informing how GenAI can be used multilingually in the classroom by combining semiotic resources and critical perspectives on GenAI, and integrating these into authentic communicative practices (Breidbach & Küster, 2014). In the following subsection, we examine the biases associated with GenAI use, which will serve as a further basis for our study.

Possible Biases in the Use of Generative AI

The role of digital media and GenAI became central to everyday meaning-making, meanwhile GenAI heavily impacts literacy teaching and learning in the foreign language classroom (Christoforou, 2025). Therefore, analysing GenAI texts has become an important dimension of literacy education. Developing literacy involves understanding how different modes contribute to meaning and how representations shape social interpretations (Yelland, 2025). Algorithms, platforms, and automated systems challenge how information is generated and distributed.

GenAI introduces additional biases to be analysed and interpreted in the classroom for multiliteracies development. Systems based on large language models (LLM) generate texts by drawing on extensive digital corpora. The data required for these systems typically include monolingual corpora, translated parallel corpora, and annotated datasets (Jouitteau, 2023). More concretely, AI needs: (i) monolingual, polished, and multimodal texts by native speakers of a specified dialect or variety, ranging from radio shows to corrections of schoolwork; (ii) trained and translated versions of the monolingual corpus, including corrected translations; and (iii) and improved versions, including syntactic-morphologic and semantic information. Languages that lack digital corpora or standardised datasets are less likely to be represented in AI systems. As a result, digital infrastructures may contribute to unequal representation of languages in computational environments (Jouitteau, 2023). In the digital era, languages that are not extensively digitised, within the existing and constructed digitality, face challenges in maintaining visibility within digital communication spaces.

Following this bias of corpora representativity, Zhang et al. (2023) conducted empirical study of ChatGPT 3.5's multilingual capabilities, comparing outputs across English, Spanish, German, French, Japanese, and Chinese. Performance in multiple-choice mathematics and logic tasks was consistently stronger in English, whilst knowledge retrieval tasks showed broadly similar results across languages. Even more strikingly, the cover letter writing task revealed a strong dependence on English, with outputs in other languages seemingly modelled on the English version. Zhang et al. (2023) attributed this English dominance to the disproportionate representation of English in the model's training corpora.

Beyond questions of multilingual corpora representation, GenAI also raises broader social and ethical issues. Kalantzis and Cope (2025) argue that "Artificial Intelligence is a new colonialism, not of material space like the old colonizers, but the colonization of social intelligence by a handful of insurgent moguls of human meaning" (p. 8). In the same train of thought, several empirical studies argue that GenAI can have biases in the representation of professionals in the images (Sobey, 2025) and broader content biases that privilege Western perspectives over those of the Global South due to the quality of the training corpora of the GenAI (Kuteeva & Andersdon, 2024). The main aspect of this new Artificial Intelligence colonialism, is the reproduction of linguistic and cultural ideologies in GenAI, ranging from Western norms to language hierarchies (Brinkmann et al., forthcoming). Therefore, contemporary AI developments are understood as a form of technological expansion that reshapes the circulation of cultural and linguistic resources.

At the same time, GenAI can function as a tool within learning environments. Research on AI-mediated learning indicates that learners use such systems in different ways, ranging from information retrieval to collaborative knowledge construction. In these contexts, GenAI may support narrative construction, language practice, and the exploration of alternative perspectives (Janfada et al., 2025; Liu et al., 2025). Rather than positioning GenAI as a substitute for learning processes, pedagogical approaches increasingly emphasise learning with and through digital systems. This perspective treats GenAI as part of an environment in which learners engage in dialogue with technological tools while developing their own interpretative capacities (Kalantzis & Cope, 2025).

In this study, we advocate for a critical exploration of GenAI's affordances in the language classroom, one that encourages students to interrogate its biases whilst drawing on their plurilingual repertoire. The following section outlines the methodology of the study.

METHODOLOGY

This chapter addresses the following research questions: (1) What similarities and differences emerge across the different language versions of the discourse analysis of a news article produced by GenAI?, and (2) How can different GenAI language versions of the same content be used to foster multiliteracies in the language classroom? In this section, we present the data collection methods, prompts, the corpus, and data analysis methods to answer the research questions.

Data Collection

The data were collected through prompts sent to ChatGPT-5.3 along with the article for analysis. For this purpose, of a ChatGPT analysis, we used the BBC article "Why has Trump attacked Venezuela and taken Maduro?" by Vanessa Buschschlüter (2026). The article reports that Donald Trump ordered military strikes on Venezuela and the capture of Nicolás Maduro, justifying the actions with claims about migration, drug trafficking, and security threats, while critics question their legality and point to geopolitical and economic reasons. Including the description of images, the text contains 1,632 words. This article was selected because it was published by a credible news source and addresses current events that can be examined from multiple perspectives, particularly those of the West and the Global South. The topic is especially relevant for Spanish language classes, as it relates to political developments in Venezuela and offers opportunities to engage with sociocultural dimensions of the school curriculum.

Although the article is written in English, the prompts used by the researchers were written in the target languages, English, Spanish, and German, and were translated into those languages by the researchers and with the help of DeepL.

To minimise variability in ChatGPT's responses, all prompts were submitted on the same day using the anonymised browser profiles of two researchers. Each prompt was entered into an individual anonymised chat session to avoid cross-contamination between languages. Because the anonymised version of ChatGPT does not allow file attachments, the article text was copied and pasted into each chat session along with the prompts. The prompts used are shown in Table 1.

Table 1. Prompts introduced to ChatGPT

Prompts in English (Researcher 2, IP in Portugal) 17.02.2026	Prompts in Spanish (Researcher 1, IP in Germany) 17.02.2026	Prompts in German (Researcher 1, IP in Germany) 17.02.2026
Please, describe the context of the text above: Scenario/Setting: Time Place Circumstances [Type and means of communication? (oral vs. written, book, newspaper, Internet, etc.)] Participants: Identities (membership in communities, groups, etc.) Relationships (e.g., power, friendship, family, etc.) Act(s)/Activity/Interaction: Speech acts (asserting, questioning, promising, etc.) Communicative acts (narrating, protesting, etc.) Social acts (cooperating, defending, etc.) Political acts (voting, governing, etc.) Social activity (visiting the doctor, attending a conference)	Por favor, describe el contexto del texto arriba: Escenario/ Setting: Tiempo Lugar Circunstancias [Tipo y Medios de comunicación? (oral vs. escrito, libro, periódico, Internet, etc.)] Participantes: Identidades (membresía de comunidades, grupos, etc.) Relaciones (p.ej., de poder, de amistad, de familia, etc.) Acto(s)/Actividad/ Interacción: Actos de habla (afirmar, preguntar, prometer, etc.) Actos de comunicación (contar, protestar, etc.) Actos sociales (cooperar, defender, etc.) Actos políticos (votar, gobernar, etc.) Actividad social (visitar el médico, atender a una conferencia)	Bitte beschreibe den Kontext des obigen Texts. Szenario/Setting: Zeit Ort Umstände [Art und Kommunikationsmittel? (mündlich vs. schriftlich, Buch, Zeitung, Internet usw.)] Teilnehmende: Identitäten (Mitgliedschaft in Gemeinschaften, Gruppen usw.) Beziehungen (z. B. Macht, Freundschaft, Familie usw.) Handlung(en)/Aktivität/ Interaktion: Sprechakte (afirmieren, fragen, versprechen usw.) Kommunikationsakte (erzählen, protestieren usw.) Soziale Akte (kooperieren, verteidigen usw.) Politische Akte (wählen, regieren usw.) Soziale Aktivität (Arztbesuch, Teilnahme an einer Konferenz)

Source: Authors' elaboration

After the prompts were designed, ChatGPT responded with the text in the language of the prompts. Here, we then analysed different responses, drawing comparisons between the answers.

Creation of the Prompts

The prompts were developed drawing on principles of CDA, which we define following Van Dijk (2015) as "a discourse analytical research that primarily studies the way socialpower abuse and inequality are enacted, reproduced, legitimated, and resisted by text and talk in the social and political context" (p. 1).

In this study, we adopt CDA following Van Dijk (2001), particularly his view that written discourse is connected to the cognitive representations of its authors. According to Van Dijk (2001), CDA is conducted from an explicit ideological position that seeks not only to understand but also to challenge social inequalities. Within this framework, GenAI is positioned as a "researcher" applying CDA to analyse the text. By comparing the analyses generated in different languages, we aim to examine whether ChatGPT constructs different discursive representations of the same article and whether it demonstrates a particular positionality toward the text.

CDA also has a strong pedagogical dimension. It has been identified as an effective tool for helping students develop critical awareness, and therefore multiliteracies, when analysing information, particularly news discourse (Dar et al., 2010). In this context, drawing on this experiment, we propose pedagogical implications for a language classroom that illustrates how GenAI can be used to perform critical analysis across multiple languages.

As an initial step, we asked ChatGPT to establish the context of the text, including its participants, circumstances, relationships, and activities, following Van Dijk (2015). Our aim was to examine potential differences in how the overall discursive context, or communicative situation, was constructed across languages. Although we formulated additional CDA-informed questions (e.g., "How are the main actors (the US and Venezuela, Trump and Maduro) referenced, both implicitly and explicitly?" and "What is the argumentation of the article based on?"), the variations observed at the level of contextual framing were already sufficiently pronounced. Therefore, for the purposes of this study, we focus exclusively on the analysis of the contextual construction of the news article, as this dimension remains sufficient to understand both the discursive structures of the text and GenAI's positionality.

Corpus of the Analysis

The corpus of analysis consists of three responses of ChatGPT-5.3 to our prompts. In total, we gathered this number of responses: 537 words or 3943 characters in English, 415 words or 2908 characters in Spanish, and 346 words or 2709 characters in German.

Data Analysis

The analysis was conducted through systematic comparisons of ChatGPT-generated responses across three language pairings: English/Spanish, English/German, and German/Spanish. The distribution of language pairings was determined by the researchers' linguistic competences, with only one of them having proficiency in German. To present the data, we translated, using DeepL, examples into English to enhance comprehension across languages. Each comparison followed a structured, step-by-step approach, examining the contextual dimensions presented in Table 2.

Table 2. Framework of prompts for CDA analysis

Category	#	Component	Examples / Description
1. Scenario / Setting	1.1	Time	—
	1.2	Place	—
	1.3	Circumstances	—
	1.4	Type & means of communication	*oral vs. written; book, newspaper, Internet, etc.*
2. Participants	2.1	Identities	*membership in communities, groups, etc.*
	2.2	Relationships	*power, friendship, family, etc.*
3. Act(s) / Activity / Interaction	3.1	Speech acts	*asserting, questioning, promising, etc.*
	3.2	Communicative acts	*narrating, protesting, etc.*
	3.3	Social acts	*cooperating, defending, etc.*
	3.4	Political acts	*voting, governing, etc.*
	3.5	Social activity	*visiting the doctor, attending a conference, etc.*

Source: Authors' elaboration

The analytical framework drew on CDA following Van Dijk (2015), with particular attention to three dimensions: (i) the omission or addition of information (e.g., in the place category in English: No reference to Maduro. Spanish: reference to Maduro when describing the place in the US: "Estados Unidos (donde es trasladado Nicolás Maduro y enfrenta cargos en Nueva York"); (ii) the organisation and structure of information (e.g., in German text, there is an additional subsection "military acts" which is absent in English and Spanish texts); and (iii) and the linguistic expression of key terms (e.g., "migration crisis" in English vs. "migration and crisis" in Spanish or "migration debate" in German). The three CDA analytical dimensions were identified inductively following an initial exploration of the data. These dimensions emerged as most relevant for capturing differences in positionality and ideological framing across the AI-generated texts in each language pairing and subsequently guided the systematic comparison of all three pairings. Findings were systematically recorded in a shared Excel table accessible to both researchers and uploaded to a repository (https://www.fdr.uni-hamburg.de/record/18689).

The analysis was divided between the two researchers: the first examined the English/German and German/Spanish pairings, while the second examined the English/Spanish pairing. Following this initial analysis, both researchers convened a virtual meeting to compare findings, discuss observed similarities and differences across the texts, and critically evaluate the consistency and logic of their interpretations. Each researcher then returned independently to the data to conduct a more detailed review. A second virtual meeting was subsequently held to discuss cross-linguistic comparisons across all three language pairings.

FINDINGS

In this section, we provide answers to the first research question. The findings differ across most components of the analysis in the three languages. In the following sections, we analyse the differences and similarities between English and Spanish, English and German and German and Spanish, before analysing the three languages together.

English and Spanish

The comparison of the English and Spanish versions revealed several key differences in how content is presented and in the amount of information provided. The word count alone reflects this disparity: the English version contains 537 words compared to 415 in Spanish, suggesting that the English text offers a more detailed account.

More specifically, the English version provided more detail across several components. In the setting component (1.3. Circumstances), the Spanish version only included "Type and Means of Communication," without describing the broader circumstances of the events covered in the article. The English version, by contrast, included general context such as the U.S. military strikes inside Venezuela and the capture of President Nicolás Maduro. A similar gap was found in the participants component (2.1. Identities): the Spanish version made no reference to Venezuelan opposition leaders (María Corina Machado, Edmundo González) or international legal experts, and provided less detail on group membership, such as the characterisation of Venezuelan migrants as a displaced population due to economic and political crisis. Overall, the Spanish version shows a pattern of some gaps in information when compared to the English one.

A second type of omission can be described as intentional rather than structural. This kind of omission can shape the reader's perception by foregrounding certain angles of the conflict while leaving others out. In the English and Spanish comparison, notable omissions were found in both versions. For instance, in the settings component (1.1. Time and 1.2. Place), the Spanish version explicitly mentioned the capture of Maduro, while the English version did not. Table 3 illustrates this in the context of component 1.1. Time.

Table 3. Example of omission of information

English	Spanish	Spanish version translated into English
Time The events are set in **late 2025 and early January 2026**. The article is dated **3 January 2026**. It takes place during **Donald Trump's second term** as US president.	⏳ **Tiempo** **Fecha:** 3 de enero de 2026. **Contexto histórico-político:** Segundo mandato de **Donald Trump** como presidente de Estados Unidos. Momento de alta tensión geopolítica entre Estados Unidos y Venezuela tras la captura del presidente venezolano.	⏳ **Time** **Date**: January 3, 2026. **Historical–political context:** Second term of **Donald Trump** as President of the United States. Moment of high geopolitical tension between the United States and Venezuela following the capture of the Venezuelan president.

Source: Authors' elaboration

Table 3 shows that in the English version, the timing is described in neutral terms, situating the events "in late 2025 and early January 2026". The Spanish version, by contrast, characterises the moment through the situation itself: "a moment of high geopolitical tension between the US and Venezuela following the capture of the Venezuelan president". Where the English reference to time is relatively neutral, the Spanish one foregrounds the US-Venezuela conflict and the capture of Nicolás Maduro.

Beyond this, certain topics appear more frequently in the English version. "Oil production" is mentioned three times in English, across the settings (1.3. Circumstances), Acts (3.2. Communicative Acts), and the overall Summary components, but only once in Spanish, in the context of participants (2.1. Relationships: "Venezuela acusa a EE. UU. de intentar apropiarse de su petróleo"). In both languages, oil is framed as a possible motive from Venezuela's perspective for the US military operation. A similar pattern is observed with "drug trafficking", which also appears more frequently in the English version.

We argue that these omissions are not coincidental. The Spanish text places greater emphasis on Venezuela and the capture of its president, while the English text focuses more on possible explanations for the US intervention. This difference in focus is especially noticeable when comparing the overall summary component of both versions, which showed the greatest number of differences between the two texts. An excerpt is provided in Table 4.

Table 4. Differences in the overall summary component

English	Spanish	Spanish version translated into English
The text is a **journalistic report** covering a dramatic geopolitical crisis in which the United States, under President Trump, has escalated from economic and political pressure to direct military intervention in Venezuela, culminating in the capture of President Nicolás Maduro. It takes place within: ● A broader **migration crisis** ● The **global drug trade debate** ● Disputes over **international law** Strategic concerns about **oil and geopolitical power**	El texto se sitúa en un **contexto de crisis política y militar internacional,** reportado por un medio periodístico escrito, donde se describen: ● Una intervención militar de EE. UU. en Venezuela. ● La captura del presidente venezolano. ● Acusaciones relacionadas con narcotráfico y migración. ● Tensiones diplomáticas y debate legal internacional.	The text is situated in a context of international political and military crisis, reported by a written journalistic outlet, where the following are described: ● A U.S. military intervention in Venezuela. ● The capture of the Venezuelan president. ● Accusations related to drug trafficking and migration. ● Diplomatic tensions and international legal debate.

Source: Authors' elaboration

The overall summary component highlights clear differences in how key terms are framed linguistically across the two versions. The "global drug trade", for instance, is presented as a "debate" in the English text but as an "accusation" in the Spanish text. A similar contrast appears with migration: in English, it is situated within "a broader migration crisis", while in Spanish, "migration" figures as one of the accusations levelled by the US against Venezuela. This pattern recurs throughout the texts more broadly, as the English version consistently uses the term "migration crisis", whereas the Spanish version opts for "massive migration" or "migration and crisis", never using that exact phrase.

Returning to the overall summary, both "U.S. military intervention" and "the capture of the Venezuelan president" are absent from the bullet points of the English text and instead appear in a preceding paragraph, where they are easier to overlook. Finally, only the English text refers to "oil and geopolitical power" in the context of "strategic concerns", which subtly lends legitimacy to the US position.

Taken together, these summaries reveal how the English text downplays the focus on Maduro's capture and instead foregrounds the three main justifications offered for the US intervention: migration, oil, and drug trafficking.

English and German

Similar to the comparison between the English and the Spanish versions, the comparison of the English and German versions revealed differences in the presentation of the content and the promotion of information, reflected in the word count with 537 words in the English version and 346 words in the German version, i.e., the German version is only 64% of the length of the English one.

The English version often omits internal political aspects of Venezuela such as the opposition and regime change, e.g., in the social acts and social activities component. It frames broader social activities mainly in terms of cross-border law enforcement and political governance. The German version, in contrast, omits military cooperation and juxtaposes military acts, in order to not include them into the political acts.

Similar to the English-Spanish comparison, the English version provides more detailed contextualisation, particularly in the setting component (1.3 Circumstances), where it explicitly links the intervention to oil, drug trafficking, and a broader pressure campaign. The German version, by contrast, relies more heavily on nominalisation and leaves actors, especially Nicolás Maduro, implicit. Moreover, this version foregrounds political contextualisation and places the conflict primarily within judicial and political international frameworks. In the same component, the English version situates the issue in a global communicative context, and frames media coverage as a combination of factual reporting and expert version, without explicitly naming the BBC as the author. In contrast, the German version uses the term "intervention" rather than "interventionism" and references the use of visual material.

The difference in contextualisation is also visible in the identities component (2.1) because the English and German versions differ in how political actors and their relationships are structured and contextualised regarding identities. An excerpt is provided in Table 5.

Table 5. Differences in the identities component

English	German	German version translated into English
Main Political Actors ● Donald Trump o US President o Holds executive and military authority ● Nicolás Maduro o President of Venezuela o Captured and indicted in New York **Other Actors** ● US military forces (15,000 troops, naval fleet) ● US government institutions (White House, DEA, CIA) ● Venezuelan armed forces ● Venezuelan opposition figures such as: o María Corina Machado o Edmundo González ● International legal experts (e.g., former ICC prosecutor) ● Venezuelan migrants ● Alleged criminal groups (e.g., Tren de Aragua) **Identities and Group Membership** ● Trump: Leader of the US federal government and commander-in-chief. ● Maduro: Leader of a socialist government (PSUV). ● Venezuelan migrants: displaced population due to economic and political crisis. ● Opposition leaders: pro-democracy activists opposing Maduro's rule.	**Zentrale Akteure** **Donald Trump** ● Rolle: US-Präsident ● Identität: Republikanischer Politiker ● Position: Oberbefehlshaber der US-Streitkräfte ● Machtposition: Initiator militärischer Maßnahmen **Nicolás Maduro** ● Rolle: Präsident Venezuelas ● Parteizugehörigkeit: PSUV (sozialistische Regierungspartei) ● Identität: Staatsoberhaupt eines autoritären Regimes ● Machtposition: Regierungschef, später Gefangener **Weitere Gruppen** ● US-Militär ● Venezolanische Streitkräfte ● Opposition (z. B. María Corina Machado) ● US-Justiz (Anklage in New York) ● Internationale Rechts- und Sicherheitsexperten ● Migranten aus Venezuela ● Drogenkartelle (z. B. „Cartel de los Soles")	**Key players** **Donald Trump** ● Role: US President ● Identity: Republican politician ● Position: Commander-in-Chief of the US Armed Forces ● Position of power: Initiator of military action **Nicolás Maduro** ● Role: President of Venezuela ● Party affiliation: PSUV (socialist ruling party) ● Identity: Head of state of an authoritarian regime ● Position of power: Head of government, later prisoner **Other groups** ● US military ● Venezuelan armed forces ● Opposition (e.g., María Corina Machado) ● US justice system (indictment in New York) ● International legal and security experts ● Migrants from Venezuela ● Drug cartels (e.g., "Cartel de los Soles")

Source: Authors' elaboration

In Table 5, we can notice differences in the structure, because the English version adds a subsection about "Identities and Group Membership" and uses subsections. On the content level, the English version distinguishes between main political actors, other actors, identities and group memberships, and their relationships, but it does not further analyse Donald Trump's position of power. Other actors connected to the US or the international context—such as Venezuelan opposition figures or drug cartels—are specified, and additional explanations are provided for groups such as Venezuelan migrants and opposition leaders. The German version also differentiates actors but organises them more explicitly according to role, identity, position, and power relations. Trump's party affiliation is mentioned, and his power position is described as that of the initiator of the military measures. Nicolás Maduro is presented first as a political leader and later as a prisoner, and he is associated with an authoritarian regime. At the same time, fewer actors are specified: only one opposition member is mentioned, without a clear linguistic connection to Venezuela, and although another drug cartel is referenced, actors related to the US or the broader international context are not further detailed.

Further differences emerge in the Relationships component (2.2). The English version subordinates' relationships to individual actors and focuses on general "conflict" and "power dynamics", without explicitly addressing international relations. In contrast, the German version conceptualises relationships more abstractly through terms such as "power relations" and "disempowerment" and explicitly situates the conflict within international law and state confrontation.

Differences are also evident in the section of acts, activities, and interactions (3.1-3.5). The English version foregrounds social acts and social activities (3.3; 3.5) such as cross-border law enforcement and governance, while also including military cooperation and sanctions. In the speech acts component (3.1), the English version distinguishes between Trump, Maduro, and legal experts. Trump's speech acts are differentiated, while legal experts appear mainly through criticism of the legality of US strikes. In contrast, the German version differentiates mainly between Trump and Maduro. In the communicative acts (3.2), the English version includes narrative and explanatory elements, focusing primarily on the content, while explicit criticism is largely absent. In the social acts (3.3), the English version includes military cooperation and sanctions. Cross-border law enforcement and political governance are treated as relevant social activities (3.5). In the German version, no legal experts appear, although Maduro's speech acts remain comparable across both analyses (3.2). In the social acts component (3.3), the German version also mentions judicial experts who criticise the situation, but omits military cooperation, and specifies the number of migrants. The social activities (3.3) in the German version include drug control, migration politics, and regime change as social activities. Regarding the political acts component (3.4), an important difference can be noticed: the German version differentiates political from military acts. Actions such as air strikes, naval deployment, the arrest of a head of state, and the destruction of military infrastructure are mentioned as military acts, while sanctions are not mentioned in either political or military acts. Disempowerment is first framed as a political act and later as a military one.

The overall summaries also differ in structure and emphasis, as can be seen in Table 6.

Table 6. Differences in the overall summary component

English	German	German version translated into English
The text is a **journalistic report** covering a dramatic geopolitical crisis in which the United States, under President Trump, has escalated from economic and political pressure to direct military intervention in Venezuela, culminating in the capture of President Nicolás Maduro. It takes place within: ● A broader **migration crisis** ● The **global drug trade debate** ● Disputes over **international law** Strategic concerns about **oil and geopolitical power**	Der Text ist: ● politisch hochbrisant ● konflikthaft ● international relevant ● analytisch und berichtend ● eingebettet in geopolitische Machtfragen Er gehört zur **politischen Krisen- und Kriegsberichterstattung** und verbindet: ● Außenpolitik ● Militärstrategie ● internationale Strafverfolgung ● Drogenpolitik ● Migrationsdebatte	The text is: ● politically highly controversial ● conflictual ● internationally relevant ● analytical and reportage-like ● embedded in geopolitical power issues It belongs to the realm of political crisis and war reporting and combines: ● foreign policy ● military strategy ● international criminal prosecution ● drug policy ● migration debate

Source: Authors' elaboration

The English version is longer and presented in continuous text, whereas the German version relies more on bullet points. In the German version, references to Venezuela and the US are not explicitly named but are largely abstracted through adjectives and thematic nouns. The English version, in contrast, includes a discussion of the oil debate, which is completely omitted in the German version and summary. Instead, the German version focuses more strongly on external political relations and military strategies. While the English summary briefly introduces the article as containing "analytical and reporting" elements and provides a short overview of its content and aims, the German version does not summarise the article itself but rather evaluates it as politically highly controversial, conflictual, internationally relevant, and embedded in broader geopolitical power issues. There are also differences across the analyses in German and in English: While English refers to "migration crisis", German refers to "migration debate" and adds concrete numbers of displaced Venezuelans.

The English version provides more detailed, actor-centered explanations and foregrounds motivations such as oil, migration, and drug trafficking, while the German version adopts a more structured and evaluative, but less explicit approach. It emphasises power relations, categorisation of political and military acts, and international legal frameworks, while omitting certain actors and topics.

German and Spanish

The comparison of the German and Spanish versions shows differences in contextualisation, categorisation, and discourse interpretation, also reflected in their word counts (346 vs. 415 words). In contrast to the German version, the Spanish version provides more explicit contextualisation within the setting components (1.1 Time; 1.2 Place; 1.3 Circumstances), situating the events within a broader geopolitical conflict between the United States (US) and Venezuela and specifying locations such as New York. In contrast to the English version, both contain pictograms or emojis.

While the German version omits contextualisations, as explained in the previous section, the Spanish version omits the description of communicative means and specifications of certain acts, concerning international, USrelated, and oppositional ones. In the time and space components (1.1; 1.2), the contextualisations in the Spanish version led to situating the event more explicitly within a broader geopolitical context by contextualising Donald Trump as the US-president and referring to the geopolitical tensions between the US and Venezuela. It explains that Nicolás Maduro has been brought to the US and explicitly names New York as the location where he is being held. The German version focuses more on the events occurring in Venezuela itself. Moreover, it places stronger emphasis on the power positions of the main actors, which becomes especially important in the identities component (2.1). Nicolás Maduro is described not only as a political leader but also explicitly as the head of an authoritarian regime, and as president and later as a prisoner. In the same component, the Spanish version, on the other hand, omits certain institutional actors such as the Venezuelan opposition and the US justice system. Instead, it introduces the journalist as an actor in the communicative process.

The versions diverge significantly in their description of the circumstances (1.3), social acts (3.3), and social activities (3.5). The German version mentions international criticism of the events and highlights regime change and the role of news reporting in conflict situations as broader social processes. It also presents a more detailed list of concrete conditions and developments, as presented in 4.2. In contrast, the Spanish version focuses on diplomatic and geopolitical conflict, as well as disputes over political legitimacy, and refers to military cooperation or conflict between actors. In the Spanish version, these social acts (3.3) appear as demonstrations within the country, whereas the German version specifies that these demonstrations are directed against Maduro. Additionally, military intervention is categorised differently: while the German version treats it as a social activity (3.5) and in a new category besides political acts (3.4), the Spanish version classifies it only as a political act (3.4).

Adding to these contrasts, an important difference appears in the interpretation of relationships between actors. An excerpt is presented in Table 7.

Table 7. Differences in the relationship component (2.2)

German	German version translated into English	Spanish	Spanish version translated into English
⚖ **Machtverhältnisse** ● Stark asymmetrisch: o USA = militärische Supermacht o Venezuela = wirtschaftlich geschwächter Staat ● Trump positioniert sich als faktischer „Verwalter" Venezuelas („run the country") ● Maduro wird entmachtet und strafrechtlich verfolgt 🌐 **Internationale Beziehungen** ● Konfrontation zwischen zwei souveränen Staaten ● Vorwurf: Verletzung des Völkerrechts ● Diskussion über „nicht-internationalen bewaffneten Konflikt"	⚖ **Power relations** ● Highly asymmetrical: o USA = military superpower o Venezuela = economically weakened state ● Trump positions himself as the de facto "administrator" of Venezuela ("run the country") ● Maduro is removed from power and prosecuted 🌐 **International relations** ● Confrontation between two sovereign states ● Allegation: Violation of international law ● Discussion about "non-international armed conflict"	🔗 **Relaciones** ● **Relación de poder internacional:** EE. UU. actúa como potencia militar interviniendo en Venezuela. ● **Relación conflictiva:** Gobierno estadounidense vs. gobierno venezolano. ● **Relación judicial:** Maduro es acusado por tribunales estadounidenses. **Relación mediática:** Periodista informa a audiencia global.	🔗 **Relationships** ● **International power relationship**: The US acts as a military power by intervening in Venezuela. ● **Conflictive relationship**: US government vs. Venezuelan government. ● **Judicial relationship**: Maduro is accused by US courts. **Media relationship**: Journalist reports to global audience

Source: Authors' elaboration

The Spanish version conceptualises relationships more directly and attributes them to the actors themselves. This is reflected in the use of the emoji of a "link", suggesting a relational connection between actors. The German version adopts a more abstract conceptualisation, using emojis of a "weight" and "abstracted world". Furthermore, the German version explicitly introduces international relationships between states, which are less emphasised in the Spanish version. Similarly, regarding speech acts, the German version attributes a broader range of actions to Maduro, presenting him as an active actor who accuses the US of imperialistic motives. The Spanish version mainly portrays him in a reactive position. In both versions, Donald Trump is mentioned more frequently than Nicolás Maduro.

Moreover, there are differences in the communicative framing. In the circumstances (1.3), the Spanish version does not mention the BBC as the media source but instead characterises the article more broadly as international news reporting and includes information about the journalistic register. The German version, by contrast, includes also contents (background analysis, quotes, political classification, references to live coverage, and image material). In terms of communicative acts

(3.2), the Spanish version highlights descriptive and explanatory functions. It focuses on the description of military operations and the reporting of political declarations, and it explicitly refers to explanatory elements such as antecedents that clarify the background of events. The German version, by contrast, emphasises the quoting of political declarations and includes the presentation of criticism by judicial experts.

In the overall conclusion (see Tables 4 and 6), both the German and the Spanish version refer to the political and military crisis. The German version is the only one evaluating the news item instead of summarising the content. While the Spanish version refers to concrete actions (presented through nominalised verbs—intervention, capture, accusations, tensions, debate) and actors or subjects (Venezuelan president, drug trafficking, migration—), the German version names only nouns (policy, strategy, prosecution, debate). The German version does not detail the actions; omitting naming the principal actors or events. The wording differs because the German version mentions "political crisis and war" in contrast to the Spanish version referring to "political and military crisis". Interestingly, in this overall conclusion, is the only time "war" is mentioned in the German version, which was never mentioned in any of the other versions, appearing here unexpectedly. Finally, the German version appears somehow less explicit in its wording of policy, debate, and strategy instead of intervention, accusation, trafficking, and tensions, found in the Spanish version.

The Spanish version offers more explicit contextualisation and actor-based descriptions of geopolitical conflict, whereas the German version focuses on power structures, categorisation, and evaluative framing. While Spanish highlights concrete actions and relationships, German prioritises interpretation, regime change, and international legal perspectives.

Overall Similarities and Differences

In this section, we point out the most important similarities and differences of the three versions. The most important differences emerge from the different word counts (see also 3.3). The English version has the highest word count, present more complete information and offering contextualisations. The Spanish version has fewer words but still contextualises the information. The German version has the lowest word count, does not offer contextualisations across the text, and is less explicit. The consequences are an increased use of bullet points and (sub)sections in the German version. All versions use numbered sections to structure the analysis. Additionally, on a semiotic level, emojis are used in the Spanish and German versions, but not in the English one. Some emojis are the same or similar, while others differ, as exemplified in the previous section.

Another important difference lies in the sections "social acts" and "social activities", which suggests that the three language versions reflect different understandings of what counts as "social". The English version does not associate migration with social issues, while the Spanish version does not mention media reporting. The German version, in turn, does not classify military cooperation as a social act or activity. However, it does refer to military interventions as a social activity, whereas the English version labels them as "military operations" and the Spanish version frames them as political acts.

Both the German and Spanish versions emphasise themes such as drug policy, migration debates, international legitimisation, and political opposition. The German version additionally introduces the notion of regime change, while the Spanish version highlights diplomatic and geopolitical conflict; both elements are absent from the English version. With regard to migration, the Spanish and German versions refer to it as a "debate", whereas the English version frames it as a "crisis". Notably, the number of 8 million migrants appears only in the German version. Another unique element in the German version is the reference to "war", which is included in the summary but not in the original text.

Another notable difference across all three versions concerns the treatment of oil, which appears repeatedly in the English version across multiple components, settings, acts, and the overall summary, yet only once in Spanish and not at all in German. Similarly, references to drug trafficking are more prominent in English and reduced in the Spanish and German versions. The one exception is the capture of the Venezuelan president, which receives greater attention in Spanish whilst being largely absent from the German version and partly from the English version.

Overall, the analysis reveals structural and lexical differences across the three versions, with English and Spanish showing greater similarity to each other than either does to German.

DISCUSSION

The findings show that a CDA of the same news articles made by ChatGPT-5.3 differs in structure and content based on the language of the prompt (here English, German, and Spanish). While the overall structure is similar across all the languages and the main analyses aspects overlap, the most striking differences are in the word count, the contextualisation, the use of and reference to key words, and the understanding of "social".

The fact that we found differences between the three versions can be based on ChatGPT's databases. As Jouitteau (2023) explained, GenAI is based on different language corpora. If these corpora are not developed enough, the results in GenAI may be less complete. In the case of English, German, and Spanish, we could observe that German leads to a less contextualised version, probably because its corpora might be less developed in this specific task. Meanwhile the English version, with a bigger word count, seems to be the most complete. This is consistent with previous studies on multilingual GenAI use, showing that the content in English can be more detailed or accurate in comparison to other languages (Zhang et al., 2023). Another argument to this point is that in the German case, some items that appear in the overall summary can be missing, such as the reinforcement of the "international" aspect of the context, or even misleading, such as appearance of new information, such as "war", which did not appear in the text. These occurrences also point out to the possible disadvantages of the German analysis, and lead us to question if these inconsistencies are related to the subject of the article centering on the US and Venezuela, or on the LLM's multilingual capabilities.

A further difference emerges when comparing the English and Spanish versions: whilst English focuses on the underlying causes of the intervention in Venezuela, such as oil production, Spanish centers on the intervention itself and the capture of the president. This difference in framing is not merely stylistic; as Van Dijk (2015) reminds us, such choices shape the cognitive representations readers construct of a conflict, and in this case, may contribute to downplaying what is, in effect, a violation of international law.

This points to a potential divergence in how the same conflict is represented across languages that are directly implicated in it—namely English and Spanish. Such divergence echoes previous findings on how GenAI outputs in English tend to reflect WEIRD perspectives (Kuteeva & Anderdson, 2024).

The comparison of the three versions offers meaningful insights for multiliteracies with a focus on CMLA, particularly regarding linguistic hierarchies and social injustices in GenAI use. The findings suggest that English dominance in the digital world is further amplified in ChatGPT, which produced the most contextualised and detailed responses. Yet the Spanish version tells a somewhat different story, foregrounding figures and events of particular significance to Venezuela, such as the capture of the foreign head of state, as central to the analysis. The German version lacks contextualisations, probably due to less developed data bases in ChatGPT, and focuses on international aspects. Taken together, these findings suggest that, under certain conditions, ChatGPT can reproduce the ideologies embedded in broader digital and spoken discourses (Brinkmann et al., forthcoming).

PEDAGOGICAL IMPLICATIONS

By testing a concrete procedure to use GenAI to develop multiliteracies with a focus on CMLA and suggesting improvements, this study aims to build pedagogical implications. We argue that the comparison between ChatGPT outcomes in different languages can be applied, in a reduced and didactised form, with students in the language classroom. Depending on the age of the students, the newspaper article can be shorter and only selected questions of CDA can be used. The examination of three languages in ChatGPT can be used to foster multiliteracies by asking students to find differences and omissions in the outcomes in different languages.

We argue that the languages to analyse the differences can be the school languages, e.g., in Germany, German, English, and Spanish or other tertiary/heritage languages of the students. By integrating students' plurilingual repertoires into such an activity in the language classroom, learning environments that challenge exclusionary structures can be created (Cummins, 2023) and social justice advanced (Kardel et al., 2025). Furthermore, students' semiotic resources can be mobilised when the structure and multimodal elements, e.g., emojis, are analysed and compared (Breidbach & Küster, 2014).

Our exploratory study shows that it is difficult to understand which version is right, rather they provide different versions of reality with different omissions and emphasis. Through such an analysis and basing on multiliteracies, students can be made aware that the same event can be related from different points of view and critical approaches are needed (New London Group, 1996). Furthermore, multiliteracies advances flexibility in learning, moving beyond the idea of only one correct result and one way to get to these results (Meyer et al., 2018). This criticality and flexibility are also required by teachers through their attitudes towards diversity and deliberation (Goossens, 2022).

With the use of the multiliteracies and critical cultural awareness, students can be led to understanding that a LLM reflects a culture connected to a language, including values, ideologies, and biases. By combining this critical cultural and a multilingual awareness (García, 2017), we hypothesize that the students can learn that their plurilingual repertoire has an exceptional value in the digitalised world, allowing them to see the same event from the different points of view.

FUTURE RESEARCH DIRECTIONS

Projections for future studies include the integration of minority languages into AI-mediated language education. In addition, further research should involve empirical investigations into learners' development of multiliteracies and particularly CMLA when this approach is implemented in AI-mediated language classrooms.

CONCLUSION

Using GenAI to analyse a news item across multiple languages reveals systematic differences that reflect the underlying structures and limitations of large language models, which are shaped by global language hierarchies. Cross-linguistic comparison of outputs reveals biases associated with the dominance of English and with differing political positioning across language contexts. Since examining such hierarchies and related social injustices is central to the multiliteracies framework, multilingual comparative analyses of GenAI's outputs offer valuable pedagogical opportunities for CMLA and critical approaches to digital, multimodal, and multisemiotic texts in the classroom.

One major limitation is that we used only three languages for the comparison and that these languages share many sociolinguistic aspects (Western European languages, national and majority languages, languages of colonisation). Furthermore, according to Alim (2010) and Fairclough (2014/1992) and the following steps of Van Dijk's (2015) CDA (personal and social cognition), the analysis is missing examinations of how the discourse of this news article, and the three versions construct social realities and legitimise or marginalise (linguistic) norms.

REFERENCES

Alim, H. S. (2010). Critical language awareness. In Hornberger, N. H., & McKay, S. L. (Eds.), *Sociolinguistics and language education* (pp. 205–231). Multilingual Matters.

Anderson, J., & Macleray, V. (2016). *Multilingual digital storytelling: Engaging creatively and critically with literacy*. Routledge. DOI: 10.4324/9781315758220

Breidbach, S., & Küster, L. (2014). Bildung, multiliteracies, and identity: Key concepts in language education in the light of sociocultural theory and dynamic system theory. In Abendroth-Timmer, D., & Hennig, E. M. (Eds.), *Plurilingualism and multiliteracies: International research on identity construction in language education* (pp. 129–144). Peter Lang. DOI: 10.3726/978-3-653-03229-1

Breuer, E. O., & Van Steendam, E. (2021). Multiple approaches to understanding and working with multilingual (multi-)literacy. In E. O. Breuer, E. Lindgren, A. Stavans, & E. Van Steendam (Eds.), *New perspectives on language and education: Vol. 85. Multilingual literacy* (pp. 1–20). Multilingual Matters.

Brinkmann, L. M., Dikilitas, K., & Tavares, V. (forthcoming). GenAI, human biases and the "return" of language and cultural ideologies. In Tavares, V. (Ed.), *The Routledge handbook of generative AI and language teacher education*. Routledge.

Buschschlüter, V. (2026, January 3). Why has Trump attacked Venezuela and taken Maduro? *BBC News*. https://www.bbc.com/news/articles/c93n4nx5yqro

Byram, M. (2021). *Teaching and assessing intercultural communicative competence. Revisited*. Multilingual Matters. DOI: 10.21832/9781800410251

Christoforou, M. (2025). Gen AI-assisted multimodal meaning design: Exercising a pedagogic metalanguage of transposition. *Pedagogies*, 1–25. DOI: 10.1080/1554480X.2025.2522884

Cope, B., & Kalantzis, M. (2013). Multiliteracies. New literacies, new learning. In Hawkins, M. R. (Ed.), *Framing languages and literacies: Socially situated views and perspectives* (pp. 105–135). Routledge. DOI: 10.4324/9780203070895

Cummins, J. (2023). Critical multilingual language awareness: The role of teachers as language activists and knowledge generators. *Language Awareness*, *32*(4), 560–573. DOI: 10.1080/09658416.2023.2285361

Dar, Z. K., Shams, M. R., & Rahimi, A. (2010). Teaching reading with a critical attitude: Using critical discourse analysis (CDA) to raise EFL university students' critical language awareness (CLA). *International Journal of Criminology & Sociological Theory*, *3*(2), 457–476. https://ijcst.journals.yorku.ca/index.php/ijcst/article/view/30585

Darvin, R. (2025). Identity and investment in the age of generative AI. *Annual Review of Applied Linguistics*, *45*, 10–27. DOI: 10.1017/S0267190525100135

Fairclough, N. (2014). Introduction. In Fairclough, N. (Ed.), *Real language series. Critical language awareness* (pp. 1–30). Taylor and Francis. (Original work published 1992) DOI: 10.4324/9781315845661-7

García, O. (2017). Critical multilingual language awareness and teacher education. In Cenoz, J., Gorter, D., & May, S. (Eds.), *Encyclopedia of language and education* (3rd ed., pp. 263–280). Springer. DOI: 10.1007/978-3-319-02240-6_30

García, O., Bartlett, L., & Kleifgen, J. (2007). From biliteracy to pluriliteracies. In P. Auer, L. Wei, W. Li, K. Knapp & G. Antos (Eds.), *Handbooks of applied linguistics: Vol. 5. Handbook of multilingualism and multilingual communication* (pp. 207–228). Mouton de Gruyter. DOI: 10.1515/9783110198553.2.207

Goossens, S. (2022). Embracing multilingualism, experiencing old tensions. Promoting and problematising language at a self-declared multilingual school. *Journal of Multilingual and Multicultural Development*, *43*(4), 309–322. DOI: 10.1080/01434632.2019.1633335

Janfada, M., Heidari, E., & Lin, A. (2025). Transcending multiliteracies pedagogies in, for, through AI-oriented learning spaces: A dialogic perspective. *Pedagogies*, 1–23. DOI: 10.1080/1554480X.2025.2563621

Jiang, L., & Gu, M. M. (2025). Advocating linguistic justice through digital multimodal composing against GenAI biases: A case study of multilingual youths in an EMI university. *Journal of Multilingual and Multicultural Development*, 1–17. DOI: 10.1080/01434632.2025.2526103

Jouitteau, M. (2023). Guide de survie des langues minorisées à l'heure de l'intelligence artificielle: Appel aux communautés parlantes [A survival guide for minority languages in the age of artificial intelligence: A call to speaking communities]. *Lapurdum*, *6*, 1–15.

Kalantzis, M., & Cope, B. (2025). Literacy in the time of artificial intelligence. *Reading Research Quarterly*, *60*(1), e591. DOI: 10.1002/rrq.591

Kardel, L., Ehmke, T., & Lemmerich, S. (2025). Exploring pre- and in-service teachers' (non-)critical cultural and multilingual awareness and responsiveness in classroom situations through voice-recorded video-based assessment. *Teaching and Teacher Education, 157*, 104962. Advance online publication. DOI: 10.1016/j.tate.2025.104962

Kuteeva, M., & Andersson, M. (2024). Diversity and standards in writing for publication in the age of AI—Between a rock and a hard place. *Applied Linguistics, 45*(3), 561–567. DOI: 10.1093/applin/amae025

Liu, G. L., Lee, J. S., & Zhao, X. (2025). Critical digital literacies, agentic practices, and AI-mediated informal digital learning of English. *System, 134*, 103797. DOI: 10.1016/j.system.2025.103797

Mahapatra, S., & Koltovskaia, S. (2025). A framework for focalising critical digital literacies in second language teacher education in the Global South. *Asian Journal of Second and Foreign Language Education, 10*(1), 44. DOI: 10.1186/s40862-025-00350-z

Meyer, O., Coyle, D., & Schuck, K. (2018). Learnscaping. Creating next-gen learning environment for pluriliteracies growth. In Bündgens-Kosten, J., & Elsner, D. (Eds.), *Bilingual education & bilingualism. Multilingual computer assisted language learning* (pp. 18–37). Multilingual Matters. DOI: 10.21832/9781788921497-004

New London Group. (1996). A pedagogy of multiliteracies: Designing social futures. *Harvard Educational Review, 66*(1), 60–92. DOI: 10.17763/haer.66.1.17370n67v22j160u

Sobey, A. (2025). The thinness of GenAI: Body size in relation to the construction of the normate through GenAI image models. *AI and Ethics, 5*(4), 4181–4196. DOI: 10.1007/s43681-025-00684-x

Van Dijk, T. A. (2001). Multidisciplinary CDA: A plea for diversity. In Wodak, R., & Meyer, M. (Eds.), *Methods of critical discourse analysis* (pp. 95–120). Sage Publications.

Van Dijk, T. A. (2015). Critical discourse analysis. In Tannen, D., Hamilton, H. E., & Schiffrin, D. (Eds.), *The handbook of discourse analysis* (pp. 466–485). Wiley. DOI: 10.1002/9781118584194.ch22

Yelland, N. (2025). Reimagining multiliteracies: The transformative influence of generative AI on pedagogies. *Pedagogies*, 1–10. DOI: 10.1080/1554480X.2025.2525270

Zhang, X., Li, S., Hauer, B., Shi, N., & Kondrak, G. (2023, December). Don't trust ChatGPT when your question is not in English: A study of multilingual abilities and types of LLMs. In *Proceedings of the 2023 conference on empirical methods in natural language processing* (pp. 7915–7927). https://doi.org/DOI: 10.18653/v1/2023.emnlp-main.491

ADDITIONAL READING

Blume, C. (2026). Approaching multiliteracies: Digitally mediated second and foreign language. In Blume, C. (Ed.), *Approaching multiliteracies: Digitally mediated second andforeign language* (pp. 1–20). Routledge. DOI: 10.4324/9781003434184

Cooper, G., Chen, J., Tang, K., & Cooper, Z. (2026). The intersection of artificial intelligence, language, and culture. ChatGPT as digital imperialist? In T. Barkatsas, W. Goff, & A. Ng (Eds.), *Exploring Cognitive, Affective, Design Thinking, Artificial Intelligence, Cybernetics and e-Learning Dimensions in Contemporary Education* (pp. 40–54). Brill. DOI: 10.1163/9789004751736_003

Cope, B., & Kalantzis, M. (2023). A multimodal grammar of artificial intelligence: Measuring the gains and losses in generative AI. *Multimodality and Society*, *4*(2), 123–152. DOI: 10.1177/26349795231221699

Darvin, R. (2026). Critical digital literacies. In W. S. E. Lam & R. Darvin (Eds.). Literacy. In C. Chapelle (Gen. Ed.), *The encyclopedia of applied linguistics*. Wiley. DOI: 10.1002/9781405198431.wbeal20282

Fairclough, A. (2010). Critical language awareness. In Hornberger, N., & McKay, S. (Eds.), *New perspectives on language and education* (pp. 205–231). Multilingual Matters.

Ortega, Y. (2024). 'Un futuro mejor para todos': Towards a critical humanizing English language teaching. *Language Teaching Research*, 13621688241262618. Advance online publication. DOI: 10.1177/13621688241262618

Tavares, V. (Ed.). (forthcoming). *Routledge handbook of generative AI and language teacher education*. Routledge.

Wan, Y., & Moorhouse, B. L. (2025). Challenges of AI in language education. In Wang, Y., Alm, A., & Dizon, G. (Eds.), *Insights into AI and language teaching and learning* (pp. 32–52). Castledown. DOI: 10.29140/9781763711600-03

KEY TERMS AND DEFINITIONS

Critical Discourse Analysis (CDA): An analysis of the ways in which events, actors, and relationships are constructed and communicated through language and other semiotic resources.

Critical Multilingual Language Awareness (CLMA): The understanding of how multiple languages interact, differ, and contribute to meaning-making in diverse communicative contexts, embedded into social and linguistic injustices.

Generative Artificial Intelligence (GenAI): A type of artificial intelligence that produces new content, such as text or images, based on patterns learned from large datasets.

Language Ideology: Beliefs and assumptions about languages, their speakers, and their social value, often shaping how linguistic differences are perceived and evaluated.

Multiliteracies: An approach to literacy that emphasizes the ability to interpret and produce meaning across multiple languages, modes, and cultural contexts.

News Framing: The process by which information is selected, organized, and presented in news discourse, influencing how audiences interpret events.

Power Relations: The ways in which authority, influence, and inequality are constructed and expressed within social and communicative contexts.

Chapter 9

AI-Generated Popular Culture Visuals, Representation, and Motivation:

A Case Study in Foreign Language Education Using the Baris Alper Yilmaz Figure

Kardelen Aslan
http://orcid.org/0000-0001-9567-2341
Mardin Artuklu University, Turkey

Kadri Nazlı
http://orcid.org/0000-0002-0373-8268
Dicle University, Turkey

ABSTRACT

This chapter examines the pedagogical impact of integrating AI-generated visuals of a culturally proximal popular figure into EFL classrooms for young learners in Türkiye. Grounded in linguistic justice perspective, the study employs a sequential explanatory mixed-methods design to investigate motivational engagement and performance patterns. Findings suggest that AI-mediated local representation functions as a motivational amplifier and performance-stabilizing element, while also raising ethical and environmental considerations regarding balanced AI integration.

DOI: 10.4018/979-8-3373-7749-0.ch009

INTRODUCTION

Motivation is not simply a matter of effort, but of identification.

The way humans process and create language has undergone a transformation over the past decade through the advent of Artificial Intelligence (AI), and Large Language Models (LLMs). Across multiple disciplines including education, healthcare and engineering, LLMs and AI have transformed passively used tools into active participants in content creation, communication, and evaluation. However, when considering the integration of AI into an educational setting, it is often viewed as a "double-edged sword". Although there is tremendous opportunity for AI to increase the instructional quality and personalization of instruction, along with the efficiency of instructional delivery, it is also fraught with risk. Younger students exposed to AI without critical thinking about its use may develop technology dependence, cognitive misalignment and decreased learner autonomy. Consequently, the pedagogical value of AI tools is largely dependent upon how they are pedagogically integrated into instructional environments and not simply based upon their existence.

The field of teaching English to young learners is a constantly evolving field that must adapt to new paradigm shifts, learner needs, and emerging technologies. Multimodal, authentic learning materials are able to support the cognitive and affective needs of children, while promoting both comprehension and engagement in the lessons. The appropriateness of advanced AI-based tools for young learners is currently a topic of much debate within the academic community. The lack of emotional intelligence in AI systems combined with ethical issues related to data usage, content exposure and moral dilemmas such as the AI use for the real human images necessitate a very cautious, age-appropriate and context-dependent pedagogical approach to the use of AI tools by young learners.

As a part of the new generation-based approach, the idea of "linguistic justice" can be used to create an environment that is more inclusive and fairer for all in a language class by engaging the justice between the cultures. In addition, using local and popular figures in instructional materials may increase students' self-awareness of their own cultural identity and may also motivate them because the material is more relevant to them. This paper examines how a well-known Turkish football player was incorporated into young learners' English lessons, using both quantitative and qualitative data collected from the students' perspective.

An overview of the current literature has shown a significant gap: little or no prior research exists which explores the combined use of AI, social media, and celebrity figures within the same English as a Foreign Language (EFL) class. Therefore, we sought to investigate the combined effect of using AI-generated visualizations of a popular culture figure (Turkish Football Player), in relation to students' motivation, attention and engagement in EFL classes at the middle school level, in this experimental study.

This research is guided by the following questions:

- **Research Question 1 (RQ1).** How influential are celebrities as a material in young learners' English as a foreign language (EFL) class?
- **Research Question 2 (RQ2).** Could AI-generated content derived from social media platforms be influential in teaching English to young learners?

As well as determining the immediate instructional impact of the use of AI-based educational materials, this chapter explores a culturally based approach to designing AI-based educational materials for young learner EFL classes. Rather than viewing AI as a tool to directly improve student academic performance, the findings indicate that culturally related visual representations generated by AI of a locally relevant pop culture icon can enhance motivation and stabilize performance when students have only limited experience with AI-educational content.

By combining the frameworks of linguistic justice, parasocial pedagogy, and multimodal engagement, this chapter presents a culturally contextualized model for the ethical use of AI-based materials in culturally responsive EFL classrooms.

The general framework and research objectives of this study have now been identified. Therefore, the next chapter will discuss the literature reviewed in order to provide the existing studies linked to the topic.

BACKGROUND

AI in ELT: Affordances and Constraints

The emergence of AI, and LLM's has dramatically impacted research on how students generate, process, and mediate language within an academic environment. With the growing use of AI/LLM technologies transitioning from being simple tools to interactive agents with the ability to create and interact with users, there is a greater need for researchers to examine the role that AI will play in education. In particular, AI technology is rapidly changing the way educators teach language and the way students learn language. The existing literature clearly identifies the role that AI will have in the language classroom as having two sides. While AI has the potential to revolutionize how teachers teach and how students learn, the implementation of AI into the classroom will also present many obstacles that must be examined critically.

Within the field of education, the existing literature presents a nuanced discussion regarding the benefits and limitations of AI-supported tools. Besides, several studies emphasize the potential of AI to enhance educational practices by improving efficiency, personalization, and instructional quality. For instance, Ali et al. (2023) argue that educational practices can be optimized through the effective use of AI technologies, particularly in terms of supporting learning processes and instructional design. From this perspective, AI tools are viewed as facilitators that can complement traditional pedagogical approaches.

As we see an increase in research about the risks of using artificial intelligence in the classroom with young learners, there is evidence to suggest that young learners' dependency on technology could result from AI's immediate feedback capabilities, increased engagement and possible long-term negative effects. The research also suggests that AI has the potential to limit the learner's ability to develop autonomy and could create a cognitive misalignment due to the way AI processes information versus humans. Calhoun and Fawcett (2023), Novawan et al. (2024), note that while AI can provide instant feedback, the risk of developing a digital addiction to AI-based applications increases with excessive or uncritical use by young learners. The research shows that it is how AI is used within a pedagogy-based approach that provides a high level of value as opposed to simply providing access to AI.

The majority of the literature also shows that AI tools can be utilized to support a wide variety of language related tasks when used in a pedagogically informed fashion. Mabuan (2024) notes that AI can help students practice a number of different language skills (reading, writing, etc.) and aid in individualized, self-paced learning; thus, AI can serve as a supplemental resource in place of traditional language instruction methods.

In addition to learner-centered perspectives, researchers have examined the role of AI tools from the standpoint of educators. Several studies suggest that AI-based platforms can assist teachers in instructional planning, material development, and the teaching of language skills and subskills. For example, Octavio et al. (2024) report that AI platforms such as ChatGPT can support language teachers in creating context-based instructional materials, thereby reducing preparation time and enabling more focused classroom interaction. However, alongside these advantages, concerns persist regarding the long-term implications of overreliance on AI tools for educators. Novawan et al. (2024) argues that excessive dependence on AI-generated content may diminish teachers' creativity and pedagogical agency in lesson preparation. Furthermore, studies by Baskara and Mukarto (2023) and Liu et al. (2023) emphasize that AI-generated materials may suffer from emotional detachment and potential inaccuracies, raising questions about the reliability and appropriateness of such content in educational contexts.

A key point from the available research is that there is a lot of opportunity for using AI tools to support foreign language education. Specifically, AI can be used by students as a tool for practicing languages and also by teachers to help plan lessons and develop educational materials. However, the opportunities provided by the use of AI tools have several associated challenges. Some of the most significant challenges include ethical concerns regarding the collection and use of data; risks of overusing or becoming addicted to AI tools; and questions about whether AI tools can provide reliable and valid information. Because of this, many researchers and authors highlight the necessity of utilizing AI tools critically and intelligently and emphasize the need for educators and students to utilize AI tools responsibly.

Young Learners and Multimodal Engagement

For many years, teaching English to young learners has been a focal point of research in the field of education; however, over time, research in this area has continuously highlighted changes in how teachers teach and the methods used to instruct young learners. Across the literature, there is general agreement that language teaching methodologies for young learners have transformed due to emerging educational paradigms, changing learner needs, and increasing technology use. More recently, as a result of the rapid growth in AI-based tools, there has been much academic discussion regarding whether or not such tools should be incorporated into ELT classrooms for young learners.

Prior research highlights the importance of authenticity and multimodality in young learners' language development. For instance, Prosic-Santovac (2017) demonstrates that authentic language input can be effectively facilitated through visual media such as cartoons, which support comprehension and engagement while aligning with the cognitive and affective characteristics of young learners. In a similar vein, Taghizadeh and Hasani Yourdshahi (2020) argue that technological tools can positively contribute to language acquisition among young learners, provided that such tools are age-appropriate, pedagogically sound, and aligned with learners' proficiency levels. These findings underscore the potential of technology-enhanced instruction when it is carefully designed and purposefully implemented.

Despite these perspectives, more recent studies raise critical concerns regarding the suitability of advanced technological tools, particularly AI-based applications, for young learners. Research suggests that the integration of such tools may pose ethical and moral challenges, especially when learners lack the cognitive maturity to critically evaluate AI-generated content. In this regard, Rao Idapalapati (2024) and Sharifuddin and Hashim (2024) caution that AI tools may not be fully appropriate for young learners due to emerging moral dilemmas related to data use, content exposure, and learner autonomy. Furthermore, Baskara and Mukarto (2023) emphasize that the absence of emotional intelligence in AI-driven systems may adversely affect young learners, whose language development is closely intertwined with affective interaction, empathy, and social engagement.

The other areas within the themes identified by the current research remain relatively under-researched and are one of the main reasons why the current study is needed. A significant reason for exploring these remaining areas includes the fact that the area of linguistic justice has been established as a way to create an environment for students that is both more equitable and inclusive in language classrooms. The focus of the current study will be on the inclusion of a Turkish soccer player in English classes for children and the impact of including this celebrity will be assessed.

Previous research has emphasized that the incorporation of local culture plays a crucial role in enabling meaningful and contextualized language teaching (Shresta, 2016). In a similar vein, Alansari (2019) and Aslan and Sirojitdinovna (2025) argue that the use of local figures in language classrooms can enhance learners' awareness of their own cultural identities by increasing relevance and a sense of connection to the learning content. Furthermore, it has been demonstrated that the use of AI and augmented reality (AR) can enrich multimodal learning environments by supporting lessons both visually and contextually (Varatharaj et al., 2024). From the perspective of linguistic justice, the literature also indicates that the inclusion of local figures can serve a balancing function in language education, counteracting the dominance of foreign figures that are frequently employed in instructional materials (Alansari, 2019; Varatharaj et al., 2024).

Nevertheless, alongside the documented advantages of integrating local figures through AI-supported approaches, several studies have also drawn attention to potential limitations. For instance, Byram (1997) and Kramsch (1998) caution that the use of local figures should be balanced, as excessive emphasis on local representations may restrict learners' exposure to global perspectives and limit the development of broader intercultural awareness. Moreover, although local figures are often regarded as motivating elements in the classroom, Dörnyei (2009) highlights that intrinsic motivation plays a more decisive role in ensuring long-term learning outcomes. From this perspective, reliance on local cultural content alone may lead to short-term engagement if it is not supported by deeper motivational mechanisms. In addition, despite the pedagogical affordances of AI and AR in introducing cultural figures into language classrooms, Selwyn (2016) warns against uncritical acceptance of technological innovations, noting that exaggerated promises of educational technology may obscure underlying inequalities and pedagogical limitations if such tools are not implemented thoughtfully.

To summarize, the current literature examining AI as a tool for teaching young learners English (in addition to expanding upon the use of AI in English Language Teaching or ELT) indicates that there are many advantages and disadvantages to using technology and AI supported tools to teach young learners English. Technology can be an effective way to increase student's interest and engagement in language development, and it provides numerous learning experiences to support students' desire for linguistic justice. However, technology has some limitations when it comes to supporting student emotional responses and addressing issues of ethics, therefore, educators need to integrate technology into the classroom with caution and a high degree of critical awareness. The previous research also supports the need for educators to take a balanced approach to integrating AI tools into the classroom, which is based on how appropriate these tools will be in terms of the type of education students receive, the well-being of students, and the educator's responsibility to educate students ethically.

Linguistic Justice and Cultural Proximity

Considering the existing literature related to teaching English to young learners and the integration of AI tools into EFL teaching, this study addresses a significant gap. The prevailing literature in ELT lacks studies investigating the synergistic influence of these three parameters (AI, social media, and celebrity) together on young learners (Murphey & Arao, 2001; Sauro, 2019). Addressing this scholarly gap, this present experimental mixed-methods study aims to empirically measure the impact of AI-generated visuals of a popular culture figure (a Turkish footballer) on middle school students' motivation, attention, and engagement in EFL classes.

Prior research establishes the foundation of the current study in three interrelated ways: (1) AI as an educational mediator that is both promising and risky; (2) the unique developmental and emotional characteristics of early learners that require multiple modes of interaction with digital content; and (3) the importance of linguistic equity in countering the effects of dominant language(s) used in the development of EFL materials. The current chapter uses a single, culturally familiar individual that has been provided through AI-generative images to explore how the motivational engagement and short-term achievement patterns of students in a specific classroom setting are related.

In this sub-chapter, we provided a review of the relevant literature and established the theoretical framework for the current study. Building upon this foundation, the following section will detail the main focus of the chapter.

MAIN FOCUS OF THE CHAPTER

Issues, Controversies, Problems

The inclusion of both AI and local, culturally relevant figures in English language teaching for young learners creates many different kinds of challenges and questions. The literature has identified a number of motivational advantages that are associated with this kind of multi-modal approach but there are also several major contradictions or conflicting demands on ELT which must be resolved in order to provide effective education and promote learner well-being.

Ethical Concerns and Cognitive Vulnerability

The use of AI tools for young learners in the classroom presents two main issues: data privacy and cognitive appropriateness. Young learners are unlikely to have developed sufficient digital literacy skills to be able to critically assess information generated by AI, which makes them vulnerable to the biases, errors or hallucinations created by Large Language Models. Additionally, a long-standing debate exists as to whether it is morally appropriate to expose children to AI-based platforms without adequate regulatory oversight, which raises questions about the children's ability to provide informed consent, the collection of data related to the children and the possible negative long-term impacts upon the development of their cognitive autonomy.

The Tension Between Engagement and Distraction

The incorporation of popular cultural figures such as prominent local athletes introduces a significant pedagogical controversy. Therefore, leveraging a beloved local figure may act as a powerful catalyst for situational engagement and aligns with the principles of linguistic justice by validating the learners' immediate cultural context. However, a problem arises when the "celebrity factor" overshadows the linguistic objectives of the lesson. Educators face the challenge of ensuring that the high-arousal stimulus of a famous figure does not lead to cognitive overload or merely superficial, short-term entertainment at the expense of deep, sustained language acquisition.

Affective Disconnect in AI-Generated Materials

Another issue is the fact that current AI programs have no emotional intelligence. The language development of early learners has strong emotional and social components; therefore, as teachers we need to be able to provide emotional scaffolding for our students through social interactions and empathy etc., which are outside of the capabilities of an artificial system. A second concern regarding the use of AI-generated educational products is whether they will create an unnatural, uncanny feeling within young learners who see and interact with the artificial representations of familiar humans. And lastly, the overuse of AI-generated educational resources could also lessen the ability of teachers to take control of their classrooms and subsequently weaken the most important relationship within a school setting, that being the one between the teacher and student.

Balancing Linguistic Justice and Global Awareness

Finally, while integrating local cultural figures promotes linguistic justice and counteracts the historical dominance of foreign entities in ELT materials, it introduces a curricular tension. The problem lies in finding the appropriate balance; an overemphasis on hyper-local representations may inadvertently restrict young learners' exposure to global perspectives. A central controversy in current ELT discourse is how to validate the learners' local identities without compromising the development of broader intercultural communicative competence, which relies on encountering and understanding diverse, global cultures.

METHODOLOGY

In order to fill the literature gap related to the AI-based materials of a locally popular celebrity in the EFL classes, we focused on a detailed design. Therefore, to fill the gap in the existing literature, an experimental study design was used.

Experimental study is a quantitative study of whether a treatment could influence the outcome of the study with two groups, one of which is provided with a treatment that could change the results (Creswell, 2009). Hence, this investigation employed an experimental mixed-methods research design, facilitating the comprehensive analysis of both quantitative and qualitative data strands. To effectively integrate these dual data sources, the study specifically adopted a sequential explanatory mixed-methods approach (Creswell, 2009). This design necessitates the initial collection and analysis of quantitative data, followed by a qualitative phase intended to elaborate upon, interpret, and provide a deeper understanding of the initial numerical findings. This methodological strategy is optimally suited to address the study's research questions by both measuring the influence of the intervention and thoroughly exploring the participants' perceptions.

Following the study's research design, the subjects were chosen based on the objective of the study. The total number of participants is 39 students from a private secondary school located in Diyarbakir, Türkiye. Participants were sampled from one private secondary school using convenience sampling because of the ease of access and the availability of institutional approval. The participants were divided into two groups as the experimental and control groups to test the practicality of the implementation process. Students in the experimental group (EG) and control group (CG) were assigned randomly after being recruited to the study. A randomized selection process was used to ensure an equal comparison of the two groups internally, while recognizing that the total sample will be limited to a specific context-based population. Evidence supporting baseline equality was provided through the almost identical pre-test mean scores observed among both groups (Etikan et al., 2016). The pre-test and post-test before the lesson implementations for the EG and CG focused on the general knowledge of the participants in terms of Simple Present Tense with 10 multiple choice questions. The pre- and post- tests were the same as depicted in Appendix 1.

The selection of Barış Alper Yılmaz was grounded in empirical and contextual considerations. The pilot study indicated a strong learner preference for him among statistically successful Turkish football players. Besides, due to his visibility during EURO 2024 with the availability of publicly shared visual materials, he became a suitable case for examining celebrity pedagogy in AI-mediated instruction. As a nationally recognized figure, his integration also served to explore the notion of linguistic justice by introducing culturally proximal representation into foreign language learning environments. Therefore, his AI-generated visuals from the official Galatasaray, his team in Türkiye, Instagram account were used to teach Simple Present Tense to the EG with the speaking activities by interpreting the pictures by asking various questions about the AI-generated photos as depicted in Appendix 2 with some pages from the experimental group's lessons.

The core intervention contrasted two 60-minute lesson plans both structurally aligned with Turkish MoNE curriculum objectives with the EG receiving instruction augmented by AI-generated multimedia visuals (featuring the popular culture figure Barış Alper Yılmaz) to enhance speaking acquisition and engagement. Conversely, the CG followed a traditional pedagogic approach relying on text-heavy activities (e.g., fill-in-the-blanks, translation exercises), strictly excluding any visual or AI-mediated input to isolate the intervention's effect. Therefore, in the CG, AI materials were isolated by engaging the learners to do the translation activities from the target language to the first language with the Grammar Translation Method. The activity for the CG focused on a foreign figure known as Alfred and his reading passage with the reading comprehension questions as shown in Appendix 3. Although the implementations for both groups were different, the focused topic was the same for both, Simple Present Tense. Therefore, for the EG and CG, the activities were based upon this grammar topic.

To ensure the content validity of the pre- and post- tests, the 10 items were meticulously aligned with the Turkish Ministry of National Education (MoNE) curriculum objectives for the Simple Present Tense. Furthermore, the test draft was reviewed by a panel of three English language teaching experts to confirm its appropriateness, difficulty level, and clarity for the target middle school age group.

Because all participants are minors, parental or legal guardian informed consent was strictly required from each participant's parent/guardian before any data collection procedures could begin. In addition to obtaining informed consent, the researchers ensured compliance with relevant ethical standards for conducting research involving minors. The demographic features of the participants are as depicted in Table 1:

Table 1. Demographic characteristics of participants

Variable	**Category**	**n**	**%**
Group	Experimental	19	48.7
	Control	20	51.3
Grade and Ages	5 (Age 11)	12	30.76
	6 (Age 12)	8	20.51
	7 (Age 13)	7	17.94
	8 (Age 14)	12	30.76

Note. Developed by the authors

Data collection was systematically phased across three weeks: Week 1 administered the topic-related pre-test immediately followed by the group interventions (executed by a single teacher to ensure instructional consistency); Week 2 involved the administration of the identical post-test to quantify achievement gains. Finally, Week 3 concluded with the qualitative strand, wherein semi-structured focus group interviews with a purposefully sampled sub-set (8 participants, 4 for both groups) were conducted to triangulate findings and gather rich, reflective data concerning the participants' subjective learning experiences and perceptions of the methodological distinctions, as shown in Table 2:

Table 2. Demographical features of interviewees

Participants	Age	Grade	Group	School
P1	11	5	Experimental	State
P2	11	5	Experimental	State
P3	11	5	Experimental	State
P4	13	7	Experimental	Private
P5	14	8	Control	State
P6	14	8	Control	State
P7	14	8	Control	Private
P8	13	7	Control	State

Note. Developed by the authors

After collecting all required data at the end of week 3, the analyses of quantitative and qualitative data were performed during week 4. All quantitative data (pre/post-test) were analyzed by use of Jamovi in order to identify whether there were statistically significant differences among experimental and control group data. A thorough content analysis was completed using NVivo (Version 15) for all qualitative data (focus group interview transcripts). NVivo is a software tool that allows the user to conduct an extensive content analysis of qualitative data; it identifies and organizes patterns within data. In this study, the patterns or "recurring themes" identified through NVivo included the most common words and phrases used by participants. It also allowed for identification of the participants' voices and the most frequent responses provided by each participant. The results from the analyses of both the quantitative and qualitative data were to be synthesized as described below. The primary purpose of synthesizing these two types of data was to ensure that the overall research findings would provide a reliable and trustworthy conclusion based on the combination of the numerical and experiential data. Therefore, the synthesis of these two types of data will allow for the triangulation of the research findings (Yıldırım & Şimşek, 2021). The findings resulting from this comprehensive analysis are reported in the subsequent section.

FINDINGS

This section provides a comprehensive discussion of both quantitative and qualitative data. The primary objective is to evaluate the motivational and pedagogical impact of integrating AI-generated visuals of a prominent local athlete into foreign language instruction. While the statistical analysis offers a robust measure of performance stability and effectiveness, the qualitative data serves to contextualize and deepen these numerical findings through the lived perspectives of the participants. Consequently, the discussion is organized into two distinct subsections: the first focusing on the quantitative outcomes, followed by a nuanced exploration of the qualitative insights.

Quantitative Findings

Before conducting the main analyses, the assumptions of parametric tests were evaluated. The Shapiro-Wilk test confirmed that the data followed a normal distribution ($W = 0.948, p = .069$). Furthermore, Levene's test indicated that the requirement for homogeneity of variances was met for both pre-test ($F(1, 37) = 0.000, p = .983$) and post-test scores ($F(1, 37) = 0.274$, $p = .604$). These results demonstrate that the data set is suitable for t-tests and ANOVA, as displayed in Table 3 and Table 4.

Table 3. Shapiro-Wilk analysis

Comparison	W	p
Pre-test correct answers vs. Post-test correct answers	0.948	.069

Note. Developed by the authors

Table 4. Homogeneity of variances test (Levene's)

Measure	F	df1	df2	p
Pre-test correct answers	0.000445	1	37	.983
Post-test correct answers	0.274	1	37	.604

Note. Developed by the authors

At the beginning of the experiment, the performance levels of the two groups were nearly identical. In the pre-tests, the experimental group (AI-athlete visuals) had a mean score of 6.11 ($SD = 2.23$), while the control group had a mean score of 6.10 ($SD = 2.20$). Within the group-comparisons, paired sample t-tests were analysed to see differences between the experimental and control groups. For the control group, a statistically significant decline was observed in the control group's performance ($t(19) = 2.90, p = .009$). The effect size for this decrease was found to be medium-to-large ($d = 0.649$), with scores dropping from 6.10 to 4.80. In contrast, the experimental group exposed to AI-generated visuals of athlete Barış Alper Yılmaz maintained their performance levels. The change from pre-test ($M = 6.11$) to post-test ($M = 5.47$) was not statistically significant ($t(18) = 1.14, p =$

.268), with a small effect size (*d* = 0.262). The descriptive statistics and the paired sample t-tests for the groups are provided in Table 5, Table 6 and Table 7.

Table 5. Descriptive statistics

Statistic	Group	Pre correct	Post correct
n	Experimental	19	19
	Control	20	20
Missing	Experimental	0	0
	Control	0	0
Mean	Experimental	6.11	5.47
	Control	6.10	4.80
Median	Experimental	6.00	6.00
	Control	6.00	4.50
Standard deviation	Experimental	2.23	2.27
	Control	2.20	2.09
Minimum	Experimental	1	2
	Control	1	2
Maximum	Experimental	9	10
	Control	9	9

Note. Developed by the authors

Table 6. Paired sample T-test for the control group

Comparison	t	df	p	Cohen's d
Pre correct vs. Post correct	2.90	19	.009	0.649

Note. Developed by the authors

Table 7. Paired sample T-test for the experimental group

Comparison	Test	Statistic	df	p	Effect Size	Value
Pre correct vs. Post correct	Student's t	2.90	19	.009	Cohen's d	0.649

Note. Developed by the authors

Additionally, a Repeated Measures ANOVA showed a significant main effect of time ($F(1, 37) = 7.42$, $p = .010$), indicating an overall change in scores across measurement points. However, the Time × Group interaction was not statistically significant ($F(1, 37) = 0.892$, $p = .351$), suggesting that the magnitude of change did not differ between the Experimental and Control Groups. Accordingly, the quantitative findings should be framed as evidence of performance maintenance rather than a differential treatment effect. To further investigate between-group differences in change, future studies might consider a direct comparison of gain scores (Δ post–pre) with corresponding effect size calculations. Repeated Measures ANOVA and the estimated marginal means for Time and Group are shown in Table 8 and Figure 1.

Table 8. Repeated measures ANOVA

Source	*Sum of Squares*	*df*	*Mean Square*	*F*	*p*
Time	18.18	1	18.18	7.447	.010
Group	2.18	1	2.18	0.892	.351
Residual	90.31	37	2.44	—	—

Note. Developed by the authors

Figure 1. Estimated marginal means for time x group

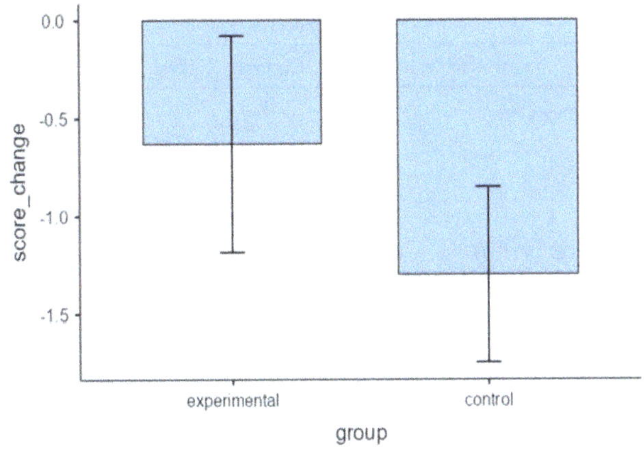

Note. Developed by the authors

To see the performance stability, we compared the mean score changes between the groups. The analysis of the score change variable revealed that the control group lost an average of 1.30 points between tests. However, the experimental group's loss was limited to only 0.63 points. It could be suggested that that the integration of AI-athlete visuals contributed to better performance stability compared to traditional methods, as the experimental group showed a less pronounced decline in scores throughout the intervention period. The descriptive statistics table and figure for the score change are provided in Table 9 and Figure 2.

Table 9. Descriptive statistics for score change

Statistic	Group	Score Change
n	Experimental	19
	Control	20
Missing	Experimental	0
	Control	0
Mean	Experimental	-0.632
	Control	-1.30
Median	Experimental	-1.00
	Control	-1.50
Standard Deviation	Experimental	2.41
	Control	2.00
Minimum	Experimental	-5
	Control	-5
Maximum	Experimental	4
	Control	2

Note. Developed by the authors

Figure 2. Score change graph

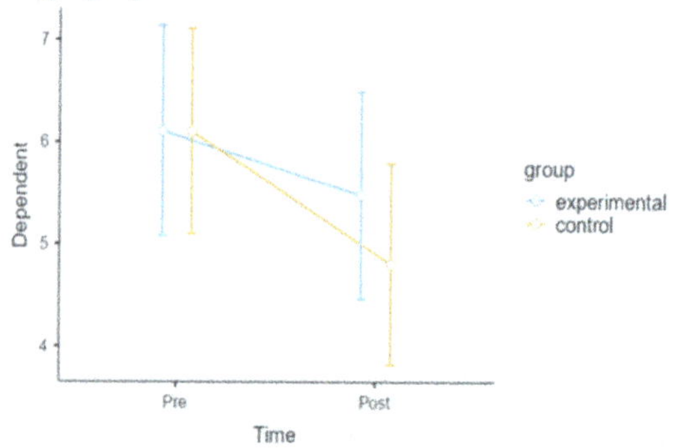

Note. Developed by the authors

Qualitative Findings

Based on the quantitative findings, eight participants were selected randomly and equally from the experimental and control groups to participate in an online semi-structured focus group interview. The demographic characteristics of the interview participants are presented in Table 2. The interviews were conducted in Turkish, the participants' mother tongue, in order to ensure clarity, depth of expression, and authentic reflection of their experiences.

A total of twelve semi-structured questions, as depicted in Appendix 4, were posed to explore participants' perspectives on motivation, learning experience, identity and representation, as well as their views on AI and ethical considerations. Sample interview questions included the following:

- With a focus on the Simple Present Tense, did you find the lesson activities motivating? Did the lesson create any sense of pressure?
- In your English classes, do you usually encounter figures from other cultures? How did seeing a local popular figure from your own culture make you feel?
- Do you think the use of AI-based visuals of a local popular figure in English classes is fair? Did these visuals influence your perspective on foreign language learning?

After the data collection process, the focus groups interviews were coded, transcribed and imported into NVivo 15 for systematic analysis. The qualitative research study used a two-step coding method for analyzing the data. Open coding (first cycle) was completed in order to find patterns that appeared across all of the transcripts. Axial coding (second cycle) was then used to categorize like codes together as higher-level themes. Additionally, to establish credibility, another researcher independently reviewed a subset of the transcripts, and a discussion was held to resolve any differences that arose. The audit trail contained the codebook structure, along with a selection of representative quotes for each theme and was kept within NVivo to provide transparency and rigorous analysis of the data. Content and thematic analysis resulted in the identification of two main themes and three primary codes, which were comprised of multiple sub-codes to allow for an in-depth understanding of participant's responses to questions. These themes and codes are listed below.

- Pedagogical and Affective Affordances
    - Cultural Proximity and Identity-Based Engagement
    - Material Design and Classroom Atmosphere
    - Perceived Instructional Benefits of AI Integration
- Perceived Risks and Ethical Reservations

- Ethical, Authenticity, and Environmental Concerns

The findings from the thematic analysis are supplied according to the quotations said by the participants. The qualitative data from that analysis is provided below.

Pedagogical and Affective Affordances

The qualitative findings revealed that the integration of a local popular figure through AI-based representations in English classes was perceived positively by participants. The reported advantages primarily centred on three interconnected dimensions: cultural proximity, the lesson process, and the perceived affordances of AI in ELT. The detailed analysis of the corresponding codes is presented below.

Cultural Proximity and Identity-Based Engagement

Participants frequently emphasized that the inclusion of a local popular figure in English lessons enhanced their motivation. This motivational effect was associated with feelings of sincerity, familiarity, and cultural relatedness. The figure was not perceived merely as a celebrity, but as someone culturally and socially proximal, which strengthened students' sense of connection to the lesson content. For instance, one student highlighted this shared identity, noting, "Since he is from the Black Sea Region and Turkish like me, I was proud to see Barış in my lessons" (P1). This sentiment of national pride and authenticity was echoed by another student who stated, "I felt the lesson was sincere, as I know he plays for our country" (P2). Furthermore, the use of AI to contextualize the footballer in a culturally familiar setting deepened this relational bond. Illustrating this in the interview, Participant 4 explained, "When I saw Barış's AI figure in his simple and typical Black Sea Region-representing house, I felt he is more than a very popular footballer. He is like a big brother making our English lessons easier" (P4).

Building upon the reflections of the experimental group, some participants further drew comparisons between the local popular figure and the character used in the control group activity, namely Alfred, when discussing their motivation during the lesson. In responding to questions related to engagement and learning experience, several participants highlighted how standard, foreign characters failed to inspire them. For instance, Participant 5 noted the lack of novelty, stating, "That lesson did not make a big change in my learning process. I always see characters like Alfred in my lessons" (P5). Underscoring the core concept of cultural proximity, another student explicitly expressed a desire for localized representation: "I wish I had seen a Turkish character in that paragraph. I would have felt a sense of belonging to that lesson if it had been like that" (P7).

To sum up, these responses suggest that the inclusion of a local figure contributed to shaping students' motivational engagement and their sense of cultural connectedness in the classroom.

Material Design and Classroom Atmosphere

Following the first code, participants further evaluated the lesson process by reflecting on the material design, presentation style, and overall classroom atmosphere. Students in the experimental group highlighted that the visually rich and colorful materials, combined with the integration of a celebrity figure, enhanced both their motivation and retention. The incorporation of the local figure was described as making the lesson more engaging and memorable, as explicitly stated by one participant,

I wasn't anxious during the class, as I know Barış Alper. The lesson was colorful and interesting. For example, the picture of Barış pulling a ball from a game machine entertained me and helped me to be engaged in the class. (P3).

In addition to the perspectives of the experimental group, participants from the control group also reflected on their learning experience. They emphasized that, rather than the conventional worksheet-based activity itself, it was the teacher's instructional style and classroom interaction that increased their engagement, as one participant expressed, "The activity is so classic for me to see. A classic worksheet! My teacher made the lesson entertaining for me. It wasn't the activity that made me more active during the class." (P8).

Overall, the participants' responses suggest that the effectiveness of the lesson process was shaped not only by the representation of instructional materials but also by the teacher's pedagogical approach.

Perceived Instructional Benefits of AI Integration

Given that the study centered on AI-based representations of a local figure, participants were also asked to reflect on the role of AI in foreign language classrooms. Students in the experimental group, who were directly exposed to AI-supported materials, evaluated their classroom experience accordingly. In contrast, participants from the control group were invited to share their perceptions and attitudes toward the potential use of AI-generated visuals in ELT contexts. Thus, the students expressed strong support for integrating these technologies. For instance, highlighting the practical advantages of material development, Participant 4 noted, "Using a local popular figure's AI visuals is logical, as they could be created easily" (P4). Others emphasized the necessity of keeping pace with modern educational tools, as Participant 1 stated, "We are in 2026. If the AI visuals are compatible with the lesson, every teacher should use it" (P1). Furthermore, students who had not yet experienced the intervention expressed a clear desire for such innovative approaches, with Participant 6 expressing, "I wish our lessons were done through the AI visuals. It is like a new breath to the process" (P6).

Accordingly, participants suggested that lessons supported by AI-based materials could represent a novel instructional approach, particularly due to their ease of integration into classroom practice.

In summary, the findings indicate that the incorporation of a local popular figure into EFL classes was perceived as both engaging and motivating. At the same time, participants emphasized that the effectiveness of the lesson was also shaped by the teacher's pedagogical approach, especially in contexts where innovative materials were not employed. Following this theme, the second main theme is presented below.

Perceived Risks and Ethical Reservations

Although both the experimental and control groups generally expressed positive views regarding the use of AI-based visuals in ELT, several participants also articulated reservations, emphasizing that such tools should be implemented cautiously. The detailed findings concerning the perceived limitations of AI in ELT are presented below.

Ethical, Authenticity, and Environmental Concerns

Some participants expressed concerns regarding the ethical implications of using AI-generated visuals of a popular figure, particularly in relation to the figure's personal stance and consent. To prevent potential misunderstandings, participants were informed that communication had been established with the footballer's manager prior to the study and that all visuals were obtained from publicly shared Instagram accounts. A selected participant clearly reflected, "It is good you took the permission. Otherwise, the celebrity would not be pleased with the intention. It is risky to use the AI-visuals, as they are not real." (P3).

In addition to these ethical considerations, another participant argued that although the AI-generated visuals were engaging and visually appealing, they lacked a sense of authenticity, as they were perceived as artificial or "manufactured." The participant further suggested that representing a local popular figure does not necessarily require AI intervention, and that excessive reliance on such technologies may contribute to reduced human effort and creativity. Illustrating this concern, Participant 2 stated, "AI reduces human efforts. Everybody could draw Barış skilfully or not. The main idea is Barış's representation, not the fancy and shiny machine-made pictures" (P2).

In addition to the perspectives expressed by the experimental group, participants from the control group also shared their views on the use of AI-generated visuals in ELT. Some raised concerns regarding the frequent use of such technologies, suggesting that large-scale reliance on AI could have potential environmental consequences in the long term, as explained by a participant,

It is interesting to be backed up by the AI-based visuals in English lessons, but we should remember that AI uses a lot of water to create the pictures or texts, so... Isn't it risky for the Earth to use them that much in the lessons? (P7).

Briefly, participants from both the experimental and control groups expressed reservations regarding the use of AI-generated visuals in ELT. These concerns primarily centred on ethical considerations, the potential reduction of human effort and creativity, and possible environmental implications associated with extensive AI use.

The following section synthesizes the quantitative and qualitative findings of the study in relation to the existing literature.

DISCUSSION

To provide an integrated interpretation of the findings, this section synthesizes the results with the previous studies. The discussion is structured around four interrelated thematic blocks, each supported by evidence derived from both data strands. These blocks are conceptualized as: Linguistic Justice and Cultural Representation, Celebrity and Parasocial Pedagogy, AI as a Double-Edged Sword, and Young Learners and Technology.

Linguistic Justice & Cultural Representation

From the perspective of linguistic justice and cultural representation, the findings demonstrate that cultural proximity functioned as a catalyst for pride, belonging, and perceived sincerity among learners. The qualitative data revealed that students experienced a heightened sense of identification when encountering a figure from their own cultural background within the English classroom. This aligns with prior scholarship suggesting that the integration of local culture enhances identity awareness and cultural relevance in language learning contexts (Alansari, 2019; Aslan & Sirojitdinovna, 2025; Shresta, 2016).

Furthermore, given that learners are frequently exposed to representations of foreign cultures in textbooks and instructional materials, the inclusion of a culturally familiar figure appears to contribute to a more balanced intercultural dynamic in the classroom. This observation resonates with Byram's (1997) argument regarding the importance of intercultural balance in language education. In a similar vein, the present findings reflect Kramsch's (1998) discussion of global–local tension, suggesting that a productive hybridity between global language content and local cultural references may enhance learner engagement.

Nevertheless, while multimodal teaching enriched by local cultural figures may promote fairness and balance within global–local representations, motivational sustainability remains contingent upon deeper internal processes. As Dörnyei (2009) emphasizes, external motivational stimuli can facilitate engagement; however, long-term success ultimately depends on intrinsic motivation. Accordingly, although the integration of a local cultural figure contributed to a sense of belonging and motivational uplift, sustained learning outcomes require the support of internally driven motivational mechanisms.

Celebrity & Parasocial Pedagogy

In addition to the results from the linguistic justice framework, this study reveals how celebrity incorporation into instruction functions as a form of pedagogy in a global English language acquisition (EAL) environment. Additionally, the data reveal that a culturally proximal celebrity can serve as an internal motivator for students in the classroom. Most notably, student responses referred to the celebrity as their "big brother" which indicated they were motivated by admiration; however, it is clear that an emotional bond was formed with the celebrity in relation to both an affective and relational level. A parasocial relationship has emerged within the classroom where familiarity and cultural proximity are contributing factors to student's emotional comfort and engagement.

These findings resonate with Murphey and Arao's (2001) assertion that elements of popular culture can be effectively incorporated into English language instruction to enhance awareness and learner attention. In the present study, however, the motivational impact appears to extend beyond attention-grabbing novelty; it is rooted in cultural familiarity and identification.

Similarly, Sauro (2019) emphasizes the role of digital media tools, such as the depicted pictures or fan products, in increasing engagement and reducing learner stress in language classrooms. The present findings support this perspective, as the integration of a culturally familiar figure mediated through digital and AI-supported visuals was associated with reduced anxiety and heightened affective involvement. Thus, celebrity integration in this context does not merely enhance attractiveness of the lesson but appears to function as an affective scaffold that facilitates pride, comfort, and sustained engagement.

AI as a Double-Edged Sword

Beyond cultural representation and celebrity integration, the findings underscore the complex role of AI in instructional material design. The data suggest that AI operates as a double-edged pedagogical tool. On one hand, participants expressed strong appreciation for AI-supported visuals, describing them as colorful, engaging, and attention-grabbing. On the other hand, they simultaneously articulated ethical and environmental reservations regarding their use.

Consistent with Ali et al. (2023) and Octavio et al. (2024), the findings indicate that AI tools may function as pedagogical supports by enhancing instructional efficiency and facilitating material development. Importantly, this interpretation is reinforced by the quantitative results: although performance declines were observed in both groups during post-testing, the experimental group demonstrated a markedly smaller decrease. In this sense, AI-mediated representation appears to have functioned not as a performance enhancer, but as a performance stabilizer, mitigating the extent of decline relative to traditional instruction.

Moreover, participants emphasized that AI-based visuals of Barış Alper Yılmaz derived from official Galatasaray social media accounts supported memory retention and vocabulary recall, as used in the lesson for the EG, particularly when accompanied by speaking-focused tasks. This observation aligns with Mabuan's (2024) argument that AI-supported tools can enhance skill-based instruction and contribute to a technologically responsive learning environment.

Nevertheless, the findings also reveal a critical dimension of learner awareness. Participants expressed concerns regarding the potential environmental consequences of excessive AI use, particularly in relation to resource consumption. Ethical considerations were also foregrounded, with students emphasizing the importance of consent and appropriate representation when integrating a celebrity figure into instructional materials. These concerns resonate with Novawan et al.'s (2024) caution regarding overreliance on AI tools and the potential reduction of human agency in educational contexts.

Furthermore, participants questioned whether AI was necessary to achieve motivational impact, suggesting that the presence of the local figure itself rather than the technological mediation was the primary driver of engagement. This perspective parallels Baskara and Mukarto's (2023) argument that AI-generated materials may lack emotional authenticity, given their manufactured nature. The qualitative data indicate that while AI enhanced visual appeal, the cultural and affective significance of the figure remained central. From this standpoint, AI appears to amplify, rather than generate, motivational value.

Ultimately, an important quantitative result is a general downward trend for the total score in both groups after the test. That said, this general decline trend merits close attention. The decrease can likely be attributed to some contextual elements, namely the limited duration of the interventions, the limited exposure, the potential for test fatigue, or the partial mismatch between multimodal instructionally based activities and the format of the assessment tool. Rather than viewing the use of AI-mediated culturally proximal representations as an educational achievement-enhancing agent, the results support the notion that AI-mediated culturally proximal representation serves as a performance stabilizer within the context of brief (short term) instruction. Longer exposure periods, distributed practice, or assessments that are structured in a way to align more closely with the format of multimodal tasks may be required to measure gains in future implementations of the interventions.

Young Learners & Technology

The final block of the discussion examines the relationship between young learners and technology within the context of AI-supported instruction. The findings indicate that students perceived technology-enhanced materials particularly those incorporating visually rich and well-designed presentations as enjoyable, motivating, and engaging. However, this positive orientation toward digital tools was accompanied by a noticeable degree of skepticism regarding the integration of AI, especially in relation to environmental concerns, ethical considerations, and perceived overuse.

The authors' dual position on the role of digital tools for young learners reflects Prosic-Santovac's (2017) conclusion that when visual tools are both developmentally appropriate and educationally relevant, they can contribute to the authenticity of a classroom environment for young learners. Similarly, Taghizadeh & Hasani Yourdshahi (2020) suggest that the successful inclusion of technology in second language learning requires that tools be age-relevant and context-specific. Consistent with these views, the findings of this study support the view that young learners react positively to technology when it is an integral part of the instructional process.

However, the views by the participants also reveal a cautionary dimension to their perceptions of technology. The participants' concerns about the potential for excessive or unguided AI use in educational settings represent some of the most general fears about the impact of technology on students as reported in the literature. In particular, while the data does not indicate that the learners studied are uniformly naive about technological innovations, it does show a developing sense of ethical awareness in response to new technologies. This is consistent with the cautions of Rao Idapalapati (2024) and Sharifuddin & Hashim (2024), noting the overreliance on new technologies can result in ethical issues and moral dilemmas in educational settings, especially if the students involved have no experience or training in how to make informed decisions about the responsible use of technology. Finally, the concerns voiced by many of the participants about the lack of human interaction and emotional detachment from the technology-based learning environment further underscores the need for teachers to remain active participants in the technology-enhanced learning environment.

Taken together, the findings suggest that young learners' engagement with technology is neither wholly enthusiastic nor wholly resistant. Instead, it reflects a nuanced and context-sensitive stance, wherein motivation coexists with ethical reflection. This indicates the emergence of an early form of critical technological consciousness, highlighting the necessity of balanced, guided, and pedagogically responsible AI integration in language education.

The discussion presents the results of both quantitative and qualitative studies as they relate to the current research and illustrates the complex roles AI-based cultural representations can take on in EFL classrooms. The integration of a culturally close to home popular figure through AI-generated images appeared to be an effective method for increasing motivation, student engagement and classroom participation with students reporting their identity and connection to a foreign language is strengthened by use of these materials. The results also indicated that visual-based and technology-based learning resources may increase student engagement if used in meaningful and intentional educational contexts.

However, the results also underscore a critical dimension. For example, learners demonstrated a nuanced awareness of the potential risks associated with AI integration, including ethical considerations, environmental concerns, and questions regarding necessity and proportionality of use. Thus, while AI-supported representations of local figures can enhance affective engagement, their pedagogical value depends on balanced, context-sensitive, and ethically informed implementation.

Synthesizing the current landscape of AI in ELT reveals that while affordances such as personalization and efficiency are significant, they must be balanced against risks of dependency and cognitive misalignment. For young learners, this balance is particularly critical; multimodal AI integration supports engagement only when developmentally appropriate and scaffolded by human mediation. Furthermore, when approached through the lens of linguistic justice, the use of AI to introduce local cultural figures serves as a transformative tool, provided that it fosters meaningful cultural representation rather than superficial technological engagement.

The following section draws upon these core insights to present the pedagogical implications and recommendations of the study.

PEDAGOGICAL IMPLICATIONS AND RECOMMENDATIONS

Drawing on the integrated findings regarding AI-generated representations of culturally proximal celebrities in EFL classrooms, several practical pedagogical implications emerge. First, teachers could develop critical AI literacy and encourage discussions about how AI materials are produced and why consent matters. Second, curriculum designers could adopt a hybrid approach that balances local familiarity with global exposure. A culturally familiar celebrity may function as a motivational "hook". Therefore, it could reduce anxiety and increase engagement through parasocial familiarity. However, this could be complemented with diverse global representations to support intercultural communicative competence. Because AI materials lack emotional authenticity, they might function as visual supports rather than instructional tools. Teachers are recommended to continue a strong pedagogical presence, providing empathy, interaction, and emotional scaffolding. Finally, while celebrity visuals stimulate initial engagement, long-term learning depends on transforming this situational motivation into intrinsic motivation through meaningful, communicative, and learner-centered language tasks.

FUTURE RESEARCH DIRECTIONS

This study examined the pedagogical implications of integrating AI-generated visuals of a culturally proximal popular figure into EFL classrooms, focusing specifically on secondary school learners due to contextual accessibility. Future research could extend this line of inquiry across broader educational levels in order to examine developmental differences in the reception and impact of culturally embedded AI-supported materials. Comparative cross-grade analyses may provide deeper insight into how age, cognitive maturity, and identity formation influence responses to local cultural representation in foreign language learning.

Given that the present study was conducted with a relatively limited sample ($n = 39$), subsequent research involving larger and more diverse participant groups would strengthen the generalizability and robustness of the findings. Expanding the demographic and institutional scope may also reveal contextual variables that mediate the motivational and performance-related outcomes observed in this research.

Furthermore, while this study explored the role of AI as a mediating tool in representing a local celebrity, future investigations may adopt a more systematic approach to examining the optimal degree and form of AI integration in language classrooms. In particular, longitudinal and design-based studies could clarify how frequency, modality, and pedagogical framing of AI-generated materials influence both cognitive outcomes and ethical perceptions among learners.

Although the current research centred on a nationally recognized football player selected through learner preference, future studies may explore the pedagogical implications of incorporating local figures from diverse professional domains, such as arts, science, or social activism. Such comparative investigations would contribute to a more nuanced understanding of whether motivational impact derives primarily from cultural proximity, celebrity status, domain relevance, or a combination of these factors.

Finally, as the present study examined short-term instructional effects, longitudinal research is needed to determine whether the stabilizing and motivational impacts identified here persist over time. Long-term investigations would be particularly valuable in assessing the relationship between culturally proximal AI-mediated materials and sustained intrinsic motivation in foreign language learning.

Overall, future research should aim to expand the developmental, contextual, and longitudinal dimensions of AI-supported culturally embedded pedagogy in EFL contexts.

CONCLUSION

The primary aim of the present research was to examine the pedagogical impact of AI-generated visuals of a culturally proximal popular figure, Barış Alper Yılmaz, in EFL classrooms. Specifically, the study investigated their influence on the motivation and academic performance of secondary school learners in a private educational context in Diyarbakır, Türkiye.

The findings demonstrate that learners, who are predominantly exposed to foreign cultural figures in EFL materials, experienced a heightened sense of pride, belonging, and engagement when encountering a local figure in their lessons. The qualitative data suggest that cultural proximity strengthened affective connection and classroom participation, particularly in skill-based activities and vocabulary retention. However, our participants also acknowledged that while the presence of a local figure enhanced engagement, it did not fundamentally alter the structural nature of the lesson itself.

Both groups experienced a decline in their scores after the post-test; however, the drop in the experimental group was significantly lower. Therefore, it seems that using AI to represent a culturally meaningful character does not improve the student's score, but helps stabilize the learning experience in the classroom. In essence, the AI is not an independent motivator of academic achievement but rather serves as a tool that enhances and supports the culturally related material that teachers provide.

The study also demonstrated the continued importance of teachers' roles in the classroom. Students stated that while the technology provided was fun and visually appealing, students felt that it was important to continue to include a human-centered, emotionally supportive pedagogy. Many students expressed skepticism about the necessity of AI mediated instruction when the motivation to engage with the material was based upon the cultural reference (i.e., the person/character) and not the technology. Students also raised questions about environmental and ethical implications such as resource usage and representation of diverse cultures.

In a nutshell, through this study, we aimed to contribute to the literature by demonstrating the potential of AI-mediated integration of culturally proximal popular figures. It has been seen that they can foster engagement and support performance stability in EFL classrooms. However, this effectiveness depends on the pedagogical framing, ethical awareness, and proportional use. The findings suggest that the true pedagogical value lies not in technological novelty, but in the meaningful alignment of global language instruction with local identity.

REFERENCES

Alansari, A. (2019). *Localizing Global English language textbooks: A critical multimodal discourse analysis of identity construction in global, regional and local editions* [PhD thesis University of Warwick]. Warwick Research Archive Portal (WRAP).

Ali, J. K. M., Shamsan, M. A., Hezam, T. A., & Mohammead, A. A. Q. (2023). Impact of ChatGPT on learning motivation: Teachers and students' voices. *Journal of English Studies in Arabia Felix*, *2*(1), 41–49. DOI: 10.56540/jesaf.v2i1.51

Aslan, E., & Sirojitdinovna, M. B. (2025). Language learning made short and sweet? Exploring student perceptions of microcelebrity teacher reels on Instagram. *Linguistics and Education*, *88*, 1–13. DOI: 10.1016/j.linged.2025.101430

Baskara, R., & Mukarto, M. (2023). Exploring the implications of ChatGPT for language learning in higher education. *Indonesian Journal of English Language Teaching and Applied Linguistics*, *7*(2), 343–358. DOI: 10.21093/ijeltal.v7i2.1387

Byram, M. (1997). *Teaching and assessing intercultural communicative competence*. Multilingual Matters.

Calhoun, K., & Fawcett, A. (2023). "They edited out her nip nops": Linguistic innovation as textual censorship avoidance on TikTok. *Language@Internet, 21*, 1–30. https://doi.org/DOI: 10.14434/li.v21.37371

Creswell, J. W. (2009). *Research design: Qualitative, quantitative, and mixed methods approaches*. Sage publications.

Dörnyei, Z. (2009). The L2 motivational self system. In Dornyei, Z., & Ushioda, E. (Eds.), *Motivation, language identity and the L2 self*. Multilingual Matters. DOI: 10.21832/9781847691293-003

Etikan, I., Musa, S. A., & Alkassim, R. S. (2016). Comparison of convenience sampling and purposive sampling. *American Journal of Theoretical and Applied Statistics*, *5*(1), 1–4. DOI: 10.11648/j.ajtas.20160501.11

Kramsch, C. J. (1998). *Language and culture*. Oxford University Press.

Liu, Y. J., Han, T., Ma, S., Zhang, J., Yang, Y., Tian, J., He, H., Li, A., He, M., Liu, Z., Wu, Z., Zhang, L., Zhu, D., Li, X., Niu, Q., Shen, D., Liu, T., & Ge, B. (2023). Summary of ChatGPT-related research and perspective towards the future of large language models. *Meta-Radiology*, *1*(2), 100017. DOI: 10.1016/j.metrad.2023.100017

Mabuan, R. A. (2024). ChatGPT and ELT: Exploring teachers' voices. [IJTE]. *International Journal of Technology in Education*, *7*(1), 128–153. DOI: 10.46328/ijte.523

Murphey, T., & Arao, H. (2001). Reported belief changes through near peer role modeling. *TESL-EJ, 5*(3). https://eric.ed.gov/?id=EJ639330

Novawan, A., Ikeda, O., & Walker, S. A. (2024). The new face of technology-enhanced language learning (TELL) with Artificial Intelligence (AI): Teacher perspectives, practices, and challenges. *Journal of English in Academic and Professional Communication JEAPCO, 10*(1), 1–18. DOI: 10.25047/jeapco.v10i1.4565

Octavio, M. M., Argüello, V. G., & Pujola, J. T. (2024). ChatGPT as an AI L2 teaching support: A case study of an EFL teacher. *Technology in Language Teaching & Learning, 6*(1), 1–25. DOI: 10.29140/tltl.v6n1.1142

Prosic-Santovac, D. (2017). Popular video cartoons and associated branded toys in teaching English to very young learners: A case study. *Language Teaching Research, 21*(5), 568–588. DOI: 10.1177/1362168816639758

Rao Idapalapati, S.Srinivasa Rao Idapalapati. (2024). AI integration in ELT as a disruptive mechanism. *International Journal of Science and Research Archive, 12*(01), 922–933. DOI: 10.30574/ijsra.2024.12.1.0941

Sauro, S. (2019). Fan fiction and informal language learning. In Dressman, M., & Sadler, R. W. (Eds.), *The handbook of informal language learning* (pp. 140–151). John Wiley & Sons Ltd. DOI: 10.1002/9781119472384.ch9

Selwyn, N. (2016). *Education and technology: Key issues and debates.* Bloomsbury Academic.

Sharifuddin, N. S., & Hashim, H. (2024). Benefits and challenges in implementing artificial intelligence in education (AIED) in ESL classroom: A systematic review (2019-2022). *International Journal of Academic Research in Business & Social Sciences, 14*(1), 146–164. DOI: 10.6007/IJARBSS/v14-i1/20422

Shresta, K. (2016). Role of (local) culture in English language teaching. *Journal of NELTA, 21*(1-2), 54–60. DOI: 10.3126/nelta.v21i1-2.20201

Taghizadeh, M., & Hasani Yourdshahi, Z. (2020). Integrating technology into young learners' classes: Language teachers' perceptions. *Computer Assisted Language Learning, 33*(8), 982–1006. DOI: 10.1080/09588221.2019.1618876

Varatharaj, A., Welch, A., Bucholtz, M., & Lee, J. S. (2024). *Teaching linguistic justice through augmented reality.* https://arxiv.org/pdf/2404.12563

Yıldırım, A., & Şimşek, H. (2021). *Sosyal Bilimlerde Nitel Araştırma Yöntemleri.* Seçkin.

ADDITIONAL READING

Apriani, E., & Supardan, D., Syafryadin, Noermanzah, & Umami, M. (2020). Independent learning: English teachers' problems in designing a good lesson plan in new normal era at MAN Rejang Lebong. *Proceeding of 1st International Conference on The Teaching of English and Literature, 1*(1), 72–78.

Aras, A. (2024). *The effects of artificial intelligence-assisted teaching on EFL vocabulary learning: A case of ChatGPT* [Master's thesis, Atatürk University].

Aydın Yıldız, T. (2023). The impact of ChatGPT on language learners' motivation. *Journal of Teacher Education and Lifelong Learning, 5*(2), 582–597. DOI: 10.51535/tell.1314355

Ballıdağ, M. (2024). *The impact of AI-based chatbots on speaking anxiety among EFL learners* [Master's thesis, İstanbul Medeniyet University].

Bryman, A. (2012). *Social research methods* (4th ed.). Oxford University Press.

Cao, M., Li, D., & Jun, W. (2020). A study of college English culture intelligence-aided teaching system and teaching pattern. *English Language Teaching, 13*(3), 77–83. DOI: 10.5539/elt.v13n3p77

Çerası, C.C. & Balcıoğlu, Y.S. (2023). AI and ethics in education: ChatGPT program example. *Uluslararası Felsefi Boyutlarıyla Teknoloji ve İletişim Sempozyumu FEBİTS*, 85–89.

Firat, M. (2023). What ChatGPT means for universities: Perceptions of scholars and students. *Journal of Applied Learning & Teaching, 6*(1), 1–22. DOI: 10.37074/jalt.2023.6.1.22

KEY TERMS AND DEFINITIONS

Artificial Intelligence (AI): The simulation of human cognitive processes by machine systems, utilized in educational contexts to generate instructional materials, facilitate language practice, and mediate multimodal content.

Cultural Proximity: The degree of cultural familiarity and shared identity between learners and the instructional content or figures, which serves to enhance emotional connection, pride, and motivation in language acquisition.

English as a Foreign Language (EFL): The study and teaching of English to non-native speakers in environments where English is not the primary or official language of communication.

Large Language Models (LLMs): Advanced artificial intelligence algorithms trained on vast datasets of text, capable of understanding, generating, and processing human language to assist in tasks such as contextual lesson planning and material design.

Linguistic Justice: An educational framework that advocates for the equitable representation of diverse local cultures and languages in instructional materials, counteracting the traditional dominance of foreign or hegemonic cultural figures.

Multimodality: An instructional approach that incorporates multiple modes of communication such as visual media, auditory input, and text often enhanced by digital tools to align with the cognitive and affective needs of learners.

Parasocial Pedagogy: The strategic educational utilization of learners' one-sided, affective relationships with public figures or celebrities to scaffold motivation, lower anxiety, and foster a supportive, comfortable learning environment.

Young Learners: Children, typically in the primary or middle school stages of education, who possess distinct developmental, cognitive, and affective characteristics that require highly engaging and context-sensitive instructional methodologies.

APPENDICES

Appendix 1: Pre- And Post- Test

1. Do you like coffee?
   A) Yes, I do.
   B) No, I like.
   C) Yes, I'd.
2. Is your brother called John?
   A) Yes, he does.
   B) Yes, he's.
   C) Yes, he is.
3. Are you happy in your new job?
   A) Yes, I'm.
   B) Yes, I am.
   C) Yes, I happy.
4. Does it snow here in winter?
   A) Yes, it does.
   B) Yes, it is.
   C) Yes, snows.
5. My brother usually _____ TV in the evening.
   A) watch
   B) watches
   C) watchs
6. They _____ to school on Saturday.
   A) doesn't go
   B) don't go
   D) goes
7. The students _____ lunch at 12:00.
   A) has
   B) have
   C) has got
8. _____ she _____ ice cream?
   A) Do / likes
   B) Does / like
   C) Is / like
9. I always _____ my homework before dinner.
   A) does
   B) do

C) doing

10. He _____ his teeth three times a day.

A) washes

B) brushs

C) brushes

APPENDIX 2

The Lesson for the EG (Some pages from the lesson material)

Figure 3.

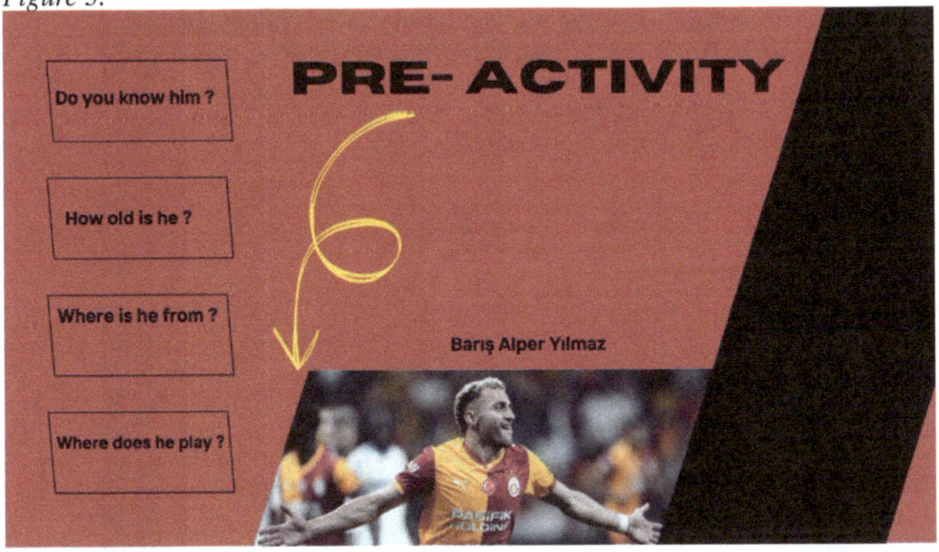

Figure 4.

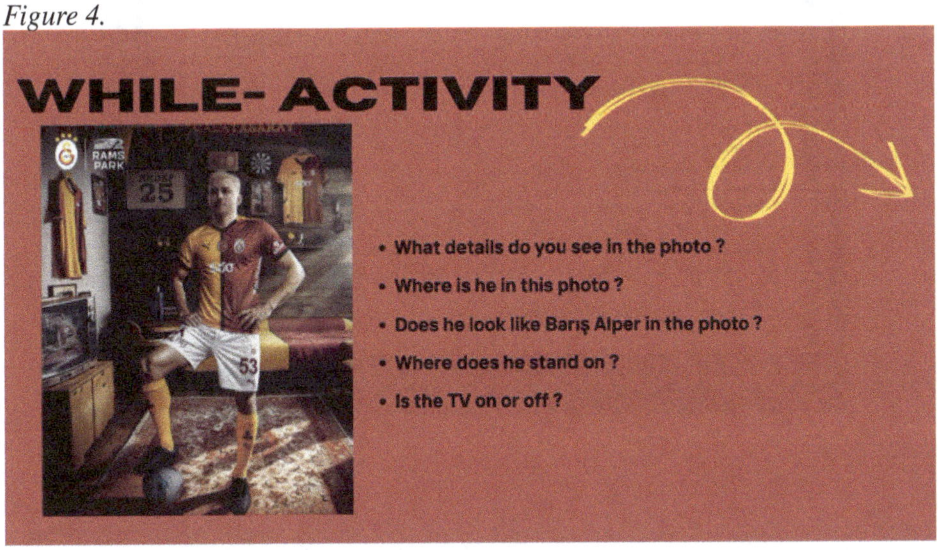

APPENDIX 3

The Lesson for CG

Figure 5.

Alfred's daily routine

Read the text carefully.

Alfred is an American boy. He lives in Los Angeles, California. He lives with his family in a modern house. He is eleven years old and he has got an older brother, David, and a younger sister, Emma.

He starts his day at about half past seven. He gets up, goes to the bathroom, takes a shower, brushes his teeth and get dressed. Then he has breakfast and at a quarter to eight he leaves home and catches the bus to school. Classes begin at half past eight. He usually has lunch at the school canteen at half past twelve. After school, at a quarter past five, he goes home. There he does his school homework and when he finishes it he helps his Mum laying the table. At half past seven the family dines together.

Alfred is a very helpful boy, so he helps his mother cleaning up everything after dinner.

He usually watches TV for a while after dinner and at about ten o'clock the most he brushes his teeth again, puts on his Spider Man pajamas and goes to bed. His parents always kiss him good night before he gets asleep. Alfred is a very happy boy!

1 True or False?

1. Alfred is an American boy. ____________
2. He lives in a modern flat. ____________
3. He is eleven years old. ____________
4. He has got two brothers. ____________
5. Alfred wakes up at eight o'clock. ____________
6. He walks to school. ____________
7. His classes begin at half past eight. ____________
8. Alfred and his family have dinner at half past seven. ____________

2 Match the antonyms.

modern •	• enters
older •	• alone
starts •	• end
leaves •	• old-fasioned
begin •	• unhappy
together •	• younger
helpful •	• finishes
happy •	• unhelpful

3 Answer the following questions.

1. Where does Alfred live? --
2. What's his sister's name? --
3. What time does he wake up? --
4. Does he have breakfast at home? --
5. What time does he leave home? --
6. Where does he have lunch? --
7. When does he return home? --
8. Does he make homework at school or at home? --
9. Is he a helpful boy? --
10. What about you? What's your daily routine like? --

APPENDIX 4

The Interview Questions

Theme 1: Motivation, Interest, and Learning Experience (SDT Dimensions)

These questions aim to uncover the reasons behind students' emotional experiences during the learning process.

- Did you generally find the activities in this Simple Present Tense unit (Barış Alper visuals/Alfred text) enjoyable? What did you enjoy the most?
- While doing these tasks, did you feel competent or successful? Which visual/text motivated you the most?
- Did you feel any pressure or tension while studying this topic? If yes, was it related to Barış Alper/Alfred in any way?

Theme 2: Identity, Representation, and Relatedness

This theme focuses on Linguistic Justice and the visibility of local identity in language learning materials.

- Were the celebrities/people you usually saw in traditional English textbooks from your own culture, or were they mostly from different cultures?
- (Experimental Group Only): How did it make you feel to see someone from Türkiye, like Barış Alper Yılmaz, in an English lesson material? Did it create a feeling such as "This lesson belongs to me"?
- (Control Group & Comparison): When you see foreign characters like Alfred or standard visuals, does your perception of the importance of English for you personally change?
- How does it make you feel to see celebrities/people from your own culture in foreign language lessons? Would it be better for you to see someone from the target language culture or from your own culture?

Theme 3: AI, Ethics, and the Future (Justice & Learner Agency)

These questions investigate students' critical awareness of AI use and how they perceive AI-generated materials.

- Did knowing that these visuals were produced by artificial intelligence (AI), rather than directly by a teacher, change your perspective on the lesson?
- Fairness: Do you think using such powerful AI-generated visuals is fair compared to other classes using standard and simpler materials? Or should everyone use the same materials?
- For the future, are there any other local figures (athletes, artists, scientists) you would like to see AI generate for English lessons? (This question measures the learner agency dimension.)
- Ethical Reflection: Do you think it is ethical to use a celebrity's (Barış Alper's) image in lesson materials, even if it is AI-generated?

Chapter 10
A Comparative Study Towards Ethical and Inclusive AI in Language Learning:
Examining Equity, Transparency, and Sustainability in Digital Language Education

I. Samuel Peter James
http://orcid.org/0000-0003-2756-8854
Shadan Women's College of Engineering, India

D. Magdalene Delighta Angeline
http://orcid.org/0000-0002-0699-9105
Joginpally B.R. Engineering College, India

T. Prabakaran
http://orcid.org/0000-0002-8458-0211
Joginpally B.R. Engineering College, India

ABSTRACT

Artificial Intelligence (AI) has transformed language education through adaptive tutoring systems, automated assessment tools, speech technologies, and generative AI applications. However, these technological advances also raise delicate ethical and equity issues, particularly regarding access, bias, and representation. This chapter offers a conceptual framework for understanding how equity and ethics are articulated in AI-driven language education across educational contexts world-

DOI: 10.4018/979-8-3373-7749-0.ch010

wide. It will examine the state of AI in language learning, from Intelligent Tutoring Systems to generative AI tools. It presents an outline focused on human-centered design, linguistic diversity, and participatory governance as part of efforts to promote fairness, transparency, and access. It also contributes to current discussions on linguistic justice, digital inclusion, and ethical AI by advancing reflections on how technology can underpin inclusive and sustainable language learning for all individuals.

INTRODUCTION

Artificial Intelligence (AI) has rapidly shifted from a background technological tool to a visible, transformative force in everyday life and education. From voice assistants such as Siri and Alexa to generative systems like ChatGPT developed by OpenAI, AI technologies now shape how individuals access information, communicate, and learn languages (Holmes & Tuomi, 2022). Since 2022, the widespread availability of generative AI (GenAI) tools has accelerated their integration into educational contexts, including language learning (Galaczi & Luckin, 2024). International policy discussions, such as the Bletchley Declaration, acknowledge both the transformative potential of AI for global wellbeing and the significant ethical risks associated with its deployment (Bengio et al., 2025).

To meaningfully examine AI in language education, it is essential to establish conceptual clarity. AI systems are broadly defined as human-designed technologies capable of perceiving environments, processing structured and unstructured data, reasoning toward goals, and adapting through learning (High-Level Expert Group on Artificial Intelligence, 2018). AI systems simulate aspects of human intelligence, enabling autonomous decision-making rather than strictly following pre-programmed instructions (Mitchell, 2020). Within this landscape, GenAI refers specifically to systems capable of producing new content—text, images, audio, or video—based on large-scale data training (UNESCO, 2023). In contrast, predictive AI systems classify, recommend, or automate decisions, often operating invisibly within digital platforms. A further discrepancy can be made between symbolic (rule-based) AI and sub-symbolic (data-driven) AI. Symbolic systems rely on explicit logic and expert-defined rules, making their decision-making processes relatively transparent and explainable. Sub-symbolic systems, such as the deep learning models underlying many generative tools, identify patterns in vast datasets but often operate as "black boxes," raising concerns about transparency and accountability. This technical distinction has significant implications for ethical and inclusive AI in language learning, particularly regarding explainability, bias, and governance.

In language education, AI-powered tools—including Intelligent Tutoring Systems (ITS), adaptive learning platforms, automated assessment tools, and generative writing assistants—offer opportunities for personalized learning, real-time feedback, and expanded access (Nguyen et al., 2023). However, these benefits are not equitably distributed. Issues such as algorithmic bias, digital divides, limited representation of minority languages, and unequal infrastructural access shape who benefits from AI integration and who remains marginalized (Coleman, 2021). Cultural under-representation and linguistic hierarchies embedded within training datasets may inadvertently reinforce global inequities (Bender et al., 2021).

This chapter proposes a conceptual framework that foregrounds human-centered design, linguistic diversity, participatory governance, and policy accountability. By examining comparative global contexts, it seeks to identify both structural challenges and actionable pathways toward ethical AI ecosystems that promote fairness, transparency, and accessibility. Ultimately, constructing inclusive AI for language learning requires collaboration among educators, policymakers, technologists, and learners themselves. Ethical AI must not only enhance efficiency and innovation but also uphold linguistic justice and digital inclusion. By aligning technological advancement with equity-driven principles, AI can serve as a catalyst for sustainable and inclusive language education worldwide.

BACKGROUND

Conceptual Framework for Ethical and Inclusive AI in Language Learning

A five-layer conceptual framework integrates technological innovation with ethical governance to ensure that AI-driven language education remains human centered, equitable, and socially responsible.

Layer 1: AI Application Layer

The AI Application Layer encompasses the core technologies deployed in language learning contexts, including ITS, adaptive learning platforms, automated assessment tools, speech and pronunciation assistants, and GenAI systems (Galaczi & Luckin, 2024; Holmes & Tuomi, 2022;). These applications represent the operational dimension of AI integration, providing personalized instruction, automated evaluation, and interactive language practice, but they also raise concerns regarding reliability, bias, environmental sustainability, and responsible deployment (Bashir et al., 2024; Bender et al., 2021; UNESCO, 2023). This layer reflects the technological infrastructure that enables data-driven learning environments.

Layer 2: Pedagogical Function Layer

The Pedagogical Function Layer articulates the educational purposes served by these technologies. AI systems contribute to personalizing learning pathways, automating feedback processes, enhancing learner engagement, diagnosing strengths and weaknesses, and generating dynamic content (Lin et al., 2019; Nguyen et al., 2023). This layer ensures that AI deployment is guided by sound pedagogical objectives rather than purely technological capability. It shifts attention from what AI can do to what AI should do in support of meaningful language learning.

Layer 3: Ethical Governance Layer

The Ethical Governance Layer introduces normative safeguards that regulate AI implementation. Core principles at this level include validity and reliability of assessment, fairness and justice in algorithmic decision-making, transparency and explainability of system processes, protection of privacy and data security, and clear accountability structures. This layer operationalizes ethical commitments, ensuring that AI systems do not compromise educational integrity or exacerbate inequality (Holmes et al., 2022; Institute for Ethical AI in Education, 2021). It serves as the moral and regulatory anchor of the framework. Broader AI ethics scholarship further underscores the need for explainable systems and safeguards against systemic bias (Bengio et al., 2025; Fjeld et al., 2020; Jenkins et al., 2020; Samek et al., 2017). Concerns about large-scale language models functioning as "stochastic parrots" reinforce the importance of transparency and responsible governance (Bender et al., 2021; Mitchell & Krakauer, 2023). The Teacher Perspectives on AI integration highlight several pedagogical and practical concerns:

- Over-reliance leading to reduced writing instruction
- Unclear scoring criteria in automated assessment
- Increased responsibility to audit AI feedback
- Need for training in AI literacy

Student perspectives reflect both opportunities and challenges associated with AI use, including the following:

- Motivation rises with interactive AI
- Confusion when AI explanations are opaque
- Frustration when accents are misrecognized
- Mixed feelings about fairness in AI scoring

Layer 4: Structural & Policy Layer

The Structural and Policy Layer addresses institutional and systemic responsibilities. Participatory governance mechanisms ensure stakeholder involvement in AI selection and evaluation. Regulatory compliance aligns AI deployment with national and international legal standards. Institutional oversight structures monitor performance, bias, and unintended consequences. Sustainability standards incorporate environmental responsibility into AI adoption decisions. This layer acknowledges that ethical AI requires not only principles but also durable governance infrastructures. International and European AI governance discussions emphasize the need for coordinated oversight mechanisms and risk-based regulation (High-Level Expert Group on Artificial Intelligence, 2018; Jenkins et al., 2020). Moreover, institutional quality management approaches in language assessment demonstrate how standards can be operationalized and monitored systematically (Saville, 2005 & 2013).

Global South and Minority Language Considerations in AI-Enhanced Language Learning

AI-driven language education does not operate uniformly across global contexts. The majority of AI systems are developed in high-resource regions, optimized for stable infrastructure, mainstream linguistic varieties, and pedagogical assumptions rooted in Global North education systems. As a result, the educational realities of the Global South where infrastructure, linguistic diversity, and resource availability differ significantly—require explicit consideration (Nguyen & Doan, 2021; UNESCO, 2023). Ethical and equitable AI design must account for these contextual disparities to prevent the deepening of global educational inequalities.

Many Global South educational environments face structural constraints that directly influence the effectiveness and fairness of AI-driven language learning tools.

1. **Unreliable electricity:** Frequent power interruptions disrupt access to cloud-based AI platforms, real-time feedback systems, and device-dependent tools, resulting in unequal learning continuity.
2. **Limited bandwidth:** High-latency or low-speed connectivity affects the performance of speech recognition, adaptive learning systems, and GenAI, creating inconsistent learning experiences across socio-economic groups.
3. **Outdated devices:** Older mobile phones or computers may not support the computational demands of modern AI platforms, excluding many learners from advanced features or entire tools.
4. **English-dominant AI tools:** AI models typically prioritize English and other major world languages, limiting support for indigenous, regional, or minority languages commonly spoken across the Global South.
5. **Lack of teacher training infrastructure:** Educators often receive limited training in AI tools, digital pedagogy, or algorithmic literacy, which restricts effective integration and may widen pedagogical inequities between well-resourced and under-resourced institutions.

These constraints highlight that technological innovation alone cannot ensure inclusive educational outcomes. Without systemic attention to infrastructure and training, AI may exacerbate rather than reduce inequalities.

Minority Language Inclusion Issues

Beyond infrastructural disparities, linguistic injustice is a core ethical concern. Many minority, regional, and native languages face structural disadvantages in AI systems due to limited digital representation (Bender et al., 2021; Mitchell & Krakauer, 2023).

1. Underrepresentation in NLP data

Most NLP datasets are dominated by Western, monolingual, and standardized language varieties, leaving minority languages and even non-standard dialects poorly represented.

2. Models penalize non-standard expressions

Automated scoring and speech recognition systems may incorrectly mark dialectal features or culturally specific expressions as errors, creating systematic disadvantage.

3. Lack of culturally relevant examples

AI-generated texts, exercises, or examples often reflect culturally Western contexts, reducing authenticity and relevance for learners whose linguistic realities differ.

4. Limited availability of speech recognition tools

ASR systems rarely include phonetic variation from indigenous or minority languages, leading to errors, misrecognition, and learner frustration (Choubey et al., 2023; Unnikrishnan & Prasad, 2021).

These issues underscore that linguistic diversity must be intentionally embedded into AI design to ensure fairness, accuracy, and cultural respect.

Actionable Solutions

Ensuring fairness for Global South and minority-language learners requires specific design and policy strategies that recognize the diversity of educational contexts.

1. Domain-specific lightweight models

Using smaller, locally optimized AI models reduces computational demands and can run on low-end devices, making AI tools accessible without requiring high-performance hardware.

2. Community-sourced datasets

Engaging local educators, linguists, and speakers in data collection supports the creation of inclusive, culturally grounded NLP datasets that represent regional language varieties.

Layer 5: Societal Outcome Layer

The Societal Outcome Layer captures the broader impacts of AI integration in language education. The digital divide in education, significantly highlighted during the COVID-19 period, underscores the risk of widening inequalities if AI systems are not designed inclusively (Coleman, 2021). When responsibly implemented, AI systems can contribute to linguistic justice, digital inclusion, equitable access to educational opportunities, and sustainable innovation (Atari et al., 2023; World Economic Forum, 2022). This layer reflects the ultimate purpose of ethical AI to enhance learning while promoting fairness, cultural responsiveness, and long-term social wellbeing.

This multi-layered model clarifies how ethical principles must operate across technical, pedagogical, and structural dimensions.

AI IN EDUCATION: CRITICAL ETHICAL CONCERNS

Artificial Intelligence (AI) is increasingly embedded across educational ecosystems, transforming how learners, teachers, institutions, and researchers engage with teaching and assessment processes. Tools such as ChatGPT and other generative systems have expanded possibilities for personalized and interactive learning, while earlier AI applications have long supported automated evaluation and adaptive instruction. These developments highlight the need for critical perspectives on both the opportunities and risks associated with generative AI in language education (Galaczi & Luckin, 2024).

Expanding Applications of AI in Education

Students benefit from AI through intelligent tutoring systems, dialogue-based learning assistants, AI-supported simulations, automated essay feedback, and adaptive accommodations for learners with special needs. Teachers utilize AI for plagiarism detection, automated grading, content curation, and formative assessment analytics. At the institutional level, AI systems are applied in admission screening, scheduling optimization, campus security, digital exam proctoring, and early identification of students at academic risk (Holmes & Tuomi, 2022).

In language learning and assessment, AI technologies have been deployed for years to support automated writing and speaking evaluation. More recent developments include automated task generation (ATG), adaptive testing with diagnostic feedback, item calibration, and detection of academic dishonesty. GenAI models further enable dynamic content creation, integration of learning analytics, and seamless blending of learning and assessment. These innovations promise greater personalization, interactive feedback, and evidence-based decision-making in language education.

AI in language learning

The integration of AI into language learning environments reflects a shift from static instructional models toward intelligent, data-driven, and learner-centered ecosystems. Figure 1 presents a structured evolution of AI applications in language education.

Figure 1. AI in language learning (Adapted from Holmes and Tuomi (2022) and Nguyen et al. (2023))

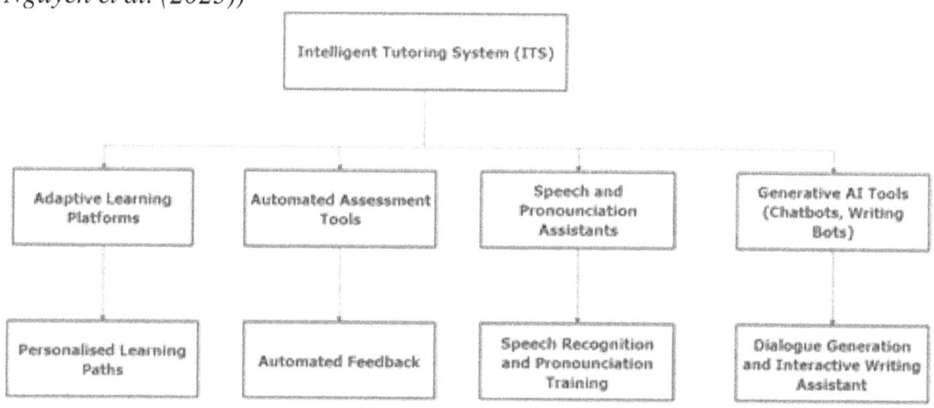

It begins with AI in Language Learning as the domain and narrows into (ITS), which further branch into four major application categories:

1. Adaptive Learning Platforms
2. Automated Assessment Tools

3. Speech & Pronunciation Assistants
4. GenAI Tools

This progression reflects the shift from rule-based instructional support systems to advanced generative models capable of producing human-like language.

Intelligent Tutoring Systems

ITS represent one of the earliest and most influential applications of Artificial Intelligence in education, laying the conceptual and technological foundation for modern adaptive and generative learning environments (Holmes & Tuomi, 2022; Lin et al., 2019). Designed to emulate key aspects of human tutoring, ITS integrate cognitive modelling, domain knowledge representation, and instructional strategies to provide structured, individualized learning support. These systems diagnose learner errors, continuously track progress, deliver targeted feedback, and adapt instructional pathways based on performance data. Unlike traditional e-learning platforms that present uniform content, ITS dynamically respond to learner input, thereby approximating the responsiveness of a skilled human instructor.

In practical language-learning contexts, ITSs are widely used for grammar tutoring, vocabulary acquisition, and the development of reading comprehension (Lin et al., 2019). For example, a grammar-focused ITS may detect repeated tense errors and provide corrective explanations along with progressively scaffolded exercises to reinforce conceptual clarity. Vocabulary training systems can adjust word difficulty levels based on recall accuracy and response time, ensuring optimal challenge. Similarly, reading comprehension modules may adapt text complexity according to demonstrated comprehension ability, gradually increasing linguistic and semantic demands as learners improve. These targeted interventions enable systematic skill development while maintaining learner engagement.

The implementation of ITS typically relies on several core technological components. Learner modelling algorithms construct dynamic profiles that represent knowledge states, misconceptions, and mastery levels. Performance analytics dashboards provide both learners and instructors with visualized insights into progression trends and areas requiring reinforcement. Knowledge tracing models—such as Bayesian Knowledge Tracing—estimate the probability that a learner has mastered a specific concept based on historical response patterns. Together, these mechanisms allow ITS to make informed instructional decisions and deliver personalized feedback with pedagogical precision.

Despite the emergence of GenAI systems, ITS remain foundational within AI-driven education. Their structured architecture, emphasis on cognitive modelling, and transparent adaptation logic continue to inform contemporary developments in personalized learning technologies. By establishing the principles of learner modelling, diagnostic assessment, and adaptive instruction, Intelligent Tutoring Systems serve as the cornerstone for more advanced AI applications in language education.

*Adaptive Learning Platforms*Adaptive learning platforms represent a significant advancement in AI-driven language education by dynamically personalizing instructional pathways according to individual learner characteristics and performance data (Dang et al., 2023). Unlike static digital content, these systems continuously analyze learner proficiency levels, engagement patterns, error frequency, and time spent on specific tasks to tailor content delivery in real time. By constructing and updating learner profiles, adaptive platforms adjust task difficulty, sequence instructional materials, and recommend targeted interventions. This data-informed responsiveness enables instruction to move beyond one-size-fits-all models toward more precise and learner-centered pedagogical design.

In practical classroom contexts, adaptive systems can identify recurring grammatical weaknesses and automatically generate focused remedial exercises. For instance, a student who consistently struggles with passive voice constructions may receive additional contextualized practice tasks, explanatory feedback, and scaffolded examples to strengthen conceptual understanding. Conversely, high-performing learners demonstrating mastery in core grammar and vocabulary may be presented with advanced writing prompts, higher-level reading passages, or analytical tasks that extend linguistic complexity. Such differentiation ensures that learners operate within their optimal developmental zone, balancing challenge and support.

The pedagogical benefits of adaptive learning platforms are substantial. By aligning task difficulty with learner readiness, these systems help reduce cognitive overload, allowing students to focus on achievable learning goals without unnecessary frustration. Immediate, personalized feedback enhances learner motivation and sustains engagement, particularly in self-directed learning environments. Furthermore, adaptive scaffolding supports incremental progression, reinforcing mastery while encouraging autonomy. Over time, these mechanisms can contribute to improved language proficiency, stronger retention, and greater confidence in communicative performance.

However, implementing adaptive systems also requires careful ethical consideration. If poorly designed, algorithmic adaptation may inadvertently reinforce existing learning gaps by persistently assigning simplified content to learners identified as lower-performing, thereby limiting exposure to more challenging material. Such practices risk entrenching inequalities rather than alleviating them. Ethical deployment, therefore, demands transparent adaptation criteria, regular bias audits, and mechanisms that ensure all learners retain opportunities for upward progression. Adaptive learning should expand educational access and support differentiated growth, not constrain learners within algorithmically determined ceilings.

Automated Assessment Tools

Automated Assessment Tools constitute a significant advancement in AI-supported language evaluation, enabling scalable, data-driven, and time-efficient assessment processes. These tools include Automated Essay Scoring (AES), Automated Writing Evaluation (AWE), diagnostic grammar scoring systems, and adaptive testing engines that dynamically adjust question difficulty based on learner responses (Link et al., 2020). By leveraging natural language processing, machine learning algorithms, and linguistic feature extraction, automated systems evaluate syntax, coherence, vocabulary richness, and structural organization with increasing sophistication. Their integration into language education reflects a broader shift toward technology-enhanced formative and summative assessment models.

In practical educational settings, automated assessment tools provide immediate feedback on writing assignments, allowing students to revise drafts iteratively before final submission. This rapid response cycle enhances formative learning by encouraging reflection and self-correction (Wang & Brown, 2022). In institutional contexts, these systems are used for placement testing in language programs, ensuring learners are assigned to appropriate proficiency levels based on diagnostic performance. Additionally, automated scoring engines are particularly valuable in high-volume examination environments, where they support efficient evaluation of large cohorts while reducing grading turnaround time (Wei et al., 2023).

Effective implementation of automated assessment tools requires rigorous validation procedures to ensure psychometric soundness. System outputs must be calibrated and validated against human raters to establish scoring accuracy and comparability. Bias testing across demographic groups is essential to prevent algorithmic inequities related to linguistic background, dialect variation, or cultural expression. Reliability metrics—such as inter-rater reliability comparisons between human and machine scoring—must be regularly assessed to confirm consistency and fairness. Without these safeguards, automated tools risk undermining the validity and credibility of language assessments.

Despite their efficiency and scalability, automated assessment systems carry inherent risks. Over-reliance on algorithmic scoring without human moderation may distort construct validity by prioritizing measurable surface-level features over deeper communicative competence, creativity, or critical thinking. Therefore, best practice recommends a hybrid assessment model in which automated tools function as supportive evaluative instruments, complemented by expert human judgment to preserve pedagogical integrity and fairness.

Speech & Pronunciation Assistants

Speech and Pronunciation Assistants represent a critical advancement in AI-enabled language learning, particularly in developing oral proficiency and listening comprehension skills. These systems are powered by Automatic Speech Recognition (ASR), phoneme-level pronunciation scoring algorithms, and prosody and fluency analysis techniques. By converting spoken input into analyzable linguistic data, the systems evaluate articulation accuracy, stress patterns, intonation contours, rhythm, and speech rate (Unnikrishnan & Prasad, 2021). Unlike traditional classroom environments where speaking practice may be limited by time constraints, AI-driven speech technologies provide continuous and individualized oral language support.

In practical applications, these assistants are widely used for accent reduction training, enabling learners to compare their pronunciation against standardized models and receive detailed phonetic feedback. Real-time pronunciation correction allows students to identify mispronounced phonemes immediately and attempt corrective repetitions. Additionally, integrated listening and speaking modules enhance communicative competence by combining auditory comprehension exercises with spoken response evaluation. Such systems are particularly beneficial in self-directed or remote learning contexts, where access to native speakers or language labs may be limited.

The pedagogical advantages of speech and pronunciation assistants are considerable. Immediate corrective feedback accelerates pronunciation refinement and prevents error stabilization. Learners can practice repeatedly in a low-pressure environment, reducing performance anxiety often associated with public speaking or classroom participation. Furthermore, scalable speaking assessment enables institutions to efficiently evaluate oral proficiency across large cohorts, supporting placement decisions and formative monitoring without excessive instructor workload.

However, these technologies present important challenges. Speech recognition systems trained on limited or homogeneous datasets may demonstrate reduced accuracy for speakers of non-standard dialects (Tatman, 2017), regional accents, or multilingual backgrounds (Choubey et al., 2023). Without diversified training data and inclusive design, such systems risk disadvantaging certain learner groups and reinforcing linguistic bias. Therefore, ethical implementation requires expanding datasets, conducting fairness testing, and continuously refining models to ensure equitable speech evaluation across diverse linguistic communities.

GenAI Tools (Chatbots & Writing Assistants)

GenAI tools represent the most recent and transformative development in AI-supported language learning. Powered by large language models and advanced neural architectures, these systems move beyond rule-based correction or structured tutoring to produce original, context-sensitive language output (Bender et al., 2021; UNESCO, 2023). Generative systems can produce essays, simulate dialogues, generate role-play conversations, provide stylistic and structural writing suggestions, and create customized vocabulary or grammar exercises. Unlike earlier AI tools that primarily evaluated learner input, GenAI actively collaborates in content creation, thereby reshaping the pedagogical dynamics of language instruction. Automated writing tools provide immediate feedback on grammar, structure, and vocabulary, though their effectiveness varies across multilingual contexts and may not fully capture nuanced writing needs (Wang & Brown, 2022; Wei et al., 2023).

In practical classroom settings, GenAI tools enable AI-powered debate simulations in which students engage with dynamically generated counterarguments to refine critical thinking and persuasive skills. Interactive conversational practice allows learners to simulate real-world communication scenarios, such as interviews, travel interactions, or professional discussions, without requiring a human interlocutor. Writing assistants provide detailed essay improvement suggestions, including organization, coherence, lexical enhancement, and tone adjustment. Additionally, teachers can use generative systems to produce customized instructional materials, comprehension passages, quizzes, and differentiated learning tasks, thereby reducing preparation time while enhancing content variety.

From a pedagogical perspective, GenAI introduces a fundamental transformation in language education. Instruction shifts from feedback-only systems toward collaborative co-writing environments, where learners interact with AI as a linguistic partner. These tools support dialogic learning by enabling continuous back-and-forth exchanges that stimulate reflection, revision, and refinement. Furthermore, exploratory learning is encouraged, as students can experiment with alternative phrasings, stylistic registers, and rhetorical structures in a supportive digital environment. This interactive flexibility expands opportunities for creativity and deeper engagement with language forms.

However, integrating GenAI also poses significant risks. Academic integrity concerns arise when students submit AI-generated content without appropriate attribution or independent effort. Over-dependence on AI-generated text may weaken authentic skill development and reduce opportunities for individual voice and identity expression (Jiang et al., 2023; Moodie, 2023). Additionally, excessive reliance on automated assistance can reduce opportunities for independent drafting, cognitive struggle, and metacognitive growth processes that are essential for long-term language mastery. To mitigate these risks, GenAI should be positioned as a guided learning companion rather than a substitute for human effort, with clear usage policies, ethical guidelines, and balanced instructional design (Galaczi & Luckin, 2024).

EMPIRICAL CLASSROOM CASE STUDIES IN AI-ENHANCED LANGUAGE LEARNING

Empirical evidence from diverse educational contexts is essential for understanding how AI systems function in real instructional settings, how learners interact with them, and how inequities emerge in practice. The following case studies illustrate actual classroom applications of adaptive learning systems, automated writing evaluation tools, speech and pronunciation technologies, and GenAI writing assistants. These examples highlight both pedagogical value and justice-related concerns such as bias, access, and cultural representation.

Case Study 1: Adaptive Grammar Learning Systems in Secondary Classrooms (Vietnam, 2023)

A secondary school in Ho Chi Minh City implemented an adaptive grammar platform designed to personalize tasks based on learner performance. As students completed grammar exercises, the system adjusted difficulty, provided targeted hints, and offered remedial lessons for repeated errors. Research on adaptive learning in EFL contexts indicates that such systems can significantly improve learner accuracy and engagement when effectively implemented (Dang et al., 2023). The findings of this study are:

- Students showed measurable improvement in accuracy and self-correction.
- Learners with older devices or slower internet experienced delays, which reduced the effectiveness of real-time adaptation.
- Students from low-income households were more likely to encounter these constraints.

Algorithmic personalization alone cannot ensure equal learning outcomes if underlying infrastructural disparities shape learners' ability to benefit from the technology.

Case Study 2: Automated Writing Evaluation in University English Courses (Türkiye, 2022)

A university introduced an Automated Writing Evaluation (AWE) tool in academic writing classes. Students submitted drafts and received immediate feedback related to coherence, lexical range, grammar, and organization. Studies on AWE systems show that while such tools enhance revision processes, their effectiveness varies across proficiency levels (Link et al., 2020; Wang & Brown, 2022). The findings of this study are:

- High-proficiency learners quickly integrated the feedback and produced improved drafts.
- Lower-proficiency students found the feedback overly abstract or linguistically advanced, and were unsure how to revise accordingly.
- In some cases, the tool's recommendations were misaligned with classroom instruction.

A single automated scoring model can inadvertently privilege stronger writers while offering less actionable support to learners who need it most, reinforcing existing proficiency gaps.

Case Study 3: Speech Recognition Challenges for Multilingual English Learners (India, 2024)

A pilot program in Karnataka implemented speech-based pronunciation assistants relying on Automatic Speech Recognition (ASR). Research has shown that ASR systems often exhibit higher error rates for speakers with regional accents and multilingual backgrounds due to limited training data diversity (Choubey et al., 2023; Unnikrishnan & Prasad, 2021). The goal was to provide individualized feedback for speaking practice. The findings of this study are

- The ASR system recorded a significantly higher error rate for students speaking Indian English influenced by regional languages such as Kannada, Telugu, and Tamil.
- Learners expressed frustration when accurate speech was marked incorrect, affecting confidence and participation.
- Teachers noted that the tool seemed calibrated toward American or British pronunciation norms.

ASR systems trained on narrow accent sets risk marginalizing multilingual learners and reinforcing linguistic hierarchies that favor Global North speech varieties.

Case Study 4: GenAI for Academic Writing Support (South Africa, 2024)

An undergraduate program used GenAI writing assistants to support argumentative essay development. Students used the tool for brainstorming, structure planning, and sentence-level refinement. Research on generative AI in language education highlights both its pedagogical potential and its cultural and epistemic limitations (Galaczi & Luckin, 2024; UNESCO, 2023). The findings of this study are

- Students appreciated the ability to test multiple argumentative framings and receive immediate stylistic suggestions.
- However, several participants reported that AI-generated examples implicitly pushed them toward Western rhetorical structures and reduced space for local communicative styles.
- Some learners relied heavily on AI suggestions, raising concerns about voice authenticity (Moodie, 2023; Mphahlele & Mashiyi, 2022).

GenAI risks homogenizing academic discourse by privileging dominant rhetorical norms and limiting culturally diverse modes of expression.

EMERGING ETHICAL AND EDUCATIONAL RISKS

Despite their potential, AI systems introduce complex risks linked to their development, deployment, and governance. Questions arise regarding who controls educational data, how student information is stored and processed, and how automated decisions affect learners' academic trajectories.

Research analyzing expert perspectives (Holmes & Tuomi, 2022) highlights recurring ethical themes:

a. **Data governance:** collection, management, ownership, and informed consent.
b. **Privacy and surveillance:** especially in e-proctoring and learning analytics systems.
c. **Bias and representation:** potential reinforcement of linguistic, cultural, or socioeconomic inequalities.
d. **Transparency and explainability:** limited intelligibility of AI-generated decisions, particularly in sub-symbolic systems.

Beyond general AI ethics, education-specific concerns emerge. The quality and integrity of educational experiences mediated by AI remain central. Ethical AI in education must address four interconnected dimensions:

a. **Purpose of Learning:** Whether AI enhances critical thinking, creativity, and meaningful engagement, or reduces learning to efficiency-driven automation.

b. **Choice of Pedagogy:** Whether AI systems align with sound pedagogical principles or impose technologically deterministic approaches.
c. **Role of Technology Relative to Teachers:** Whether AI supports and augments educators or risks marginalizing professional expertise.
d. **Equitable Access:** Whether AI widens or narrows digital divides across socio-economic and global contexts.

Implications for Ethical and Inclusive Language Education

In language learning, these concerns are particularly pronounced. AI-generated feedback may privilege dominant languages or standard varieties, potentially marginalizing minority linguistic identities (Bender et al., 2021; UNESCO, 2023). Automated systems may inadequately capture cultural nuance, pragmatic competence, or communicative authenticity. Furthermore, reliance on opaque algorithms in assessment contexts raises fairness concerns when decisions affect learners' academic progression (Holmes et al., 2022; Mitchell, 2023).

Thus, while AI offers transformative opportunities for innovation in language education, its implementation demands critical scrutiny. Ethical and inclusive AI must prioritize transparency, accountability, pedagogical integrity, and equitable access. Addressing these concerns is essential to ensuring that AI functions not merely as a tool for efficiency, but as a catalyst for fair, human-centered, and socially responsible educational development (Bengio et al., 2025).

Acknowledging the wide range of concerns expressed by governments, researchers, educators, learners, and technology developers, significant efforts have been made to codify ethical principles to guide AI applications—particularly in education. These initiatives aim to translate abstract ethical concerns into practical frameworks that can inform policy, procurement, implementation, and evaluation.

While comprehensive, subsequent analyses—particularly by Holmes and Tuomi (2022)—noted that these general AI principles require further contextualization to address the specific pedagogical and institutional realities of education. Responding to this need for sector-specific clarity, Nguyen and colleagues (2023) conducted a systematic review of educational policy documents and identified seven common principles tailored explicitly to ethical AI in education. Their framework integrates broader AI ethics concerns with educational priorities such as learner wellbeing, pedagogical integrity, equitable access, and professional responsibility. Collectively, these underscore the growing recognition that ethical AI in education requires both universal normative standards and context-sensitive application grounded in educational values and practices.

Ethical Principles in Language Learning and Assessment

As the uses of language assessments expand—particularly for admissions, employment, and migration—ethical considerations have evolved beyond traditional fairness toward broader concerns of equity, diversity, inclusion, and social justice. Within this context, six interrelated principles have been identified in prior research and policy frameworks to guide ethical AI in language learning and assessment (European Commission, 2018; Holmes et al., 2022; UNESCO, 2023):

a. Validity and Reliability
b. Fairness, Equity and Justice
c. Consent, Privacy and Data Security
d. Transparency and Explainability
e. Accountability
f. Sustainability

These principles are also reflected in emerging institutional frameworks for ethical AI in language education (Cambridge English, forthcoming 2025). These principles collectively ensure that AI applications do not compromise educational integrity while supporting innovation (ILTA, 2002/2018; Nguyen et al., 2023; Pastorino-Campos & Galaczi, 2025).

Validity and Reliability

Language learning and assessment systems that incorporate AI must remain valid and reliable for their intended purposes and uses (Bachman & Palmer, 1996).

a. Validity refers to whether an assessment accurately measures the intended construct (i.e., the specific language knowledge, skills, or abilities it is designed to evaluate).
b. Reliability refers to the consistency and dependability of the measurement, ensuring that decisions based on results are trustworthy across different contexts and administrations (Bachman & Palmer, 1996).

This principle applies across contexts, including high-stakes proficiency examinations and classroom-based formative assessments integrated into learning programs (Joint Committee on Testing Practices, 2002; Saville, 2013).

Fairness, Equity and Justice in AI-Enhanced Language Education

AI-enabled language learning and assessment systems must not perpetuate bias, discrimination, or structural inequalities. They should be intentionally designed to promote fairness across cultural, linguistic, and socio-economic backgrounds and contribute to socially just outcomes (Saville, 2010).

Algorithmic bias represents a critical ethical challenge in AI-driven language learning and assessment. When AI systems—particularly those based on large-scale, internet-derived datasets—are trained on uncurated data, they risk reproducing historical inequalities and dominant cultural narratives. As Bender et al. (2021) caution, large, unfiltered datasets often encode hegemonic perspectives, amplifying structural disadvantages faced by marginalized groups. Without deliberate dataset curation and transparent documentation, such biases may become embedded in automated scoring, feedback generation, or content creation systems.

Ensuring fairness, equity, and justice is foundational to the ethical use of AI in language learning. These principles require more than the absence of bias—they demand proactive design choices, inclusive governance, and socio-technical awareness that acknowledge historical inequalities embedded in education systems. In language education, fairness connects directly to learners' academic mobility, employment pathways, and participation in civic life. Thus, AI systems in this domain must be designed, implemented, and monitored with particular care, given the high-stakes outcomes associated with language proficiency.

Structural Inequities in AI-Mediated Language Learning

AI tools are often developed using datasets dominated by high-resource languages, standardized varieties, and Global North linguistic norms. This creates systemic disadvantages for learners whose identities or linguistic features fall outside these dominant categories. Speech recognition systems frequently misrecognize accented English, tonal languages, or multilingual speech patterns, while automated writing scoring systems sometimes penalize rhetorical structures common in non-Western traditions (Choubey et al., 2023; Galaczi & Luckin, 2024).

These inequities are not merely technical flaws; they reflect broader historical and sociopolitical dynamics. Learners from low-income households may lack stable internet access, quality devices, or conducive learning environments. Without deliberate correction, AI systems may amplify these disadvantages by allocating less advanced content, misclassifying ability levels, or producing feedback that fails to account for linguistic diversity. Fairness, therefore, requires confronting both algorithmic bias and structural disadvantage simultaneously.

Equality of Access and Opportunity

Equitable AI access requires examining multiple layers given in Figure 2:

- **Physical access**: Devices, connectivity, electricity stability
- **Digital literacy**: Ability to use AI tools effectively
- **Linguistic access**: Representation of dialects, accents, minority languages
- **Pedagogical access**: Designing AI so all learners can benefit equally

Figure 2. Equality of access and opportunity (Author's representation adapted from OECD (2022) and UNESCO (2021) frameworks on equitable access to digital and AI-enabled education)

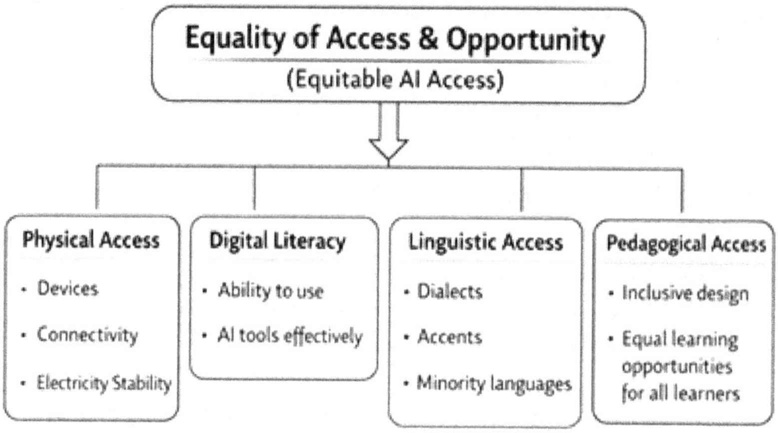

In many countries, AI-enabled tools assume uninterrupted broadband, updated operating systems, and user familiarity with digital platforms. However, learners in rural regions, low-resource schools, or marginalized communities often lack these prerequisites. As a result, AI can inadvertently widen rather than close attainment gaps.

Justice Beyond Bias: Societal and Institutional Implications

Language assessments frequently function as gateways to higher education, migration, and employment. When AI-generated decisions influence these pathways, justice requires:

- Transparency around how decisions are made

- Explainability of scoring criteria
- Mechanisms for appeals
- Protection from discrimination
- Consideration of societal impact

The ethical requirement is not only to avoid harm but to actively dismantle inequitable structures reinforced by traditional language assessments.

Fairness in GenAI Use

GenAI introduces new justice considerations:

- Generated examples may reinforce Western norms of argumentation or discourse.
- Writing assistance may privilege learners with higher digital fluency.
- AI-generated feedback may misinterpret cultural nuance.
- Students may become dependent on suggestions aligned with dominant linguistic patterns, marginalizing local identity and voice.

Ensuring justice means designing AI that respects linguistic plurality and supports learner agency.

Inclusive Governance and Participatory Decision-Making

Equitable AI requires governance models that involve:

- Teachers in tool evaluation and selection
- Learners in usability testing
- Local communities in decisions about linguistic representation
- Independent oversight committees for auditing bias
- Clear accountability structures

Participatory governance ensures that marginalized voices shape how technology is used.

Consent, Privacy and Data Security

AI-enabled language learning and assessment systems must safeguard individuals' privacy rights and ensure responsible data governance. Users must be clearly informed about what data is collected, how it is stored, how it will be used, and for what purposes—including research, validation, or content development. Explicit and informed consent must be obtained before collecting sensitive data. In addition, providers bear responsibility for securing all data against unauthorized access, breaches, or misuse.

In educational contexts, data may include not only demographic information but also speech recordings, writing samples, behavioral analytics, biometric data (e.g., in e-proctoring), and learning progress indicators. Such data are sensitive because they relate directly to learners' identities, abilities, and opportunities.

Transparency and Explainability

AI systems used in language learning and assessment must be designed, developed, and deployed in ways that enable meaningful oversight and governance. Both the outputs of the system (what decision was made) and the processes behind those outputs (how and why the decision was made) should be communicated in forms understandable to stakeholders with varying levels of technical expertise.

Transparency ensures that users are aware of AI involvement, while explainability enables them to understand and evaluate its decisions. Together, these elements are central to building trust and accountability in AI-mediated educational processes.

Accountability

Clear accountability structures must underpin the development, deployment, and ongoing management of AI systems in language learning and assessment. Assessment providers must explicitly define who is responsible for decision-making, oversight, monitoring, and corrective action. Establishing accountability ensures that when errors, harms, or ethical breaches occur, responsibility is neither diffused nor displaced onto the technology itself.

AI systems cannot be moral agents. Responsibility always remains with human actors and institutions. Therefore, governance frameworks must specify:

a. Who approves the use of AI in assessment processes.
b. Who validates and monitors system performance.
c. Who responds to complaints, appeals, or identified biases.
d. Who ensures compliance with legal and ethical standards.

Without clear lines of responsibility, ethical principles such as fairness, transparency, and privacy cannot be effectively enforced.

Participatory Governance in AI-Driven Language Education

Participatory governance serves as a critical implementation layer for the ethical integration of Artificial Intelligence into language education. While ethical principles such as fairness, transparency, accountability, and sustainability define normative standards, participatory governance operationalizes these principles through inclusive decision-making processes. In the context of AI-driven language learning, governance should not remain solely in the hands of technology developers or institutional administrators. Instead, it must actively involve teachers, learners, policymakers, researchers, and community stakeholders in the design, evaluation, and oversight of AI systems. Such collaborative engagement ensures that technological innovation remains aligned with pedagogical values, cultural contexts, and educational priorities rather than being driven exclusively by market or efficiency considerations. The key components:

a. Teacher involvement in AI system selection
b. Student feedback integration in AI deployment
c. Community consultation for linguistic representation
d. Institutional ethics review committees
e. Continuous bias monitoring

These components help identify unintended consequences, including discriminatory outcomes or unequal access, before they become structurally embedded.

ENVIRONMENTAL SUSTAINABILITY IN AI-DRIVEN LANGUAGE EDUCATION

Environmental sustainability is an emerging and essential dimension of ethical AI use in language education. Large language models (LLMs) and other deep learning systems require considerable computational power during both training and inference, resulting in significant energy consumption and associated carbon emissions (Bashir et al., 2024). Training state-of-the-art generative models may require thousands of GPU hours, and the ongoing deployment of such systems across millions of learners amplifies their cumulative environmental impact. As educational institutions increasingly integrate AI-driven learning platforms, sustainability considerations must be evaluated alongside pedagogical and ethical goals. The key factors are:

- Compute cost of AI models
- Carbon intensity of cloud datacentres

- Lightweight alternatives
- Energy-efficient inference techniques
- Proportional-use design

A key concern is the compute cost of AI models. Larger models generally deliver more fluent language output and more sophisticated feedback, but they also demand vastly greater computational resources. This raises the question of proportionality: whether the pedagogical benefits justify the environmental cost. In many language learning scenarios, lightweight or domain-specific models can provide adequate instructional support without relying on energy-intensive architectures. Another factor is the carbon intensity of cloud datacenters that host AI services. Energy sources used by these facilities differ significantly across regions. Educational institutions operating in areas with coal-dependent energy grids may inadvertently contribute to higher emissions when deploying cloud-based AI systems. Transparent reporting of datacenter energy profiles and carbon footprint metrics is therefore essential for informed decision-making.

Sustainable deployment also requires exploring lightweight alternatives, such as distilled models or smaller transformer architectures optimized for educational tasks. Distillation reduces computational complexity while maintaining functional accuracy, enabling institutions to adopt AI tools with lower energy demands. Similarly, the use of energy-efficient inference techniques such as quantization, caching, and batch processing can substantially reduce the environmental impact of real-time interactions with AI tools. Finally, sustainable AI integration in language education should follow a proportional-use design approach, ensuring that the complexity of the model aligns with actual pedagogical needs. High-stakes automated assessment or advanced writing support may justify the use of larger models, but routine tasks (e.g., grammar checking, vocabulary scaffolding, or pronunciation feedback) can be served by less resource-intensive solutions. Aligning model choice with instructional purpose not only lowers carbon emissions but also reduces institutional costs and promotes responsible use of educational technology.

Environmental sustainability thus forms a crucial part of equitable and ethical AI ecosystems. Considering energy use, carbon impact, and model proportionality ensures that AI contributes not only to effective learning but also to long-term social and ecological responsibility.

FUTURE RESEARCH DIRECTIONS

The future of AI in language learning is expected to extend beyond adaptive feedback and generative assistance toward more immersive, ethical, and sustainable educational ecosystems. As technological capabilities expand, research and development will increasingly focus on multimodal integration, emotional intelligence, cultural inclusivity, interpretability, and environmental responsibility. These directions collectively signal a transition from efficiency-driven AI systems to human-centered, socially responsible innovation in language education.

Multimodal AI Learning Environments

Future AI systems will move toward multimodal integration, combining text processing, speech recognition, gesture detection, facial expression analysis, and real-time translation within unified learning platforms. Such environments will enable learners to interact using multiple communicative channels simultaneously, closely mirroring authentic human communication. For example, pronunciation feedback could be combined with facial expression monitoring to assess articulation effort, while gesture recognition could support immersive role-play simulations. Real-time translation systems may facilitate cross-linguistic interaction among global learners. These developments may lead to fully immersive AI-driven language laboratories where learners engage in simulated real-world environments enhanced by augmented or virtual reality technologies. Multimodal AI thus holds the potential to bridge the gap between classroom learning and authentic learning.

Emotion-Aware Learning Systems

Emerging research suggests that future AI systems may incorporate affective computing capabilities to detect emotional states, such as frustration, confusion, boredom, and high engagement. By analyzing speech tone, response latency, facial micro-expressions, and interaction patterns, AI systems could adjust instructional pacing, task difficulty, or feedback style in real time. For instance, prolonged hesitation might prompt additional scaffolding, while sustained engagement could lead to progression to advanced challenges. Emotion-aware systems would enable more empathetic digital tutoring environments, support learner motivation and reducing dropout risk. However, ethical data governance and privacy safeguards will be critical when implementing affect-sensitive technologies.

Culturally Responsive AI

The next phase of AI development must prioritize cultural and linguistic inclusivity. Historically, many AI systems have been trained on datasets dominated by Western linguistic norms, which can marginalize diverse dialects and communicative styles. Future culturally responsive AI must incorporate diverse linguistic datasets, support minority and endangered languages, and reflect non-Western discourse conventions. This includes recognizing varied politeness strategies, rhetorical patterns, and sociolinguistic contexts. Such initiatives align with principles of linguistic justice, ensuring equitable representation and preventing systemic bias. By embedding cultural responsiveness into model training and evaluation, AI in language learning can become more globally inclusive and pedagogically fair.

Explainable AI in Assessment

As AI becomes more deeply embedded in assessment processes, explainability will become a central research priority. Future developments will focus on interpretable deep learning models that provide transparent reasoning for scoring decisions. Transparent scoring dashboards may present feature-level explanations, highlighting grammar usage, coherence measures, lexical diversity, and structural organization. Confidence interval reporting could indicate the certainty level of automated evaluations, supporting informed decision-making. Additionally, human–AI collaborative evaluation systems are likely to emerge, combining algorithmic efficiency with expert human judgment to enhance construct validity and fairness. Explainable AI will thus strengthen trust, accountability, and regulatory compliance in educational assessment.

Sustainable AI Deployment

Environmental sustainability will increasingly shape AI development strategies. Large-scale language models require substantial computational energy, raising concerns about carbon emissions and long-term ecological impact. Future AI systems must prioritize reduced computational energy demands, the use of smaller domain-specific models tailored for educational contexts, and proportional AI usage principles that match model complexity to pedagogical needs. Sustainable design practices may include model compression, energy-efficient training techniques, and lifecycle carbon auditing. Over time, environmental sustainability is likely to become a formal evaluation metric in AI adoption decisions within educational institutions.

CONCLUSION

AI has become deeply integrated into language education, but its value depends not only on technological sophistication but also on the principles guiding its implementation. While AI can personalize instruction, enhance feedback, and expand access, it can also reinforce bias, privilege dominant linguistic norms, and deepen existing inequities if left unchecked. Therefore, an equity-centred perspective is essential.

The framework presented in this chapter demonstrates that ethical AI requires alignment across application, pedagogy, governance, policy, and societal outcomes. Empirical classroom evidence highlights the importance of real-world evaluation, as learners' experiences reveal limitations invisible in conceptual models. Centering fairness and justice transforms AI from a neutral tool to an active mechanism for promoting inclusion, linguistic diversity, and equal opportunity. Ensuring ethical practice requires continuous monitoring, teacher-student participation, transparent decision-making, sustainable deployment, and global awareness of diverse contexts. AI must support—not substitute—human judgment, empathy, and cultural understanding. As the field evolves, research must prioritize fairness auditing, cross-cultural inclusivity, sustainable design, and community-based governance.

AI's future in language education must be built around human dignity and linguistic justice. When designed and deployed responsibly, AI can democratize learning opportunities, amplify learner agency, and support a more just and inclusive educational ecosystem. The goal is not merely to integrate AI, but to ensure that its benefits extend equitably to all learners, across cultures, languages, and contexts.

REFERENCES

Atari, M., Xue, M. J., Park, P. S., Blasi, D. E., & Henrich, J. (2023). Which humans? *PsyArXiv*. https://doi.org/DOI: 10.31234/osf.io/5b26t

Bachman, L. F., & Palmer, A. S. (1996). *Language testing in practice: Designing and developing useful language tests* (Vol. 1). Oxford University Press.

Bashir, N., Donti, P., Cuff, J., Sroka, S., Ilic, M., Sze, V., Delimitrou, C., & Olivetti, E. (2024). *The climate and sustainability implications of generative AI*. An MIT Exploration of Generative AI. https://doi.org/DOI: 10.21428/e4baedd9.9070dfe7

Bender, E. M., Gebru, T., McMillan-Major, A., & Shmitchell, S. (2021). On the dangers of stochastic parrots: Can language models be too big? In *Proceedings of the 2021 ACM Conference on Fairness, Accountability, and Transparency (FAccT '21)* (pp. 610–623). https://doi.org/DOI: 10.1145/3442188.3445922

Bengio, Y., Mindermann, S., Privitera, D., Besiroglu, T., Bommasani, R., Casper, S., Choi, Y., Fox, P., Garfinkel, B., Goldfarb, D., Heidari, H., Ho, A., Kapoor, S., Khalatbari, L., Longpre, S., Manning, S., Mavroudis, V., Mazeika, M., Michael, J., . . . Zeng, Y. (2025). *International AI safety report* (DSIT 2025/001). https://l1nq.com/9Mf4e

Cambridge English. (Forthcoming 2025). *Principles of good practice.*

Choubey, L., Shrivastava, A., & Mohanty, A. (2023). Accent bias and fairness challenges in speech recognition systems for Indian English users. *IEEE Access : Practical Innovations, Open Solutions*, *11*, 54621–54633. DOI: 10.1109/ACCESS.2023.3276617

Coleman, V. (2021). *Digital divide in UK education during COVID-19 pandemic: Literature review. Cambridge Assessment Research Report.* Cambridge Assessment.

Dang, T. K. A., Nguyen, H. T., & Le, T. T. (2023). Adaptive learning technologies in Asian EFL classrooms: A systematic review. *Education and Information Technologies*, *28*(6), 7421–7445. DOI: 10.1007/s10639-022-11481-y

Fjeld, J., Achten, N., Hilligoss, H., Nagy, A., & Srikumar, M. (2020). *Principled artificial intelligence: Mapping consensus in ethical and rights-based approaches to principles for AI*. SSRN Electronic Paper Collection. https://doi.org/DOI: 10.2139/ssrn.3518482

Galaczi, E., & Luckin, R. (2024). *Generative AI and language education: Opportunities, challenges and the need for critical perspectives*. https://sl1nk.com/1k48i8d

High-Level Expert Group on Artificial Intelligence. (2018). *A definition of AI: Main capabilities and scientific disciplines*. European Commission. https://sl1nk.com/a1z8cpg

Holmes, W., Porayska-Pomsta, K., Holstein, K., Sutherland, E., Baker, T., Shum, S. B., Santos, O. C., Rodrigo, M. T., Cukurova, M., Bittencourt, I. I., & Koedinger, K. R. (2022). Ethics of AI in education: Towards a community-wide framework. *International Journal of Artificial Intelligence in Education, 32*(3), 504–526. DOI: 10.1007/s40593-021-00239-1

Holmes, W., & Tuomi, I. (2022). State of the art and practice in AI in education. *European Journal of Education, 57*(4), 542–570. DOI: 10.1111/ejed.12533

ILTA. (2002/2018). *Code of ethics*. https://www.iltaonline.com/page/CodeofEthics

Institute for Ethical AI in Education. (2021). *The ethical framework for AI in education*. Institute for Ethical AI in Education. https://l1nq.com/cLnaq

Jenkins, O. C., Lopresti, D., & Mitchell, M. (2020). *Next wave artificial intelligence: Robust, explainable, adaptable, ethical, and accountable*. https://sl1nk.com/gkychk7

Jiang, L., Li, H., & Sun, T. (2023). Generative AI in academic writing: Impacts on learner agency and writing development. *Computers & Education: Artificial Intelligence, 4*, 100128. DOI: 10.1016/j.caeai.2023.100128

Joint Committee on Testing Practices. (1988/2002). *Code of fair testing practices in education*. https://www.apa.org/science/programs/testing/fair-testing.pdf

Lin, C. H., Warschauer, M., & Blake, R. (2019). Language learning through adaptive systems: A review of technologies and pedagogical implications. *Computer Assisted Language Learning, 32*(1–2), 1–25. DOI: 10.1080/09588221.2018.1485708

Link, S., Dursun, A., Karakaya, K., & Hegelheimer, V. (2020). Towards automated writing evaluation for Turkish EFL learners: System performance and learner perceptions. *ReCALL, 32*(3), 269–288. DOI: 10.1017/S0958344020000010

Mitchell, M. (2020). *Artificial intelligence: A guide for thinking humans*. Pelican.

Mitchell, M. (2023). AI's challenge of understanding the world. *Science, 382*(6671), eadm8175. Advance online publication. DOI: 10.1126/science.adm8175 PMID: 37943939

Mitchell, M., & Krakauer, D. C. (2023). The debate over understanding in AI's large language models. *Proceedings of the National Academy of Sciences of the United States of America, 120*(13), e2215907120. DOI: 10.1073/pnas.2215907120 PMID: 36943882

Moodie, G. (2023). Academic writing, voice, and identity in African higher education: Challenges in the age of AI. *Journal of Higher Education in Africa, 21*(1), 57–79.

Mphahlele, N., & Mashiyi, N. (2022). Digital writing practices and cultural identity among South African undergraduate students. *Reading & Writing Journal of the Reading Association of South Africa, 13*(1), 1–10. https://doi.org/DOI: 10.4102/rw.v13i1.309

Nguyen, A., Ngo, H. N., Hong, Y., Dang, B., & Nguyen, B.-P. T. (2023). Ethical principles for artificial intelligence in education. *Education and Information Technologies, 28*(4), 4221–4241. DOI: 10.1007/s10639-022-11316-w PMID: 36254344

Nguyen, M. A., & Doan, S. T. (2021). Digital inequality in Vietnamese classrooms: Impacts on technology-supported English language learning. *Asia Pacific Journal of Education, 41*(2), 187–203. DOI: 10.1080/02188791.2020.1756734

Pastorino-Campos, C., & Galaczi, E. (2025). Ethical AI for language assessment: Considerations and principles. *Annual Review of Applied Linguistics*. Advance online publication. DOI: 10.1017/S0267190525100081

Samek, W., Wiegand, T., & Müller, K.-R. (2017). *Explainable artificial intelligence: Understanding, visualizing and interpreting deep learning models*. https://doi.org//arXiv.1708.08296DOI: 10.48550

Saville, N. (2005). Setting and monitoring professional standards: A QMS approach. *Research Notes, 22*, 2–5. https://sl1nk.com/moBVk

Saville, N. (2010). Developing a model for investigating the impact of language assessment. *Research Notes, 42*, 2–8. https://sl1nk.com/BBdkh

Saville, N. (2013). Using standards and guidelines. In *The companion to language assessment* (Vol. II, Part 7: Assessment development). https://doi.org/DOI: 10.1002/9781118411360.wbcla105

Tatman, R. (2017). Gender and dialect bias in YouTube's automatic captions. *Proceedings of ACL Workshop on Ethics in NLP*, 53–59. DOI: 10.18653/v1/W17-1606

UNESCO. (2023). *Guidance for generative AI in education and research*. UNESCO. https://l1nq.com/05WWX

Unnikrishnan, R., & Prasad, R. (2021). Multilingual learners and the challenges of ASR in educational settings. *International Journal of Speech Technology, 24*(3), 549–560. DOI: 10.1007/s10772-021-09815-5

Wang, Y., & Brown, D. (2022). The affordances and limitations of automated feedback for multilingual university writers. *Assessing Writing*, *52*, 100616. DOI: 10.1016/j.asw.2022.100616

Wei, J., Wang, Y., & Yang, H. (2023). Effects of Automated Writing Evaluation on EFL learners: A meta-analysis. *Journal of Second Language Writing*, *62*, 101021. DOI: 10.1016/j.jslw.2023.101021

World Economic Forum. (2022). *Artificial intelligence for children toolkit*. World Economic Forum. https://l1nq.com/idh6m3c

ADDITIONAL READING

Cong, W., Pek, L. S., Yuchen, Z., Latif, I. N. A., Bo, Z., & Ming, L. (2025). Integrating generative AI in language education: A systematic review of pedagogical, ethical, and technological themes. *International Journal of Learning. Teaching and Educational Research*, *25*(2), 577–595. DOI: 10.26803/ijlter.25.2.26

He, M., Abbasi, B. N., & He, J. (2025). AI-driven language learning in higher education: Self-reflection, creativity, anxiety, and emotional resilience in EFL learners. *Humanities & Social Sciences Communications*, *12*(1), 1525. DOI: 10.1057/s41599-025-05817-5

Li, J., Yan, Y., & Zeng, X. (2025). Exploring artificial intelligence in inclusive education: A systematic review of empirical studies. *Applied Sciences (Basel, Switzerland)*, *15*(23), 12624. DOI: 10.3390/app152312624

Sailer, M., & Homner, L. (2020). Educational technology and learner motivation: A review. *Educational Psychology Review*, *32*, 1–28.

Yan, W., Li, B., & Lowell, V. L. (2025). Integrating artificial intelligence and extended reality in language education: A systematic review (2017–2024). *Education Sciences*, *15*(8), 1066. DOI: 10.3390/educsci15081066

KEY TERMS AND DEFINITIONS

Adaptive Learning: An educational model where AI systems adapt to learner performance and progress gradually by modifying content complexity, pacing and feedback.

Algorithmic Bias: Systematic and unfair discrimination embedded in AI systems due to biased training data, flawed design, or unequal representation.

Artificial Intelligence (AI): Artificial Intelligence refers to systems that can compute and solve problems that are usually handled by the human mind, i.e., learning, reasoning, problem-solving, perception and understanding language.

Automated Assessment: AI algorithms that analyze the answers provided by learners (e.g., multiple choice, speech, essays, etc.) and automatically produce scores or feedback.

Fairness in AI: AI systems must not engage in unfair discrimination and should not treat various demographic groups unfairly.

GenAI: A subset of AI systems capable of producing new content such as text, speech, images, or code, based on patterns learned from large datasets.

Intelligent Tutoring System (ITS): A computer-based instructional system that provides personalized guidance, feedback, and adaptive support to learners without direct human intervention.

Participatory Governance: A policy perspective where educators, learners, researchers, and stakeholders are engaged in the decision-making procedure concerning the implementation of AI.

Personalization: The customization of learning content, feedback and learning pathways to the needs, abilities and preferences of individual learners.

Speech Recognition Technology: This is an AI-based tool that transcribes spoken language into text and evaluates the pronunciation, fluency, and accuracy of the voice recognition.

Chapter 11
Fostering Linguistic Identities and Educational Justice Through AIALL:
Insights From the Pluridentities Project

Cristina A. Huertas-Abril
http://orcid.org/0000-0002-9057-5224
Universidad de Córdoba, Spain

ABSTRACT

Linguistic capital, understood as the set of competencies and resources that enable individuals and communities to participate effectively in social contexts, plays a key role in shaping the identity of the European Union. However, it faces several challenges, including the dominance of English as a global language that often marginalizes other languages. Similarly, the growing presence of non-EU languages within citizens' repertoires is not always reflected or valued in educational practices. The Pluridentities project (Horizon Europe Grant 101178914) examines how educational policies influence linguistic identities, attitudes toward languages, and the protection of linguistic capital in the EU. It also explores the impact of technology on student motivation and educational practices. This chapter, result of the second phase of Pluridentities, highlights how AIALL tools offer new opportunities for language teaching and learning, as well as to raise awareness on the importance of multilingualism, equity, equality and social justice in current global education.

DOI: 10.4018/979-8-3373-7749-0.ch011

INTRODUCTION

Linguistic capital encompasses the competencies, repertoires, and linguistic resources available to individuals and communities that enable them to interact, participate, and position themselves effectively across diverse social, cultural, and educational contexts. As such, it represents a fundamental component in the construction and consolidation of the identity of the European Union (EU) (Surmont et al., 2025). Within the European context, linguistic capital encompasses not only proficiency in different languages but also the ability to mobilize linguistic knowledge strategically in multilingual environments. In this sense, it functions as a key mechanism through which individuals and groups negotiate meaning, access opportunities, and engage with the broader socio-political structures that shape European society.

In a milieu characterized by profound linguistic and cultural diversity, the significance of linguistic capital becomes particularly relevant. The EU is home to a wide array of languages, dialects, and communicative traditions, which together form a complex linguistic ecosystem (European Commission, 2026). Within such a setting, linguistic capital operates not merely as a practical means of communication but also as a symbolic and social resource that reflects power relations, cultural recognition, and patterns of mobility. Consequently, the distribution and development of linguistic capital influence individuals' capacity to participate fully in public life, educational systems, and transnational networks across Europe.

Furthermore, linguistic capital plays a crucial role in fostering social justice, equity, democratic participation, and cultural cohesion within the European Union. By enabling individuals to engage across linguistic boundaries, it supports intercultural dialogue and mutual understanding among diverse populations. At the same time, policies and educational initiatives aimed at strengthening linguistic repertoires contribute to reducing inequalities and promoting equitable access to social, cultural, and economic opportunities. For these reasons, linguistic capital is increasingly recognized as a central element in the promotion of multilingualism and intercultural competence within European institutions and policy frameworks (Council of Europe, 2014).

This chapter examines the relevance of linguistic identities and linguistic capital within the European context as a starting point for exploring the relationships between multilingualism, educational policies, and social justice, considering the advances of AI. In doing so, it situates these dimensions within broader discussions on equity, equality, and justice in language education, particularly considering the growing presence of digital and AI-Assisted Language Learning (AIALL). For this, the theoretical and conceptual foundation for the Pluridentities project (Horizon Europe Project Ref. 101178914) will be examined, analyzing the core pillars of the project through a critical lens. It must be noted that the Pluridentities project, bringing together researchers and educators from across Europe, examines the role of linguistic capital learning environments, language policies, and technology in secondary education (i.e., students aged 14-18) while promoting collaborative Research–Practice Partnerships (RPPs), a long-term collaboration between researchers and practitioners that co-designs, implements, and evaluates evidence-informed solutions to address real educational challenges.

Subsequently, the chapter highlights how the critical integration of digitalization and technologies applied to language learning and teaching, paying special attention to AI-enhanced educational tools, can contribute to the development of more equitable learning environments. When implemented from an inclusive and ethically informed perspective, such technologies have the potential to broaden opportunities for participation, facilitate more equitable access to knowledge, and support the holistic development of learners' linguistic and cultural identities across the European Union. The chapter concludes by reflecting on the implications of these perspectives for language education and European linguistic policies in increasingly fair digital and technologically mediated educational contexts.

THEORETICAL BACKGROUND

Linguistic Repertoires, Linguistic Capital and Linguistic Identities

Although the concepts of 'linguistic repertoire' and 'plurilingual repertoire' are closely related, they differ in scope and emphasis. A linguistic repertoire refers to the complete set of linguistic resources an individual possesses and mobilizes to communicate, including languages, dialects, registers, styles, and semiotic resources, regardless of their level of proficiency. In contrast, a plurilingual repertoire specifically emphasizes the dynamic integration and interaction of multiple languages within an individual's communicative competence. In the context of the Pluridentities project and this chapter, the focus will be on the linguistic repertoire, considered as the breadth of available communicative resources, beyond the plurilingual repertoire which highlights the ability to draw flexibly on those resources across languages. In this context, the concept of linguistic repertoires has become central in contemporary sociolinguistic research for understanding how individuals and communities use language in increasingly multilingual and multicultural societies. Rather than being limited to clearly separated "languages," repertoires include a wide range of linguistic features, varieties, registers, styles, and communicative practices that individuals acquire through socialization, education, mobility, and everyday interaction. This perspective highlights the fluid and dynamic nature of language use, emphasizing that speakers do not simply switch between bounded linguistic systems but instead mobilize flexible and interconnected resources depending on context, interlocutor, and communicative purpose (García & Otheguy, 2020).

As affirmed by Surmont et al. (2025), from a broad perspective, linguistic capital refers to the value attributed to individuals' linguistic repertoires. A linguistic repertoire encompasses the full range of languages, linguistic varieties, registers, and communicative resources that an individual possesses and can mobilize across different contexts (Finegan, 2012). It therefore includes not only one's first or primary language(s), but also additional languages that have been learned, as well as sociolects, registers, and communicative styles developed through social interaction and experience. Linguistic capital thus refers to the value—whether real or perceived—that is associated with such repertoires within specific social contexts (Bourdieu, 1977, 1986).

Bourdieu (1977) argues that linguistic competence can be understood as a form of capital whose value is determined within a social "market," that is, a system of relations structured by authority, legitimacy, and symbolic power. Within such a framework, the use and recognition of particular languages or varieties are not neutral, but rather embedded in broader social dynamics that shape which forms of linguistic expression are considered legitimate, prestigious, or valuable. Consequently, languages cannot be understood merely as technical instruments for communication; they also function as symbolic and social resources that may influence individuals' access to opportunities and their positioning within social structures. Linguistic capital is thus often unequally distributed, leading to symbolic violence and the marginalization of individuals with non-standard linguistic repertoires (Bettney, 2022; Chen & Manosuthikit, 2025; Mallinson, 2024), as it is usually shaped by the societal valuation of specific dialects and language varieties, which frequently functions to reinforce existing social hierarchies (Ja'afreh & Al-Saudi, 2024).

Despite this, and considering that the use of certain languages may contribute to the reproduction of power structures and social inequalities (Bourdieu, 1986), current research on multilingualism often employs the concept with a somewhat different emphasis. Linguistic capital should be used to highlight the social and economic value (real or perceived) of broad linguistic repertoires and to stress that linguistic competencies and communicative strategies can function as valuable resources rather than mechanisms of social exclusion (López Blanco, 2025; Zschomler, 2019). From this perspective, multilingualism is not merely a descriptive characteristic of contemporary societies but also a potential asset that can enhance individuals' participation in social, cultural, and economic life.

In this light, the Council of Europe (2007, 2014) explicitly links linguistic and cultural diversity to key democratic and social objectives. According to the Council of Europe (2007), the recognition and promotion of linguistic diversity are closely associated with social cohesion, the reduction of marginalization and exclusion, and the strengthening of democratic citizenship, including participation in public life. In this sense, linguistic diversity is framed not as a barrier but as a resource that can contribute to more inclusive and participatory societies. Within the European educational landscape—including increasing linguistic, cultural, and migratory diversity—the analysis of linguistic capital and linguistic identities therefore becomes a central analytical lens for understanding processes of socialization, participation, and identity construction.

Linguistic identities are deeply intertwined with an individual's sense of self and their capacity to participate fully in social and educational spheres (Ignatius, 2025; Soare, 2025). Consequently, they should be understood as dynamic and situated constructions that emerge through communicative practices, social experiences, and the power relations in which individuals participate: rather than being conceived as singular, fixed, or essentialist entities, linguistic identities are multiple and evolving (Fisher et al., 2024). They develop and transform over time in response to changing social, educational, and cultural contexts, as well as to individuals' personal and collective trajectories (Cummins, 2015; Li et al., 2022). Linguistic identities are then continuously negotiated in everyday interactions and shaped by the recognition (or lack thereof) granted to particular linguistic practices within institutional and social settings.

The literature on linguistic capital and linguistic identities reveals a complex interplay between language, power, and self-perception, particularly within educational settings, migration contexts, and emerging digital landscapes. In educational contexts, linguistic identities are particularly shaped through processes of recognition, legitimization, and valuation of students' linguistic repertoires and, consequently, their linguistic capital. When students' languages and linguistic varieties are acknowledged as legitimate and valuable resources for learning and communication, this recognition can foster the development of positive linguistic identities and strengthen students' sense of belonging within both the school environment and the broader social community. Conversely, the devaluation, marginalization, or invisibilization of certain linguistic repertoires may generate processes of exclusion and stigmatization. Such dynamics can negatively affect learners' linguistic self-esteem and restrict their opportunities for full participation in educational processes (Beljić, 2015; García & Wei, 2014).

For these reasons, contemporary research increasingly emphasizes the importance of adopting inclusive and multilingual perspectives in education that recognize the complexity and richness of learners' linguistic repertoires. By acknowledging linguistic diversity as a valuable pedagogical and social resource, educational systems can contribute to fostering more equitable and participatory learning environments. In the EU context, where linguistic and cultural diversity continue to expand, understanding the interplay between linguistic capital, linguistic identities, and educational practices is therefore essential for promoting inclusive forms of participation, equitable access to learning opportunities, and the development of democratic and socially cohesive societies.

Equity and Social Justice in (Language) Educational Practices

Achieving equity requires a critical re-evaluation of standard language-related practices. Monoglossic language-in-education policies are identified as a form of epistemic injustice that diminishes learners' abilities to make valid knowledge contributions (Kerfoot & Bello-Nonjengele, 2023). For instance, standardized testing often fails to accurately measure the intelligence or capabilities of linguistically diverse students, penalizing them for diverging from dominant linguistic norms (Wang et al., 2021).

There is no doubt that language and educational policies play a fundamental role in shaping linguistic identities and in advancing (or, conversely, limiting) equity and social justice in access to educational and social opportunities (Norton, 2013; Pavlenko & Blackledge, 2004). Language policies embedded in educational systems influence not only which languages are taught, but also how linguistic diversity is framed, valued, and legitimized within institutional settings.

Educational social justice therefore requires critically questioning entrenched linguistic hierarchies and promoting pedagogical and policy approaches that recognize linguistic plurality as a constitutive element of teaching and learning processes. Rather than treating linguistic diversity as an obstacle to be managed, socially just educational frameworks emphasize the need to view multilingualism as a valuable resource that reflects the complex sociolinguistic realities of contemporary societies (Xiao, 2024). From this perspective, education should be oriented toward the recognition, validation, and legitimization of diverse linguistic repertoires, fostering learning environments in which *all* students can develop positive linguistic identities and participate meaningfully in academic and social life. When students' linguistic resources are acknowledged as legitimate components of the educational process, they are more likely to experience a stronger sense of belonging, engagement, and agency within the school community.

In this context, a dominant pedagogical approach emerging to combat linguistic racism (Allweiss & Al-Adeimi, 2025), understood as the denial of fundamental human rights in institutional and noninstitutional settings based on language use (Figueroa, 2024). is translanguaging (García, 2009; Lasagabaster & García, 2014), the process by which multilingual individuals flexibly and strategically draw on their entire linguistic repertoire (instead of treating languages as separate and bounded systems) to construct meaning, facilitate communication, and engage in cognitive and social practices within multilingual contexts. Translanguaging is consistently framed as a powerful mechanism for enacting social justice in multilingual settings due to its flexible use of linguistic and modal resources, and its pedagogical use advocates for the active integration of learners' full linguistic and meaning-making repertoires (Siahaan et al., 2026). Moreover, rather than viewing translanguaging merely as a scaffolding tool, the literature positions it as a political stance (Wei, 2022), as it challenges monolingual norms and the pressure of standardization, promoting inclusivity and cultural relevance (Pande, 2025).

Advancing equity in language education involves recognizing and valuing the diverse linguistic resources that students bring with them to educational settings. These include heritage and family languages, regional and minority languages, linguistic varieties, and everyday communicative practices that form part of learners' lived experiences and social identities. By acknowledging these linguistic practices as legitimate expressions of students' linguistic capital, educational institutions can contribute to more inclusive and equitable learning environments that both validate students' identities and support fuller participation in educational processes.

Educational Justice Through AIALL: Challenges and Opportunities

The rapid integration of technology in language education introduces new dimensions to the social justice discourse, and the connections between educational Justice and Artificial Intelligence-Assisted Language Learning (AIALL) reveal a complex interplay between technological advancements, equity, and pedagogical approaches.

Challenges for Equity and Social Justice in AIALL

Despite the potential of AIALL to expand access to language education, several structural challenges must be considered when assessing its contribution to equity and educational justice. One major concern is unequal accessibility (Wang et al., 2023). The effective use of AI tools often depends on access to digital devices, reliable internet connectivity, and the financial resources required to obtain and maintain technological infrastructure (Godwin-Jones, 2021; Hockly, 2023). These requirements can create barriers for learners in under-resourced educational contexts or economically disadvantaged communities, thereby limiting the inclusive potential of AI-enhanced learning environments (Huertas-Abril & Palacios-Hidalgo, 2025).

Another risk associated to AIALL relates to the linguistic scope of many AI systems. AI-driven language tools are typically trained on large datasets that prioritize standardized or dominant language varieties (Chung & Bong, 2022; Katsarou et al., 2023). As a result, they may not adequately reflect the diversity of real-world linguistic practices, including regional dialects, multilingual interactions, or non-standard varieties. This imbalance can reduce the effectiveness of AI tools for learners whose linguistic repertoires differ from these standardized norms, potentially reinforcing existing linguistic hierarchies (Crompton & Burke, 2023; Shaikh et al., 2023). At the same time, and considering that AIALL tools cannot imitate human-human interaction (Huertas-Abril & Palacios-Hidalgo, 2025), many AI systems are not yet fully adapted to the diverse needs of all users. Accessibility challenges remain particularly relevant for older adults and individuals with specific needs when technologies are not designed according to inclusive design principles (Kent, 2020; Peña-Acuña & Crismán-Pérez, 2022).

As educational institutions increasingly adopt artificial intelligence, a central theme emerging from the research is the critical need to address algorithmic equity and implement rigorous algorithmic bias mitigation to ensure these technologies serve as instruments for justice rather than tools that perpetuate existing inequalities (Ketere, 2025; Lewis, 2025). Ethical concerns related to academic integrity and the potential misuse of AI-generated content raise important questions about responsible use in (language) education (Godwin-Jones, 2021; Shaikh et al., 2023). Similarly, there is a risk that excessive reliance on AIALL technologies could reduce students' engagement with traditional learning processes if these tools are used as substitutes rather than complements to human teaching (Karaca & Kılcan, 2023).

Opportunities for Advancing Educational Justice through AIALL

One of the principal strengths of AIALL from a social justice perspective lies in its potential to expand access to high-quality language practice, particularly in contexts where formal instruction or opportunities to interact with proficient or native speakers are limited or unavailable (Godwin-Jones, 2021; Lin & Mubarok, 2021). By leveraging adaptive technologies, AIALL systems can provide learners with individualized practice opportunities (Huang et al., 2023; Belda-Medina & Calvo-Ferrer, 2022) that would otherwise be difficult to access due to geographical, socioeconomic, or institutional constraints. AIALL tools can thus have the potential to reduce certain structural barriers to language education and contribute to more equitable access to linguistic resources.

Similarly, technological tools such as chatbots and intelligent virtual agents, for example, can create safe and low-pressure environments for language practice, enabling learners to experiment with language use without the fear of negative evaluation that often accompanies traditional classroom interactions (Zhai & Wibowo, 2023). These environments, especially those using machine learning (Huertas-Abril, 2025), can support the development of learner autonomy by allowing students to practice at their own pace, receive immediate feedback, and engage in repeated communicative exchanges. As a result, such tools may help reduce language learning anxiety and foster greater confidence in language use, particularly among learners who might otherwise feel marginalized or hesitant to participate in face-to-face communicative contexts (Belda-Medina & Calvo-Ferrer, 2022).

Furthermore, emerging research suggests that artificial intelligence can contribute to more equitable educational outcomes by supporting the early identification of students who may be at risk of academic disengagement or failure. Through the analysis of learning patterns and performance data, AI systems can help educators detect difficulties at an early stage, enabling timely pedagogical interventions that may prevent cumulative learning gaps and reduce dropout rates (Godwin-Jones, 2021; Huang et al., 2023). When implemented responsibly and ethically, such predictive capabilities can support more inclusive and responsive educational practices. In this light, AI-based technologies offer significant potential for enhancing accessibility for learners with disabilities (Jeon et al., 2023; Youn, 2023). AI-powered communicative tools—including speech recognition systems, text-to-speech technologies, and adaptive interfaces—can facilitate more inclusive forms of participation by enabling learners with diverse needs to engage more fully in language learning activities. By providing alternative modes of interaction and personalized support, these technologies can help remove barriers that have historically limited participation in language education, thereby contributing to more inclusive and equitable learning environments.

PLURIDENTITIES: RESEARCH-PRACTICE PARTNERSHIPS

As discussed in previous sections, the challenges associated with multilingualism, educational social justice, and the use of AI affect, in different ways, the protection of linguistic capital in Europe, which constitutes the core focus of the Pluridentities project (Horizon Europe Project Ref. 101178914). This project investigates how multilingual identities can be protected, strengthened, and promoted through inclusive educational policies and classroom practices across diverse European contexts. Bringing together universities and educational stakeholders from five countries (Aruba, Belgium, the Netherlands, Spain and Sweden), the project adopts an interdisciplinary and evidence-informed approach to examine the relationships among linguistic diversity, language education, digital technologies, and social inclusion. More specifically, Pluridentities have three key objectives: (i) to identify the role of education policies in promoting multilingualism and preserving languages; (ii) to identify the impact of multilingual education programs on attitudes and perceptions towards languages and to provide solutions to safeguard the EU's linguistic capital; and (3) to identify the impact of technology on multilingualism and secondary students' motivation to learn languages.

Through the analysis of issues related to linguistic capital, learning environments, linguistic policies and the role of technology, together with close collaboration with schools and local stakeholders, Pluridentities seeks both to understand the factors underlying the current situation and to identify sustainable solutions that benefit all parties involved. Specifically, Pluridentities aims to examine the role of educational policies in promoting multilingualism and preserving languages, as well as to identify good practices and barriers shaping linguistic identities in the EU, including those related to digitalization, technology, and AI use. It also investigates the impact of multilingual education programs on attitudes towards languages and explores ways to safeguard linguistic capital, including the diverse linguistic repertoires of many (new) European citizens. Finally, it analyses the influence of technology on multilingualism and student motivation for language learning, providing the educational sector with guidance to address emerging challenges such as artificial intelligence, machine translation, and speech technologies in pedagogical practice.

Pluridentities adopts an educational action-research design characterized by the iterative development of solutions aimed at addressing complex, practice-based educational problems (McKenney & Reeves, 2014). Following an initial phase of analysis and exploration of needs and challenges related to multilingualism in secondary education, the research advances to the design and development of interventions, which are subsequently evaluated and subjected to critical reflection. This cyclical progression facilitates both the refinement and maturation of the intervention and a deeper understanding of the underlying and emerging theoretical frameworks. Central to this approach is the use of RPPs, through which researchers and practitioners collaborate closely in the co-design and implementation of solutions to contemporary educational challenges. RPPs are conceptualized as sustained, systematic collaborations between researchers and practitioners aimed at improving schools and educational systems through research (Farrell et al., 2021). Elaborating on this definition, Coburn et al. (2013) identify five distinguishing characteristics of RPPs: they are (1) long-term in orientation, (2) centered on problems of practice, (3) grounded in principles of mutualism, (4) supported by deliberate strategies to cultivate and maintain the partnership, and (5) oriented toward the production of original analyses.

Within Pluridentities' Work Package 5, led by Universidad de Córdoba and focused on technology, one of the RPPs is specifically oriented towards promoting the ethical use of AI(ALL) in secondary education, focusing mainly on language learning or multilingual education. This RPP brings together researchers, teachers, and other educational stakeholders (i.e., students, school leaders, families, future teachers) to collaboratively explore how AI(ALL) tools can be integrated into teaching and learning processes in ways that are pedagogically meaningful, socially responsible, and ethically grounded. Particular attention is given to supporting both teachers and students in developing critical awareness of AI technologies, their affordances, and their potential risks.

The following section thus puts forward a set of proposals for the ethical use of AIALL. These proposals are informed not only by considerations of responsible and transparent use of AI, but also by a commitment to safeguarding and promoting the values associated with multilingualism. Emphasis is placed on ensuring that AI applications do not marginalize linguistic diversity but rather contribute to its recognition and enhancement within educational settings.

PRACTICAL PROPOSALS TO FOSTER LINGUISTIC IDENTITIES AND EDUCATIONAL JUSTICE THROUGH AIALL

Building on the need identified within one of the Pluridentities' RPPs to promote the ethical use of AI among both students and teachers, this section suggests real uses of tools that situate AI literacy within broader pedagogical and social objectives. It should be noted that the practical activities presented in this section are hypothetical proposals rather than classroom interventions that have already been implemented. They were developed as illustrative examples to demonstrate how the needs identified through the needs analysis conducted within the RPPs could be addressed in educational settings. As such, these activities are intended to bridge research findings and pedagogical practice by offering adaptable, evidence-informed ideas that teachers may tailor to their own contexts. Future stages of the project will evaluate the implementation and effectiveness of these proposals in authentic classroom environments.

In this context, it is necessary to emphasize the importance of equipping educational communities with the critical skills required to engage with AI(ALL) technologies in a responsible, reflective, and informed manner, particularly in contexts where such tools are increasingly embedded in everyday teaching and learning practices. Moreover, the proposals provided here highlight the importance of protecting and valuing the diverse linguistic identities present in the classroom. Ethical AI use in language education must take into account learners' linguistic repertoires and cultural backgrounds, fostering inclusive practices that respect and empower all students. In doing so, the expected results from this RPP seek to align technological innovation with broader educational goals related to equity, inclusion, and the preservation of linguistic capital.

Storybooks for Thought

AI-generated storybooks represent a promising pedagogical tool within AIALL, particularly in secondary education, where they can simultaneously support (foreign) language development and foster critical engagement with ethical issues related to artificial intelligence. By generating customizable, context-sensitive narratives, AI allows educators to design storybooks that reflect learners' linguistic repertoires and identities, cultural backgrounds, and proficiency levels. This adaptability enables the creation of multilingual texts that incorporate multiple languages, dialects, and communicative styles, thereby validating linguistic diversity and promoting inclusive language learning environments.

Students can then interact with narratives dynamically, co-construct stories, or modify existing texts, thus promoting active learning and learner autonomy. Moreover, such storybooks can be used to expose learners to authentic and varied linguistic input, including minority or heritage languages that are often underrepresented in traditional teaching materials. In this way, AI-generated narratives can contribute to a more equitable representation of linguistic diversity and support the development of positive linguistic identities. Gemini Storybook (often known as Gemini AI Storybook or simply Storybook) is a free Google GenAI tool which automatically creates, illustrates, and narrates personalized stories that can be used for this purpose. An illustrative example of a prompt to be used with Gemini's Storybooks, designed to generate an AI-based multilingual storybook for pedagogical and critical reflection purposes, is provided below:

Write an engaging anime-style illustrated storybook for readers aged 14–18 that explores the theme "Equity, Equality, and Justice in AI-Enhanced Language Education." The story should follow a diverse group of students in a modern classroom where AI tools help them learn languages, but where they gradually discover that true learning and fairness depend on valuing each classmate's linguistic repertoire—including accents, dialects, multilingual identities, and cultural expressions. Through relatable characters, emotional moments, and visually vivid scenes typical of anime storytelling, show how respecting and integrating different ways of speaking becomes essential to building equity, fostering equality, and achieving social justice in the classroom. The narrative should balance entertainment with reflection, encouraging readers to see linguistic diversity not as a problem to fix but as a powerful resource for collective learning and inclusive AI-supported education.

The prompt presented above can serve as a template for developing additional AI-generated storybooks aimed at raising awareness of linguistic diversity. When introducing this prompt, Gemini Storybook creates the images and text for the story (see Figure 1). The complete Gemini Storybook created with the aforementioned prompt is available at the following link: https://share.gemini.google/OzFBA10wNbo3. As can be seen, the beginning of the story, titled "The Heart of the Code," illustrates a clear case of algorithmic bias, as the AI system equates "correct" language use with a single standardized norm, thereby implicitly devaluing linguistic variation. Amara's pronunciation, shaped by her family and cultural background, is shown as an error rather than as a legitimate expression of linguistic diversity. This way, the learners and the teacher can reflect how AI may enforce a homogenizing model of language that privileges dominant or "neutral" varieties while marginalizing others, revealing how supposedly neutral technologies can reproduce existing hierarchies and discriminatory practices.

Figure 1. Gemini-generated storybook to raise awareness about AI biases related to multilingualism

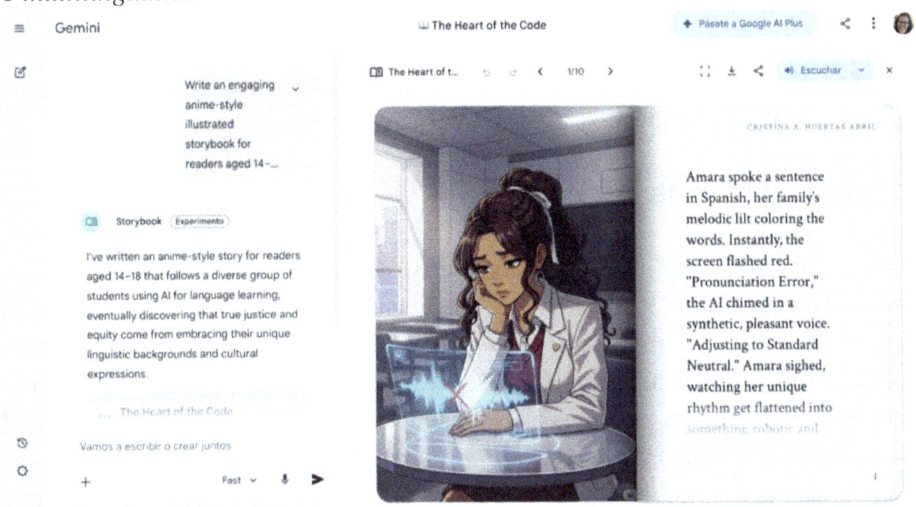

Source: Author's own elaboration using Storybooks (experiment) by Gemini

From a pedagogical perspective, a storybook like this highlights the risk of using AIALL tools uncritically. The storybook underscores the need for teachers to foster critical AI literacy, ensuring that students understand how such systems may embed biases and normative assumptions about language. Moreover, it calls for the integration of inclusive teaching practices that recognize and value diverse linguistic repertoires, rather than suppressing them. Educators should therefore mediate AIALL, contextualizing its feedback and encouraging reflection, so that technology should support rather than undermine equity, identity, and the preservation of linguistic diversity in the classroom. In fact, the story ends with the following sentences:

The other students began to whisper, realize that their own "errors" were actually hidden treasures. Yuki looked at Kenzo and smiled. They hadn't just achieved equality; they had found justice. They had proven that AI-enhanced education is only truly "smart" when it honors the full spectrum of human identity. In the heart of the code, they found that diversity wasn't a problem to be solved, but the very language of progress.

Following the reading of this excerpt, students could engage in a guided reflective activity exploring the distinction between equality and justice in AI-assisted language learning. Working individually or in small groups, they could discuss questions such as: "why were the students' 'errors' described as hidden treasures?," "how can AI systems unintentionally overlook or devalue linguistic diversity?," and "what responsibilities do educators and learners have to ensure that AI promotes inclusion rather than uniformity?" As a concluding task, students could write a brief reflection identifying one way in which AI tools could better recognize and value diverse linguistic repertoires. This activity encourages critical digital literacy while fostering awareness of linguistic identities, multilingualism, and the ethical implications of AI in education

Multilingual Hymns

AI-based song creation tools offer innovative possibilities for reinforcing AIALL in secondary education while simultaneously addressing ethical issues related to AI, particularly in multilingual contexts. By enabling students to generate lyrics, melodies, and performances through AI systems, these tools can create engaging, creative, and participatory learning environments in which language use is embedded in meaningful and expressive practices. Song creation encourages repetition, pronunciation practice, and vocabulary acquisition, while also supporting the development of rhythm, intonation, and fluency in the target language. For the example presented in Table 1 of a 'multilingual anthem,' we began by generating the song lyrics with the assistance of ChatGPT, obtaining the lyrics in three languages and polishing them before generating the hymn. More specifically, the prompts in ChatGPT were:

Write the lyrics for a song about the importance of multilingualism and respect for linguistic diversity in today's society, and then set them to music. Write the song in English, but include other European languages.

Now adapt it so that the primary language is Spanish.

Now adapt it to French.

In the case of Suno, the prompts, replicated for the three languages, were:

Create an uplifting, catchy anthem using the lyrics provided. Modern pop with subtle folk and cinematic influences, designed to feel inspiring, emotional, and energetic. Strong build-ups leading to powerful choruses, driving drums, and

acoustic guitar. Dynamic female lead vocals with layered harmonies, joined by a choir in the final chorus to create a sense of unity and celebration. The multilingual phrases should stand out naturally and be clearly articulated. The overall feeling should be hopeful, inclusive, and empowering.

Table 1. Trilingual version of a multilingual hymn

Spanish Version	English Version	French Version
Verse 1 Nacimos en mil lugares, diferentes sonidos al hablar Desde nanas susurradas hasta historias junto al mar Cada palabra es memoria, cada acento es hogar Diferentes lenguas, mismo pulso al respirar **Pre-Chorus** Dijeron "habla igual para entender" Pero es mejor la diversidad **Chorus** *Hello,* hola, *bonjour, ciao* Somos lenguas, somos culturas, *Guten Tag, olá, hej, salut* Cada lengua tiene su luz Diferentes voces, una canción En cada idioma hay conexión Déjalas volar, sin olvidar Bajo el mismo cielo van a sonar **Verse 2** ¿Perdidos al traducir? No, nos volvemos a encontrar En *chaque mot*, en *every word*, en cada forma de amar Del ritmo del español a la elegancia del *français* Y la fuerza del *Deutsch* que dice lo que no ves **Pre-Chorus** Ninguna voz lo puede contar Solo juntas lo pueden lograr **Chorus**	**Verse 1** We were born in different places, different sounds upon our lips From whispered lullabies to stories on the wind's soft drift Every word a piece of history, every phrase a living flame Different tongues, but hearts that echo just the same **Pre-Chorus** They said "Speak the same to understand" But I learned more when I could expand **Chorus** *Hello, hola, bonjour, ciao* We're more alike than we know now *Guten Tag, olá, hej, salut* Every language holds the truth Different words, one human song In every voice, we all belong Raise them high, let them fly All our voices share one sky **Verse 2** Lost in translation? No, we're found in every way *In κάθε λέξη [káthe léxi], in chaque mot* we say From the rhythm of español to the grace of français To the strength in Deutsch that carries what we can't convey **Pre-Chorus** No single voice can tell it all But together we stand tall **Chorus**	**Verse 1** Nés en mille endroits, avec des sons à partager Des berceuses murmurées aux histoires à raconter Chaque mot porte un passé, chaque accent une identité Langues différentes, même cœur pour vibrer **Pre-Chorus** On disait "parle pareil pour comprendre" Mais j'ai appris en laissant les voix s'étendre **Chours** *Hello, hola, bonjour, ciao* On est plus proches qu'on ne croit *Guten Tag, olá, hej, salut* Chaque langue porte une vertu Des mots divers, une chanson Dans chaque voix, une union Laisse-les vivre, laisse-les croire Sous le même ciel, une histoire **Verse 2** Perdus en traduction ? Non, on se retrouve autrement *In every word,* en chaque mot, dans chaque sentiment Du rythme de l'espagnol à la grâce du français Et la force du Deutsch qui dit ce qu'on ne sait **Pre-Chorus** Aucune voix ne peut tout dire Mais ensemble, on peut construire **Chorus**

Source: Author's own elaboration using ChatGPT

To create the hymns, Suno, an AI-based music generation platform, was used to create the songs from textual prompts. Although Suno can also generate the lyrics, they were provided and Suno was used to generate the melodies, vocals, and instrumental arrangements (see Figure 2). Users can provide a structured textual prompt specifying parameters such as thematic content, genre, mood, and linguistic features, upon which the system autonomously generates a complete musical composition in seconds.

Figure 2. Process of creation the multilingual hymns

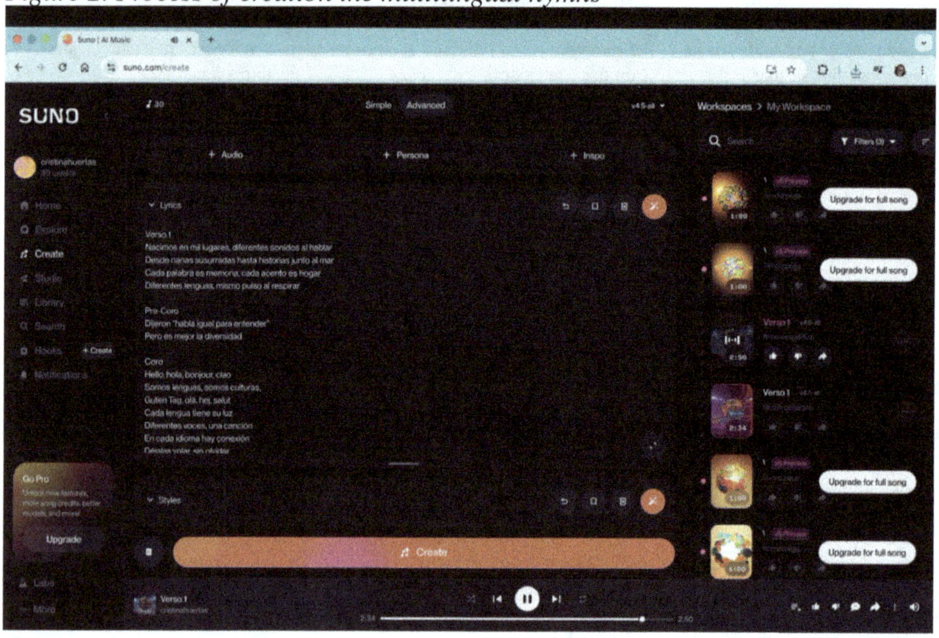

Source: Author's own elaboration using Suno

Suno can be extensively utilized across creative, educational, and experimental domains, as it significantly reduces the technical barriers associated with music production while enabling the rapid prototyping and iteration of musical concepts. In the context of language teaching and learning, these AI-supported affordances facilitate the creation of customized, linguistically rich musical materials that can enhance vocabulary acquisition, pronunciation practice, and intercultural awareness. By allowing learners and educators to generate songs in multiple languages and tailored to specific pedagogical objectives, the technology promotes active engagement, multimodal learning, and creative expression, thereby enhancing motivation and fostering deeper linguistic competence through the integration of language, digital technologies, and artistic practices.

Following the multilingual hymn, students could participate in a critical discussion examining language representation and linguistic hierarchies in AI-generated content. Students could be invited to identify which languages are included in the hymn and, more importantly, which are absent, before reflecting on possible reasons behind these choices. Guiding questions might include: "why are these particular languages represented?," "whose voices and identities are missing?," and "how might AI training data influence these linguistic choices?" As a follow-up task, students could collaboratively redesign the hymn by incorporating minority, regional, migrant, or Indigenous languages represented in their own communities, discussing how these additions change the message of the song. This activity promotes critical AI literacy by encouraging learners to question linguistic prestige, colonial legacies, and the power structures that shape AI-generated outputs, while reinforcing the value of linguistic diversity and social justice in multilingual education.

FUTURE RESEARCH DIRECTIONS

In the context of AIALL, multilingualism, and educational justice, several avenues for future research can be identified to advance both theoretical understanding and pedagogical practice. On the one hand, further research is needed to examine how AIALL tools can be designed and implemented in ways that genuinely promote equity and inclusion, rather than reproducing existing linguistic and social hierarchies. This may include investigating how AI(ALL) systems can better accommodate diverse linguistic repertoires, including minoritized languages, dialects, and non-standard varieties, and how these tools can be adapted to different sociocultural and educational contexts. Consequently, empirical studies exploring learners' experiences across diverse settings would be especially valuable.

On the other hand, there is also a need for in-depth research on the ethical dimensions of AIALL in language education. This includes issues related to algorithmic bias, linguistic representation, data privacy, and academic integrity. Future studies should explore how students and teachers understand and negotiate these ethical challenges, as well as how pedagogical interventions (i.e., AI-generated storybooks or song creation activities) can foster critical AI literacy and ethical awareness, particularly in multilingual classrooms. In this light, research should also further investigate the pedagogical potential of creative AI applications, such as AI-generated narratives and songs, in supporting both language development and identity formation. This includes examining how such tools can enhance learner engagement, motivation, and intercultural competence, as well as how they can be used to validate students' linguistic identities and promote positive attitudes toward linguistic diversity.

Taken together, these research directions highlight the importance of interdisciplinary, critical, and context-sensitive approaches to AIALL, with a strong emphasis on equity, multilingualism, and social justice in increasingly digital educational environments.

CONCLUSION

The integration of AI-assisted language learning (AIALL) within multilingual educational contexts presents both significant opportunities and critical challenges for advancing equity, equality, and social justice. These issues constitute one of the central areas of inquiry within the Pluridentities project, which examines how multilingual identities can be fostered through inclusive educational policies, innovative pedagogical practices, and collaborative RPPs. Linguistic capital and linguistic identities remain central to understanding how learners engage with language education, particularly in an increasingly diverse European context. While AI tools have the potential to expand access to language learning, personalize instruction, and foster more inclusive and flexible learning environments, they also risk reproducing existing inequalities if issues such as the digital divide, linguistic bias, and unequal access are not adequately tackled.

At the same time, the pedagogical use of creative AI applications, such as storybooks and song generation, demonstrates how AI can be harnessed not only as a tool for language development but also as a means of fostering critical awareness and ethical reflection on linguistic diversity and social educational justice. Within the Pluridentities project, these resources are conceived as illustrative pedagogical proposals emerging from the needs identified through the RPPs, where researchers and practitioners collaboratively explored how AI could support multilingual education while promoting inclusion and ethical digital practices. By engaging learners in the analysis of linguistic representation, authorship, and power in AI-generated content, educators can promote critical digital literacy and encourage students to reflect on broader questions of linguistic justice, multilingualism, and inclusion. These approaches align with socially just educational frameworks that seek to validate diverse linguistic repertoires and support the development of positive and diverse linguistic identities.

Ultimately, the contribution of AIALL to more equitable language education may depend on how these technologies are conceptualized, implemented, and critically examined within educational systems. The collaborative nature of the RPPs provides an appropriate framework for this process by enabling researchers and practitioners to co-design, reflect upon, and refine pedagogical approaches grounded in the realities of classroom practice. It is thus essential to adopt a balanced and reflexive approach that leverages the strengths of AIALL while remaining attentive to its limitations and ethical implications. By placing equity, multilingualism, and social justice at the center of AIALL, educators, researchers, and policymakers can work toward more inclusive, participatory, equal, and linguistically diverse learning environments.

ACKNOWLEDGMENT

This chapter has been developed within the Project 'Pluridentities: Protecting and stimulating plurilingual identities in learners in Europe via inclusive policies and classroom practices,' granted by the European Union's Horizon Europe research and innovation program (Grant No. 101178914).

REFERENCES

Allweiss, A., & Al-Adeimi, S. (2025). Addressing imperial evasion: Toward an anti-imperialist pedagogy in teacher education. *Teaching in Higher Education, 30*(2), 308–326. DOI: 10.1080/13562517.2024.2350016

Belda-Medina, J., & Calvo-Ferrer, J. R. (2022). Using chatbots as AI conversational partners in language learning. *Applied Sciences (Basel, Switzerland), 12*(17), 8427. DOI: 10.3390/app12178427

Beljić, I. (2015). La construcción de las identidades lingüísticas: El caso de la variedad andaluza del español y las modalidades meridionales del serbio [The construction of linguistic identities: The case of the Andalusian variety of Spanish and the southern varieties of Serbian]. *Verba Hispanica, 23*(1), 87–105. DOI: 10.4312/vh.23.1.87-105

Bettney, E. (2022). Examining hegemonic and monoglossic language ideologies, policies, and practices within bilingual education in Colombia. *Íkala, Revista de Lenguaje y Cultura [Íkala, Journal of Language and Culture], 27*(1), 249–270. DOI: 10.17533/udea.ikala.v27n1a12

Bourdieu, P. (1977). The economics of linguistic exchanges. *Social Sciences Information. Information Sur les Sciences Sociales, 16*(6), 645–668. DOI: 10.1177/053901847701600601

Bourdieu, P. (1986). The Forms of Capital. En J. Richardson (Ed.), *Handbook of Theory and Research for the Sociology of Education* (pp. 241–258). Greenwood.

Chen, C., & Manosuthikit, A. (2025). Persistent invisibilities: Discourses, identities, and investment in English as a Foreign Language among Yi minority college students in contemporary China. *LEARN Journal: Language Education and Acquisition Research Network., 18*(2), 264–287. DOI: 10.70730/PDJO8958

Chung, B., & Bong, H. K. M. (2022). A study on the intelligibility of Korean-accented English: Possibilities of implementing AI applications in English education. *The Journal of AsiaTEFL, 19*(1), 197–215. DOI: 10.18823/asiatefl.2022.19.1.12.197

Coburn, C., Penuel, W., & Geil, K. (2013). *Research-Practice Partnerships: A Strategy for Leveraging Research for Educational Improvement in School Districts.* William T. Grant Foundation. https://eric.ed.gov/?id=ED568396

Council of Europe. (2007). From linguistic diversity to plurilingual education: Guide for the Development of Language Education Policies in Europe. Language Policy Unit, Council of Europe. https://rm.coe.int/16802fc1c4

Council of Europe. (2014). *Languages for democracy and social cohesion. Diversity, equity and quality. Sixty years of European co-operation.* Language Policy Unit, Council of Europe. https://rm.coe.int/languages-for-democracy-and-social-cohesion-diversity-equity-and-quali/168069e7bd

Crompton, H., & Burke, D. (2023). Artificial intelligence in higher education: The state of the field. *International Journal of Educational Technology in Higher Education, 20*(1), 22. DOI: 10.1186/s41239-023-00392-8

Cummins, J. (2015). Intercultural education and academic achievement: A framework for school-based policies in multilingual schools. *Intercultural Education, 26*(6), 455–468. DOI: 10.1080/14675986.2015.1103539

European Commission. (2026). *Languages in the EU – why multilingualism matters.* https://translation.ec.europa.eu/languages-eu-why-multilingualism-matters_en

Farrell, C., Penuel, W., Coburn, C., Daniel, J., & Steup, L. (2021). *Research-practice partnerships in education: The state of the field.* William T. Grant Foundation. https://eric.ed.gov/?id=ED615899

Figueroa, M. (2024). Language development, linguistic input, and linguistic racism. *Wiley Interdisciplinary Reviews. Cognitive Science, 15*(3), e1673. DOI: 10.1002/wcs.1673 PMID: 38297101

Finegan, E. (2012). Language: Its structure and use. (6th ed.). Wadsworth Cengage learning.

Fisher, L., Evans, M., Forbes, K., Gayton, A., Liu, Y., & Rutgers, D. (2024). Language experiences, evaluations and emotions (3Es): Analysis of structural models of multilingual identity for language learners in schools in England. *International Journal of Multilingualism, 21*(1), 418–438. DOI: 10.1080/14790718.2022.2060235

García, O. (2009). *Bilingual education in the 21st Century: A global perspective.* Wiley/Blackwell.

García, O., & Otheguy, R. (2020). Plurilingualism and translanguaging: Commonalities and divergences. *International Journal of Bilingual Education and Bilingualism, 23*(1), 17–35. DOI: 10.1080/13670050.2019.1598932

García, O., & Wei, L. (2014). *Translanguaging: Language, bilingualism and education*. Palgrave Macmillan. DOI: 10.1057/9781137385765

Godwin-Jones, R. (2021). Big data and language learning: Opportunities and challenges. *Language Learning & Technology, 25*(1), 4–19. https://bit.ly/414kkFl. DOI: 10.64152/10125/44747

Hockly, N. (2023). Artificial intelligence in English language teaching: The good, the bad and the ugly. *RELC Journal, 54*(2), 445–451. DOI: 10.1177/00336882231168504

Huang, X., Zou, D., Cheng, G., Chen, X., & Xie, H. (2023). Trends, research issues and applications of artificial intelligence in language education. *Journal of Educational Technology & Society, 26*(1), 112–131. DOI: 10.30191/ETS.202301_26(1).0009

Huertas-Abril, C. A. (2025). Machine Learning. In McCallum, L., & Tafazoli, D. (Eds.), *The Palgrave Encyclopedia of Computer-Assisted Language Learning*. Palgrave Macmillan. DOI: 10.1007/978-3-031-51447-0_104-1

Huertas-Abril, C. A., & Palacios-Hidalgo, F. J. (2025). Artificial intelligence–assisted language learning for *all* in the new global context: Threats and opportunities. In Wei, W., & Schnell, J. (Eds.), *The Routledge Handbook of Endangered and Minority Languages* (pp. 355–376). Routledge. DOI: 10.4324/9781003439493-27

Ignatius, D. (2025). *Language, Identity, and Integration: From the Tower of Babel to Contemporary Indian Language Policy*. BITS – Journal of Business, IT, and Social Science. DOI: 10.51470/BITS.2025.04.02.34

Ja'afreh, H., & Al-Saudi, J. (2024). Language variation, regional identities, and social perceptions of Karak and Amman dialects in Jordan: A comparative study. International *Journal of Linguistics. Literature and Translation, 7*(9), 70–78. DOI: 10.32996/ijllt.2024.7.9.9

Jeon, J., Lee, S., & Choe, H. (2023). Beyond ChatGPT: A conceptual framework and systematic review of speech-recognition chatbots for language learning. *Computers & Education, 206*, 104898. DOI: 10.1016/j.compedu.2023.104898

Karaca, A., & Kılcan, B. (2023). The adventure of artificial intelligence technology in education: Comprehensive scientific mapping analysis. *Participatory Educational Research, 10*(4), 144–165. DOI: 10.17275/per.23.64.10.4

Katsarou, E., Wild, F., Sougari, A.-M., & Chatzipanagiotou, P. (2023). A systematic review of voice-based intelligent virtual agents in EFL education. [iJET]. *International Journal of Emerging Technologies in Learning*, *18*(10), 65–85. DOI: 10.3991/ijet.v18i10.37723

Kent, D. (2020). A room with a VUI – voice user interfaces in the TESOL classroom. *Teaching English with Technology*, *20*(3), 96–124.

Kerfoot, C., & Bello-Nonjengele, B. O. (2023). Towards epistemic justice: Constructing knowers in multilingual classrooms. *Applied Linguistics*, *44*(3), 462–484. DOI: 10.1093/applin/amac049

Ketere, C. (2025). Decolonizing Artificial Intelligence: Reducing Algorithmic Biases in African Educational and Linguistic Contexts. *Journal of Contemporary Issues in Open Distance and E-Learning*, *2*(1), 18–37. DOI: 10.71060/7qk9nd52

Lasagabaster, D., & García, O. (2014). Translanguaging: Towards a dynamic model of bilingualism at school. *C&E, Cultura y Educación*, *26*(3), 557–572. DOI: 10.1080/11356405.2014.973671

Lewis, A. A. (2025). Unpacking cultural bias in AI language learning tools: An analysis of impacts and strategies for inclusion in diverse educational settings. *International Journal of Research and Innovation in Social Science*, *9*(1), 1878–1892. DOI: 10.47772/IJRISS.2025.9010151

Li, J., Xu, M., & Chen, J. (2022). A Bourdieusian analysis of the multilingualism in a poverty-stricken ethnic minority area: Can linguistic capital be transferred to economic capital? *Journal of Multilingual and Multicultural Development*, *43*(2), 122–139. DOI: 10.1080/01434632.2020.1733585

Lin, C.-J., & Mubarok, H. (2021). Learning analytics for investigating the mind map-guided AI chatbot approach in an EFL flipped speaking classroom. *Journal of Educational Technology & Society*, *24*(4), 16–35. https://www.jstor.org/stable/48629242

López Blanco, J. D. (2025). Do languages open doors? A theoretical model of linguistic capital and (im)mobility and its application in Spanish youth migration. *Journal of Ethnic and Migration Studies*, *51*(3), 565–582. DOI: 10.1080/1369183X.2024.2359676

Mallinson, C. (2024). Linguistic variation and linguistic inclusion in the US educational context. *Annual Review of Linguistics*, *10*(1), 37–57. DOI: 10.1146/annurev-linguistics-031120-121546

McKenney, S., & Reeves, T. C. (2014). Methods of evaluation and reflection in design research. *Zeitschrift für Berufs-und Wirtschaftspädagogiek, 27*, 141–153. https://research.utwente.nl/en/publications/methods-of-evaluation-and-reflection-in-design-research/

Norton, B. (2013). *Identity and language learning: Extending the conversation* (2nd ed.). Multilingual Matters. DOI: 10.21832/9781783090563

Pande, M. H. (2025). Translanguaging Pedagogy: A Tool for Social Justice and Equity in the Language Classroom. *Language, Literature, and Interdisciplinary Studies (LLIDS), Social Justice Special Issue,* 2.65–2.78, DOI: 10.71106/AIUT8526

Pavlenko, A., & Blackledge, A. (Eds.). (2004). *Negotiation of identities in multilingual contexts.* Multilingual Matters. DOI: 10.21832/9781853596483

Peña-Acuña, B., & Crismán-Pérez, R. (2022). Research on Papua, a digital tool with artificial intelligence in favor of learning and linguistic attitudes towards the learning of the English language in students of Spanish language as L1. *Frontiers in Psychology, 13*, 1019278. DOI: 10.3389/fpsyg.2022.1019278 PMID: 36389452

Shaikh, S., Yayilgan, S. Y., Klimova, B., & Pikhart, M. (2023). Assessing the usability of ChatGPT for formal English language learning. *European Journal of Investigation in Health, Psychology and Education, 13*(9), 1937–1960. DOI: 10.3390/ejihpe13090140 PMID: 37754479

Siahaan, S., Saputro, I. E., Yulianingsih, L., Faizin, M., Sinaga, J. B., & Ardhi, M. A. (2026). Writing as Transformative. In S. Siahaan, I. E. Saputro, L. Yulianingsih, M. Faizin, J. B. Sinaga, & M. A. Ardhi (Eds.), *Transformative Learning and Literature in Writing: Theory, Pedagogy, and Practice* (pp. 85–98). PT. Harmoni Anak Negeri.

Soare, I. L. (2025). Language, Identity, and Cognitive Equity: Rethinking Multilingualism in Migrant-Inclusive EFL Pedagogy. *Analele Universită ii „Dunărea de Jos" din Gala i, Fascicula XX, Sociologie [The Annals of "Dunărea de Jos" University of Galaţi. Fascicle XX, Sociology], 20*(1), 153–167. https://www.ceeol.com/search/article-detail?id=1385816

Surmont, J., Van Oss, V., D'Hulster, M., Mijts, E., Van Donselaar, B., Van den Branden, K., Buelens, K., Sylvén, L. K., Olsson, E., Segura Hudson, M., Wakelkamp, I., Van de Guchte, M., Palacios-Hidalgo, F. J., Huertas-Abril, C. A., Luque-González, R., Husárová, B., & Curado-Toledano, N. (2025). *Pluridentities: Theoretical Framework on Languages, Identity, and Policy.* Pluridentities. DOI: 10.5281/zenodo.17949143

Wang, S., Lang, N., Bunch, G. C., Basch, S., McHugh, S. R., Huitzilopochtli, S., & Callanan, M. (2021). Dismantling Persistent Deficit Narratives About the Language and Literacy of Culturally and Linguistically Minoritized Children and Youth: Counter-Possibilities. *Frontiers in Education*, *6*, 641796. DOI: 10.3389/feduc.2021.641796

Wang, X., Liu, Q., Pang, H., Tan, S. C., Lei, J., Wallace, M. P., & Li, L. (2023). What matters in AI-supported learning: A study of human-AI interactions in language learning using cluster analysis and epistemic network analysis. *Computers & Education*, *194*, 104703. DOI: 10.1016/j.compedu.2022.104703

Wei, L. (2022). Translanguaging as a political stance: Implications for English language education. *ELT Journal*, *76*(2), 172–182. DOI: 10.1093/elt/ccab083

Xiao, G. (2024). The power of language ideologies: creating heteroglossic implementational spaces in a practical English class. *Working Papers in Educational Linguistics, 38,* 48–66. https://repository.upenn.edu/handle/20.500.14332/60632

Youn, S. J. (2023). Test design and validity evidence of interactive speaking assessment in the era of emerging technologies. *Language Testing*, *40*(1), 54–60. DOI: 10.1177/02655322221126606

Zhai, C., & Wibowo, S. (2023). A systematic review on artificial intelligence dialogue systems for enhancing English as foreign language students' interactional competence in the university. *Computers & Education*, *4*, 100134. DOI: 10.1016/j.caeai.2023.100134

Zschomler, S. (2019). 'Language Is Your Dignity': Migration, Linguistic Capital, and the Experience of Re/De-Valuation. *Languages (Basel, Switzerland)*, *4*(3), 64. DOI: 10.3390/languages4030064

ADDITIONAL READING

Huertas-Abril, C. A., & Palacios-Hidalgo, F. J. (2023). New possibilities of artificial intelligence-assisted language learning (AIALL): Comparing visions from the East and the West. *Education Sciences*, *13*(12), 1234. DOI: 10.3390/educsci13121234

Huertas-Abril, C. A., Palacios-Hidalgo, F. J., Curado-Toledano, N., & Husárová, B. (2025). *Technology & Plurilingualism in Spanish Secondary Education: Preliminary Qualitative Results (Pluridentities Working Paper 14a)*. Pluridentities. DOI: 10.5281/zenodo.17912978

Palacios-Hidalgo, F. J. (2025). AI for the Democratization of Language Learning. In McCallum, L., & Tafazoli, D. (Eds.), *The Palgrave Encyclopedia of Computer-Assisted Language Learning. Palgrave.* Macmillan. DOI: 10.1007/978-3-031-51447-0_98-1

Palacios-Hidalgo, F. J., & Huertas-Abril, C. A. (2024). AIALL and queer language education to prevent gender-based violence: Using artificial intelligence for lesson planning. In Buenestado-Fernández, M., Jiménez-Millán, A., & Palacios-Hidalgo, F. J. (Eds.), *Comprehensive sexuality education for gender-based violence prevention* (pp. 189–210). IGI Global. DOI: 10.4018/979-8-3693-2053-2.ch011

Palacios-Hidalgo, F. J., & Huertas-Abril, C. A. (2025). Impact of technology use on the construction of identity in language learners: A 2020–2024 systematic literature review. *International Journal of Multilingualism*, 1–19. DOI: 10.1080/14790718.2025.2546506

Palacios-Hidalgo, F. J., Huertas-Abril, C. A., Husárová, B., & Curado-Toledano, N. (2025). *Technology & Plurilingualism in Spanish Secondary Education: Preliminary Quantitative Results (Pluridentities Working Paper 12a).* Pluridentities. DOI: 10.5281/zenodo.18536041

Tafazoli, D. (2024). Exploring the potential of generative AI in democratizing English language education. *Computers and Education: Artificial Intelligence*, *7*, 100275. DOI: 10.1016/j.caeai.2024.100275

Tafazoli, D., Daneshrah, A., Ranjbaran Madiseh, F., Tabatabaei, F. S., Mozafarianpour, A., Ranjbar, M., Zainuddin, N., Gonzalez Vidal, T., Roe, J., Dabir, S., Omrani, B., Behboodzade, H., Talebi-Dastenaei, M., & Mokhatebi Ardakani, M. (2026). Language teacher AI competence self-efficacy, emotion regulation, and mindfulness in relation to teacher digital burnout: A mediation model. *Computer Assisted Language Learning*, 1–32. DOI: 10.1080/09588221.2026.2640091

Üvek, N., & Solmaz, O. (2026). Balancing Support and Autonomy in ELT Master Students' Use of AI for Academic Writing. In A. Sorayyaei Azar, R. K. Ghosh, E. Çela, D. Flett (Klosi) (Eds.), *Leveraging AI for Future-Ready Writing Education* (pp. 165-190). IGI Global. DOI: 10.4018/979-8-3373-5601-3.ch008

KEY TERMS AND DEFINITIONS

Artificial Intelligence–Assisted Language Learning (AIALL): pedagogical and technological approach that integrates artificial intelligence (AI) techniques into language education to support, enhance, and personalize the language learning process. In academic contexts, it is typically seen as an evolution of Computer-Assisted Language Learning (CALL), extending it by incorporating intelligent systems capable of adapting instruction, analyzing learner behavior, and generating dynamic linguistic input and feedback.

Linguistic Capital: social value of language skills within a particular society. In fields such as Sociolinguistics, it describes how knowledge of certain languages or language varieties can provide individuals with social, cultural, or economic advantages, such as better access to education, employment, and social opportunities.

Linguistic Identities: ways in which individuals understand and express who they are through their use of language. This dynamic concept describes how language choices, varieties, and practices can reflect and shape a person's social, cultural, and personal identity within different communities and contexts.

Linguistic Repertoire: range of languages, language varieties, and communicative resources that an individual can use to communicate. It includes all the linguistic knowledge and skills a person draws on in different social and cultural contexts.

Pluridentities: Horizon Europe research project (Grant No. 101178914) that investigates the development of multilingual identities within the school context, considered a key site for fostering linguistic diversity and social inclusion. The project proposes a framework based on four central components that shape multilingualism and identity formation in education: linguistic capital, the learning environment, language policy, and technology. Through this approach, Pluridentities examines how educational systems can promote multilingual competence while strengthening students' identification with European values.

Research-Practice Partnership (RPP): Sustained and systematic collaborations between researchers and practitioners designed to improve educational institutions and systems through the use of research. RPPs are characterized by a long-term orientation, a focus on problems of practice, a commitment to mutualistic relationships, the use of deliberate strategies to develop and sustain collaboration, and an emphasis on the production of original analyses.

Social Justice: in language learning and teaching, social justice refers to the principle of promoting equity, inclusion, and equal opportunities for all learners regardless of their linguistic, cultural, or socioeconomic backgrounds. In this field, it involves recognizing and valuing linguistic diversity, reducing inequalities in access to language education, and adopting pedagogical practices that empower learners and support fair participation in educational and social contexts.

Translanguaging: process by which multilingual individuals flexibly and strategically draw on their entire linguistic repertoire, instead of treating languages as separate and bounded systems, to construct meaning, facilitate communication, and engage in cognitive and social practices within multilingual contexts.

Compilation of References

Abdelrady, A. H., Ibrahim, D. O. O., & Akram, H. (2025). Unveiling the role of Copilot in enhancing EFL learners' writing skills: A content analysis. *World Journal of English Language, 15*(8), 174–185. DOI: 10.5430/wjel.v15n8p174

Ait-Hroch, A., & Ibrahimi, A. (2025). Integrating AI Tools in Blended Language Training: Enhancing Language Skills Development in University Students. In *Supporting Personalized Learning and Students' Skill Development With AI* (pp. 343-368). IGI Global Scientific Publishing. DOI: 10.4018/979-8-3693-8965-2.ch017

Al Nuaimi, H. (2024). Anxiety and task-based language teaching in second language acquisition. *Research Studies in English Language Teaching and Learning*, 2(4), 251–267. DOI: 10.62583/rseltl.v2i4.56

Alam, A. (2023a). The secret sauce of student success: Cracking the code by navigating the path to personalized learning with educational data mining. In *2023 2nd International Conference on Smart Technologies and Systems for Next Generation Computing (ICSTSN)* (pp. 1-8). IEEE. DOI: 10.1109/ICSTSN57873.2023.10151558

Alam, A. (2023b). Media multitasking with M-learning technology in real-time classroom learning: Analysing the dynamics in formal educational settings for the future of E-learning in India. In *2023 2nd International Conference on Smart Technologies and Systems for Next Generation Computing (ICSTSN)* (pp. 1-6). IEEE. DOI: 10.1109/ICSTSN57873.2023.10151509

Alam, A., & Mohanty, A. (2022). Facial analytics or virtual avatars: competencies and design considerations for student-teacher interaction in AI-powered online education for effective classroom engagement. In *International Conference on Communication, Networks and Computing* (pp. 252-265). Cham: Springer Nature Switzerland. DOI: 10.1007/978-3-031-43145-6_21

Alam, A., & Mohanty, A. (2023a). Learning on the move: a pedagogical framework for state-of-the-art mobile learning. In *International Conference on Data Management, Analytics & Innovation* (pp. 735-748). Singapore: Springer Nature Singapore. DOI: 10.1007/978-981-99-1414-2_52

Alam, A., & Mohanty, A. (2023b). From bricks to clicks: The potential of big data analytics for revolutionizing the information landscape in higher education sector. In *International Conference on Data Management, Analytics & Innovation* (pp. 721-732). Singapore: Springer Nature Singapore. DOI: 10.1007/978-981-99-1414-2_51

Alam, A. (2023c). Leveraging the power of 'modeling and computer simulation' for education: An exploration of its potential for improved learning outcomes and enhanced student engagement. In *2023 International Conference on Device Intelligence, Computing and Communication Technologies (DICCT)* (pp. 445-450). IEEE. DOI: 10.1109/DICCT56244.2023.10110159

Alam, A., & Mohanty, A. (2023c). Developing 'happiness engineering' subject for the schools in India: Designing the pedagogical framework for a sustainable happiness curriculum. *Qubahan Academic Journal, 3*(4), 1–20. DOI: 10.48161/qaj.v3n4a145

Alam, A., & Mohanty, A. (2023d). Implications of virtual reality (VR) for school teachers and instructional designers: An empirical investigation. *Cogent Education, 10*(2), 2260676. DOI: 10.1080/2331186X.2023.2260676

Alam, A., & Mohanty, A. (2024). Framework of Self-Regulated cognitive engagement (FSRCE) for sustainable pedagogy: A model that integrates SRL and cognitive engagement for holistic development of students. *Cogent Education, 11*(1), 2363157. DOI: 10.1080/2331186X.2024.2363157

Alansari, A. (2019). *Localizing Global English language textbooks: A critical multimodal discourse analysis of identity construction in global, regional and local editions* [PhD thesis University of Warwick]. Warwick Research Archive Portal (WRAP).

Al-Azawei, A., Serenelli, F., & Lundqvist, K. (2016). Universal Design for Learning (UDL): A content analysis of peer-reviewed journal papers from 2012 to 2015. *The Journal of Scholarship of Teaching and Learning, 16*(3), 39–56. DOI: 10.14434/josotl.v16i3.19295

Albedah, F. (2025). Artificial intelligence in language education: A systematic review of multilingual applications, large language models, and emerging challenges. *Language Teaching Research Quarterly, 49*, 247–268. DOI: 10.32038/ltrq.2025.49.13

Albeihi, H. H. M., & Rice, M. F. (2025). Generative AI and language diversity: Implications for teachers and learners. *Arab World English Journal*, *16*(1), 43–54. DOI: 10.24093/awej/vol16no1.3

Ali, J. K. M., Shamsan, M. A., Hezam, T. A., & Mohammead, A. A. Q. (2023). Impact of ChatGPT on learning motivation: Teachers and students' voices. *Journal of English Studies in Arabia Felix*, *2*(1), 41–49. DOI: 10.56540/jesaf.v2i1.51

Alim, H. S. (2010). Critical language awareness. In Hornberger, N. H., & McKay, S. L. (Eds.), *Sociolinguistics and language education* (pp. 205–231). Multilingual Matters.

Allen, L. K., & Kendeou, P. (2023). ED-AI Lit: An interdisciplinary framework for AI literacy in education. *Policy Insights from the Behavioral and Brain Sciences*, *11*(1), 3–10. DOI: 10.1177/23727322231220339

Allweiss, A., & Al-Adeimi, S. (2025). Addressing imperial evasion: Toward an anti-imperialist pedagogy in teacher education. *Teaching in Higher Education*, *30*(2), 308–326. DOI: 10.1080/13562517.2024.2350016

Alm, A., & Watanabe, Y. (2023). Integrating ChatGPT in Language Education: A Freirean Perspective. *Iranian Journal of Language Teaching Research*, *11*(3), 19–30. DOI: 10.30466/IJLTR.2023.121404

Almegren, A., Almegren, R. M., Hazaea, A. N., Mahdi, H. S., & Mohammed Ali, J. K. (2025). AI powered ELT: Instructors' transformative roles and opportunities. *PLoS One*, *20*(5), e0324910. DOI: 10.1371/journal.pone.0324910 PMID: 40440266

Almuhanna, M. (2024). Teachers' perspectives of integrating AI-powered technologies in K-12 education for creating customized learning materials and resources. *Education and Information Technologies*, *30*(8), 10343–10371. DOI: 10.1007/s10639-024-13257-y

Almutairi, H., Alfaifi, A. A., & Saleem, M. (2026). Writing accuracy: How AI-assisted writing instruction can support EFL undergraduate students. *Information (Basel)*, *17*(2), 157. DOI: 10.3390/info17020157

Alper, M. (2017). *Giving voice: Mobile communication, disability, and inequality*. MIT Press. DOI: 10.7551/mitpress/10771.001.0001

Amirova, N. (2025). Traditional vs. non-traditional teaching in secondary education: A comparative analysis. *Porta Universorum*, *1*(3), 101–109. DOI: 10.69760/portuni.010309

Anderson, J., & Macleray, V. (2016). *Multilingual digital storytelling: Engaging creatively and critically with literacy*. Routledge. DOI: 10.4324/9781315758220

Anshari, A., & Asrifan, A. (2026). AI-Enhanced Language Acquisition: Transforming the Learning Experience. In *AI in Literary Education and Language Learning* (pp. 117-146). IGI Global Scientific Publishing. DOI: 10.4018/979-8-3373-6330-1.ch005

Anya, U. (2011). Connecting with communities of learners and speakers: Integrative ideals, experiences, and motivations of successful black second language learners. *Foreign Language Annals*, *44*(3), 441–466. DOI: 10.1111/j.1944-9720.2011.01142.x

Ariel, L., & Hayak, M. (2025). The paradox of AI in ESL instruction: Between innovation and oppression. *Educational Theory*, *75*(4), 646–660. DOI: 10.1111/edth.70034

Aslan, E., & Sirojitdinovna, M. B. (2025). Language learning made short and sweet? Exploring student perceptions of microcelebrity teacher reels on Instagram. *Linguistics and Education*, *88*, 1–13. DOI: 10.1016/j.linged.2025.101430

Atari, M., Xue, M. J., Park, P. S., Blasi, D. E., & Henrich, J. (2023). Which humans? *PsyArXiv*. https://doi.org/DOI: 10.31234/osf.io/5b26t

Atherton, P. (2025). AI agents of change? Generative AI (GAI) and teacher agency. *EDULEARN25 Proceedings*, 768–775. IATED. https://library.iated.org/view/ATHERTON2025AIA

Aubrey, S. (2022). The relationship between anxiety, enjoyment, and breakdown fluency during second language speaking tasks: An idiodynamic investigation. *Frontiers in Psychology*, *13*, 968946. DOI: 10.3389/fpsyg.2022.968946 PMID: 36118455

Australian framework for artificial intelligence in higher education. Australian Centre for Student Equity and Success. https://bit.ly/4rmtubb

Aydın Yıldız, T. (2025). Sustainability Education in L2 Writing: AI-Based Multimodal Awareness and Engagement. *Sustainability (Basel)*, *17*(21), 9376. DOI: 10.3390/su17219376

Bachman, L. F., & Palmer, A. S. (1996). *Language testing in practice: Designing and developing useful language tests* (Vol. 1). Oxford University Press.

Bacon-Shone, J., Bolton, K., & Luke, K. K. (2015). *Language use, proficiency and attitudes in Hong Kong*. Social Sciences Research Centre, HKU.

Bacon-Shone, J., Bolton, K., & Lee, S. L. (2025). Researching Hong Kong's Multilingual Landscape. In Durk, G., & Cenoz, J. (Eds.), *The handbook of linguistic landscapes and multilingualism* (pp. 309–336). John Wiley & Sons., DOI: 10.1002/9781394231805.ch20

Bahari, A., & Liu, Y. (2025). AI integration in EFL teacher development: A mixed-methods evaluation of digital competency, professional trajectories, and pedagogical innovation within adaptive learning ecosystems. *Interactive Learning Environments*, ●●●, 1–17. DOI: 10.1080/10494820.2025.2591251

Bai, B., Wang, J., & Zhou, H. (2020). An intervention study to improve primary school students' self-regulated strategy use in English writing through e-learning in Hong Kong. *Computer Assisted Language Learning*, *35*(9), 2265–2290. DOI: 10.1080/09588221.2020.1871030

Bang, J., & Lee, S. M. (2024). Addressing bias for equity in AI-driven customized learning systems. *Multimedia-Assisted Language Learning*, *27*(4), 70–86. DOI: 10.15702/mall.2024.27.4.70

Barocas, S., Hardt, M., & Narayanan, A. (2019). *Fairness and machine learning: Limitations and opportunities*. http://fairmlbook.org

Bashir, N., Donti, P., Cuff, J., Sroka, S., Ilic, M., Sze, V., Delimitrou, C., & Olivetti, E. (2024). *The climate and sustainability implications of generative AI*. An MIT Exploration of Generative AI. https://doi.org/DOI: 10.21428/e4baedd9.9070dfe7

Baskara, R., & Mukarto, M. (2023). Exploring the implications of ChatGPT for language learning in higher education. *Indonesian Journal of English Language Teaching and Applied Linguistics*, *7*(2), 343–358. DOI: 10.21093/ijeltal.v7i2.1387

Basturkmen, H. (2012). Languages for specific purposes curriculum creation and implementation in Australasia and Europe. *Modern Language Journal*, *96*(s1), 59–70. DOI: 10.1111/j.1540-4781.2012.01297.x

Belda-Medina, J., & Calvo-Ferrer, J. R. (2022). Using chatbots as AI conversational partners in language learning. *Applied Sciences (Basel, Switzerland)*, *12*(17), 8427. DOI: 10.3390/app12178427

Beljić, I. (2015). La construcción de las identidades lingüísticas: El caso de la variedad andaluza del español y las modalidades meridionales del serbio [The construction of linguistic identities: The case of the Andalusian variety of Spanish and the southern varieties of Serbian]. *Verba Hispanica*, *23*(1), 87–105. DOI: 10.4312/vh.23.1.87-105

Bendarkawi, J., Ponce, A., Mata, S. C., Aliu, A., Liu, Y., Zhang, L., & Monroy-Hernández, A. (2025, April). ConversAR: Exploring Embodied LLM-Powered Group Conversations in Augmented Reality for Second Language Learners. In *Proceedings of the Extended Abstracts of the CHI Conference on Human Factors in Computing Systems* (pp. 1-11). DOI: 10.1145/3706599.3720162

Bender, E. M., Gebru, T., McMillan-Major, A., & Shmitchell, S. (2021). On the dangers of stochastic parrots: Can language models be too big? *Proceedings of the 2021 ACM Conference on Fairness, Accountability, and Transparency*, 610–623. DOI: 10.1145/3442188.3445922

Bengio, Y., Mindermann, S., Privitera, D., Besiroglu, T., Bommasani, R., Casper, S., Choi, Y., Fox, P., Garfinkel, B., Goldfarb, D., Heidari, H., Ho, A., Kapoor, S., Khalatbari, L., Longpre, S., Manning, S., Mavroudis, V., Mazeika, M., Michael, J., . . . Zeng, Y. (2025). *International AI safety report* (DSIT 2025/001). https://l1nq.com/9Mf4e

Benjamin, R. (2019). *Race after technology: Abolitionist tools for the new Jim Code*. Polity Press.

Bettney, E. (2022). Examining hegemonic and monoglossic language ideologies, policies, and practices within bilingual education in Colombia. *Íkala, Revista de Lenguaje y Cultura [Íkala, Journal of Language and Culture], 27*(1), 249–270. DOI: 10.17533/udea.ikala.v27n1a12

Bhowmik, M. K. (2014). Ethnic minority students' education in Hong Kong: Rhetoric, issues and priorities. *International Journal of Comparative Education and Development, 16*, 126–140.

Bhowmik, M. K. (2017). Equitable and quality educational opportunities for Hong Kong's ethnic minorities: The challenges to achieve SDG4. *Curriculum Perspectives, 37*(2), 191–196. DOI: 10.1007/s41297-017-0030-x

Biagini, G. (2025). Towards an AI-literate future: A systematic literature review exploring education, ethics, and applications. *International Journal of Artificial Intelligence in Education, 35*(4), 2616–2666. DOI: 10.1007/s40593-025-00466-w

Biesta, G. J. J. (2015). *Beautiful risk of education*. Routledge. DOI: 10.4324/9781315635866

Bitchener, J., & Ferris, D. R. (2012). *Written corrective feedback in second language acquisition and writing*. Routledge., DOI: 10.4324/9780203832400

Blodgett, S. L., Barocas, S., Daumé Iii, H., & Wallach, H. (2020, July). Language (technology) is power: A critical survey of "bias" in NLP. In *Proceedings of the 58th annual meeting of the association for computational linguistics* (pp. 5454-5476). DOI: 10.18653/v1/2020.acl-main.485

Bocevska, A., Savoska, S., Ristevski, B., & Blazheska-Tabakovska, N. (2018). Analysis of accessibility of the e-learning platforms according to the WCAG 2.0 standard compliance. *Proceedings of the 8th International Conference on Applied Internet and Information Technologies*, 26–31. https://doi.org/DOI: 10.20544/AIIT2018.P06

Bolton, K., & Lee, S. L. (2020). A socio-historical approach to multilingualism in Hong Kong. In P. Siemund, & J. Leimgruber (Eds.), *Multilingual global cities: Hong Kong, Singapore, and Dubai* (pp. 38–62). Routledge. https://doi.org/DOI: 10.4324/9780429463860-4

Bolton, K., Bacon-Shone, J., & Lee, S. L. (2020). Societal multilingualism in Hong Kong. In P. Siemund, & J. Leimgruber (Eds.), *Multilingual global cities: Dubai, Hong Kong and Singapore* (pp. 160–184). Routledge. https://doi.org/DOI: 10.4324/9780429463860-12

Boudadi, N. A., Gutierrez-Colon, M., & Rodriguez, M. U. (2024). A Gamified learning environment (Moodle) to enhance English language learning at university level. *International Journal of Instruction*, *17*(4), 483–502. DOI: 10.29333/iji.2024.17427a

Bourdieu, P. (1986). The Forms of Capital. En J. Richardson (Ed.), *Handbook of Theory and Research for the Sociology of Education* (pp. 241–258). Greenwood.

Bourdieu, P. (1977). The economics of linguistic exchanges. *Social Sciences Information. Information Sur les Sciences Sociales*, *16*(6), 645–668. DOI: 10.1177/053901847701600601

Breidbach, S., & Küster, L. (2014). Bildung, multiliteracies, and identity: Key concepts in language education in the light of sociocultural theory and dynamic system theory. In Abendroth-Timmer, D., & Hennig, E. M. (Eds.), *Plurilingualism and multiliteracies: International research on identity construction in language education* (pp. 129–144). Peter Lang. DOI: 10.3726/978-3-653-03229-1

Breuer, E. O., & Van Steendam, E. (2021). Multiple approaches to understanding and working with multilingual (multi-)literacy. In E. O. Breuer, E. Lindgren, A. Stavans, & E. Van Steendam (Eds.), *New perspectives on language and education: Vol. 85. Multilingual literacy* (pp. 1–20). Multilingual Matters.

Brinkmann, L. M., Dikilitas, K., & Tavares, V. (forthcoming). GenAI, human biases and the "return" of language and cultural ideologies. In Tavares, V. (Ed.), *The Routledge handbook of generative AI and language teacher education*. Routledge.

Brown, H. D., & Lee, H. (2025). *Principles of language learning and teaching: A course in second language acquisition*. Taylor & Francis., DOI: 10.4324/9781003494294

Bryfonski, L., Ku, Y. Y., & Mackey, A. (2024). Research methods for IDs and TBLT: A substantive and methodological review. *Studies in Second Language Acquisition*, *46*(3), 617–643. DOI: 10.1017/S0272263124000135

Budiman, A., & Liu, X. (2025). Beyond standard English: How Global Englishes enhances creativity, reduces language anxiety, and increases willingness to communicate. *Frontiers in Psychology*, *16*, 1611630. DOI: 10.3389/fpsyg.2025.1611630 PMID: 40606868

Bulathwela, S., Pérez-Ortiz, M., Holloway, C., Cukurova, M., & Shawe-Taylor, J. (2024). Artificial intelligence alone will not democratise education: On educational inequality, techno-solutionism and inclusive tools. *Sustainability (Basel)*, *16*(2), 781. DOI: 10.3390/su16020781

Buschschlüter, V. (2026, January 3). Why has Trump attacked Venezuela and taken Maduro? *BBC News*. https://www.bbc.com/news/articles/c93n4nx5yqro

Butler, Y. G., & Huang, B. H. (Eds.). (2022). *Research methods for understanding child second language development*. Taylor & Francis., DOI: 10.4324/9780367815783

Byram, M. (1997). *Teaching and assessing intercultural communicative competence*. Multilingual Matters.

Byram, M. (2021). *Teaching and assessing intercultural communicative competence. Revisited*. Multilingual Matters. DOI: 10.21832/9781800410251

Caldwell-Harris, C. L., & Ayçiçeği-Dinn, A. (2009). Emotion and lying in a non-native language. *International Journal of Psychophysiology : Official Journal of the International Organization of Psychophysiology*, *71*(3), 193–204. DOI: 10.1016/j.ijpsycho.2008.09.006 PMID: 18929603

Calhoun, K., & Fawcett, A. (2023). "They edited out her nip nops": Linguistic innovation as textual censorship avoidance on TikTok. *Language@Internet, 21*, 1–30. https://doi.org/DOI: 10.14434/li.v21.37371

Cambridge English. (Forthcoming 2025). *Principles of good practice*.

Campbell, E. (2004). Ethical bases of moral agency in teaching. *Teachers and Teaching*, *10*(4), 409–428. DOI: 10.1080/1354060042000224142

Canagarajah, A. S. (2013). *Translingual practice: Global Englishes and cosmopolitan relations*. Routledge. DOI: 10.4324/9780203120293

Caruana, L. F., & Żammit, J. (2024). Exploring beliefs, motivations and emotions: Insights from learning Maltese as a second language. *Language Teaching Research, 13621688241289724*, 13621688241289724. Advance online publication. DOI: 10.1177/13621688241289724

Carvalho, R. (2020, August 30). Academic marginalisation of Hong Kong's ethnic minority groups increases amid coronavirus pandemic. *South China Morning Post*. https://n9.cl/x8bxrt

Casal-Otero, L., Catalá, A., Fernández-Morante, C., Taboada, M., Cebreiro, B., & Barro, S. (2023). AI literacy in K-12: A systematic literature review. *International Journal of STEM Education, 10*(1), 1–17. DOI: 10.1186/s40594-023-00418-7

CAST. (2024). *CAST Universal Design for Learning Guidelines version 3.0*. CAST. https://udlguidelines.cast.org

Cercas Curry, A., Bhatt, U., & Prabhakaran, V. (2024). The AI gap: How socioeconomic status affects language technology interactions. *arXiv preprint*. https://arxiv.org/abs/2505.12158

Chaitani, H. (2026). Artificial intelligence, ideology, and literacy: A multilectal framework for empowering criticality in adult education. In S. Kadry & B. S. (Eds.), *Artificial intelligence in education: Creating an equitable, creative, and effective learning environment*. IntechOpen. DOI: 10.5772/intechopen.1013545

Chaovanapricha, K., & Chaturongakul, P. (2020). Interdisciplinary teacher collaboration in English for specific purposes subjects in a Thai university. *English Language Teaching, 13*(5), 139–148. DOI: 10.5539/elt.v13n5p139

Chee, H., Ahn, S., & Lee, J. (2024). A competency framework for AI literacy: Variations by different learner groups and an implied learning pathway. *British Journal of Educational Technology*. Advance online publication. DOI: 10.1111/bjet.13556

Chen, L. (2023, June 23). Hong Kong rolls out first AI curriculum for junior secondary students, including lessons on ChatGPT, with 'lives definitely affected by artificial intelligence'. *South China Morning Post*. https://n9.cl/2phugf

Chen, A., Zhang, Y., Jia, J., Liang, M., Cha, Y., & Lim, C. P. (2025). A systematic review and meta-analysis of AI-enabled assessment in language learning: Design, implementation, and effectiveness. *Journal of Computer Assisted Learning, 41*(1), e13064. DOI: 10.1111/jcal.13064

Chen, C., & Manosuthikit, A. (2025). Persistent invisibilities: Discourses, identities, and investment in English as a Foreign Language among Yi minority college students in contemporary China. *LEARN Journal: Language Education and Acquisition Research Network.*, *18*(2), 264–287. DOI: 10.70730/PDJO8958

Cheng, J. K. (2015). Enhancing the Chinese writing skills of non-Chinese speaking students. *SpringerPlus*, *4*(S2), O1. DOI: 10.1186/2193-1801-4-S2-O1

Cheng, L. (2023). Delving into the role of mindfulness on the relationship among creativity, anxiety, and boredom of young EFL learners. *Heliyon*, *9*(2), e13733. Advance online publication. DOI: 10.1016/j.heliyon.2023.e13733 PMID: 36873160

Cherbow, K., & McNeill, K. L. (2022). Planning for student-driven discussions: A revelatory case of curricular sensemaking for epistemic agency. *Journal of the Learning Sciences*, *31*(3), 408–457. DOI: 10.1080/10508406.2021.2024433

Cheung, H. T. (2019). The effect of age of arrival to the development of Cantonese narrative in ethnic minority children of Hong Kong. In J. Wakefield (Ed.), *Cantonese as a second language: Issues, experiences and suggestions for teaching and learning*, (pp. 232–250). Routledge.

Chiu, T. K. F., Xia, Q., Zhou, X., Chai, C. S., & Cheng, M. (2023). Systematic literature review on opportunities, challenges, and future research recommendations of artificial intelligence in education. *Computers and Education: Artificial Intelligence*, *4*, 100118. DOI: 10.1016/j.caeai.2022.100118

Choubey, L., Shrivastava, A., & Mohanty, A. (2023). Accent bias and fairness challenges in speech recognition systems for Indian English users. *IEEE Access : Practical Innovations, Open Solutions*, *11*, 54621–54633. DOI: 10.1109/ACCESS.2023.3276617

Christensen, H., Cunningham, S., Fox, C., Green, P., & Hain, T. (2012). A comparative study of adaptive, automatic recognition of disordered speech. *Proceedings of Interspeech*, *1–4*, 1776–1779. Advance online publication. DOI: 10.21437/Interspeech.2012-484

Christoforou, M. (2025). Gen AI-assisted multimodal meaning design: Exercising a pedagogic metalanguage of transposition. *Pedagogies*, 1–25. DOI: 10.1080/1554480X.2025.2522884

Chu, M. K. (2023, August 15). [Nurturing ethnic minority youth Develop valuable human resources]. *Mingpao Daily*.

Chung, B., & Bong, H. K. M. (2022). A study on the intelligibility of Korean-accented English: Possibilities of implementing AI applications in English education. *The Journal of AsiaTEFL, 19*(1), 197–215. DOI: 10.18823/asiatefl.2022.19.1.12.197

Chu, T., & Wang, W. (2025). Exploring EFL teachers' epistemic agency and its influencing factors in an AI-integrated context through the double stimulation model. *The Asia-Pacific Education Researcher, 34*(4), 1267–1275. DOI: 10.1007/s40299-024-00940-4

Cintrón-Valentín, M. C., & Ellis, N. C. (2016). Salience in second language acquisition: Physical form, learner attention, and instructional focus. *Frontiers in Psychology, 7*, 1284. DOI: 10.3389/fpsyg.2016.01284 PMID: 27621715

Coburn, C., Penuel, W., & Geil, K. (2013). *Research-Practice Partnerships: A Strategy for Leveraging Research for Educational Improvement in School Districts.* William T. Grant Foundation. https://eric.ed.gov/?id=ED568396

Coker, H., Kalsoom, Q., & Mercieca, D. (2023). Teachers' use of knowledge in curriculum making: Implications for social justice. *Education Sciences, 14*(1), 3. DOI: 10.3390/educsci14010003

Coleman, V. (2021). *Digital divide in UK education during COVID-19 pandemic: Literature review. Cambridge Assessment Research Report*. Cambridge Assessment.

Collier, S., Burston, B., & Rhodes, A. (2016). Teaching STEM as a second language: Utilizing SLA to develop equitable learning for all students. *Journal for Multicultural Education, 10*(3), 257–273. DOI: 10.1108/JME-01-2016-0013

Cong-Lem, N., Van Bui, C. N., Nguyen, N. P. N., & Huynh, M. Q. (2025). Bridging or breaking? A systematic review of how generative AI shapes equity in foreign language education. *International Journal of Applied Linguistics*, ijal.70052. Advance online publication. DOI: 10.1111/ijal.70052

Cope, B., & Kalantzis, M. (2013). Multiliteracies. New literacies, new learning. In Hawkins, M. R. (Ed.), *Framing languages and literacies: Socially situated views and perspectives* (pp. 105–135). Routledge. DOI: 10.4324/9780203070895

Cosgrove, J., & Cachia, R. (2025). *DigComp 3.0: European Digital Competence Framework* (5th ed.). Publications Office of the European Union. DOI: 10.2760/0001149

Costanza-Chock, S. (2020). *Design justice: Community-led practices to build the worlds we need.* MIT press., DOI: 10.7551/mitpress/12255.001.0001

Couldry, N., & Mejias, U. A. (2023). The decolonial turn in data and technology research: What is at stake and where is it heading? *Information Communication and Society*, *26*(4), 786–802. DOI: 10.1080/1369118X.2021.1986102

Council of Europe. (2001). *Common European framework of reference for languages: Learning, teaching, assessment.* Council of Europe Publishing.

Council of Europe. (2007). From linguistic diversity to plurilingual education: Guide for the Development of Language Education Policies in Europe. Language Policy Unit, Council of Europe. https://rm.coe.int/16802fc1c4

Council of Europe. (2014). *Languages for democracy and social cohesion. Diversity, equity and quality. Sixty years of European co-operation.* Language Policy Unit, Council of Europe. https://rm.coe.int/languages-for-democracy-and-social-cohesion-diversity-equity-and-quali/168069e7bd

Council of Europe. (2020). *Common European framework of reference for languages: Learning, teaching, assessment — Companion volume.* Council of Europe Publishing.

Crenshaw, K. (1989). Demarginalizing the intersection of race and sex: A Black feminist critique of antidiscrimination doctrine, feminist theory and antiracist politics. *University of Chicago Legal Forum*, *1989*, 139–167. https://chicagounbound.uchicago.edu/uclf/vol1989/iss1/8

Crenshaw, K. (2013). Demarginalizing the intersection of race and sex: A black feminist critique of antidiscrimination doctrine, feminist theory and antiracist politics. In Maschke, K. (Ed.), *Feminist legal theories* (pp. 23–51). Routledge.

Crenshaw, K. W. (1991). Mapping the margins: Intersectionality, identity politics, and violence against women of color. *Stanford Law Review*, *43*(6), 1241–1299. DOI: 10.2307/1229039

Crenshaw, K. W. (1994). Mapping the margins: Intersectionality, identity politics, and violence against women of color. In Fineman, M. A. (Ed.), *The public nature of private violence: Women and the discovery of abuse* (pp. 93–118). Routledge.

Creswell, J. W. (2009). *Research design: Qualitative, quantitative, and mixed methods approaches.* Sage publications.

Crompton, H., & Burke, D. (2023). Artificial intelligence in higher education: The state of the field. *International Journal of Educational Technology in Higher Education*, *20*(1), 22. DOI: 10.1186/s41239-023-00392-8

Crookes, G. V. (2021). Critical language pedagogy: An introduction to principles and values. *ELT Journal*, *75*(3), 247–255. DOI: 10.1093/elt/ccab020

Cucchiarini, C., Neri, A., & Strik, H. (2009). Oral proficiency training in Dutch L2: The contribution of ASR-based corrective feedback. *Speech Communication*, *51*(10), 853–863. DOI: 10.1016/j.specom.2009.03.003

Cui, W., & Zhang, J. (2025). AI applications in language learning: Improving speaking fluency and pronunciation using chatbots and speech feedback. *Interactive Learning Environments*. Advance online publication. DOI: 10.1080/10494820.2025.2546634

Cummins, J. (2015). Intercultural education and academic achievement: A framework for school-based policies in multilingual schools. *Intercultural Education*, *26*(6), 455–468. DOI: 10.1080/14675986.2015.1103539

Cummins, J. (2023). Critical multilingual language awareness: The role of teachers as language activists and knowledge generators. *Language Awareness*, *32*(4), 560–573. DOI: 10.1080/09658416.2023.2285361

Daher, R. (2025). Integrating AI literacy into teacher education: A critical perspective paper. *Discover Artificial Intelligence*, *5*(1), 217. Advance online publication. DOI: 10.1007/s44163-025-00475-7

Dalton, B., & Strangman, N. (2006). Improving struggling readers' comprehension through scaffolded hypertexts and other computer-based literacy programs. In McKenna, M. C., Labbo, L. D., Kieffer, R. D., & Reinking, D. (Eds.), *International handbook of literacy and technology* (Vol. 2, pp. 75–92). Lawrence Erlbaum Associates.

Dang, T. K. A., Nguyen, H. T., & Le, T. T. (2023). Adaptive learning technologies in Asian EFL classrooms: A systematic review. *Education and Information Technologies*, *28*(6), 7421–7445. DOI: 10.1007/s10639-022-11481-y

Darling-Hammond, L. (2017). Teacher education around the world: What can we learn from international practice? *European Journal of Teacher Education*, *40*(3), 291–309. DOI: 10.1080/02619768.2017.1315399

Darvin, R. (2025). Identity and investment in the age of generative AI. *Annual Review of Applied Linguistics*, *45*, 10–27. DOI: 10.1017/S0267190525100135

Darvin, R., & Norton, B. (2015). Identity and a model of investment in applied linguistics. *Annual Review of Applied Linguistics*, *35*, 36–56. DOI: 10.1017/S0267190514000191

Dar, Z. K., Shams, M. R., & Rahimi, A. (2010). Teaching reading with a critical attitude: Using critical discourse analysis (CDA) to raise EFL university students' critical language awareness (CLA). *International Journal of Criminology & Sociological Theory*, *3*(2), 457–476. https://ijcst.journals.yorku.ca/index.php/ijcst/article/view/30585

Davin, K. J., Kissau, S., Haudeck, H., Ade-Thurow, B., Gómez-Pereira, D., Oon, P. T., & Dornburg, A. (2026). Global and educational disparities in AI integration: A study of L2 teacher training and usage patterns. *System, 136*, 103901. DOI: 10.1016/j.system.2025.103901

Davoodi, A. (2024). EQUAL AI: A framework for enhancing equity, quality, understanding and accessibility in liberal arts through AI for multilingual learners. *Language, Technology, and Social Media, 2*(2), 178–203. DOI: 10.70211/ltsm.v2i2.139

De Bot, K., Lowie, W., & Verspoor, M. (2005). *Second language acquisition: An advanced resource book*. Psychology Press., DOI: 10.4324/9780203446416

de la Fuente, M. J., & Goldenberg, C. (2022). Understanding the role of the first language (L1) in instructed second language acquisition (ISLA): Effects of using a principled approach to L1 in the beginner foreign language classroom. *Language Teaching Research, 26*(5), 943–962. DOI: 10.1177/1362168820921882

de Sousa Santos, B. (2014). *Epistemologies of the South: Justice against epistemicide*. Routledge.

Decreto-Lei n.º 79/2014, de 14 de maio [Decree-Law No. 79/2014 of 14 May]. *Diário da República*, 1.ª série, n.º 92.

Decreto-Lei n.º 9-A/2025, de 14 de fevereiro [Decree-Law No. 9-A/2025 of 14 February]. *Diário da República*, 1.ª série, n.º 32, Suplemento.

DeFrancis, J. (1984). *The Chinese language: Fact and fantasy*. University of Hawaii Press. DOI: 10.1515/9780824840303

Delgado, R., & Stefancic, J. (2023). *Critical race theory: An introduction* (4th ed.). New York University Press.

Derakhshan, A., Teo, T., Saeedy Robat, E., Janebi Enayat, M., & Jahanbakhsh, A. A. (2024). Robot-assisted language learning: A meta-analysis. *Review of Educational Research, 00346543241247227*. Advance online publication. DOI: 10.3102/00346543241247227

Derakhshan, A., & Zare, J. (2023). The impact of altruistic teaching on English as a foreign language (EFL) learners' emotion regulation: An intervention study. *Brain Sciences, 13*(3), 458. DOI: 10.3390/brainsci13030458 PMID: 36979269

Desai, H. (2025). What's worth measuring? The future of assessment in the AI age. Retrieved March 25, 2026, from UNESCO website: https://www.unesco.org/en/articles/whats-worth-measuring-future-assessment-ai-age#:~:text=AI%20detection%20tools%20have%20proven,means%20is%20likely%20closing%20permanently

Dewaele, J. M. (2005). Investigating the psychological and emotional dimensions in instructed language learning: Obstacles and possibilities. *Modern Language Journal, 89*(3), 367–380. DOI: 10.1111/j.1540-4781.2005.00311.x

Dewaele, J. M., Özdemir, C., Karci, D., Uysal, S., Özdemir, E. D., & Balta, N. (2022). How distinctive is the foreign language enjoyment and foreign language classroom anxiety of Kazakh learners of Turkish? *Applied Linguistics Review, 13*(2), 243–265. DOI: 10.1515/applirev-2019-0021

DGEEC. (2025). Inscritos no Ensino Superior Resultados do Inquérito Registo de Alunos Inscritos e Diplomados do Ensino Superior (RAIDES). In *E.* https://www.dgeec.medu.pt/api/ficheiros/68d54caac94dd8ed9f2a4992

DGEEC. (2025, September 26). *Inscritos em mobilidade internacional de grau.* Direção Geral de Estatísticas Da Educação e Ciência. https://www.dgeec.medu.pt/art/ensino-superior/estatisticas/vagas-e-inscritos/65772c531c5ebb42fe23c8c5

Dixon, L. Q., Zhao, J., Shin, J. Y., Wu, S., Su, J. H., Burgess-Brigham, R., Gezer, M. U., & Snow, C. (2012). What we know about second language acquisition: A synthesis from four perspectives. *Review of Educational Research, 82*(1), 5–60. DOI: 10.3102/0034654311433587

Dörnyei, Z. (2009). The L2 motivational self system. In Dornyei, Z., & Ushioda, E. (Eds.), *Motivation, language identity and the L2 self.* Multilingual Matters. DOI: 10.21832/9781847691293-003

Douglas Fir Group. (2016). A transdisciplinary framework for SLA in a multilingual world. *Modern Language Journal, 100*(S1), 19–47. DOI: 10.1111/modl.12301

Driver, M. (2022). Emotion-laden texts and words: The influence of emotion on vocabulary learning for heritage and foreign language learners. *Studies in Second Language Acquisition, 44*(4), 1071–1094. DOI: 10.1017/S0272263121000851

Driver, M. Y. (2023). Measuring and understanding linguistic insecurity in heritage and foreign language contexts: Design and validation of a novel scale. *Journal of Multilingual and Multicultural Development,* •••, 1–20. DOI: 10.1080/01434632.2023.2265901

Du, J., & Daniel, B. K. (2024). Transforming language education: A systematic review of AI-powered chatbots for English as a foreign language speaking practice. *Computers and Education: Artificial Intelligence, 6,* 100230. DOI: 10.1016/j.caeai.2024.100230

Dunkel, P. (1991). Listening in the native and second/foreign language: Toward an integration of research and practice. *TESOL Quarterly*, *25*(3), 431–457. DOI: 10.2307/3586979

Ebadi, S., Velayati, S., Ramezanzadeh, A., & Salman, A. R. (2025). Exploring the impact of AI-powered speaking tasks on EFL learners' speaking performance and anxiety: An activity theory study. *Acta Psychologica*, *259*, 105391. DOI: 10.1016/j.actpsy.2025.105391 PMID: 40812259

Education Bureau. (2026, April 20). *[Chinese language education]*. Education Bureau. https://n9.cl/yvdl5

Ekizer, F. N. (2025). Exploring the impact of artificial intelligence on English language teaching: A meta-analysis. *Acta Psychologica*, *260*, 105649. DOI: 10.1016/j.actpsy.2025.105649 PMID: 41066858

Ellis, R., & Sheen, Y. (2006). Reexamining the role of recasts in second language acquisition. *Studies in Second Language Acquisition*, *28*(4), 575–600. DOI: 10.1017/S027226310606027X

Elsayed, A. M., Kholikov, A., Abdullayeva, I., Al-Farouni, M., & Wodajo, M. R. (2024). Teacher support in AI-assisted exams: An experimental study to inspect the effects on demotivation, anxiety management in exams, L2 learning experience, and academic success. *Language Testing in Asia*, *14*(1), 53. DOI: 10.1186/s40468-024-00328-7

Engh, D. (2013). Why use music in English language learning? A survey of the literature. *English Language Teaching*, *6*(2), 113–127. DOI: 10.5539/elt.v6n2p113

Esmaeilzadeh, F., Ghahari, S., & Rohani, G. (2025). Artificial intelligence in language teaching and assessment: A systematic review of research (2020-2024). *The Asian Journal of Applied Linguistics*, *9*(1), 1222–1222. DOI: 10.25442/hku.30888980

Etikan, I., Musa, S. A., & Alkassim, R. S. (2016). Comparison of convenience sampling and purposive sampling. *American Journal of Theoretical and Applied Statistics*, *5*(1), 1–4. DOI: 10.11648/j.ajtas.20160501.11

Eubanks, V. (2018). *Automating inequality: How high-tech tools profile, police, and punish the poor*. St. Martin's Press.

European Center for Not-for-Profit Law. (2025, November 11). *Blueprint for rights-centered AI in public participation*. European Center for Not-for-Profit Law. https://bit.ly/4sDhnHF

European Commission. (2021). *Digital Education Action Plan (2021–2027)*. Publications Office of the European Union. https://n9.cl/nk38l

European Commission. (2026). *Languages in the EU – why multilingualism matters.* https://translation.ec.europa.eu/languages-eu-why-multilingualism-matters_en

European Commission/EACEA/Eurydice. (2021). *Teachers in Europe: Careers, development and well-being*. Publications Office of the European Union. https://n9.cl/36ql1g

European Parliament and Council of the European Union. (2024). Regulation (EU) 2024/1689 of the European Parliament and of the Council of 13 June 2024 laying down harmonised rules on artificial intelligence (Artificial Intelligence Act). *Official Journal of the European Union*, 1689. https://n9.cl/k1ka6

Fairclough, N. (2014). Introduction. In Fairclough, N. (Ed.), *Real language series. Critical language awareness* (pp. 1–30). Taylor and Francis. (Original work published 1992) DOI: 10.4324/9781315845661-7

Farahani, M., & Ghasemi, G. (2024). Artificial intelligence and inequality: Challenges and opportunities. *International Journal of Innovation in Education*, *9*, 78–99. DOI: 10.32388/7HWUZ2

Farrell, C., Penuel, W., Coburn, C., Daniel, J., & Steup, L. (2021). *Research-practice partnerships in education: The state of the field.* William T. Grant Foundation. https://eric.ed.gov/?id=ED615899

Farrelly, T., & Baker, N. (2023). Generative artificial intelligence: Implications and considerations for higher education practice. *Education Sciences*, *13*(11), 1109. DOI: 10.3390/educsci13111109

Farrow, J., Farrow, M. J., & Zhang, C. (2025). Advancing Translational Science Through AI-Enhanced Teacher Learning for Early Language and Composing. *Education Sciences, 15*(11), 1496. DOI: 10.3390/educsci15111496

Fataar, A. (2025, October 29). *Decolonising the algorithm: Teaching for justice in age of AI.* University World News. https://bit.ly/4upYaLg

Ferris, D. (2011). *Treatment of error in second language student writing*. University of Michigan Press., DOI: 10.3998/mpub.2173290

Fettes, M., & Karamouzian, F. M. (2018). Inclusion in education: Challenges for linguistic policy and research. In *Language policy and language acquisition planning* (pp. 219–235). Springer International Publishing., DOI: 10.1007/978-3-319-75963-0_13

Feuerriegel, S., Hartmann, J., Janiesch, C., & Zschech, P. (2024). Generative AI. *Business & Information Systems Engineering, 66*(1), 111–126. DOI: 10.1007/s12599-023-00834-7

Figueroa, M. (2024). Language development, linguistic input, and linguistic racism. *Wiley Interdisciplinary Reviews. Cognitive Science, 15*(3), e1673. DOI: 10.1002/wcs.1673 PMID: 38297101

Filiz, O., Kaya, M. H., & Adiguzel, T. (2025). Teachers and AI: Understanding the factors influencing AI integration in K-12 education. *Education and Information Technologies, 30*(13), 17931–17967. DOI: 10.1007/s10639-025-13463-2

Finegan, E. (2012). Language: Its structure and use. (6th ed.). Wadsworth Cengage learning.

Fisher, L., Evans, M., Forbes, K., Gayton, A., Liu, Y., & Rutgers, D. (2024). Language experiences, evaluations and emotions (3Es): Analysis of structural models of multilingual identity for language learners in schools in England. *International Journal of Multilingualism, 21*(1), 418–438. DOI: 10.1080/14790718.2022.2060235

Fjeld, J., Achten, N., Hilligoss, H., Nagy, A., & Srikumar, M. (2020). *Principled artificial intelligence: Mapping consensus in ethical and rights-based approaches to principles for AI*. SSRN Electronic Paper Collection. https://doi.org/DOI: 10.2139/ssrn.3518482

Flores, N., & Rosa, J. (2015). Undoing appropriateness: Raciolinguistic ideologies and language diversity in education. *Harvard Educational Review, 85*(2), 149–171. DOI: 10.17763/0017-8055.85.2.149

Florian, L., & Black-Hawkins, K. (2011). Exploring inclusive pedagogy. *British Educational Research Journal, 37*(5), 813–828. DOI: 10.1080/01411926.2010.501096

Fraschini, N. (2023). Language learners' emotional dynamics: Insights from a Q methodology intensive single-case study. *Language, Culture and Curriculum, 36*(2), 222–239. DOI: 10.1080/07908318.2022.2133137

Fraser, N. (2008). Abnormal justice. *Critical Inquiry, 34*(3), 393–422. DOI: 10.1086/589478

Fraser, N. (2010). Injustice at intersecting scales: On 'social exclusion'and the 'global poor'. *European Journal of Social Theory, 13*(3), 363–371. DOI: 10.1177/1368431010371758

Freiermuth, M. R. (2020). Introduction and overview: the inescapable confluence of technology, psychology and second language learners and users. In *Technology and the psychology of second language learners and users* (pp. 3–32). Springer International Publishing., DOI: 10.1007/978-3-030-34212-8_1

Freire, P. (1970). Pedagogy of the Oppressed (trans. MB Ramos). *New York: Continuum, 2005.*

Freire, P. (1970). *Pedagogy of the oppressed.* Herder & Herder.

Fricker, M. (2007). *Epistemic Injustice: Power and the Ethics of Knowing.* Oxford University Press. DOI: 10.1093/acprof:oso/9780198237907.001.0001

Fryer, L. K., Li, C., Guo, Z., Liang, L., & Zhong, Y. (2025). Self-efficacy's role within learning a new language during formal education: Systematic review, critical evaluation of past research and paths forward for research and practice. *Studies in Second Language Learning and Teaching, 15*(2), 251–278. DOI: 10.14746/ssllt.48234

Galaczi, E., & Luckin, R. (2024). *Generative AI and language education: Opportunities, challenges and the need for critical perspectives.* https://sl1nk.com/1k48i8d

Gallegos, I. O., Rossi, R. A., Barrow, J., Tanjim, M. M., Kim, S., Dernoncourt, F., Yu, T., Zhang, R., & Ahmed, N. K. (2024). Bias and fairness in large language models: A survey. *Computational Linguistics, 50*(3), 1097–1179. DOI: 10.1162/coli_a_00524

Gao, F., & Gube, J. (2020). Multicultural education: How are ethnic minorities labelled and educated in post-handover Hong Kong? *Migration and Language Education, 2*(3), 51–59. DOI: 10.29140/mle.v1n2.363

García, O., Bartlett, L., & Kleifgen, J. (2007). From biliteracy to pluriliteracies. In P. Auer, L. Wei, W. Li, K. Knapp & G. Antos (Eds.), *Handbooks of applied linguistics: Vol. 5. Handbook of multilingualism and multilingual communication* (pp. 207–228). Mouton de Gruyter. DOI: 10.1515/9783110198553.2.207

García, O. (2009). *Bilingual education in the 21st Century: A global perspective.* Wiley/Blackwell.

García, O. (2017). Critical multilingual language awareness and teacher education. In Cenoz, J., Gorter, D., & May, S. (Eds.), *Encyclopedia of language and education* (3rd ed., pp. 263–280). Springer. DOI: 10.1007/978-3-319-02240-6_30

García, O., & Otheguy, R. (2020). Plurilingualism and translanguaging: Commonalities and divergences. *International Journal of Bilingual Education and Bilingualism, 23*(1), 17–35. DOI: 10.1080/13670050.2019.1598932

García, O., & Wei, L. (2015). Translanguaging in education: Principles, implications and challenges. In *Translanguaging: Language, bilingualism and education* (pp. 119–135). Palgrave Macmillan UK., DOI: 10.1057/9781137385765_8

Gass, S. M., & Mackey, A. (2014). Input, interaction, and output in second language acquisition. In *Theories in second language acquisition* (pp. 194–220). Routledge., DOI: 10.4324/9780203808184

Georgiou, G. P. (2026). Envisioning the futures of language education in the era of artificial intelligence. *Journal of Futures Studies*, 1–14. https://bit.ly/46VE01E

Ghiasvand, F., & Seyri, H. (2025). A collaborative reflection on the synergy of Artificial Intelligence (AI) and language teacher identity reconstruction. *Teaching and Teacher Education, 160*, 105022. DOI: 10.1016/j.tate.2025.105022

Gilmore, A. (2007). Authentic materials and authenticity in foreign language learning. *Language Teaching, 40*(2), 97–118. DOI: 10.1017/S0261444807004144

Giroux, H. A. (2020). *On critical pedagogy*. Bloomsbury. DOI: 10.5040/9781350145016

Godfroid, A., & Andringa, S. (2023). Uncovering sampling biases, advancing inclusivity, and rethinking theoretical accounts in second language acquisition: Introduction to the special issue SLA for all? *Language Learning, 73*(4), 981–1002. DOI: 10.1111/lang.12620

Godwin-Jones, R. (2021). Big data and language learning: Opportunities and challenges. *Language Learning & Technology, 25*(1), 4–19. https://bit.ly/414kkFl. DOI: 10.64152/10125/44747

Godwin-Jones, R. (2022). Partnering with AI: Intelligent writing assistance and instructed language learning. *Language Learning & Technology, 26*(2), 5–24. DOI: 10.64152/10125/73474

Godwin-Jones, R. (2023). Emerging spaces for language learning: AI bots, ambient intelligence, and the metaverse. *Language Learning & Technology, 27*(2), 6–27. https://hdl.handle.net/10125/73501. DOI: 10.64152/10125/73501

Goetze, J., & Driver, M. (2022). Is learning really just believing? A meta-analysis of self-efficacy and achievement in SLA. *Studies in Second Language Learning and Teaching, 12*(2), 233–259. DOI: 10.14746/ssllt.2022.12.2.4

Golonka, E. M., Bowles, A. R., Frank, V. M., Richardson, D. L., & Freynik, S. (2012). Technologies for foreign language learning: A review of technology types and their effectiveness. *Computer Assisted Language Learning, 27*(1), 70–105. DOI: 10.1080/09588221.2012.700315

Gómez, D. C. (2020). The third digital divide and Bourdieu: Bidirectional conversion of economic, cultural, and social capital to (and from) digital capital among young people in Madrid. *New Media & Society*, *23*(9), 2534–2553. DOI: 10.1177/1461444820933252

Gonzales, S. (2024). AI literacy and the new digital divide-A global call for action. *Paris, France: UNESCO. Retrieved March*, *30*, 2025.

Google. (2021). *Project Euphonia: Improving speech recognition for non-standard speech*. Google. https://sites.research.google/euphonia/about/

Goossens, S. (2022). Embracing multilingualism, experiencing old tensions. Promoting and problematising language at a self-declared multilingual school. *Journal of Multilingual and Multicultural Development*, *43*(4), 309–322. DOI: 10.1080/01434632.2019.1633335

Gorski, P. (2016). Rethinking the role of "culture" in educational equity: From cultural competence to equity literacy. *Multicultural Perspectives*, *18*(4), 221–226. DOI: 10.1080/15210960.2016.1228344

Gregersen, T., MacIntyre, P. D., & Meza, M. (2016). Positive psychology exercises build social capital for language learners: Preliminary evidence. DOI: 10.2307/jj.30945667.9

Gruba, P. (2004). Computer assisted language learning (CALL). The handbook of applied linguistics, 623-648. DOI: 10.1002/9780470757000.ch25

Guerriero, S. (Ed.). (2017). *Pedagogical knowledge and the changing nature of the teaching profession* (Educational Research and Innovation). OECD Publishing. DOI: 10.1787/9789264270695-en

Gu, J., & Liu, Q. (2025). Enhancing Chinese EFL university students' self-regulated learning through AI chatbot intervention: Insights from achievement goal theory. *Learning and Motivation*, *92*, 102191. DOI: 10.1016/j.lmot.2025.102191

Gumiero, R., & de Araújo, K. (2019). Contribuition of Paulo Freire and Célestin Freinet to the process of teaching-learning. *Acta Scientiarum. Education*, •••, 41.

Hajizadeh, S., Salman, A. R., & Ebadi, S. (2023). Evaluating language learning applications from efl learners' perspectives: The case of mondly. DOI: 10.21203/rs.3.rs-3011332/v1

Hamilton, L. S., Kaufman, J. H., & Diliberti, M. (2020). *Teaching and leading through a pandemic: Key findings from the American Educator Panels COVID-19 studies*. RAND Corporation., DOI: 10.7249/RRA168-2

Harasim, L. (2017). Learning Theory and Online Technologies. In *Learning Theory and Online Technologies* (2nd ed.). Routledge., DOI: 10.4324/9781315716831-6

Hargreaves, E., Buchanan, D., & Quick, L. (2025). *Children's life-histories in primary schools: Imagining schooling as a positive experience*. Palgrave Macmillan. DOI: 10.1007/978-3-031-69445-5

Hejazi, S. Y., Sadoughi, M., & Peng, J. E. (2023). The structural relationship between teacher support and willingness to communicate: The mediation of L2 anxiety and the moderation of growth language mindset. *Journal of Psycholinguistic Research, 52*(6), 2955–2978. DOI: 10.1007/s10936-023-10026-9 PMID: 37935808

Helm, P., Gábor, B., Koch, G., & Giunchiglia, F. (2024). Diversity and language technology: How language modeling bias causes epistemic injustice. *Ethics and Information Technology, 26*(8), 8. Advance online publication. DOI: 10.1007/s10676-023-09742-6

High-Level Expert Group on Artificial Intelligence. (2018). *A definition of AI: Main capabilities and scientific disciplines*. European Commission. https://sl1nk.com/a1z8cpg

Hoang, V. Q. (2024, November). Fostering Willingness to Communicate in Online Educational Environments: Opportunities and Challenges. In *The 2nd International Conference: Resiliency by Technology and Design (RTD 2024)* (pp. 272-286). Atlantis Press. DOI: 10.2991/978-94-6463-583-6_13

Ho, C. S. M., & Lee, J. C.-K. (2025). From intuition to action: Exploring teachers' ethical awareness in the use of AI tools in education. *Computers and Education: Artificial Intelligence, 9*, 100502. DOI: 10.1016/j.caeai.2025.100502

Hockly, N. (2023). Artificial intelligence in English language teaching: The good, the bad and the ugly. *RELC Journal, 54*(2), 445–451. DOI: 10.1177/00336882231168504

Hofer, B. K., & Pintrich, P. R. (1997). The development of epistemological theories: Beliefs about knowledge and knowing and their relation to learning. *Review of Educational Research, 67*(1), 88–140. DOI: 10.3102/00346543067001088

Holliday, A. (2015). Native-speakerism: Taking the concept forward and achieving cultural belief. In *(En) countering native-speakerism: Global perspectives* (pp. 11–25). Springer.

Holmes, W., Porayska-Pomsta, K., Holstein, K., Sutherland, E., Baker, T., Shum, S. B., Santos, O. C., Rodrigo, M. T., Cukurova, M., Bittencourt, I. I., & Koedinger, K. R. (2021). Ethics of AI in education: Towards a community-wide framework. *International Journal of Artificial Intelligence in Education, 32*(3), 504–526. DOI: 10.1007/s40593-021-00239-1

Holmes, W., & Tuomi, I. (2022). State of the art and practice in AI in education. *European Journal of Education, 57*(4), 542–570. DOI: 10.1111/ejed.12533

Hong Kong Government. (2016). *The Hong Kong poverty situation report on ethnic minorities*. Census and Statistics Department, Hong Kong Government. https://n9.cl/3mn1sh

Hong Kong Government. (2021). *Population census*. Census and Statistics Department, Hong Kong Government. https://n9.cl/fg5adc

Hong Kong Policy Research Institute. (2019, March 1). *The study for Chinese language proficiency of the non-language subjects textbooks used in primary and secondary schools*. Hong Kong Policy Research Institute. https://n9.cl/wu8h0l

Hong Kong Unison. (2018, January 1). *A comprehensive review of learning and teaching of Chinese for ethnic minority students in Hong Kong 2006-2016*. Hong Kong Unison.

Hong, X., & Guo, L. (2025). Effects of AI-enhanced multi-display language teaching systems on learning motivation, cognitive load management, and learner autonomy. *Education and Information Technologies, 30*(12), 1–35. DOI: 10.1007/s10639-025-13472-1

Horwitz, E. K. (2020). *Becoming a language teacher: A practical guide to second language learning and teaching*. Castledown Publishers., DOI: 10.29140/9780648184416

Huang, F., Wang, Y., & Zhang, H. (2024). Modelling Generative AI Acceptance, Perceived Teachers' Enthusiasm and Self-Efficacy to English as a Foreign Language Learners' Well-Being in the Digital Era. *European Journal of Education, 59*(4), e12770. DOI: 10.1111/ejed.12770

Huang, X. (2019). Understanding Bourdieu - Cultural Capital and Habitus. *Review of European Studies, 11*(3), 45. Advance online publication. DOI: 10.5539/res.v11n3p45

Huang, X., Wu, Y., & Dou, A. (2024). AI-enhanced task-based language teaching: Fostering personalized college English learning. *Frontiers in Educational Research, 7*(10). Advance online publication. DOI: 10.25236/FER.2024.071033

Huang, X., Zou, D., Cheng, G., Chen, X., & Xie, H. (2023). Trends, research issues and applications of AI in language education. *Journal of Educational Technology & Society*, *26*(1), 112–131. DOI: 10.30191/ETS.202301_26(1).0009

Hubbard, P., & Schulze, M. (2025). AI and the future of language teaching: Motivating sustained integrated professional development. [IJCALLT]. *International Journal of Computer-Assisted Language Learning and Teaching*, *15*(1), 1–17. DOI: 10.4018/IJCALLT.378304

Huertas-Abril, C. A. (2025). Machine Learning. In McCallum, L., & Tafazoli, D. (Eds.), *The Palgrave Encyclopedia of Computer-Assisted Language Learning*. Palgrave Macmillan. DOI: 10.1007/978-3-031-51447-0_104-1

Huertas-Abril, C. A., & Palacios-Hidalgo, F. J. (2025). Artificial intelligence–assisted language learning for all in the new global context: Threats and opportunities. In Wei, W., & Schnell, J. (Eds.), *The Routledge handbook of endangered and minority languages* (pp. 355–376). Routledge. DOI: 10.4324/9781003439493-27

Hung, H. T. (2017). Design-based research: Redesign of an English language course using a flipped classroom approach. *TESOL Quarterly*, *51*(1), 180–192. DOI: 10.1002/tesq.328

Hutchinson, T., & Waters, A. (1987). *English for specific purposes: A learning-centred approach*. Cambridge University Press. DOI: 10.1017/CBO9780511733031

Hwang, W. Y., Luthfi, M. I., & Liu, Y. F. (2024). AI-enhanced video drama-making for improving writing and speaking skills of students learning English as a foreign language. *Innovation in Language Learning and Teaching*, •••, 1–18. DOI: 10.1080/17501229.2024.2437655

Hyland, K. (2019). *Second language writing*. Cambridge university press., DOI: 10.1017/9781108635547

Hyland, K. (2022). English for specific purposes: What is it and where is it taking us? *ESP Today*, *10*(2), 202–220. DOI: 10.18485/esptoday.2022.10.2.1

Ignatius, D. (2025). *Language, Identity, and Integration: From the Tower of Babel to Contemporary Indian Language Policy*. BITS – Journal of Business, IT, and Social Science. DOI: 10.51470/BITS.2025.04.02.34

ILTA. (2002/2018). *Code of ethics*. https://www.iltaonline.com/page/CodeofEthics

Ilyashenko, L., Markova, S., Mironov, A., Vaganova, O., & Smirnova, Z. (2019). Ambiente educativo como recurso de desarrollo para el proceso de aprendizaje |Educational environment as a development resource for the learning process. *Amazonia Investiga, 8*(11), 303–312. https://amazoniainvestiga.info/index.php/amazonia/article/view/312/287

Ingram, M. (2025). The role of AI in language preservation and revitalization. In Ardalan, I. D., Banifatemi, A., Gonzalez, F., Ingram, M., Moradinezhad, R., & Williams, L. (Eds.), *AI for community: Preserving culture and tradition* (pp. 55–80). Chapman and Hall/CRC. DOI: 10.1201/9781003517115-5

Institute for Ethical AI in Education. (2021). *The ethical framework for AI in education*. Institute for Ethical AI in Education. https://l1nq.com/cLnaq

Ironsi, C. S., & Bostanci, H. B. (2026). Enhancing the reading comprehension and autonomy of foreign language students using generative AI-integrated assistant. *Frontiers in Education, Volume 11-2026*. Retrieved from https://www.frontiersin.org/journals/education/articles/10.3389/feduc.2026.1763238

Islam, M. K., Sarker, M. F. H., & Islam, M. S. (2022). Promoting student-centred blended learning in higher education: A model. *E-Learning and Digital Media, 19*(1), 36–54. DOI: 10.1177/20427530211027721

Ismayilli, F. (2025). The Role of Positive Emotional Atmosphere in Enhancing Foreign Language Acquisition. *Porta Universorum, 1*(3), 186–213. DOI: 10.69760/portuni.010316

Ja'afreh, H., & Al-Saudi, J. (2024). Language variation, regional identities, and social perceptions of Karak and Amman dialects in Jordan: A comparative study. International *Journal of Linguistics. Literature and Translation*, *7*(9), 70–78. DOI: 10.32996/ijllt.2024.7.9.9

Janfada, M., Heidari, E., & Lin, A. (2025). Transcending multiliteracies pedagogies in, for, through AI-oriented learning spaces: A dialogic perspective. *Pedagogies*, 1–23. DOI: 10.1080/1554480X.2025.2563621

Jantakoon, T., Jantakun, T., Jantakun, K., Pongpanich, W., Pasmala, R., Wannapiroon, P., & Nilsook, P. (2025). The effectiveness of artificial intelligence in English instruction for speaking and listening skills: A meta-analysis. *Contemporary Educational Technology, 17*(4), ep596. Advance online publication. DOI: 10.30935/cedtech/17310

Jelson, A., Manesh, D., Jang, A., Dunlap, D., Kim, Y.-H., & Lee, S. W. (2025). An empirical study to understand how students use ChatGPT for writing essays. *ArXiv Preprint ArXiv:2501.10551.*

Jenkins, O. C., Lopresti, D., & Mitchell, M. (2020). *Next wave artificial intelligence: Robust, explainable, adaptable, ethical, and accountable.* https://sl1nk.com/gkychk7

Jeon, J., Lee, S., & Choe, H. (2023). Beyond ChatGPT: A conceptual framework and systematic review of speech-recognition chatbots for language learning. *Computers & Education, 206*, 104898. DOI: 10.1016/j.compedu.2023.104898

Jesudas, R. (2025, June). Empowering language learning: The role of AI in enhancing language skills. In. AIP Conference Proceedings: Vol. 3306. *No. 1* (p. 050023). AIP Publishing LLC., DOI: 10.1063/5.0278362

Jiang, L., & Gu, M. M. (2025). Advocating linguistic justice through digital multimodal composing against GenAI biases: A case study of multilingual youths in an EMI university. *Journal of Multilingual and Multicultural Development*, 1–17. DOI: 10.1080/01434632.2025.2526103

Jiang, L., Li, H., & Sun, T. (2023). Generative AI in academic writing: Impacts on learner agency and writing development. *Computers & Education: Artificial Intelligence, 4*, 100128. DOI: 10.1016/j.caeai.2023.100128

Joint Committee on Testing Practices. (1988/2002). *Code of fair testing practices in education.* https://www.apa.org/science/programs/testing/fair-testing.pdf

Jouitteau, M. (2023). Guide de survie des langues minorisées à l'heure de l'intelligence artificielle: Appel aux communautés parlantes [A survival guide for minority languages in the age of artificial intelligence: A call to speaking communities]. *Lapurdum, 6*, 1–15.

Junta de Andalucía. (2005). *Plan de Fomento del Plurilingüismo en Andalucía [Plan to Promote Multilingualism in Andalusia].* Junta de Andalucía. https://n9.cl/w5jc66

Junta de Andalucía. (2016). *Plan Estratégico de Desarrollo de las Lenguas en Andalucía. Horizonte 2020 [Strategic Plan for Language Development in Andalusia. Horizon 2020].* Junta de Andalucía. https://n9.cl/dt2r7

Junta de Andalucía. (n.d.). *Transformación digital educativa [Digital transformation in education].* Junta de Andalucía. https://n9.cl/98465

Kahn, P., Carrigan, M., Smith, P., Murtagh, L., Liu, R., & Song, F. (2025). Teacher agency and generative artificial intelligence: Teaching in higher education as a responsive, cultural activity. *Learning, Media and Technology*, •••, 1–12. DOI: 10.1080/17439884.2025.2575993

Kalantzis, M., & Cope, B. (2025). Literacy in the time of artificial intelligence. *Reading Research Quarterly*, *60*(1), e591. DOI: 10.1002/rrq.591

Kangas, S. E. (2014). When special education trumps ESL: An investigation of service delivery for ELLs with disabilities. *Critical Inquiry in Language Studies*, *11*(4), 273–306. DOI: 10.1080/15427587.2014.968070

Kang, O., & Hirschi, K. (2025). Bias and stereotyping: Human and artificial intelligence (AI). *Annual Review of Applied Linguistics*, *45*, 69–84. DOI: 10.1017/S026719052500008X

Kannadhasan, M. (2025). Next-Gen language pedagogy: Leveraging generative AI to support inclusive English language learning. *International Journal of Teaching. Learning and Education*, *4*(5), 638368. DOI: 10.22161/ijtle.4.5.7

Karaca, A., & Kılcan, B. (2023). The adventure of artificial intelligence technology in education: Comprehensive scientific mapping analysis. *Participatory Educational Research*, *10*(4), 144–165. DOI: 10.17275/per.23.64.10.4

Karakaya, K., & Bozkurt, A. (2022). Mobile-assisted language learning (MALL) research trends and patterns through bibliometric analysis: Empowering language learners through ubiquitous educational technologies. *System*, *110*, 102925. DOI: 10.1016/j.system.2022.102925

Kardel, L., Ehmke, T., & Lemmerich, S. (2025). Exploring pre- and in-service teachers' (non-)critical cultural and multilingual awareness and responsiveness in classroom situations through voice-recorded video-based assessment. *Teaching and Teacher Education*, *157*, 104962. Advance online publication. DOI: 10.1016/j.tate.2025.104962

Kasneci, E., Sessler, K., Küchemann, S., Bannert, M., Dementieva, D., Fischer, F., Gasser, U., Groh, G., Günnemann, S., Hüllermeier, E., Krusche, S., Kutyniok, G., Michaeli, T., Nerdel, C., Pfeffer, J., Poquet, O., Sailer, M., Schmidt, A., Seidel, T., & Kasneci, G. (2023). ChatGPT for good? On opportunities and challenges of large language models for education. *Learning and Individual Differences*, *103*, 102274. Advance online publication. DOI: 10.1016/j.lindif.2023.102274

Katsarou, E., Wild, F., Sougari, A.-M., & Chatzipanagiotou, P. (2023). A systematic review of voice-based intelligent virtual agents in EFL education. [iJET]. *International Journal of Emerging Technologies in Learning*, *18*(10), 65–85. DOI: 10.3991/ijet.v18i10.37723

Kennedy, K. J., & Castek, J. M. (2025). Empowering ELA teachers: Recommendations for teacher education in the AI era. *Contemporary Issues in Technology & Teacher Education*, *25*(1), 1–31. https://citejournal.org/volume-25/issue-1-25/english-language-arts/empowering-ela-teachers-recommendations-for-teacher-education-in-the-ai-era

Kent, D. (2020). A room with a VUI – voice user interfaces in the TESOL classroom. *Teaching English with Technology*, *20*(3), 96–124.

Kerfoot, C., & Bello-Nonjengele, B. O. (2023). Towards epistemic justice: Constructing knowers in multilingual classrooms. *Applied Linguistics*, *44*(3), 462–484. DOI: 10.1093/applin/amac049

Kerr, R. C., & Kim, H. (2025). From prompts to plans: A case study of pre-service EFL teachers' use of generative AI for lesson planning. *English Teaching*, *80*(1), 95–118. DOI: 10.15858/engtea.80.1.202503.95

Kersten, K., & Winsler, A. (Eds.). (2022). *Understanding variability in second language acquisition, bilingualism, and cognition: A multi-layered perspective*. Taylor & Francis., DOI: 10.4324/9781003155683

Kessler, G., & Bikowski, D. (2011). The influence of SLA training in curricular design among teachers in preparation. *CALICO Journal*, *28*(2), 522–545. DOI: 10.11139/cj.28.2.522-545

Ketere, C. (2025). Decolonizing Artificial Intelligence: Reducing Algorithmic Biases in African Educational and Linguistic Contexts. *Journal of Contemporary Issues in Open Distance and E-Learning*, *2*(1), 18–37. DOI: 10.71060/7qk9nd52

Khari, M. A. (2026). Beyond the algorithm: Educational justice for plurilingual students in AI-assisted classrooms. In Rousoulioti, T., Pitsou, C., Saglam, A., & Finch, K. (Eds.), *Language education and human rights in democratic educational settings* (pp. 405–444). IGI Global Scientific Publishing. DOI: 10.4018/979-8-3373-2670-2.ch015

Khlaif, Z. N., Alkouk, W. A., Salama, N., & Abu Eideh, B. (2025). Redesigning Assessments for AI-Enhanced Learning: A Framework for Educators in the Generative AI Era. *Education Sciences*, *15*(2), 174. Advance online publication. DOI: 10.3390/educsci15020174

Kildė, L. (2025). Humanising digital language education 5.0 through a Freirean lens. *Acta Paedagogica Vilnensia,* (54), 157–169. https://bit.ly/4szm2u8

Kim, N.-Y., Cha, Y., & Kim, H.-S. (2019). Future English learning: Chatbots and artificial intelligence. *Multimedia-Assisted Language Learning*, *22*(3), 32–53. DOI: 10.15702/mall.2019.22.3.32

Knouse, S. M., Bessy, M., & Longest, K. C. (2021). Knowing who we teach: Tracking attitudes and expectations of first-year postsecondary language learners. *Foreign Language Annals*, *54*(1), 50–72. DOI: 10.1111/flan.12510

Koehler, M. J., Mishra, P., Kereluik, K., Shin, T. S., & Graham, C. R. (2013). The technological pedagogical content knowledge framework. In *Handbook of research on educational communications and technology* (pp. 101–111). Springer., DOI: 10.1007/978-1-4614-3185-5_9

Koenecke, A., Nam, A., Lake, E., Nudell, J., Quartey, M., Mengesha, Z., Toups, C., Rickford, J. R., Jurafsky, D., & Goel, S. (2020). Racial disparities in automated speech recognition. *Proceedings of the National Academy of Sciences of the United States of America, 117*(14), 7684–7689. DOI: 10.1073/pnas.1915768117 PMID: 32205437

Kohnke, L., & Zou, D. (2025). Artificial intelligence integration in TESOL teacher education: Promoting a critical lens guided by TPACK and SAMR. *TESOL Quarterly*, *59*(S3), S267–S278. DOI: 10.1002/tesq.3396

Kontra, E. H. (2020). The L2 motivation of learners with special educational needs. In *The Palgrave handbook of motivation for language learning* (pp. 495–513). Springer International Publishing., DOI: 10.1007/978-3-030-28380-3_24

Kormos, J. (2016). *The second language learning processes of students with specific learning difficulties*. Routledge., DOI: 10.4324/9781315692371

Kormos, J. (2020). Specific learning difficulties in second language learning and teaching. *Language Teaching*, *53*(2), 129–143. DOI: 10.1017/S0261444819000442

Kormos, J., & Smith, A. M. (2023). *Teaching languages to students with specific learning differences* (Vol. 18). Channel View Publications., DOI: 10.21832/KORMOS8615

Kramsch, C. (2000). Second language acquisition, applied linguistics, and the teaching of foreign languages. *Modern Language Journal*, *84*(3), 311–326. DOI: 10.1111/0026-7902.00071

Kramsch, C. (2009). *The multilingual subject.* Oxford University Press.

Kramsch, C. J. (1998). *Language and culture*. Oxford University Press.

Küçükuncular, A., & Ertugan, A. (2025). Teaching in the AI era: Sustainable digital education through ethical integration and teacher empowerment. *Sustainability (Basel)*, *17*(16), 7405. DOI: 10.3390/su17167405

Kuhfeld, M., Soland, J., Tarasawa, B., Johnson, A., Ruzek, E., & Lewis, K. (2020). Projecting the potential impact of COVID-19 school closures on academic achievement. *Educational Researcher*, *49*(8), 549–565. DOI: 10.3102/0013189X20965918

Kuteeva, M., & Andersson, M. (2024). Diversity and standards in writing for publication in the age of AI—Between a rock and a hard place. *Applied Linguistics*, *45*(3), 561–567. DOI: 10.1093/applin/amae025

Lam, H. C. (2011). A critical analysis of the various ways of teaching Chinese characters, *Electronic Journal of Foreign Language Teaching*, *8*, 57–70. https://n9.cl/qr0k7s

Lantolf, J. P., & Thorne, S. L. (2006). *Sociocultural theory and the genesis of second language development*. Oxford University Press.

Lardiere, D. (2017). *Ultimate attainment in second language acquisition: A case study*. Routledge., DOI: 10.4324/9781315084480

Lasagabaster, D., & García, O. (2014). Translanguaging: Towards a dynamic model of bilingualism at school. *C&E, Cultura y Educación*, *26*(3), 557–572. DOI: 10.1080/11356405.2014.973671

Lee, S. L. (2019). Teaching and learning Cantonese as a second language: Learners' attitudes and learning hurdles. In J. Wakefield (Ed.), *Cantonese as a second language: Issues, experiences and suggestions for teaching and learning* (pp. 47–66). Routledge. https://doi.org/DOI: 10.4324/9781351184250

Lee, B. J. (2024). Reimagining language learning: AI-driven innovations for engagement and growth. *Technology in Language Teaching & Learning*, *6*(3), 102773–102773. DOI: 10.29140/tltl.v6n3.102773

Lee, M. T. N., Tse, S. K., & Loh, E. K. Y. (2011). The impact of the integrative perceptual approach on the teaching of Chinese characters in a Hong Kong kindergarten. *Early Child Development and Care*, *181*(5), 665–679. DOI: 10.1080/03004431003768006

Lee, S. L. (2023). Teaching literacy skills to Cantonese learners. In Lee, S. L. (Ed.), *The learning and teaching of Cantonese as a second language* (pp. 67–86). Routledge. DOI: 10.4324/9781003054696

Lee, S. L., & Chen, Y. (2024). Discussions of using AI in language education in Hong Kong. In Pan, F. (Ed.), *AI in language teaching, learning, and assessment* (pp. 133–148). IGI Global Scientific Publishing., DOI: 10.4018/979-8-3693-0872-1.ch007

Lee, Y.-J., & Jeong, S.-H. (2026). Implementing AI-integrated English writing: University English language learners writing strategies and perceptions. *International Journal of Evaluation and Research in Education, 15*(1), 805–814. DOI: 10.11591/ijere.v15i1.35461

Leijen, Ä. (2023). Supporting and assessing professional agency of student teachers in initial teacher education. In Tierney, R. J., Rizvi, F., & Ercikan, K. (Eds.), *International Encyclopedia of Education* (4th ed., pp. 339–345). Elsevier., DOI: 10.1016/B978-0-12-818630-5.04090-2

Le-Khanh, H., Do, K., & Tran-Thanh, V. (2024). EFL writing teachers' agency in response to AI emergence from an ecological perspective. In Bui, H. P., & Namaziandost, E. (Eds.), *Innovations in Technologies for Language Teaching and Learning* (pp. 79–94). Springer Nature Switzerland., DOI: 10.1007/978-3-031-63447-5_5

Leonardi, V. (2010). *The role of pedagogical translation in second language acquisition: From theory to practice*. Peter Lang., DOI: 10.3726/978-3-0351-0071-6

Lewis, A. A. (2025). Unpacking cultural bias in AI language learning tools: An analysis of impacts and strategies for inclusion in diverse educational settings. *International Journal of Research and Innovation in Social Science, 9*(1), 1878–1892. DOI: 10.47772/IJRISS.2025.9010151

Ley Orgánica 3/2020, de 29 de diciembre, por la que se modifica la Ley Orgánica 2/2006, de 3 de mayo, de Educación [Organic Law 3/2020, of December 29, amending Organic Law 2/2006, of May 3, on Education]. *BOE* no. 340, 30 December 2020, 122868–122953. https://n9.cl/4sf5b

Li, B., Tan, Y. L., Wang, C., & Lowell, V. (2025). Two years of innovation: A systematic review of empirical generative AI research in language learning and teaching. *Computers and Education: Artificial Intelligence, 9*, 100445. DOI: 10.1016/j.caeai.2025.100445

Li, D. C. S., & Chuk, J. Y. P. (2015). South Asian students' needs for Cantonese and written Chinese in Hong Kong: A linguistic study. *International Journal of Multilingualism, 12*(2), 210–224. DOI: 10.1080/14790718.2015.1009375

Lightbown, P. M. (2000). Anniversary article. Classroom SLA research and second language teaching. *Applied Linguistics, 21*(4), 431–462. DOI: 10.1093/applin/21.4.431

Light, J., & McNaughton, D. (2015). Designing AAC research and intervention to improve outcomes for individuals with complex communication needs. *Augmentative and Alternative Communication : AAC, 31*(2), 85–96. DOI: 10.3109/07434618.2015.1036458 PMID: 25904008

Li, J., Huang, J., Wu, W., & Whipple, P. B. (2024). Evaluating the role of ChatGPT in enhancing EFL writing assessments in classroom settings: A preliminary investigation. *Humanities & Social Sciences Communications, 11*(1), 1268. DOI: 10.1057/s41599-024-03755-2

Li, J., Xu, M., & Chen, J. (2022). A Bourdieusian analysis of the multilingualism in a poverty-stricken ethnic minority area: Can linguistic capital be transferred to economic capital? *Journal of Multilingual and Multicultural Development, 43*(2), 122–139. DOI: 10.1080/01434632.2020.1733585

Li, M., & Noori, A. Q. (2024). Exploring the nexus of attitude, contextual factors, and AI utilization intentions: A PLS-SEM analysis among primary mathematics teachers in China. *Asian Journal for Mathematics Education, 3*(3), 289–311. DOI: 10.1177/27527263241269060

Lin, C. H., Warschauer, M., & Blake, R. (2019). Language learning through adaptive systems: A review of technologies and pedagogical implications. *Computer Assisted Language Learning, 32*(1–2), 1–25. DOI: 10.1080/09588221.2018.1485708

Lin, C.-J., & Mubarok, H. (2021). Learning analytics for investigating the mind map-guided AI chatbot approach in an EFL flipped speaking classroom. *Journal of Educational Technology & Society, 24*(4), 16–35. https://www.jstor.org/stable/48629242

Lin, H. C. K., Chao, C. J., & Huang, T. C. (2015). From a perspective on foreign language learning anxiety to develop an affective tutoring system. *Educational Technology Research and Development, 63*(5), 727–747. DOI: 10.1007/s11423-015-9385-6

Link, S., Dursun, A., Karakaya, K., & Hegelheimer, V. (2020). Towards automated writing evaluation for Turkish EFL learners: System performance and learner perceptions. *ReCALL, 32*(3), 269–288. DOI: 10.1017/S0958344020000010

Lippi-Green, R. (1997). *English with an accent: Language, ideology and discrimination in the United States.* Routledge., DOI: 10.4324/9780203348802

Lipponen, L., & Kumpulainen, K. (2011). Acting as accountable authors: Creating interactional spaces for agency work in teacher education. *Teaching and Teacher Education, 27*(5), 812–819. https://www.sciencedirect.com/science/article/abs/pii/S0742051X11000023?via%3Dihub. DOI: 10.1016/j.tate.2011.01.001

Li, S. (2016). The construct validity of language aptitude: A meta-analysis. *Studies in Second Language Acquisition, 38*(4), 801–842. DOI: 10.1017/S027226311500042X

Li, S., Hiver, P., & Papi, M. (2022). Individual differences in second language acquisition: Theory, research, and practice. In *The Routledge handbook of second language acquisition and individual differences* (pp. 3–34). Routledge., DOI: 10.4324/9781003270546-2

Liu, G. L., Lee, J. S., & Zhao, X. (2025). Critical digital literacies, agentic practices, and AI-mediated informal digital learning of English. *System, 134*, 103797. DOI: 10.1016/j.system.2025.103797

Liu, J., Sihes, A. J. B., & Lu, Y. (2025). How do generative artificial intelligence (AI) tools and large language models (LLMs) influence language learners' critical thinking in EFL education? A systematic review. *Smart Learning Environments, 12*(1), 48. Advance online publication. DOI: 10.1186/s40561-025-00406-0

Liu, M., Moore, Z., Graham, L., & Lee, S. (2002). A look at the research on computer-based technology use in second language learning: A review of the literature from 1990–2000. *Journal of Research on Technology in Education, 34*(3), 250–273. DOI: 10.1080/15391523.2002.10782348

Liu, W. (2023). The theory of second language development for international students. *Journal for multicultural. Education, 17*(3), 367–378. DOI: 10.1108/JME-08-2022-0106

Liu, X., & Xiao, Y. (2024). Chinese university teachers' engagement with generative AI in different stages of foreign language teaching: A qualitative enquiry through the prism of ADDIE. *Education and Information Technologies, 30*(1), 485–508. DOI: 10.1007/s10639-024-13117-9

Liu, Y. J., Han, T., Ma, S., Zhang, J., Yang, Y., Tian, J., He, H., Li, A., He, M., Liu, Z., Wu, Z., Zhang, L., Zhu, D., Li, X., Niu, Q., Shen, D., Liu, T., & Ge, B. (2023). Summary of ChatGPT-related research and perspective towards the future of large language models. *Meta-Radiology, 1*(2), 100017. DOI: 10.1016/j.metrad.2023.100017

Liu, Z. (2022). Introducing a multimodal perspective to emotional variables in second language acquisition education: Systemic functional multimodal discourse analysis. *Frontiers in Psychology, 13*, 1016441. DOI: 10.3389/fpsyg.2022.1016441 PMID: 36324780

Li, X. (2022). The significance of Q-methodology as an innovative method for the investigation of affective variables in second language acquisition. *Frontiers in Psychology, 13*, 995660. DOI: 10.3389/fpsyg.2022.995660 PMID: 36059765

Lo, C. K., Yu, P. L. H., Xu, S., Ng, D. T. K., & Jong, M. S. (2024). Exploring the application of ChatGPT in ESL/EFL education and related research issues: A systematic review of empirical studies. *Smart Learning Environments, 11*(1), 50. DOI: 10.1186/s40561-024-00342-5

Lodge, J. M., Bower, M., Gulson, K., Henderson, M., Slade, C., & Southgate, E. (2025). *Australian Framework for Artificial Intelligence in Higher Education.* Australian Centre for Student Equity and Success. https://bit.ly/4rmtubb

Loewen, S., & Sato, M. (2017). Instructed second language acquisition (ISLA): An overview. *The Routledge handbook of instructed second language acquisition*, 1-12. DOI: 10.4324/9781315676968-1

Loewen, S. (2020). *Introduction to instructed second language acquisition.* Routledge., DOI: 10.4324/9781315616797

López Blanco, J. D. (2025). Do languages open doors? A theoretical model of linguistic capital and (im)mobility and its application in Spanish youth migration. *Journal of Ethnic and Migration Studies, 51*(3), 565–582. DOI: 10.1080/1369183X.2024.2359676

Lopez-Gazpio, I. (2025). Integrating large language models into accessible and inclusive education: Access democratization and individualized learning enhancement supported by generative artificial intelligence. *Information (Basel), 16*(6), 473. Advance online publication. DOI: 10.3390/info16060473

Lynch, S. (2025). How AI is leaving non-English speakers behind. Retrieved March 28, 2026, from https://news.stanford.edu/stories/2025/05/digital-divide-ai-llms-exclusion-non-english-speakers-research

Mabuan, R. A. (2024). ChatGPT and ELT: Exploring teachers' voices. [IJTE]. *International Journal of Technology in Education, 7*(1), 128–153. DOI: 10.46328/ijte.523

Macaro, E., Handley, Z., & Walter, C. (2012). A systematic review of CALL in English as a second language: Focus on primary and secondary education. *Language Teaching, 45*(1), 1–43. DOI: 10.1017/S0261444811000395

MacIntyre, P. D., & McGillivray, M. F. (2023). The inner workings of anxiety in second language learning. *Annual Review of Applied Linguistics*, *43*, 88–104. DOI: 10.1017/S0267190523000065

Mackey, A. (2014). Practice and progression in second language research methods. *AILA Review*, *27*(1), 80–97. DOI: 10.1075/aila.27.04mac

Mackey, A. (2020). *Interaction, feedback and task research in second language learning: Methods and design*. Cambridge University Press., DOI: 10.1017/9781108589284

Mack, K., McDonnell, E., Jain, D., Wang, L. L., Froehlich, J. E., & Findlater, L. (2021). What do we mean by "accessibility research"? A literature survey of accessibility papers in CHI and ASSETS from 1994 to 2019. *Proceedings of the 2021 CHI Conference on Human Factors in Computing Systems*, 371. https://doi.org/ DOI: 10.1145/3411764.3445412

Mahapatra, S. (2024). Impact of ChatGPT on ESL students' academic writing skills: A mixed methods intervention study. *Smart Learning Environments*, *11*(1), 9. DOI: 10.1186/s40561-024-00295-9

Mahapatra, S., & Koltovskaia, S. (2025). A framework for focalising critical digital literacies in second language teacher education in the Global South. *Asian Journal of Second and Foreign Language Education*, *10*(1), 44. DOI: 10.1186/s40862-025-00350-z

Mallinson, C. (2024). Linguistic variation and linguistic inclusion in the US educational context. *Annual Review of Linguistics*, *10*(1), 37–57. DOI: 10.1146/annurev-linguistics-031120-121546

Markl, N. (2022). Language variation and algorithmic bias: understanding algorithmic bias in British English automatic speech recognition. *ACM International Conference Proceeding Series*, 521–534. DOI: 10.1145/3531146.3533117

Marras, A., Fornara, F., & Pasqualotto, A. (2026). Harnessing AI for inclusive teaching: Professional development strategies for early educators. In *AI in Early Education: Integrating Artificial Intelligence for Inclusive and Effective Learning* (pp. 267–290). wiley. DOI: 10.1002/9781394352821.ch16

Matjie, M. A., Nethavhani, A., & Matlakala, M. (2026). AI and the digital divide in education. *Frontiers in Computer Science, Volume 8-2026*. Retrieved from https://www.frontiersin.org/journals/computer-science/articles/10.3389/fcomp .2026.1759027

Mazzi, F. (2024). Authorship in artificial intelligence-generated works: Exploring originality in text prompts and artificial intelligence outputs through philosophical foundations of copyright and collage protection. *The Journal of World Intellectual Property*, *27*(3), 410–427. DOI: 10.1111/jwip.12310

McCrocklin, S. (2020). Exploring the effectiveness of structured language learning experiences for bilinguals in a language acquisition course. *TESOL Journal*, *11*(2), e477. DOI: 10.1002/tesj.477

McKenney, S., & Reeves, T. C. (2014). Methods of evaluation and reflection in design research. *Zeitschrift für Berufs-und Wirtschaftspädagogiek*, *27*, 141–153. https://research.utwente.nl/en/publications/methods-of-evaluation-and-reflection-in-design-research/

McLoughlin, C., & Lee, M. J. W. (2010). Personalised and self regulated learning in the Web 2.0 era: International exemplars of innovative pedagogy using social software. *Australasian Journal of Educational Technology*, *26*(1), 28–43. DOI: 10.14742/ajet.1100

McManus, K. (2024). Replication studies in second language acquisition research: Definitions, issues, resources, and future directions: Introduction to the special issue. *Studies in Second Language Acquisition*, *46*(5), 1299–1319. DOI: 10.1017/S0272263124000652

McPhee, S. W., & Jerowsky, M. (2025). Beyond technical skills: A pedagogical perspective on fostering critical engagement with generative AI in university classrooms. *Frontiers in Education*, *10*, 1–7. DOI: 10.3389/feduc.2025.1593278

Mehrabi, N., Morstatter, F., Saxena, N., Lerman, K., & Galstyan, A. (2021). A survey on bias and fairness in machine learning. *ACM Computing Surveys*, *54*(6), 1–35. DOI: 10.1145/3457607

Mehta, V., Selvakumar, P., Anute, N. B., Gandhimathi, S., Seelam, P. K., & Manjunath, T. C. (2025). Second Language Acquisition Support Through Media Literacy and Digital Media Platforms. In *Supporting Linguistic Differences Through Literacy Education* (pp. 361–388). IGI Global Scientific Publishing., DOI: 10.4018/979-8-3373-3496-7.ch011

Meyer, O., Coyle, D., & Schuck, K. (2018). Learnscaping. Creating next-gen learning environment for pluriliteracies growth. In Bündgens-Kosten, J., & Elsner, D. (Eds.), *Bilingual education & bilingualism. Multilingual computer assisted language learning* (pp. 18–37). Multilingual Matters. DOI: 10.21832/9781788921497-004

Miao, F., & Cukurova, M. (2024). *AI competency framework for teachers*. UNESCO. https://n9.cl/kyua4

Microsoft. (2023). *Immersive reader documentation*. Microsoft. https://learn.microsoft.com/en-us/azure/ai-services/immersive-reader/

Midigo, J. (2025). AI-Powered Innovations for Documenting and Revitalizing African Languages. *Cultural Arts Research and Development*, *5*(2), 26–41. DOI: 10.55121/card.v5i2.517

Mignolo, W. (2025). Entrevista a Walter Mignolo (segunda parte): Pensar a partir de lo destituido que sea relevante política y éticamente en el presente [Interview with Walter Mignolo (part two): Thinking from the dismissed that is politically and ethically relevant in the present]. *Revista de Filosofía (La Plata)*, *55*(1), e120. DOI: 10.24215/29533392e120

Mignolo, W. D. (2011). *The darker side of western modernity: Global futures, decolonial options*. Duke University Press.

Mignolo, W. D., & Walsh, C. E. (2018). *On decoloniality: Concepts, analytics, praxis*. Duke University Press.

Mikroyannidis, A., Perifanou, M., & Economides, A. A. (2025). Enhancing Language Learning with Generative AI: The Case of the OpenLang Network Platform. *Computers*, *14*(12), 546. DOI: 10.3390/computers14120546

Mills, C. (2008). Reproduction and transformation of inequalities in schooling: The transformative potential of the theoretical constructs of Bourdieu. *British Journal of Sociology of Education*, *29*(1), 79–89. DOI: 10.1080/01425690701737481

Mimoudi, A., & Mokhtari, K. (2025). 'AIA-PCEK': A new framework for teaching with AI. *Cogent Education*, *12*(1), 2563171. Advance online publication. DOI: 10.1080/2331186X.2025.2563171

Mishra, P., & Koehler, M. J. (2006). Technological pedagogical content knowledge: A framework for teacher knowledge. *Teachers College Record*, *108*(6), 1017–1054. DOI: 10.1111/j.1467-9620.2006.00684.x

Mitchell, M. (2020). *Artificial intelligence: A guide for thinking humans*. Pelican.

Mitchell, M. (2023). AI's challenge of understanding the world. *Science*, *382*(6671), eadm8175. Advance online publication. DOI: 10.1126/science.adm8175 PMID: 37943939

Mitchell, M., & Krakauer, D. C. (2023). The debate over understanding in AI's large language models. *Proceedings of the National Academy of Sciences of the United States of America, 120*(13), e2215907120. DOI: 10.1073/pnas.2215907120 PMID: 36943882

Moeller, A. K., & Catalano, T. (2015). Foreign language teaching and learning. DOI: 10.1016/B978-0-08-097086-8.92082-8

Mohamed, S., Png, M. T., & Isaac, W. (2020). Decolonial AI: Decolonial theory as sociotechnical foresight in artificial intelligence. *Philosophy & Technology, 33*(4), 659–684. DOI: 10.1007/s13347-020-00405-8

Mohebbi, A. (2025). Enabling learner independence and self-regulation in language education using AI tools: A systematic review. *Cogent Education, 12*(1), 2433814. DOI: 10.1080/2331186X.2024.2433814

Molla, T., & Nolan, A. (2020). Teacher agency and professional practice. *Teachers and Teaching, 26*(1), 67–87. DOI: 10.1080/13540602.2020.1740196

Monib, W. K., Qazi, A., De Silva, L., & Mahmud, M. M. (2024). Exploring Learners' Experiences with ChatGPT in Personalized Learning. *2024 6th International Workshop on Artificial Intelligence and Education (WAIE)*, 66–70. IEEE. DOI: 10.1109/WAIE63876.2024.00019

Monib, W. K. (2025). Sentiment and SWOT analyses of DeepSeek AI: Insights from media, self-perceptions, user perceptions, and literature. *SAGE Open, 15*(4), 21582440251395224. DOI: 10.1177/21582440251395226

Monib, W. K., Qazi, A., Apong, R. A., Azizan, M. T., De Silva, L., & Yassin, H. (2024). Generative AI and future education: A review, theoretical validation, and authors' perspective on challenges and solutions. *PeerJ. Computer Science, 10*, e2105. DOI: 10.7717/peerj-cs.2105 PMID: 39650462

Monib, W. K., Qazi, A., Jain, J., & Ponniah, L. (2025). A comprehensive scientometric analysis of ChatGPT research global trends and future prospects. *TechTrends, 69*(6), 1–19. DOI: 10.1007/s11528-025-01110-z

Monib, W. K., Qazi, A., & Mahmud, M. M. (2025). Exploring learners' experiences and perceptions of ChatGPT as a learning tool in higher education. *Education and Information Technologies, 30*(1), 917–939. DOI: 10.1007/s10639-024-13065-4

Moodie, G. (2023). Academic writing, voice, and identity in African higher education: Challenges in the age of AI. *Journal of Higher Education in Africa, 21*(1), 57–79.

Mphahlele, N., & Mashiyi, N. (2022). Digital writing practices and cultural identity among South African undergraduate students. *Reading & Writing Journal of the Reading Association of South Africa, 13*(1), 1–10. https://doi.org/DOI: 10.4102/rw.v13i1.309

Murphey, T., & Arao, H. (2001). Reported belief changes through near peer role modeling. *TESL-EJ, 5*(3). https://eric.ed.gov/?id=EJ639330

Namaziandost, E. (2025). Integrating flipped learning in AI-enhanced language learning: Mapping the effects on metacognitive awareness, writing development, and foreign language learning boredom. *Computers and Education: Artificial Intelligence, 100446*, 100446. Advance online publication. DOI: 10.1016/j.caeai.2025.100446

Namaziandost, E., Behbahani, H. K., & Naserpour, A. (2024). Peer support in language learning: Mitigating anxiety, enhancing achievement, cultivating growth mindsets, and increasing enjoyment. *Journal of Applied Learning and Teaching, 7*(2), 296–313. DOI: 10.37074/jalt.2024.7.2.40

Nedungadi, P., Tang, K.-Y., & Raman, R. (2024). The transformative power of generative artificial intelligence for achieving the sustainable development goal of quality education. *Sustainability (Basel), 16*(9779), 9779. Advance online publication. DOI: 10.3390/su16229779

New London Group. (1996). A pedagogy of multiliteracies: Designing social futures. *Harvard Educational Review, 66*(1), 60–92. DOI: 10.17763/haer.66.1.17370n67v-22j160u

Nguyen, A., Ngo, H. N., Hong, Y., Dang, B., & Nguyen, B.-P. T. (2023). Ethical principles for artificial intelligence in education. *Education and Information Technologies, 28*(4), 4221–4241. DOI: 10.1007/s10639-022-11316-w PMID: 36254344

Nguyen, M. A., & Doan, S. T. (2021). Digital inequality in Vietnamese classrooms: Impacts on technology-supported English language learning. *Asia Pacific Journal of Education, 41*(2), 187–203. DOI: 10.1080/02188791.2020.1756734

Niazai, H., & Monib, W. K. (2025a). AI for personalized learning in medical education. In *Teaching in the Age of Medical Technology* (pp. 91–122). IGI Global Scientific Publishing. DOI: 10.4018/979-8-3373-1519-5.ch004

Niazai, H., & Monib, W. K. (2025b). The role of generative AI in curriculum development and its impact on well-being. *Advances in Computational Intelligence and Robotics, 229*, 229–252. Advance online publication. DOI: 10.4018/979-8-3373-3316-8.ch009

Noble, S. U. (2018). *Algorithms of oppression: How search engines reinforce racism*. New York University Press. DOI: 10.18574/nyu/9781479833641.001.0001

Norton, B. (2013). *Identity and language learning: Extending the conversation* (2nd ed.). Multilingual Matters. DOI: 10.21832/9781783090563

Novawan, A., Ikeda, O., & Walker, S. A. (2024). The new face of technology-enhanced language learning (TELL) with Artificial Intelligence (AI): Teacher perspectives, practices, and challenges. *Journal of English in Academic and Professional Communication JEAPCO, 10*(1), 1–18. DOI: 10.25047/jeapco.v10i1.4565

Nussbaum, M. C. (2011). Perfectionist liberalism and political liberalism. *Philosophy & Public Affairs, 39*(1), 3–45. DOI: 10.1111/j.1088-4963.2011.01200.x

O'Dowd, R. (2025). Issues of equity and inclusion in Virtual Exchange. *Language Teaching, 58*(1), 44–56. DOI: 10.1017/S026144482300040X

O'Neil, C. (2016). *Weapons of math destruction: How big data increases inequality and threatens democracy*. Crown.

Octavio, M. M., Argüello, M. V. G., & Pujolà, J.-T. (2024). ChatGPT as an AI L2 teaching support: A case study of an EFL teacher. *Technology in Language Teaching & Learning, 6*(1), 1142. DOI: 10.29140/tltl.v6n1.1142

OECD. (2023). *Education at a glance 2023: OECD indicators*. OECD Publishing. DOI: 10.1787/e13bef63-

Okada, A., Sherborne, T., Panselinas, G., & Kolionis, G. (2025). Fostering transversal skills through open schooling supported by the care-know-do pedagogical model and the UNESCO AI competencies framework. *International Journal of Artificial Intelligence in Education, 35*(4), 1953–1998. DOI: 10.1007/s40593-025-00458-w

Oliver, M. (1990). *The politics of disablement: A sociological approach*. Macmillan. DOI: 10.1007/978-1-349-20895-1

Ortega, L. (2014). *Understanding second language acquisition*. Routledge., DOI: 10.4324/9780203777282

Overdeck Family Foundation. (2025). 2025 AI strategy update. Retrieved March 3, 2026, from https://overdeck.org/news-and-resources/article/2025-ai-strategy-update/#:~:text=2,for%20collaborative%20learning%20and%20innovation

Overdeck Family Foundation. (2026, January 27). What we learned: Exploring the role of educators in the age of AI. Retrieved February 24, 2026, from Overdeck Family Foundation website: https://overdeck.org/news-and-resources/article/what-we-learned-exploring-the-role-of-educators-in-the-age-of-ai/#:~:text=1,not%20end%20users%2C%20of%20AI

Owenby, M. A. D., & O'Dowd, R. (2018). In This Together. In *Teachers' Experiences with Transnational, Telecollaborative Language Learning Projects*. Peter Lang Verlag. DOI: 10.3726/b14311

Oxfam Hong Kong. (2020). *A study on the challenges faced by mainstream schools in educating ethnic minorities in Hong Kong*. Oxfam. https://n9.cl/yyiv3

Oyetade, K., & Zuva, T. (2025). Advancing equitable education with inclusive AI to mitigate bias and enhance teacher literacy. *Educational Process: International Journal, 14*, e2025087. DOI: 10.22521/edupij.2025.14.87

Palacios-Hidalgo, F. J. (2025a). AI for the democratization of language learning. In McCallum, L., & Tafazoli, D. (Eds.), *The Palgrave encyclopedia of computer-assisted language learning* (pp. 1–4). Palgrave Macmillan Cham. DOI: 10.1007/978-3-031-51447-0_98-1

Palacios-Hidalgo, F. J. (2025b). Critical language pedagogy: Revisiting the concept. In Palacios-Hidalgo, F. J., & Huertas-Abril, C. A. (Eds.), *Redefining language education through critical language pedagogy* (pp. 1–22). IGI Global Scientific Publishing. DOI: 10.4018/979-8-3693-5421-6.ch001

Pande, M. H. (2025). Translanguaging Pedagogy: A Tool for Social Justice and Equity in the Language Classroom. *Language, Literature, and Interdisciplinary Studies (LLIDS), Social Justice Special Issue*, 2.65–2.78, DOI: 10.71106/AIUT8526

Pang, W., & Wei, Z. (2025). Shaping the future of higher education: A technology usage study on generative AI innovations. *Information (Basel), 16*(2), 95. Advance online publication. DOI: 10.3390/info16020095

Paris, D. (2012). Culturally sustaining pedagogy: A needed change in stance, terminology, and practice. *Educational Researcher, 41*(3), 93–97. DOI: 10.3102/0013189X12441244

Pastorino-Campos, C., & Galaczi, E. (2025). Ethical AI for language assessment: Considerations and principles. *Annual Review of Applied Linguistics*. Advance online publication. DOI: 10.1017/S0267190525100081

Patterson, J. (2025, September 2). *Multilingual artificial intelligence often reinforces bias*. Johns Hopkins University. https://bit.ly/4rvAeDJ

Pavlenko, A., & Blackledge, A. (Eds.). (2004). *Negotiation of identities in multilingual contexts*. Multilingual Matters. DOI: 10.21832/9781853596483

Pawlak, M., & Waniek-Klimczak, E. (2015). Issues in teaching, learning and testing speaking in a second language. DOI: 10.1007/978-3-642-38339-7

Peña-Acuña, B., & Crismán-Pérez, R. (2022). Research on Papua, a digital tool with artificial intelligence in favor of learning and linguistic attitudes towards the learning of the English language in students of Spanish language as L1. *Frontiers in Psychology*, *13*, 1019278. DOI: 10.3389/fpsyg.2022.1019278 PMID: 36389452

Perry, B., & Stewart, T. (2005). Insights into effective partnership in interdisciplinary team teaching. *System*, *33*(4), 563–573. DOI: 10.1016/j.system.2005.01.006

Pfenninger, S., & Polz, S. (2018). Foreign language learning in the third age: A pilot feasibility study on cognitive, socio-affective and linguistic drivers and benefits in relation to previous bilingualism of the learner. *European Second Language Association. Journal*, *2*(1), 1–13. DOI: 10.22599/jesla.36

Pham, V. P. H., Lian, A., White, J., & Lian, A. (2025). Overview of Empowering Educators: Integrating AI Tools for Personalized Language Instruction. In *Empowering Educators: Integrating AI Tools for Personalized Language Instruction* (pp. 1-8). Cham: Springer Nature Switzerland. DOI: 10.1007/978-3-032-01348-4_1

Phillipson, R. (1992). *Linguistic imperialism*. Oxford University Press.

Phillipson, R., & Meighan, P. (2025). Resisting linguistic imperialism: A conversation with Robert Phillipson on linguistic human rights, multilingualism, and Indigenous and minority languages. *Journal of Education for Multilingualism*, *2*(1), 131–151. https://bit.ly/47rkDh2

Piechurska-Kuciel, E. (2008). Input, processing and output anxiety in students with symptoms of developmental dyslexia. *Language learners with special needs. An international perspective*, 86-109. DOI: 10.2307/jj.27710857.8

Piechurska-Kuciel, E. (2011). The relationship between language anxiety and the development of the speaking skill: Results of a longitudinal study. *Speaking and instructed foreign language acquisition*, 200-212. DOI: 10.2307/jj.29308412.17

Pinto-Llorente, A. M., & Izquierdo-Álvarez, V. (2024). Digital Learning Ecosystem to Enhance Formative Assessment in Second Language Acquisition in Higher Education. *Sustainability (Basel)*, *16*(11), 4687. DOI: 10.3390/su16114687

Poehner, M. E., & Lu, X. (2024). Sociocultural theory and corpus-based English language teaching. *TESOL Quarterly*, *58*(1), 1–12. DOI: 10.1002/tesq.3282

Poon, H. F. (2014). *Interactive online self-access learning package for 'Chinese writing skills'*. The Hong Kong Institute of Education. https://n9.cl/0ibze

Proctor, C. P., Dalton, B., & Grisham, D. L. (2007). Scaffolding English language learners and struggling readers in a Universal Literacy Environment with embedded strategy instruction and vocabulary support. *Journal of Literacy Research*, *39*(1), 71–93. DOI: 10.1080/10862960709336758

Prosic-Santovac, D. (2017). Popular video cartoons and associated branded toys in teaching English to very young learners: A case study. *Language Teaching Research*, *21*(5), 568–588. DOI: 10.1177/1362168816639758

Raghavendra, P., Wood, D., Newman, L., & Lawry, J. (2012). Why aren't you on Facebook? Patterns and experiences of using the internet among young people with physical disabilities. *Technology and Disability*, *24*(3), 149–162. DOI: 10.3233/TAD-2012-0343

Ramezanzadeh, A., & Ebadi, S. (2025). AI-generated storytelling for socially just EFL pedagogy: Exploring learner emotions through Fraser's justice theory. *System*, *129*, 103588. DOI: 10.1016/j.system.2024.103588

Ramos HolguĆn, B., & Aguirre Morales, J. (2014). Materials Development in the Colombian Context: Some Considerations about Its Benefits and Challenges. *How*, *21*(2), 134-150. DOI: 10.19183/how.21.2.8

Rao Idapalapati, S.Srinivasa Rao Idapalapati. (2024). AI integration in ELT as a disruptive mechanism. *International Journal of Science and Research Archive*, *12*(01), 922–933. DOI: 10.30574/ijsra.2024.12.1.0941

Rao, K., & Torres, C. (2017). Supporting academic and affective learning processes for English language learners with universal design for learning. *TESOL Quarterly*, *51*(2), 460–472. DOI: 10.1002/tesq.342

Rasooli, A., Zandi, H., & DeLuca, C. (2019). Conceptualising fairness in classroom assessment: Exploring the value of organisational justice theory. *Assessment in Education: Principles, Policy & Practice*, *26*(5), 584–611. DOI: 10.1080/0969594X.2019.1593105

Redecker, C., & Punie, Y. (2017). *European framework for the digital competence of educators: DigCompEdu*. Publications Office of the European Union. DOI: 10.2760/178382

Regan, P., & Jesse, J. (2019). Ethical challenges of edtech, big data and personalized learning: Twenty-first century student sorting and tracking. *Ethics and Information Technology*, *21*(3), 167–179. DOI: 10.1007/s10676-018-9492-2

Ricaurte, P. (2023, May 13). *AI ethics for the majority world: The question of violence at scale* [Transcript]. Goethe-Institut. https://bit.ly/46VJVnq

Richardson, J. E. (2017). *Analysing newspapers: An approach from critical discourse analysis*. Bloomsbury Publishing.

Robinson, P. (2001). *Task complexity, cognitive resources, and syllabus design: A triadic framework for examining task influences on SLA* (pp. 287-318). na. DOI: 10.1017/CBO9781139524780.012

Robinson, P. (2011). Second language task complexity, the Cognition Hypothesis, language learning, and performance. In *Second language task complexity: Researching the cognition hypothesis of language learning and performance* (pp. 3–38). John Benjamins Publishing Company., DOI: 10.1075/tblt.2.05ch1

Rodriguez-Saavedra, M. O., Barrientos-Alfaro, A. R., Málaga-Dávila, C. P., Chávez-Quiroz, F. G., & Arguedas-Catasi, R. W. (2025). Ethics and biases in the use of ChatGPT for academic research. *International Journal of Innovative Research and Scientific Studies, 8*(1), 874–885. DOI: 10.53894/ijirss.v8i1.4432

Román Mendoza, E. (2025). La inteligencia artificial generativa en la enseñanza de español: Una aproximación desde la pedagogía crítica [Generative artificial intelligence in Spanish language education: A critical pedagogy approach]. *Culture Crossroads, 29*, 211–229. DOI: 10.55877/cc.vol29.654

Romele, A. (2020). Technological capital: Bourdieu, postphenomenology, and the philosophy of technology beyond the empirical turn. *Philosophy & Technology, 34*(3), 483–505. DOI: 10.1007/s13347-020-00398-4

Rosa, J., & Flores, N. (2017). Unsettling race and language: Toward a raciolinguistic perspective. *Language in Society, 46*(5), 621–647. DOI: 10.1017/S0047404517000562

Rose, D. H., & Meyer, A. (2002). *Teaching every student in the digital age: Universal Design for Learning*. ASCD.

Rosell-Aguilar, F. (2005). Task design for audiographic conferencing: Promoting beginner oral interaction in distance language learning. *Computer Assisted Language Learning, 18*(5), 417–442. DOI: 10.1080/09588220500442772

Ryding, K. C. (2013). Second-language acquisition. *The Oxford handbook of Arabic linguistics*, 392-411. DOI: 10.1093/oxfordhb/9780199764136.013.0017

Sailer, M., Maier, R., Berger, S., Kastorff, T., & Stegmann, K. (2024). Learning activities in technology-enhanced learning: A systematic review of meta-analyses and second-order meta-analysis in higher education. *Learning and Individual Differences, 112*, 102446. DOI: 10.1016/j.lindif.2024.102446

Samek, W., Wiegand, T., & Müller, K.-R. (2017). *Explainable artificial intelligence: Understanding, visualizing and interpreting deep learning models*. https://doi.org//arXiv.1708.08296DOI: 10.48550

Sangwa, S., & Mutabazi, P. (2025). AI-powered multilingual degrees in higher education: Postcolonial insights on linguistic justice and disruptive innovation. *Open Journal of AI, Ethics & Society (ISSN: 3105-3076), 1*(1).

Sanz, C. (2014). Contributions of study abroad research to our understanding of SLA processes and outcomes: The SALA Project, an appraisal. In *Language acquisition in study abroad and formal instruction contexts* (pp. 1–14). John Benjamins Publishing Company., DOI: 10.1075/aals.13.01ch1

Sauro, S. (2019). Fan fiction and informal language learning. In Dressman, M., & Sadler, R. W. (Eds.), *The handbook of informal language learning* (pp. 140–151). John Wiley & Sons Ltd. DOI: 10.1002/9781119472384.ch9

Saville, N. (2005). Setting and monitoring professional standards: A QMS approach. *Research Notes, 22*, 2–5. https://sl1nk.com/moBVk

Saville, N. (2010). Developing a model for investigating the impact of language assessment. *Research Notes, 42*, 2–8. https://sl1nk.com/BBdkh

Saville, N. (2013). Using standards and guidelines. In *The companion to language assessment* (Vol. II, Part 7: Assessment development). https://doi.org/DOI: 10.1002/9781118411360.wbcla105

Schneider, B., & Oliveira, M. (2025). Developing critical AI language literacy—Prompting experiments on raciolinguistic bias to understand large language models as cultural artefacts. *AI & Society*. Advance online publication. DOI: 10.1007/s00146-025-02727-7

Schofield, A. (2025). Opinion: Hidden biases, discrimination in AI decision-making. Retrieved March 28, 2026, from https://redlineproject.news/2025/03/20/opinion-the-hidden-biases-and-discrimination-in-ai-decision-making/#:~:text=For%20instance%2C%20a%C2%A0study%20published%20in,generated%20harmful%20and%20racist%20stereotypes

Schuler, D., & Namioka, A. (Eds.). (1993). *Participatory design: Principles and practices*. Lawrence Erlbaum Associates.

Seale, J., Colwell, C., Coughlan, T., Heiman, T., Kaspi-Tsahor, D., & Olenik-Shemesh, D. (2021). 'Dreaming in colour': Disabled higher education students' perspectives on improving design practices that would enable them to benefit from their use of technologies. *Education and Information Technologies, 26*(2), 1687–1719. DOI: 10.1007/s10639-020-10329-7

Segler, T. M., Pain, H., & Sorace, A. (2002). Second language vocabulary acquisition and learning strategies in ICALL environments. *Computer Assisted Language Learning, 15*(4), 409–422. DOI: 10.1076/call.15.4.409.8272

Selvi, A. F. (2025). Meet your new AI teacher: Hypes, promises, and realities in AI-powered language education platforms. *Applied Linguistics Review*. Advance online publication. DOI: 10.1515/applirev-2025-0224

Selwyn, N. (2011). Education and technology: Key issues and debates. *Continuum.*

Selwyn, N. (2016). *Education and technology: Key issues and debates*. Bloomsbury Academic.

Selwyn, N. (2019). *Should robots replace teachers? AI and the future of education*. Polity Press.

Shaikh, S., Yayilgan, S. Y., Klimova, B., & Pikhart, M. (2023). Assessing the usability of ChatGPT for formal English language learning. *European Journal of Investigation in Health, Psychology and Education, 13*(9), 1937–1960. DOI: 10.3390/ejihpe13090140 PMID: 37754479

Shao, K., Pekrun, R., & Nicholson, L. J. (2019). Emotions in classroom language learning: What can we learn from achievement emotion research? *System, 86*, 102121. DOI: 10.1016/j.system.2019.102121

Sharifuddin, N. S., & Hashim, H. (2024). Benefits and challenges in implementing artificial intelligence in education (AIED) in ESL classroom: A systematic review (2019-2022). *International Journal of Academic Research in Business & Social Sciences, 14*(1), 146–164. DOI: 10.6007/IJARBSS/v14-i1/20422

Sharma, P., Nimma, D., Punithaasree, K. S., & Faizal, M. M. (2024, October). AI Tools for Enhanced English Learning: Leveraging Machine Learning for Improved Outcomes. In *2024 IEEE 1st International Conference on Green Industrial Electronics and Sustainable Technologies (GIEST)* (pp. 1-6). IEEE. DOI: 10.1109/GIEST62955.2024.10959829

Shepperd, L. (2022). Including underrepresented language learners in SLA research: A case study and considerations for internet-based methods. *Research Methods in Applied Linguistics, 1*(3), 100031. DOI: 10.1016/j.rmal.2022.100031

Shi, H., Chai, C. S., Zhou, S., & Aubrey, S. (2025). Comparing the effects of ChatGPT and automated writing evaluation on students' writing and ideal L2 writing self. *Computer Assisted Language Learning*, •••, 1–28. DOI: 10.1080/09588221.2025.2454541

Shresta, K. (2016). Role of (local) culture in English language teaching. *Journal of NELTA, 21*(1-2), 54–60. DOI: 10.3126/nelta.v21i1-2.20201

Shum, M. S.-k., Tai, C.-p., & Shi, D. (2016). The effectiveness of using 'reading to learning to write' pedagogy in teaching Chinese to non-Chinese speaking students in Hong Kong. *International Journal of Bilingual Education and Bilingualism, 21*, 43–60. https://n9.cl/p3mjfj

Shum, M. S., Shi, D., Huang, X., Tai, C., & Yung, W. (2019). Using the genre-based approach in teaching Chinese written composition to South Asian Ethnic minority students in Hong Kong. *Writing & Pedagogy, 11*(2), 253–283. DOI: 10.1558/wap.36916

Siahaan, S., Saputro, I. E., Yulianingsih, L., Faizin, M., Sinaga, J. B., & Ardhi, M. A. (2026). Writing as Transformative. In S. Siahaan, I. E. Saputro, L. Yulianingsih, M. Faizin, J. B. Sinaga, & M. A. Ardhi (Eds.), *Transformative Learning and Literature in Writing: Theory, Pedagogy, and Practice* (pp. 85–98). PT. Harmoni Anak Negeri.

Sins Invalid. (2019). *Skin, tooth, and bone: The basis of movement is our people.* Sins Invalid.

Skehan, P. (1991). Individual differences in second language learning. *Studies in Second Language Acquisition, 13*(2), 275–298. DOI: 10.1017/S0272263100009979

Skutnabb-Kangas, T. (2000). *Linguistic genocide in education—or worldwide diversity and human rights?* Routledge. DOI: 10.4324/9781410605191

Skutnabb-Kangas, T., & Dunbar, R. (2010). *Indigenous children's education as linguistic genocide and a crime against humanity? A global view.* Gáldu Čála.

Skutnabb-Kangas, T., & Phillipson, R. (Eds.). (2022). *The handbook of linguistic human rights.* John Wiley & Sons. DOI: 10.1002/9781119753926

Soare, I. L. (2025). Language, Identity, and Cognitive Equity: Rethinking Multilingualism in Migrant-Inclusive EFL Pedagogy. *Analele Universită ii „Dunărea de Jos" din Gala i, Fascicula XX, Sociologie [The Annals of "Dunărea de Jos" University of Galaţi. Fascicle XX, Sociology], 20*(1), 153–167. https://www.ceeol.com/search/article-detail?id=1385816

Sobey, A. (2025). The thinness of GenAI: Body size in relation to the construction of the normate through GenAI image models. *AI and Ethics*, *5*(4), 4181–4196. DOI: 10.1007/s43681-025-00684-x

Son, J.-B., Ružić, N. K., & Philpott, A. (2025). Artificial intelligence technologies and applications for language learning and teaching. *Journal of China Computer-Assisted Language Learning*, *5*(1), 94–112. DOI: 10.1515/jccall-2023-0015

Spada, N., & Lightbown, P. M. (1993). Instruction and the development of questions in L2 classrooms. *Studies in Second Language Acquisition*, *15*(2), 205–224. DOI: 10.1017/S0272263100011967

Sudina, E. (2021). Study and scale quality in second language survey research, 2009–2019: The case of anxiety and motivation. *Language Learning*, *71*(4), 1149–1193. DOI: 10.1111/lang.12468

Sudina, E. (2023). Scale quality in second-language anxiety and WTC: A methodological synthesis. *Studies in Second Language Acquisition*, *45*(5), 1427–1455. DOI: 10.1017/S0272263122000560

Sun, J., & Wang, Y. (2025). Fuzzy-set qualitative comparative analysis (fsQCA) in second language acquisition: An applied example of writing engagement. *Research Methods in Applied Linguistics*, *4*(1), 100193. DOI: 10.1016/j.rmal.2025.100193

Surmont, J., Van Oss, V., D'Hulster, M., Mijts, E., Van Donselaar, B., Van den Branden, K., Buelens, K., Sylvén, L. K., Olsson, E., Segura Hudson, M., Wakelkamp, I., Van de Guchte, M., Palacios-Hidalgo, F. J., Huertas-Abril, C. A., Luque-González, R., Husárová, B., & Curado-Toledano, N. (2025). *Pluridentities: Theoretical Framework on Languages, Identity, and Policy*. Pluridentities. DOI: 10.5281/zenodo.17949143

Szabó, F., & Szoke, J. (2024). How does generative AI promote autonomy and inclusivity in language teaching? *ELT Journal*, *78*(4), 478–488. DOI: 10.1093/elt/ccae052

Taff, S. D., & Lazzaro, C. V. B. (2025). Critical pedagogy: Praxis and social reform through education. In *Routledge Companion to Occupational Therapy: Theories, Concepts and Models* (pp. 639–650). Taylor and Francis. DOI: 10.4324/9781003526766-51

Taghizadeh, M., & Hasani Yourdshahi, Z. (2020). Integrating technology into young learners' classes: Language teachers' perceptions. *Computer Assisted Language Learning*, *33*(8), 982–1006. DOI: 10.1080/09588221.2019.1618876

Tang, L., Zhang, C. A., & Cui, Y. (2024). A multigroup SEM analysis of mediating role of enjoyment, anxiety, and boredom in the relationships between L2 motivational self-system, L2 proficiency, and intercultural communication competence. *Language Teaching Research, 13621688241265211*, 13621688241265211. Advance online publication. DOI: 10.1177/13621688241265211

Tanksley, T. C. (2024). "We're changing the system with this one": Black students using critical race algorithmic literacies to subvert and survive AI-mediated racism in school. *English Teaching, 23*(1), 36–56. DOI: 10.1108/ETPC-08-2023-0102

Tatman, R. (2017). Gender and dialect bias in YouTube's automatic captions. *Proceedings of ACL Workshop on Ethics in NLP*, 53–59. DOI: 10.18653/v1/W17-1606

Tatman, R., & Kasten, R. (2017). Effects of talker dialect, gender and race on accuracy of Bing Speech and YouTube automatic captions. *Proceedings of Interspeech, 934–938*, 934–938. Advance online publication. DOI: 10.21437/Interspeech.2017-1746

Teimouri, Y., Goetze, J., & Plonsky, L. (2019). Second language anxiety and achievement: A meta-analysis. *Studies in Second Language Acquisition, 41*(2), 363–387. DOI: 10.1017/S0272263118000311

Thao, L. T., Thuy, P. T., Thi, N. A., Yen, P. H., Thu, H. T. A., & Tra, N. H. (2023). Impacts of emotional intelligence on second language acquisition: English-major students' perspectives. *SAGE Open, 13*(4), 21582440231212065. DOI: 10.1177/21582440231212065

Thapa, M. B., & Shrestha, K. (2026). Empowering teachers through ChatGPT: Perceptions and experiences in English as a foreign or second language (EFL/ESL) classrooms as a form of community service. *ASEAN Journal of Community Service and Education, 5*(1), 21–32. https://ejournal.bumipublikasinusantara.id/index.php/ajcse/article/view/812

The Zubin Foundation. (2018). *Securing a good start for students of Chinese as an additional language in kindergarten*. The Zubin Foundation.

Thorne, S. L. (2024). Generative artificial intelligence, co-evolution, and language education. *Modern Language Journal, 108*(2), 567–572. DOI: 10.1111/modl.12932

Tomlinson, B. (Ed.). (2016). *SLA research and materials development for language learning* (pp. 3–22). Routledge., DOI: 10.4324/9781315749082

Topol, E. (2024, September 11). *Dr. Eric Topol on how AI is transforming health and medicine clinical center news*. https://www.cc.nih.gov/news/2024/nov-dec/eric-topol-ai

Torkhani, D. (2025). AI-enhanced language learning: The impact of Talkpal. AI on EFL undergraduate students' English-speaking skills. *American Journal of STEM Education, 11*, 69–82. DOI: 10.32674/232w1188

Towell, R., & Hawkins, R. D. (1994). *Approaches to second language acquisition*. Multilingual Matters., DOI: 10.21832/9781800418271

Truong, U. T. (2024). Writing Classes in the AI Era: Redefining English Teachers' Roles. *Proceedings - 2024 6th International Workshop on Artificial Intelligence and Education, WAIE 2024*, 50–55. Institute of Electrical and Electronics Engineers Inc. DOI: 10.1109/WAIE63876.2024.00016

UNESCO. (2021). *Recommendation on the ethics of artificial intelligence*. UNESCO. https://n9.cl/4zoy2m

UNESCO. (2023). *Global education monitoring report 2023: Technology in education — A tool on whose terms?* UNESCO. DOI: 10.54676/UZQV8501

UNESCO. (2023). *Guidance for generative AI in education and research*. UNESCO. https://l1nq.com/05WWX

UNESCO. (2024). Generative AI: UNESCO study reveals alarming evidence of regressive gender stereotypes. Retrieved March 25, 2026, from https://www.unesco.org/en/articles/generative-ai-unesco-study-reveals-alarming-evidence-regressive-gender-stereotypes#:~:text=their%20content%20can%20significantly%20amplify,Member%20States%20in%20November%202021

UNESCO. (2025a). *Report of the Independent Expert Group on artificial intelligence and culture*. Retrieved from https://www.unesco.org/sites/default/files/medias/fichiers/2025/09/CULTAI_Report%20of%20the%20Independent%20Expert%20Group%20on%20Artificial%20Intelligence%20and%20Culture%20%28final%20online%20version%29%201.pdf

UNESCO. (2025b). What you need to know about AI and the right to education. Retrieved March 3, 2026, from https://www.unesco.org/en/articles/what-you-need-know-about-ai-and-right-education#:~:text=One%20major%20challenge%20is%20that,ensuring%20the%20right%20to%20education

UNESCO. (2025c). *AI and the Future of Education: Disruptions, Dilemmas and Directions*. UNESCO. https://www.unesco.org/en/articles/ai-and-future-education-disruptions-dilemmas-and-directions

Universidade NOVA de Lisboa. (2024). *Mestrado de Ensino de Inglês no 3.º ciclo do Ensino Básico e no Ensino Secundário [Master's Degree in Teaching English in Lower Secondary and Upper Secondary Education]*. Faculdade de Ciências Sociais e Humanas. https://n9.cl/k0lrr

Unnikrishnan, R., & Prasad, R. (2021). Multilingual learners and the challenges of ASR in educational settings. *International Journal of Speech Technology, 24*(3), 549–560. DOI: 10.1007/s10772-021-09815-5

Ututalum, C.Charisma S. Ututalum. (2025). Transformative potential of generative AI in higher education teaching practices. *Environment and Social Psychology, 10*(9). Advance online publication. DOI: 10.59429/esp.v10i9.3291

Vafaee, P., & Suzuki, Y. (2020). The relative significance of syntactic knowledge and vocabulary knowledge in second language listening ability. *Studies in Second Language Acquisition, 42*(2), 383–410. DOI: 10.1017/S0272263119000676

Valdés, G. (2001). Heritage language students: Profiles and possibilities. In Peyton, J. K., Ranard, D. A., & McGinnis, S. (Eds.), *Heritage languages in America: Preserving a national resource* (pp. 37–77). Delta Systems.

Valdivieso, T., & González, O. (2025). Generative AI Tools in Salvadoran Higher Education: Balancing Equity, Ethics, and Knowledge Management in the Global South. *Education Sciences, 15*(2), 214. Advance online publication. DOI: 10.3390/educsci15020214

Vallejo, C. (2018). Translanguaging: Language, bilingualism and education. *Bellaterra – Journal of Teaching & Learning Language & Literature, 11*(1), 85–95. https://doi.org/DOI: 10.5565/rev/jtl3.764

Van Dijk, T. A. (2001). Multidisciplinary CDA: A plea for diversity. In Wodak, R., & Meyer, M. (Eds.), *Methods of critical discourse analysis* (pp. 95–120). Sage Publications.

Van Dijk, T. A. (2015). Critical discourse analysis. In Tannen, D., Hamilton, H. E., & Schiffrin, D. (Eds.), *The handbook of discourse analysis* (pp. 466–485). Wiley. DOI: 10.1002/9781118584194.ch22

Vanmassenhove, E., Shterionov, D., & Gwilliam, M. (2021). Machine Translationese: Effects of Algorithmic Bias on Linguistic Complexity in Machine Translation. *Proceedings of the 16th Conference of the European Chapter of the Association for Computational Linguistics,* 2213. https://aclanthology.org/2021.eacl-main.188.pdf

Varatharaj, A., Welch, A., Bucholtz, M., & Lee, J. S. (2024). *Teaching linguistic justice through augmented reality*. https://arxiv.org/pdf/2404.12563

Varsik, S., & Vosberg, L. (2024). *The potential impact of Artificial Intelligence on equity and inclusion in education*. OECD Publishing.

Veldhuis, A., Lo, P., Kenny, S., & Antle, A. N. (2024). Critical artificial intelligence literacy: A scoping review and framework synthesis. *International Journal of Child-Computer Interaction, 43*, 100708. DOI: 10.1016/j.ijcci.2024.100708

Viberg, O., Kizilcec, R., Wise, A. F., Jivet, I., & Nixon, N. (2024). Advancing equity and inclusion in educational practices with AI-powered educational decision support systems (AI-EDSS). *British Journal of Educational Technology, 55*(5), 1974–1981. DOI: 10.1111/bjet.13507

Vidhya Lakshmi, C. N., Kumar, S., Varghese, G. G., Jenefa, L., & Nandhini, P. U. (2026). Strategies for training educators in AI literacy and implementation. In Abdelaal, R. M. S., & Kayyali, M. (Eds.), *AI-powered pedagogy, academic transformation, and faculty empowerment* (pp. 383–404). IGI Global Scientific Publishing., DOI: 10.4018/979-8-3373-9220-2.ch016

Villarreal, D. (2024). Sociolinguistic auto-coding has fairness problems too: Measuring and mitigating overlearning bias. *Linguistics Vanguard : Multimodal Online Journal, 10*(1), 679–692. DOI: 10.1515/lingvan-2022-0114

Vipperla, R., Renals, S., & Frankel, J. (2010). Ageing voices: The effect of changes in voice parameters on ASR performance. *EURASIP Journal on Audio, Speech, and Music Processing, 2010*, 1–10. DOI: 10.1155/2010/525783

Vygotsky, L. S. (1978). *Mind in society: The development of higher psychological processes*. Harvard University Press.

W3C. (2018). *Web Content Accessibility Guidelines (WCAG) 2.1*. https://www.w3.org/TR/WCAG21/

Walter, Y. (2024). Embracing the future of Artificial Intelligence in the classroom: The relevance of AI literacy, prompt engineering, and critical thinking in modern education. *International Journal of Educational Technology in Higher Education, 21*(1), 15. DOI: 10.1186/s41239-024-00448-3

Wang, S., Lang, N., Bunch, G. C., Basch, S., McHugh, S. R., Huitzilopochtli, S., & Callanan, M. (2021). Dismantling Persistent Deficit Narratives About the Language and Literacy of Culturally and Linguistically Minoritized Children and Youth: Counter-Possibilities. *Frontiers in Education, 6*, 641796. DOI: 10.3389/feduc.2021.641796

Wang, X., Liu, Q., Pang, H., Tan, S. C., Lei, J., Wallace, M. P., & Li, L. (2023). What matters in AI-supported learning: A study of human-AI interactions in language learning using cluster analysis and epistemic network analysis. *Computers & Education*, *194*, 104703. DOI: 10.1016/j.compedu.2022.104703

Wang, Y. (2024). A review of emotions in second language acquisition from a positive psychology perspective. *International Journal of Education and Humanities*, *4*(3), 287–296. DOI: 10.58557/(ijeh).v4i3.241

Wang, Y., & Brown, D. (2022). The affordances and limitations of automated feedback for multilingual university writers. *Assessing Writing*, *52*, 100616. DOI: 10.1016/j.asw.2022.100616

Warschauer, M. (2004). *Technology and social inclusion: Rethinking the digital divide*. MIT Press.

Wedlock, J., & Wilson, N. (2024). Inclusion in the learning game: Applying considerations from cognitive neuroscience, educational psychology, and SLA to language learning activity and materials design. *TESOL in Context*, *33*(1), 58–81. DOI: 10.21153/tesol2024vol33no1art2014

Wei, J., Wang, Y., & Yang, H. (2023). Effects of Automated Writing Evaluation on EFL learners: A meta-analysis. *Journal of Second Language Writing*, *62*, 101021. DOI: 10.1016/j.jslw.2023.101021

Wei, L. (2018). Translanguaging as a practical theory of language. *Applied Linguistics*, *39*(1), 9–30. DOI: 10.1093/applin/amx039

Wei, L. (2022). Translanguaging as a political stance: Implications for English language education. *ELT Journal*, *76*(2), 172–182. DOI: 10.1093/elt/ccab083

Wei, L., & García, O. (2022). Not a first language but one repertoire: Translanguaging as a decolonizing project. *RELC Journal*, *53*(2), 313–324. DOI: 10.1177/00336882221092841

Wenden, A. L. (2002). Learner development in language learning. *Applied Linguistics*, *23*(1), 32–55. DOI: 10.1093/applin/23.1.32

Weng, Z., & Fu, Y. (2025). Generative AI in language education: Bridging divide and fostering inclusivity. *International Journal of Technology in Education*, *8*(2), 395–420. DOI: 10.46328/ijte.1056

Williamson, B., & Eynon, R. (2020). Historical threads, missing links, and future directions in AI in education. [Taylor & Francis.]. *Learning, Media and Technology*, *45*(3), 223–235. DOI: 10.1080/17439884.2020.1798995

World Economic Forum. (2022). *Artificial intelligence for children toolkit*. World Economic Forum. https://l1nq.com/idh6m3c

Xiao, G. (2024). The power of language ideologies: creating heteroglossic implementational spaces in a practical English class. *Working Papers in Educational Linguistics, 38,* 48–66. https://repository.upenn.edu/handle/20.500.14332/60632

Xiao, Y. (2025). The impact of AI-driven speech recognition on EFL listening comprehension, flow experience, and anxiety: A randomized controlled trial. *Humanities & Social Sciences Communications*, *12*(1), 1–14. DOI: 10.1057/s41599-025-04672-8

Xiong, M., & Teo, T. (2025). Unveiling the effects of GenAI on motivation of learning English as a second/foreign language: Evidence from meta-analysis. *Educational Research Review*, *49*, 100744. DOI: 10.1016/j.edurev.2025.100744

Yelland, N. (2025). Reimagining multiliteracies: The transformative influence of generative AI on pedagogies. *Pedagogies*, 1–10. DOI: 10.1080/1554480X.2025.2525270

Yıldırım, A., & Şimşek, H. (2021). *Sosyal Bilimlerde Nitel Araştırma Yöntemleri.* Seçkin.

Yıldız, T. A. (2023). The impact of ChatGPT on language learners' motivation. *Journal of Teacher Education and Lifelong Learning*, *5*(2), 582–597. DOI: 10.51535/tell.1314355

Yingsoon, G. Y., Zhang, S., Chua, N. A., & Xiaoyao, T. (2025). Empowering Multicultural Literacies: Fostering Second Language Acquisition With Media and Digital Platforms. In *Supporting Cultural Differences Through Literacy Education* (pp. 77-108). IGI Global Scientific Publishing. DOI: 10.4018/979-8-3693-9271-3.ch004

Young, I. (2011). *Responsibility For Justice* (Freeman, S., Ed.). Oxford University Press. DOI: 10.1093/acprof:oso/9780195392388.001.0001

Youn, S. J. (2023). Test design and validity evidence of interactive speaking assessment in the era of emerging technologies. *Language Testing*, *40*(1), 54–60. DOI: 10.1177/02655322221126606

Yusmaliana, D., Abubakari, M. S., Monib, W. K., & Shafik, W. (2026). Between Independence and Supervision: A Reflective Account of a PhD Student in the Era of AI. In Irham, I., Huda, M., & Yaqin, L. N. (Eds.), *International Student Narratives in Globalized Higher Education* (pp. 305–334). IGI Global Scientific Publishing., DOI: 10.4018/979-8-3373-4212-2.ch012

Zakaria, A., & Aryadoust, V. (2024). A scientometric analysis of applied linguistics research (1970–2022): Methodology and future directions. *Applied Linguistics Review, 15*(4), 1595–1619. DOI: 10.1515/applirev-2022-0210

Zare, J., Karimpour, S., & Delavar, K. A. (2022). The impact of concordancing on English learners' foreign language anxiety and enjoyment: An application of data-driven learning. *System, 109*, 102891. DOI: 10.1016/j.system.2022.102891

Zawacki-Richter, O., Marín, V. I., Bond, M., & Gouverneur, F. (2019). Systematic review of research on artificial intelligence applications in higher education – where are the educators? *International Journal of Educational Technology in Higher Education, 16*(1), 39. Advance online publication. DOI: 10.1186/s41239-019-0171-0

Zhai, C., & Wibowo, S. (2023). A systematic review on artificial intelligence dialogue systems for enhancing English as foreign language students' interactional competence in the university. *Computers & Education, 4*, 100134. DOI: 10.1016/j.caeai.2023.100134

Zhang, X., Li, S., Hauer, B., Shi, N., & Kondrak, G. (2023, December). Don't trust ChatGPT when your question is not in English: A study of multilingual abilities and types of LLMs. In *Proceedings of the 2023 conference on empirical methods in natural language processing* (pp. 7915–7927). https://doi.org/DOI: 10.18653/v1/2023.emnlp-main.491

Zhang, Y., & Dong, C. (2024). Exploring the digital transformation of generative ai-assisted foreign language education: A socio-technical systems perspective based on mixed-methods. *Systems, 12*(11), 462. DOI: 10.3390/systems12110462

Zhang, Y., & Samsudin, M. A. (2026). From familiarity to criticality: Cultivating EFL teachers' AI literacy through an AI-integrated genre-based pedagogy. *Education Sciences, 16*(1), 150. DOI: 10.3390/educsci16010150

Zhao, Z. J., Li, J., Hong, Y., & Yun, T. Y. (2025). Lesson study as an approach to facilitate the integration of Gen-AI into EFL curriculum design in higher education. *International Journal for Lesson and Learning Studies, 14*(3), 253–279. DOI: 10.1108/IJLLS-01-2025-0029

Zheng, L., & Yang, Y. (2024). Research perspectives and trends in artificial intelligence-enhanced language education: A review. *Heliyon, 10*(19), e38617. Advance online publication. DOI: 10.1016/j.heliyon.2024.e38617 PMID: 39416824

Zhong, Y., Tan, S., Xu, X., Shao, Z., & Liu, Q. (2024). Second language learners' academic emotions in grammar learning with explicit attention to grammatical complexity. *Journal of Multilingual and Multicultural Development*, •••, 1–19. DOI: 10.1080/01434632.2024.2407042

Zhu, M., & Wang, C. (2025). A systematic review of AI in language education: Current status and future implications. *Language Learning & Technology*, *29*(1), 1–29. DOI: 10.64152/10125/73606

Zschomler, S. (2019). 'Language Is Your Dignity': Migration, Linguistic Capital, and the Experience of Re/De-Valuation. *Languages (Basel, Switzerland)*, *4*(3), 64. DOI: 10.3390/languages4030064

Zulianti, H., Nurchurifiani, E., Hastomo, T., Maximilian, A., & Ajeng, G. D. (2025). Enhancing novice EFL teachers' competency in AI-powered tools through a TPACK-based professional development program. *World Journal of English Language*, *15*(3), 117–131. DOI: 10.5430/wjel.v15n3p117

About the Contributors

Francisco Javier Palacios-Hidalgo (él/he/him), Associate Professor, belongs to the Department of English and German Studies of the Universidad de Córdoba (Spain), where he teaches at the Faculty of Education Sciences and Psychology. He is a member of the Research Group HUM-1122 'Research in Languages, Technology and Education' (RELATED). His research focuses on the teaching of English as a foreign language, language and bilingual education teacher training, educational technologies, teacher digital literacy and queer pedagogy.

Carlos Lindade is a Portuguese-Canadian Assistant Professor at the Faculty of Arts and Humanities, University of Porto (FLUP) and an experienced professional in English Language Teaching (ELT). He has a long record of training both pre- and in-service English Foreign Language teachers (EFL) and contributing to coursebook development for Portuguese learners of English. His research centers on ELT materials development, the pedagogical use of artificial intelligence in EFL teacher education, and technology-enhanced language learning (TELL). He combines classroom teaching, teacher training and research to support evidence-informed innovation in language education.

***

Ashraf Alam is currently serving as an Assistant Professor in the Department of Education at NIT Calicut, Kerala, India. He has been recognised among the World's Top 2% Scientists by Stanford University and Elsevier. His academic contributions include more than 75 Scopus-indexed publications and over 100 conference presentations delivered at national and international academic forums. His work has appeared in reputed research publication platforms including Elsevier, Springer, Taylor & Francis, CRC Press, Routledge, Atlantis Press, Springer Nature, Palgrave Macmillan, and IEEE. He earned his Ph.D. from IIT Kharagpur, where his research engaged with foundational concerns in educational policy, curriculum design, educational technology, philosophy of education, innovation in education, educational administration, governance, and pedagogical transformation. His work is grounded in a transdisciplinary orientation that draws from educational sciences, digital pedagogy, curriculum theory, learning analytics, sustainability education, instructional design, artificial intelligence, ethics of technology, and socio-technical studies. Dr. Ashraf's scholarship strives to interrogate and expand the boundaries of educational thought by examining the epistemological, ethical, and social dimensions of digital and post-digital pedagogies. His work critically engages with the changing nature of knowledge production, learner agency, pedagogical mediation, and institutional transformation in technologically saturated educational environments. He is particularly invested in advancing inclusive digital learning, gamified instructional strategies, AI-mediated educational ecosystems, and ethically governed technology integration in education. His research agenda is animated by the pursuit of design-oriented, ethically attuned, and contextually responsive frameworks that can support meaningful educational reform. Through his work, he seeks to contribute to the development of pedagogical models that are not only technologically innovative but also socially just, epistemically inclusive, developmentally sensitive, and aligned with the broader goals of sustainable and human-centred education.

Kardelen Aslan completed her undergraduate education in English Language Teaching and obtained her master's degree in the field of English Language Education / Teaching English as a Foreign Language. She currently works as a lecturer at the School of Foreign Languages at Mardin Artuklu University. Her academic interests include AI-supported foreign language teaching, EFL material design for young learners, learner motivation and classroom participation, technology-assisted teaching approaches, and the use of social media and popular culture elements in language teaching. Her research mainly focuses on the effects of AI-assisted visuals and digital materials on the foreign language learning process. She has presented papers at national and international academic events and conducts academic studies on innovative teaching designs, new teaching methods, and technology-based pedagogical practices. She continues her academic career in the field of foreign language education.

Lisa Marie Brinkmann is a research assistant at the University of Hamburg and holds a PhD in learners' investment and portfolio work in the French language classroom. Her research interests include methods to promote plurilingualism in education, such as the use of portfolios or linguistic landscapes, and critical pedagogies, including decolonial approaches and intercultural learning in language education.

Cristina A. Huertas-Abril, Full Professor, belongs to the Department of English and German Studies of the Universidad de Córdoba (Spain), where she teaches at the Faculty of Education Sciences and Psychology. She is the principal investigator of the Research Group HUM-1122 "Research in Languages, Technology and Education" (RELATED). Her research mainly focuses on Computer-Assisted Language Learning (CALL), Collaborative Online International Learning (COIL), Teaching English as a Foreign Language, bilingual education and teacher training.

Vidhya Lakshmi C N is an experienced ELT (English Language Teaching) and soft skills trainer with a strong foundation in LSRW (Listening, Speaking, Reading, Writing) skills, creative thinking, and clear articulation. She holds a Ph.D. in ELT and certifications such as Train the Trainer (VSkills), TESOL (ITTT), and IELTS Teacher Training, among others. With over two decades of experience, she has served as an Assistant Professor of English, Skill Development Cell Head, and Soft Skills Trainer at various prestigious institutions, including Hindustan Institute of Technology & Science and Peri Institute of Technology. Her contributions include publishing a patent in ELT, several academic journals, and textbooks, along with presenting papers at national and international conferences. A firm advocate of activity-based teaching, Dr. Vidhya also brings international exposure through her volunteering experiences in the USA, enhancing her dynamic approach to education and skill development.

Isabele Lavado holds a PhD in Language Sciences from the University of Porto and is an English Language Lecturer at the Polytechnic Institute of Castelo Branco, Portugal. Her research focuses on English for Specific Purposes (ESP), academic English, and Integrated Content and Language in Higher Education (ICLHE). She is particularly interested in interdisciplinary collaboration between content and language teachers and in promoting language awareness in higher education. Her current work explores the use of Artificial Intelligence (AI) in higher education, particularly Large Language Models (LLMs) for language teaching, translation, and research enhancement. She collaborates with the Working CLIL research group (CETAPS – University of Porto and Universidade Nova de Lisboa).

Siu-lun Lee is Principal Lecturer at the Chinese University of Hong Kong. He is an experienced teacher and administrator of Chinese language programmes, with extensive involvement in curriculum development and linguistic research. His academic interests include AI in education, applied linguistics, Cantonese studies, Chinese linguistics, language teaching pedagogy, multilingualism, and sociolinguistics. He is editor of The learning and teaching of Cantonese as a second language and author of the Modern Cantonese series published by Routledge.

Wali Khan Monib received the UBD Graduate Scholarship (UGS) to pursue his Ph.D. at the Centre for Lifelong Learning, Universiti Brunei Darussalam. He has worked as a faculty member at Shaikh Zayed University (SZU), Khost, Afghanistan since 2014. He was director of the research center at SZU from 2020-2022. He served as an instructor for the Legal Education Support Program-Afghanistan (LESPA) with the University of Washington School of Law from 2014 to 2018. He received the World Bank (HEDP) scholarship for his M.Ed. in Teaching English as a Second Language from Universiti Teknologi Malaysia, Johor, Malaysia. He holds a B.A. in English Language and Literature from Nangarhar University, Nangarhar, Afghanistan. He has presented at international conferences, published in peer-reviewed journals, and serves as a peer reviewer for SCI- and SSCI-indexed journals. He has also been invited to act as an editor for manuscripts submitted to SAGE Open. His research interests center around Technology in Education, AI, Discourse Analysis, Sentiment Analysis, EFL/ESL, Microlearning, Innovative Teaching and Learning Methods, Curriculum Studies and Lifelong Learning.

Kadri Nazlı works as an Assistant Professor (Doctor Lecturer) in the Department of Turkish Language and Literature, Department of Modern Turkish Language, at the Faculty of Literature, Dicle University. He completed his undergraduate education at the Faculty of Letters, Department of Western Languages and Literatures at Istanbul University. He received his master's degree from the Institute of Social Sciences at Dicle University in the Department of Turkish Language and Literature. He also completed his doctoral studies at the same institute. His academic research interests include humour, linguistics, language usage studies, sociolinguistics, and discourse analysis. Between 2007 and 2023, he worked at the School of Foreign Languages at Dicle University. Since 2023, he has continued his academic work in the Department of Turkish Language and Literature.

Liudmila Shafirova is a researcher at the Research Centre on Didactics and Technology in the Education of Trainers (CIDTFF), Education and Psychology department of the University of Aveiro, Portugal. Her work explores the intersections of plurilingual education, computer-mediated language learning, informal learning contexts, and multiliteracies, with a focus on innovation in language pedagogy.

Gibin Varghese is a research scholar in Hindustan Institute of Technology and Science.

Index

A

B

C

D

E

N

P

S

T

www.ingramcontent.com/pod-product-compliance
Lightning Source LLC
LaVergne TN
LVHW062327300926
849161LV00007B/1602
9798337377490